URBAN SOCIETY

Sixth Edition

URBAN SOCIETY

Noel P. Gist University of Missouri-Columbia
Sylvia Fleis Fava Brooklyn College of the City University of New York

Thomas Y. Crowell
HARPER & ROW, PUBLISHERS
New York Hagerstown Philadelphia San Francisco London

URBAN SOCIETY, Sixth Edition

Copyright © 1974 by Harper & Row, Publishers, Inc.

Published simultaneously in Canada by Fitzhenry &
Whiteside, Ltd., Toronto.

Library of Congress Cataloging in Publication Data

Gist, Noel Pitts, 1899-
   Urban society.

   First–4th ed. (1933-56) by N. P. Gist and L. A. Hal-
bert.
   Includes bibliographies.
   1. Sociology, Urban. 2. Sociology. 3. Social
psychology. 4. Urbanization. I. Fava, Sylvia Fleis,
1927-   joint author. II. Title.
HT151.G53 1974   301.36   74-9942
ISBN 0-690-00493-1

Preface

The first edition of *Urban Society* appeared in 1933. Successive editions recorded and analyzed some of the important changes that have occurred in cities and in the processes of urbanization. The wide acceptance of the book by classroom teachers indicates that it has contributed to the education of several college generations of students as well as others immediately involved with problems and issues in urban communities. While the book has obviously been concerned with many problems of city life, it has not attempted to advocate solutions to these problems. That task more appropriately falls within the province of others.

Those conversant with the book in its several editions are certainly aware of the changes over the years in the contents of the volume. Perhaps the most important change is the shift from a distinctly American focus, characteristic of the first edition, to increasing emphasis on urbanism and city life from a global perspective. Cities and the entire panorama of urbanization are no longer confined to a single country or region. In the book, therefore, cross-national and cross-cultural comparisons have been made, although comparative materials have necessarily been restricted because of limitations of space or because relevant data are not readily available. But even with increasing emphasis on cross-national comparisons and analyses, the book is heavily weighted with materials on American society.

The book is not concerned solely with cities *per se;* it is also about entire societies whose institutions may bear the imprint, in varying degrees, of urbanism in all its manifestations. In this respect we have dichotomized these societies as urban-industrial (or industrial) and developing (or nonindustrial) countries. The former model applies to those countries or regions in which most of the people reside in urban communities and are engaged in nonagricultural occupational pursuits. Such countries are urbanized in both a demographic and cultural sense—demographic in that a high proportion of the population are urban dwellers; cultural in that the entire population of the country, or at least most of it, whether urban or rural, has been greatly influenced by the values, forms of organization, and lifestyles characteristic of cities.

Developing countries, as used here, are societies in which most of the

v

people live in villages and open-country communities and are generally engaged in primary occupations, such as agriculture, or in occupations related to agriculture. Although such countries may have large and small cities, urban influence has been less pervasive, so far as most of the nonurban people are concerned, than cities in urban-industrial regions. It may be noted that more attention has been directed to the urbanization of developing societies than was the case in earlier editions.

In all six editions considerable emphasis has been placed on ecological patterns and processes, but certainly not to the exclusion of the structural and functional aspects of urban institutions or of the interaction of groups and individuals in an urban setting. It is commonplace that all aspects of cities, or of the societies in which they are located, have undergone and are undergoing change. In writing the book we have attempted to record many of these changes and to analyze their significance and relevance to current issues. While we have not intended the book to be a history of cities, nevertheless the historical backgrounds of urbanization and city life are emphasized in some chapters, especially those concerned with the origins and development of cities.

Several new chapters have been introduced in the present edition, and other chapters retaining the same titles have been largely re-written or had additional data incorporated into the analyses. The discussion of contemporary urbanization in world perspective has been expanded to two chapters in order to afford sufficient space for such an important subject. The chapter on classes and types of cities has been omitted, and in its place are two chapters with an ecological focus, namely, the "inner city" and the "suburbs." Another change is the omission of the chapter on intergroup relations in cities, but much of the subject matter originally subsumed under the heading is considered, when appropriate, in other chapters.

We have not presented the book as an original contribution to sociological theory pertaining to urban community life. Rather, using an eclectic approach, we have drawn on the researches and theories of many persons engaged in the sociological enterprise. Hopefully, the intellectually curious and energetic reader will obtain a better understanding of the city and its meaning in human society. To those whose researches and ideas we have utilized in the organization of this book we are grateful; their contributions are acknowledged in footnotes or other references. We owe special thanks to Maynard Robison for his assistance in preparing material for the housing and planning chapters and to our editors, Herman Makler and Susan Bass, for their skill and patience in transforming the manuscript into a book. For sins of omission or commission the authors are solely responsible.

January 1974   NOEL P. GIST

SYLVIA F. FAVA

Contents

THE ORIGIN AND GROWTH OF CITIES

THE SOCIAL PSYCHOLOGY OF URBAN LIFE

SOCIAL ASPECTS OF URBAN HOUSING AND REDEVELOPMENT

Tables, Figures, and Illustrations

TABLES

FIGURES

ILLUSTRATIONS

THE ORIGIN AND GROWTH OF CITIES

1 • The Origin of Cities

 Because cities are linked with a particular kind of social organization, commonly called "civilization," they cannot be adequately described or explained by geography, engineering, or architecture, but require analysis by the social sciences. The term "civilization" as it is used here does not carry the implication that civilization is better than other types of social organization; rather, it refers to a complex social system that involves its participants in a different set of interactions than do noncivilized societies.

Urbanism may be defined in two ways: as a "way of life" and as a settlement pattern.[1] As a way of life urbanism is characterized by complex social organization; as a settlement pattern it is exemplified by the city as a relatively permanent habitation for a large heterogenous population that is densely settled and not engaged in producing its own food. These two aspects of urbanism are analytically separable, and later in this book we shall deal with situations where urban settlement and urban social life do not coexist. For example, the chapters on world urbanization describe numerous very large contemporary cities in underdeveloped countries which are not highly urban in a social sense. Even in industrial countries there are enclaves within cities whose residents follow a way of life that differs little from their previous farm or village life. Such enclaves are described in the chapters on ecology, on the adjustment of migrants, and on the various forms within the city of such social institutions as the family.

The Recent Origin of Cities

The most impressive fact about the origin of cities is that they appeared so recently in the history of mankind. This is true despite the fact that the first cities appeared about five or six thousand years ago, that is,

[1] See Louis Wirth, "Urbanism as a Way of Life", *American Journal of Sociology*, 64 (July 1938), 3–24.

3000-4000 B.C.[2] Although this span encompasses all of written history, for record-keeping emerged only with cities, it is very short when compared either with the half-million years the human species has been on earth or with the 40,000 years that physically modern man, *Homo sapiens*, has existed. Put another way, the 6,000 years of man's urban existence represent only slightly more than one percent of his total existence on earth and only about 10 percent of his existence as physically modern man.

The earliest cities in the world appeared approximately 3500 B.C. in the Middle East in what is now southern Iraq. One other area is generally accepted as a core area for the origin of urbanism. The best current evidence indicates that cities arose independently in the New World in Central Mexico about 300 B.C., and from there the crucial inventions diffused to other parts of the Americas. Cities in the New World emerged later than those in the Old World, but they apparently developed independently, without being influenced by areas already urban.

The Causes of Urban Development

There appear to have been two requirements in order for cities to emerge. The first was the existence of a surplus of food and other necessities. In other words, levels of productivity had to be high enough so that a person produced more than he and his immediate dependents needed for survival. The surplus would allow some people to live in settlements where they were not concerned with the actual physical provision of their own supply of food and other material goods. Therefore, these settlements could be relatively large, densely populated, and permanent.

The second requirement was the addition of other forms of social organization to those based on family and kinship. The sheer existence of a surplus is not sufficient to insure that it will be concentrated and

[2] Because of the absence of written records, the scarcity of archeological remains, problems of classifying the surviving artifacts, and conceptual problems (that is, what constitutes agriculture, village life, and the like), there is great confusion and uncertainty over the dating of all events before historic times. Wide variations exist for all the dates employed here. For example, many authorities would assign a date of 700,000 to a 1,000,000 years for the appearance of the human species on earth. Authorities also differ on the dates for the beginning of the Neolithic in various parts of the world, the first emergence of cities, of metal-working, and so on. All of the dates employed in this chapter should, therefore, be regarded as tentative and subject to revision, pending further investigation and classification. In general we have followed the dating suggested in Robert Braidwood and Gordon Willey, eds., *Courses Toward Urban Life* (1962); Grahame Clark and Stuart Piggott, *Prehistoric Societies* (1965); and David R. Harris, "New Light on Plant Domestication and the Origins of Agriculture: A Review," *Geographical Review*, 57 (January 1967), 90–107.

distributed to people living apart from the original producers. It requires a social system in which people owe loyalty and obligation to groups other than the family and kin.

The Agricultural Revolution

It was impossible to accumulate a surplus of life necessities during all but the most recent past of mankind. Man has spent most of his history on earth as a nomad, a wanderer without any settled habitation. This lack of permanent settlement was related to an extremely unproductive

FIGURE 1.1 ● Agriculture—where it began and how it spread. The domestication of plants and animals occurred independently in the Mideast area of the Old World and in central Mexico in the New World. Independent development may also have occurred in ancient China. From these nodal areas agriculture gradually spread throughout the world, with the addition of locally developed crops in various regions. Source: The map follows the data and sequence given in David R. Harris, "New Light on Plant Domestication and the Origins of Agriculture: A Review," *Geographical Review* LVII (January 1967). © 1967 by *The New York Times*. Reprinted by permission.

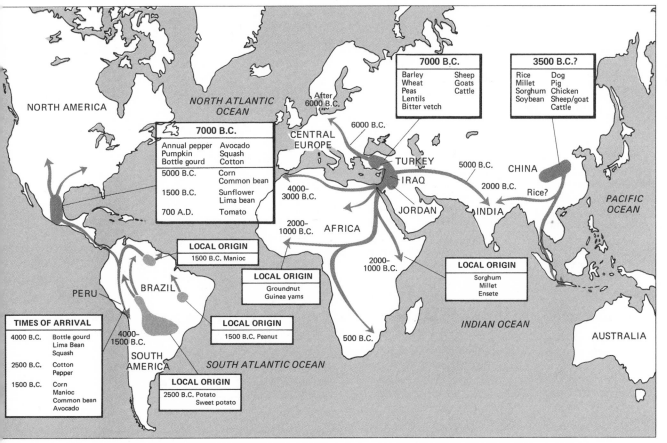

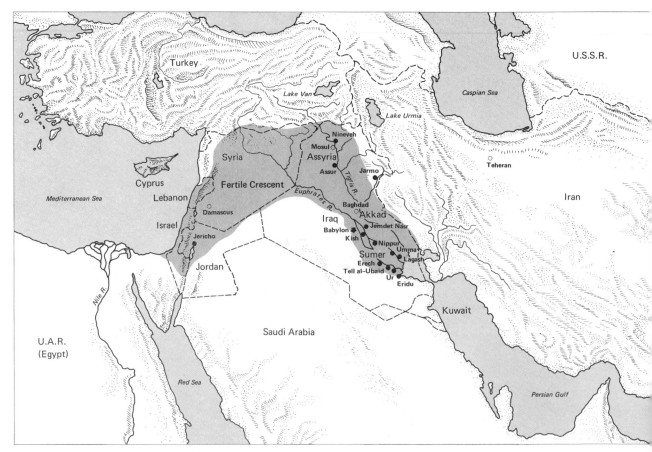

FIGURE 1.2 • The Fertile Crescent. Black dots indicate ancient cities and villages; all of those shown did not exist at the same time. The modern Tigris and Euphrates rivers flow along different routes than the ancient courses shown. Open dots indicate present-day cities. National boundaries shown are also modern. Source: Adapted with permission from Robert Braidwood, "Agricultural Revolution." Copyright © 1960 by Scientific American, Inc. All rights reserved.

level of technology. Men had only crude unpolished stone tools and subsisted by hunting wild animals and gathering edible plants. And because the yield from this method of exploiting the environment was low and erratic, the quest for food was the full-time occupation of the entire group, which was also compelled to follow the food supply as the seasons changed or a given area's supply of animals and growth of plants was exhausted. A more precise name for this technological level is the Old Stone Age or Paleolithic (from *paleo*, old: *lith*, stone). From man's beginnings 500,000 years ago until about 9000 B.C., all human groups lived at this technological level, with only small improvements in tools and skills occurring over long intervals. There are still a few groups today who live at a Paleolithic level.[3] For example, although most of Australia's aborigines now reside in cities or in government settlements, a few groups in the "outback" desert areas still follow a stone-age style of life.

Important environmental forces were also at work between 500,000 and 9000 B.C. to inhibit the emergence of cities. During this period, which geologists call the Pleistocene, glaciers several times covered, receded, and then covered again the areas of the world that are now Canada, the northern United States, northern Europe, and northern

[3] See, for example, M. G. Bicchieri, ed., *Hunters and Gatherers Today* (1972).

Asia. During most of the Pleistocene, man was additionally handicapped in coping with his environment, for he had not attained his fully modern physical and mental characteristics; physically modern man emerged about 40,000 B.C. The Pleistocene came to an end about 9000 B.C., when the glaciers finally retreated, and the great changes in climate, wild life, and rainfall that were ushered in on most of the world's surface necessitated a readjustment of man's way of living. We must, however, guard against invoking environmental determinism in explaining the origin of cities, because major changes of climate and environment had occurred several times before but had never been responded to technologically and socially as they now were. The environmental changes brought about by the melting of the glaciers were not uniform. In northern areas, such as northern Europe, these changes marked the extinction of herds of woolly mammoth, hairy rhinoceros, giant bear, and other big game; instead, forests grew on what had been tundra, and small game flourished. Some parts of the world were inundated by the release of waters from the melting glaciers. Other areas, such as the Sahara, became semiarid as the rainbelts shifted. Some areas were relatively unaffected.

In one part of the world, a hospitable environment and a major technological breakthrough combined to provide the basis for the first human communities based on food production rather than food-gathering. This phenomenon took place in the so-called Fertile Crescent—the hilly uplands of what is now Israel, Lebanon, Jordan, Syria, northern Iraq, and western Iran.

Environmentally the Fertile Crescent was an area of benign climate where the wild ancestors of barley, wheat, sheep, goats, and cattle were found. About 7000 B.C. these species of plants and animals, and later others, began to be cultivated rather than hunted or gathered in the wild state. It is hard for us to realize that the domestication of plants and animals is an invention and has become part of man's life only comparatively recently. The implications of domestication were in fact revolutionary although their impact was felt gradually. At first techniques of agriculture and animal husbandry were very primitive and people still relied heavily on hunting and gathering. Tools were still made of stone, although techniques of grinding were developed to give them a sharper edge. (The invention of metal-working techniques was several thousand years in the future.) Other technological advances were added over time and enhanced the usefulness of agricultural production. Clay was shaped and fired to harden it and produce pottery, which was very useful for storage. Weaving was invented, thus increasing the productive use of some animals and plants by providing man with clothing, bed coverings, floor mats, and the like, other than those made of animal skin. Wheeled transport was invented only about 3000 B.C. and was, of course, invaluable in transporting people and goods.

The various technological inventions reinforced one another in enabling man to control his environment and exploit its potential more fully. This vital period in man's history, when he combined refined stone tools with domestication of plants and animals, has been called the Neolithic (New Stone Age) Revolution or the Agricultural Revolution. The "revolution" was neither rapid nor tumultuous, as we customarily think of revolutions, but was indeed revolutionary in the sense that it formed the base for stability of residence and resources.

Jarmo, a Neolithic Village

Excavations at Jarmo in the Fertile Crescent show that it was inhabited as an agricultural village for several hundred years around 6500 B.C.[4] Jarmo was a permanent, year-round settlement with about two dozen several-roomed, rectangular, mud-walled houses that showed signs of frequent repair and rebuilding, so that the excavations revealed about a dozen distinct levels of occupancy. The people of Jarmo grew domesticated barley and wheat and kept domesticated goats, dogs, and possibly sheep. Evidences of other Neolithic inventions were also found at the site—tools and stone objects of fine workmanship based on new stone-working techniques, weaving, and pottery. The pottery objects were found only in the upper, hence later, levels of the excavations.

Other aspects of life in Jarmo are indicated in the finding of large numbers of clay figurines used as religious cult objects. The people of Jarmo may also have done some trading, for they had tools of obsidian, a volcanic glass with a cutting edge much sharper and harder than stone. The nearest source of obsidian was 200 miles away. There were many other Neolithic villages in the Fertile Crescent, particularly by 5000 B.C., but Jarmo was among the very earliest of these farming villages.

Some indication of the importance of agriculture and other Neolithic technological advances is shown by comparing the size of Neolithic settlements with earlier ones. Estimates are that stone-using, hunting-gathering technology (Paleolithic) supported human populations of about one-half to one human being per square mile, while stone-using, agricultural (Neolithic) technology supported densities of 30 or more per square mile.[5] For example, it is probable that one square mile was needed to support each individual of the peoples with an advanced Paleolithic technology who produced the well-known cave paintings of the Spanish peninsula.[6] In contrast it has been calculated that approxi-

---

[4] This description is based on Robert Braidwood and Bruce Howe, "Southwestern Asia beyond the Land of the Mediterranean Littoral," in Braidwood and Willey, *op. cit.*, pp. 132–46: and Robert Braidwood, "The Agricultural Revolution," *Scientific American*, 203 (September 1960), 130–52.

[5] V. Gordon Childe, "The Urban Revolution," *Town Planning Review*, 21 (April 1950), 4–5.

[6] Luis Pericot, "The Social Life of Spanish Paleolithic Hunters as Shown by Levantine Art," in S. Washburn, ed., *The Social Life of Early Man* (1961), p. 210.

mately 150 people lived at Jarmo at a density of 27 people per square mile.[7]

By 5000 B.C. the Fertile Crescent and nearby areas to which agricultural practices had diffused were studded with agricultural villages like Jarmo. These were *not* cities, either in terms of settlement pattern or way of life. Although Neolithic villages marked a sharp departure in technology from hunting-gathering nomads, both were precivilized— that is, simple rather than complex—social orders. Hunting-gathering groups and Neolithic farm-villages were alike in being small, even though the latter were, of course, larger than the former. Both were self-contained, for virtually all the group needed was obtained within its own confines. They were homogeneous, for even though the Neolothic allowed permanent settlement, both of these technological levels required every individual to devote full attention to obtaining food; thus, the major distinctions were those of age and sex, since all individuals had the same occupation and attendant property and wealth. In all Stone Age societies, kinship was very important and the family, performing economic, socialization, leadership, and other functions, was the major social unit. Finally, religion and art reinforced the values of this small world, as in the cave paintings to magically insure success in the hunt, or in the "fertility goddesses" of much of the Neolithic Near East.

The individuals constituting such societies shared the same experiences and expectations, and were thus primarily knit together by similar sentiments and points of view. Redfield contrasts this kind of social bond with the social bonds resting on impersonal, specialized relations which

result from mutual usefulness, from deliberate coercion, or from the mere utilization of the same means. In [this] . . . order men are bound by things, or are themselves things. They are organized by necessity or expediency. Think, if you will, of the orderly way in which automobiles move in response to the traffic light or the policeman's whistle, or think of the flow of goods, services, and money among the people who together produce, distribute, and consume some commodity such as rubber.[8]

Over time the Neolithic villages developed efficient material culture with advanced agriculture. There was increasing abundance in Fertile Crescent villages but there was no technological determinism—no inevitability—to the development of cities solely on the basis of the surplus eventually produced by the agricultural villages. Material abundance was a necessary precondition for urban development, but it was not sufficient. Many of the peasant societies of the Near East remained at

[7] Braidwood, *op. cit.*, p. 143.

[8] Robert Redfield, *The Primitive World and Its Transformations* (1953), p. 21. Redfield's formulation is similar to Durkheim's contrast between mechanical and organic solidarity, to Cooley's distinction between primary and secondary groups, and to such typologies as *Gemeinschaft-Gesellschaft*, which are described in Chapter 2 of this text.

that level, while their neighbors, starting from a similar economic and environmental base, became urban civilizations.

Social Structure in the Earliest Cities—Southern Mesopotamia

Complex social organization was the additional element necessary for agricultural societies to develop into urban societies. What set the process in motion? In the last analysis, "Exceptional and unpredictable combinations of circumstances and persons brought about one of the manifestations of human achievement which we call civilization."[9] The available evidence suggests that new religious or political allegiances motivated and obligated people to a wider, more interdependent network of relationships. In any event, the earliest cities had centralized religious and governmental authorities which were organized in formal, bureaucratic, and specialized ways in contrast to the more personal and informal ways employed by the family and kin group.

The world's first cities appeared in incipient form about 3500 B.C. and were well developed by 3000-2500 B.C. They appeared in that section of the Fertile Crescent variously called southern Mesopotamia, Sumer, Babylonia, and, now, southern Iraq. This area was not in the hilly uplands where the domestication of plants and animals had begun, but in the more level portion of the Crescent lying between the Tigris and Euphrates rivers, which flooded and thus fertilized much of the lowlands every year. Some of the early cities were Eridu, Ur, Ubaid, Nippur, Lagash, and, somewhat later, Babylon and Nineveh. Jericho, on the opposite end of the Fertile Crescent in modern Jordan, apparently was another very early city.

Two major social inventions were manifest in these early cities. The first was the development of a system of writing and numerical notation, which enabled man to keep exact records, accumulate knowledge, and preserve literature, poetry, philosophy, and other intellectual products. The second social innovation was the emergence of full-time specialists—persons whose regular occupation was a craft, trading, administration, a profession, or a service.[10] Literacy and a complex division of labor released man's many abilities and talents.

The ancient cities of southern Mesopotamia illustrate complexity and the civilized quality of life within them. Full-time specialists, such as draftsmen, transport workers, officials, and priests, exchanged their services for food produced by the farmers, although it was not a direct exchange but one mediated by other agencies. The priests, for example, were fed, housed, and clothed by the temple administration, which in

[9] Clark and Piggott, *op. cit.*, p. 184.
[10] Cf. Childe, *op. cit.*

turn obtained these items from the tithes collected from farmers. Great art was produced by full-time specialists in the field, while others invented writing and numerical notation, which were vital in keeping the records and accounts so prominent in the many indirect transactions now necessary. Sumerian writing, a cuneiform script incised on clay tablets, was used mainly for documentary purposes, such as temple accounts, inventories, receipts, and records of land transferral. The exact and predictive sciences, such as arithmetic, geometry, and astronomy, were invented by the literate segment of society and served to help plan major projects. The Sumerians used time calculations based on astronomy to determine the appropriate time for irrigating their fields, and their temples could not have been constructed without advanced mathematics.

Although cities had emerged, only a small portion of the population lived in cities or engaged in specialized urban tasks. Farm technology still produced only a small surplus, and hence it was impossible for more than a tiny minority to be relieved of growing or gathering their own subsistence. Estimates are that only about five percent of the labor force of ancient Sumer was employed in specialized occupations, and, at a somewhat later period in Sumerian development, less than 20 percent were so employed.[11]

Sumerian cities are judged to have included between 7,000 and 20,000 people, although Uruk extended over 1,100 acres and contained possibly 50,000 people.[12] The general layout of Sumerian cities is indicated by several well-excavated sites.

Radiating out from the massive public buildings . . . toward the outer gates, were streets, unpaved and dusty, but straight and wide enough for the passage of solid-wheeled carts or chariots. Along the streets lay the residences of the well-to-do citizenry, usually arranged around spacious courts and sometimes provided with latrines draining into sewage conduits below the streets. The houses of the city's poorer inhabitants were located behind or between the large multiroomed dwellings. They were approached by tortuous, narrow alleys, were more haphazard in plan, were less well built and very much smaller. Mercantile activities were probably concentrated along the quays of the adjoining river or at the city gates. The marketplace or bazaar devoted to private commerce had not yet appeared.

Around every important urban center rose the massive fortifications that guarded the city against nomadic raids and the usually more formidable campaigns of neighboring rulers. Outside the walls clustered sheepfolds and irrigated tracts, interspersed with subsidiary villages and ultimately disappearing into the desert. And in the desert dwelt only the nomad, an object of mixed fear and scorn to the sophisticated court poet.[13]

[11] Robert Adams. "The Origin of Cities," *Scientific American*, 203 (September 1960), 168.
[12] *Ibid.*, p. 166; and Childe, *op. cit.*, p. 9.
[13] Adams, *op. cit.*, p. 10.

Sumerian cities originated as city-states, were welded about 2400 B.C. into a short-lived empire under Sargon of Akkad, and later suffered from warfare and shifts of political hegemony to the Babylonians and finally to the Assyrians. The formation of the state underscores the point that society was organized on the basis of residence instead of, or on top of, a basis of kinship. Taxes were a function of the allegiance and duties the individual owed to the state. In ancient Sumer the state was a theocracy, combining religious and civil administration and authority, a circumstance which has fostered speculation about the possible role of religion in ushering in urban complexity. Wheatley has suggested that "whenever . . . we trace back the characteristic urban form to its beginnings we arrive not at a settlement that is dominated by commercial relations,

Reconstruction of ancient Babylon in the time of Nebuchadnezzar. A royal procession passes through the Ishtar Gate on its way to the palace, on whose roof (right) the famous "Hanging Gardens" can be seen. In the distant background (upper right) is the pyramid-shaped *ziggurat,* or temple, the Tower of Babel. The main features of Babylon are characteristic of ancient Mesopotamian cities. (Oriental Institute, University of Chicago)

a primordial market, or at one that is focused on a citadel, an archetypical fortress, but rather at a ceremonial complex for religious expression."[14] In any event, in ancient Mesopotamia the populace paid tribute or taxes to a religious-secular administration, thus allowing for the concentration of the surplus product. Without centralized authority, the tiny surplus of individual producers would not have added up to effective working capital. In Sumerian society, the temple authorities were important in performing this function.

The monumental public buildings of cities symbolized the society's surplus product and also the new foci of allegiance. Sumerian cities were focussed on the *Ziggurat* or raised platform and temple, which towered above the flat plains. A class-structured society emerged from the unequal distribution of more plentiful property and from specialized activities. The elite contributed important functions to the society— usually religious, political, or military—but nevertheless the gap between their life and that of the peasant-farmer was very wide. The magnificent jewelry, household objects, musical instruments, and other items found in the royal tombs at Ur, an important Sumerian city mentioned in the Bible, testify not only to the high aesthetic and technical level of the culture but also to the luxuries enjoyed by the privileged.[15]

More abstractly, the complex differentiated social structure of even the earliest urban civilized society is evident in several dimensions. Institutional diversity is shown in the emergence of authority structures—especially the state—with full-time personnel and distinct buildings separate from the family and kinship group which formerly organized the individual's life. Occupational diversity adds another dimension, for now people differ greatly in their training and life styles and begin to develop loyalty to their craft group, trade interest, or professional standards. Social-class differences add a vertical dimension to diversity. Interpersonal relations also take on a new dimension, for now some associations among people are indirect, impersonal, and specialized. Finally, social control and integration are achieved through the interdependence of diverse groups. All of these new complex aspects of social organization are in addition to, not replacements for, the previous simpler forms. The family and kinship group remain an important organizing institution. Intensely personal, unspecialized primary-group contacts remain, as does social control through similarity of points of view.

---

[14] Paul Wheatley, *The Pivot of the Four Quarters,* (1971), p. 225.

[15] For a description of the city by its chief excavator, see Sir Leonard Woolley, *Ur of the Chaldees* (1929).

Independent Urban Development
in the Western Hemisphere

Agriculture was invented independently in the New World and here, too, it ultimately provided, in certain environments and among certain peoples, the material basis for cities. Domestication of plants began about 7000 B.C. in Central Mexico, about the same time as in the Middle East, but the crops were different and the pace and content of change were far different.[16] Agriculture in Central Mexico was not immediately or rapidly a complete economic success, and hunting-gathering remained the main sources of food supply for thousands of years after agriculture was known. Cultivated food replaced hunting-gathering only very gradually. It was not until about 1500 B.C. that settled agricultural villages appear in Central Mexico.

Despite differences in the background of urban development in ancient Mesopotamia and Central Mexico, a study of these two earliest urban societies concluded that "the parallels . . . in the forms that institutions ultimately assumed, as well as in the processes leading to them, suggest that both instances are most significantly characterized by a common core of regularly occurring features."[17] The most basic feature, according to Adams, was the organization of society along hierarchical political lines rather than solely on the basis of kinship. Cities in both ancient Mesopotamia and Central Mexico emerged as theocracies, rather rapidly became militaristic, and developed into the capitals of far-flung empires, an even more complex form of political organization. Another common feature of the development of complex urban social structure in ancient Mesopotamia and Central Mexico was the gradual emergence of social classes and social placement unrelated to kinship and other ascriptive criteria. Adams deals only with the earliest history of cities in these two regions, which have since experienced varied changes. However, his analysis is important because it indicates that the crucial factor in the origin and maintenance of the two earliest, independently evolved urban societies was the development of a complex social organization rather than the build-up of technology.

One of the early civilizations produced in the New World, that of the Maya, is a paradoxical one. The Maya had an agriculture based on maize and other plants, but domesticated few if any animals; nor did they invent the plough, which meant they had to rely entirely on human labor to clear and plant the tropical rain-forests of Central Mexico and modern Guatemala where their civilization reached its height. The Maya developed a form of hieroglyphic writing and an elaborate and very accurate calendar. They were also accomplished astronomers and mathemati-

---

[16] Clark and Piggott, *op. cit.*, pp. 171ff.; Harris, *op. cit.*, pp. 101–4.

[17] Robert McC. Adams, *The Evolution of Urban Society: Early Mesopotamia and Prehispanic Mexico* (1966), pp. 174–75.

cians, even employing the concept of zero, but they never invented the wheel or discovered the use of metals. Mayan astronomy and calendrics were developed for religious purposes since the Maya regulated virtually all aspects of life by involved reckonings of celestial time. The Maya were masters of monumental stone architecture and representational art in carving and painting. The ruins of the "Governors' Palace," in Uxmal, Yucatan, have been compared in artistic and technical perfection with the Parthenon in Athens.

Mayan religion was based on nature worship, and by 1000 B.C. their raised mounds surmounted by temples which, along with related ceremonial buildings, were the major features of Mayan cities began to appear. Cities grew up between 300 B.C. and A.D. 300. At its height, between A.D. 300 and 900, Mayan civilization covered a vast territory encompassing Central Mexico, the Yucatan peninsula, and Guatemala. The Maya still flourished on the Yucatan peninsula at the time of the Spanish conquest, but they had already lost their position of prominence.

A derivative civilization was later formed in the valley of Mexico by the Aztecs, whose religion was based on human sacrifice. The Aztec cities and their capital, Tenochtitlan, with a population of 100,000,

Ruins of Teotihuacan. Shown are the Avenue of the Dead running about a mile from the ceremonial Pyramid of the Moon (foreground), past the Temple of the Sun (left), which stands about 22 stories high, to the remains of the vast administrative complex at the far end. Teotihuacan was inhabited from about 150 B.C. to A.D. 750 and at its peak had a population of 85,000. It is situated about 35 miles northeast of present-day Mexico City. (Georg Gerster, Rapho Guillumette Pictures)

much impressed the Spanish under Cortez, who conquered the Aztecs and their ruler, Montezuma II, in 1519. Tenochtitlan was located on the site now occupied by Mexico City.

The only other indigenous New World civilization was that of the Inca in the Central Andes, in what is now Peru, Bolivia, and Chile. Although agricultural practices were diffused to the Central Andes after 2500 B.C. from the north, ultimately from the Maya, the South American civilization was very different from the Mayan. After 750 B.C., agricultural practices and village life were well established along the Peruvian coast. The Inca developed a system of numerical notation in the *quipu*, a knotted string, but they never developed a system of writing. This lack probably also accounts for their failure to develop very far in such sciences as calendrics, astronomy, or mathematics.

The Inca cities clustered around stone temple pyramids covered with beaten gold in honor of the sun god. The Inca conquered various independent local kingdoms between A.D. 1100 and 1400 and formed a vast empire. The tremendous area, five times the size of Europe, was linked together administratively by a centralized governmental bureaucracy under a god-king and by a stupendous 10,000-mile system of highways.[18] The Inca capital was located at Cuzco, in present-day Ecuador. The modern city of the same name stands on the site of the old capital and has many buildings constructed with stones from ruined Inca buildings. Inca wealth, power, and "welfare statism" were reflected in their elaborate public works such as bridges, canals, and terrace systems, as well as in their large-scale social and economic planning such as resettlement projects, "valley authorities," and city-planning. In contrast to the Maya, the Inca had discovered metal-working at an early date. A few centuries before Christ they used gold, silver, and soon thereafter copper, and by A.D. 1000 were working in bronze. The Inca were conquered by the Spanish led by Pizarro in 1532.

Other Early Urban Development

Agriculture, animal domestication, and other technologies spread from the originating section of the Middle East to Asia, Africa, and Europe, and in some cases were followed by the emergence of cities.

Agricultural practices diffused eastward into Asia after 5000 B.C., and by 2500 B.C. a fully developed urban civilization is found in northwest India in the Indus River Valley of present-day West Pakistan. The major cities of the Indus civilization, Mohenjo-daro and Harappa, were 350 miles apart on the Indus River and appear to have been the twin capitals

[18] Victor Von Hagen, *Highway of the Sun* (1955), p. 295.

of a huge empire covering a territory 950 by 700 by 550 miles.[19] Each of the cities covered at least a square mile and probably contained a population of 20,000. The civilization they headed is characterized as having been highly controlled and planned, and very stable for a period of a thousand years. For example, a standard system of weights and measures existed and was applied to bricks, pottery, and other items which were uniform over the whole territory of the empire. Mohenjo-daro and Harappa themselves were built on identical plans. On the western edge of the city a citadel, about 1,200 feet by 600 feet, was located, built atop a raised mud-brick platform roughly 30 feet high. The complex included ceremonial and public buildings such as a public bath, a large pillared hall, a large building suggesting study activity, and another building, probably a temple. In each city, streets, shops, and the homes of the main population lay below the citadel and were laid out in a grid pattern of blocks of approximately equal size. It is likely that different sections of the city were set aside for particular groups—workers, artisans, merchants, and the ruling group. Large public granaries and flour-mills were found on the outskirts of the cities, indicating centralized control of food production. There is evidence that the Indus society traded with Sumerian cities and possibly other areas.[20] The script

[19] This description is based on Stuart Piggott, *Prehistoric India* (1950).

[20] As a result of the recent apparent discovery along the Persian Gulf of the ruins of Dilmun, a major urban maritime trading kingdom noted in Assyrian records and in the Gilgamesh Epic, new light may soon be available on the Indus Valley civilization and on its relationship to the ancient Mesopotamian cities. See Geoffrey Bibbey, *Looking for Dilmun* (1969).

FIGURE 1.3 • The world's earliest cities first evolved from villages in lower Mesopotamia, where plants and animals had previously been domesticated (see Figure 1.1). Thereafter cities also arose in similar river valleys to which agriculture had spread: the Nile valley, the Indus valley, and along the Yellow River. The cities of Mesoamerica developed independently, as had their agriculture. Source: Gideon Sjoberg, "The Origin and Evolution of Cities." Copyright © 1965 by Scientific American, Inc. All rights reserved.

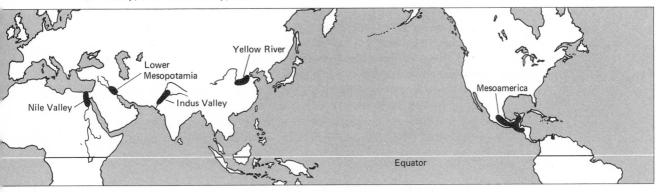

of the Indus River Valley civilization has not yet been deciphered, but the civilization is also enigmatic on other grounds. There are no clear indications of who its founders were or when or from where they came; its ending is also obscure, although it appears to have been violently conquered about 1500 B.C.

Further east in Asia, events are unclear and dating is unreliable before 2500 B.C. By that date civilized urban societies are found in the Yellow River Valley of China. Before then, perhaps about 3500 B.C., agriculture had been established in the area, but whether agriculture was independently invented in China or was diffused from the Middle East—or some combination of the two processes—is not known.[21]

Early Cities in Egypt

The evidence for the diffusion of agriculture and other aspects of Neolithic technology southwest from the Fertile Crescent down the Nile Valley of Egypt is very clear; the domesticated crops and animals have no antecedents in Africa and appear substantially later in Egypt than in Sumer. The transition to settled agricultural communities appears to have taken place around 4000 B.C. in Egypt, and about 3300 B.C. cities and civilization emerged there.

The transition in Egypt . . . to civilization was not, however, the inevitable result of the adoption of these new technologies. . . . The transition was effected in Egypt and probably within a comparatively few generations, by the establishment of the ascendancy of a single ruler, god on earth, as Pharaoh of Upper and Lower Egypt. With the beginning of the first dynasty we move into Egyptian history, and through the media of literature and monumental art perceive a civilization and a constitution wholly unlike that of contemporary Sumer save in its economic and technological basis—an African and not a western Asiatic world.[22]

Egyptian cities were not generally as large or densely settled as those of Sumer, but they suffered from fewer conquests and reconquests and rested on a civilization remarkable for surviving several thousand years with relatively few changes. Egyptian society revolved around the concept of the god-king, or pharaoh, whose capitals were such cities as Memphis and Thebes. In contrast, in Mesopotamia, civil and religious rule, although interrelated, were not identical. Also the religious functionaries were regarded as representatives of the god, not as gods themselves. Power was further fragmented by dispersal of the population in feuding city-states rather than in a unified nation. In Egypt most of the full-time specialists were attached to the god-king or his temple-court, where they produced masterpieces of sculpture, painting, and

[21] Cf. Wheatley, *op. cit.*
[22] Clark and Piggott, *op. cit.*, p. 221.

architecture. Most notable are the Sphinx and great pyramids, the largest of which, built in 2600 B.C., rises 480 feet above the desert. The god-king was also the head of an elaborate centralized civil service. This bureaucracy had at its service clerks, or scribes, trained in hieroglyphic writing; paper (papyrus) and ink, which the Egyptians invented; and the world's first calendar, also an Egyptian invention and similar to the 365-day calendar we use today. The bureaucracy conducted an annual census, collected taxes, and maintained a system of courts. The Egyptians were skilled in the medical sciences and produced treatises on anatomy, surgery, and pharmacy.

Urban Development in Sub-Saharan Africa

Agriculture gradually spread to the rest of Africa, reaching the northwest about 4000-3000 B.C. and East and West Africa between 2000-1000 B.C. The southern areas were introduced to agriculture about 500 B.C. via the expansion of Bantu-speaking peoples from West and Central Africa, who conquered or displaced the existing hunting-gathering peoples.[23]

Early urban development south of the Sahara has been little studied until recent times and large gaps in the archeological record still exist.[24] The urban civilizations of the western Sudan region were among the earliest to emerge, in part under the influence of migration from other regions of Africa and of the Islamic religion which penetrated this part of Africa about this time. Strategically situated between the desert to the north and the forest areas to the south, the area consists of grassy plains and savannahs, and has several very large navigable rivers—the Niger, the Senegal, and the Benue. All of the urban economies that developed were based on extensive trade, particularly in gold from the south and salt from the north. The inland empire of Ghana (whose borders differ from those of modern Ghana) flourished from A.D. 700 to A.D. 1200, and was succeeded by Mali (A.D. 1200–1500), which absorbed Ghana and extended its domination westward. The most important of Mali's cities was Timbuctoo, whose contemporary condition scarcely reflects its earlier glory as the center of trade, scholarship, and empire.[25] Mali was gradually overcome by the Songhoi empire, which reached its zenith between 1350 and 1600. Thereafter the region was increasingly subject to North African and European influence.

The best known of the kingdoms to have flourished in the forest belt south of the savannahs were the Yoruba, the Benin, and the Ashanti. The Yoruba organized their inland city-states about A.D. 1100, reaching

---

[23] Harris, *op. cit.*, pp. 97-101.

[24] The following account is based on Basil Davidson, *African Kingdoms*, (1966), and his *The Lost Cities of Africa* (1959).

[25] Horace Miner, *The Primitive City of Timbuctoo* (1953), pp. 3–12.

the peak of their power with the state of Oyo between 1600 and 1700, although the Yoruba kingdom persisted until British annexation at the end of the nineteenth century. The Benin kingdom, a powerful trading state, ruled from about the twelfth century on in what is now southern Nigeria. The Benin produced the naturalistic bronze heads and figures of their kings which created an artistic and technical sensation when they were exhibited in Europe early in the twentieth century. After 1600 the Ashanti ruled parts of what is now Ghana, the Ivory Coast, and Togo. Their capital, Kumasi, impressed the first Europeans who saw it in the early nineteenth century "by its wide streets, clean houses and sanitary facilities that included such things as built-in plumbing."[26]

Turning to east and south Africa one finds, among many others, the city of Kilwa, situated on an island off the coast of modern Tanzania. Kilwa reached its major prosperity between A.D. 1150–1500, based on trade across the Indian Ocean with Arabia, India, and China. Gold, ivory, iron, and tortoise shell were among the major export items of cities like Kilwa. Trading was so extensive in this Bantu-speaking region that Arabic influences became important in religion and in language. Further south there were kingdoms like those of the Buganda in Uganda, whose king, Mutesa, was visited by Henry Stanley, the British explorer, in 1875. Still further south, the inland Monomotapa empire, a large confederacy of tribes, spread over much of modern Rhodesia. This empire, which flourished between the fifteenth and eighteenth centuries, has left the ruins of a major center, Zimbabwe, remarkable for its monumental stone work in buildings and encircling walls and for its hillside terracing. Many of these kingdoms had no written language but have otherwise been compared in level of civilization with medieval Europe.[27]

Urban Development in Europe

Agriculture, cities, and civilization were relatively late in becoming established in Europe and clearly derived their impetus, although not their content, from the Middle East.[28] The explanation lies partly in environment, for the final retreat of the ice sheets from northern Europe and Britain did not occur until 8300–7900 B.C. When agriculture based on plants domesticated in the Middle East was brought to Europe, it was established earliest—by about 6000 B.C.—in southeastern Europe where

[26] Davidson, *African Kingdoms*, p. 197.

[27] For another point of view, see Gideon Sjoberg, *The Preindustrial City* (1960), p. 33. Sjoberg holds that despite other manifestations of social complexity, the settlements of groups that lacked written languages, such as the Ashanti and the Yoruba in Africa and the Inca in South America, could only be classed as "quasi-urban."

[28] This account is based on Clark and Piggot, *op. cit.*, pp. 244-331, and Sjoberg, *op. cit.*, pp. 56ff.

climate, soil, and topography were most similar to conditions in the Middle East. Agriculture did not reach the heavily forested areas of central Europe with their cold, damp growing conditions until 5000 B.C., and the earliest beginnings of agriculture in Britain date to about 4000 B.C. European agriculture required many adjustments, and effective agricultural production sufficient to maintain Neolithic villages occurred several thousand years after these dates.

The establishment of European cities followed roughly the same sequence. The European areas closest to the Middle East were those that developed cities earliest, by easy contact with the "idea of the city" and also by the actual movement of people. Between 2300 and 1900 B.C. there were disruptions in the established kingdoms of Mesopotamia and Egypt partly because of invasions by "barbarians" (that is, uncivilized, nonurban groups). About this time the earliest cities in Europe began to form. They were the cities of the Mycenaean Greeks on mainland Greece and those of the Minoans on the island of Crete, two interrelated civilizations which emerged about 2000 B.C. The Mycenaeans were great traders—and raiders—whose influence in Europe extended widely, reaching as far as Britain where Mycenaean style is evident in the ruins of Stonehenge.

Between 1200 and 1000 B.C., barbarian war bands, including some tribes from Europe, repeatedly attacked the urban settlements in south-

FIGURE 1.4 ● The sequence of urban evolution begins with the first cities of Mesopotamia, makes its next appearance in the Nile valley, then extends to the Indus, to the eastern Mediterranean region, and to China. Cities emerged later, but independently, in the New World. In each area cities rose and fell but urban life, once established, never wholly disappeared. Source: Gideon Sjoberg, "The Origin and Evolution of Cities." Copyright © 1965 by Scientific American, Inc. All rights reserved.

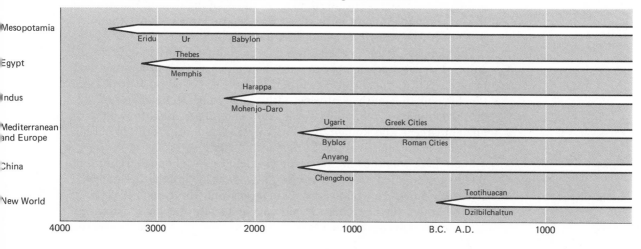

eastern Europe and the Middle East. One result was the further spread into southern Europe of the ideas, techniques, and material goods of city life and civilization. By the seventh century B.C., civilized, urban Europe in the Mediterranean area—the Dorian Greeks in Greece, the Etruscans in central Italy, and the Phoenician-established centers in Spain—contrasted with the nonurban area north of the Alps.

THE ROMAN EMPIRE AND CITIES OF MEDIEVAL EUROPE   About 500 B.C., Rome freed itself from the Etruscans and began the imperial consolidation which was to bring stability to large areas of Europe for hundreds of years. Rome also benefited greatly from the urban culture of classical Greece, which was at its zenith in the fifth and fourth centuries B.C. and included such ideas as the rights of the individual urban citizen and certain other universalistic principles. Rome was the largest ancient city in the Western world, capital of an empire extending over Europe, the British Isles, Asia Minor, and North Africa. The Romans established cities in England and in western Europe as far as the Rhine, as well as in central Europe and the Balkans. (Scandinavia and northern Europe remained nonurban and initial urbanization there dates only to A.D. 1100).

The population of Rome at its peak has been variously estimated at from 250,000 to 1,000,000 inhabitants. Certainly it was the largest European city until the rise of Constantinople and London. With the decline of the empire came the eclipse of the city itself as a great administrative capital. Rome had been the hub of a vast network (52,000 miles) of well-maintained, well-policed roads which facilitated the free movement of goods and people throughout the empire. As the empire slowly disintegrated under invasions and internal troubles, surplus production could no longer be drawn from a wide territory nor, concomitantly, could specialists and others be maintained apart from the soil. It is difficult to assign a specific date to the "fall" of the Roman Empire, but the last Roman emperor in the West was deposed in A.D. 476. Gradually, Rome itself became little more than a straggling town.

The demise of the Roman Empire was followed by a long period of cultural and economic stagnation when cities ceased to flourish over large parts of Europe. During the period of the so-called Dark Ages, from the fifth to the tenth centuries, cities generally declined, trade languished, and intellectual life was at a low ebb. The glories of the cities of ancient Greece and Rome faded into the past, and urbanization did not continue to develop again in Europe until after A.D. 1100.

Feudalism was the characteristic political and economic structure of the European Middle Ages. The orientation was toward the soil and local self-sufficiency. The many petty kingdoms and the constant warfare between them further inhibited contacts and trade over great distances. These conditions prevented concentration of effective surpluses and the support of a specialized division of labor. Significantly, the Roman Catholic Church, the one most nearly universal institution in Europe at this time, and the one resting on a literate specialized clergy, was also an important means of preserving the heritage of Western civilization.

The ruralism of the Middle Ages was gradually transformed under the impact of increasing trade and expanding intellectual horizons. Much long-distance trade was generated by the movement of thousands of Crusaders back and forth across Europe from 1096 to 1291. Their need for food, clothing, shelter, and transportation had to be met at numerous places en route. The Crusaders also brought back new objects, new wants, and new ideas.

Beginning with the eleventh century, cities along the Mediterranean felt the effects of renewed commercial activities. Florence, Genoa, Venice, Pisa, and other cities of the Italian peninsula were among the first to enjoy the benefits of a commercial renaissance. Along the northwest coast of Europe and in the Baltic area, city growth increased under the stimulation of trade. In central Europe growth was slower, but there was growth nevertheless.

As commerce flourished, a merchant class grew in power and ultimately gained ascendancy over the feudal nobility. The merchants represented a way of life based on craft and service specialization, on the concentration of surplus production, and on living apart from the farms. Thus, they constituted a stimulus for the large-scale reappearance of cities in Europe. Another was the rediscovery of the high artistic and intellectual achievements of the urban cultures of classical Greece and the Roman Empire.

Summary

By the early centuries of the Christian era, cities had been established on all of the world's continents except Australia. In each case they were the result of profound technological and social transformations, represented by efficient agriculture and by a differentiated social organization with a new division of labor based on full-time nonagricultural occupational specialization. But these cities were tiny beginnings in an overwhelmingly nonurban and even preurban world; they were small, seldom reaching over 5,000 or 10,000 in size, and included only a small fraction of the total population of the area in which they were located. The vast majority of the world's population still lived as peasants in agricultural villages and a considerable proportion still lived as nomads, hunting and gathering without permanent settlement. Many of the nonurban and preurban groups actively resisted urbanization when they were exposed to it, indicating once again that there was no automatic evolution toward urbanization.

Despite their structural similarities, the early cities and their civilizations show broad cultural variation. All are complex, but the emphases and substance of complexity vary. Even the earliest cities suggest there are many ways to be urban.

In the next chapter we will deal with the so-called Industrial Revolution, which introduced profound changes into the nature of urban development, especially so in Europe where the revolution originated.

Selected Bibliography

BOOKS

Adams, Robert McC., *The Evolution of Urban Society: Early Mesopotamia and Prehispanic Mexico*. Chicago: Aldine, 1966.

Bibbey, Geoffrey, *Looking for Dilmun*. New York: Knopf, 1969.

Braidwood, Robert, and Gordon Willey, eds., *Courses Toward Urban Life*. Viking Fund Publications in Anthropology, #32, 1962. Distributed by the Aldine Publishing Company, Chicago.

Childe, V. Gordon, *Man Makes Himself*. New York: The New American Library, 1951.

Clark, Grahame, and Stuart Piggott, *Prehistoric Societies*. New York: Knopf, 1965.

Coulborn, Rushton, *The Origin of Civilized Societies*. Princeton: Princeton University Press, 1959.

Davidson, Basil, *The Lost Cities of Africa*. Boston: Little, Brown, 1959.

Frankfort, Henri, *The Birth of Civilization in the Near East*. Bloomington: Indiana University Press, 1951.

Fustel de Coulanges, N. D., *The Ancient City*. Garden City, N. Y.: Doubleday Anchor Books, 1955.

Hammond, Mason, assisted by Lester J. Bartson, *The City in the Ancient World*. Cambridge: Harvard University Press, 1972.

Kraeling, Karl, and Robert Adams, eds., *City Invincible: A Symposium on Urbanization and Cultural Development in the Ancient Near East*. Chicago: University of Chicago Press, 1960.

Lampard, Eric, "Historical Aspects of Urbanization," in Philip M. Hauser and Leo F. Schnore, eds., *The Study of Urbanization*. New York: Wiley, 1965.

Redfield, Robert, *The Primitive World and Its Transformation*. Ithaca: Cornell University Press, 1953.

Scientific American, "The Earliest Cities," Part I of *Cities: Their Origin, Growth and Human Impact*, with introductions by Kingsley Davis. San Francisco: W. H. Freeman, 1973.

Singer, Charles, E. J. Holmyard, and A. R. Hall, *A History of Technology*. Vol. 1, *From Early Times to Fall of Ancient Empires*. New York and London: Oxford University Press, 1954.

Sjoberg, Gideon, *The Preindustrial City*, chs. 2 and 3. Glencoe, Ill.: The Free Press, 1960.

Steward, Julian, "Development of Complex Societies: Culture Causality and Law: A Trial Formulation of the Development of Early Civilization," in Julian Steward, ed., *The Theory of Culture Change.* Urbana, Ill.: University of Illinois Press, 1955.

Wheatley, Paul, *The Pivot of the Four Quarters: A Preliminary Enquiry into the Origins and Character of the Ancient Chinese City.* Chicago: Aldine, 1971.

Willis, F. Roy, *Western Civilization: An Urban Perspective.* Vol. 1, *From the Rise of Athens to the Seventeenth Century.* Lexington, Mass.: D. C. Heath, 1973.

ARTICLES

Adams, Robert M., "The Origin of Cities," *Scientific American*, 203 (September 1960), 153–72.

Armillas, Pedro, "Urban Revolution." Part III, "The Concept of Civilization," in David L. Sills, ed., *International Encyclopedia of the Social Sciences*, vol. 16, pp. 218–21. New York: Macmillan Company and The Free Press, 1968.

Bascom, William, "The Urban African and His World," *Cahiers D'Études Africaines* (1963), 163–83.

Blumberg, Rae L., and Robert F. Winch, "Societal Complexity and Familial Complexity: Some Evidence for the Curvilinear Hypothesis," *American Journal of Sociology*, 77 (March 1972), 898–921.

Braidwood, Robert, "The Agricultural Revolution," *Scientific American*, 203 (September 1960), 130–52.

Childe, V. Gordon, "The Urban Revolution," *Town Planning Review*, 21 (April 1950), 3–17.

Freeman, Linton C., and Robert Winch, "Societal Complexity: An Empirical Test of a Typology of Societies," *American Journal of Sociology*, 62 (March 1957), 461–66.

Harris, David R., "New Light on Plant Domestication and the Origins of Agriculture: A Review," *Geographical Review*, 57 (January 1967), 90–107.

Solheim, Wilhelm G. "An Earlier Agricultural Revolution," *Scientific American*, 226 (April 1972), 34–41.

Wirth, Louis, "Urbanism as a Way of Life," *American Journal of Sociology*, 44 (July 1938), 3–24.

2 • The Preindustrial City and the Industrial Revolution

 Two great series of technological developments, called "revolutions" for purposes of simplicity, underlie urban development. The first of these, the Agricultural Revolution, described in the previous chapter, ultimately enabled cities to emerge in various parts of the world. The second, the Industrial Revolution, enabled cities to grow to very large size, and in many instances the city population eventually became the majority population of entire nations. It may be said that the Agricultural Revolution made it possible for cities to exist and that the Industrial Revolution made it possible for cities to dominate the world. The date 1750 is usually assigned as the "beginning" of the Industrial Revolution in England where it originated. Obviously any precise date is somewhat arbitrary.

The preindustrial world was characterized by the small percentage of population living in cities and the small size of preindustrial cities. In countries where cities existed, usually no more than 10 percent and often less than five percent of the population were able to live in urban settlements. The best available figures indicate that in 1800 only 2.4 percent of the world's population lived in cities (defined as communities of at least 20,000 inhabitants).[1] In the preindustrial period cities of 100,000 or more were rare, although under certain social as well as economic conditions some surpassed even this size. Rome in the second century A.D., Constantinople as the later political successor to Rome, Baghdad before A.D. 1000, the cities of Sung China between A.D. 1100 and 1300, and Edo (Tokyo), Kyoto, and Osaka in seventeenth- and eighteenth-century Japan all had populations well above 100,000, and in some cases, possibly even a million. However, most preindustrial cities, including many important ones, had populations of five to ten thousand.[2]

[1] Kingsley Davis, "The Origin and Growth of Urbanization in the World," *American Journal of Sociology*, 60 (March, 1955), 433.

[2] These statements are based on Gideon Sjoberg, *The Preindustrial City* (1960), pp. 82–85.

Social Change in Post-medieval Europe

Urban development in Western civilization advanced not only in response to the technological aspects of industrialization but also as a consequence of a transformation of the social structure. Major debates still rage in the social sciences about the precise role of technological and nontechnological factors in social change. Although we cannot pinpoint the relative contribution of each set of factors, there is no doubt that social organization of a certain type was a precondition for the emergence of urban industrial communities in Europe and North America. An important question is whether a similar type of social structure is necessary for cities to develop successfully in the little-urbanized parts of the world.

Modern city growth in Europe was stimulated by the demise of feudal systems of government and by the emergence of new ideals and forms in political, social, and intellectual life. Nationhood gained currency, first in monarchical and later in democratic forms. Large areas were unified under the impetus of nationalism, with a resultant expansion of areas covered by common coinage, long transportation systems, absence of frequent customs and toll collection, and the like. The social system was marked by the increasing influence of a major new middle class—merchants and others whose interests and wealth were not based on agriculture or land ownership. The religious unity of Europe under Roman Catholicism was shattered by the Protestant Reformation in the sixteenth century. New views also arose concerning the position and rights of the individual. The invention of the printing press by Gutenberg in 1455 enabled knowledge and ideas to be disseminated on a much broader base than ever before in history. Columbus' discovery of the New World in 1492 opened up major new commercial opportunities as well as avenues of social mobility.

According to Mumford, the modern state began to take form during the fourteenth century, and epitomized the principles of uniformity and centralization.[3] Under their impetus the dispersed feudal estates were consolidated; power and population were no longer scattered. Cities with royal courts typically embodied central economic as well as political power, for the nobility were a major group of consumers and also the source of capital for economic enterprises. "After the sixteenth century, accordingly, . . . about a dozen towns quickly reached a size not attained in the Middle Ages even by a bare handful: in a little while London had 250,000 inhabitants, Naples, 240,000, Milan over 200,000, Palermo and Rome, 100,000, Lisbon, port of a great monarchy, over 100,000, similarly, Seville, Antwerp, and Amsterdam; while Paris in 1594 had 180,000."[4]

[3] Lewis Mumford, *The City in History* (1961), pp. 351–56.
[4] *Ibid.*, p. 355.

Religious as well as political factors helped lay the foundation for modern Western societies. In the Renaissance a major shift in social values turned men's attention to the things of this world. The Renaissance marked the freeing of man's intellect from the medieval outlook. The consequences of the Renaissance were profound not only for the arts and literature but also for all fields of human endeavor. A spirit of inquiry affected the growth of the sciences, and the philosophy of humanism spurred the understanding and well-being of man. All of these values went into building a civilization more complex and more far-flung than any that had preceded it. An intellectual milestone was the elaboration by Copernicus between 1513 and 1543 of a new system of astronomy postulating that the earth rotated around the sun. This heliocentric theory was in direct contrast to the so-called Ptolemaic or geocentric theory, which placed the earth at the center of the universe, a view that had been held since ancient times.

Max Weber has pointed out how certain features of the Protestant Reformation were conducive to the expansion of technology and production.[5] Weber noted that the puritan aspects of Protestantism fostered economic rationality. High value is placed on an active rather than a contemplative life, unremitting labor is moral virtue and duty, and the more productive the labor is the more it signifies that the individual performing it had found favor in the eyes of God. Hence success, profit, and wealth are not necessarily evil. They are vices only if they lead to idleness and dissipation.

Such an outlook was a powerful motivation to work; it also placed a high moral value on the material consequences of one's work. It was a set of beliefs consonant with the technological innovations of industrial capitalism. Weber did not hold that he had proved a causal relationship between Protestantism and the rise of modern industrial society. However, it has been noted that although the ideology of the "Protestant Ethic" originated with small religious sects in the sixteenth century, it spread throughout Western civilization among all religious groups and coincided with the productive expansion of the Industrial Revolution.

Industrial Technology and City Growth

Technology had made steady although slow advances before the Industrial Revolution, the processes of metal-working becoming especially

[5] Max Weber, *The Protestant Ethic and the Spirit of Capitalism*, tr. Talcott Parsons (1958). This work was originally published in 1905. Critiques of Weber's thesis include N. Birnbaum, "Conflicting Interpretations of the Rise of Capitalism: Marx and Weber," *British Journal of Sociology*, 4 (June 1953), 125–41: Kurt Samuelsson, *Religion and Economic Action: A Critique of Max Weber* (1961, originally published in Swedish, 1957); and Alvin Gouldner and R. Peterson, *Notes on Technology and the Moral Order* (1962).

important, but these advances did not transform the carrying capacity of the economy as radically as the Industrial Revolution did.[6]

Essentially the Industrial Revolution consisted in the substitution of machines for tools and in the replacement of inanimate sources of energy for animate sources. For the first time in history man had machines—objects capable of operating separately from him—rather than tools, which were basically an extension of his limbs. For the first time, too, man had available sources of energy other than those of his own body and of domesticated animals such as oxen, horses, mules, camels, llamas, and elephants. (Water power, the one major source of inanimate energy before the Industrial Revolution, was by its nature limited in location and usefulness.) The first major new source of inanimate energy was coal, which was used to propel steam engines. Later, oil, gas, and then hydroelectric and nuclear power were used to run a variety of machines.

[6] Copper was the first useful metal man discovered, and by approximately 3000 B.C. bronze, an alloy of copper and tin, was in use. Tools such as axes, ploughs, and hoes made of bronze were much more efficient and durable than those of stone, wood, or bone. The invention of techniques of iron-working about 1000 B.C. brought even more efficient tools into being and still further enhanced man's ability to obtain sustenance from the environment. These dates refer to the discovery of the processes, not to the period during which their use was widespread or common.

FIGURE 2.1 ● World use of coal, oil, and gas has boomed in a single century. The substitution of inanimate sources of energy for the work energy of men and animals is one of the hallmarks of industrialism. Used to propel machines, these new sources of energy have enormously increased productivity. Source: *Population Bulletin* (April 1971), p. 10. Based on data from Political and Economic Planning, *World Population and Resources,* London: George Allen and Unwin, Ltd., 1964; and United Nations, *World Energy Supplies,* New York: Issues for 1958 (#1), 1960 (#3), and 1970 (#13).

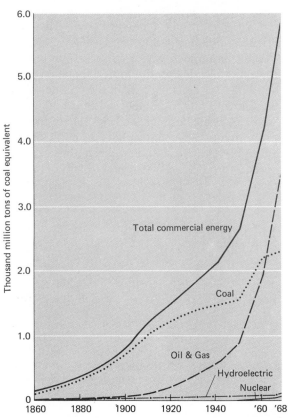

The significance of the Industrial Revolution was that it immensely broadened the economic capacity of society. With the application of new and revolutionary forms of technology to manufacturing, transportation, and warfare, the basis was laid for the growth of cities larger than the world had ever seen before. Steam power harnessed to the factory machine made possible the production of far more commodities than could be fabricated in a handicraft technology. With the increase in factory output and the intensification of commercial activities to dispose of fabricated commodities, more and more workers were needed to tend the machines or perform the various tasks related to trade. As the cities of Europe and America became increasingly industrialized, they drew to them vast numbers of country and village folk. The die was thus cast for a new type of community in the Western world—the mass-production city. Manchester and Birmingham in England and Pittsburgh in the United States were to become symbols of the pervasive economic changes based on the new technology.

The Factory System

As long as industry was in the handicraft stage there was no reason why concentration of population for industrial purposes alone should take place on a very large scale. Certainly the advantages of concentration were outweighed by disadvantages: transportation facilities were not adequate for the distribution of fabricated commodities; sufficient food and shelter for a concentrated population could not be provided; the labor supply was inadequate, for workers were characterized more by their immobility than mobility. Even during the period when factories were operated by water-driven machinery, the geographical location of cities usually forbade any great expansion of industries. Only when the steam-driven engine came into universal use did workers concentrate in large numbers in industrial centers.

As the Industrial Revolution in Europe and America gained headway, new labor-saving devices appeared, and these in turn were instrumental in transferring all kinds of home industries to the factory and thereby accentuating the concentration of population in the industrial centers.

The modern industrial town or city is, therefore, partly a product of steam and, more recently, electrical power. By its very nature steam is economical when applied to large manufacturing units concentrated within a small area. Consequently, the power-driven machine drew manufacturing out of the home and placed it in a centralized location.

As the factory system expanded to meet the needs and demands of a growing population, more workers were required to tend the machines and dispose of the finished products. To the factories in towns and cities, then, flocked rural people, attracted not only by the novelty of city life but also by the possibilities of greater economic rewards. Here they crowded into stuffy and unsanitary quarters near the industrial plants.

City growth in England represents very well the relationship between manufacturing and urbanization. The technological revolution as applied to industry got under way in England earlier than in any other country, and at a time when the world's natural resources were virtually untouched. Vasts amounts of raw materials were brought to the British Isles to feed the maws of the machinery, whose insatiable appetites were forever increasing. To the factories and mills came people in search of work, settling in towns and cities close to the places of employment. Thus such cities as Birmingham, Leeds, Manchester, and Sheffield became vast concentrations of factories surrounded by the homes of the people who manned the machines.

The Mechanization of Agriculture

While steam and electricity were being utilized to turn the wheels of factories in the great industrial centers, mechanical energy and scientific knowledge were being applied to agriculture to increase the output of farm and ranch. But, while the revolution in industry and the expansion of commerce demanded more workers, the revolution in agriculture made it possible for fewer people to supply the basic needs of an expanding population. The result was a gradual divorcement of men from the soil.

In 1750 the great majority of the labor force—about 85 to 90 percent—in what was to become the United States was engaged in agriculture. These percentages steadily declined to 80 percent by 1805 and 70 percent by 1830.[7] In 1870 over half (50.3 percent) of the United States' labor force was employed in agriculture, while in 1970 less than five percent of the employed were engaged in agricultural occupations—farmers and farm managers, farm foremen, and laborers.[8] In 1970 this small group produced not only enough food to maintain the United States as one of the best-fed nations, but great quantities of food and raw materials were shipped abroad, and staggering surpluses piled up in storage bins. This has come about not only through mechanization but also through the application of scientific knowledge to increase soil fertility, improve plant and animal strains, and reduce wastage in various ways.

[7] The accuracy and sources of these figures are discussed in Sidney Aronson, *Status and Kinship in the Higher Civil Service* (1964), ch. 3.

[8] Frederick J. Dewhurst and Associates, *America's Needs and Resources* (1955), p. 732; and *Statistical Abstract of the United States* (1970), p. 226.

Sociological Analysis of Urban-Industrial Development

A variety of conceptual approaches has been applied to determine the essential social characteristics and dynamics of urban-industrialism. These approaches include the formulation of typologies and the presentation of evolutionary frameworks, approaches that are often related. The detailing of social complexity is a key feature of the analyses and is dealt with in several major ways. Another important methodological problem is the separation conceptually and, if possible, empirically of the social effects of urbanism and industrialism.

The Ideal Type

The concept of an "ideal type" has been applied to communities as it has to other social phenomena. This conceptual device is a constructed proposition which designates the hypothetical characteristics of a "pure" or "ideal" type. As used in this sense the terms *pure* or *ideal* have nothing to do with subjective evaluations of the phenomena being studied. The concept merely hypothesizes certain qualities or characteristics of the phenomenon in question, in this instance the community. Actually, no single city or town would conform absolutely to the ideal type that is postulated, but the concept has the value of providing a focus for the study of community life. A problem for the social scientist is to examine empirically the attributes of particular communities from the standpoint of the ideal type that has been hypothesized. This procedure clearly implies a comparative analysis, since communities may be compared on the basis of their actual as well as hypothesized attributes.

In the following discussion, some ideal types of communities will be considered. For the purposes of this book, only the most abbreviated and elementary analysis is possible.

REDFIELD'S FOLK-URBAN TYPOLOGY   Robert Redfield, the anthropologist, has provided a typology of a folk society or community which is by implication the polar opposite of an urban community.[9] The folk community (or society) as Redfield views it is "small, isolated, nonliterate, and homogeneous, with a strong sense of group solidarity. . . . Behavior is traditional, spontaneous, uncritical, and personal; there is no legislation or habit of experiment and reflection for intellectual ends. . . . The sacred prevails over the secular, the economy is one of status rather than of the market."[10] This, clearly, is stated as an ideal type; it may not conform precisely to any particular community.

[9] Robert Redfield, "The Folk Society," *American Journal of Sociology*, 52 (January, 1947), 293–308. Redfield initially developed this idea in his *Tepoztlan: A Mexican Village* (1930). Subsequently, he modified this theory somewhat in his *The Little Community* (1955).

[10] Redfield, "The Folk Society," p. 297.

Redfield never specified clearly the characteristics of the urban portion of the typology; by implication urban life was characterized by the opposite traits of the folk community. However, he did define the peasant in a way which suggests that the urban end of the typology could be subdivided. To a limited extent Redfield enlarged on this theme in his later work, but major reformulation in this direction was done by Gideon Sjoberg. According to Redfield, "There were no peasants before the first cities. . . . The peasant is a rural native whose long established order of life takes important account of the city. . . . Peasantry then is . . . that style of life which prevailed outside of cities yet within their influence during the long period between the urban revolution and the industrial revolution."[11]

A criticism of the folk-urban concept of community has been made by Lewis, who restudied the Mexican town of Tepoztlan some years after Redfield had conducted research in the same community and formulated his well-known typology. It is Lewis' criticism that the folk-urban concept "focuses attention primarily on the city as a source of change, to the exclusion or neglect of other factors of an internal or external nature," and that "culture change may not be a matter of a folk-urban progression, but rather an increasing or decreasing heterogeneity of culture elements in the society at large," and that the incorporation of these elements do not necessarily make the community more "urban."[12]

Sjoberg finds the concept of "folk" community acceptable provided it is not applied to relatively complex communities. He would reserve the concept of "feudal" community for those units that include a relatively large peasant population and a small elite. Such communities, as he views them, are more heterogeneous, more stratified, and more occupationally differentiated than folk communities. They contain a small corps of literate persons, a government apparatus, and a priestly class. The folk community as the term is applied by Redfield may be more appropriate for tribal communities than for communities that are made up of peasants "who have a fairly complex form of social organization and who have fairly frequent contacts with the outside world."[13] Sjoberg has, in effect, substituted for Redfield's folk-urban dichotomy a three-part typology: folk (nonurban), preindustrial urban (feudal, peasant), and industrial urban. Sjoberg's distinctions between the two types of urbanism are detailed later in this chapter.

A similar distinction is noted by Foster,[14] whose concept of "peasant" community is similar to that of Sjoberg's feudal community. The typical

[11] Robert Redfield, *The Primitive World and its Transformation* (1953), pp. 31, 53.

[12] Oscar Lewis, "Tepoztlan Restudied," *Rural Sociology*, 18 (June, 1953), 130–31.

[13] Gideon Sjoberg, "Folk and 'Feudal' Societies," *American Journal of Sociology*, 58 (November 1952), 231–40.

[14] George M. Foster, *Traditional Cultures: The Impact of Technological Change* (1962), pp. 46–49.

tribal community, according to Foster, is self-sufficient both ec ly and culturally. It produces its own food and artifacts, ma own indigeneous social system, and exists in a state of cultu tion—or has done so until recent times. The peasant communi other hand, "represents the rural expression of large, class-st economically complex, preindustrial civilizations, in which t commerce and craft specializations are well developed, in whicl is commonly used, and in which market disposition is the goal fo of the producer's effort."[15] The peasant (or feudal) community new type; it has existed for thousands of years, and exists i numbers today, mainly in the underdeveloped areas of the world. Vestiges of such communities remain even in the industrial societies of the West. Although the peasant community represents a distinct way of life, its contacts with the city, however tenuous they may be, have served as channels for the diffusion of urban culture into the smaller community.

OTHER TYPOLOGIES   Many other typologies have been developed to focus on the nature of modern urbanism. Often these have taken the form of dichotomies or polar types, but are readily reformulated into continua in which the characteristics under review are cast into a range of variation. Polar typologies and continua are one kind of ideal type; they are not intended to represent reality but are guides to the study of empirical data.

Major polar typologies dealing with the community include Ferdinand Tönnies' *Gemeinschaft-Gesellschaft;* Emile Durkheim's mechanical versus organic solidarity; Henry Maine's status-contract; Howard P. Becker's sacred-secular; Max Weber's traditional versus rational authority; and Charles Cooley's primary-nonprimary groups. We shall briefly describe some of these typologies in the following paragraphs.

Despite their diversity these typologies have in common the contrast between simple and more complex societies, although they differ in terms of the aspect of social complexity on which they focus. More recently theorists have preferred the term *differentiation* to *complexity.* Modern urban-industrial societies are the most complex and differentiated of all, with cities manifesting the largest concentration of institutional specialization, diversity of roles, and impersonal relationships.

Tönnies' ideal types, *Gemeinschaft* and *Gesellschaft,* were presented in a book of that title in 1887, and have no precise equivalents in English. *Gemeinschaft* represents a kind of behavior in which calculation, efficiency, and specific goals are subordinated to the social relationships themselves. The interactions between parent and child, between husband and wife, and among kinsmen are examples, as in interaction among residents of a common locality such as the immediate neighborhood. In these cases the participants share a "community of feeling . . .

[15] *Ibid.,* pp. 47–48.

that results from likeness and from shared life-experience."[16] In contrast, *Gesellschaft* relationships are characterized by the separation of means from ends. The end or goal, the task to be performed, whether on an industrial assembly line, in a retail store, or in an office bureaucracy, is paramount, and personal relationships are subordinate. Human contacts thereby become instrumental to the effective achievement of the overall purpose. Examples of *Gesellschaft* relationships are those in the factory or the army. Obviously no relationships are solely *Gemeinschaft* or solely *Gesellschaft* and the two kinds of interaction have existed throughout human history; however, *Gesellschaft* relationships are more characteristic of city life. Indeed, Tönnies indicated that there was a progressive shift from societies based on *Gemeinschaft* to those based on *Gesellschaft*, with the expansion of city life playing a key part in the shift.

Durkheim's ideal-type constructs of mechanical and organic solidarity present contrasting bases of social integration. Mechanical solidarity is characteristic of societies which are simple in the sense that their social unity derives from similarity and homogeneity; social unity is mechanical and automatic in that the parts of society are interchangeable. Durkheim noted that in such societies law tends to be criminal law and is repressive because it focuses mainly on punishing criminal acts against society from which the individuals, being similar to one another in values and beliefs, cannot readily be distinguished. In contrast, organic solidarity characterizes complex societies in which the diversity of individual positions and life experiences is associated with a social unity based on the interdependence of specialized parts. In such societies, Durkheim indicated that civil law predominates since legal concerns dealing with contractual and other limited obligations between dissimilar individuals become more numerous; punishment takes the form of restitution and compensation rather than physical repression, violence, and vengeance.

As with Tönnies' *Gemeinschaft-Gesellschaft*, Durkheim's typology was viewed as a continuum of gradual evolution in which there was a progressive shift to societies dominated by organic solidarity. He associated the dynamics of the change with the increasing size and density of population, the ease and rapidity of communication, and especially with the increase in the division of labor. All of these traits are linked with the growth of cities, and are greatly accentuated by the development of industrial cities. Although Durkheim formulated no specifically urban theory, the shifting balance of mechanical and organic solidarity is clearly part of the process of change toward an urban society.

[16] Horace Miner, "Community-Society Continua," *International Encyclopedia of the Social Sciences* (1968), vol 3, p. 175.

SHORTCOMINGS OF THE TYPOLOGICAL APPROACH While it is doubtless already evident that the concepts embodied in such terms as folk-urban, *Gemeinschaft-Gesellschaft*, and mechanical versus organic solidarity are so broad that they are invariably vague, it is our view in this book that they do provide a perspective and that even with their limitations they are valuable conceptual tools. In any case, a community typology should be considered a "first step" in community analysis. It must be kept in mind that these typologies are essentially hypotheses rather than proved end-results of research.

The major criticisms of the typologies center around four problems. (1) The unit of analysis is unclear. Thus, sometimes it is the total society and sometimes the city; often it shifts within the same typology. In Redfield's analysis, for example, one cannot pinpoint when the analysis refers to urban society and when to the city itself. In such circumstances the role of the city is virtually impossible to untangle. (2) Although the typologies tend to focus on one variable, there is little analytic separation of variables. A crucial instance is the lack of analytic separation of the effects of industrialism from those of urbanism, a topic to be discussed more fully later in this chapter. (3) Even when they assume the form of continua, the typologies fail to deal adequately with the range of cities. (4) The typologies also fail to deal with the range of variation in urban (and nonurban) characteristics *within* cities.

Parsons' Neoevolutionary System

In his earlier work, Talcott Parsons developed a four-fold typology for classifying societies.[17] The two key "pattern variables" were particularism-universalism and ascription-achievement. The first pair of variables refers to whether the interaction of individuals is governed by standards developed for that relationship among *particular* individuals (for example, as Parsons notes, a man falls in love with a particular blonde not the category blondeness) or whether the relationship is governed by universal standards (for example, "all men are equal before the law"). The second pair refers to whether the basic placement of the individual in society is a result of characteristics over which he or she has little control such as lineage, sex, age, race (ascription) or a result of characteristics he or she has "earned" such as education and skills (achievement). The two sets of variables, in Parsons' analysis, yield four types of society—particularistic-ascriptive; particularistic-achievement; universalistic-ascriptive; and universalistic-achievement. As Parsons noted, contrast-

[17] Talcott Parsons, *The Social System* (1951), pp. 58–67; see also Talcott Parsons, R. F. Bales, and E. A. Shils, *Working Papers in the Theory of Action* (1953), and Talcott Parsons, "Pattern Variables Revisited: A Response to Robert Dubin," *American Sociological Review,* 25 (August 1960), 467–83.

ing the first and fourth types yields constructs similar to the familiar dichotomies such as *Gemeinschaft-Gesellschaft*.[18] Particularistic-ascriptive societies are those in which the family and kinship are the chief organizing structure; they are also nonurban. Universalistic-achievement societies are represented by highly industrialized societies. Although by no means a definitive test of Parsons' scheme, it is certainly true that the social changes of the Industrial Revolution were in the direction of more inclusive norms and of the impersonal judgment of performance.

Although the evolutionary implications of Parsons' analysis of social change are evident in the four-fold typology, they are fully developed in his most recent work,[19] which is much more sophisticated and larger in scope than those cited previously. While still subject to detailed evaluation,[20] Parsons' evolutionary scheme is an important attempt at providing a complete framework for the analysis of modern industrial society. For the purposes of this book its main shortcoming is a lack of focus on the city and urbanism, even though these are subsumed in his analysis.

Parsons' scheme is neoevolutionary in that it is multilinear and does not involve the idea of *necessary* progression from one evolutionary stage to another. In this brief review we can highlight only the most relevant aspects of his scheme, particularly his analysis of differentiation within societies. Differentiation involves the separation, specificity, and specialization of the roles, institutions, and activities of a society, the results of which are the increasing autonomy and further development of each of the separate "parts" and the consequent necessity for new integrative mechanisms. In Parsons' own terms:

A unit, sub-system, or category of units or sub-systems having a single, relatively well-defined place in the society divides into units or systems (usually two) which differ *both* in structure and functional significance for the wider system. To take a familiar example . . . , the kinship-organized household in predominantly peasant societies is *both* the unit of residence and the primary unit of agricultural production. In certain societies, however, most productive work is performed in specialized units, such as workshops, factories, or offices manned by people who are *also* members of family households. Thus two sets of roles and collectivities have become differentiated, and their functions separated.[21]

The three evolutionary stages Parsons describes differ in their degree of differentiation. (1) *Primitive* societies are the least differentiated and

[18] Parsons, Bales, and Shils, *op cit.*, p. 207.
[19] Talcott Parsons, *Societies: Evolutionary and Comparative Perspectives* (1966); Talcott Parsons, *The System of Modern Societies* (1971); and Victor Lidz and Talcott Parsons, eds., *Readings in Premodern Societies* (1972).
[20] See, for example, the review symposium by Wolf Heydebrand and Jackson Toby in *Contemporary Sociology*, 1 (September 1972), 387–401.
[21] Parsons, *Societies: Evolutionary and Comparative Perspectives*, p. 22.

contain no cities. (2) All *intermediate* societies are characterized by the emergence of written language and major differentiation but are of several subtypes, including the *archaic*, which is associated with the earliest cities;[22] the *"historic" intermediate empires* of China, India, Islam, and Rome; and the *"seedbed"* societies (ancient Israel and Greece). (3) The *modern* societies of northern Europe and the United States all have as a distinguishing feature a legal system that is both based on universalistic principles and autonomous in the sense that executive and legislative powers are separate. Parsons emphasizes the importance of such a legal system in serving to integrate and legitimate the increasingly differentiated modern society.

Parsons does not view the Industrial Revolution mainly in its technological or narrow economic sense but as part of the trend "which involved new orders of differentiation and increased organic solidarity in Durkheim's sense . . . in that vast increases in economic productivity entailed immense extension of the division of labor in the social sense."[23] A key element in increasing economic differentiation was the gradual extension of the market system, that is, the production of items for monetary sale, to include a wider range of products. Before the Industrial Revolution few products were sold for money; at most, foodstuffs grown in the immediate area might be exchanged at a local "market" town for handicraft products.

Economic differentiation in the Industrial Revolution was also importantly manifested in the separation of the functions of production, labor, capital, and management, each of which became organized in a separate set of bureaucracies. The contrast between the artisan who combines all four functions in himself and the modern factory worker is extreme. Economic differentiation occurred slowly and piecemeal. Thus, the "family firm" is a still-existing, although relatively unimportant type; the family owns and manages the company, which may be quite large, and is already highly bureaucratized in terms of production technology and the hiring and organization of workers.

In addition to the Industrial Revolution, Parsons saw two other major sets of causes for the new levels of differentiation in modern society: the changing place of religion in the seventeenth century and the "democratic" revolution of the eighteenth century. The Protestant Reformation, which had its roots in the doctrines Martin Luther promulgated in the early sixteenth century, not only shattered the religious unity of Western Europe but also, in time, led to further religious diversity as many ´Protestant denominations came into existence. Most fundamentally religion was no longer the basis of social unity, and ethnic, territorial, and governmental organization no longer coincided with

---

[22] *Ibid,* p. 52.
[23] Parsons, *The System of Modern Societies,* p. 74.

religious membership. In Parsons' terms a greater differentiation developed among religion, government, and nongovernmental secular culture. The democratic revolution encouraged further differentiation between the broad norms of society and the government: the "subject" of a monarchy became a "citizen" in a democracy with rights which the government was to protect.

DIFFERENTIATION IN THE BRITISH COTTON INDUSTRY   Neil Smelser, a student of Parsons, provides a specific case of the differentiation process that took place in the Industrial Revolution, namely the way in which the factory production of cotton cloth was linked with changes in the family division of labor and family consumption patterns.[24] Smelser's analysis supports Parsons' contention that

[t]he critical development was the differention of labor (or, more technically, of services) from the diffuse matrix in which it had been imbedded. This differentiation involved distinguishing the work-role complex from the family household and also increased the "mobility of labor"—the readiness of households to respond to employment opportunities by changing residences or learning new skills. These changes affected the structures of family systems and local communities profoundly. Many features of the modern form of nuclear-family kinship structure gradually emerged during the nineteenth century. And industrial society became urbanized by a degree never before known in history.

These processes established what sociologists call the *occupational role*, specifically contingent upon status in an employing organization structurally distinct from the household. Usually the employing organization has only one member in common with the household; it also has premises, disciplines, authority systems, and property distinct from those of the household. Typically the employed person receives (according to his employment status and role performance) a money income that is the main source of his household's access to the market for consumer goods. The employing organization markets its product and pays the employee wages or a salary, whereas the typical peasant or artisan sold his own products. The organization thus comes between the worker and the consumer market.[25]

Smelser's anaylsis indicates that just prior to the Industrial Revolution the British cotton industry was a "putting out" system,[26] that is, the raw cotton was "put out" to be spun into thread and then woven into cloth. This was typically a rural family operation carried on at home in the winter while the family farmed during the summer. Spinning and other steps in the process were performed by the wife and children and the husband did the weaving. The work was all done manually on the spinning wheel and hand loom. This "cottage industry" enabled the

---

[24] Neil J. Smelser, *Social Change in the Industrial Revolution: An Application of Theory to the British Cotton Industry, 1770–1840* (1959).

[25] Parsons, *The System of Modern Societies*, p. 77.

[26] The following description is based on Smelser, *op. cit.*

Textile production was transformed from a family enterprise carried on at home to factory production by individuals and currently is highly automated. (Merrimack Valley Textile Museum—top and middle; J.P. Stevens & Co., Inc.—bottom)

family to combine economic activities with the supervision and training of its children. It was also compatible with rural residence and with the running of a farm. The major forms of differentiation under the "putting out" system were that the spinners and weavers did not own or control the raw cotton and they did not control the distribution of the finished cloth. Thus, actual production had begun to be separated from the decisions bearing on production, distribution, and control of capital.

Beginning about 1760, a series of changes in the British cotton industry culminated in urban factory production of cloth and in the demise of the family as the production unit. Smelser points out that, although his analysis focuses on the technological aspects of the Industrial Revolution, many other features of British society enabled technology to change: the social stratification system, political arrangements, and a series of dissatisfactions which were legitimated by the dominant religious and other value systems.

Technologically, the major changes began in the 1760's and 1770's with the introduction of the spinning jenny, the water frame, and the carding machine. Until about 1790, the impact of these changes was mainly to transform spinning from a home to a mill operation. This increased the differentiation between the actual production process and the control of production, which was now in the hands of mill owners. However, even in the mills the family was still the production unit. A widespread pattern, as Smelser's statistics show, was for the father and/or mother to be employed in the operation of the mill machinery, with their children serving as assistants.

As spinning production increased, so did the pressure for more productivity in the weaving process. Cartwright invented the power loom in 1785 and it gradually replaced the hand loom, which meant that weaving became a full-time occupation rather than the part-time job of the male head of the farm. Steam power also began to be applied to spinning, which resulted, over several decades, in the construction of large factories in which women and boys tended the machinery, an operation not requiring great strength or training. The number of assistants required as machines became larger and more productive grew beyond the capacity of the family to supply them from among their own children and relatives. Spinning and weaving were combined in single factories and this further increased the size of the firms.

The large steam-driven factories were no longer country mills; rather, they were now urban installations where large amounts of labor, raw materials, and capital were centralized. Manchester, a leading center of cotton production in Britain, grew by 22 percent between 1801 and 1811, by 40 percent between 1811 and 1821, and by 47 percent between 1821 and 1831.[27] By 1831 its population was almost 228,000, probably the first industrially based city in history.

[27] *Ibid.*, pp. 188, 193.

The overall effect of the mechanization of spinning and weaving in these factories on the family was twofold. First, the family itself was no longer the productive unit—the work of family members had been differentiated. The family members were employed as individuals at separate tasks, and often the male breadwinner was not even employed in the cotton factory but in another urban occupation. Second, since the family no longer worked together, its work activities had become differentiated from its other functions, primarily socialization.

Several events in Britain in the first half of the nineteenth century underscore the several aspects of family differentiation. A series of laws were passed limiting children's work hours and requiring them to attend school. Such legislation was necessary to protect the child from exploitation at work where family supervision was no longer available and also indicated the necessity of the child to have more complex training than he could receive at home. Trade unions and the so-called "friendly societies" became increasingly important as mediators between individual family members and industry. To protect the family in its new industrial environment, such institutions as savings banks, loan societies, "poor laws" (a form of welfare), and cooperative societies also developed.

Although Smelser's analysis emphasizes the differentiation of family functions in the Industrial Revolution, he does note that many other aspects of differentiation could be discussed: the differentiation of education from religious training through the secularization of schools; the separation of political parties from aristocratic family cliques; and the replacement of political and class patronage by a merit system in the military and in the civil service.

Urbanization and Industrialization

As we noted earlier of the typological approach, a major problem in analyzing the social effects of industrialization is separating its consequences from those of urbanization. As yet there are no definitive empirically based statements, but several fruitful approaches to the problem have been developed. Attempts to formulate the essential characteristics of urbanism under different economic conditions include the broad typologies of Sjoberg, Wirth, and Shevky and Bell. Another approach focuses on the individual, examining the impact of differing amounts of urban and/or industrial experience. A third approach, often subsumed under the two just mentioned but analytically separable from them, involves the cross-cultural comparison of cities and industrial systems. The efforts to clarify the basic features of urbanism and industrialism have intensified in recent years, partly because of the availability of a greater range of data, and partly because of increased interest. As both urbanism and industrialism spread in varying degrees to all corners of the world, there is more than theoretical interest in the question of whether either or both of these conditions necessarily involve Westernization in a social sense.

Sjoberg's Study of Preindustrial Social Structure

It has been suggested that certain features of social organization are common to all preindustrial cities, thus emphasizing that cities depend for their existence on an adequate social base, as well as on technological and environmental factors. This does not mean that all preindustrial cities have identical social structures; rather, their diversity is a series of variations on the same theme.

Sjoberg's pioneering study of preindustrial cities, both old and relatively new, Western and non-Western in culture, concluded that these cities are characterized by particular systems of social stratification, family and kinship, political organization, religion, education, and communication.[28]

Some of the characteristic differences which Sjoberg and others have observed are considered below.

1. In industrial or modern cities the loosely organized nuclear family is predominant. The extended or joint family system, with members of a larger kinship group commonly residing in a single household, is characteristic of preindustrial cities.

2. The class system in industrial cities tends to be flexible, social mobility occurs frequently, and the characteristic feature of the system is a large middle class whose members are not readily distinguishable from those of higher or lower classes. The social structure of the preindustrial city is relatively rigid, social mobility between strata is slow or infrequent, and a small, easily recognizable elite class is sharply separated from the masses.

3. A symbol of industrial cities is the complex machine whose application has helped to accelerate social change and create a society oriented toward mass production and distribution of goods and services. In preindustrial cities, most of the manual work is performed by man or beast; technology consists mainly of simple tools which may be used by craftsmen for limited production of finished articles.

4. In modern industrial cities, economic units tend to be large, and prices, weights and measures, marketing procedures, and the quality of

---

[28] Gideon Sjoberg, *The Preindustrial City* (1960), pp. 323–38. Sjoberg's formulation of the preindustrial city concept has been considered too broad by some; see, for example, Oliver Cox, "The Preindustrial City Reconsidered," *The Sociological Quarterly,* 5 (Spring 1964), 133–44.

products are usually standardized. The characteristic economic establishment in preindustrial cities is the small retail shop or cottage
industry. Neither measures nor products are extensively standardized.

5. In modern cities, at least in democratic societies, governmental
functionaries are commonly selected on the basis of expertise, experience, competence, or voter appeal, and community issues are often
settled by mass expression or public sentiment. The political system of
preindustrial cities is usually dominated by a "ruling clique" representing a small elite class, and positions in government are usually filled on
the basis of tradition or personal influence, with little effective expression of public opinion on community problems or issues.

As Sjoberg defines them, preindustrial cities existed not only in earlier
periods of history but they are also found in certain regions of the world
today, notably in parts of Asia, Africa, and the Middle East. Many cities
exhibit characteristics of both the modern and the preindustrial types,
indicating that urban centers are undergoing a transition toward modernization. Thus, many of today's preindustrial cities possess some
attributes usually thought to be characteristic of industrial cities, such
as local newspapers, radio stations, and modern schools and universities.

"Urbanism as a Way of Life"

Whereas Sjoberg attempted to codify the characteristics of the preindustrial city, Wirth attempted to codify the characteristics of the large
modern city. In a famous essay, "Urbanism as a Way of Life,"[29] Wirth
stated that among the distinguishing features of the metropolis, aside
from large size and relative density of population, are heterogeneity of
people and cultures; anonymous, transitory, and impersonal relationships; occupational specialization; secularization of thought; and the
predominance of segmental and secondary contact. These features are
elaborated on in Table 2.1. This concept of the metropolis is, like that of
Sjoberg's preindustrial city, manifestly an ideal construct, and shares
many features with the typologies discussed earlier.

Wirth's thesis on the social consequences of urban size, density, and
heterogeneity has generated much discussion and research. Morris, a
British sociologist, has recently analyzed a number of propositions Wirth
derived from these three characteristics and has concluded that "Wirth's
theory has proved much more applicable to industrial that to preindustrial cities."[30] Morris argues that Wirth implicitly assumed an urban
society in which economic rationality is highly valued and in which large
pure bureaucracies are possible.

[29] *American Journal of Sociology*, 44 (July 1938).
[30] R. N. Morris, *Urban Sociology* (1968), p. 169.

Preindustrial versus industrial cities. On the facing page, above, a general
view of Sofara, in Mali, a newly independent African nation with a long
preindustrial history as part of the vast Sudanic empires. Below is Assisi, Italy,
a well-preserved example of the walled cities that dotted medieval Europe.
Note the striking contrast of Assisi with modern industrial Kansas City, on this
page. (facing page: United Nations—top; Italian Government Travel Office—
bottom; this page: Missouri Tourism Commission)

TABLE 2.1: Louis Wirth's Sociological Definition of the City in Relation to Size, Density, and Heterogeneity

A Schematic Version

SIZE An increase in the number of inhabitants of a settlement beyond a certain limit brings about changes in the relations of people and changes in the character of the community	Greater the number of people interacting, greater the potential differentiation
	Dependence upon a greater number of people, lesser dependence on particular persons
	Association with more people, knowledge of a smaller proportion, and of these, less intimate knowledge
	More secondary rather than primary contacts; that is, increase in contacts which are face to face, yet impersonal, superficial, transitory, and segmental
	More freedom from the personal and emotional control of intimate groups
	Association in a large number of groups, no individual allegiance to a single group
DENSITY Reinforces the effect of size in diversifying men and their activities, and in increasing the structural complexity of the society	Tendency to differentiation and specialization
	Separation of residence from work place
	Functional specialization of areas—segregation of functions
	Segregation of people: city becomes a mosaic of social worlds
HETEROGENEITY Cities products of migration of peoples of diverse origin Heterogeneity of origin matched by heterogeneity of occupations Differentiation and specialization reinforces heterogeneity	Without common background and common activities premium is placed on visual recognition: the uniform becomes symbolic of the role
	No common set of values, no common ethical system to sustain them: money tends to become measure of all things for which there are no common standards
	Formal controls as opposed to informal controls. Necessity for adhering to predictable routines. Clock and the traffic signal symbolic of the basis of the social order
	Economic basis: mass production of goods, possible only with the standardization of processes and products
	Standardization of goods and facilities in terms of the average
	Adjustment of educational, recreational, and cultural services to mass requirements
	In politics success of mass appeals—growth of mass movements

SOURCE: Eshref Shevky and Wendell Bell, *Social Area Analysis,* Stanford Sociological Series # 1 (Stanford, Calif., Stanford University Press, 1955), pp. 7-8.

THE SCALE OF INDUSTRIAL SOCIETY   Building upon the work of Wirth and others, Eshref Shevky and Wendell Bell have formulated a theory applying to very large cities in industrial societies.[31] They contend that the most important feature of such societies is an increase in "scale," that is, an increase in "the scope of social interaction and dependency."[32] Increases in scale are manifested in changes in the range and intensity of relations, in further differentiation of function, and in more complexity of social organization. Among the specific changes that occur are those in which the city is involved in a greater range of economic and social relations, through the centralization of the functions of coordination, control, and promotion. "We should see the city, then, as dominant always in relation to a system of interaction, interdependence, and control which embraces the total society. So today, as the 'free market' ceases to be the major type of control system and its place is taken by formal (public and private) governmental functions, these relations remain centered in the cities. As society increases in scale it ceases to be organized chiefly in autonomous local units and becomes organized in terms of a far-flung web or organization, whose points of convergence are typically urban."[33]

Shevky and Bell stress the transforming societal effects, including the role of cities, of industrialization. In commenting on the shortcomings of Wirth's theory, they emphasize that "*it is not the city which is an underlying 'prime mover' in the recent transformation of Western society, but the necessities of economic expansion itself.*"[34] Shevky and Bell's theory of scale provides, in sum, an analysis of industrial urbanism. As such it stands in useful contrast to Sjoberg's construct of preindustrial urban society.[35]

Paradoxical as it may seem, the city as a type of community may be less important in the modern world than it was in earlier periods, despite the fact that most industrial societies are becoming increasingly urbanized in a cultural and social-psychological sense. The justification for such a proposition stems from the fact that communities—rural and urban alike—are enmeshed in the institutional network of the larger society and are no longer detached or semi-isolated units related to the

[31] Eshref Shevky and Wendell Bell, *Social Area Analysis* (1955), esp. ch. 2.

[32] *Ibid,* p. 7.

[33] *Ibid.,* p. 12.

[34] *Ibid,* p. 8 (italic emphasis in original).

[35] Comparison of cities in two societies with low-scale positions—Accra in Ghana and Abidjan in the Ivory Coast—with Rome and San Francisco as cities representative of societies with high-scale positions shows that the former cities have much less differentiation of population and spatial areas than the latter cities. This confirms the thesis that cities in preindustrial societies differ in urban structure from cities in industrialized societies. See Remi Clignet and Joyce Sween, "Accra and Abidjan: A Comparative Examination of the Theory of Increase in Scale," *Urban Affairs Quarterly,* 4 (March 1969), 297–324.

outside world by only tenuous connections. Morris and the Shevky-Bell theory suggest that Wirth's description of the social consequences of city life will apply less well to distinguish cities in fully developed metropolitan societies since these are in many ways mass societies with relatively few urban-rural differences.[36] In such societies rural areas are in many ways urban.

Modernity and the City

One of the most fascinating and fruitful ways to examine the distinction between the impact of industrialization and that of urbanization is to determine whether urban residents think and behave differently from nonurban residents. If there are such differences, then the problem becomes one of determining whether industrial or urban experiences have brought them about. Several broadly based studies have recently examined this question.

Modernity is the term applied to describe the attitudes and behavior of Western industrial people. Inkeles defines it as

(1) openness to new experience, both with people and with new ways of doing things such as attempting to control births; (2) the assertion of increasing independence from the authority of traditional figures like parents and priests and a shift of allegiance to leaders of government, public affairs, trade unions, cooperatives, and the like; (3) belief in the efficacy of science and medicine, and a general abandonment of passivity and fatalism in the face of life's difficulties; and (4) ambition for oneself and one's children to achieve high occupational and educational goals. Men who manifest these characteristics (5) like people to be on time and show an interest in carefully planning their affairs in advance. It is also part of this syndrome to (6) show strong interest and take an active part in civic and community affairs and local politics; and (7) to strive energetically to keep up with the news, and within this effort to prefer news of national and international import over items dealing with sports, religion, or purely local affairs.[37]

These characteristics may be seen as the psychological correlates of the complex differentiated structure of urban-industrial society, described earlier in this chapter. A "modern man" in Inkeles' terms would feel at ease and function efficiently in such a society, whereas a "traditional man" would be better adapted to life in a preindustrial urban society.

Inkeles and his colleagues administered a tested standardized ques-

---

[36] Morris, *op. cit,* p. 171; see also Janet Abu-Lughod, The City is Dead—Long Live the City: Some Thoughts on Urbanity," in Sylvia F. Fava, ed., *Urbanism in World Perspective: A Reader* (1968), pp. 154–65; and Herbert Gans, "Urbanism and Suburbanism as Ways of Life: A Re-evaluation of Definitions," in *ibid.,* pp. 63–81.

[37] Alex Inkeles, "Making Men Modern: On the Causes and Consequences of Individual Change in Six Developing Countries," *American Journal of Sociology,* 75 (September 1969), 208–25.

tionnaire measuring modernity to young men in six countries—Argentina, Chile, India, Israel, Nigeria, and East Pakistan (now Bangladesh). The young men covered the range of residential types from farmers to newly arrived urban migrants to established city residents of various occupations. In each country, groups of men were classified as modern by the questionnaire results. The proportions varied from country to country but since the sample was not random these differences are not definitive. However, they are in the expected direction, with a traditional, predominantly rural society such as Bangladesh having a low percentage of "modern men." It is important to note that the modernity is not just verbal and attitudinal; those who scored high on modernity were also those who behaved in a modern way by joining voluntary organizations, reading newspapers, contacting officials about public issues, and discussing politics with their wives.

Not unexpectedly, both urban and industrial experience were related to modernism. Urban residence of itself[38] has some effect, but apparently the major modernizing impact of the city operates through the greater availability of formal schooling in the city. At least this is highly indicated by Inkeles' data and also by a similar study among Turkish women,[39] both studies showing that modernism is most highly correlated with formal schooling. This helps explain why some rural residents become modern by access to educational opportunities. Since such opportunities are more limited in rural areas, proportionately fewer rural individuals become modern. Significantly, Inkeles points out that the school curriculum is probably not the underlying modernizing influence but, rather, the institution of the school as a rational organization.[40] The school, by offering a course of study based on individual comprehension, observation, and logic, "teaches" attitudes and values about women, nature, time, God, fate, and politics which serve to orient the student in a modern way to the people and world around him.

The modernizing effect of factory experience was the second most important predictor of modernity in Inkeles' study. In fact, the slogan of the project became "The factory can be a school—a school for modernization."[41] Again, it appears to be the factory as a rational organization which brings about modernization, rather than the technology learned in

---

[38] Thus, the Turkish data referred to below show that regardless of education, women with urban experience are more modern. The urban impact is also cumulative—the more urban experience the more modern.

[39] Allan Schnaiberg, "The Modernizing Impact of Urbanization: A Causal Analysis," *Economic Development and Cultural Change,* 20 (October 1971), 80–104.

[40] There is little reason to doubt this assertion. One consequence is that schools not run as rational organizations, but as centers for the learning of traditional, usually religious, wisdom, would not be associated with modernism. Such is the case with the educational system of preindustrial urban societies, particularly those of the past.

[41] Inkeles, *op. cit,* p. 213.

the factory. "We reasoned that work in a factory should increase a man's sense of efficacy, make him less fearful of innovation, and impress on him the value of education as a general qualification for competence and advancement."[42]

These results suggest that both the city and industrial experience effect changes in man's beliefs and behavior. The changes occur not through the individual's simple presence in the city or factory, but by the fact that such presence is likely to involve him in a network of rational complex organizations.

Summary

In this chapter we have reviewed the course of cities since the Industrial Revolution, and have indicated some of the factors and conditions that have given rise to an unprecedented growth of urban communities. Since the medieval period there has been a complex interlocking of economic, technological, and social factors which transformed Europe and engendered the rise of the urban-industrial city. We have also considered some of the theories developed to explain the significant features of industrial urbanism, particularly the ideal types formulated by Redfield, Tönnies, and Durkheim. Parsons' addition of a neoevolutionary framework to the concept of differentiation represents another way of approaching the structure of industrial society. Finally, the work of Sjoberg and Wirth was used to contrast the preindustrial city with the industrial city. More precise methods of disentangling the effects of urbanism and industrialism, involving the measurement of "modernity" among people in various communities and work situations, were also described.

In the following chapter, we focus the discussion on the urbanization of the United States, indicating some of the important trends that have transformed the country from a predominantly agricultural society to a country of many cities, both large and small, all within the course of two centuries, and mainly since the turn of the twentieth century.

Selected Bibliography

BOOKS

Chandler, Tertius, and Gerald Fox, *3000 Years of Urban Growth*. New York; Seminar Press, 1973.

[42] *Ibid*, p. 213.

Foster, George, *Traditional Societies and Technological Change*, 2d ed. New York: Harper and Row, 1973.

Hauser, Philip, "Observations on the Urban-Folk and Urban-Rural Dichotomies as Forms of Western Ethnocentrism," in Philip Hauser and Leo Schnore, eds., *The Study of Urbanization*. New York: Wiley, 1965.

Hoselitz, Bert, "Interaction between Industrial and Pre-industrial Stratification Systems," in Neil Smelser and Seymour M. Lipset, eds., *Social Structure and Mobility in Economic Development*. Chicago: Aldine, 1966.

Lerner, Daniel, and Lucille Plevsner, *The Passing of Traditional Society*. Glencoe, Ill: The Free Press, 1958.

Lewis, Oscar, "Further Observations on the Folk-Urban Continuum and Urbanization with Special Reference to Mexico City," in Philip Hauser and Leo Schnore, eds., *The Study of Urbanization*. New York: Wiley, 1965.

Marshall, Leon, "The Emergence of the First Industrial City: Manchester 1780–1850," in Caroline Ware, ed., *The Cultural Approach to History*. New York: Columbia University Press, 1940. Reissued in 1965 by Kennikat Press, Port Washington, N. Y.

Mumford, Lewis, *The City in History*. New York: Harcourt, Brace and World, 1961.

Nisbet, Robert, *The Social Philosophers: Community and Conflict in Western Thought*. New York: Thomas Y. Crowell, 1973.

Pahl, R. E., "The Emergence of Industrial Urbanism in Britain," in his *Patterns of Urban Life*. New York: Humanities Press, 1970.

Parsons, Talcott, *Societies: Evolutionary and Comparative Perspectives*. Englewood Cliffs, N. J.: Prentice-Hall, 1966.

———, *The System of Modern Societies*. Englewood Cliffs, N.J.: Prentice-Hall, 1971.

Pirenne, Henri, *Medieval Cities*, trans. Frank Halsey. Garden City, N. Y.: Doubleday Anchor Books, 1956.

Sennett, Richard, ed., *Classic Essays on the Culture of Cities*. New York: Appleton-Century-Crofts, 1969.

Singer, Charles, E. J. Holmyard, A. R. Hall, and T. L. Williams, eds., *A History of Technology*, vols 2–5. New York: Oxford University Press, 1957–58.

Sjoberg, Gideon. "The Rural-Urban Dimension in Preindustrial, Transitional, and Industrial Societies," in R. E. L. Faris, ed., *Handbook of Modern Sociology*. Chicago: Rand McNally, 1964.

———, "Theory and Research in Urban Sociology," in Philip Hauser and Leo Schnore, eds., *The Study of Urbanization*. New York: Wiley, 1965.

Weber, Adna, *The Growth of Cities in the Nineteenth Century*. Ithaca, N.Y.: Cornell University Press, 1963. Originally published in 1899.

Weber, Max, *The Protestant Ethic and the Spirit of Capitalism*, trans. Talcott Parsons. New York: Scribner, 1958.

ARTICLES

Cox, Oliver, "The Preindustrial City Reconsidered," *Sociological Quarterly*, 5 (Spring 1964), 133–44.

Eisenstadt, Shmuel, "Social Evolution," in David L. Sills, ed., *International Encyclopedia of the Social Sciences*, vol. 5, pp. 228–34. New York: Macmillan Company and The Free Press, 1968.

Form, William F., "The Accommodation of Rural and Urban Workers to Industrial Discipline and Urban Living: A Four Nation Study," *Rural Sociology*, 36 (December 1971), 488–508.

———, "Technology and Social Behavior of Workers in Four Countries: A Sociotechnical Perspective," *American Sociological Review*, 37 (December 1972), 727–39.

Miner, Horace, "Community-Society Continua," in David L. Sills, ed., *International Encyclopedia of the Social Sciences*, vol. 3, pp. 174–80. New York: Macmillan Company and The Free Press, 1968.

Schwartz, Richard R., and James Miller, "Legal Evolution and Social Complexity," *American Journal of Sociology*, 70 (September 1964), 159–69.

3 • The Urban Transformation of the United States

In the several hundred years since the Pilgrims' landing in 1519, the territory that became the United States has been transformed from the Indians' homeland to a nation in which 73 percent of the population are urban. Its cities are of such size that in 1970 the urban segment of the nation, that is, almost three-quarters of the total population, occupied only 1.53 percent of the nation's land area, a territory roughly equal to the size of Florida.[1]

The United States has become the world's leading urban-industrial society and is in many ways the "model" for this form of urban development, either to be emulated or to be examined for mistakes to be avoided by the rest of the world. Although the urban transformation of the United States was rapid, there were major sequences of development, which will be described below, to indicate the nature of the sweeping social, economic, and technological changes that have occurred.

The Three Stages of Urban Development in the United States

For purposes of our discussion and analysis we will divide the urban community development of the United States into three periods: preindustrial, urban-industrial, and metropolitan. There is an emergent fourth stage which we may call "megalopolitan."

The dates assigned in any such schematic presentation must necessarily be approximate. The first period was the longest, lasting from the establishment of the colonies in what was to become the United States until about 1850, or, if one prefers the reference points of wars as

---

[1] *HUD Newsletter*, 3 (July 3, 1972), p. 3.

watersheds, until the Civil War. By the midnineteenth century the preindustrial city was fast fading from the American scene. The urban-industrial period was a late-nineteenth-century phenomenon extending to the early part of the twentieth century. It encompassed the period between 1850 and 1900 or 1920 or, in martial reckoning, between the Civil War and World War I. The metropolitan period, the current urban era, began after 1900, perhaps 1920 or after World War I; it is a twentieth-century phenomenon. At the present time there are signs indicating further fundamental changes underway in community forms in the United States, suggesting that a fourth period may soon need description and analysis. The emergent fourth period dates from the midtwentieth century after World War II. Signs of major urban changes were clearly apparent by the 1960's and 1970's. Obviously there is variation among individual cities and the regions of the United States in the dates and the extent to which they experienced the transformations.

In applying the three-part description of American urban development, one must bear in mind the purpose for which it was intended. It is a description of dominant community forms, those that are characteristic of a particular period. It is not a description of all communities in a particular period nor the way all Americans lived at a particular time. Thus, in the current metropolitan period a considerable number of Americans still live on farms or in isolated sections such as Appalachia.

Preindustrial, Urban-Industrial, and Metropolitan Periods

In this section we shall provide a brief overview of the sequence of the development of the United States.

THE PREINDUSTRIAL PERIOD   In the preindustrial period urban residents made up a small percentage of the total population and cities were small in size. The leading cities were East Coast seaports. The importance of water transportation in the preindustrial period is reflected in the building of many canals to broaden the trading hinterland. Water power was also a source of work energy, although domestic animals were the chief source. The occupations of city residents were in commerce and trade, administration, service, and the small-scale hand production of "manufactured" goods. Mechanized production in the United States had its beginnings only in the 1820's, when the first textile mills were set up in New England using the spinning and weaving machines that had been invented somewhat earlier in England. Most people were farmers, but even city residents were overwhelmingly rural in background and experience. The internal structure of cities in the preindustrial period was relatively undifferentiated into separate areas for separate activities, for the cities were small enough so that people could easily walk or ride (by horseback or by horse and wagon) to the variety of available facilities. Thus, houses, shops, and public buildings were typically interspersed; often the tradesman or artisan lived above or behind his store.

The preindustrial city in the United States retained a social organization based on personal communication and contact. An important example was the provision of what we now regard as municipal services. Individual families or private organizations provided their own water supplies, disposal of sewage and garbage, and "welfare" and health facilities. For a time fire-fighting and police protection were also provided on a volunteer basis; traces of this system survive today in the so-called volunteer fire departments of outlying communities. Life in the preindustrial American city was far from idyllic but it did present a coherent picture, one in which the cities served the needs of a rural agricultural society.

THE URBAN-INDUSTRIAL PERIOD   The urban-industrial period in the United States was a time of transition to a society dominated by large cities organized on a new basis. Cities of 100,000 in population, or even over a million, appeared with increasing frequency. As they increased their proportion of the total population, they extended their influence in other ways as well. The cities that grew up or prospered in this period were tied to locations along the railroad lines that extended further and further across the nation; consequently they played a major role in the "opening up" of the vast central and western areas of the United States. Occupationally the urbanites were now employed in substantial proportion at factory jobs tending machines. Work energy was increasingly provided by inanimate sources of power—steam, electricity, and gas—rather than by men and domestic beasts of burden. Agricultural occupations and productivity were also altered dramatically as machines began to replace hand labor and the horse-drawn plow.

The internal structure of the American city acquired the characteristic high-rise downtown, which is still an American hallmark, during the urban-industrial era. As the cities grew larger with the advent of large-scale factories, the subareas of the city began to become more specialized into retail, wholesale, industrial, administrative, and tourist and entertainment areas; ethnic and social class neighborhoods clearly emerged, especially in the larger cities. In the smaller centers the equivalents were "Main Street" and "the other side of the tracks." The specialized activities were especially concentrated in the central business district, with local railroads, trolleys, and el and subway lines converging on this point so that the city's residents could carry on their various activities and then be transported back to the several types of resident̄al areas strung out along the transportation lines.

Socially, the urban-industrial period witnessed a shift to a more

Chicago over 100 years. In 1831, Chicago was just emerging as a settlement, but by the late 1880's it was a burgeoning railroad and manufacturing center, and by 1936 a modern metropolis. (Courtesy Chicago Historical Society)

differentiated, more *Gesellschaft*-oriented, larger-scale society, to employ some of the classificatory terms introduced in the previous chapter. Large specialized impersonal organizations became more and more frequent not only in industrial production but also in the bureaucratization of many other activities such as the school and welfare. The city gradually took on the responsibility of providing more and more services—water, sanitation, and some welfare and health services—as well as the beginnings of regulating and setting standards in fields like housing. All of these activities became reflected in full-time, paid occupations requiring their own training and expertise, for example, the creation of municipal fire and police forces. The social changes were reflected in ambivalent attitudes toward the city—on the one hand, recognition of the unparalleled opportunity structure provided by industrial growth; on the other, concern with the unmet problems and human misery generated by the new social order.

THE METROPOLITAN PERIOD   The metropolitan period represents a community form whose significance is still somewhat unclear, particularly in social terms, despite the fact that we already seem to be moving toward a fourth period of development. The metropolis is the characteristic city form of a mature industrial society. Such cities have a greater range of location than did those in the previous periods since they depend on the long-distance highway and superhighway rather than the railroad or major water transport for access to them. Technologically they are also creatures of advanced industrialism in that they often depend on such inventions as air-conditioning and the long-distance movement of water, as witness the phenomenal growth of Los Angeles and Phoenix. The metropolis represents the sprawl and explosion of the city, in both numerical and geographic terms. Metropolises of multimillion inhabitants are common and often extend their hegemony over a radius of 50 miles or more.

The automobile, the truck, the bus, and the telephone are only the most visible signs of the "second industrial revolution" which underlies metropolitan growth. The most basic change is the thoroughgoing mechanization of industry, which has resulted in enormous gains in productivity by factory labor so that most Americans are now employed in service industries rather than in agricultural or factory jobs.

The internal structure of the metropolis is far different from that of the city of the urban-industrial period, especially in the form and function of the downtown section. In the urban-industrial period the central business district coordinated the city's activities through actual physical centralization of the city's basic activities; residential neighborhoods and the facilities serving them—local schools, daily shopping, religious institutions, and the like were the major activities located outside the central area. Hence, these neighborhoods were strung along the trolley and subway lines and commuter railroads that led into the downtown area. The new flexibility in location engendered by metropolitan technology—not only rubber-wheeled transportation but also the shorter work week, mass production applied to housing, and widespread electrification—affected both the downtown area and the residential areas of the metropolis. There was a selective decentralization of the specialized parts of the central business district. Large shopping centers, drive-in movies, and industrial parks became scattered throughout the metropolis, while the central area retained office jobs—particularly the "front offices" of major corporations and the major financial, legal, and governmental institutions—activities that coordinate the actual production and distribution of goods now taking place at sites scattered throughout the metropolis. Residential neighborhoods have also decentralized—or, as it is usually termed, *suburbanized*—into a variety of locations often outside the legal city limits, where they achieved a lower density than in the city neighborhoods of the urban-industrial period. One consequence of downtown and residential decentralization beyond the legal city limits has been the creation of a host of urban problems: erosion of the city tax base; increased racial segregation of blacks and other minorities who lack the opportunity to participate fully in the suburban movement; physical erosion of sections of the downtown and residential areas, including abandonment in some cases; and the concentration of the poor, rejected, unwanted, or deviant individuals in the central city.

When delineating the metropolitan period, it becomes difficult to make meaningful rural-urban distinctions, for the metropolis is influential far beyond even its extensive physical borders. The metropolis represents a national or "mass" society in which consumer goods are designed and marketed by nationwide firms; radio and television networks present news and entertainment simultaneously to crossroads hamlets and high-rise apartments; and books, magazines, recordings, and machine-

TABLE 3.1:   Urban Population of the United States: 1790–1970

	Percent of Total Population
Current urban definition	
1970	73.5
1960	69.9
1950	64.0
Previous urban definition	
1960	63.0
1950	59.6
1940	56.5
1930	56.1
1920	51.2
1910	45.6
1900	39.6
1890	35.1
1880	28.2
1870	25.7
1860	19.8
1850	15.3
1840	10.8
1830	8.8
1820	7.2
1810	7.3
1800	6.1
1790	5.1

SOURCE: *U. S. Census of Population, 1970. Number of Inhabitants. United States Summary*. Final Report PC(1)–A1, p. 42.

produced copies of everything from great art to a movie star's favorite wig are widely and inexpensively available. The content and distribution of these goods and ideas are typically directed by the large corporations, banks, insurance companies, and governmental bodies quartered in the downtown areas. In a very real sense, then, America is metropolitan America.

In attempting to apply the three-stage developmental scheme to an understanding of individual cities in the United States, one must be aware of when a city underwent its major growth. Cities that had their heyday in an earlier period will tend to have retained more characteristics from that period, especially in their physical form, than cities that experienced their major growth in the current metropolitan period. Thus, one would not expect to find the full range of metropolitan traits in Charleston, South Carolina, which was the fifteenth largest city in the United States in 1850 but was not even included on the 1900 list of the country's 50 largest cities. On the other hand, Los Angeles had a population of only 1,600 in 1850, 50,000 in 1890, and 2.8 million by 1970, making it the third largest city in the United States. Some cities, of course, have experienced major growth in all three periods. These are located exclusively on the East Coast since there were few sizable American cities elsewhere in the preindustrial period. Thus, New York, Philadelphia, and Boston are contemporary mixes of all three periods.

Rural-Urban Distribution

The statistics on the rural-urban distribution of population in the United States show the total nature of the change in community distribution. According to the first census in 1790, only about 5 percent of the population was classified as urban, while the 1970 census shows that 73.5 percent of the population was so classified. Detailed figures are presented in Figure 3.1 and Table 3.1. Thus, in 180 years a nation in which more than nine out of ten Americans lived in rural areas became a nation in which three out of four Americans lived in cities. Inclusion of rural-urban data prior to the first census would, of course, heighten this contrast.

Viewing the span of data indicates three major types of rural-urban distribution in the history of the American population. The first, which lasted until the midnineteenth century, saw the rural population as dominant. In 1850 the urban population was only 15.3 percent of the total, and in 1860, on the eve of the Civil War, still only 19.8 percent. During this preindustrial period in the United States, urban population was not only a distinct minority of the whole, but cities themselves were small in size. In colonial times the leading cities, all East Coast seaports, were Philadelphia, Boston, Charleston (South Carolina), and Newport (Rhode Island); in 1743 Boston was the largest of these with a population of slightly over 16,000. In 1775, just before the American Revolution, Philadelphia's 40,000 population made it the largest city, while New York, with 25,000, was second.[2]

By 1800 there were only six cities in the United States with more than 8,000 inhabitants, Philadelphia leading with almost 70,000, followed by New York (Manhattan) with 60,000 and Boston with 25,000.[3] By 1850 there were several large cities: New York with over 600,000 residents, Philadelphia with 408,000, Baltimore with 169,000, and Boston with 137,000; but cities with over 100,000 residents made up only six percent of the American population at this time.[4] Nevertheless, these cities signaled the urban-industrial era to come. In 1850 London already had a population of over 2 million and Paris of over a million.

The second period of urbanization in the United States coincided with the industrialization of the nation and encompassed the major growth of American cities as well as their increasing importance in American life. By 1900 the urban percentage of the population had risen to 39.7 percent, and after World War I the 1920 census showed that the urban

[2] Carl Bridenbaugh, *Cities in Revolt: Urban Life in America, 1743–1776* (1955), pp. 5, 216.
[3] Adna Weber, *The Growth of Cities in the Nineteenth Century* (originally published 1899, reissued 1953), pp. 21–22.
[4] *Ibid.*, pp. 39, 450.

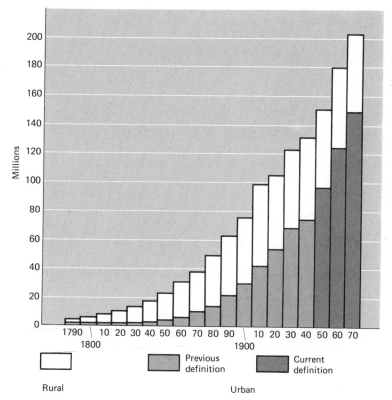

FIGURE 3.1 ● Urban and rural population: 1790–1970. The gradual growth of urban population in the United States transformed a predominantly rural nation into a predominantly urban one. In making historical comparisons one must keep in mind the new urban definition used since 1950. Source: U.S. Bureau of the Census, U.S. Census of Population:1970, *Number of Inhabitants*. Final Report PC (1)-A1. United States Summary.

Rural

Previous definition

Current definition

Urban

population was a statistical majority—51.2 percent of the total. Since then the urban proportion of population has continued to rise.

In the urban-industrial period a new kind of city rose to prominence. Some of the cities of the preindustrial period such as Philadelphia, New York, and Boston added an industrial base to their commercial economies and remained in leading positions, while others such as Charleston, not so favorably situated, declined in importance. The archetype of the American industrial city is Chicago, which was founded only in 1837 and had a population of 16,000 by 1847, 30,000 in 1850, 300,000 in 1870, and a million in 1890.[5] The crucial factors in Chicago's growth were the convergence of rail lines there—the first mile of track in Chicago was laid in 1848—and the city's proximity to the expanding agricultural settlement areas of the Midwest. The city functioned as an entrepôt for the trans-shipment of goods into the rural areas and the processing and shipping of agricultural products from the rural hinterland to the urban populations of the United States. Chicago also developed important industries, especially steel mills and the manufacture of farm machinery.

St. Louis, Cleveland, Detroit, Pittsburgh, Cincinnati, Kansas City, Minneapolis-St. Paul and scores of lesser centers grew to prominence in the latter half of the nineteenth century, as did, with some time lag, the cities of the Southwest and Far West—Houston, Fort Worth, Dallas, Seattle, Portland, Salt Lake City, Denver, and San Francisco. By 1890 the United States had 28 cities of at least 100,000 inhabitants, which in the aggregate accounted for over 15 percent of the United States population.[6]

The urban growth in the second half of the nineteenth century was the accompaniment of the industrialization of the United States. Adna Weber has pointed out that the manufacturing increase, as measured by the amount of capital invested, average number of employees per factory, and net value of product, was especially marked in the decade of 1880–1890.[7] As city populations expanded, they also provided an increasing market for their own goods and services. Men and women were drawn to the cities not only to build and staff the factories but also to build and staff the infrastructure of the city: the streets, bridges, and transportation network; the energy supply (first steam, later electricity) to run the machines; the water supply and sewage system; and the hospitals, schools, and public installations. This was an era of basic city-building unparalleled in American history. It was also an era of major social change as, over a comparatively few decades, millions of migrants and immigrants sought to adjust to cities. For all, urban-born

[5] Harold M. Mayer and Richard C. Wade, with the assistance of Glen E. Holt, *Chicago: Growth of a Metropolis* (1969), pp. 30, 35.

[6] Weber, *op cit.*, pp. 22, 39.

[7] *Ibid*, p. 27.

or not, it was a period of forging a new set of social relationships and institutions suited to urban life on a vastly increased scale.

In the third period of rural-urban population distribution, approximately since the turn of the century, the rural-urban categories are no longer the most accurate description of the settlement patterns of Americans. By 1970, 73.5 percent of the population was classified as urban. However, a larger and larger proportion of those so classified were living in very large cities which were no longer functionally contained within their municipal boundaries; the cities now organized and coordinated their daily activities in a surrounding suburban "ring." Los Angeles is the archetype of the American metropolis, epitomizing not only its physical form but also the new life styles of an established industrial nation. By the midtwentieth century, metropolises housed the majority of the urban population. The 1970 census revealed that for the first time the suburban population of the metropolitan areas exceeds that of their central-city residents. The suburban population is now the largest component (but not the majority) of the American population, heralding the close of the metropolitan era as we know it.

A New Urban Definition

The accuracy of a definition of "rural" and "urban" is not innate or fixed, but depends on the usefulness of the resulting categories. If businessmen, politicians, government, and researchers find that rural-urban classifications do not help in analyzing or predicting community events, then the definition is not valid no matter how precise it may be.

Typically, rural-urban definitions achieve their utility by a very simple method. The definition consists only of some easily measurable items such as size, density, or legal community status. These simple items are assumed to be associated, in ways that may or may not be fully understood, with more complex items such as socioeconomic behavior. Therefore, by employing the definition based on the simple items one has an index to the more complex items. Lack of validity (hence utility) in the definition results when changes occur in the association between the simple and the complex items. Then the definition cannot serve as a valid (useful) index.

This is precisely what happened in the United States in the three or four decades preceding 1950. One of the major changes was that rapid transportation and communication, especially the automobile and telephone, enabled many people to live an urban existence without living in places that were large, densely settled, or legally incorporated as cities. Accordingly, the censuses from 1950 on are based on a new urban definition that tries to reflect the changed conditions.

For some time, census officials and others were in agreement that the official definition of "urban" as an incorporated place of 2,500 or over

TABLE 3.2:   United States Population by Residence: 1950–1970

| | URBAN | | | | | |
| | Urbanized Areas | | Other Urban Places | | Total | |
Year	Thousands	Percent	Thousands	Percent	Thousands	Percent
1950*	69,249	45.8	27,598	18.2	96,847	64.0
1960	95,848	53.5	29,429	16.4	125,269	69.9
1970	118,447	58.3	30,878	15.2	149,325	73.5

| | RURAL | | | | | |
| | Farm | | Nonfarm | | Total | |
Year	Thousands	Percent	Thousands	Percent	Thousands	Percent
1950*	23,048	15.2	31,431	20.8	54,479	36.0
1960	15,635	8.7	38,419	21.4	54,054	30.1
1970	9,712	4.8	44,175	21.7	53,887	26.5

*Excludes Hawaii and Alaska.
SOURCE: Office of the President, *Report on National Growth* (1972), p. 15.

was unrealistic. In 1950 the Bureau of the Census changed the definition to include as urban unincorporated settlements of 2,500 or more,
and, under certain conditions, to classify as urban incorporated or
unincorporated settlements of less than 2,500. This classification was
achieved by the introduction of the concept of "Urbanized Area" in 1950.
The Urbanized Area consists of a city (or "twin cities") of at least 50,000
in size (the "central city") and its surrounding closely settled territory.
All population in Urbanized Areas is classified as urban, regardless of its
corporate status or size. Outside of Urbanized Areas, only places with
2,500 inhabitants or more were classified as urban but the settlements
need not be incorporated. The new 1950 definition was retained in the
1960 and 1970 censuses.

The change in rural-urban definitions had the effect of increasing the
urban population in the 1950 and succeeding censuses over the figure
that would have been obtained by the old definition and correspondingly
reducing the rural population. Comparison of the percentages according
to the "old" and "new" definitions are included in both Figure 3.1 and
Table 3.1. Table 3.2 presents urban and rural population for 1950 to
1970, showing the relative proportion of Urbanized Area population in
the total urban population; the components of the rural population are
also shown in detail.

The new urban definition makes a greater difference in the highly
urbanized states than in most of the states that are predominantly rural.
This is so because of the shift of large numbers of persons to the suburbs
and other outlying areas of cities. A great many of these people would
have been classified as rural under the old definition.

Standard Metropolitan Statistical Areas

The new urban classification, utilizing the concept of Urbanized Area, is essentially an attempt to include the metropolitan population as urban. The Urbanized Area definition measures the extent of dense settlement around large cities (50,000 or more in size) and classifies that population as urban, regardless of the legal status of the political community. The Urbanized Area is based on urban land use around large cities as the major criterion of metropolitan character.

In 1950, along with Urbanized Area, the census also introduced another new definition of metropolitan, the Standard Metropolitan Area, retitled Standard Metropolitan Statistical Area for the 1960 and 1970 censuses.

Both Urbanized Area and SMSA are measures of the characteristic midtwentieth century American "city"—a large city whose influence extends far beyond the legal city limits and whose central urban core serves as a coordinating center for a complex network of surrounding residential and industrial suburbs, commercial and office installations, outlying shopping malls, and entertainment and recreational facilities. Both Urbanized Area and SMSA are measures of the immediate geographic extent of the influence of the metropolitan areas. Neither is a "better" measure than the other; they were developed for different purposes. One must be careful to check, however, which definition of metropolitan area is being used in a particular research study or discussion. The Urbanized Area is a more accurate measure of the territorial extent of daily metropolitan influence and contact. Presumably it is for this reason that all Urbanized Area population is classified as urban. But because Urbanized Area boundaries conform so well to the area of actual metropolitan settlement, the boundaries seldom conform to other data series and, in any event, the Urbanized Area boundaries necessarily change from census to census as the spread of built-up settlements expands. SMSA's, since they are based on county units, can be coordinated with a whole array of other data series. The more general use of SMSA's in studies of metropolitan areas results from this fact. Usually SMSA boundaries are larger than those of Urbanized Area boundaries. All SMSA population is classified as metropolitan by the census, but in the rural-urban count some may be classified as rural.

The specific criteria used in the 1970 census to designate SMSA's are detailed below. They represent only minor changes from the 1950 and 1960 criteria.

LARGE POPULATION NUCLEUS Each SMSA has as its starting point the *county*[8] containing a city (or cities) of at least 50,000 inhabitants. This

[8] In New England the town unit is used rather than the county.

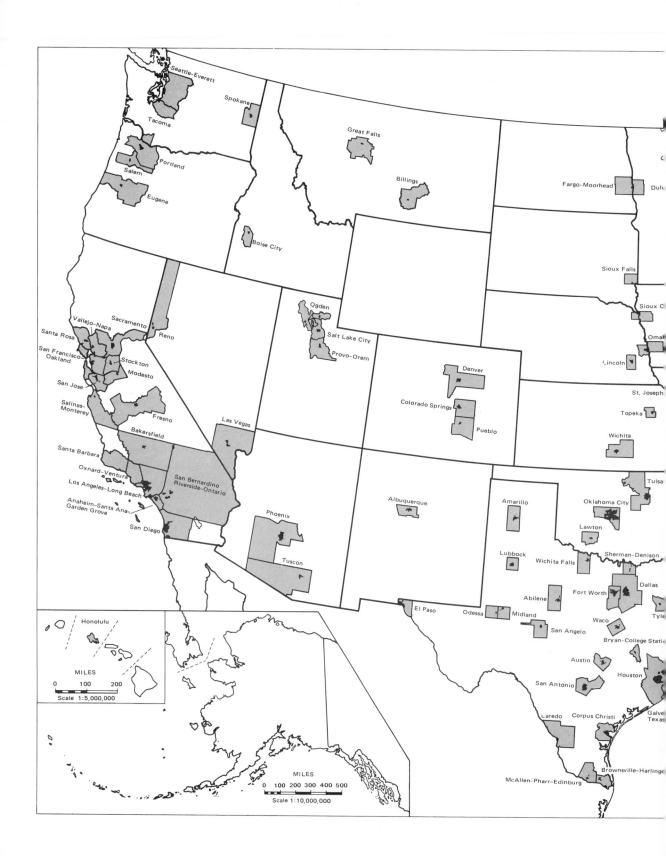

Seattle–Everett
Spokane
Tacoma
Portland
Salem
Eugene
Boise City
Vallejo–Napa
Sacramento
Santa Rosa
San Francisco–
Oakland
Stockton
Modesto
San Jose
Salinas–
Monterey
Fresno
Bakersfield
Santa Barbara
Oxnard–Ventura
Los Angeles–Long Beach
Anaheim–Santa Ana–
Garden Grove
San Diego
Reno
Las Vegas
San Bernardino
Riverside–Ontario
Phoenix
Tuscon
Great Falls
Billings
Ogden
Salt Lake City
Provo–Orem
Denver
Colorado Springs
Pueblo
Albuquerque
El Paso
Fargo–Moorhead
Duluth
Sioux Falls
Sioux C
Omal
Lincoln
St. Joseph
Topeka
Wichita
Tulsa
Amarillo
Oklahoma City
Lawton
Lubbock
Wichita Falls
Sherman–Denison
Abilene
Fort Worth
Dallas
Odessa
Midland
San Angelo
Waco
Tyle
Bryan–College Statie
Austin
Houston
San Antonio
Laredo
Corpus Christi
Galve
Texas
McAllen–Pharr–Edinburg
Brownsville–Harlinge

Honolulu

MILES
0   100   200
Scale 1:5,000,000

MILES
0 100 200 300 400 500
Scale 1:10,000,000

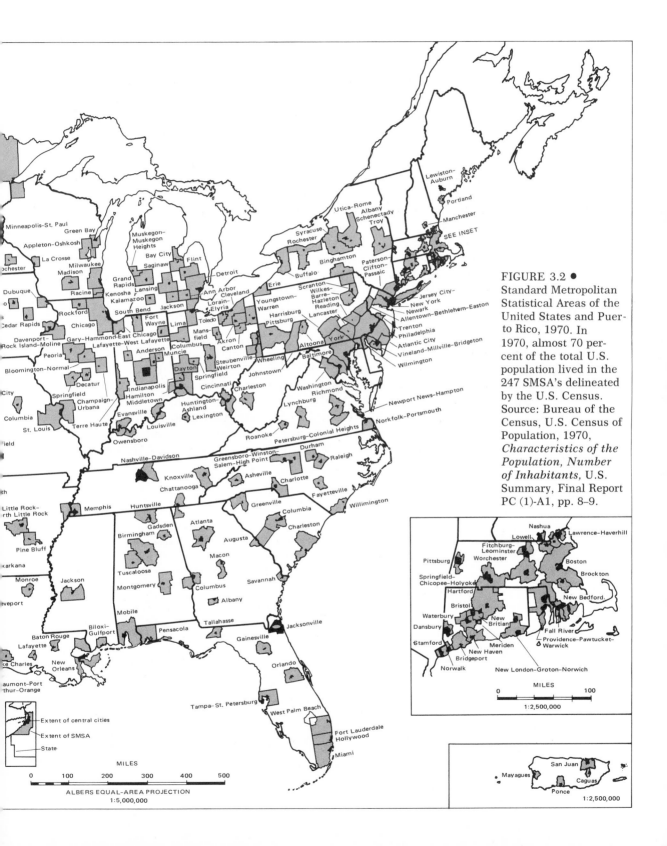

FIGURE 3.2 •
Standard Metropolitan
Statistical Areas of the
United States and Puer-
to Rico, 1970. In
1970, almost 70 per-
cent of the total U.S.
population lived in the
247 SMSA's delineated
by the U.S. Census.
Source: Bureau of the
Census, U.S. Census of
Population, 1970,
*Characteristics of the
Population, Number
of Inhabitants,* U.S.
Summary, Final Report
PC (1)-A1, pp. 8–9.

Extent of central cities
Extent of SMSA
State

MILES
0   100   200   300   400   500
ALBERS EQUAL-AREA PROJECTION
1:5,000,000

MILES
0   100
1:2,500,000

1:2,500,000

contrasts with the Urbanized Area concept in which the starting point, while also a city of at least 50,000 in size, does not include the county in which the city is located but adds territory according to the actual settlement pattern.

RELATED CONTIGUOUS COUNTIES   The SMSA uses counties as its "building blocks," and counties surrounding the central-city county may be included as part of the SMSA. The county need not be in the same state as the central-city county nor is there any limit to the number of counties that may be included, provided they meet the qualifying criteria. To qualify the county must (1) serve as a place of work or as a home for a concentration of nonagricultural workers[9] and (2) maintain regular social and economic contacts that integrate it with the city containing the central-city county.[10] The assumption is that counties meeting the above criteria are not agricultural hinterlands but function as part of the urban network focused on the central-city county.

Applying these criteria, the 1970 census designated a total of 243 SMSA's in the 50 states and an additional four in Puerto Rico. The metropolitan population totaled over 139 million, constituting 68.6 percent of the total 1970 United States population of 203 million.[11] The United States is truly a land of metropolitan communities as the 1970 SMSA's shown in Figure 3.2 indicate. The Bureau of the Census has continued to refine the SMSA concept and to designate new or revised SMSA's as the criteria apply. Early in 1973 a total of 267 SMSA's was listed.[12]

[9] Criteria are as follows: At least 75 percent of the labor force of the county must be in the nonagricultural sector, and at least one of the following conditions must also be met: (a) the county must have 50 percent or more of its population living in contiguous minor civil divisions with a density of at least 150 persons per square mile, in an unbroken chain of minor civil divisions with such density radiating from a central city in the area; or (b) the number of nonagricultural workers employed in the county must equal at least 10 percent of the number of nonagricultural workers employed in the county containing the largest city in the area, or be the place of employment of 10,000 nonagricultural workers; or (c) the nonagricultural labor force living in the county must equal at least 10 percent of the nonagricultural labor force living in the county containing the largest city in the area, or be the place of residence of a nonagricultural labor force of 10,000. U.S. Bureau of the Budget, *Standard Metropolitan Statistical Areas* (1967), p. 2.

[10] Criteria of integration are that 15 percent of the workers living in the county work in the county or counties containing central cities of the area, *or* that 25 percent of those working in the county live in the county or counties containing central cities of the area.

[11] *U. S. Census of Population: 1970. Number of Inhabitants, United States Summary*, Final Report PC(1)–A1, pp. XII, 206.

[12] *HUD Newsletter*, 4 (May 28, 1973), p. 4.

Standard Consolidated Areas

Even the SMSA concept is inadequate to deal with the largest metropolitan complexes. This is in keeping with our contention that further changes in community form are underway in metropolitan America. In 1960 the two largest metropolitan areas in the United States, New York and Chicago, were designated by the Bureau of the Census as Standard Consolidated Areas. Four SMSA's and two additional counties were included in the New York-Northwestern New Jersey Standard Consolidated Area for a total population of over 16 million in 1970. The Chicago-Northwestern Indiana Standard Consolidated Area includes two SMSA's and had a total population in 1970 of 7.6 million. The territory included in these Standard Consolidated Areas was the same in 1970 as in 1960.

Economic and Technological Changes

Economic and technological factors were not determinative in the successive development of American cities, but they were necessary in order to support ever-increasing numbers of urbanites. Chief among the economic changes was the reordering of occupational distribution. In the preindustrial period, most workers in the United States were employed in so-called primary occupations, mainly agriculture, but also forestry, hunting, and fishing. Because all of these occupations depend on the direct utilization of natural resources and thus have to be carried out where the resources are located, they are therefore associated with rural living. The lack, or limited mechanization, of the primary occupations during the preindustrial period in the United States precluded the possibility of supporting large urban populations. It has been estimated that in 1800 one farmer's work was sufficient to feed five people on the farm and only one-half person in the city.[13]

The urban-industrial period is associated with the so-called secondary or goods-producing occupations, those in which materials are processed into transportable goods. These occupations are those of industrial manufacturing and in order to employ a substantial proportion of the labor force they require a large-scale economy with a substantial capital investment and a high degree of organization.

The metropolitan period is associated with the tertiary occupations, those whose personnel produce services rather than goods. Examples of the many tertiary occupations are editors, actors, truck drivers, tele-

[13] William F. Ogburn, "The Social Impact of Technological Changes," in Elizabeth Briant Lee and Alfred McClung Lee, eds., *Social Problems in America,* rev. ed. (1955), p. 53.

phone operators, teachers, secretaries, hairdressers, physicians, law-yers, accountants, judges, salesmen, managers, and administrators.

In the colonial and early federal periods, the vast majority of Ameri-cans were farmers, the main primary occupation. In 1850, 67 percent were in primary occupations, and even as late as 1870, over half, 55 percent, were so employed.[14] The proportion in primary occupations declined rapidly as urban-industrial growth proceeded, and by 1900 barely 40 percent of the labor force was engaged in primary occupations. Concomitantly the proportion in secondary occupations rose from 16 percent in 1850 to about 30 percent of the total labor force between 1910 and 1920. Thereafter the relative proportion in the secondary occupa-tions leveled off, while the proportion in tertiary occupations steadily increased until, sometime between 1930 and 1940, the United States became the first nation in history to have more than half its labor force in tertiary occupations. The percentage was 53.5 in 1940, and by 1970, 64.4 percent of the total United States labor force was in the service-producing fields. These trends are graphically portrayed in Figure 3.3. This astonishing economic transformation underlies the urban trans-formation of the United States. In the space of little more than a century, a nation which had been primarily agricultural, with two-thirds of its

[14] Figures for 1850 are drawn from Reinhard Bendix and Seymour Martin Lipset, *Social Mobility in Industrial Society* (1959), p. 84. Figures for 1870 and later dates were computed from data in *The Office Industry: Patterns of Growth and Location.* A Report of the Regional Plan Association, prepared by Regina Belz Armstrong and edited by Boris Pushkarev (1972), p. 16.

FIGURE 3.3 ● Economic transforma-tion of the United States is reflected in the changing proportions of the labor force in major types of occupa-tion. As industrialism advanced, jobs in tertiary occupations (services) in-creased, while those in primary oc-cupations (agriculture) and those in secondary occupations (factory pro-duction) declined. A majority of Americans now work in tertiary oc-cupations, with an even larger pre-ponderance predicted by the year 2000. Source: *"The Office Industry": Patterns of Growth and Location.* New York: Regional Plan Association, 1972.

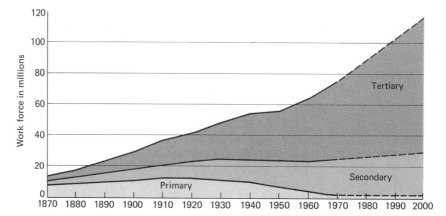

labor force employed in primary occupations in 1850, had become, by 1970, a nation in which two-thirds of the labor force was employed in tertiary occupations.

The predominance of tertiary occupations in the labor force is characteristic of advanced industrial nations. By 1970 the United States had been joined by five other countries—Canada, Britain, Belgium, The Netherlands, and Sweden—in having a predominantly tertiary labor force, and Japan and France are likely to have such distributions soon.[15] In contrast, underdeveloped countries typically have very high percentages of their labor forces in primary occupations, often 70 or 80 percent.[16] In Brazil in 1950, almost two-thirds of the males over ten years of age were employed in agriculture, mining, or forestry.[17]

In the contemporary world, industrial and urban development have sometimes become "out of step" with one another. There are an increasing number of highly urbanized countries which have low levels of industrialization. By high levels of urbanization we mean that these countries have large percentages of their total population living in cities, not simply that they contain large cities. For example, many nations of tropical and middle South America have very large percentages of their total populations living in cities; yet, however one measures industrialization, these regions are not highly industrialized.[18] Other areas of the world, especially in Asia and Africa, are also experiencing "runaway urbanism," and the economic and social ramifications of urbanization under these circumstances are discussed at length in Chapters 4 and 5.

In the United States, the shift from a preindustrial economy to an industrial one went hand in hand with urban expansion because, with mechanization, agricultural productivity rose, thus "freeing" farmers to leave the land for the cities where factory employment was readily available. The data in Table 3.3 are indicative of the sharp decline over time in the number of man hours needed to produce basic crops in the United States. By 1920 only 30.2 percent of the American population lived on farms, indicating the magnitude of the shift to industrial occupations and urban residence. By 1970 the highly mechanized, large-scale farms, "factories in the field," claimed less than five percent of the total population. The industrialization of the United States during the latter half of the nineteenth century rested on the firm foundation of the mechanization of agriculture.

[15] Constance Sorrentino, "Comparing Employment Shifts in 10 Industrialized Countries," *Monthly Labor Review* (October 1971), 3–11. Because of the definitions and data she employs, Sorrentino's list differs somewhat from other compilations.

[16] P. Sargant Florence, *Economics and Sociology of Industry: A Realistic Analysis of Development*, rev. ed. (1969), pp. 6–7.

[17] T. Lynn Smith, *Brazil: People and Institutions*, 4th ed. (1972), p. 91.

[18] For an elaboration of this point, see Benjamin Higgins, "Urbanization, Industrialization, and Economic Development," in Glenn Beyer, ed., *The Urban Explosion in Latin America* (1967).

TABLE 3.3: Changes in the Average Amount of Labor Required to Produce Three Basic Crops in the United States

Years	Man Hours per Unit*		
	Corn for grain	Wheat	Cotton
1800	344	373	601
1935–39	108	67	209
1965–69	7	11	30

*Per 100 bushels for corn and wheat; per bale for cotton.
SOURCE: Office of the President, *Report on National Growth* (1972), p. 16.

TABLE 3.4: Some Inventions Affecting Development of the Office Industry

Energy supply and application
  1834　Electric motor (M. H. von Jacobi)
  1854　Hydraulic passenger elevator (E. G. Otis)
  1879　Electric lamp (T. A. Edison)
  1881　First commercial electric power plant (Pearl Street, New York)
  1887　First successful electric street railway (F. J. Sprague, Richmond)
  1887　First electric elevator

Information transmission
  1833　Electromagnetic telegraph (F. Gauss and W. Weber)
  1866　First successful transatlantic telegraph cable
  1876　Telephone (A. G. Bell)
  1878　First commercial telephone switchboard (New Haven)

Information handling
  1837　Stenography (Pitman)
  1874　Commercial adaptation of the typewriter (Remington)
  1888　Stenography (Gregg)
  1894　Commercial adaptation of the mechanical calculator (W. S. Burroughs)

Building construction
  1884　Steel frame (Home Insurance Co. Building in Chicago, ten floors, by William Le Baron Jenney)
  1889　First steel frame high-rise building in New York (Tower Building at 50 Broadway, eleven floors, by Bradford L. Gilbert)

SOURCE: *The Office Industry: Patterns of Growth and Location.* A Report of the Regional Plan Association, prepared by Regina Belz Armstrong, edited by Boris Pushkarev, Cambridge, Mass: MIT Press (1972), p. 9.

The process of increasing productivity was repeated in the build-up of industrial productivity during the urban-industrial period. These gains resulted in part from the increased work energy available to manufacturing workers. In 1869 the labor of the average manufacturing worker was aided by 1.1 horsepower of mechanical energy: by 1909 the amount had risen to 2.9 horsepower and by 1929 to 4.9.[19] A host of new inventions augmented and mobilized productivity. These involved the supply and application of energy, the increased speed and fidelity of

[19] Florence, *op. cit.*, p. 14. In 1963 the figure was 12.7 horsepower per manufacturing worker.

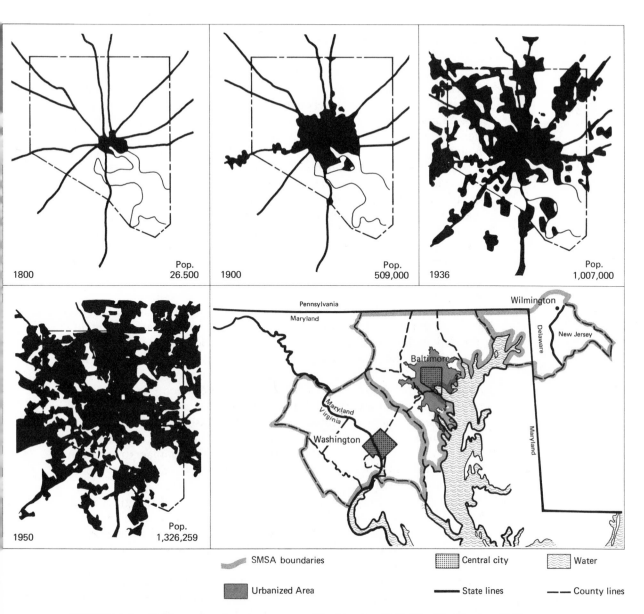

| Pop. 26.500 | Pop. 509,000 | Pop. 1,007,000 |
| 1800 | 1900 | 1936 |

| Pop. 1,326,259 |
| 1950 |

Pennsylvania
Maryland

Wilmington

Delaware

New Jersey

Baltimore

Maryland
Virginia

Washington

Maryland

SMSA boundaries   Central city   Water

Urbanized Area   —— State lines   — — County lines

FIGURE 3.4 • Baltimore's expansion over a century and a half is shown in four maps above. The effects of economic and technological change are apparent in the transition from a compact "walkable" city to a star-shaped pattern, which then blurs as the automobile age comes into its own. The 1970 Baltimore Urbanized Area and SMSA boundaries, shown in the map on the lower right, indicate that the five-county Baltimore SMSA is now part of the southern portion of the great eastern megalopolis stretching from north of Boston to south of Washington, D.C. The Washington, D.C., SMSA includes two counties in Maryland and four in Virginia, while the Wilmington SMSA includes one county each in Delaware, New Jersey, and Maryland. Sources: U.S. Bureau of the Census, *Census of Population: 1970, General Population Characteristics,* Final Report PC (1)-B22 Maryland, p. 31; and U.S. Bureau of the Census, *Characteristics of the Population, Number of Inhabitants,* Vol. II, Part A, report issued 1972.

information transmission and handling, and advancements to building construction. Important aspects of these changes are detailed in Table 3.4. As industries became larger and more interdependent, these inventions were utilized to deal with the mounting paper work and to house in high-rise office buildings and retail emporia the enlarging numbers of clerical, professional, and managerial employees. Advances in transportation technology also went toward maximizing industrial productivity as the trolley, railroads (both long-distance and commuter), and el and subway lines were able to move goods and people faster and further than the horse-drawn vehicles, pedestrian traffic, and water transport of the preindustrial period. The American urban-industrial city took on a star-shaped pattern as growth proceeded along these fixed tracks of transportation. The ecological changes over time are discussed in detail in Chapters 6–11.

As industrial productivity rose, industrial urbanism carried with it the seeds of its own transformation. Industrial work became so highly productive that within a few decades proportionately fewer workers were needed and the labor force shifted to predominantly tertiary employment. City patterns were transformed by some of the effects of mature industrialization: the work week was shortened;[20] income levels rose; ownership of automobiles and telephones became widespread; and the horizontal factories suited to mechanized assembly-line production and located in outlying areas far from their head offices came into existence. Figure 3.4 shows the contrast among the compact urban form of Baltimore in 1800, the star-shaped pattern of the city's urban-industrial era, and the "spread city" of 1970.

By 1970 primary occupations made up only four percent of the United States labor force, secondary occupations 31.5 percent, and tertiary occupations 64.4 percent.[21] Our review has indicated this is the current result of successive mechanization and reorganization of agriculture and other raw materials-producing occupations and the goods-producing occupations. Some of the service-producing occupations are now experiencing similar productivity gains through the application of electronic computers, whose number in the United States has jumped from 214 in 1955 to an estimated 107,000 in 1971.[22] Consequently, we may expect still further economic and related community transformations in the United States.

[20] The average nonagricultural work week was 60.0 hours in 1870, 50.3 in 1910, and 38.8 in 1950. M. Gendell and H. Zetterberg, *A Sociological Almanac for the United States*, 2d ed. (1964), p. 68.

[21] Computed from data in *The Office Industry* . . . , p. 16.

[22] *Ibid.*, p. 11.

Social Aspects of Community Change

Since the social causes and consequences of urbanization are the chief subject of urban sociology, succeeding chapters of this book will present detailed analyses of the social organization characteristic of various types of urban communities in the United States. Tertiary occupations, for example, tend to assume a professional or semiprofessional status and expertise, a subject discussed in Chapter 15. Increased leisure, "a blessing or a bane," available now to a broad spectrum of the urban population in particular, has emerged as a new field of urban study; some of the findings are detailed in Chapter 16. The family in the city, community and political participation, and urban status systems are among other aspects of social behavior discussed in later chapters. Nevertheless, it may be well to summarize here some of the major social trends of the three stages of urban development in the United States.

RURAL-URBAN RELATIONSHIPS   In the preindustrial period in the United States, even the cities were part of an economy and belief system that was primarily rural and agricultural. The city was the "handmaiden" of the rural society, a view articulated by Thomas Jefferson.[23] In any event, differences in rural and urban life styles, economy, and outlook were less sharp in the preindustrial period than in the urban-industrial era.[24] True, urban-industrial expansion was a "gateway" for rural and agricultural settlement of the Midwest and Far West, but as cities grew in size and number, in occupational, organizational, and human diversity, their populations shared fewer and fewer experiences and interests with the rural population. In the metropolitan period, the cities were the nerve centers of a national society, and once again it is difficult to draw rural-urban distinctions. Now, however, the direction comes from the cities whose huge size and geographic extension are insufficient to indicate their role in American society. Thus, cities now direct even the content of many aspects of rural life—through policy-making with respect to agricultural products, through corporate ownership of large farms run by highly trained managers, through the marketing of standard brands as readily available in rural areas as they are in cities, and through urban development of textbooks and curricula for rural students. Rural-urban distinctions are also relatively unimportant because, in the midtwentieth century, all communities, large and small, are involved in a network of governmental regulation and financing at the federal and state levels. To a large extent this has come about precisely because the legally bounded municipality has been superseded by the

[23] For an elaboration of this point, see Chapter 21, "The Image of the City."

[24] Arthur M. Schlesinger presents the point of view that rural-urban contrasts were greatest in the late nineteenth century. See his *The Rise of the City: 1878–1898* (1933, reissued 1971).

metropolis, which is not, except in very rare cases, a unit of government. Despite the overriding importance of metropolitan cities in our national life, our attitudes are often antiurban, suggesting that our mental picture of the United States has not kept pace with reality.[25]

SOCIAL CLASS, SOCIAL MOBILITY, AND STYLE OF LIFE   Industrial urbanism is associated with high standards of living, a fact as true for the United States as for other countries of the world. Florence has calculated that the ten highest income countries all had less than one-quarter of their labor forces in agriculture, while the ten lowest income countries all had well over half of their labor forces in agriculture.[26] The average family income in the United States is now the highest in the world.

The vast economic restructuring of the United States has brought about changed distributions of occupation, education, and income, three quantitative measures of social class. These changes have had the effect of "built-in" social mobility for large segments of the American population. Thus, in 1900, 17.8 percent of the labor force were farm laborers, and an additional 12.4 percent were laborers in urban occupations; by 1970 the percentages in these low-ranking occupations had dropped to less than two percent for the farm laborers and to about six percent for the urban laborers. At the other end of the occupational "ladder," only 4.2 percent of the labor force in 1900 were employed in the professional and technical occupations, but by 1970 the percentage had more than tripled to over 14 percent.

Although changes in social class and social mobility have occurred throughout American society, such changes are more pronounced in the cities. For example, increasing levels of education are associated more with urban than with rural occupations. In 1970 the median number of school years completed by urban adults (those 25 years of age or over) was 12.1, indicating that more than half these men and women had had some college training.[27] The farm population's median was 10.7 years, indicating that half the farm adults had had less than three years of high school education. Both these medians have risen appreciably since 1900 when the average American completed only elementary school.

The effects of industrialism on social class are evident in ways that are less obvious but as equally important as the quantitative measures of income, occupation, and education. In the midnineteenth century the increasing availability of factory-produced items of consumption profoundly altered the "taste" of large segments of American society.[28] In the 1830's and 1840's, objects for the home, which previously had been

[25] See Chapter 21.
[26] Florence, *op. cit.*, pp. 6–7.
[27] *U.S. Census of Population: 1970. General Social and Economic Characteristics. United States Summary.* Final Report PC(1)–C1, Table 75.
[28] This theme is developed in Russell Lynes, *The Tastemakers* (1954).

hand-made and usually custom-made, began to be mass produced: for example, "fancy weaving" by machine; machine-printed wallpapers; and power-loomed ingrain, Brussels, and tapestry carpets. Between 1840 and 1860, the output of factory-made furniture and upholstery quadrupled. Art and decorative objects also began to be mass produced: Currier and Ives lithographs began to be distributed in 1834, and the so-called Rogers' groups of sculpture were available in the 1860's and 1870's. Stimulated by the Civil War need for uniforms, clothing had begun to be manufactured by patterns to standard sizes, a practice transferred to the manufacture of civilian clothing after the war. The era of mass circulation magazines began about 1875, with publication of *Harper's Bazaar.* One by one, the hallmarks of privilege, status, and elitism could be purchased for a modest sum by a considerable part of the population, a consequence of which has been the continual search for new marks and levels of "taste" and distinction.

Consumption patterns are only one aspect of life style. Other aspects such as family interaction patterns and leisure pursuits are covered in Chapters 14 and 16, respectively. Life styles vary considerably in the city even within the same economic and occupational groups, and Chapter 12, "Urban Status Systems," and Chapter 15, "The Urban World of Work," provide some insight into this process. There is little doubt that the variation in life styles has increased over time in the United States, as a direct result of the broader choices which abundant material goods and less physically demanding occupations have made possible. The search for alternative life styles, whether in youth communes or in retirement villages, suggests that social mobility and material success are not necessarily satisfying to all groups in the population. As the "megalopolitan" period develops more fully, we shall most likely see increased emphasis on alternative life styles, often associated with particular subareas of the megalopolis.

VOLUNTARY AND FORMAL ASSOCIATIONS   As was pointed out in Chapter 2, the growth of large-scale industry is accompanied by increasing "scale" in the society as a whole. This is particularly true in cities, where the number of potentially interacting individuals is largest and the variety of specialized interests and needs greatest. One consequence of increased scale is the proliferation of voluntary and formal organizations to serve a variety of special purposes. Many, but by no means all, urbanites now participate in one or more such organizations, a topic whose implications for the local neighborhood and for political life are described in Chapters 13 and 17.

A measure of the role of specialized formal associations in the increasing scale of society is provided by the number of nationally organized formal associations. Before 1800 only 14 such organizations existed in the United States and they were concerned with trade and business, agriculture, religion, veterans' and patriotic affairs, and fraternal and ethnic interests. By 1850 the number had increased to only 33 nationally organized associations, but by 1900 there were 331. To the earlier types were added, first, associations concerned with labor, science and technology, health and medicine, governmental, legal, and civic affairs, and social welfare, and, later, associations dealing with hobbies and sports and athletics.[29] By 1960 there were over 6,000 nationally or regionally organized associations, and by 1971 almost 12,000.[30]

The development of social work illustrates the consequences of the shift from informal to formal structure. Hillman, who studied the development of social work in Chicago, noted that there, as in other American cities, "social work . . . is in large measure a product of urbanization, not only in the volume and nature of problems, but also in the fact of organization and in the methods adopted. These latter are in accord with the more impersonal social relationships of urban life as compared with rural life."[31] As social work became formally organized, it became a full-time occupation, a "business," staffed by professionals, graduates of schools of social work, who gradually outnumbered the volunteers and those not formally trained. Social work agencies became specialized in a particular problem—youth, the aged, adoption, the handicapped, and so forth. The need to coordinate activities arose from specialization and also from the need to systematize the flow of information in a large city. "Umbrella" organizations have arisen in social work to coordinate and supervise the efforts of the host of social work bureaucracies. As federal funding of social welfare[32] has accelerated, the addition of this new level of organization has become more pronounced. In most other fields of organized endeavor—professional groups, unions, college student groups, law enforcement agencies, art retailers—the metropolitan period has witnessed a similar proliferation of "super" organizations to coordinate the activities of autonomous but interrelated bureaucracies.

SOCIAL CONTROL   As might be anticipated, social control in the American city has undergone "sea changes" in the transition from preindustrial to metropolitan society.[33] The larger numbers of people and the impersonal nature of much urban contact have been accompanied by

[29] *Encyclopedia of Associations.* Vol. 1, *National Organizations of the United States (1961),* cited in Amos Hawley, *Urban Society* (1971), pp. 130–31.

[30] *Encyclopedia of Associations.* Vol. 1, *National Organizations of the United States,* 8th ed. (1973).

[31] Arthur Hillman, "Urbanization and the Organization of Welfare Activities in the Metropolitan Community of Chicago," in Ernest W. Burgess and Donald J. Bogue, eds., *Contributions to Urban Sociology* (1964), p. 246.

[32] Comparative figures of federal funding to 1963–1964 are given in Harold Wilensky and Charles Lebeaux, *Industrial Society and Social Welfare* (1965), p. vi.

[33] Specific aspects of social control are discussed in Chapters 19 and 20.

increases in impersonal means of control—legislation, clocks, signs, railings, traffic lights, and an increasingly professional and technically equipped police force. The problems of social control have been complicated by the fact that many of the activities to be controlled are new, so that no previous informal norms pertaining to them existed. Thus, the processing in factories of most food items for home consumption raises problems of standards and inspection; the need to protect the consumer barely arises in preindustrial societies but is most urgently required in metropolitan societies where affluence raises levels of consumption of all kinds of goods. In addition, social control in industrial societies and especially in metropolitan societies must deal with the multiplicity of normative standards in the population and the rapidity of change. Whose standards should be observed and enforced? Problems of enforcement are, of course, also magnified by physical mobility.

Social control in the urban context includes not merely deviance, which is increasingly difficult to define in the metropolitan situation with its proliferation of life styles, but also includes regulation in the sense of coordination. Although communication and consensus remain problems in industrial society, two major thrusts toward coordination are evident. For one, an increased range of responsibilities have been defined as subject to federal regulation and standardization. Some of these—airport regulation, pollution control, car safety—obviously do not correspond to any local jurisdiction. Others, particularly the agglomeration of the poor and blacks in central cities, are locally concentrated, but there is increasing recognition that these are national problems which will only respond to massive regional or national efforts. Second, the metropolis serves as the "switchboard" to coordinate both public and private organizational efforts, a function already evident in the concentration there of industrial main offices and headquarters of national organizations. About two-thirds of the central offices of even agricultural organizations are now located in metropolitan areas,[34] presumably because they too must be close to the sources of information on price supports, marketing conditions, and labor projections.

Contemporary Urbanization in the United States

The vastness and virgin character of the United States at its beginning led to earlier development near the initial points of colonization, especially since technology limited accessibility. Consequently, urban development proceeded unevenly. The several sections of the United States moved at various dates and rates through the three stages

---

[34] Hawley, *op. cit.*, p. 230.

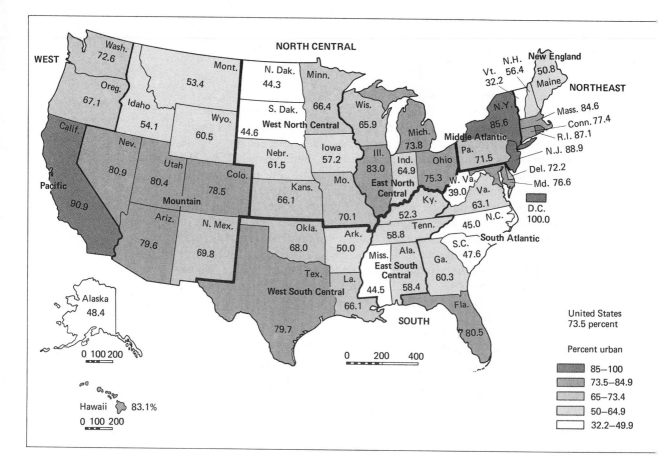

FIGURE 3.5 ●
Percentage of population
urban by state, 1970,
shows that urbanization is
unevenly distributed. Re-
gional and divisional
boundaries for the United
States are also shown, enabling further comparison
of areas of high and low
urbanization, especially in
conjunction with Table
3.5. Source: U.S. Bureau
of the Census, *Statistical
Abstract of the U.S.,*
1972, p. xii; and *U.S.
Census of Population,
1970, Number of Inhabi-
tants,* Final Report
PC(1)-A1, p. 32.

presented above, a fact that is still reflected in current regional variation
in urbanization.

Regional Differences in Urbanization

Since the northeastern region was the center of early industrial and
commercial developments, that area was highly urbanized as early as
the turn of the century. (The discussion of regional and state urbanization that follows utilizes the census definition of urban and the municipally bounded city, rather than Urbanized Areas and SMSA's.) The 1970
census reveals, as Table 3.5 shows, that during the 1960's this lead was
finally overcome and the Northeast has lost its historic position as the
country's most urbanized region. With the shift of population and
industry to the South and West, these sections of the country have
experienced especially rapid gains in urbanization. The Pacific area,
including Alaska and Hawaii, is now the most urban of the geographic
subdivisions of the United States, with 86 percent of the population
classified as urban. The Northeast remains a highly urban region and
contains a concentration of very urbanized states, as is apparent from
Figure 3.5. The Northeast has in fact already entered upon a new phase
of urban development which we will discuss later in this chapter.

The South and West are setting the pace in rate of urban growth at the present time. Florida, Arizona, Nevada, Colorado, and California have experienced an especially rapid urban expansion. Alaska and Hawaii are also undergoing major urban growth, Hawaii having already reached a very high level. With the exception of Texas and Florida, the South still lags behind other sections in terms of its level of urbanization, but its urban growth rate is very high and its future clearly urban. The percentage of the population classified as urban in the component subdivisions of the four regions of the United States in 1970 are listed in Table 3.5. Data for individual states are listed in Figure 3.5.

TABLE 3.5: Percentage of United States Population Classified as Urban by Region: 1970

Region	Percent
NORTHEAST	
New England	76.4
Middle Atlantic	81.7
NORTH CENTRAL	
East North Central	74.8
West North Central	63.7
SOUTH	
South Atlantic	63.7
East South Central	54.6
West South Central	72.6
WEST	
Mountain	73.1
Pacific	86.0

SOURCE: *U.S. Census of Population, 1970. Number of Inhabitants, United States Summary.* Final Report PC(1)–A1. Table 6.

The rapid growth of cities in the South and West appears to bear both cause and effect relationships to significant changes that have occurred, or are occurring, in the country. Perhaps the most important change has been the industrialization of these sections. Until fairly recently the economy of southern and western cities was dominated by trade, but as early as the 1920's their manufacturing activities sharply increased. During World War II the location of numerous military bases and defense industries in the South and West had the effect of drawing population to cities in those areas, and the postwar years witnessed a continuation of the same trend. Proximity to a labor supply, sources of raw materials, and an enlarging body of consumers appear to be the principal reasons for industrial developments in these sections, although the spread of affluence and emphasis on leisure and outdoor activity in contemporary life styles have also played a part.

Although prospects of industrial employment were one of the principal lures of cities in these regions, some areas like Arizona, Florida, and California widely publicized their climatic assets. No doubt part of urban growth in the South and West has been a result of the attractiveness of certain cities as popular playgrounds, health resorts, or places of permanent retirement. During the 1950–1960 decade, Fort Lauderdale's population increased by 130 percent and by an additional 66 percent between 1960 and 1970. Las Vegas had a population increase of 94 percent in the 1960–1970 period, while Colorado Springs grew by 91 percent and Hollywood, Florida, by 206 percent in that same period. Houston's spectacular growth in the last few decades reflects its commercial expansion as the main seaport and financial capital of Texas, as well as the main center of the space industry. In 1960 Houston became, for the first time, one of the ten most populous cities in the United States; by 1970 Houston's population of 1.2 million ranked it as the sixth largest city in the country.

New England presents the opposite side of the picture. Many cities in this area have lost population in recent years, and even greater numbers have had only minor increases. Boston's population declined by eight percent between 1960 and 1970, causing the city to drop to sixteenth in size among United States cities, and Providence's population declined from 207,000 to 179,000 during that period. Industrial dispersal from New England, especially the shift of textile and leather manufacturing to southern or midwestern locations, has exerted a considerable population drain on the cities. After World War II, New England had little share in the defense industry, one of the important contributors to recent urban growth. In some sections of New England, however, especially Vermont and New Hampshire, the growing trend toward ownership of second homes and the popularity of winter sports has become an important new "industry."

City Growth by States

By 1850 the major patterns of urban settlement were fairly well established in the northeastern states, whereas in the remaining regions of the United States urbanization did not really get under way until considerably later. In Indiana, for example, it was not until 1840 that any settlement was large enough to be classified as a city. At the turn of the century, only eight states, of which six were in the Northeast, had a majority of their population in cities. During the first three decades of the present century, thirteen states moved into this category.

Between 1930 and 1940 there was a slump in the urban trend, and no additional state increased its proportion of city residents beyond the 50 percent mark. But during the 1940's and 1950's, a period of wartime and postwar activity, the rate of urbanization was sharply accelerated. By 1970, 41 of the 50 states had more than half of their populations living in cities, and 16 had three-quarters or more of their populations living in cities. The most urban state in 1970 was California with nine of ten residents classified as urban; Rhode Island, New York, and New Jersey almost reached that level with percentages of 87.1, 85.6, and 88.9, respectively, of their populations classified as urban.

Just as the states vary greatly as to proportions of urban residents, so do they differ widely in rate of increase of the urban population. All 50 states except Vermont and West Virginia showed increases of urban population between 1960 and 1970. For the United States as a whole the urban population increased by 19.2 percent. Generally speaking, states with a high percentage of urban population had a low rate of increase, and vice versa, although there were exceptions like California. Five states, three of them in the Northeast, had an urban increase of less than 10 percent between 1960 and 1970. On the other hand, of the four states with the highest rates of urban increase, all except Florida were west of the Mississippi River.

The most significant gain is probably that of California, which added the largest *number* of urban residents—almost 5 million—during the 1960–1970 decade. In the previous decade it had also experienced an urban population increase of about 5 million, so that between 1950 and 1970 California added approximately 10 million urban people. This vast increase of urbanites, most of them migrants from other states, swelled California's total population so that by the winter of 1962–1963 California surpassed New York as the most populous state. One result of California's population increase was its gain of eight seats in the national House of Representatives as a result of the reallocation following the 1960 census and an additional five following the 1970 census.

The nine states still predominantly rural are Alaska, Arkansas, Mississippi, North Carolina, South Carolina, North Dakota, South Dakota, Vermont, and West Virginia.

Even in preponderantly rural states the population has become increasingly urbanized. In 1900, less than 10 percent of the population was urban in six states—Idaho, North Dakota, Oklahoma, Mississippi, Arkansas, and North Carolina. Seventy years later none of these states had less than 44 percent of its population living in cities, and 68 percent of Oklahoma's people was classed as urban and 54 percent of Idaho's.

The most rural of the 50 states are now Vermont with 32.2 percent of its population living in cities and West Virginia with 39 percent so classified. Vermont was one of the few states experiencing a percentage increase in rural population between 1960 and 1970. New Hampshire and Connecticut experienced a similar increase, an indication of the popularity of second homes and, in Connecticut at least, the outer fringes of suburban growth. States with large rural farm populations continue to show substantial declines of rural population. Thus, North Dakota's rural population declined by 16 percent between 1960 and

1970, South Dakota's by 10.8 percent, and Mississippi's by 9.4 percent.

These trends presage further declines in the rural proportion of the population, although we may be approaching a limit in terms of the magnitude of the declines that have already occurred. In 1970 the rural population was 26.5 percent of the total United States population whereas it was 30.1 percent in 1960.[35] From 1960 to 1970 the absolute numbers of the rural population also declined, continuing a trend first revealed in the 1960 census. It marked the first time since census-taking was begun in 1790 that the rural population actually decreased. Before 1960 rural population had always increased at a lower rate than the urban population, but nevertheless it increased.

Metropolitan America

As we indicated earlier, the most important recent development in the United States has been the growth of numerous metropolitan communities, to the extent that today the majority of Americans live in census-defined metropolitan areas. Thus, it is more accurate to speak of metropolitan, rather than urban, America.

The metropolitan community is an extensive geographic unit whose social and economic activities form a more or less integrated system centering around a large city. Metropolitan development differs from previous urban development in that the community is much larger in both area and population, and the linkages among the specialized territorial components are more complex. No segment of a metropolitan community is self-sufficient in its day-to-day activities. For this reason there is constant and intense movement among the various parts of the metropolis. The travel of commuters from "dormitory suburbs" to "downtown"; "local" deliveries of mail, newspapers, and department-store merchandise over a wide area; the trucking of produce from near-by farms and of manufactured goods from outlying factories—all testify to the interdependence among the various segments of the metropolitan community.

METROPOLITAN GROWTH   In 1970 over two-thirds (68.6 percent) of the population of the United States lived in the Standard Metropolitan Statistical Areas delineated by the census.[36] Using the boundaries of the SMSA's as defined in 1970, we find the following percentages of the United States population living in SMSA's over the past thirty years: 1970, 68.6 percent; 1960, 63 percent; 1950, 58 percent; and 1940, 49 percent.

[35] By no means all, and possibly not even a majority, of these ruralites were members of farm families. Our earlier discussion of changing community forms in the United States has indicated the difficulties these changes create in the meaning of rural-urban designations.
[36] See pp. 67–70 above for the census definition of SMSA.

The 1970 SMSA's ranged in size from 56,000 in Meriden, Connecticut, to 11.5 million for the New York SMSA. In 1970 three states, Alaska, Vermont, and Wyoming, had no metropolitan areas, and the recognition in 1971 by the Bureau of the Census of the Greater Anchorage SMSA left only the last two without metropolitan centers. At the other extreme, California, the most metropolitan state, had 93 percent of its population living in metropolitan areas.

TABLE 3.6: Percentage Increase in Population in the United States, in Metropolitan Areas and in Area Outside of Metropolitan Areas: 1910–70

	1960–70	1950–60	1940–50	1930–40	1920–30	1910–20
Total U.S. population	13.3	18.5	14.5	7.2	16.1	14.9
All metropolitan areas reported	16.6	26.4	22.0	8.1	28.3	26.9
Central cities	0.1*	1.5*	13.9	5.1	22.3	25.2
Suburban areas	33.1*	61.7*	35.6	15.1	44.0	32.0
Area outside metropolitan areas	6.8	7.1	6.1	6.5	7.9	9.6

*These figures are corrected for population changes due to annexation of territory between 1950 and 1960 and between 1960 and 1970. Almost all of the central-city growth in recent decades is accounted for by annexation; thus, it is important to refer to the corrected figures.
SOURCES: W. S. Thompson, "The Growth of Metropolitan Districts in the United States: 1900–1940," U. S. Government Printing Office, 1947; *U. S. Census of Population: 1950. Number of Inhabitants*, vol. 1, PA; *U. S. Census of Population: 1960. Number of Inhabitants. United States Summary.* Final Report PC(1)–1A, p. XXV and Table Q. *U. S. Census of Population: 1970. Number of Inhabitants. United States Summary.* Final Report PC(1)–A1, Tables 9, 34, 40, 42. The student should keep in mind that the criteria defining metropolitan districts from 1900 to 1940 differ somewhat from those used in defining metropolitan areas since 1950.

Metropolitan development in the United States is essentially a twentieth-century phenomenon. Table 3.6 indicates that the metropolitan areas have grown faster than the rest of the United States in every decade since the turn of the century. In 1970, for example, the metropolitan-area population increased by 16.6 percent over that of 1960, while that of the United States as a whole increased by only 13.3 percent, and that of population in nonmetropolitan areas by only 6.8 percent. Streams of migrants have been leaving rural farm areas, villages, and small towns and flocking to the supercities so that most of the population growth is taking place in metropolitan areas.

THE DECLINE OF THE CENTRAL CITY   The metropolis as a whole has gained enormously in population, but this growth is not distributed evenly within the metropolitan area. The central cities of metropolitan areas have grown relatively little and in some cases have actually lost population. Some of the many reasons for this decline include the sheer unavailability of space for further building, the obsolescence of housing and industrial plants in core areas, programs of urban renewal and redevelopment deliberately aimed at reducing population density, the availability of rapid, cheap methods of communication and transportation, and the spread of relatively affluent life styles centered on the family and leisure. Table 3.6 shows that the suburban ring of the metropolitan area has consistently grown at a much higher rate than the central cities, with the result that the suburban population eventually outnumbered the central-city population. This major reversal of the numerical dominance of the central city occurred in the late 1960's, and by 1970 the suburban population constituted the largest segment of the total American population—37.2 percent. The percentages for the central city and for population not living in SMSA's are shown below, as are the corresponding percentages for 1960.

	Inside SMSA's		Outside SMSA's
	Central City	Suburbs	
1970	31.4	37.2	31.4
1960	33.4	33.3	33.3

Figure 3.6 shows the percentages for 1970 of population living in central-city and suburban locations for all SMSA's having one million or more in population.

One-third of the central cities of SMSA's actually lost population in the 1960–1970 decade, continuing a trend that had first been significantly revealed in the 1960 census. These losses do not usually reflect economic decline but rather the decentralization of population and institutions within the metropolitan area. In most cases population decline in the central city was accompanied by population growth in the rest of the SMSA. Losses were particularly marked in the cities of SMSA's in the north central and northeastern regions. Of the ten largest SMSA's, only the New York and Los Angeles central cities did not show a decline in population. In some of the central cities such as Detroit, Pittsburgh, and St. Louis, the decline in central-city population exceeded 10 percent.[37]

THE CHANGING COMPOSITION OF CENTRAL-CITY POPULATION   The vast migration to the suburban portions of metropolitan areas has not encompassed all segments of the population equally. The poor, the black, the aged, the single and the divorced, and the foreign born are disproportionately concentrated in the central cities.[38] By 1970, 13.4 percent of the central-city population of metropolitan areas was composed of people

[37] Figures computed from *U.S. Census of Population and Housing: 1970. General Demographic Trends for Metropolitan Areas, 1960 to 1970.* United States Summary. Final Report PHC(2)–1, Table 11.

[38] For important variations and changes in these concentrations, as well as an elaboration of this social implications, see Chapters 10 and 11, "The Inner City" and "The Suburbs," respectively.

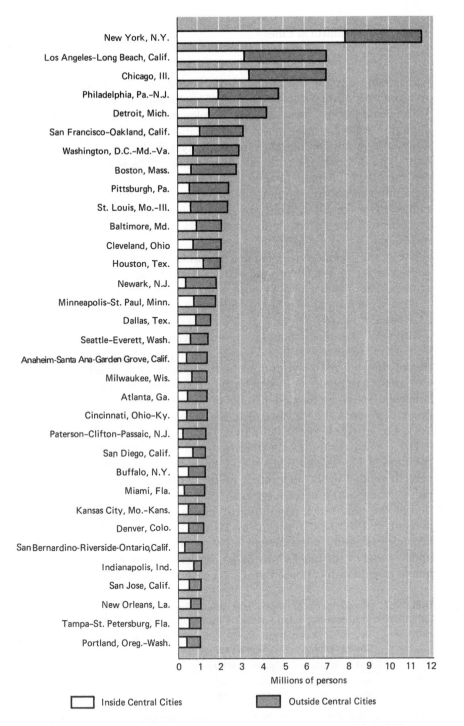

FIGURE 3.6 ● SMSA's of one million or more, ranked by size, 1970, and showing population inside central cities and outside central cities. Most of the largest metropolitan areas in the United States now have a majority of their populations living in the suburban area outside the central cities. Source: U.S. Bureau of the Census, *Census of Population, 1970, U.S. Summary, Number of Inhabitants*, p. 36.

with incomes below the poverty line, whereas only 7.2 percent of the suburban population was composed of such individuals.[39]

The trend toward "two societies" is even more marked in terms of the changing color composition of central cities and suburbs. On the one hand, the small increases in central-city population are due almost entirely to the increase of the black population. The white population in central cities declined by 600,000 during the 1960's, but the black population grew (through natural increase and in-migration) by over 3.2 million. One result is that the blacks increased considerably as a proportion of the nation's total central-city population, from 16 percent in 1960 to 21 percent in 1970.

The great population expansion in suburban portions of the metropolitan areas, on the other hand, was overwhelmingly the result of white growth. The number of whites in suburbs grew by 15.5 million in the 1960's. Whites make up the vast majority of the suburban population, 94.1 percent in 1970.

Although the black population also grew in suburban areas, the numerical increase of 800,000 was insufficient to alter the black proportion of the suburban population. In 1970, as in 1960, blacks comprised just under five percent of all suburban residents. Most of the new black suburbanites were located in one of the twelve largest metropolitan areas, and more than a third of them were in just three SMSA's—New York, Los Angeles, and Washington, D.C.

The overall results of these growth patterns for the residential distribution of blacks and whites have been substantial. By 1970 only 28 percent of the white population of the United States lived in central cities, whereas the percentage was 33 in 1960. In contrast, the proportion of the total black population living in central cities rose from 53 percent in 1960 to 58 percent by 1970. Thus, the black population is becoming steadily more urbanized than the white population, a fact underscored by the blacks' proportionate decline from 32 to 26 percent in nonmetropolitan locations. Details are provided in Table 3.7.

TABLE 3.7: Percentages of Black and White Population Living in Central-City, Suburban, and Nonmetropolitan Locations in the United States: 1970 and 1960

| | INSIDE METROPOLITAN AREAS | | | | OUTSIDE METROPOLITAN AREAS | |
| | Central City | | Suburbs | | | |
	Black	White	Black	White	Black	White
1970	58	28	16	40	26	32
1960	53	33	15	35	32	32

SOURCE: *U. S. Census of Population and Housing, General Demographic Trends for Metropolitan Areas, 1967–1970.* Final Report. PHC(2)–1 United States, p. 6.

[39] Office of the President, *Report on National Growth* (1972), p. 22.

Megalopolis: The Urban Future

The large-scale movement of population into the outer rings of metropolitan areas may be ushering in a new phase of metropolitan development. In regions where there are many Standard Metropolitan Statistical Areas, as the outer ring of one metropolitan area expands it often overlaps with the outer ring of another metropolitan area. The result is a continuous band of urban and suburban development, sometimes stretching for hundreds of miles. This phenomenon has been called variously "strip city," "city region," "supermetropolis," "megalopolis," and "galaxy."

The largest and most intensively studied megalopolis is that of the northeastern seaboard.[40] The main axis of the northeastern megalopolis extends about 600 miles from southern New Hampshire to northern Virginia and extends inland 30 to 100 miles from the Atlantic shore to the Appalachian foothills. The total area, over 53,000 square miles, had a population of about 37 million in 1960, approximately one-fifth of the total population of the United States. This megalopolis encompasses all of Massachusetts, Rhode Island, Connecticut, New Jersey, Delaware, and the District of Columbia, most of Maryland, large chunks of New York State and Pennsylvania, and slices of New Hampshire and Virginia.[41]

Gottmann describes megalopolis and its meaning for future urban life as follows:

As one follows the main highways between Boston and Washington, D.C., one hardly loses sight of built-up areas, tightly woven residential communities, or powerful concentrations of manufacturing plants. Flying this same route one discovers, on the other hand, that behind the ribbons of densely occupied land along the principal arteries of traffic, and in between the clusters of suburbs around the old urban centers, there still remain large areas covered with woods and brush alternating with some carefully cultivated patches of farmland. These green spaces, however, when inspected at closer range, appear stuffed with a loose but immense scattering of buildings, some of them residential but some of industrial character. That is, many of these sections that look rural actually function largely as suburbs in the orbit of some city's downtown. Even the farms, which occupy the larger tilled patches, are seldom worked by people whose only occupation and income are properly agricultural. And yet these farm areas produce large quantities of farm goods!

Thus the old distinctions between rural and urban do not apply here any

---

[40] Jean Gottmann, *Megalopolis: The Urbanized Northeastern Seaboard of the United States* (1961). Gottmann, a French geographer, directed an extensive research of this area in the 1950's.

[41] *Ibid.*, pp. 25–26.

more. . . . In this area, then, we must abandon the idea of the city as a tightly settled and organized unit in which people, activities, and riches are crowded into a very small area clearly separated from its nonurban surroundings. Every city in this region spreads out far and wide around its original nucleus; it grows amidst an irregularly colloidal mixture of rural and suburban landscapes; it melts on broad fronts with other mixtures, of somewhat similar though different texture, belonging to the suburban neighborhoods of other cities. . . . This region serves thus as a laboratory in which we may study the new evolution reshaping both the meaning of our traditional vocabulary and the whole material structure of our way of life.

. . . So great are the consequences of the general evolution heralded by the present rise and complexity of Megalopolis that any analysis of this region's problems often gives one the feeling of looking at the dawn of a new stage in human civilization. . . . Indeed, the area may be considered the cradle of a new order in the organization of inhabited space. . . .

Separation between place of work and place of residence creates within the area the system of daily "tidal" movements involved in commuting. Over these are superimposed other currents, some seasonal and some irregularly recurrent. These reflect relations between different parts of Megalopolis that stem from more complicated needs than the simple journey from home to work. These other needs grow more complicated and more general as average family income rises and both goods and activities that were once considered dispensable come to be regarded as necessary by large number of Megalopolitans. . . .

New *patterns of intense living* that have become normal in Megalopolis affect not only land use. They also exert a strong influence on the economic and social foundations of society. . . . The density of activities and of movement of all kinds is certainly the most extraordinary feature of Megalopolis, more characteristic even than the density of population and of skyscrapers. It has become a means of maintaining economic growth and stabilizing society; but how far can it go without destroying itself? . . . The self-defeating effect of dense concentrations may be observed also in other fields than transportation. . . .

It is easier to accept responsibility for solutions than to provide them. The many millions of people who find themselves *neighbors in Megalopolis*, even though they live in different states and hundreds of miles from one another, are barely becoming aware of the imperatives of such a "neighborhood." . . . Responsible public opinion is becoming conscious of the problems involved, and the struggle to find solutions has started. It is especially difficult because no one problem can be tackled without affecting others. Transportation, land use, water supply, cultural activities, use and development of resources, government and politics—all are interrelated. . . .

Megalopolis stands indeed at the threshold of a new way of life, and upon solution of its problems will rest civilization's ability to survive.[42]

THE YEAR 2000   Recent projections on American population growth and distribution indicate that by the year 2000, 85 percent of the American population will be metropolitan.[43] The exact number of Americans living

[42] *Ibid.*, pp. 5–16 *passim*, Reprinted by permission.
[43] *Population and the American Future.* Report of the Commission on Population Growth and the American Future (1972), pp. 34ff.

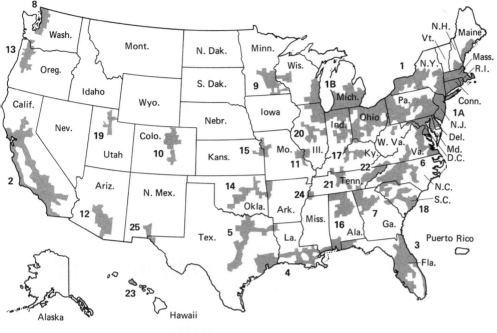

FIGURE 3.7 ● Urban regions in the year 2000. Projections indicate that 85 percent of the American people will be living in vast metropolitan agglomerations by the year 2000. These projections should be compared with the 1970 metropolitan distribution shown in Figure 3.2. Source: Jerome P. Pickard, "U.S. Metropolitan Growth and Expansion, 1970–2000, with Population Projections," p. 143 in U.S. Commission on Population Growth and the American Future. *Population Distribution and Policy.* Sara Mills Mazie, ed., Vol. V of the Commission research reports, Washington, D.C.: Government Printing Office.

in metropolitan areas will depend mainly on whether the average family has two or three children. Projections on the basis of the two-child family indicate 225 million people in metropolitan areas by the year 2000, while projections based on the three-child family would yield 273 million metropolites by that year.

The authors of these projections point out that the bulk of this metropolitan growth will be in urban regions, that is, "areas of one million people or more comprised of a continuous zone of metropolitan areas and intervening counties within which one is never far from a city.[44] This is the concept of megalopolis. By 2000 it is estimated that

[44] *Ibid.*, p. 36.

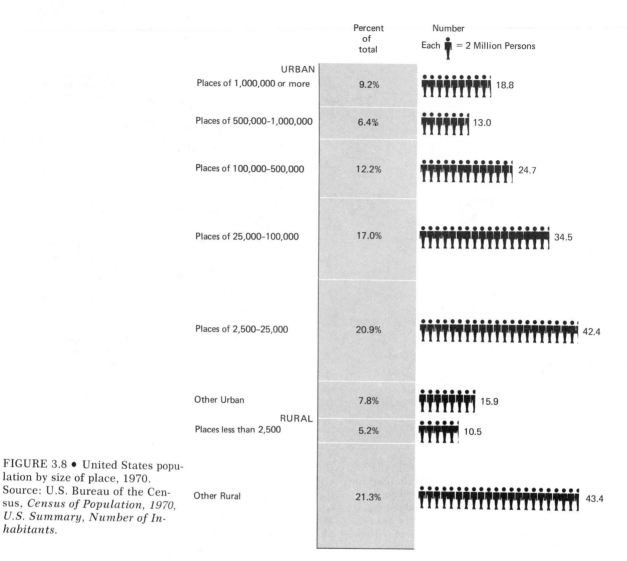

Percent
of
total

Number

Each ♟ = 2 Million Persons

URBAN
Places of 1,000,000 or more — 9.2% — 18.8

Places of 500,000–1,000,000 — 6.4% — 13.0

Places of 100,000–500,000 — 12.2% — 24.7

Places of 25,000–100,000 — 17.0% — 34.5

Places of 2,500–25,000 — 20.9% — 42.4

Other Urban — 7.8% — 15.9

RURAL
Places less than 2,500 — 5.2% — 10.5

Other Rural — 21.3% — 43.4

FIGURE 3.8 • United States population by size of place, 1970. Source: U.S. Bureau of the Census, *Census of Population, 1970, U.S. Summary, Number of Inhabitants.*

five-sixths of the American people will be living in 25 urban regions, which are shown in Figure 3.7. According to these projections, 54 percent of all Americans will be living in the two largest urban regions; 41 percent in the metropolitan galaxy extending along the Atlantic seaboard and westward past Chicago, while another 13 percent will be in the California region lying between San Francisco and San Diego. It is important to note that these projections are "essentially the outcome of trends now observable—but not . . . a prediction of what will happen or what is desirable."[45]

One myth about the urban future should be laid to rest, namely, that masses of people will be living "piled on top of one another." The urban densities of the United States have been declining at least since 1880.[46]

[45] *Ibid.*, p. 37.
[46] *Report on National Growth*, pp. 18–19.

This has been the result of the more rapid geographic expansion of urban areas than of population growth within them. As Elazar has pointed out, most Americans live in relatively small-sized places.[47] The distribution of the American population by size of place is shown in Figure 3.8. While it is true that most of these people are, or will be, within the "orbit" of large metropolitan galaxies, nevertheless the actual social and civic reality of their daily lives is of a smaller compass. The megalopolis and urban region are real in the sense that they represent interdependence but they may impinge only indirectly on the individual's routine activities.

Americans continue to prefer living in the open country or a small town or city (64 percent) as opposed to medium- or large-sized cities or suburbs (36 percent).[48] The expansion of small, low-density communities in the context of megalopolitan growth may represent one way of combining the American antiurban bias with the economic realities of the late twentieth century. It leaves unresolved such major questions as the availability of natural resources to sustain such a pattern and whether the opportunity for choice will be extended to all Americans.

Selected Bibliography

BOOKS

Baltzell, E. Digby, ed., *The Search for Community in Modern America.* New York: Harper and Row, 1968.

Bell, Daniel, *The Coming of Post-Industrial Society.* New York: Basic Books, 1973.

Bollens, John C., and Henry J. Schmandt, *The Metropolis: Its People, Politics, and Economic Life.* New York: Harper and Row, 1965.

Bridenbaugh, Carl, *Cities in the Wilderness: The First Century of Urban Life in America, 1625–1742.* New York: Ronald Press, 1938.

———, *Cities in Revolt: Urban Life in America, 1743–1776.* New York: Knopf, 1955.

Davis, Kingsley, and F. G. Styles, eds., *California's Twenty Million.* Berkeley, Calif.: Institute of International Studies, Population Monograph # 10, University of California, 1971.

Duncan, Beverly, and Stanley Lieberson, *Metropolis and Region in Transition.* Beverly Hills, Calif.: Sage Publications, 1970.

Ferriss, Abbott L., ed., *Research and the 1970 Census.* Oak Ridge, Tenn.: Southern Regional Demographic Group, Oak Ridge Associated Universities, 1972.

[47] Daniel Elazar, "Smaller Cities in Metropolitan Society: The New American 'Towns'," Center for the Study of Federalism, Temple University, Working Paper # 9 (c. 1969).

[48] *Population and the American Future*, p. 34.

Gottmann, Jean, *Megalopolis*. New York: Twentieth Century Fund, 1961.

Green, Constance McLaughlin, *American Cities in the Growth of the Nation*. New York: Harper and Row, 1965.

———, *The Rise of Urban America*. New York: Harper Colophon Books, 1965.

Hansen, Niles M., *Rural Poverty and the Urban Crisis*. Bloomington: University of Indiana Press, 1970.

Hawley, Amos, *Urban Society*. New York; Ronald Press, 1971.

Hirsch, Werner Z., ed., *Los Angeles: Viability and Prospects for Metropolitan Leadership*. New York: Praeger, 1971.

Hughes, Helen MacGill, ed., *Cities and City Life*. Sociological Resources for the Social Studies Series, American Sociological Association. Boston: Allyn and Bacon, 1970.

Mayer, Harold, and Richard C. Wade, *Chicago: Growth of a Metropolis*. Chicago: University of Chicago Press, 1969.

McKelvey, Blake, *The Urbanization of America, 1860–1915*. New Brunswick, N. J.: Rutgers University Press, 1963.

———, *The Emergence of Metropolitan America, 1915–1966*. New Brunswick, N. J.: Rutgers University Press, 1968.

Population and the American Future. The Report of the Commission on Population Growth and the American Future. Washington, D.C.: U.S. Government Printing Office. 1972.

Schlesinger, Arthur M., *The Rise of the City, 1878–1898*. New York: Macmillan, 1933; reissued Chicago: Quadrangle Paperback, 1971.

von Eckardt, Wolf, *The Challenge of Megalopolis. A Graphic Presentation of the Urbanized Northeastern Seaboard of the United States, Based on the Original Study of Jean Gottmann*. New York: Macmillan, 1964.

U. S. Bureau of the Census, *Current Population Reports*, Series P23, No. 37, "Social and Economic Characteristics of Population in Metropolitan and Nonmetropolitan Areas, 1970 and 1960." Washington, D.C.: U.S. Government Printing Office. 1971.

———, *People of the United States in the 20th Century*, by Irene B. Taeuber and Conrad Taeuber (Census Monograph). Washington, D.C.: U.S. Government Printing Office, 1971.

Wade, Richard C., *The Urban Frontier: The Rise of Western Cities, 1790–1830*. Cambridge: Harvard University Press, 1959.

Warner, Sam Bass, *The Private City: Philadelphia in Three Periods of Its Growth*. Philadelphia: University of Pennsylvania Press, 1968.

———, *The Urban Wilderness: A History of the American City*. New York: Harper and Row, 1972.

Warren, Roland, *The Community in America*, 2d ed. Chicago: Rand McNally, 1972.

Wilensky, Harold, and C. Lebeaux, *Industrial Society and Social Welfare*, with a new introduction by Harold Wilensky. New York: The Free Press, 1965.

ARTICLES

Aronson, Sidney, "The Sociology of the Telephone,: "*International Journal of Comparative Sociology*, 12 (September 1971), 153–67.

Clawson, Marion, "The Future of Nonmetropolitan America," *American Scholar*, 42 (Winter 1972–73), 102–9.

Elazar, Daniel J., "The Metropolitan Frontier: A Perspective on Change in American Society." General Learning Press Module, 1973.

Glenn, Norval D., and J. L. Simmons, "Are Regional Cultural Differences Diminishing?" *Public Opinion Quarterly*, 31 (Summer 1967), 176–93.

Goldmark, Peter, "Communication and the Community," *Scientific American*, 227 (September 1972), 143–50.

Hauser, Philip M., "The Census of 1970," *Scientific American*, 225 (July 1971), 17–25.

Kemeny, John, "The City and the Computer Revolution," in *Governing Urban America*, Monograph #7, *Annals of the American Academy of Political and Social Science*, 1967.

Shryock, Henry, "The Natural History of Standard Metropolitan Areas," *American Journal of Sociology*, 63 (September 1957), 163–70.

4 • Contemporary Urbanization in World Perspective: I

In this and the following chapter we shall use the term *urbanization* in a demographic rather than a cultural and social sense. It will apply especially to the changes in the numerical size of designated sectors of a population, such as the urban and rural components. At the same time, for comparative purposes we shall consider the growth and expansion of individual cities, and of that portion of the total population designated as urban and rural. We shall also consider urbanization in both the industrialized countries of the world and those in which industrialization is relatively underdeveloped. Most highly industrialized countries are also highly urbanized, and by the same token, most of the industrially underdeveloped countries are still predominantly rural.

In this chapter and the next we shall present a comparative analysis of urbanization and the growth of cities, utilizing data from various cultures and countries. Such an approach, we feel, makes it possible to view the contemporary development of cities from a global perspective. The phenomenon of world urbanism should therefore assume a significance not apparent in an analysis limited to a single country or region. But such a procedure has its limitations, for a comprehensive presentation would not be possible within the confines of a few chapters. For the purposes of this volume, then, the discussion may be considered merely an introduction to world urbanization.

Since our discussion is focused on the demographic aspects of urbanization, we cannot, within the limits of these chapters, provide an analysis of other important features of city life on the world scene. Therefore, such important matters will be considered in other chapters, again being restricted by limitations of space and often inadequate data pertaining to important urban phenomena. Inasmuch as discussion of contemporary urbanization involves considerable quantitative data in tabulated form, it is important that the reader examine the accompanying tables.

The Dichotomy between Industrial and Developing Countries

For this discussion we shall dichotomize the world's countries as "industrial" and "developing." Industrialized countries are those in which most of the people reside in sizable communities and are engaged in nonagricultural occupations, whereas in developing countries, most of the population resides in small communities and is engaged in agriculture or other forms of primary production. This dichotomy of industrial and developing countries is obviously an oversimplification; taking the world as a whole there are degrees or levels of industrial or nonagricultural developments. But allowing for these variations, the dichotomy is useful in providing a short-cut to our analysis. The countries of western Europe and northern America, for example, are highly industrialized and urbanized, whereas in most of the countries of Asia and Africa a low level of industrialization and urbanization prevails.

Urbanization and Networks of Cities and Towns

One of the important developments related to urbanization is the emergence of networks of cities and towns that function to relate them to each other in economic, political, and cultural matters. In industrial societies neither the city nor the small town is any longer an island unto itself. As people become more and more aware of the increasing interdependence of cities and towns, organizations emerge which provide the formal bonds that give meaning to this interdependency. In many countries and states there exist, for example, leagues or associations of municipalities which are concerned with various problems and issues considered important to the communities, as well as organizations of mayors, city managers, and other elected or appointed administrators from municipalities of varying size. On another level there are the formal arrangements between industrial or commercial firms with operations in more than one city. On still another level there are the networks of voluntary associations representing a wide variety of personal and group interests and activities. Finally, there are the informal networks that bind together friends and relatives who live in different communities. All of these, taken together, comprise what might be called an "urban social system."

In developing societies, formal and informal networks do exist between and among cities, and others are emerging, but cities and towns in such areas are still more isolated than those in industrial countries having the advantages of modern forms of technology and organization. It is not unusual, in developing countries, for small towns to exist in a state of social and cultural isolation from other communities, a situation that scarcely exists in industrial countries.

Methods of Measuring
Urban Trends

Because precise and complete data are not available for all countries, and because census enumerations are often made at different dates and by different criteria, it is necessary, in demographic surveys, to make use of estimates, extrapolations, and population projections. Kingsley Davis, for example, selected three dates (1950, 1960, and 1970), making projections from data obtained mainly in the 1950's and 1960's. Projections have also been made by demographers for future dates such as 1980 and the year 2000. It should be noted that such projections are not predictions of the precise size of a given population at a designated future date; rather, they are indications of what is *probable* if certain known trends of the present and recent past are projected into the future. Such projections are always expressed in terms of probabilities, and may exceed or fall short of the projected size of a given population.

To clarify the application of methods of measuring urban population changes we shall distinguish between three procedures. The first is to determine the *rate* of growth (or decline) of an individual city. If, for instance, a city of 150,000 increased in population by 25,000 over a designated period of time, say between 1960 and 1970, its rate of growth for this period, expressed as a percentage, would be 16.6. But we must remember that the actual *size* of the city has a definite bearing on the rate of growth. If the city mentioned above had a population of 500,000 in 1960 and increased by 25,000 during the following decade, its rate of growth would be only five percent. For example, Melbourne, Australia, with a population of slightly over 2 million in 1970, experienced a 19 percent increase over the preceding decade, although the actual population increase amounted to 350,000. On the other hand, Brisbane's increase of 200,000 persons over the same period (from 600,000 to 800,000) represented an increase of 33 percent.

The same principle applies if we consider the *increase* (or *decrease*) in the population of a country. The urban population of France, for example, grew by nearly 7 million between 1960 and 1970 for an increase of 24 percent, but the Federal Republic of Germany, with a larger urban population base, increased by almost 8 million, or only 18 percent.

The third measure we shall consider is the proportion of a population classified as urban or rural and the change in the proportion over a designated length of time, which we shall refer to as the *level* and *rate* of urbanization. In 1960, Austria's urban population accounted for exactly half of the total number of inhabitants; in 1970 this ratio had increased to only 51 percent. On the other hand, Australia's urban population represented 77 percent of the total in 1960, but a decade later the percentage had increased sharply to 84.

Because the official distinction between "urban" and "rural" varies greatly among the nations of the world, it is not possible to make a precise comparison of countries concerning the degree or level of urbanization they have attained. Most countries have established, for their own purposes, a rural-urban dividing line between 2,000 and 5,000 inhabitants, and some have even used 20,000 as the dividing line, since this figure can be uniformly applied in most countries. This division will be followed in our discussion of comparative world developments, although it may differ from the rural-urban distinctions made within many countries. The United Nations criterion of 20,000 persons, however, has the effect of placing the level of urbanization lower than would be the case if various national distinctions were employed. In the United States, for example, the rural-urban dividing point has been established by the federal Bureau of the Census at 2,500. In delineating large cities, it is common practice to use the figure of 100,000 as an index of metropolitanization, not merely urbanization. References in the literature to "great cities," or sometimes "city," usually mean cities of 100,000 inhabitants or more.

The Changing Tempo of Urbanization: Industrial Countries

As we have discussed in Chapter 2, industrialization in the Western world has had the effect of increasing the rate of urbanization, especially in the early stages of industrial development. The most rapid urbanization of both England and the United States occurred in the nineteenth century, and the twentieth century has witnessed an acceleration of this process in many other industrial countries. In England, according to Davis, it took about 79 years for the inhabitants of cities over 100,000 to increase from 10 to 30 percent of the total population, 66 years in the United States, 48 years in Germany, 36 years in Japan, and 26 in Australia.[1] These differences are due in considerable measure to the periods of time in which intensive industrialization actually got under way. Japan and Australia were relatively late arrivals on the industrial scene.

[1] Kingsley Davis, "Urbanization of the Human Population," *Scientific American*, 213 (September 1965), 43.

If the present trend continues in the industrialized countries, it seems almost inevitable that the rate of urbanization will decline and the urban-rural ratio eventually become stabilized. This has already happened in England, where a high proportion of the population has resided in cities since the turn of the present century. Technology associated with both industrialism and agriculture has meant the release of agricultural workers who often migrate to the cities in order to find suitable employment and other advantages. This drain on the rural population has been going on in these countries for a long time and has now reached a point in which the pool of rural-farm migrants is "drying up."

That the entire world is becoming increasingly urbanized is generally known. Over the span of seven decades preceding 1970, the world's population doubled, from less than 2 billion to about 3.6 billion. But the urban population increased much more rapidly, from about 224 million in 1900 to one and one-third billion by 1970, a six-fold increase. In this connection it is important to realize (1) the difference between the rate of growth of individual cities, (2) the rate of growth of the entire population of a country (or even the entire world) residing in cities, and (3) the increase or decrease in the proportion of a country's population in the urban or rural sectors. A country experiencing a low rate of urbanization may also have cities in which the growth rate is extremely high.

The Beginnings of Industrialism and Urbanism as a Dominant System

Although cities have existed through many centuries, as we discussed at some length in Chapter 1, it was not until the Industrial Revolution occurred in the Western world that the beginnings of urbanism appeared as a phenomenon developing entire societies. In a sense, Manchester, England, stands as a symbol of emergent industrialism, for it was in this city that the factory system very early came to dominate the life of the community and eventually the entire society.[2] In Manchester we see the convergence, in a single city, of a developing technology with new forms of social, political, and economic organization. It was a development that was destined to affect the lives of countless millions of people all over the world. Up to this time, even in England, most of the world's people earned a living as small shopkeepers or craftsmen, or were engaged in agriculture or other forms of primary production. Manchester became the prototype for developments in many countries.

Most highly urbanized countries of the world are, as we have noted, the most highly industrialized, and almost all of them are located in the

[2]Leon S. Marshall, "The Emergence of the First Industrial City: Manchester, 1780–1850," in Caroline Ware, ed., *The Cultural Approach to History*, (1940).

Aerial view of London. Modern office skyscrapers, like the one in the foreground, have multiplied recently, altering the profile of London. Such structures represent an intensive use of space, which is expensive and at a premium. Increasing numbers of white collar workers have created a need for such facilities. (British Tourist Authority, N. Y.)

temperate climatic zones. To provide a time perspective of their development, they may be placed in two categories: the early established urban-industrial countries and the newly industrialized societies. A third category, emerging urbanized countries, will be considered later.

England has the distinction (some consider it dubious) of being the first major country to become industrialized and urbanized, but many others were to follow that country in fairly rapid sucession: the United

103

States, Canada, The Netherlands, Scandinavia, France, Germany, Switzerland, Belgium, Australia, and New Zealand. By the end of the nineteenth century, all of these countries were well on the road to a high level of urbanization and a social order that has had far-reaching ramifications for almost every aspect of community life.

Somewhat later in this timetable, in the early years of the twentieth century, other countries began to emulate this pattern of society. Many of the countries in this category form a belt across southern and eastern Europe—Spain, Italy, Hungary, Poland, Rumania, Greece, the Soviet Union, Czechoslovakia, and Yugoslavia. Also included in this category is South Africa, as is Japan, the only non-Western country that has become highly industrialized and urbanized. Much of Japan's and Russia's urban-industrial development has occurred since World War II. Among the countries that are highly urbanized, although sometimes considered "developing" societies, are Venezuela, Chile, Uruguay, and Argentina; but they, too, are moving fairly rapidly toward the goal of extensive industrialization.

It seems unlikely, however, that many countries can ever attain the saturation stage that some of the urban-industrial regions have reached, or are likely to reach before the end of the present century. This would appear to be especially true of numerous Asian and African countries which are predominantly rural and whose economic and technological development is still on a relatively low level. In a few countries the urban-rural ratio changes very slowly; a kind of stablized balance between the rural and urban population has been attained although falling far short of high-level urban saturation.

The slowing down of the rate of urbanization in a particular country, or even no increase at all, does not mean that cities in that country have ceased to grow. On the contrary, cities in highly urbanized societies may continue to grow even though the proportion of population already living in cities is very high.

One reason that the growth of cities in highly urbanized societies is slowing down is that fewer rural people are available to migrate to them, unless migrants from other countries are attracted to them. In Australia, for example, only about 12 percent of the population resides in rural communities (in villages and on farms); in the United Kingdom, 21 percent; in West Germany, 18 percent; in Japan, 17 percent; and in the United States and Canada, about 25 percent. When the rural population in these countries is subclassified by occupation, the figures become even more meaningful. In the United States the farm population reached an all-time low in the 1960's, or only seven percent of the total population, while in England there were only 500,000 farm residents, representing less than three percent of the working population. Obviously, some countries are "scraping the bottom of the rural barrel," traditionally the principal source of urban-bound migrants. Today, one agricultural worker in the technologically developed societies may produce ten times as much as his counterpart a century ago. But it is obvious that the number or proportion of agricultural producers can never be reduced to near zero, unless a country is able or willing to import all the food and other materials it needs to sustain its population.

Urbanization in Developing Countries

Industrial and Developing Countries Compared

Any comparison of urbanization in industrial and developing countries must take into account the varied conditions under which these developments have occurred. In industrial countries, cities developed *pari passu* with urban and rural technology and forms of organization adaptable to a changing milieu. Even as early as the nineteenth century, technological innovations in agriculture resulted in increased productivity and therefore a surplus of agricultural products. These innovations, when applied, meant that fewer and fewer people were necessary to do the work; the "surplus" were therefore free to move to the cities and obtain employment in the expanding urban economies. Generally speaking, farmers who remained on the land prospered, or at least were able to purchase many of the things produced in the cities, thus providing a domestic market for the products of urban factories and mills. Those who did not prosper were inclined to pull up stakes and head for the urban Promised Land or another country.

Quite a different situation has prevailed in the developing countries. In these areas agriculture has not benefited maximally by the application of modern technology; methods of agricultural production remain relatively primitive, producing only a small exportable surplus over and beyond what is needed for home consumption. Most of the rural population has remained on, or only slightly above, the subsistence level, with spendable incomes insufficient to purchase many city-produced things. Thus they have provided only a slim market for urban-manufactured goods. Furthermore, the high birth rates characteristic of these countries produce a surplus of people to be "exported" to the cities. And unlike most industrial countries, whose rural populations have been declining or growing slowly, the developing countries continue to have a growing rural population even though vast numbers forsake the land.

There is some tendency to view urbanization in developing countries as a latter-day version of what occurred earlier in countries that are now highly industrialized and urbanized. However, conditions under which urbanization and industrialization occurred in the industrial societies are in many respects quite different from conditions that prevail in developing countries. Functions performed by cities in developing societies are different in certain respects from the functions of cities in industrialized regions. Some of these may be summarized:

1. Most contemporary developing societies were, at one time or another, subject to colonial domination, and many have only recently emerged from the status of a colony which was exploited by the colonial powers. Indeed, cities such as Bombay, Calcutta, Singapore, Jakarta, Colombo, Cairo, and Shanghai were actually created by colonial powers to serve their own economic, political, and military interests.

Raw materials produced in the colonies were usually transported to the occupying country to supply its urban factories and mills and therefore provide employment for city dwellers. People in the colonies were thus denied the benefits of extensive industrialization except as many became, almost literally, laborers in the vineyard, producing materials to be shipped abroad for processing. Many of the Western industrial societies were colonial powers whose dynamic economic development was in some measure a legacy of colonial rule in which they were the chief beneficiaries. Nor were the foundations of city growth the same for the colonial powers and their overseas possessions. Colonial domination in its many manifestations left an almost indelible imprint on these

Most large cities have sharp contrasts of poverty and affluence, commonly indicated by extremes of housing accommodations, especially in developing countries. The accompanying photographs show these extremes in Bombay, India. Left is a family of "street sleepers" without any housing shelter; right is a fashionable apartment district in the same city. (David Channer, Nancy Palmer—left; Noel P. Gist—right)

countries and thus became a serious handicap to modernization even after independence was achieved.[3]

2. Inasmuch as the colonial powers did not sponsor or promote extensive industrial development in their colonies, but instead siphoned off the raw materials for processing in their own establishments, industrialism did not play a major role in the growth of cities in the colonial areas. Only recently, mainly since World War II, have these countries emphasized the development of industry and the expansion of the economy in general.

3. The burgeoning populations in most of the developing countries have made it increasingly difficult in recent years for rural people engaged in agriculture or related occupations to earn a livelihood, or at least maintain a standard of living commensurate with their rising expectations. Hence, many forsake the land and move to the cities, hoping to find jobs and a better way of life. In India, for example, farms

---

[3] For a relevant discussion, see especially Philip Hauser, ed., *Urbanization in Latin America* (1961), a report of proceedings of an international conference on urbanization, and published by UNESCO.

have been so fragmented that the average size of a farm (around two acres) cannot adequately support the families of many farm operators, not to mention the hordes of landless farm laborers who also depend on farm owners for a livelihood, as well as village craftsmen and other workers whose occupations are tied to agriculture. Of the 400 million rural persons in India directly or indirectly dependent on agriculture, many are almost literally pushed off the land. All over the nonindustrial world the picture, with many variations, is similar.

Most of the developing countries are presently experiencing an annual increase of the total population of between two and a half and three percent. This increase is due not only to high birth rates but also to the decline of mortality made possible by the application of modern technical and medical innovations and facilities. With agricultural technology still comparatively primitive, and industrial technology and organization relatively underdeveloped, these countries are more efficient in producing a surplus of people than a surplus of agricultural and industrial products. Such conditions result in unemployment, underemployment, and nonproductive employment, which means a heavy burden of poverty for the many persons trapped in this situation. The escapist flight to the cities commonly means a leap from the proverbial rural frying pan into the urban fire. The urban economies are simply not expanding rapidly enough to absorb all the locally born residents, not to mention in-migrants in search of jobs. As a United Nations report states it, many of them become "hangers-on and odd-job men who live on the rim of starvation in the rundown slums and miserable fringe settlements of the great urban jungles."[4] In Nigeria, for example, it has been estimated that the expanding modern sector of the economy "cannot absorb more than one-third of those who seek employment in it."[5]

Comparative Levels and Rates of Urbanization

Countries and regions vary greatly in the proportion of population residing in urban communities, or in cities of varying size. Although every region of the world is experiencing increasing urbanization, some have approached the maximum level while others have only a small proportion of population living in cities. The differences are most pronounced between industrial and developing countries. In Australia, for example, almost nine out of ten persons live in urban communities, and six out of ten reside in large cities of 100,000 or over; it is one of the most

[4] Report of the United Nations Committee on Housing, Building, and Planning. New York: United Nations, July 24, 1969, p. 29.

[5] F. H. Harbison, "The Generation of Employment in Newly Developing Countries," in James R. Sheffield, ed., *Education, Employment, and Rural Development* (1967), p. 181.

TABLE 4.1: Countries Representing Extremes of High and Low Urbanization by Percentage of Population in Cities over 20,000 and Large Cities over 100,000

Country	High Urbanization*	Large Cities†	Country	Low Urbanization*	Large Cities†
Belgium	87	28	India	19	10
Australia	86	65	Ceylon	19	11
Uruguay	81	53	Indonesia	17	12
England and Wales	78	71	Zaire (Congo)	16	7
Netherlands	78	45	Laos	15	7
Venezuela	76	37	Sudan	12	3
Chile	76	37	Kenya	10	7
United States	74	58	Ethiopia	10	3
Japan	72	55	Uganda	8	4
Israel	72	55	Tanzania	5	3

SOURCES: *United Nations, *Demographic Yearbook* (1971), Table 5. †Population Reference Bureau, Inc., *1972 World Population Data Sheet*. Census data for 1970 and 1971, or most recent figures available.

urbanized and metropolitanized countries in the world. But as Table 4.1 indicates, others are not far behind.

If one shifts the geographic focus a different picture emerges. At the lower end of the urbanization level are countries that have less than 10 percent of their population located in cities, notably such countries as Yemen, Saudi Arabia, Afghanistan, Chad, Uganda, Kenya, Ethiopia, Nepal, and the Sudan, all of which are relatively small in total population. But there are many developing countries whose level of urbanization ranges between 10 and 30 percent—countries like India, Pakistan, Indonesia, and Thailand.

Obviously, most of the world's countries fall somewhere between the two extremes shown in Table 4.1, if they are arranged on a continuum in terms of the level of urbanization. All of the countries of southern and eastern Europe are moderately urbanized, as are the nations of the Middle East and most of Latin America. Most of Africa, excluding South Africa and countries facing the Mediterranean Sea, might be considered the least urbanized continent, but Asia (excluding Japan) is also low on the urbanization scale.

Among the countries that got an early start on the road to urbanism there has generally been a slowing down both in numerical increase and in annual rates of growth, in urban as well as in rural sectors. For the most part, these are the countries we repeatedly refer to as industrial or urban-industrial. Countries that got a late start, mainly in nonindustrial regions, have experienced a relatively rapid growth of cities and a moderate growth rate of rural population. A survey conducted in the 1960's by the United Nations reveals differences when regions are classified by recency of urbanization:[6]

[6] Adapted from United Nations, Department of Economic and Social Affairs, *Urbanization: Development Policies and Planning* (1968), p. 15.

1. *Early urbanized*: Regions at least 25 percent urbanized by 1920 (western and northern Europe, northern America, temperate South America, and Australia and New Zealand).

2. *Recently urbanized*: Regions at least 25 percent urbanized by 1960 but not by 1920 (southern and eastern Europe, Japan, northern Africa, southern Africa, tropical South America, and Middle America).

3. *Least urbanized*: Regions under 25 percent urban in 1960 (mainland east Asia, south and southeast Asia, the Middle East, southwest Africa, the Caribbean, and tropical Africa).

The average annual rates of population growth between 1920 and 1960 for these three stages expressed as percentages are as follows:

	Urban	Rural and Small Town
Early urbanized regions	1.8	0.4
Recently urbanized regions	3.2	0.6
Least urbanized regions	3.8	1.0

Rapid and Slow Urbanization

Countries vary widely as to trends in urbanization when gauged by the changing proportions of the urban population calculated from the base of the total population. Paradoxically, the growth of a country's total population may be rapid, and the cities may be growing rapidly, but the level of urbanization may actually be low. In any case, the percentage of the urban population may be high or low, and the country may be highly industrialized or underdeveloped. The marked differences among countries with high and low urbanization patterns are indicated in Table 4.2, which contains a representative sample of countries. In the "low" column the United Kingdom and Ceylon have identical urbanization rates for the two decades between 1950 and 1970 , although the United Kingdom is one of the most industrialized countries in the world and Ceylon one of the least industrialized. In the "high" column, the Soviet Union, extensively industrialized, is urbanizing at about the same speed as Yugoslavia and Chile, and all three more rapidly than the United States.

Paradoxically, countries that are becoming urbanized slowly often generate the rapid growth of cities. A relevant example is India, where the rate of urbanization has been slow in recent years, less than one percent a decade. In 1950, 17.1 percent of the population resided in cities (as defined by the Indian census); two decades later, the percentage was 18.8. Yet some of the world's fastest growing cities are in that country. What, then, is the explanation for this discrepancy? It is that the rural population is increasing at about the same percentage rate as the urban population. But since the rural population is at least four times as large as the urban, the very magnitude of the rural base results in a low

TABLE 4.2: Urbanization Trends, 1950 to 1970, Stated as Change in Proportion of Urban Population to Total Population in Rapidly Urbanizing and Slowly Urbanizing Countries

Country	HIGH Percent Urban			Country	LOW Percent Urban		
	1950	1970	Change		1950	1970	Change
Japan	37.4	83.3	+45.9	Indonesia	12.3	17.9	+5.6
Uruguay	56.6	84.2	+27.6	Bolivia	20.4	25.3	+4.9
Yugoslavia	17.2	38.7	+21.5	Kenya	5.2	9.2	+4.0
Soviet Union	42.5	62.3	+29.8	Thailand	10.0	13.0	+3.0
Chile	54.3	73.7	+19.4	Netherlands	70.5	72.2	+1.7
Australia	72.1	88.5	+16.4	Ceylon	15.0	16.6	+1.6
Canada	61.7	74.7	+13.0	United Kingdom	77.5	79.1	+1.6
United States	64.0	75.2	+11.2	Israel	79.8	81.3	+1.5

SOURCE: Adapted from projections in Kingsley Davis, *World Urbanization, 1950–1970*, vol. I (1969), Table C.

percentage increase although vast numbers of persons forsake the farms and villages for urban centers; hence, the rapid growth of existing individual cities although the urban-rural ratio is not greatly altered. Other countries such as Thailand, the Philippines, Indonesia, and Cambodia have experienced a comparably low rate of urbanization and a rapid growth of individual cities for much the same reason.

Urbanization and the Growth of Cities of Varying Size

In considering city growth, one should keep in mind that the mere size of a city's population is a limiting factor on the rate of growth when expressed as a percentage. A large city may have a lower rate of growth than a small city, even though the increase in numbers of inhabitants may be about the same for the two communities. Very large cities often have a low rate of increase, even though the numerical increase of the population may be very great; and by the same token, a decrease in the rate of a city's growth does not usually mean an actual decline in numbers of inhabitants. With these comments in mind, we shall examine data concerning some of the large cities of the world.

Viewing the growth of great cities from a global perspective, we find that, for the world as a whole, an estimated 23 percent of the population resided in cities of 100,000 or more in 1972, compared with about 19 percent in 1960 and 16 percent in 1950[7]. The trend toward metropolitanization, as well as urbanization, appears to be universal, or almost so. The proportion of population living in large cities varies, as one might

[7] Population Reference Bureau, Inc., *1972 World Population Data Sheet*, and Kingsley Davis, *World Urbanization*, 1950–1970, vol. II (1972), p. 187.

expect, from one region or country to another. Generally the highly industrialized countries have a higher proportion of population living in large cities than do the developing countries, although there are exceptions.

A United Nations report estimated the existence in the late 1960's of 351 cities of a half-million or more inhabitants, predicting that by 1980 the number of great cities of this size would be about 725.[8] Davis estimated in 1959 that the number of metropolitan centers of 100,000 population or over in the world had reached 1,064.[9] A decade later he updated this figure, estimating the existence of 1,037 cities from 100,000 to 500,000 inhabitants, 172 with populations from 500,000 to 1,000,000, and 165 in the million class—a total of 1,374.[10] Truly this is an age of giant cities. Unless some unprecedented catastrophe should befall modern civilization, it seems likely that this number will increase considerably by the year 2000, which is less than three decades in the future. The global nature of this trend is clear.

Comparison of Central Cities and Metropolitan Areas

The comparative ranking of large cities by size is often misleading because the criteria employed for determining size may differ from one country to another. When such terms as "metropolitan area," "greater," or "agglomeration" are employed descriptively, the "city" may include suburban or satellite communities along with the "central city" or the "city proper." The central city of Buenos Aires, for example, has a population of about 3 million, but Greater Buenos Aires has over 8 million inhabitants. Obviously, the size of a "city proper" depends in part on the location of the municipal boundary lines. Table 4.3 represents top-ranking cities, ranked by size of the city proper and by estimated size of the larger metropolitan area.

Among the world's largest central cities, Shanghai, with nearly 11 million inhabitants, is the largest, having almost 2 million more than the central city of Tokyo, which for a number of years claimed to be the world's largest city. But when the unit is the entire metropolitan area, or urban agglomeration, the picture changes. With a population of some 16 million, New York is the world's largest metropolitan area. Tokyo, with over 14 million, is in second place while Paris, with over 9 million, ranks third. Metropolitan Calcutta ranks ninth among the world's great urban agglomerations, and the central city of Calcutta, with some 5 million inhabitants, also ranks ninth.

---

[8] United Nations, *Urbanization: Development Policies and Planning*, p. 18.
[9] Kingsley Davis, *The World's Metropolitan Areas* (1959).
[10] *World Urbanization 1950-1970*, vol. I (1969), Table B.

TABLE 4.3: The Ten Largest World Cities and Metropolitan Areas by Size of Population in 1970 or 1971 or most Recent Available Data

City Proper	Size (millions)	Metropolitan Area	Size (millions)
Shanghai	10.8	New York	16.2
Tokyo	8.8	Tokyo	14.7
New York	7.9	Paris	9.2
Peking	7.5	Mexico City	8.5
London	7.4	Buenos Aires	8.4
Moscow	6.9	Los Angeles	8.3
São Paulo	5.9	London	8.1
Bombay	5.7	São Paulo	8.0
Calcutta	5.0	Calcutta	7.2
Cairo	4.9	Moscow	7.2

SOURCES: United Nations, *Demographic Yearbook*, (1971), Table 9; and Kingsley Davis, *World Population 1950–1970*, vol. II (1972), Table F. Both Shanghai and Peking have a larger central-city population than was estimated or reported before China was admitted to the United Nations. They are not included in the column on metropolitan areas because such data were not available at this writing.

The Growth of Small Cities

More is known about the growth of large cities than small ones. Major cities have attracted much attention not only because of their size but also because of their economic, political, and cultural influence. Yet there are thousands of small and medium-sized cities—the exact number is not known, at least on a worldwide basis. The proportion of a country's total population living in urban centers under 100,000 varies considerably from one area to another. In 1970, several countries had more than one-fourth of their total populations living in small cities.[11] Among these were Finland, Denmark, Belgium, West Germany, Venezuela, Sweden, Mexico, Chile, the Soviet Union, Japan, Poland, Canada, and Switzerland. At the other end of the spectrum were countries with less than 10 percent of their respective populations in small cities, among them Thailand, India, the Philippines, China, Syria, Ceylon, and Burma. It would appear, then, that the urban-industrial countries generally have a larger proportion of the population in small and medium-sized cities than is the case of developing countries. A striking exception, however, is the United Kingdom.

Yet in most major geographic regions the large-city population in recent years has grown more rapidly than the small-city population. For each of the two decades between 1950 and 1970, large cities increased in size more rapidly than small cities in 14 of 17 major regions of the world, and less rapidly in three areas. This does not mean that the small-city population is declining, nor is there any reason to believe that a decline

[11] Calculated from *ibid.*, Table C.

will occur in the forseeable future. Indeed, the pattern may be reversed at some time in the future if large cities repel more people and institutions than they attract. One of the reasons that the large-city population appears to grow more rapidly than the small-city population is that some urban centers may be reclassified as large cities when their population, at a particular point in time, exceeds 100,000, or whatever size is used to designate "largeness." In these instances the small-city population declines by the corresponding figure.

The Metropolitan Galaxy

The growth of great metropolitan or regional clusters has been a striking feature of the urban process in many industrial countries. These may be termed *metropolitan galaxies* or *regions*, although the term *megalopolis*, meaning a kind of supermetropolis, has also come into wide usage.[12]

In Japan, Tokyo and Yokohama become the foci of a megalopolis which includes, within that area, numbers of satellite cities and towns. The Osaka-Kyoto galaxy is somewhat smaller. On the western part of The Netherlands is the *Randstad* (literally rim city), which includes Amsterdam, The Hague, Rotterdam, Utrecht, Leiden, and many smaller cities and towns, all within a short distance of each other in an almost continuous settlement. The Ruhr Valley in western Germany, center of a major iron and steel industry, has produced a major galaxy—Essen, Dortmund, Düsseldorf, and many smaller places. These three major cities and their satellites form an almost unbroken urban belt.

The London metropolitan galaxy covers over 700 square miles and includes, in addition to the major city, many others that make up this gigantic complex. Farther north Manchester and Liverpool are centers of a comparable, though smaller, complex of cities that are more or less integrated into an overall system of interrelated communities. As was indicated in Chapter 3, such vast metropolitan galaxies have also been a feature of urbanization in the United States.

Although these gigantic clusters tend to be more characteristic of industrial than of nonindustrial societies, many of them have emerged in developing countries. Metropolitan Calcutta, for example, includes numerous suburbs and satellite communities, but there is no megalopolis in the entire country comparable to, say, the built-up area that extends in an almost continuous series of communities from Boston to Washington, D.C. It may well be, however, that with continued industrialization, involving modern technology and social organization applicable to large-scale urban development, the Western type of metropolitan galaxies will evolve.

[12] Jean Gottmann, *Megalopolis*, (1961).

Growth Rates of Metropolitan Centers

The Industrial World

In the Western Hemisphere, one of the most rapidly growing cities is metropolitan Paris. Although its rate of growth was only moderately high (18 percent for the 1960–1970 decade), almost 1.5 million were added to the population, and more than a million during the preceding decade. Metropolitan Rome increased in population between 1950 and 1970 by 38 percent, which represented an addition of some 900,000 persons. Metropolitan Athens grew by 30 percent during the same decade, an increase of some 600,000 residents. The great port of Rotterdam grew by 40 percent, with about 400,000 additions to the population. Metropolitan Tokyo had a moderate increase of 23 percent, but this represented 2.5 million persons. Metropolitan Detroit's increase of 23 percent meant the addition of about 900,000 to the city's population. Houston had a three-fold population increase over two decades.

The rate of growth of individual cities varies considerably from one country to another, and from one point in time to another. Of the 57 cities with over 100,000 inhabitants in the United Kingdom, all except five increased in population between 1950 and 1970. Yet the increase was exceptionally slow. Such major cities as London, Birmingham, Manchester, Glasgow, and Liverpool increased annually less than one percent in each of the two decades, a pattern that prevailed in most of the other metropolitan centers. Similarly, cities in Belgium, Austria, and East Germany grew by less than one percent annually between 1950 and 1970. But such low rates of increase were not universal in the industrial countries. Most of the cities of France increased in population from two to four percent annually during the same period, and the same was true of The Netherlands, Switzerland, and several eastern European countries.

The Developing World

Rapid growth of great cities is particularly characteristic of developing countries. Over the short span of two decades between 1950 and 1970, some major cities even doubled in size, including Baghdad, Istanbul, Manila, Beirut, and Taipei. Some of them trebled in size in the same period, including Karachi, Bangkok, Teheran, and Djakarta. Cairo's population in 1950 was about 2.5 million, but by 1970 some 3 million persons had been added, more than doubling its size and making it the largest metropolis in Africa.

The situation in Latin America is similar. Lima had about 500,000 residents in 1940, but by 1970 had increased five-fold. Mexico City reached the 1,000,000 point about 1930; by 1970 it had grown to about 6

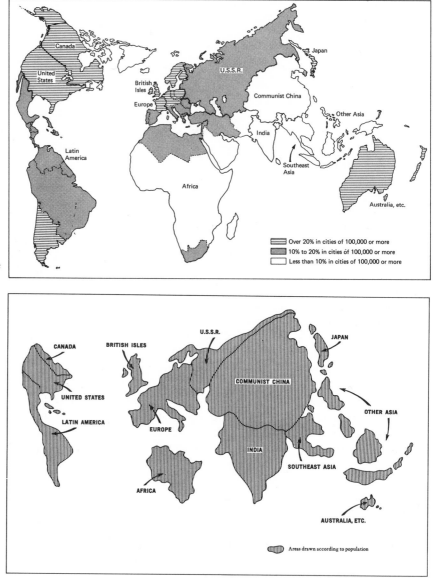

FIGURE 4.1 • Upper map, showing degrees of urbanization in major world regions in 1970, indicates that highly urbanized countries are concentrated in North America and Europe. Lower map, showing areas of the world drawn to scale according to total population in 1970, indicates why the study of cities must include those in non-Western, less urbanized areas. Many of the least urbanized countries have enormous populations and hence already contain large numbers of urban dwellers. Source: Upper map is based on the cumulative index of urbanization for 22 world regions, K. Davis, *op. cit*, part II, Table 60; lower map is adapted from *The New York Times*, p. 3, 1962, p. E11. © 1962 by The New York Times Company, reprinted by permission.

million, with prospects it will be over 7 million by 1980. Brasilia, the new capital of Brazil, had only 12,000 residents in 1957; 13 years later it had increased to 500,000 . In 1941, Caracas had a population of 359,000; in 1970 its population exceeded the 2 million mark. The "boom town" of Latin America is metropolitan São Paulo; with over 8 million residents, it is one of the largest metropolitan centers of that continent. Over the two decades following 1950, the population increased two and one-half times, adding some 6 million people during this period. In addition to the relatively high birth rate of São Paulo's population, vast numbers of immigrants from abroad and migrants from the interior flocked to the city. In 1959, the population of São Paulo was about equal to that of Rio de Janeiro, but in the next decade it forged ahead and now exceeds the population of the capital city by nearly 1,000,000 inhabitants.

The 35 countries of tropical Africa are fairly representative of the nonindustrial or developing regions. Whereas the annual average rate of total population growth in these countries is around three percent, the urban population is increasing at twice that rate, and in some of the

Aerial view of São Paulo, Brazil, a rapidly growing metropolis that now ranks among the three largest metropolitan centers in Latin America, even surpassing Rio de Janeiro, the capital of Brazil. São Paulo draws its population from various regions of Brazil and also from European and other Latin American countries. (Consulate General of Brazil, New Orleans)

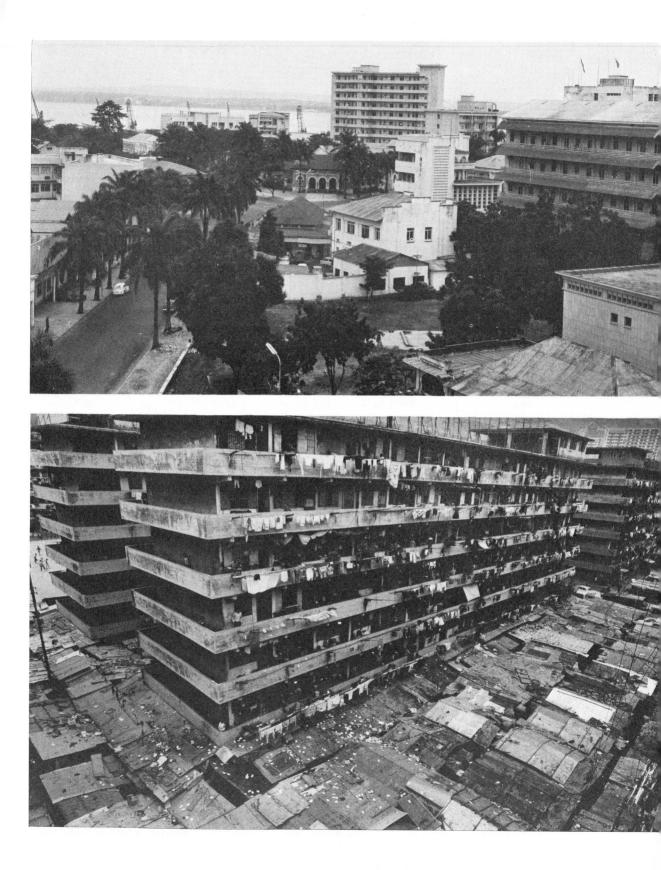

Kinshasa (formerly Leopoldville) in Zaire (formerly The Congo) is the capital, having a population of a half million. In some respects it is as modern as Western cities, as indicated by the buildings in the top photograph. In less than a half century it has grown from a straggling town to a major metropolis. (Louise E. Jefferson)

Swarms of refugees from Mainland China have at times almost inundated Hong Kong. As a result the Hong Kong municipality has been hard pressed to provide housing for them. The bottom photograph shows an apartment built for refugees, and in the foreground are shacks hastily constructed for the overflow. (Peter Martens, Nancy Palmer)

countries even higher. Furthermore, the relatively high rate of increase in the rural population is not likely to decline soon, which means that the influx of urban-bound migrants will continue for the indefinite future. Moreover, the majority of these migrants are drawn to the large cities. Rosser estimates that in 1970, about 70 percent of the total *urban* population was concentrated in cities of 100,000 or more inhabitants.[13] At the beginning of the present century there was only one city in tropical Africa with a population of 100,000 or over; in the early 1960's there were 57 large cities, 23 of which were in Nigeria. In the 1940–1950 decade, Nairobi, in Kenya, doubled in size, then doubled again in the 1950–1960 period, keeping up this rate of increase through the 1960's, attaining a population of more than 500,000 by 1970. Kinshasa (formerly Leopoldville), in Zaire (formerly the Congo), was a country town of 34,000 in 1930; by 1970, it had more than 500,000 inhabitants.

Some of the world's largest cities have grown as a result, in large part, of the influx of refugees. Hong Kong, for example, had a prewar population of about 1.5 million. Following a sharp decline of population during World War II there came an influx of refugees from mainland China, as many as 10,000 a week; by 1950 Hong Kong's population had increased to more than 2 million; by 1961 to about 3 million;[14] and by 1970 to 4 million—a dramatic example of metropolitan growth running

[13] Colin Rosser, *Urbanization in Tropical Africa* (1973), p. 17.
[14] T. D. Vaughan and D. J. Dwyer, "Some Aspects of Population Growth in Hong Kong," *Economic Geography*, 42 (January 1966), 37–52.

far ahead of industrialism. The heavy influx of refugees into Seoul, Calcutta, Delhi, Karachi, and other cities accounts for part of the swollen populations of these cities. Some 2 million refugees, fleeing from combat zones in Vietnam, has been chiefly responsible for the doubling of Saigon's population in the 1960's.

Some cities that underwent spectacular growth during World War II have experienced a decline in the rate of growth since then, although certainly not a numerical decrease. Davis reports that the average population increase of five major Indian cities (Calcutta, Bombay, Hyderabad, Delhi, and Bangalore) declined from 52 percent between 1941 and 1951 to 33 percent between 1951 and 1961.[15] Delhi alone dropped from a 107 percent growth rate in the 1941-1951 period to 63 percent in the 1951–1961 decade, while Bangalore declined from 90 percent to 29 percent. This decline continued through the decade preceding 1970, when the average percentage growth rate of the five cities, taken together, declined to 24.

Summary

In this chapter we have considered two types of societies, industrial and developing. Industrial societies, typical of such regions as western Europe and northern America, have generally experienced extensive urbanization and now have a large proportion of population living in cities. Most industrial societies utilize advanced technology and large-scale organization. Developing societies are predominantly agricultural, although they, too, often have large cities that are modern in many respects. We have noted the major urban trends in both types of society, and have described methods of measuring or otherwise ascertaining such trends. One important fact stands out: In all countries, whether industrial or developing, the movement is toward increasing urbanization, although the conditions of such growth may vary considerably from one country or region to another.

The growth of large metropolitan communities throughout the world has created difficulties in making international comparisons because of differences in official definitions of a "city" and of where the boundary lines are to be drawn. The metropolitan area may be much larger or even more populous than the city proper because of the growth of suburban or satellite communities. Furthermore, great clusters of cities, which we

---

[15] Kingsley Davis, "Urbanization in India: Past and Future," in Roy Turner, ed., *India's Urban Future* (1961), p. 10. These figures have been challenged by Jakobson and Prakash, who state that a major change in the census definition of "urban" for the 1951–1961 decade may have meant a higher growth rate for this decade and for the preceding one. See Leo Jakobson and Ved Prakash, "Urbanization and Regional Planning in India," *Urban Affairs*, 2 (March 1967), 39.

have designated as "galaxies" or "metropolitan regions," are in the process of formation in numerous countries. Wherever these galaxies have developed, the country's population has been drawn increasingly toward them, usually at the expense of rural areas or small towns. In developing countries particularly, although certainly not entirely, there has been, in the past half-century, an unprecedented but rapid growth of large cities, and this trend seems likely to continue into the foreseeable future.

Selected Bibliography

Bibliography applicable to this chapter is applicable to Chapter 5 as well, and is therefore appended to that chapter (pp. 144–45).

5 • Contemporary Urbanization in World Perspective: II

Comparative High and Low City Growth Rates

Just as countries and regions vary greatly as to the rate of growth of the urban population, and also of the rate of urbanization, so do individual cities vary widely. Among the world's large cities it would appear that the most rapid growth is occurring in developing countries, whereas the growth of cities in industrial regions has been comparatively slow in recent years. Table 5.1 exhibits the wide disparity in the growth rate of metropolitan centers over two decades.

As we noted in the previous chapter, the rate of population increase or decrease, calculated as a percentage, is influenced by the size of the base. London, for example, has recently had a much greater numerical increase of population than Naples, although the rate of growth was lower. But one fact stands out in the table: the growth rate of individual cities is generally larger in developing countries than in industrialized regions. All of the rapid-growth cities listed in the table more than doubled in population during the two decades, but such cities as Vienna and Hamburg scarcely gained in size.

There are various reasons for this disparity in growth, but one important factor is the volume of rural-urban migrations. In most industrial countries the rural population base has been declining, both proportionally and in absolute numbers, for a number of years. If, for example, in a country of 100 million inhabitants, the size of the rural sector has declined to about 10 million, the reservoir of potential migrants is relatively small. Assuming that five percent of the rural population migrates each decade, the volume would be about 500,000 persons settling in the cities. But if in a developing country with, say, a total population of 200 million, the rural sector accounts for 150 million

TABLE 5.1: Selected Cities Showing High and Low Growth Rates between 1950 and 1970

High Percentage Increase		Low Percentage Increase	
Accra	333	Naples	32
Bogota	328	Budapest	29
São Paulo	243	Amsterdam	28
Montevideo	253	Copenhagen	27
Seoul	218	Moscow	22
Djakarta	213	Prague	13
Taipei	187	London	10
Istanbul	165	Brussels	under 1
Manila	130	Vienna	under 1
Cairo	128	Hamburg	under 1

SOURCE: Adapted from Kingsley Davis, *World Urbanization 1950–1970*, vol. I (1969), Table E.

people, of which five percent migrate each decade, then about 7.5 million persons would be added to the urban population. Many of them will head for the large cities, swelling the population of these metropolitan areas. To these numbers may be added the natural increase of the existing urban population. In most of the nonindustrial countries the rural population continues to increase in size, thus assuring a continuous stream of rural-urban migrations and a consequent piling-up of people in these centers. With a relatively high birth rate in both the rural and urban sectors of these countries, there is no indication that this situation will significantly change in the foreseeable future.

Table 5.2 may be examined from several perspectives. These data indicate (1) that rates of total population growth in industrial countries are usually lower than in developing societies; (2) that the rates of growth of the urban population are likewise generally lower in the former than in the latter type of society, excepting Japan; and (3) that the rural population in industrial countries is declining or approaching a stationary level in contrast to the rural sectors of developing societies. Actually, in most industrial countries the rural population has exhibited an absolute decline as well as a proportional decrease.

Among the industrial countries listed in Table 5.2, Japan has experienced the most pronounced urban growth for the two decades 1950 to 1970, and at the same time the sharpest decline of rural population. These demographic changes have been closely associated with Japan's phenomenal industrial growth since the end of World War II. At the other end of the spectrum is the United Kingdom, where the rate of urban growth is only slightly higher than the increase in the total population, and the rural population seems to have reached or approached a stationary level. Among the nonindustrial countries included in the table, Nigeria's total population more than doubled over the twenty-year period, the rural sector of the country increased almost as much, while the urban population increased by two and one-half times. In all of the

TABLE 5.2: Estimated Percentage Rates of Growth or Decline of Total Population, and Urban and Rural Sectors, in Representative Industrial and Developing Countries, 1950–1970

Industrial Countries	Total	Urban	Rural	Developing Countries	Total	Urban	Rural
Australia	50	84	-38	Nigeria	116	245	97
Soviet Union	36	97	-11	Mexico	96	168	43
United States	36	60	-6	Philippines	89	120	81
France	23	56	-14	Thailand	88	136	77
Japan	23	174	-67	Brazil	80	166	31
West Germany	22	40	-21	Turkey	69	140	49
Spain	18	42	-.05	Egypt	64	123	36
Norway	18	54	-7	South Africa	61	107	31
Italy	15	34	-.05	Indonesia	56	126	46
United Kingdom	11	13	00	India	54	68	49

SOURCE: Calculated from Kingsley Davis, *World Urbanization, 1950–1970*, vol. I (1969), Table A.

developing countries, except India, the urban population more than doubled. The very fact that the rural population in these countries continues to grow, and fairly rapidly at that, indicates that rapid urban growth will continue into the indefinite future.

India's rate of growth, for example, either for the total population or the urban sector, is smaller than in the other countries in the table, but this is due in part to the numerical size of the population. Although India's population increased by about 200 million (from about 350 to 550 million) over the two decades, and the urban population increased by about 42 million (from 60 to 102 million), the proportional increases were less than in the other countries, all of which had smaller populations. In the final analysis, however, it is the increasing (or decreasing) *numbers* of people that are important. When, for example, the population of India's cities increase by more than 40 million in the course of two decades, the social, political, and economic effects are very great indeed. It should be remembered, also, that India's rural population increased by about 150 million during the same period, thus creating an oversupply of people in the rural sectors and therefore an abundance of potential migrants to the cities.

The Recent Urbanization of Two Populous Countries

The Soviet Union

The Soviet Union is a land of many cities, among them some of the world's largest. The rapid industrialization of the country is paralleled by increasing urbanization and the rapid growth of metropolitan centers, especially those associated with heavy industry which attracts workers from the outside. In 1970, there were 221 cities each having more than 100,000 inhabitants, and of these ten were in the million class, including Moscow with nearly 7 million and Leningrad with slightly under 4 million.[1] The Soviet Union ranks among the five countries with the greatest number of large cities, the others being the United States, Japan, India, and the People's Republic of China.

The trend toward urbanization of the Soviet Union has been continuous for a century, except for short interruptions such as World War II, when many of its cities were either destroyed or evacuated by the inhabitants under conditions of crisis. Taking the year 1920 as a point in time, some 21 million persons, or 15 percent of the population, were then classed as urban residents; a half-century later, in 1970, an estimated 134 million persons were classified as residents of cities, or 56 percent of the total population.[2] Although the total population of the country almost doubled during this period, the urban population increased six-fold, and the rural population actually declined by about 12 million. In the decade between 1959 and 1970, this phenomenal urban increase was especially apparent; during this period the total population grew by 16 percent, but the urban growth rate was 36 percent, while the rural population declined by three percent. Of the 36 million persons added to the urban population in this decade, Harris estimates that 41 percent resulted from a "natural increase," 45 percent from in-migration, and 14 percent from administrative and boundary changes. At its present rate of urbanization, within two or three decades the Soviet Union will rank with other highly industrialized countries in the proportion of population living in cities. In fact, the level of urbanization at present is roughly comparable to the level attained by the United States some three decades ago.

The People's Republic of China

Like the Soviet Union, mainland China is also a land of many cities. This much is known, although precise census data on China's population are not available. Indeed, most of the data are based partly on estimates, extrapolations, and projections from various sources of information.[3] Ullman estimates that in 1957 some 13 percent of China's population was classified as urban, compared with 11 percent in 1949. The 1969 estimates by Davis place the urban figure at approximately 23 percent,

[1] Chauncey D. Harris, "Urbanization and Population Growth in the Soviet Union, 1959–1970," *Geographical Review*, 61 (January 1971), 102–25.

[2] Chauncey D. Harris, *Cities of the Soviet Union* (1970), p. 232.

[3] Two surveys on which this discussion is mainly based are Morris B. Ullman, "Cities of Mainland China, 1953–1959," in *International Population Reports*, U. S. Bureau of the Census, Foreign Manpower Research Office, August 1969 (reprinted in Gerald Breese, ed., *The City in Newly Developing Countries* [1969]); and Kingsley Davis, *World Urbanization 1950–1970*, vol. I, (1969), Table E.

Two views of Shanghai, China. At top is a photograph of government housing, built since 1955 on a reclaimed slum area on the northwestern outskirts of the metropolis. Picture at bottom is a general view of a central section of the city, a busy seaport. Shanghai is reputed to be the world's largest city, with Peking a close second among major Chinese cities. (Paolo Koch, Rapho Guillumette)

compared with 11 percent in 1950. The number of cities over 100,000 in 1953, according to Ullman, was 102, which accounted for eight percent of the total population and 54 percent of the urban population. Davis identified 140 cities over 100,000 in 1970, or 60 percent of the urban population and 14 percent of the total. Ullman listed nine cities in the million class in 1953, but seventeen years later the number, according to Davis, had risen to 31. Of the ten largest cities in the world, two— Shanghai and Peking—are in China. Clearly, the Ullman and Davis data show some variations, but they appear to provide a reasonably accurate overall picture of China's population trend and condition. Inasmuch as China is officially committed to a national program of industrialization, the trend toward urbanization there will undoubtedly continue.

Primate Cities and
Their Problems

Wherever city growth has occurred, past or present, so-called primate cities have developed to a point in which one, or possibly two or three, centers in each country exceed all others in size, perhaps even in influence and prestige. Such primacy might be expected, since disparities in both size and rates of growth are probably inevitable. In many countries, however, the gap between the largest city and the next largest is so vast as to create an imbalance in the urban system. Vienna, for example, exceeds the population of Linz seven times over, and Budapest is ten times as large as Miskolc, the second largest Hungarian city. On the other hand, Rotterdam is about the same size as Amsterdam, although at its present rate of growth it will surpass Amsterdam in a few years.

A somewhat simplified picture of urban primacy may be obtained by calculating the ratio of the population size of the largest city to that of the second city in size. A ratio of 3, for example, means that the largest city is three times as large as the next city in size. Among the urban-industrial countries there is, of course, considerable variation in primacy ratios. The following cities are representative of high primacy and low primacy as of 1970.

TABLE 5.3: Selected Cities Showing High and Low Primacy Ratios, 1970

High		Low	
Lima	13.1	Istanbul	2.1
Buenos Aires	11.5	New York	1.7
Manila	11.6	Moscow	1.7
Budapest	10.5	Rome	1.6
Santiago	8.6	Calcutta	1.5
Copenhagen	7.7	Johannesburg	1.3
Vienna	7.4	Sydney	1.2
Paris	7.1	São Paulo	1.2
Teheran	6.5	Rotterdam	1.0
Havana	6.0	Belgrade	1.0

SOURCE: Calculated from Kingsley Davis, *World Urbanization, 1950–1970*, vol. I (1969), Table E.

Davis has employed a different technique for gauging the extent of urban primacy. He refers to his method as the Four-City Index, which he considers more meaningful than comparisons of the largest and next largest cities in a country. The index is obtained by dividing the population of the largest city by the combined population of the next three cities.[4] An index of, say, 3.00 for any country simply means that the largest city is three times as big as the combined population of the next three in size. An index of .5 indicates that the primate city has only half the population of the combined total of the next three. Although metropolitan Paris, for example, is seven times as large as the second city in France, the Four-City Index of 3.1 indicates that it is only three times as large as the combined population of Lyon, Marseille, and Bordeaux. Copenhagen is almost eight times as large as the second city in Denmark, but the Four-City Index gives it a rating of 3.5. By this procedure, Italy, Canada, Poland, and The Netherlands, among other industrial countries, have an index considerably less than 1. Davis' Four-City Index, when applied to cities of developing countries, yields contrasting ratios. Peru and the Philippines have high primacy indexes of 5.3 and 4.6, respectively. At the other extreme are China and Nigeria, with indexes of .51 and .57, respectively.

Another aspect of primacy is the proportion of a country's population that lives in a single metropolitan community. In Latin America in the 1960's, for example, 16 of 22 countries each had half or more of the population living in one great metropolitan center. Greater Bangkok accounts for about 56 percent of Thailand's population. These are extreme examples, of course, but they do indicate a tendency toward pronounced primacy.

[4] Davis, *op. cit.*, pp. 242–46.

Conditions and Effects
of Urban Primacy

Urban primacy is the consequence of various combinations of interrelated factors, and each country or region is more or less unique as to the conditions that produce high or low primacy. It would appear, however, that high primacy tends to be especially characteristic of societies in which the level of urbanization is low, though there are exceptions. Small countries more than large and populous ones are also likely to have a primate metropolis several times the size of any other city in the country. In such countries the primate city is generally the cultural, economic, and social "capital."

Most commonly, the primate city is also the political capital, although there are numerous exceptions, such as Washington, Rio de Janeiro, Ottawa, Canberra, and The Hague. Most primate cities have grown rapidly in recent years, especially if they are political or economic capitals. As headquarters of national political power, or as cultural centers, they have an attractiveness for potential migrants that extends even beyond whatever economic advantages exist there. Over the two decades 1947 to 1967, for example, Bangkok's population more than tripled, and there seems to be no immediate cessation to the momentum it has achieved.

If a political capital has built-in economic and cultural features, such a city may grow to great magnitude and also be supreme both in political influence and prestige: London, Paris, Brussels, Madrid, Stockholm, Copenhagen, Moscow, Tokyo, and Vienna are typical. In more than one sense these cities function as a national "headquarters." The impetus they receive from a combination of factors, including a long and impressive history, gives them a head start that other cities are unable to overcome.

Similarly, in developing societies, such great cities as Mexico City, Bangkok, Buenos Aires, Lima, Rangoon, Teheran, Caracas, Seoul, and Istanbul overshadow in size, economic dominance, and cultural resources all other cities in their respective countries. Again there are exceptions. Shanghai is China's primate city, but the political and cultural capital, Peking, is somewhat smaller though growing rapidly. Rio de Janeiro is the political and cultural capital of Brazil, but it has recently been surpassed in size by São Paulo. Delhi is the political capital of India, but is outdistanced in size by both Bombay and Calcutta. Karachi is the major city and former political capital of Pakistan, but the capital has recently been moved to Islamabad, a small city, and Lahore is generally considered the cultural capital of the country.

High primacy has both advantages and disadvantages. On the positive side, the primate city may function as a force for national integration, especially in smaller countries and particularly in developing societies.

Brussels and Ankara. The large building (top photo) houses various European
organizations headquartered in Brussels. This city is the political, economic,
and cultural capital of Belgium. Ankara, the political capital of Turkey, has
numerous skyscrapers, one of which is shown here (bottom photo). The economic and cultural capital of Turkey is Istanbul. (Belgian Consulate General,
N. Y.—top; Turkish Information Office, N. Y.—bottom)

Its concentration of limited cultural, economic, and technological resources may be more functional than if the resources were widely
distributed among other cities. Concentration of such resources in a
single capital metropolis may reinforce and stimulate innovations in
almost every sphere of national life. A small country like Uruguay might
well be at a disadvantage if its extensive resources were widely dispersed, away from Montevideo.

From a negative standpoint, high primacy may stifle economic or other
developments seriously needed in smaller regional cities. The lure of the
primate metropolis may be so powerful that a never-ending stream of
people is drawn to it. Hoselitz notes that high primacy may be parasitic,
that is, such cities receive an undue share of the national investment,
attract excessive manpower, and have a high consumption rate as
compared to a production rate.[5]

The conclusions of the authors of a United Nations report concerned
with developing countries reinforce the negative aspect of high primacy.

As long as the few large centers continue to attract a disproportionate share
of the existing industry or commercial activity, professional people, and modernizing institutions, the gap between metropolis and the remaining institutions of a nation will widen, for there will be proportionately fewer industrial
jobs, educational opportunities, or chances to learn new skills in the outlying
areas. There will be proportionately fewer doctors and administrators, lawyers,
teachers and so on able to handle the service and organizational apparatus of
the smaller cities of the rural regions.[6]

One sociologist has argued that the overconcentration of population in
a few major cities creates an imbalance in which the lesser cities are
unable to develop adequately because they are overshadowed by one or

[5] Bert F. Hoselitz, "Urbanization and Economic Growth in Asia," paper presented at the
   Congress for Cultural Freedom Conference on Problems of Economic Growth, Tokyo, 1957.
[6] United Nations, Department of Economic and Social Affairs, *Urbanization: Development
   Policies and Planning* (1968), p. 85.

more metropolitan giants.[7] This is essentially the problem of many major cities. The case of Egypt is illustrative. Two cities, Cairo and Alexandria, had one-fourth of the entire Egyptian population in 1970, and about half of the urban inhabitants. A large part of the country's manufacturing, communication, transportation, and financial institutions is centered in these two cities, which also have a virtual monopoly on the cultural and political institutions of the country. But whatever the theoretical explanation of urbanization, the consequences are fairly clear. As a result of the massive movement of population to these cities, the economic resources and facilities have not been equal to the task of absorbing the in-migrants into the economy and providing them with jobs and services. Added to these strains is the natural increase of residents which results in a mass entrance into the labor market, each month or year, of adults who compete for jobs and services with the in-migrants.

Overurbanization

The rapid growth of cities all over the world and the emergence of various problems associated with urbanism have engendered the concept of "overurbanization." Although efforts have been made to define specifically the concept and to provide supporting empirical evidence for it, it remains a somewhat nebulous and ambiguous notion, not greatly different from "overpopulation" or "optimum population." Yet the idea of overurbanization, when viewed evaluatively, has considerable value.

Two approaches have been followed in dealing with the nature and extent of overurbanization. One, proposed by Davis and Golden, employed a statistical measure to distinguish between countries that are overurbanized and those that are not.[8] Davis and Golden calculated the percentage of males engaged in nonagricultural occupations in a large number of countries, in or about 1950, which they defined as an index of industrialization; they also obtained the percentage of population in cities over 100,000, a ratio representing the degree of urbanization. The coefficient of correlation between the two variables, degree of industrialization and degree of urbanization, was .86. The relationship between the two variables was presented in a regression curve, and those countries that exceeded markedly this pattern were overurbanized in that the degree of urbanization was greater than would be expected from the existing level of industrialization. By and large, the developing countries included in the sample tended to be overurbanized by this criterion.

[7] Janet L. Abu-Lughod, "Urbanization in Egypt: Present State and Future Prospects," *Economic Development and Cultural Change*, 13 (April 1965), 314–44.

[8] Kingsley Davis and Hilda H. Golden, "Urbanization and the Development of Pre-Industrial Areas," *Economic Development and Cultural Change*, 3 (October 1954), 16–30.

Another approach, presented in a seminar held in Bangkok in 1956 and sponsored by the United Nations Educational, Scientific, and Cultural Organization (UNESCO), emphasized the historical and normative aspects of overurbanization.[9] In this procedure, four industrial countries (United States, Canada, France, and Germany) were considered as a norm, and the relations between the variables of industrialization and urbanization at various dates were considered a measure of normality. Marked deviations from this pattern were interpreted as "abnormal." "Thus Asia," according to the seminar report, "can be said to be comparatively overurbanized in relation to its degree of economic development [that is, industrialization]."

Apparently the assumption in both the Davis and Golden and UNESCO approaches was that overurbanization results when the pressures on land and other natural resources are so great that people flock to the cities and therefore create a serious imbalance, particularly in the industrially underdeveloped regions. An Indian demographer, critical of this assumption, has observed that in some countries judged overurbanized by these criteria there is little serious pressure on land resources; he also notes that in the Asian countries there has for many years been increasing pressure on the land, but only during the past few decades has the headlong rush to the cities been so spectacular, resulting in what has come to be viewed as overurbanization.[10] What is needed, Sovani insists, are more refined and reliable procedures for determining the causes and consequences of overurbanization, but the problem remains an important one.

The Social and Economic Implications of Overurbanization

Whatever may be the validity or invalidity of existing interpretations of overurbanization, or the methods devised for its measurement, it can scarcely be denied that in some countries the growth of cities has in recent decades been much more rapid than the economic expansion necessary to provide the necessities of life for the people who live in them. And by whatever criteria are employed, developing countries tend to be overurbanized to a greater degree than industrial countries. Stated in nonstatistical terms, countries may be overurbanized if the economic system is not expanding rapidly enough to provide employment and incomes for the employable urban inhabitants, whether locally born or immigrants, and if urban institutions are unable to provide adequate housing, education, sanitation, medical care, and other basic needs. But by these criteria, countries that appear to be overurbanized may also be

[9] Philip M. Hauser, ed., *Urbanization in Asia and the Far East*, Bangkok, (1957).
[10] N. V. Sovani, "The Analysis of 'Over-Urbanization'," *Economic Development and Cultural Change*, 12 (January 1964), 113–22.

overruralized in the sense that the rural communities and their institutions also fail to provide the things that are needed or expected, such as jobs and income. The fact is that conditions of life in the countryside may impose as extreme hardships on the people who live there as people in cities endure, although these conditions may be less photogenic than those in the cities. Basically, then, the phenomenon of overurbanization is the result of massive population growth in an entire society, not in just the cities, when conditions for economic and technological growth to support the society's entire population are unfavorable.

Overurbanization is not necessarily confined to developing countries, although in their present stage of development it is more evident there than in most urban-industrial societies. Throughout much of the nineteenth century, and even into the twentieth, cities in many Western countries exhibited conditions similar to the characteristics of many cities in today's developing societies. The miserable living and working conditions existing in London around the turn of the twentieth century might be interpreted as overurbanization if viewed in terms of the human and social consequences of existing conditions.[11]

The Case of Calcutta

What are the effects, in a concrete sense, of overurbanization on those who live and work in such a city? If we assume that India, for example, is overurbanized, by such criteria as those previously mentioned, one may then focus on the conditions that prevail in Indian cities as a consequence of overurbanization, and Calcutta may be cited as the end-product of excessive urbanization. Between 1950 and 1970, metropolitan Calcutta increased by some 2 million people, an average of over 100,000 a year for the two decades. This massive growth resulted from a natural increase (balance of births over deaths) and in-migrations from villages and other cities. Most of the in-migrants were destitute, without any marketable occupational skills. As a result there has been a piling up of people in the slums, most of them unemployed or eking out a bare existence from charitable handouts or incomes derived from part-time or nonproductive jobs. An estimated 300,000 residents are homeless "street sleepers," and nearly half of the families live in a single room.

The economy of Calcutta, like that of the entire country, has not been expanding rapidly enough to afford full employment for those entering the labor market, nor have other institutions been capable of providing shelter and sanitation, or educational, health, and welfare services, to meet increasing needs. Most of the existing institutions are burdened beyond their capacity, and sufficient funds are not available to expand

---

[11] See especially Charles Booth, *The Life and Labour of the People of London*, 3 vols. (1892–1897).

the services. Eventually, many do find employment and are able to afford some of the desired amenities and services, but others are forced into beggary, or dependence on the assistance of friends or relatives. Still they come, by the tens of thousands. Truly, this represents overurbanization by almost any criteria, but it stems in part from the inability of the land and institutions to support the burgeoning rural and urban population. What is true of Calcutta is also true, in varying degrees, of many other cities of the developing world.

The Urban Future: Projections

Projections of population changes may vary according to the method followed. In projecting the rate of urbanization in various countries and regions, Davis presents two methods.[12] One he calls the "constant-rate" projection, in which the assumption is made that the same rate of change will continue throughout a given span of time, say 1970 to 1985. The difficulty with this procedure is that the rate of change may not remain constant in the future, just as it has fluctuated in the past. The second method is based on the assumption that the urbanization of developing countries will exhibit patterns of change similar to the "urban transition" that occurred in industrial countries such as the United States and the United Kingdom; that is, the developing countries, by this method of projection, will at some time in their national history go through the urban transition characterized by a decline in the rate of urbanization and the growth of cities. The second type of projection yields somewhat more conservative results than the first. Some of these estimates are shown in Table 5.4.

TABLE 5.4: Projected Percentage of World Urban Population, and Numbers of Urban Residents, for Designated Dates

Date	Percent Urban (Over 20,000)	Number of Urban Residents (In billions)	Percent Large Cities (Over 100,000)	Number of Residents in Large Cities (In billions)
1970	39	1.4	24	.8
1975	42	1.7	26	1.0
1985	49	2.3	32	1.5
2000	61	3.9	42	2.7

SOURCE: Kingsley Davis, *World Urbanization, 1950–1970*, vol. II (1972). The "constant-rate" method of calculating increase is employed here, using a weighted average of urban and rural trends. Percentages are rounded. (Method I–A, pp. 126–27.)

It should be remembered that these figures are projections, and are valid only so long as the urban trends on which they are based continue.

[12] *World Urbanization 1950–1970*, vol. II (1972).

The size and distribution of the urban population may exceed or fall short of the projections, but they do provide a view of what the future is likely to be. Some features of these data stand out. Although slightly under 40 percent of the world's population was urban in 1970, by 1985 the projected percentage is 49, and at the end of the century it is estimated that well over half of the world's population will be urban residents. In round numbers, then, the urban population will have increased from about 1.3 billion in 1970, to 2.3 billion in 1985, and finally to 3.9 billion at century's end—about equal to the total world population in 1970.

Much the same future is projected for large cities over 100,000. In 1970, slightly less than one-fourth of the world's population resided in metropolitan centers, but by the end of the century, thirty years later, the proportion is projected to about two-fifths. In terms of numbers, the increase will be from 863 million in 1970 to about 2.7 billion in the year 2000.[13]

Other Projections

If one examines the projections for the *number* of large cities (over 100,000), similar trends are apparent. Davis' estimates of the number of large cities in 1975 place the number at 1,983; by 1985, 2,600; and at the end of the century, 3,814. The number of large cities will thus likely double over the three decades following 1970. Not only will the large cities increase in numbers, but they will grow larger in size. The average size of the large cities in 1970 was calculated by Davis at about 500,000 inhabitants; thirty years later the average size is projected to be about 648,000.[14] But this does not accurately reveal the whole picture: The number of small cities moving into the large-city category each year tends to keep the average size fairly low. Cities that are already large, say in the million class, will get even larger. What the maximum size will be there is no way of knowing, but it is possible that some cities will attain a population of 20 million or more by the end of the century.

Hauser has also projected the future growth of world cities.[15] If the rate of urbanization between 1900 and 1950 continues to 1975, the population in cities of 20,000 or over during this twenty-five-year period will have more than doubled, increasing from approximately 502 million in 1950 to 1.2 billion in 1975, somewhat less than the 1.7 billion projected by Davis. The world urban population at that date, according to Hauser's projection, will be about eleven times the present total

[13] *Ibid.*, p. 143.

[14] *Ibid.*, p. 145.

[15] Philip M. Hauser, "The Social, Economic , and Technological Problems of Rapid Urbanization," in Bert F. Hoselitz and Wilbert E. Moore, eds., *Industrialization and Society* (1966), p. 201.

population of the United States. Population in large cities of over 100,000 will also double between 1950 and 1975, reaching a total of about 745 million, or almost four times the present American population. This figure is also somewhat lower than the Davis projection. As we noted in Chapter 3, metropolitan expansion in the United States is projected to continue.

The United Nations projections made in 1968 for urban population growth from 1960 to 1980 are similar.[16] In the "more developed regions" (industrial countries) the proportion of population living in cities of over 20,000 will have increased from 44 percent to an estimated 53 percent, representing a numerical growth from 433 million in 1960 to 623 million in 1980. Thus, the urban population will increase by about 190 million, but the rural and small-town population will experience an increase of only 22 million. In the "less developed" or "developing" countries, however, the number of urban residents will increase from 319 million to 737 million, more than double the 1960 figure. At the same time, the rural and small-town population will reach a total of 2.3 billion, an increase of about 400 million persons in the two decades.

Another way of viewing future urban prospects in various countries is to examine the projections that indicate the number of years in which the population in a particular country will double. These projections indicate clearly that the number of years necessary for the doubling of a population, at the rate of increase in 1972, is far greater for industrial countries than for developing societies.[17] At or near one end of the spectrum are such countries as Sweden, 174; the United Kingdom, 139; France, 99; Italy, 99; the United States, 70; and Japan, 58. At or near the

[16]United Nations, *Urbanization: Development Policies and Planning*, p. 19.
[17]Population Reference Bureau, Inc., *1972 Population Reference Sheet*.

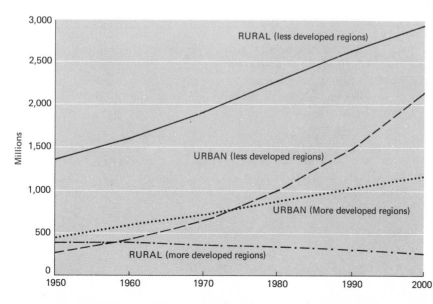

FIGURE 5.1 • Projections for rural and urban population growth to the year 2000. This graph indicates that population increase, both rural and urban, will be greater in developing than in industrial regions, taken as a whole. Source: *Population Bulletin* (April 1971), p. 12. Based on data from United Nations, *A Concise Summary of the World Population Situation in 1970,* New York: United Nations, 1971.

other end are India, 28; Egypt, 25; Brazil, 25; Thailand, 21; and Mexico, 21. Such projections would mean, for example, that the population of France would not be doubled until the year 2071, and the United States, not until 2042. On the other hand, India's population would double its 1972 size in the year 2000, while Mexico's would double in 1993. If the present rate of growth of the urban population continues or increases, it is readily apparent that the numbers of people piling into the cities will be very large indeed, and in the developing societies it is doubtful if these populations, urban and rural alike, can be sustained. The crisis for them is not very far in the future.

Prospects and Implications

United Nations demographers have more recently provided similar views of the future. Their projections indicate that the world population will double between 1971 and 2006, a period of thirty-five years. This will represent an increase from 3.7 billion to 7.4 billion people.[18] At the anticipated rates of rural and urban growth, based on population changes in recent years, the size of the urban population (cities of over 20,000) will be in excess of 3 billion and the aggregate population of large cities will exceed 2 billion. The important question is: Can the world feed, clothe, house, educate, and provide employment and medical facilities for so many urbanites, in addition to the billions who will reside in rural communities? The prospects are not very encouraging.

Prospects for Industrial Countries

Unless some major catastrophe such as global or atomic warfare occurs, the prospects are that cities will continue to grow in most countries throughout the present century, and even beyond. It seems almost certain, also, that the urban proportion of the population in many countries will likewise increase. However, in countries that are already highly urbanized and industrialized, the rate of city growth will probably continue to decline although the numbers of people in cities will probably continue to grow indefinitely, if for no other reason than the excess of births over deaths.

But these countries appear to be moving toward a "saturation" level of urbanization, following the experience of England. A saturation point is reached when the rural population has so diminished that there is no appreciable "surplus" of people and therefore little or no net migration to the cities. Cities can now receive migrants mainly from villages and

[18] United Nations, *Demographic Yearbook* (1971).

small towns, or other cities. Such industrial countries as the United States, The Netherlands, Belgium, Great Britain, Switzerland, Germany, Japan, Australia, and Canada are experiencing this trend. In such countries the future growth of cities will depend increasingly on a natural increase of population—the balance of births over deaths.

Economic and technological developments in industrial countries have apparently achieved a momentum which has the potential for economic expansion and therefore a comparatively high standard of living for the masses. Continued expansion may make jobs available for an expanding urban population, possibly at an increasingly higher standard of living, which actually means increased consumption of available resources. Yet the prospects for continuing prosperity are by no means assured.

One matter commonly overlooked or ignored in an urban-industrial society is the accelerated consumption of natural resources when the supply of those resources is usually finite. The relatively high standard of living in urban-industrial countries may lead, sooner or later, to the exhaustion of those resources. When and if this occurs, some of the economic advantages associated with urbanism may disappear or be greatly reduced. Consumption of numerous natural resources in highly urbanized countries has already exceeded their replacement or renewal. Declining energy sources—oil and gas, for example—may well lead to revolutionary and not altogether welcome changes in the daily lives of urban people in these countries. Some Western countries have been dubbed as wasteful "throwaway" societies, an observation based on the widespread practice of discarding as junk or garbage resources that are no longer wanted or useful. Mountainous garbage heaps and used-car

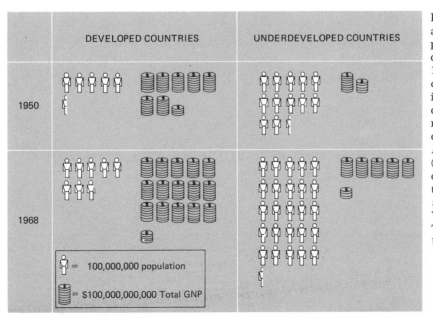

FIGURE 5.2 • Population and income growth compared for industrial and developing countries, 1950–1968. Population increase was small and income growth large in industrial regions, but the reverse was true in developing regions. Source: *Population Bulletin* (April 1971), p. 26. Based on data from United Nations, *Yearbook of National Account Statistics,* Vol. II: International Tables, 1969, New York: United Nations, 1970.

"cemeteries" in or near cities attest to the pressures on a country's resources.

The accelerated consumption of natural resources resulting from urbanization and industrialization has also created problems of environmental pollution which are seriously jeopardizing the quality of life. What were once considered symbols of progress—factory chimneys belching out clouds of grimy smoke, automobiles emitting poisonous fumes—are the built-in features of industrialism, which can be altered effectively only at considerable cost in money and life styles. Whether the peoples benefiting from industrialism and urbanism will be willing to assume these costs before pollution becomes a serious threat to actual survival remains to be seen.

One of the characteristics of Western cities is "urban sprawl." Modern transportation technology has made it possible for city people to live farther and farther from the city's center or the place of employment. If, as seems likely, fuel for privately owned automotive vehicles becomes increasingly scarce and expensive, the prevailing mode of transportation may of necessity become modified, or for many persons abandoned altogether. Indeed, such changes in transportation may well involve major changes in the suburban way of life and work.

Prospects for Developing Countries

For the less developed countries, the United Nations has estimated the percentage increase in urban population over the two decades, 1960 to 1980, to be from about 15 to 24 percent of the total population.[19] Although the rural population is declining proportionally, it nevertheless will experience an estimated increase, during this period, in absolute numbers of about 645 million rural and small-town inhabitants, while the numerical increase of the urban population is estimated at 418 million. The irony of these figures is that the rural population in the developing countries, taken as a whole, is already so large that vast numbers of rural dwellers will continue to flow into the cities; indeed, the projected increase of the urban population for the two decades, 418 million, will continue, for the foreseeable future, and cities will be jammed with rural migrants because in many countries the countryside cannot continue to support all of the growing nonurban populations.

The declining rate of growth of many large cities in developing societies in recent years should not obscure the fact that the growth rate is still high, and if these rates continue the cities will double their populations about every fifteen or twenty years. Davis has cogently stated the crisis the developing societies face: "The poor countries thus

[19] United Nations, *Urbanization: Development Policies and Planning*, p. 19.

confront a grave dilemma. If they do not substantially step up the exodus from the rural areas, these areas will be swamped with underemployed farmers. If they do step up the exodus, the cities will grow at a disastrous rate."[20] It may even be disastrous if the rural exodus or the inflow of people from abroad continues at the *present* rate.

Why "disastrous"? The prospects are that the increase in industrial productivity may not be rapid enough to support or provide employment for the large numbers of people who will, in the foreseeable future, continue their movement to the cities in search of jobs. Nor does it seem likely that agricultural production can increase rapidly enough in numerous countries to feed both the growing rural populations and the urban as well.

For one thing, there is the demographic "explosion." If mortality rates continue to decline in South Asia, according to Irene Taeuber, and if birth rates remain unchanged, the population will increase from 858 million in 1960 to 2.6 billion in the year 2000, or a three-fold increase.[21] This single region's population would be larger than the population that inhabited the entire earth in 1950. If, say, 20 percent of that population live in cities, the number of urban residents would be in excess of 500 million. To increase productivity to the level that such a population, rural and urban, could be adequately employed, fed, housed, clothed, and educated would be virtually impossible. It is unlikely, however, that the urban population of South Asia will grow to this size—the Malthusian scourges of disease and starvation will see to that if contraceptive methods fail to achieve population control. Further, several demographers have also observed that a different fertility pattern seems to be emerging in Latin America, where the gap between urban and rural rates is being narrowed as a result of the rising fertility of city people. If this trend should continue and become widespread, it would complicate the problems already intensified by mass migration to the cities.

In most developing countries the demands of a burgeoning population, both urban and rural, on the limited resources are usually heavy, especially in the densely populated regions. The inhabitants are increasing in numbers but their productivity is generally low. Consequently, there is a severely limited surplus of both consumable products and the monetary values they represent. Agricultural people in these countries usually consume most of what they produce and produce most of what they consume.

Most of the cities in developing countries do not have the advantage of relatively abundant surpluses, as do cities in industrial societies. Econo-

---

[20] Kingsley Davis, "The Urbanization of the Human Population," *Scientific American*, 213 (September 1963), 51.

[21] Irene B. Taeuber, "Demographic Instability: Resolution or Retrogression in Asia," Office of Population Research, Princeton, N. J. Paper presented at a sociology seminar at the University of Missouri, 1965.

mic expansion is generally slow, and what does occur may be mainly for the benefit of an already advantaged elite. Even when incomes of the masses do increase, inflationary trends in most countries tend to cancel out any real financial gains. A workingman's income generally does not permit savings sufficient to make personal investments or purchases of any magnitude, or yield tax revenue in any considerable amount.[22] Not only are incomes low but jobs are scarce. Cities, and the countries in which they are located, therefore find it difficult or impossible to raise the necessary capital for extensive economic development or for investment in other essentials of modern life.

There is no evidence that the surplus of rural people in developing countries will decline soon or rapidly enough to prevent a human inundation of the cities and make possible a comfortable standard of living for both the rural and urban masses. Under the conditions that prevail, both urban and rural unemployment, or nonproductive employment, seems destined to remain high for the foreseeable future; at the same time, under these conditions, the levels of living for most of the people, urban and rural alike, are almost certain to remain low. The "vicious circle" will be difficult to break. The gap between the industrial and developing countries, which is already wide, will probably become wider if measured by economic and social well-being. The momentum

[22]Gunnar Myrdal estimates that the average per capita income of south and southeast Asian countries in the 1960's ranged, in United States dollar equivalents, from about 40 to 160 dollars a year. See his *Asian Drama* (1968), vol. I, p. 535.

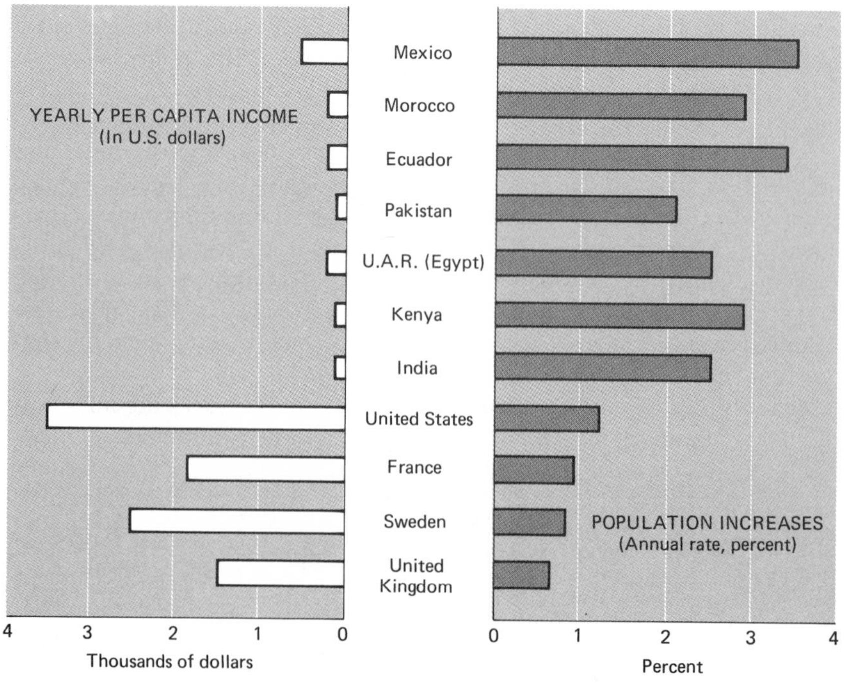

FIGURE 5.3 • Annual population rates of increase and increase in per capita incomes, 1970, for eleven countries. Those with low per capita incomes have high population growth rates. The reverse is true of high-income regions. Source: *Population Bulletin* (April 1971), p. 27. Based on data from United Nations, *United Nations Statistical Yearbook,* and *United Nations Demographic Yearbook,* New York: United Nations, 1970 (both); and Population Reference Bureau, Inc., *1970 World Population Data Sheet,* April 1970.

YEARLY PER CAPITA INCOME (In U.S. dollars)

Mexico
Morocco
Ecuador
Pakistan
U.A.R. (Egypt)
Kenya
India
United States
France
Sweden
United Kingdom

POPULATION INCREASES (Annual rate, percent)

4 3 2 1 0
Thousands of dollars

0 1 2 3 4
Percent

achieved by the industrial countries will undoubtedly carry them farther along the road of industrialism and urbanism.

As Hoselitz has observed, the Industrial Revolution in the West coincided with technological change in agriculture that not only made possible a surplus of food but also a surplus of labor,[23] both of which were of benefit to the urban sector. In developing countries, however, urbanization has commonly been accompanied by severe shortages in agricultural production and therefore a serious food problem in the cities. Countries unable to provide food for the urban or rural population or both must of necessity spend their foreign exchange on the importation of food supplies, thus reducing the funds needed for providing institutional or other facilities for the population. In some instances, only the assistance of countries with a surplus of food has alleviated food shortages.

Summary

While continuing the discussion of urban trends on the world scene begun in Chapter 4, considering some relatively recent data on urbanization in the Soviet Union and the People's Republic of China, we have been mainly concerned in this chapter with the social and economic implications of urbanization and especially with the piling up of population in large metropolitan centers. The trend toward the emergence of so-called primate cities was emphasized, and the advantages or disadvantages of urban primacy discussed. Also, we examined the concept of overurbanization and considered its consequences, especially in developing countries.

What does the future hold for urbanism? Taking several demographic projections into account, we noted that all point to a doubling of the world's urban population within the next few decades, and to a continued growth of the rural population in some developing countries, which has not been the case in industrial countries. These projections provided us with a tentative picture of the size of the world's population, and of some individual countries, for specified dates as far ahead as the year 2000. Finally, the consequences of this massive growth of population to the survival of modern man or to his mode of life and work were considered. The prospects do not appear very favorable.

In Part II which is designated "Urban Ecology" we shall consider varied aspects of the spatial patterning of cities, the processes of social change that have created these patterns, and the problems that such changes have produced.

[23] Bert Hoselitz, "The Role of Urbanization in Economic Development," in Roy Turner, ed., *India's Urban Future* (1962), p. 169.

Selected Bibliography

BOOKS

Beckinsale, R. P., and J. M. Houston. *Urbanization and Its Problems.* Oxford: Basil Blackwell, 1968.

Beyer, Glenn H., ed., *The Urban Explosion in Latin America.* Ithaca: Cornell University Press, 1967.

Breese, Gerald, ed., *The City in Newly Developing Countries.* Englewood Cliffs, N. J.: Prentice-Hall, 1969.

Davis, Kingsley, *World Urbanization, 1950–1970.* vol. I: *Basic Data for Cities, Countries, and Regions* (1969); vol. II: *Analysis of Trends, Relationships, and Development* (1972). Institute of International Studies, University of California, Berkeley.

Dickinson, Robert, *The City Region in Western Europe.* New York: Humanities Press, 1967.

Hanna, William J., and Judith Hanna, *Urban Dynamics in Black Africa.* Chicago: Aldine-Atherton Press, 1971.

Harris, Chauncy D., *Cities of the Soviet Union.* Chicago: Rand McNally, 1970.

Harris, Walter D., Jr., *The Growth of Latin American Cities.* Athens: Ohio University Press, 1971.

Hauser, Philip M., and Leo F. Schnore, eds., *The Study of Urbanization.* New York: Wiley, 1967.

Hauser, Philip M., ed., *Urbanization in Asia and the Far East.* Calcutta: UNESCO, 1957.

——, *Urbanization in Latin America*, Paris and New York: UNESCO, 1961.

Mabogunje, A., *Urbanization in Nigeria.* N. Y.: Africana Publishing Co., 1969.

Meadows, Paul, and Ephraim H. Mizruchi, eds., *Urbanism, Urbanization and Change: A Comparative Perspective.* Reading, Mass: Addison-Wesley, 1969.

Miner, Horace, ed., *The City in Modern Africa.* New York: Praeger, 1967.

Morse, Richard, ed., *The Urban Development of Latin America, 1750–1920.* Stanford: Center for Latin American Studies, Stanford University, 1971.

Rosser, Colin, *Urbanization in Tropical Africa.* New York: International Urbanization Survey, Ford Foundation, 1973.

Stone, Leroy D., *Urban Development in Canada.* Ottawa: Dominion Bureau of Statistics, 1972.

Turner, Roy, ed., *India's Urban Future.* Berkeley and Los Angeles: University of California Press, 1962.

United Nations, *Demographic Yearbook.* New York (annual reports dealing in part with urban data).

——, *Growth of the World's Urban and Rural Population.* New York: United Nations, 1969.

——, Department of Economic and Social Affairs, *Urbanization: Development Policies and Planning*, International Social Development Review, No. 1. New York: United Nations, 1968.

UNESCO, *Social Implications of Industrialization and Urbanization in Africa South of the Sahara.* New York: United Nations, 1966.

Yazaki, Takeo, *Social Change and the City in Japan: From Earliest Times through the Industrial Revolution*, trans. Donald Swain. San Francisco and New York: Japan Publications Trading Co., 1968.

ARTICLES

Abu-Lughod, Janet, "Urbanization in Egypt: Present State and Future Prospects," *Economic Development and Cultural Change*, 13 (April 1965), 314–44.

Bose, Nirmal Kumar, "Calcutta: A Premature Metropolis," *Scientific American*, 213 (September 1965), 91–102.

Boulding, Kenneth E., "The City as an Element in the International System," *Daedalus*, 97 (Fall 1968), 1111–23.

Browning, Harley, "Recent Trends in Latin American Urbanization," *Annals of the Academy of Political and Social Science*, 316 (March 1958), 111–20.

Chang, Sen-dou, "Peking: The Growing Metropolis of Communist China," *Geographical Review*, 55 (April 1965), 313–29.

Davis, Kingsley, "Urbanization of the Human Population," *Scientific American*, 213 (September 1965), 41–53. (The entire issue is devoted to articles on cities.)

Durand, John, and C. Pelaez, "Patterns of Urbanization in Latin America," *Milbank Memorial Fund Quarterly*, 43 (October 1965), 166–96.

El-Shakhs, Salah, "Development, Primacy, and Systems of Cities," *Journal of Developing Areas* (October 1972), 11–37.

Epstein, A. L., "Urbanization and Social Change in Africa," *Current Anthropology*, 8 (1967), 275–96.

Frolic, B. M., "The Soviet Study of Soviet Cities," *Journal of Politics* (1970), 675–95.

Gibbs, Jack, and Leo F. Schnore, "Metropolitan Growth: An International Study," *American Journal of Sociology*, 66 (September 1960), 160–70.

Ginsburg, Norton S., "The Great City in Southeast Asia," *American Journal of Sociology*, 60 (March 1955), 455–62.

Harris, Chauncy D., "Urbanization and Population Growth in the Soviet Union," *Geographical Review*, 61 (January 1971), 102–25.

Hoyt, Homer, "Growth and Structure of Twenty-one Great World Cities," *Land Economics*, 42 (February 1966), 53–64.

Kornhauser, D. H., "Urbanization and Population Pressure in Japan," *Pacific Affairs*, 31 (September 1960), 275–85.

Lewis, Robert A., and Richard Rowland, "Urbanization in Russia and the USSR: 1897–1966," *Annals of the Association of American Geographers*, 59 (December 1969), 776–96.

Linsky, Arnold S., "Some Generalizations Concerning Primate Cities," *Annals of the Association of American Geographers*, 55 (September 1965), 501–13.

Murphey, Rhoads, "Urbanization in Asia," *Ekistics*, 21 (January 1966), 8–17.

Schnore, Leo F., "Metropolitan Development Problems in the United Kingdom," *Economic Geography*, 38 (July 1962), 215–33.

Sjoberg, Gideon, "The Preindustrial City," *American Journal of Sociology*, 60 (March 1955), 438–45.

Sovani, N. V., "The Analysis of 'Over-Urbanization'," *Economic Development and Cultural Change*, 12 (January 1964), 113–22.

Taeuber, Irene, "Urbanization and Population Change in the Development of Modern Japan," *Economic Development and Cultural Change*, 9 (October 1958), 1–28.

URBAN ECOLOGY

6 • The Ecological Approach

"Everything is connected to everything else."[1] This is the basic principle of ecology, whether applied to limited sets of phenomena—such as in plant ecology, animal ecology, urban ecology—or to a total analysis of the hundreds of species and processes on earth. Ecology is concerned with systems. The ecological approach describes and analyzes the *system of interdependence* among different elements in a common setting. In plant and animal ecology interdependence is among different species that mutually adjust in the same environment. In human ecology there is only one species but there are numerous important group differences within the species that are related to economic, social, and cultural factors. Human ecology is also complicated by man's ability to transform the world around him to a much greater degree than other species.

In a system of interrelated parts, "everything must go somewhere" and "there is no such thing as a free lunch."[2] These additional principles of ecology indicate that in an ecological system every action has consequences, some occurring quickly in closely related parts of the system and others manifesting themselves more slowly, often in unintended and unexpected ways. Many people were alerted to the complex interconnections in ecological systems by Rachel Carson's *Silent Spring*,[3] a vivid, well-documented description of the destructive effects, especially on birds, of widespread spraying of chemical pesticides, such as DDT, which eventually found their way into the birds' food supply. *Silent Spring* also illustrated that the components of an ecological system are in "balance" even though the size of particular components may vary from time to time. The system will continue to function so long as there are enough representatives of a given component to contribute its

[1] Barry Commoner, *The Closing Circle: Nature, Man, and Technology* (1971), p. 39.

[2] *Ibid.*, pp. 39–46.

[3] Rachel Carson, *Silent Spring* (1962). A detailed account of the response to her book by industry, government, scholars, and the public is given in Frank Graham, Jr., *Since Silent Spring* (1970).

function to the maintenance of the whole. Ecological systems typically oscillate, with one of their components thriving more than the others for a period, but there is a point beyond which recovery of balance is not possible. Many conservationists, citizen's organizations and legislative bodies have begun seeking action to prevent collapse of various ecological systems.

Urban Ecology

While human ecology is concerned with the interrelationships among men in their spatial setting, urban ecology is specifically concerned with these interrelationships as they manifest themselves in the city. Urban ecology includes the study of such external expressions of ecological interrelationships as the distribution of cities[4] or their internal structure and composition.[5] Because urban ecology devotes much attention to the description of these external manifestations, the fact that its main concern is the system producing these external patterns, rather than the patterns themselves, is sometimes obscured. Michelson has pointed out that this confusion has been increased by the tendency to reduce the *discipline* of urban ecology to a particular ecological *method*, namely mapping the distribution of social phenomena in the city to produce ecological correlations.[6]

Much of the sociological literature on ecology is concerned with the distribution in space of people and institutions, but spatial distribution is only a starting point in ecological analysis. Human ecology goes further than merely determining where designated groups are located or where they perform particular functions. It is also concerned with interactive relationships between individuals and groups and the way these relationships influence, or are influenced by, particular spatial patterns and processes. It is concerned with cultural, racial, economic, and other differences insofar as preferences and prejudices associated with these differences serve to bring people socially or spatially together or keep them apart. It is concerned with social organization insofar as the organization of human activities influences, or is influenced by, the spatial distribution of people or of institutions. Above all, it is concerned with the dynamics of the social order insofar as change in the structure and functions of institutions, or changes in patterns of human relationships, bring about ecological changes and vice versa.

[4] Two very different examples of this broad application of urban ecology are Otis Dudley Duncan, "Social Organization and the Ecosystem," in R. E. L. Faris, ed., *Handbook of Modern Sociology* (1964), and Brian B. J. Berry, ed., *City Classification Handbook* (1972).

[5] This chapter, as well as Chapters 7–11, will deal with the second type of application, the description and analysis of areas within the city.

[6] William Michelson, *Man and His Urban Environment* (1970), p. 12.

It should be kept in mind that urban ecology as a science does not deal with individuals as individuals; rather, it is concerned with groups of individuals having some common characteristic such as age, sex, income, education, race, marital status, and the like. Nor does urban ecology deal with individual business firms or industries, but with types such as financial institutions, light manufacturing, service enterprises, and so on. The concern of urban ecology with categories of people or institutions arises from its attempt to describe the system of interrelationships underlying the visible city. Single individuals or commercial enterprises are not self-sufficient but dependent on others who in turn are dependent on them. Accruing from this interdependency is a complex interplay of forces. Furthermore, the properties of the interrelated whole are different than the properties of the component parts. For these reasons, urban ecology is always concerned with collectivities.

Elements of the Ecological System

The ecological system has been described as having four elements: population, organization, environment, and technology.[7] A fifth element, social-psychological factors, is added in this discussion. These five elements may easily be recalled by the acronym P.O.E.T.S.

POPULATION Human ecology always deals with a specific concrete population of human beings. Population groups have characteristics which affect their adjustment. Thus, a population has a rate of increase or decrease which helps determine the degree of competition for space. For example, houses and apartments were easier to find in the 1930's when urban marriage and birth rates were low and few people migrated to cities than in the post-World War II period when marriage and birth rates and immigration were at high levels. Populations can also be described in terms of their density or other aspects of their distribution.

Movement, another characteristic of populations that is relevant to urban ecology, may be of various types: permanent or transitory, within the city or between cities, or between city and countryside. For example, such phenomena as migration and immigration, commuting, moving from one address to another, the summer exodus from the city, the "rush hour," and holiday and weekend travel have definite regularity and meaning. The daily ebb-and-flow movement in the city, resulting from the separation of work place and place of residence which is a significant aspect of modern urbanization, offers an interesting example. The

---

[7] Otis Dudley Duncan, "Human Ecology and Population Studies," in Philip Hauser and Otis Dudley Duncan, eds., *The Study of Population* (1959), pp. 681–84. This presentation is broadly based on Duncan's analysis, except that he does not include the fifth element.

daily urban ebb and flow of workers is characterized by main currents, countercurrents, and crosscurrents of movements. Some move laterally across the city. Others, perhaps the majority, move centripetally to the center of the city during morning hours. More and more, however, commuting has taken on a centrifugal direction as workers commute to outlying work places, either from the city or from other parts of suburbs. Some movements are short, possibly a few minutes' walk, others are long, often as far as forty or fifty miles in the larger metropolitan areas.

ENVIRONMENT   Populations exist in a given natural environment, which is broadly defined here to include location, climate, natural resources, flora and fauna, topography, natural disasters, and geologic change. The population must cope with this environment to exist, and environments differ in the resources they offer for survival. Environment may set ultimate limits to the size and density of the population, but the process of adjustment is continuous and reciprocal because man in turn modi-

Views of Positano, Regina, and Sydney, show the influence of the natural setting on ecological patterns, in the contrast between hilly terrain, very flat plains, and location on a major ocean. Positano, a town near Naples, also has a long preindustrial history while Regina, capital of Saskatchewan, in Canada, and Sydney, largest city in Australia, are more recently established and represent industrial-urban development. (Italian Government Tourist Office—left; Joe Fartak/Color Productions Ltd.—top; © American Airlines Photo—bottom)

fies the environment via his technology and culture.[8] The transformed environment may then support populations at entirely different levels, as a comparison of present-day Manhattan or Chicago with those same areas when occupied by the Indian readily shows.

In the city, man's modification of the natural environment reaches a high level. Most native plants and animals are destroyed and new ones introduced intentionally (the English sparrow) or unintentionally (the brown rat). Waters are polluted by sewage and industrial wastes and the air by smoke and smog. The terrain is altered by roads, railroads, swamp drainage, the construction of reservoirs and canals, the development of golf courses and beaches, and by bombing and other war damage.[9]

Despite man's increased ability to cope with the natural environment, it is still a factor to be reckoned with in analyzing cities, as the following discussion of two aspects of the natural environment—terrain and rivers—indicates.

If all cities were located on level plains, completely removed from waterways, hills, and mountains, their ecological patterning would be mainly the result of man-made factors unhampered by topographic characteristics. But few cities are located on sites devoid of surface irregularities. Indeed, an irregular terrain has often been selected for initial settlement because of the advantages it offered for defense or transportation, as in the case of many early European and American settlements that later grew into urban centers. It is the viewpoint of this book that topographic conditions are not so much direct causes of particular ecological configurations as they are limiting factors to which some kind of ecological adjustment can be made.

Cities located on waterways, especially rivers, make a rather typical ecological adjustment to this physical fact. Probably most cities on rivers were initially located on one side of the bank; but as they grew in size and became more specialized in their functions, they tended to spill over the river to the opposite bank. Population and institutions on one side of the river are commonly quite different from those on the other. One side, especially if it is on low ground and considered less desirable for residential purposes, may be devoted mainly to heavy manufacturing. East St. Louis, North Kansas City, and Camden, New Jersey, are examples of highly industrialized developments on opposite sides of

[8] Michelson's recent work emphasizes that environment does not act simply in human ecology but interacts in far-reaching and subtle ways with other aspects of ecology. Specifically he criticizes urban ecology for its failure to deal adequately with the interrelationships between the physical environment and social factors. He believes the failure stems from (1) too simple a conceptualization of the physical environment; (2) too exclusive a focus on aggregates so that the range of variation within a given group is unexplained; (3) separation of urban ecology from other ecological fields; and (4) the emergence of large-scale conscious intervention in the city, particularly by government, after urban ecology had already emerged. Michelson, *op. cit.*, pp. 17–25.

[9] Lee Dice, *Man's Nature and Nature's Man* (1955), pp. 77–78.

major rivers in the United States. On the right bank of the Rhine, at Cologne, is a similar development. Budapest is likewise a city divided by a river: Buda on the hill side of the Danube, Pest on the flat plains on the opposite side of the stream.[10] Buda is an old town with winding streets; the hill is the historical nucleus of the city. Pest is modern in layout and contains most of the commercial and industrial establishments and residences of the workers. Cities on irregular terrain show the effect of topographic irregularities in the pattern of growth. Wedged between Lake Superior and a high escarpment is Duluth, whose expansion can occur in only two directions, along the waterfront. The result is a city stretching for twenty or more miles along the lake but extending scarcely a half-mile back from the shore line. The extreme density of population in Bombay is partly due to the fact that the city is located on an island and cannot expand territorially beyond the water's edge.

TECHNOLOGY   The adjustment of a population to its environment is obviously conditioned by the available technology. This is implied in what we have said about man's modification of the natural environment. The carrying power of a given environment varies according to the means man has developed to make use of it. The city as we know it—the industrial city—depends on a complex specialized technology which makes it possible for a considerable proportion of the population to live apart from direct concern with agriculture.

   The internal spatial patterns of cities are also, to a very considerable extent, the creation of technology, especially the technology of factory and transportation. As technological changes have taken place, the ecology of the city has correspondingly undergone changes. Wherever cities are characterized by small-scale manufacturing and distributive enterprises, the place of work and place of residence are unseparated for many families. This pattern prevailed in early European and American cities, and is still widespread in cities of economically underdeveloped countries such as those of the Orient. Dual functions are carried out in the same building. A retail merchant may operate his business on the first floor and house his family in the rear of the building or on the second floor; or a craftsman may carry out his operations in the rear of a structure which also houses his family. Sometimes the same structure is used for three purposes: residence, manufacturing, and merchandising. Increased mechanization that required factories altered these locational patterns.

   In the early days of the Industrial Revolution, factories were located in the inner zones of cities; or, perhaps more accurately, cities tended to develop around the factories, with workers residing close to the place of employment. The result was high residential density, families stacked on families in crowded tenements occupied by workers and their depen-

[10] Robert F. Dickinson, *The West European City* (1951), p. 209.

dents. But as transportation technology changed, as the speed and size of vehicles increased, workers tended to break the ties that bound them to the vicinity of a factory site. Later changes in the size and layout of factories (large and requiring a single level for assembly-line production) forced such establishments to move to open land more cheaply available at the city's outskirts. And as residence spread into the suburbs, commercial services diffused as well.

With the growth of large-scale industrial and commercial organizations in many countries of the world, the detachment of the work place from the place of residence became more and more a distinguishing feature of city life. On the basis of the 1970 census, of the 58 million wage earners in American cities, only 1.9 percent worked at home.[11] Long-distance commuters in smaller cities as well as in metropolitan areas shuttle back and forth between their place of work and their residence. Almost 17 percent of the urban workers in the United States reported that they worked in a county that is not the one they live in.

Obviously technological developments have greatly affected the ecology of cities not only with reference to the distribution of business and industry but also with reference to the distribution of people. As technological changes continue, there can be no doubt that other ecological changes will occur.[12]

ORGANIZATION   A crucial element in the ecological complex is organization. For human beings organization is always *social* because they cannot exist on a sustaining basis apart from other human beings. As interdependent creatures, it is necessary that they organize, that is, make their activities regular and systematic when they are living in the same group, whether that group be as small as the family or as large as the metropolis or the nation. Without some form of organization, chaos would result, as sometimes happens in times of disaster, revolution, rapid social change, or other instances where the social order is temporarily disrupted.

Urban ecology is, of course, concerned with those aspects of social organization which impinge upon the community level. Foremost among these is the division of labor, for the network of occupational interdependence is very extensive and we are often unaware of many of its ramifications. Thus, the feasibility of staggered working hours to reduce rush-hour congestion hinges on whether studies can uncover what kinds of business can operate for part of the day without the services of other types of enterprise. There is no point in having type "A" firms begin work at 8:30 A.M. while type "B" firms begin at 9:00 A.M., if the former cannot function without the latter.

[11] *U. S. Census of Population 1970. General Social and Economic Characteristics. United States Summary.* Final Report PC(1)-C1, Table 87.

[12] See Chapters 3, 9, 10, and 11 for discussions of the specific ways in which transportation technology has affected American cities.

The ramifications of interdependence are often brought to light during a prolonged strike. Typographers would seem far removed from retailing, the theater and entertainment, fashion, cafe society, charity balls, and real estate and employment agencies. Yet, the lengthy strike by the typographers union against the leading New York City's leading newspapers in 1962–1963 ultimately had serious adverse effects on all of these groups, who were without their customary advertising and publicity.

Since much organization of human activities in the city is embodied in economic organization, it is inevitable that urban ecology devotes much of its attention to cost and to the locational factors affecting cost, namely, time and distance. Economic exchange, since it does not require personal contact or acquaintance, is well suited to the large populations of the city. Economic organization, however, is only part of social organization; social organization also involves such concepts as status, position, and role. Thus, we cannot understand the occupational division of labor in Western society, for example, without recognizing the status of women or youth or the position of blacks and immigrants within society.

The physical pattern of the city mirrors some of the organizing principles of social structure. Is the skyline dominated by the cathedral, the fortress, or the office skyscraper? Do groups occupy separate residential areas on the basis of race, religion, ethnic affiliation, wealth, caste, occupation, social class, or other criteria? Is movement within the city unimpeded or is it restricted by such governmental controls as curfews, passes, ghettos, police, and check-points? To what extent is commercial or residential location a matter of laissez-faire, and to what extent is it directed by the government through zoning laws, building restrictions, subsidized housing, rights of eminent domain, and so on?

THE SOCIAL-PSYCHOLOGICAL ELEMENT   As we said at the beginning of this section, a fifth element, the social-psychological aspect of human ecology, must be added to the four ecological elements posited by Duncan. If man is anything at all, he is a creature of wits and sentiments. He is a purposive animal, capable of making choices of his own volition, capable of certain action patterns in accordance with the sentiments and values he has acquired. Commonly he is a person of prejudice, and his likes and dislikes of other individuals and groups influence the character of his associational life and frequently affect his position in the ecological structure of the community.

Preferences, values, attitudes, and beliefs must be common to a significant number of individuals who act or are willing to act on them in order to qualify as social-psychological elements in human ecology; purely idiosyncratic individual tastes are unimportant.

Several examples, of which the pattern of black residential segregation in American cities is noteworthy, illustrate the social-psychological element in human ecology. Spatial segregation of Negroes in slums is only in part related to their limited economic means, and even their generally low economic position is in turn related to many social-psychological factors such as attitudes, prejudice, motives, public opinion, rumor, gossip, and propaganda. Taeuber's analysis of residential racial segregation in American cities indicated that low incomes and the desire to live together accounted for some degree of racial segregation, but that discrimination by whites was certainly the most important.[13]

Firey's study in central Boston indicated that two social-psychological factors were at work in determining land use there, in addition to the expected economic competition. (1)"Space . . . also [has] an additional property, *viz.*, that of being at times a symbol for certain cultural values that have become associated with a certain spatial area." (2) "Locational activities are not only economizing agents but may also bear sentiments which can significantly influence the locational process."[14] Sentiment and symbolism may supersede other considerations and result in non-economic, "nonrational" use of land. Thus, Beacon Hill, with its historical, literary, and "old-family" associations, has remained a fashionable residential area, despite the fact that its central location would bring much higher financial return if it were put to commercial use. The Boston Common, several colonial burying-grounds, and historic churches and meeting houses stand in the heart of Boston. The retention of these landmarks is expensive, but public opinion runs high against demolishing the edifices in which major events of the Revolution took place.

Firey points out that sentimental and symbolic attachment to spatial location is not restricted to historic or upper class areas. The foreign-born Italian immigrants tend to remain in the North End of Boston even when their means permit them to move elsewhere, for the North End provides the traditional Italian community life not available in other sections of the city.

A study of zoning in Austin, Texas, also demonstrates the role of values and volition in human ecology.[15] Analysis of the proceedings of the Austin City Planning Commission and the commission's Zoning Committee for 1956–1960 and interviews with the participants revealed that the central problem in urban zoning was resolution of the conflict among competing values and beliefs about effective land use. Willhelm describes three major sets of opposing values: economic versus protective values; collective versus individual values; and present-time versus future-time values. The differences between those emphasizing eco-

---

[13] Karl Taeuber, "Residential Segregation," *Scientific American*, 213 (August 1965), 2–9.

[14] Walter Firey, "Sentiment and Symbolism as Ecological Variables," *American Sociological Review*, 10 (April 1945), 141.

[15] Sidney Willhelm, *Urban Zoning and Land-Use Theory* (1962). The title of this volume belies its general relevance for the study of human ecology.

nomic values as opposed to those emphasizing protective values are most fundamental. Thus, decision-makers who approached the zoning process from an economic point of view held that zoning should maximize profit and that residential and nonresidential uses of land should compete with one another, with the economic market determining the use of land. In contrast, those decision-makers with a protective point of view held that zoning should be based first on protecting residential use of land and that other types of land use and the profit motive should be secondary in zoning decisions. Those with the protective orientation often described themselves as "people-oriented."[16] The current debates about "exclusionary" zoning in suburbs undoubtedly offer opportunity for analysis in terms of the differing value orientations with which various groups approach the zoning process. It is not known whether Willhelm's particular set of value contrasts is the most appropriate description in this type of zoning.

Interrelationships of the Ecological Elements

Environment, population, technology, organization, and social-psychological elements all mutually modify one another, an interaction that can be seen clearly if the elements are expressed schematically. The case of suburban expansion of American cities after World War II may serve as an example. The symbols P, O, E, T, and SP, respectively, stand for population, organization, environment, technology, and social-psychological elements.

Few residential buildings were constructed in American cities during the Depression of the 1930's and World War II, and many of the earlier industrial and residential structures were built in a period of rapid growth and industrialization with minimum restriction and planning. Thus, by the mid-1940's the central areas of many American cities were characterized by polluted air and by little open space for parks or recreation or for further industrial or residential expansion (O,SP, T→E). During this same period, most immigrant groups had been assimilated into the middle class; increased mechanization drew more people to cities, the proportion of the labor force in unskilled jobs was reduced, the amount of leisure time available increased, and values about early marriage and child-bearing changed. All of this resulted in a rapidly expanding, prosperous, middle class, urban population with many young children (O,SP, T, → P). The change in the size and composition of the urban population pressed on the already crowded city cores which were undesirable in terms of middle class amenities for children, thereby complicating the adjustment of urban middle class living (P → E, O, SP).

[16] *Ibid.*, pp. 94–96, 217.

Ownership of cars and homes (especially since mass-production techniques had been applied to housing) was widely possible for the middle class and made possible an explosion of residential suburbs which replaced farms or relatively open land on the outskirts of American cities. ($O \longleftrightarrow T \rightarrow E$).

The new communities, based, as we have noted, on a series of adaptations and new interrelationships among the five ecological elements, set still further changes in motion. Social scientists have been particularly interested in the organizational and social-psychological changes resulting from these new communities ($E, P, T, O_1, SP_1 \rightarrow O_2, SP_2$). These include the drive for a metropolitan form of government, the concern among politicians with the shift of many voters to areas outside the city limits, the research studies and debates about the quality of religious and family life in suburbs, discussion of the values exemplified by suburbia, and proposals to control urban sprawl by zoning and better planning.

This schematic analysis indicates that the systemic interrelations underlying the ecological community are in a constant cycle of adaptation and re-adaptation.

The Social Component
in Human Ecology

Although all human ecologists have recognized the importance of social factors, various schools of thought differ sharply in the relative position they assign to such factors within the ecological framework. One recent survey of human ecology has classified these schools of thought as the "classical," the "neo-orthodox," and the "sociocultural."[17]

The so-called classical position, exemplified by Robert Park and Ernest Burgess, includes an emphasis on cultural elements as separate from and, to a large extent, dependent upon, the noncultural ecological elements. The classical ecologists used many concepts such as *competition*, *natural area*, *biotic community*, and *symbiosis*, which are derived from plant and animal ecology and from Social Darwinism.

Beginning in the late 1930's, the classical position was criticized and modified. Generally speaking the more recent schools of thought have assigned social factors a more central position in human ecology. The so-called neo-orthodox approach has done this either by retaining the emphasis on the noncultural elements but indicating they can only be understood in terms of culture (James Quinn) or by concentrating on

---

[17] George A. Theodorson, "Introductions" to Parts I and II in George A. Theodorson, ed., *Studies in Human Ecology* (1961). Rather similar distinctions are made in Willhelm, *op. cit.*, chs. 2 and 3. Willhelm uses the terms, "traditional materialism," "neoclassical materialism," and "cultural" to describe the three major types of emphasis on social factors in human ecology.

those cultural elements reflected in the economic aspects of community structure (Amos Hawley).

The sociocultural position is the only view of human ecology to assign cultural factors a major causative influence. Walter Firey, an important exponent of this point of view, notes in his study of Boston that sentiment and symbolism often resulted in inefficient or uneconomic uses of land, and further notes that other types of ecological approaches do not account for such land uses.

Although this presentation is oversimplified, it does serve to suggest the variety of ways in which the social factor may be conceptualized in human ecology. All of these approaches have produced research results and, except for the strict classical position, are currently being used.

Ecological Patterns of Urban Growth

Are there uniformities in the ecological patterning of cities and if so what is the nature of such patterns? If such uniformities exist, can they be presented in the form of principles or generalizations? A number of urban ecologists have attempted to go beyond mere description to the formulation of a set of theories or hypotheses concerning the ecological pattern of the city. In their efforts to formulate systematic principles, they are aware of the fact that scientific theories are generalizations which may not fit all the details of each individual city. Theoretical constructs concerning ecological structure postulate a kind of ideal type which may not actually exist in all details but which may approximately describe the recurring patterning of cities. If the theoretical construct departs too far from what actually exists, its validity is open to question, or at least has limited applicability. On the other hand, a theory of urban ecology may have validity without having a universal application; if it is designed to apply only to cities of a certain country or region, or to cities of a particular type, then it may be valid, provided it is accurately descriptive of the spatial configurations that actually exist.

Three theories of urban ecology patterns have been particularly interesting to sociologists. The first is the "concentric zone theory" of urban growth, formulated many years ago by Ernest Burgess. The second is the "sector theory" of city growth, developed later by Homer Hoyt. The third is C. D. Harris and Edward Ullman's "multiple nuclei theory." Each theory is, in a sense, an ideal construct, a set of generalizations. Burgess is particularly explicit in noting that his concentric zone theory has no reference to any particular city but that it is an abstraction representing a kind of generalized ecological profile of cities, presumably American communities. Each of the theories is concerned with ecological change and with the spatial patterns that have emerged from these changes.

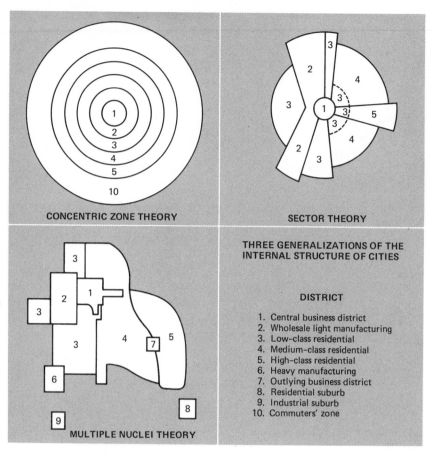

FIGURE 6.1 • Schematic illustration of three early theories of city growth. These are probably more applicable to cities in ur- ban-industrial than in de- veloping countries. Source: C. D. Harris and Edward L. Ullman, *An- nals*, 242 (November 1945), 7–17.

Each was developed on the basis of knowledge concerning the ecology and growth of American cities. Whether their authors intended them to apply to cities in other countries is not clear, but whatever validity they possess is higher for American communities than for cities outside the United States. As we shall observe later in this volume, certain cities in Latin America, the Orient, and Africa differ quite markedly from American cities in their ecological configurations.

Burgess' Concentric Zone Theory

Writing in the early 1920's, chiefly on the basis of the then-unfolding knowledge of the structure of the city of Chicago, Burgess suggested that urban expansion causes a modern city to assume a pattern of concentric zones, each characterized by a typical land use.[18] These zones, according to Burgess, are idealized concepts; no city conforms absolutely to his scheme. Physical barriers such as rivers, lakes, hills, and gulches tend to distort the zonal pattern of a community. Lines of transportation, such as railroads and automobile highways, divide the zones into smaller sections.

[18] Ernest W. Burgess, "The Growth of the City," in Robert E. Park and Ernest W. Burgess, *The City* (1925), p. 51.

A. THE CENTRAL BUSINESS DISTRICT The first or inner zone, according to the Burgess theory, comprises the "central business district," the area where skyscrapers, department stores, cheap variety emporia, hotels, restaurants, theaters, and motion-picture houses are concentrated to meet the needs of downtown shoppers or transients. The inner zone is essentially an area of retail trade, light manufacturing, and commercialized recreation. In Chicago it is called the "Loop," in New York the "Midtown" and "Downtown" areas, and in Pittsburgh the "Golden Triangle." In American cities, at least, the central business district occupies a relatively small proportion of the entire area of the community.

B. THE ZONE OF TRANSITION The zone surrounding the central business district was designated by Burgess as the "zone of transition," because, being in the immediate path of business and industrial expansion, it has an ephemeral character. Unlike the business district, which is a nonresidential area for the most part, the zone of transition tends to be heavily populated by the lower income classes, by Old World immigrants and rural migrants, by unconventional folk, and by social outcasts such as criminals and prostitutes. Typically, the zone of transition also contains some high-cost luxury housing—the "Gold Coast."

C. THE ZONE OF WORKINGMEN'S HOMES The third area in Burgess' scheme was designated the "zone of workingmen's homes." Superior to the area of transition in physical appearance, but falling short of the residential districts of the middle classes, it is populated largely by workers whose economic status enables them to have many of the comforts and even some of the luxuries the city has to offer.

D. THE ZONE OF MIDDLE CLASS DWELLERS Beyond the zone occupied by the working classes is a broad area populated mainly by professional people, owners of small businesses, the managerial group, clerical forces, and the like. In this area, there are hotels and apartment houses, and detached residences with spacious yards and gardens.

E. THE COMMUTER'S ZONE On the outer periphery of the city is the "commuter's zone," an area beyond the political boundaries of the city consisting of satellite towns and suburbs that exist in a mutually dependent relationship with the metropolis. These towns and hamlets, dubbed by some writers "bedroom communities," may house many of the city's workers by night but are largely vacated during the day.

Burgess gave empirical support to his hypothesis by presenting sociological data, mainly from Chicago, which in their distributive patterns take the form of a series of gradients. He showed that, in passing from the center or Loop of Chicago to the periphery, delinquency rates, sex ratios, and percentages of foreign-born persons tended to decrease, while home ownership was inclined to increase.[19] In certain instances the gradients were uniformly continuous. These gradients were also observed by Shaw and McKay[20] in their ecological studies of delinquency and by Faris and Dunham[21] in a study of the ecology of insanity in Chicago.

Hoyt's Sector Theory of Urban Growth

On the basis of data provided during the depression by real-property inventories of 142 American cities, Hoyt formulated the sector theory of urban development.[22] Briefly, the theory holds that high-rent areas tend to be located on the outer fringes of one or more sectors or quadrants of the city, and that in some sectors the low-rent districts assume the shape of a cut of pie, extending from the center to the city's periphery. As cities grow in population, the high-rent areas move outward along one sector; districts thus abandoned by the upper-income groups become obsolete and frequently deteriorate, and are inherited by people of lower economic status. Instead of forming a concentric zone around the periphery of the city, Hoyt insists, the high-rent areas are ordinarily located on the outer edge of one or more sectors. Furthermore, industrial areas develop along river valleys, water courses, and railroad lines instead of forming a concentric zone around the central business district. In recent decades there has been a tendency for factories to locate on outerbelt lines near the edge of the city. Hoyt likened the pattern of the American city to an "octopus" with tentacles extending in various directions along the transportation lines.

Hoyt observed that the high-rent residential areas tend to be located along established transportation routes, usually on high ground and away from the "flats." In some cities these districts are situated on attractive waterfronts not used for industrial purposes. Chicago, for example, has a high-rent area stretching along the lake front from the Loop to the northern city limits; beyond the city's northern boundaries is a string of upper-class suburbs which follows the lake shore for thirty or forty miles and is connected with Chicago by rapid transit lines. A similar pattern of development may be noted in Madison, Wisconsin, a much smaller city, where the two areas of maximum rentals are along the shore of Lake Mendota, near the eastern and western extremities of the metropolitan district.

[19] "The Determination of Gradients in the Growth of a City," *Publications of the American Sociological Society*, 21 (1927), 178–84.

[20] Clifford Shaw and Henry McKay, *Juvenile Delinquency and Urban Areas* (1942).

[21] R. E. L. Faris and H. Warren Dunham, *Mental Disorders in Urban Areas* (1939).

[22] Homer Hoyt, *The Structure and Growth of Residential Neighborhoods in American Cities* (1939), ch. 6. See also his article, "The Structure of American Cities in the Post-War Era," *American Journal of Sociology*, 48 (January 1943), 475–92.

Harris and Ullman's
Multiple-Nuclei Theory

Harris and Ullman's theory differs from both the Burgess and Hoyt theories in that it postulates not one center for the city, but several.[23] Each of the centers tends to specialize in a particular kind of activity—retailing, wholesaling, finance, government, recreation, education, and the like. Several centers may have existed from the beginning of the city, or many have developed later in a division from one center. London is an example of the first type, where the financial and governmental centers were separate from the inception of the town. Chicago illustrates the second type, for while heavy industry was originally concentrated in the downtown area, it later tended to concentrate in an area of its own in the extreme southeast of the city.

Multiple centers develop for the following reasons: (1) Certain activities require specialized facilities and concentrate where these facilities occur. Thus heavy industry requires large acreage and long-distance connections, in contrast to retailing which requires much less space and easy local accessibility. (2) Similar activities benefit from location close to one another. For example, the clustering of retail establishments concentrates potential customers. (3) Certain dissimilar activities may be disadvantageous to one another. Industry which requires large space and may have "nuisance" features is incompatible both with retailing which depends on heavy pedestrian and street traffic and with high-class residential development. (4) For some urban activities a downtown location is too expensive and would not be the most advantageous site in any case.

The major urban activities often form subnuclei on the following pattern. The central business district contains the major retail shopping area, but, especially in large cities, financial and governmental districts may form separate concentrations within it. "Automobile row" may also be a separate part of the central business district. Wholesaling, light manufacturing, heavy industry, high-class and low-class residences— each tends to occupy separate nuclei apart from the central business district. The Harris and Ullman approach suggests that seeking an "ideal" urban pattern may be fruitless, since historic and not necessarily predictable factors may create the nuclei and their locational distribution.

Limitations of the Theories

A general criticism of the concentric-zone theory was offered by Alihan, who declared that a zone can have significance only if its boundaries

[23] C. D. Harris and Edward L. Ullman, "The Nature of Cities," *The Annals*, 242 (November 1945), 7–17.

mark a distinction between gradients.[24] If, as the term implies, gradients are continuous, zonal lines can be drawn arbitrarily at any radius from the center. In other words, it would be as logical to have twenty zones as five. Apparently, however, the Burgess theory, according to Alihan, implies a certain homogeneity of phenomena within a particular concentric zone, and the same idea appears to be implicit in the sector theory. Alihan's analysis of the shortcomings of the zonal pattern was part of her more basic critique of the logic and coherence of the classical ecological approach developed by Park and Burgess. Specifically, Alihan contended that this approach did not take account of the impact of sociocultural factors in the ecological process.

In a penetrating critique, based upon a study of land use in Boston, Firey found both the concentric-zone and sector theories inadequate for that city.[25] The distribution of particular population groups in Boston shows much greater variability than either the Burgess or Hoyt schemes permit. Firey points out, for example, that Beacon Hill and the West End, situated in what would be the zone of transition, are populated by sharply contrasting people. One part of Beacon Hill is a fashionable residential district; adjacent to it, within the same concentric zone, is a low-income area populated in the main by lower-class immigrants and their descendants. These two contiguous areas have for the past century and a half been sharply set off from one another in terms of class status, population characteristics, housing, and reputation. Furthermore, Firey observed, the two adjacent areas do not represent a "gradation" in accordance with the Burgess and Hoyt theories, but are in certain respects "polar opposites." Firey pointed out, as noted earlier in this chapter, that the persistence of these areas could not be explained in economic terms, thus requiring modification of the dynamics of the Burgess theory in particular. Firey thereby confirmed with empirical data the kind of inadequacies that Alihan had earlier pointed out, namely the absence of sociocultural factors in the Park-Burgess ecological approach.

Firey also demonstrates that the distribution of income classes, based upon rentals, does not conform to the concentric-zone hypothesis. In the inner zone are both the highest and lowest rental areas. Similarly, the outermost zone includes low-rent and high-rent areas. "Not a single concentric zone reveals any homogeneity in its rental classes."[26] Firey found that the "sector" lying southwest of Boston was characterized both by upper-class and lower-class residents and could not therefore be considered homogeneous. The working-class towns in the metropolitan district do not conform to the sector theory, with the exception of the North Shore, but are distributed at random.

[24] Milla Alihan, *Social Ecology* (1938), p. 225.
[25] Walter Firey, *Land Use in Central Boston* (1947), pp. 41–86.
[26] *Ibid.*, p. 77.

Recent Advances in
Ecological Theory

The most fundamental criticism of the concentric zone, the sector, and, to a lesser extent, the multiple-nuclei theories was that they assumed a single distributive dimension. More recent ecological studies have indicated that ecological distribution is multidimensional and each dimension may be distributed differently. For example, one study demonstrates that both the Hoyt and Burgess descriptions have some validity, but for different aspects of urban life.[27] This conclusion was drawn from a study of residential areas in four United States cities ranging in population between 200,000 and 500,000—Akron, Dayton, Indianapolis, and Syracuse. It was found that areas characterized by many apartment buildings, families with few young children, and families in which the wife works were most frequent near the city center and gradually declined in relative frequency toward the periphery. In other words, these traits were distributed in a concentric zonal fashion. On the other hand, characteristics associated with the prestige of residential areas, as measured by the education and occupations of the inhabitants, were distributed in sector fashion, although the position of the sector varied from one city to another. In each of the four cities there was a segment of territory that extended from the center to the periphery and was inhabited with a higher proportion of people with at least a high school education and with nonmanual jobs than the rest of the city.

The Shevky-Bell-Williams Method

The first attempt to ascertain the several dimensions of American cities and the resultant spatial distribution was the trail-blazing study of Los Angeles County by Shevky and Williams.[28] Later studies by Shevky and Bell applied the approach to San Francisco Bay region data for 1940 and 1950 and elaborated many of the concepts and procedures.[29] The particular problem to which the studies addressed themselves was the development of a procedure for delineating "social areas," going beyond the methods commonly used in delineating relatively homogeneous "ecological areas." If carefully delineated, such areas could not only indicate the general ecological structure of a city but could also be used effectively as a basis for comparative studies, either of areas within a particular city or between different cities.

---

[27] Theodore Anderson and Janice Egeland, "Spatial Aspects of Social Area Analysis," *American Sociological Review*, 26 (June 1961), 392–98.

[28] Eshref Shevky and Marilyn Williams, *The Social Areas of Los Angeles* (1949).

[29] Eshref Shevky and Wendell Bell, *Social Area Analysis* (1955), and Wendell Bell, "The Social Areas of the San Francisco Bay Region," *American Sociological Review*, 18 (February 1953), 39–47.

Shevky, Williams, and Bell employed three indexes: (1) "social rank" (also called "economic status"), representing measures of occupation and education; (2) "urbanization" ("family status"), representing measures of fertility, gainfully employed women, and single-dwelling or multiple-dwelling residence; and (3) "segregation" ("ethnic status"), representing measures of ecological segregation of ethnic or racial groups. The census tracts of Los Angeles and San Francisco were then typed according to their characteristics as related to these three basic indexes.

It is important to note that Shevky, Williams, and Bell defended the three indexes in terms of a general theory of the increased "scale" or specialization of urban society. This is their version of the ecological system. There is considerable debate as to whether there are precisely three dimensions to urban society, whether the indexes Shevky, Williams, and Bell have constructed are adequate to measure these dimensions, and, indeed, what the dimensions should be called.[30] Despite these caveats, social area analysis is a major advance in research on the areal dimensions of American cities.

The Application of
Social Area Analysis

In social area analysis, first the researcher takes data from the census and computes composite indexes for each census tract to indicate social rank and family and ethnic status of the tract. The typology of urban "social space" is constructed in the Shevky-Williams-Bell method by dividing the census tract scores on social rank (economic status) into four parts from high to low; urbanization scores (family status) are also divided into four parts.[31] Since a census tract's score in one dimension is separate from its score in the other dimension, application of this process yields a potential of 16 different types of census tract, as in Figure 6.2.

In Figure 6.2 the number represents economic status and the key letter represents family status. The census tracts in type 1D, for example, contain populations scoring low on the social rank dimension (economic status), that is, they have low rents, contain many persons with blue-

[30] The major evaluations of social area analysis are Amos Hawley and Otis Dudley Duncan, "Social Area Analysis: A Critical Appraisal," *Land Economics*, 33 (November 1957), 337–44; M.D. Van Ardsol, Jr., S. Camillieri, and C. Schmid, "An Investigation of the Utility of Urban Typology," *Pacific Sociological Review*, 4 (1961), 26–32; T. R. Anderson and L. L. Bean, "The Shevky-Bell Social Areas: Confirmation of Results and a Reinterpretation," *Social Forces*, 40 (1961), 119–24; and Janet Abu-Lughod, "Testing the Theory of Social Area Analysis: The Ecology of Cairo, Egypt," *American Sociological Review*, 34 (April 1969), 198–212.

[31] Other dividing points for census tract scores may be chosen, of course. The application described here is based on Wendell Bell, "Social Areas: Typology of Urban Neighborhoods," in Marvin Sussman, ed., *Community Structure and Analysis* (1959).

	High			
	1A	2A	3A	4A
	1B	2B	3B	4B
FAMILY STATUS	1C	2C	3C	4C
	1D	2D	3D	4D
	Low			
	Low	ECONOMIC STATUS		High

FIGURE 6.2 • Social Area Key based on economic status (numbers 1–4) and family status (letters A–D). Source: Wendell Bell, "The Utility of the Shevky Typology for the Design of Urban Subarea Field Studies," *Journal of Social Psychology,* 47 (February 1958) p. 73.

collar occupations, and many persons with no more than a grade-school education. Type 1D tracts also score low on the urbanization dimension (family status), that is, they have low fertility ratios (few children under five in relation to the number of women aged 15–44); many woman are in paid employment rather than at home as housewives and mothers; and they have few single-family detached homes. Contrasting social area type 4D with type 1D, we find that the family status of the two groups of census tracts is the same (both are low in this dimension), but social area type 4D contains tract populations high in economic status while 1D tract populations are low in economic status.

The third dimension, ethnic status or segregation, is typically divided into "high," those tracts with proportionately larger numbers of American racial and nationality minority groups, and "low," those tracts with relatively few such residents. Added to the 16 types already constructed on the economic and family dimensions, this yields a total of 32 possible social area types. This allows for the fact that in addition to the variety of combinations of economic and family status already described, these characteristics may be found in highly segregated or in less-segregated census tracts.

All 32 possible areal types are not necessarily found in a city. Figure 6.3 indicates their actual distribution in the San Francisco Bay region. It should be noted that although there is a tendency for the highly

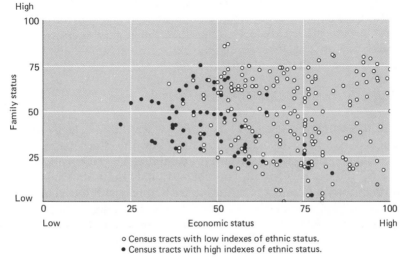

o Census tracts with low indexes of ethnic status.
• Census tracts with high indexes of ethnic status.

FIGURE 6.3 • Distribution of census tracts in the social areas of the San Francisco Bay Region. The three social area dimensions are relatively independent of each other, as shown by the existence of tracts with various combinations of family, economic, and ethnic status, although the highly segregated areas tend to predominate at the lower end of the economic dimension. This actual distribution of census tracts should be compared with the theoretical model of possible types (two dimensions only) shown in Figure 6.2. Source: Bell, *op. cit.,* p. 74.

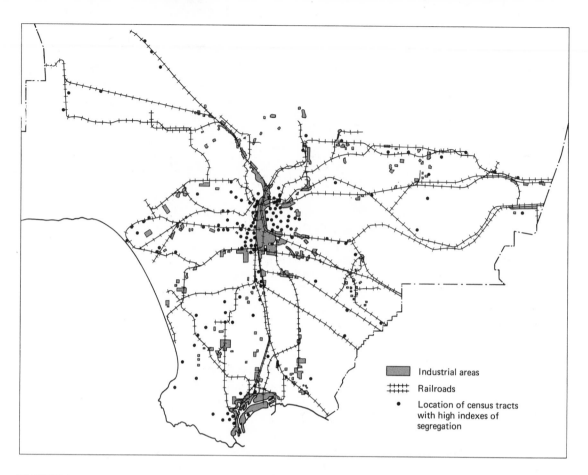

Industrial areas

Railroads

Location of census tracts with high indexes of segregation

FIGURE 6.4 • Ecological segregation in Los Angeles. Dots show location of census tracts having high indexes of segregation. Note that such tracts tend to be located near industrial districts. Source: Eshref Shevky and Marilyn Williams, *The Social Areas of Los Angeles*. Originally published by The University of California Press; reprinted by permission of The Regents of the University of California.

segregated areas to cluster toward the low end of the economic dimension, exceptions are numerous.

On the whole, Figure 6.3 indicates, as is confirmed by statistical correlations, that the three dimensions are relatively independent of each other. This is one reason why the geographic distribution of social area types combining the three dimensions does not show any uniform pattern such as zonal or sector. Even a single dimension may not show a simple pattern. Figure 6.4 shows that the highly segregated census tracts of Los Angeles, mainly blacks and Mexican-Americans in that city, are located near industrial areas.

The Utility of Social Area Analysis

Bell has employed the grid shown in Figure 6.2 to select four census tracts in San Francisco in order to study how the character of an area is related to various aspects of urban social life. The tracts chosen are all low in ethnic status but vary in economic and family status: (1) Mission, a tract in social area type 2C in Figure 6.2, has both low economic and low family status and is a low-rent, rooming-house area; (2) Pacific Heights, in social area type 4D, is a high-rent apartment house area, high on economic status but low on family status; (3) Outer Mission, an area of small houses and average income families, is in social area type 2B and is relatively higher on family status than on economic status; (4) St. Francis Wood, high on both economic and family status, represents social area type 4B and is characterized by well-to-do families in large single-family houses. Bell interviewed a sample of 701 male residents drawn from the four census tracts. Patterns of social participation varied significantly, indicating the distinctiveness of the areas delineated by the economic, family, and ethnic status dimensions. For example, men in the high economic status neighborhoods, Pacific Heights and St. Francis Wood, belong to a larger number of formal associations than men in the low economic status neighborhoods. In neighborhoods high in family status (St. Francis Wood and Outer Mission), men have more informal group contact and neighboring.[32]

A somewhat similar study utilizing social areas was conducted in Los Angeles by Greer.[33] By studying only census tracts that had the same rank on economic and ethnic status, Greer focused on the variation in social participation related to family status. He found the higher the tract ranked on family status the more neighboring occurred among residents and the greater the locality-orientation. The degree to which "urbanism as a way of life" characterizes the behavior of people in the city is therefore differentially linked to the characteristics of the various people who make up the urban environment. Ecological analysis enables us to examine these critical variations.

Factorial Ecology

The most recent development in urban ecology has been the application of factor analysis, a sophisticated method that allows greater precision in determining the several dimensions of urban structure. It is, in this sense, an elaboration of the social area analysis approach.

Factor analysis involves producing mathematical constructs (factors) which will account for the maximum amount of variation in a set of data with a minimum number of factors. As in social area analysis, in factorial ecology the basic unit is the census tract or ward and its indices on each of the specified variables, such as median rent or percentage of the population married. Correlations are computed for each unit with every other unit on each of the variables. Factors are extracted statistically from this data matrix to account for measurable amounts of the matrix's variance. "A factor is, therefore, a hypothetical 'force' underly-

---

[32] Wendell Bell and M. Force, "Urban Neighborhood Types and Participation in Formal Associations," *American Sociological Review*, 21 (February 1956), 25–34; and Wendell Bell and M. Boat, "Urban Neighborhoods and Informal Social Relations," *American Journal of Sociology*, 62 (January 1957), 391–98.

[33] Scott Greer, "Urbanism Reconsidered: A Comparative Study of Local Areas in a Metropolis," *American Sociological Review*, 21 (February 1956), 19–25.

ing and presumably accounting for the variance *common* to several variables which are highly intercorrelated. A separate general or group factor is hypothesized to account for each relatively independent cluster of intercorrelated variables."[34] The parsimony achieved by factor analysis in reducing the number of explanatory variables is very great. For example, it is reported that 20 to 70 variables have been reduced to a range of three to ten factors.[35]

While factor analysis is a powerful tool, the nature of the method requires an "intuitive leap"[36] from the rotation of the data matrix to the identification and interpretation of the factors. Various computational techniques have been suggested to overcome this difficulty, but the problem remains a fundamental one.[37] There will undoubtedly be further improvements in the technical aspects of factorial ecology. The application of factor analysis to urban ecology dates only from the 1950's, and many of the important studies, such as those of Helsinki and Boston by Frank Sweetser and Abu-Lughod's study of Cairo, date only from the mid-1960's. It is much too early for a total assessment of the contribution of factorial ecology.

FACTORIAL ECOLOGY OF PREINDUSTRIAL AND INDUSTRIAL CITIES   One of the major results of factorial ecology has been the in-depth study of the dynamics of preindustrial urban ecological systems as contrasted with industrial systems. Nonfactorial studies had already uncovered important contrasts between the spatial structure of preindustrial and industrial cities.[38] For example, cities whose major street patterns and public buildings were set down in the industrial period tend to be centered on a "downtown" dominated by high-rise commercial enterprises that are surrounded by a decaying "zone in transition," while the higher socioeconomic groups live far from the city center—generally progressively further as their socioeconomic level is higher. In cities whose major growth was in the preindustrial period, the content of this distribution is to some extent reversed: the city center is dominated by religious and governmental structures although the major commercial markets are also present. The urban elite live immediately adjacent to the city core and the lower socioeconomic groups live progressively further from the central area. In the many cities, such as European

---

[34] Janet Abu-Lughod, *Cairo: 1001 Years of the City Victorious* (1971), p. 185.

[35] Duncan Timms, *The Urban Mosaic: Towards a Theory of Residential Differentiation* (1971), pp. 56–58.

[36] *Ibid.*, p. 52.

[37] Alfred A. Hunter, "Factorial Ecology: A Critique and Some Suggestions," *Demography*, 9 (February 1972), 107–17.

[38] Leo F. Schnore, "On the Spatial Structure of Cities in the Two Americas," in Philip M. Hauser and Leo F. Schnore, eds., *The Study of Urbanization* (1965); and Gideon Sjoberg, *The Preindustrial City* (1960), ch. 4.

capitals, whose major development took place in both preindustrial and industrial periods, the ecological patterns tend to reflect a "mix."[39]

Factorial ecology studies suggest that despite the differences in the visible city, the same dimensions (factors) may underlie preindustrial and industrial cities. The best current evidence suggests that the two most fundamental urban dimensions are socioeconomic status and family type, with the ethnic composition and mobility characteristics (transiency) of the population as additional possible dimensions.[40] The similarity of these dimensions to those suggested by social area analysis is apparent.

The imbedding of these dimensions in a preindustrial versus an industrial *system* has quite different consequences for the ecology of the city. In industrial cities the dimensions become increasingly differen-

Caracas has outer ring of slum shanties, an ecological pattern common in developing nations, and contrasting with the decentralized location of higher socioeconomic groups in advanced industrial societies. (Courtesy Mary D. Howard)

[39] For descriptions of London, Paris, Vienna, and Stockholm, see Francis L. Hauser, "Ecological Patterns of European Cities," in Sylvia F. Fava, ed., *Urbanism in World Perspective: A Reader* (1968), pp. 193–216.

[40] See, for example, Timms, *op cit.*, pp. 54–63 and ch. 5; and R. J. Johnston, *Urban Residential Patterns* (1971), pp. 330–53.

tiated, that is, the locational effects of economic rank, family cycle, and ethnic affiliation become increasingly independent and separable. Thus, cities in industrial societies will have groups at each economic level with varying types of families and ethnic affiliations, and the resulting spatial distribution will display the complex interweaving of these factors.[41] In contrast, in preindustrial societies the dimensions may not be greatly differentiated from one another, resulting in a spatial structure that differs from that of the industrial city. Timms has commented that

> in the pre-modern city the simplicity of the social and ecological systems is reflected in that of the resulting spatial pattern. Self-contained quarters and a general zonal arrangement, with central-city location being the preserve of the elite, provide the basic plan. In the modern city a more complicated spatial order is apparent. Each differentiating property tends to follow its own distinct spatial pattern. The need to be within reasonable access to work and the attraction of the elite areas are reflected in the sectoral distribution of social rank. Once identified with a particular rank, developments in a given direction tend to perpetuate that identity. The attraction of new suburbs, with new houses and new standards of amenities, is reflected in a zonal arrangement of family status. The younger the area, the more young people; the older the area, the more old people and the fewer families with young children. The zones in transition around the central business district and on the rural-urban periphery provide a haven for despised minorities and an attractive location for all those who welcome the anonymity and freedom from traditional social controls characteristic of the urban way of life. Since each set of differentiating properties is, to a greater or lesser extent, independent of all the others, the resulting spatial pattern is highly complex. It is unlikely that any simple model, stressing the influence of one or other spatial arrangement, will provide an acceptable description of the modern city.[42]

Berry and Rees have formulated a preliminary scheme of the various ways in which the underlying urban dimensions may be differentiated from one another.[43] Their review of the factorial analyses of cities of varying cultural backgrounds and degree of industrialization indicates at least six combinations of the three dimensions: socioeconomic status, family status (labeled "stage-in-life cycle" or "urbanization" by some authors), and minority groups.[44] An important source of the variation was the extent to which family status and/or minority-group segregation were associated with socioeconomic rank. Cities of the least industrialized region of the United States, the South, showed, for example, a greater association of the ethnic dimension with the economic dimen-

---

[41] Some approximation of these processes is evident in the results of social area analysis, as indicated in Figures 6.2 and 6.3 above.

[42] Timms, *op. cit.*, p. 252.

[43] Brian J. L. Berry and Philip H. Rees, "The Factorial Ecology of Calcutta," *American Journal of Sociology*, 74 (March 1969), 445–91. The title belies the broad relevance of this article for factorial ecology.

[44] *Ibid.*, pp. 467–69.

sion. In northern cities the ethnic and economic dimensions became more differentiated, so that in Chicago, for example, members of the minority group (blacks) were residentially segregated but were found in substantial numbers at every point in the economic dimension, although the tendency for them to be overrepresented at the bottom economic ranks still existed.

THE FACTORIAL ECOLOGY OF CALCUTTA AND CHICAGO   Detailed study of Calcutta, a rapidly growing metropolis of over 7 million inhabitants, leads Berry and Rees to view its ecological structure as exemplifying both preindustrial and industrial ecological features, indicating to them that Calcutta is a city in transition. Comparison of the social areas of Chicago and Calcutta, diagrammed in Figure 6.5, indicates that both are similar in that socioeconomic status and family cycle are separate dimensions. Social areas of type "A" are those occupied by groups characterized by high socioeconomic status and low familism. In both cities such areas exist and are located fronting the special amenities—Lake Michigan in Chicago and the Maidan, a large park, in Calcutta. The distribution of the "D" social areas—those inhabited by groups combining the lowest socioeconomic status with high familism (young

FIGURE 6.5 • Generalized social areas of Chicago and Calcutta. Comparison of the ecological distribution of social and economic groups in these cities indicates both preindustrial-urban and urban-industrial characteristics in Calcutta. The outer ring of residential areas of low socioeconomic status and high fertility (type D) is characteristic of preindustrial cities, while an emerging modern residential area of high socioeconomic status and low fertility (type A) is characteristic of industrial cities. Key—Type of residential area: A-high economic status, low fertility; B-high economic status, high fertility; C-low economic status, low fertility; D-low economic status, high fertility. Source: Brian J. L. Berry and Phillip H. Rees, "The Factorial Ecology of Calcutta," *American Journal of Sociology*, 74 (March 1969), p. 488. Reprinted with permission of The University of Chicago Press.

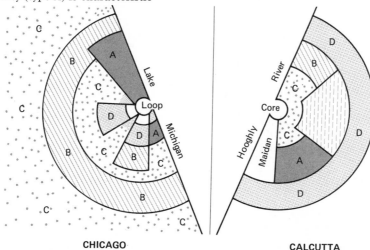

CHICAGO   CALCUTTA

age groups, many children)—clearly indicate some preindustrial aspects of Calcutta. In Calcutta the "D" social areas encircle the periphery of the city; in Chicago they are found near the city center. Social area type "B" represents areas high in both socioeconomic status and familism. In Chicago these areas are located in a suburban ring, but not in Calcutta. Social area type "C" represents areas low in both familism and socioeconomic status; in Chicago they are located in both a middle-city position and a vast belt beyond the suburbs, the latter reflecting the more efficient transportation and communication of the modern metropolis. Figure 6.5 cannot portray adequately the much greater importance of the ethnic dimension in Calcutta, where ethnic origin and caste are strongly linked to occupation and other economic indicators. Berry and Rees note that in this regard Calcutta resembles the ecological model of cities of the American South.

THE FACTORIAL ECOLOGY OF CAIRO   Abu-Lughod's monumental factorial analysis of Cairo, Egypt, demonstrates another way in which ecological factors may be related.[45] Cairo exemplifies a preindustrial system in a particular cultural context, with modern elements increasingly present.

[45] This discussion is based on her *Cairo: 1001 Years of the City Victorious* and "Testing the Theory of Social Area Analysis: The Ecology of Cairo, Egypt."

FIGURE 6.6 • The thirteen "subcities" of Cairo, Egypt, as delineated by factor analysis. These areas represent a wide variation in life styles, ranging from the most traditional to modern Western forms. Source: Janet Abu-Loghod, *Cairo: 1001 Years of the City Victorious* (copyright © 1971 by Princeton University Press), Map 17, p. 187. Reprinted by permission of Princeton University Press.

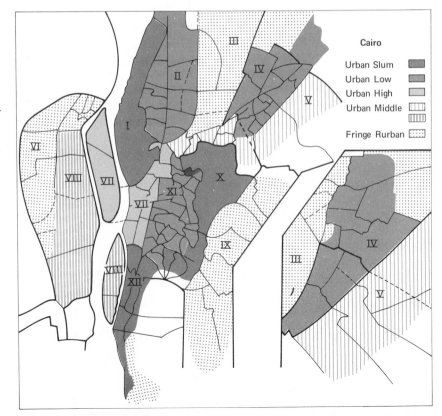

The city's ecological structure is simple in that few dimensions are needed to describe it, and these dimensions are not greatly differentiated from one another. Abu-Lughod reduced the number of factors to three: life style, settlements of unattached migrant males, and social pathology. Her most important finding is that the first of these factors explained over half of the statistical variation in her analysis of the census tracts of Cairo in 1947 and again in 1960. Abu-Lughod indicates that life style encompasses both the economic rank and familism; thus, in Cairo, economic rank and familism are not yet separate ecological dimensions. This reflects a modernizing society in which class and family patterns are still linked. High economic status is associated with a modern, Western kind of life style, including important changes in the role of women and in family size; low economic status is associated with traditional family roles and high fertility. As Abu-Lughod puts it:

Thus census tracts with high Factor I scores are characterized by commodious housing accommodations, by a highly literate population having low rates of dependency and unemployment, and by the presence of resident domestic servants. These are economic aspects of a life style which, in today's Cairo, is increasingly finding expression in more "modern" family patterns of female education, delayed age at marriage, and lower fertility. . . . At the opposite extreme are the tracts scoring lowest in Factor I. House overcrowding often reaches astronomical heights, most residents are illiterate, and females seldom attend school or commute to paid employment. Here the traditional patterns of female exclusion from the educational system mesh with marriage at a very young age and a post-nuptial life of high, sustained, and generally uncontrolled fertility.[46]

On the basis of Factor I, life-style, Abu-Lughod delineated 13 major "subcities" of contemporary Cairo, each different in population characteristics, physical appearance, the kinds of housing and shopping facilities available, and "even in the dominant dress that adorns the inhabitants and perhaps symbolizes their belief systems."[47] These areas are shown in Figure 6.6. Abu-Lughod believes these areas exemplify three major types of population in Cairo: the rural, the traditional urban, and the modern or industrial urban.[48] The "rural" population of Cairo does not consist of farmers but of impoverished urban residents, many of them migrants to the city, whose way of life, except occupationally, differs little from the agricultural villages of Egypt. This population is concentrated in a loose ring on the outskirts of Cairo in subcities III, IX, XIII, and VI, and constituted about 14 percent of the total population of Cairo in 1960. The traditional urban population, that is, those who follow the "economic activities, forms of social relationships, and systems of

[46] Abu-Lughod, "Testing the Theory of Social Area Analysis: The Ecology of Cairo, Egypt," pp. 205, 207.

[47] Abu-Lughod, *Cairo: 1001 Years of the City Victorious*, p. 188.

[48] *Ibid.*, pp. 218–20.

values which were once typical within the Cairo of a hundred years ago,"[49] are concentrated in three inner city slum areas—I, X, XII—that in 1960 made up 30 percent of Cairo's population. The modern urban-industrial population is concentrated in one high-income area, VII, and one middle-income area, V, and accounted for 9 percent of the population. The remainder of Cairo's population, about 46 percent, is found in areas II, IV, VIII, XI, which represent various low- and middle-income levels and various combinations of traditional and modern life styles.

Comparison of Figure 6.6 with Figure 6.5 for Chicago and Calcutta shows the preindustrial nature of Cairo in the peripheral band of low-income, high-fertility areas on the outskirts of the city, similar to area "D" in Calcutta. The "A" areas of Chicago and Calcutta are most similar to the modern urban areas of Cairo, which occupy desirable locations on the Nile just as their counterpart areas in Chicago and Calcutta occupy especially attractive sites. Areas corresponding to the "B" and "C" types of Chicago and Calcutta do not exist in Cairo, since the economic and family dimensions are not separate, although they may emerge from among the transitional areas in which 46 percent of contemporary Cairenes live. As this chapter has indicated, whether and where such ecological areas will emerge depends on systematic change in Egyptian society.

Summary

In this chapter we have been concerned with some of the theoretical aspects of human ecology as it is manifest in the city. We have discussed some of the processes of human ecology and have provided some theoretical models that may help to explain some of the spatial characteristics of cities. It should be emphasized at this point that no single theoretical model fits all cities; there is a wide diversity of types of cities and of the ecological characteristics they manifest. The ecological features and processes of urban communities will be considered more descriptively in the following chapters. We now turn our discussion to the phenomenon of ecological segregation, which seems to be a feature of most if not all cities, although varying widely in the forms it takes and the social implications of the segregation process.

[49] *Ibid.*, p. 219.

Selected Bibliography

BOOKS

Abu-Lughod, Janet, *Cairo: 1001 Years of the City Victorious.* Princeton, N. J.: Princeton University Press, 1971.

Commoner, Barry, *The Closing Circle: Nature, Man, and Technology.* New York: Knopf, 1971.

Ehrlich, Paul R., and Anne H. Ehrlich, *Population, Resources, Environment: Issues in Human Ecology*, 2d ed.. San Francisco: W. H. Freeman, 1972.

Faris, Robert E. L., *Chicago Sociology, 1920–1932.* San Francisco: Chandler, 1967.

Hadden, Jeffrey, and Edgar F. Borgatta, *American Cities: Their Social Characteristics.* Chicago: Rand McNally, 1965.

Hawley, Amos, ed., *Roderick McKenzie on Human Ecology.* Chicago: University of Chicago Press, 1968.

——, *Urban Society: An Ecological Approach.* New York: Ronald Press, 1971.

Johnston, R. J., *Urban Residential Patterns.* London: G. Bell and Sons, 1971.

Michelson, William, *Man and His Urban Environment.* Reading, Mass: Addison-Wesley, 1970.

Park, Robert E., Ernest W. Burgess, and Roderick D. McKenzie, with an Introduction by Morris Janowitz, *The City.* Chicago: University of Chicago Press, 1967; originally published 1925.

Park, Robert E., *Collected Papers.* Vol. II, *Human Communities: The City and Human Ecology.* Glencoe, Ill.: The Free Press, 1952.

Schnore, Leo F., *The Urban Scene: Human Ecology and Demography.* New York: The Free Press, 1965.

Short, James F., Jr., ed., *The Social Fabric of the Metropolis: Contributions of the Chicago School of Urban Sociology.* Chicago: University of Chicago Press, 1971.

Suttles, Gerald D., *The Social Order of the Slum.* Chicago: University of Chicago Press, 1968.

Theodorson, George, ed., *Studies in Human Ecology*, Evanston, Ill.: Row Peterson, 1961.

Timms, Duncan, *The Urban Mosaic: Toward a Theory of Residential Differentiation.* Cambridge, England: Cambridge University Press, 1971.

ARTICLES

Abu-Lughod, Janet, "The City Is Dead—Long Live the City: Some Thoughts on Urbanity," in Sylvia F. Fava, ed., *Urbanism in World Perspective: A Reader*, pp. 154–65. New York: Thomas Y. Crowell, 1968.

——, "Testing the Theory of Social Area Analysis: The Ecology of Cairo, Egypt," *American Sociological Review*, 34 (April 1969), 198–212.

Anderson, Theodore, and Janet Egeland, "Spatial Aspects of Social Area Analysis," *American Sociological Review*, 26 (June 1961), 393–98.

Berry, Brian B. J., ed., "Comparative Factorial Ecology," special issue of *Economic Geography*, 47 Supplement (June 1971), 209–367.

——, and Philip R. Rees, "The Factorial Ecology of Calcutta," *American Journal of Sociology*, 74 (March 1969), 445–91.

Duncan, Otis Dudley, "Social Organization and the Ecosystem," in R. E. L. Faris, ed., *Handbook of Modern Sociology*, pp. 37–83. Chicago: Rand McNally, 1964.

Firey, Walter, "Sentiment and Symbolism as Ecological Variables," *American Sociological Review*, 10 (April 1945), 140–48.

Goist, Patrick Dixon, "City and 'Community': The Urban Theory of Robert Park," *American Quarterly*, 23 (Spring 1971), 46–59.

Guest, Avery M., "Retesting the Burgess Zonal Hypothesis: The Location of White Collar Workers," *American Journal of Sociology*, 76 (May 1971), 1095–1108.

Duncan, Otis Dudley, and Leo F. Schnore, "Cultural, Behavioral and Ecological Perspectives in the Study of Social Organization," *American Journal of Sociology*, 65 (September 1959), 132–46.

Hawley, Amos, "Human Ecology," *International Encyclopedia of the Social Sciences*, vol. 4, pp. 328–337. New York: Macmillan Company and The Free Press, 1968.

Haggerty, Lee J., "Another Look at the Burgess Hypothesis: Time as an Important Variable," *American Journal of Sociology*, 76 (May 1971), 1084–94.

Hunter, A., "The Ecology of Chicago: Persistence and Change, 1930–1960," *American Journal of Sociology*, 77 (November 1971), 425–45.

Molotch, Harvey J., "Toward a More Human Human Ecology: An Urban Research Strategy," *Land Economics*, 43 (August 1967), 336–44.

Orleans, Peter, "Robert Park and Social Area Analysis: A Convergence in Urban Sociology," *Urban Affairs Quarterly*, 1 (1966), 5–19.

Schnore, Leo F., "On the Spatial Structure of Cities in the Two Americas," in Philip M. Hauser and Leo F. Schnore, eds., *The Study of Urbanization*, pp. 347–98. New York: Wiley, 1965.

7 • Ecological Segregation

 Ecological segregation stems from the fact that city people, like people elsewhere, differ from one another. But they are also interdependent. In the competition both for status and for desirable spatial location in the city, these differences and interdependencies determine what space people consider desirable and their ability to obtain it. The result is ecological segregation—the clustering together in the same residential area of people with similar characteristics.

Segregation is one visible expression of the systematic ecological interrelationships we have described in Chapter 6. The varied physically segregated areas of the city represent the positions of various urban groups in this linked system. Since the system is manifold, there are many bases of segregation and no "pure" segregated areas. In this chapter we will describe the major kinds of residentially segregated areas in America cities. Some material will be provided on segregated areas in foreign cities, but we have not attempted a total analysis of the complex bases of segregation in societies other than the United States.

The Nature of Segregation

From the ecological point of view, the most important differences and interdependencies are those that affect large numbers of people, for these will have the greatest impact on the spatial structure of the city. Consequently, the differences and interdependencies embodied in the socioeconomic structure will have the greatest relevance to understanding ecological segregation. Differences of social class, religion, ethnic origin, and race are among the major characteristics toward which social attitudes, beliefs, and customs are directed. It is no accident that our major types of residential areas follow these lines—Gold Coast and exclusive suburb, Black Belt and Chinatown, Little Italy and Swedetown, and the like.

The division of labor and social differences often reinforce one another. A given racial, ethnic, or class group is associated, sometimes by preference and sometimes by social pressure, with a particular occupation—black laborers, Chinese laundrymen, low-caste leather workers, Italian fruit-sellers, white Ivy League executives of corporations or banks, Jewish merchants or professionals. Occupying these positions has, in turn, implications for income, power, and social standing, as well as other factors differentiating groups from one another.

Voluntary and Involuntary Segregation

Some aspects of ecological segregation are matters of choice or planning, while others are unplanned or involuntary. Voluntary segregation occurs when the individual, on his own initiative, seeks to live with others of his own kind and apart from those who are different in what he considers to be some fundamental respect. Motives may vary from one individual, group, or area to another. Certain individuals may elect to live with others of similar characteristics because of the prestige such residence accords them; some may choose to live in a segregated area because such residence may afford them a sense of security or otherwise provide satisfactions not attainable elsewhere; others may select such a residential location because they know or imagine that they are not welcome in areas occupied by persons who are different. These reasons are not mutually exclusive; any or all of them may apply to a particular individual.

With its emphasis on preference and not prejudice, this is the psychologically positive aspect of segregation. If, however, those identified with a particular group regard with hostility or fear another group whose members are different in certain respects, it is unlikely they will choose the same residential neighborhood unless forced to do so by economic or other circumstances. The tensions that result from living among people whom one dislikes or considers inferior, or the anxieties provoked by the awareness that one is not wanted in a particular neighborhood or district, are sufficient to provide the basis for much residential separation reflecting human differences.

Involuntary segregation may occur in two ways. An individual or family may be required by law or custom, or both, to reside in a designated area, or may be prevented from living in an area occupied by others who are different in certain respects.

Involuntary segregation also occurs through the operation of impersonal economic forces. Individuals or families tend to seek their own economic level; ordinarily they live in areas where they can afford to live, not necessarily where they would like to live. Obviously a family with a two-thousand-dollar-a-year income cannot live on the Gold Coast

or Park Avenue whatever their aspirations might be. They are forced by sheer economic circumstances to confine their choice to areas occupied by people of middle or low incomes.

These two forms of involuntary segregation, like the three forms of voluntary segregation, are also not mutually exclusive. An individual or family may be forced by custom, law, and economic circumstances to live in, or apart from, a particular district. Economic pressure sometimes becomes a technique for enforcing segregation. An individual or family forced by economic circumstances to reside in a particular area might have selected the area anyway, irrespective of economic considerations.

Street scene in the Bowery, New York City. Many large American cities have such districts occupied mainly by unattached men segregated ecologically from the mainstream of society. (Margaret Miner)

Limited Segregation

The process of segregation does not necessarily result in the formation of areas inhabited solely by persons of a certain race or culture. More often than not there is a mixture, particularly on the fringes. Recent studies of 12 of the largest cities in the United States showed that from 22 to 78 percent of the white population lived in census tracts that were classified as "mixed."[1] It is probably true, however, that some of these areas

[1] Davis McEntire, *Residence and Race* (1960), Table 6.

were mixed because they were in the process of changing to predominantly black occupancy.

One of the Seattle districts, designated by Hatt as a "polyethnic" area,
showed a considerable variety of ethnic types living side by side: Gentile
whites, Jews, Chinese, Japanese, Filipinos, and blacks.[2] The mixed
block with no single type occupying more than half the dwelling units
was the most frequent pattern. Blocks with a preponderance of a single
type were not necessarily contiguous, indicating that whole blocks, or
even groups of blocks, were skipped by the population in the course of
residential changes.

Similarly, a study of an Italian area in Boston showed that only 42
percent of the population were first- or second-generation Italians, 10
percent were first-generation Jewish immigrants, 9 percent were of
Polish background, 8 percent were of "other Slavic" background, 5
percent were of Irish ancestry, and the remaining quarter was distributed among a variety of ethnic groups.[3]

Segregation and Social Relations

The segregation of population, whether voluntary or involuntary, may
affect the entire fabric of relationships among people in a community.
People who do not associate intimately with each other because they
differ in certain fundamental respects tend to live apart from those who
are different. Obviously this segregation does not always occur, but there
is a tendency in that direction.

Similarly, social isolationism is reinforced by spatial isolationism; the
more people are spatially segregated, the less likely they are to come into
intimate contact with those who have different characteristics. At least
the possibilities of close relationships on the basis of social equality are
greatly reduced. Instead, contacts tend to be formalized, confined principally to the market place or the work situation. People who work together
on the job, or who have contacts of a strictly economic character, may
live in entirely different social and ecological worlds.

An example is provided by Mack in an analysis of an industrial port
located on Lake Erie.[4] During the rapid industrial expansion of the city
in the late nineteenth century, there was a heavy influx of Swedes and
Finns, who became collectively categorized as "the Swedes." Their
residential locality, called "Swedetown," was situated near the docks
and railroad repair yards. Around the turn of the century an influx of

[2] Paul Hatt, "Spatial Patterns in a Polyethnic Area," *American Sociological Review*, 10
(June 1945), 352–56.

[3] Herbert Gans, *The Urban Villagers* (1962), pp. 8–10.

[4] Raymond W. Mack, "Ecological Patterns in an Industrial Shop," *Social Forces*, (May 1954),
351–56.

Italians occurred. Since the Italians also found employment at the docks and yards, they initiated an invasion of Swedetown that ended in complete succession, although the original name was still retained in common usage. The Swedes, considering the Italians their social inferiors, moved into another area that came to be known as "the Harbor." These two areas, as Mack points out, were not only ecologically separate but were also distinct sociological communities, membership in which was determined by the ethnic label. If one was a Swede (or Finn), he could not become a member of the Italian community, and vice versa.[5]

This pattern of social and ecological segregation was carried over into work relationships in the same city. At the time of the study (the early 1950's), both Italians and Swedes were employed in the railroad car repair shop. By agreement with management, only Italians were assigned to light repair work and only Swedes to heavy repair work in which railroad cars were dismantled and rebuilt. Working on different sides of the yard, the "lights" and "heavies" formed two distinct groups, with different tests of admittance, different roles, and different norms of relations among the members, They were kept apart not so much by ethnic differences as such as by prevailing prejudices and stereotypes.

Residential Segregation and Government Control

Governmental actions affect residential segregation in several ways. Sometimes these actions are deliberately designed to further the segregation process. On the other hand, while government in the United States has acted to ban residential segregation by race, such segregation appears to be increasing because a larger proportion of the black population is concentrated in very large cities and because the low socioeconomic position of blacks limits their range of residential choice. Sometimes governmental action with respect to housing segregation is unintended. Subsidized housing in the form of "projects" for low-income groups or tax-abated developments for middle-income groups were designed to provide more and better housing, but the imposition of income and other restrictions may increase residential segregation along these lines. Urban renewal programs, often involving wholesale demolition of neighborhoods, may disperse voluntarily segregated groups. For example, the West End in Boston, a low-income Italian area, was razed in the city's urban redevelopment program and replaced by luxury apartment buildings.[6]

[5] *Ibid.*, p. 352.
[6] Gans, *op.cit.*, pp. 281ff.

Types of Segregation in Cities of the United States

The principal types of segregated areas in American cities reflect the major differences customarily recognized and acted on in American society—race, ethnic affiliation, and occupation—and underscore the fundamental point that ecological segregation is not random or the result of merely personal preferences and individual motivation, but reflects the position of groups in a network of interdependence, some of whose ramifications may be obscure to the participating individuals. It is for this reason that human ecology always involves social organization as well as social psychology.

Race and Ethnicity

The significance of "race" as a factor in ecological segregation of population in American cities is well illustrated in the case of blacks and Puerto Ricans in New York City.[7] Both of these minorities have tended to cluster, but there is relatively little mixing in black-Puerto Rican residential areas. Although most of the Puerto Ricans are Spanish-speaking and have a style of life that distinguishes them from English-speaking whites of a different cultural background, and although around 10 percent are classified as black, they nevertheless have gained access to housing that is commonly unavailable to blacks who may even have a higher income level. For this and other reasons, Puerto Ricans are more widely dispersed than blacks. It seems likely that the Puerto Rican minority in cities may experience, with the passing of time, an assimilative-integrative process somewhat comparable to that of earlier immigrants from European countries.

There is some evidence that residential segregation of ethnic or nationality groups is not declining as rapidly as many believe. While there has certainly been a scattering of "ethnics" in American cities, especially native-born persons of foreign or mixed parentage, nevertheless many have strong sentimental ties to the neighborhoods occupied mainly by others of their own cultural heritage. Glazer and Moynihan have observed this in New York City,[8] and Gans has also described a similar phenomenon among Boston's Italians.[9]

In a study of interethnic segregation in the New York metropolitan area, Kantrowitz concluded that such separation remains fairly high, even into the second generation.[10] In his research he included eleven

[7] Jean Gottmann, *Megalopolis* (1961), pp. 705–7.

[8] Nathan Glazer and Daniel Patrick Moynihan, *Beyond the Melting Pot,* 2d ed. (1970).

[9] Gans, *op. cit.*

[10] Nathan Kantrowitz, "Ethnic and Racial Segregation in the New York Metropolis," *American Journal of Sociology,* 74 (May 1969), 685–96.

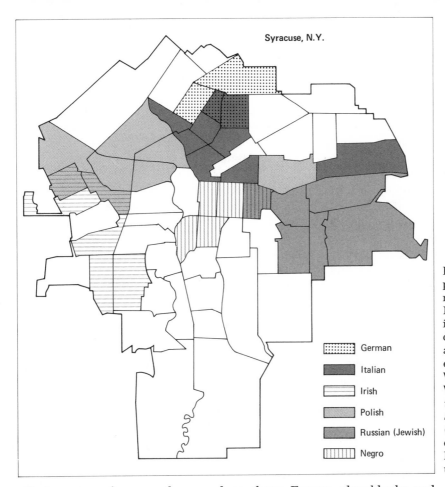

Syracuse, N.Y.

German

Italian

Irish

Polish

Russian (Jewish)

Negro

FIGURE 7.1 • Ecological patterning of six ethnic minorities in Syracuse, New York. American cities vary in the residential distribution of residents according to race and ethnicity. Source: Charles Willie and Morton Wagenfeld, *Socio-Economic and Ethnic Areas, Syracuse and Onondago Counties, N.Y., 1960.* Syracuse University Youth Development Center. Figures 14–19.

ethnic groups from northern and southern Europe plus blacks and Puerto Ricans. As one might expect, segregation indexes of the eleven European ethnic groups from blacks and Puerto Ricans were high, ranging from 78 to 88 (with 100 representing total segregation). Most of the European ethnics were mutually separated by segregation indexes ranging from 40 to 70, with 11 out of 55 combinations less than 40. These indexes are indicative of moderate segregation. The average segregation index of the northern Europeans was almost identical to that of the southern Europeans. Persistence of these patterns of segregation in the New York region may or may not be representative of other American cities, but it seems probable that in the larger centers, at least, birds of a cultural feather often flock together if the members are proud of their heritage and find satisfaction in living close together.

Recent Immigrants and Segregation

Immigration to American cities since World War II has been different in certain respects from earlier population movements. Cuban political refugees, probably a half-million or more, have settled largely in cities of Florida. Because of language and cultural patterns that distinguish them from the majority of people in those cities, and especially because they have a commonality of unhappy experiences under an authoritarian dictatorship, they have tended to congregate in certain sections of communities. Large areas of Miami, for example, are now populated almost solidly by Cubans seeking refuge in the United States. Just as ethnic areas in northern cities were once referred to as "Little Polands" or "Little Sicilies," areas in the major cities of Florida are sometimes popularly labelled "Little Cubas." In these areas Spanish, not English, is the *lingua franca.*

But by no means all of the recent immigrants from other countries gravitate to ethnic islands. Many of these immigrants have considerable education and marketable occupational skills. Consequently they have less economic need to locate near or among other persons of their own ethnic background, in contrast to earlier immigrants, who sought the assistance and companionship of persons having a similar language and culture. Many of the recent arrivals possessed professional or business experience that enabled them from the beginning to find lucrative employment and therefore to have a wide range of residential choices. Even before World War II, large numbers of Jewish immigrants who escaped the Nazi terror in Germany were well-educated persons having occupational skills in considerable demand. There was certainly no reason, except possibly sentimental, why they should choose to live in a segregated ghetto. Many recent immigrants from Asian countries are for the same reasons widely scattered in American cities.

Residential Separation of Occupational Groups

The social and economic differences between occupational groups are reflected in the tendency for people in the same broad occupational group to cluster together residentially. A study of the 22-county New York metropolitan region employed an index of residential specialization to measure the degree to which an occupational group's residential distribution differed from the overall distribution of residences.[11] The metropolitan region was also divided into four rings differing in distance and accessibility to Manhattan, which was the first ring. The index of residential specialization was applied to determine whether a given occupational group's homes were over- or underrepresented in any of the rings or were the same as that of homes in general.

It was found that the homes of those in upper white collar occupations (professionals and managers) were overrepresented in the third ring, the suburban commuting zone, about 20 to 30 miles from Manhattan. To some extent, the upper white collar groups were also overrepresented in

[11] Edgar M. Hoover and Raymond Vernon, *Anatomy of a Metropolis* (1959), pp. 154–76.

the high rent areas of Manhattan. The lower white collar groups (clerks and sales personnel) were concentrated in the second ring, the New York city boroughs, and one New Jersey county that borders Manhattan. This area is served by subway and elevated train and has many apartment and attached single-family houses. The blue collar workers were over-represented in the fourth or outer ring, a diverse area beyond the regular commuting distance, composed of industrial satellite communities, spacious suburbs, and resorts. Within the fourth ring, subgroups of blue collar workers were further segregated residentially—craftsmen and foremen preferred suburbanlike communities while semiskilled workers and laborers tended to live in industrial sections. Finally, the service workers (domestics, barbers, elevator operators, and the like) were heavily concentrated in the first ring, Manhattan itself. Obviously, people of every occupation lived in almost every type of area, but these were the broad features of residential specialization.

A study of the Chicago metropolitan area also observed the tendency of the various occupational groups to live apart from one another. Various measures of segregation were applied to the residential distribution of eight occupational groups. One of the major findings of the study was that the top and bottom occupational groups are the most residentially segregated from the rest of the labor force and from one another. Segregation indexes were highest for the professionals and for laborers, and gradually declined toward the center of the occupational hierarchy. "This finding suggests that residential segregation is greater for those occupational groups with clearly defined status than for those groups whose status is ambiguous."[12]

Like the New York metropolitan study, the Chicago study also found that while differences in income among the occupational groups accounted for some of the variation in residential distribution, it did not account for all. For example, the clerical workers, who generally had lower incomes than the craftsmen and foremen, nevertheless tended to live among other white collar groups rather than among blue collar families. Social prestige and community of interest were evidently more determinative of residence than income. The study also shed some light on even more underlying factors in the ecological process. Dissimilarity in residential distribution was more highly associated with the occupational status of one's father than with one's own present socioeconomic status.

Chinatowns as Ethnic Segregation

During the latter part of the nineteenth century many Chinese settled in American cities, mainly on the West Coast and in the Rocky Mountain

[12] Otis Dudley Duncan and Beverly Duncan, "Residential Distribution and Occupational Stratification," *American Journal of Sociology*, 60 (March 1955), 493–503.

area. According to Lee,[13] since women were relatively scarce in these cities, some of the Chinese men performed "women's work," that is, cooking, washing, and domestic service. Others were employed as laborers in lumbering, railroad construction, and mining. The majority were located in smaller cities, and as technological and economic changes reduced their occupational security, they tended to migrate to metropolitan centers in which there was a demand for their services. The result has been that Chinatowns in small cities have either declined in population or have disappeared altogether. More and more, the Chinese are being concentrated in great metropolises like Chicago, New York, and San Francisco.

The present-day Chinatown illustrates the principles of interdependence in the ecological community. According to Lee, China-

[13] Rose Hum Lee, "The Decline of Chinatowns in the United States," *American Journal of Sociology*, 54 (March 1949), 422–32.

Street scene in San Francisco's Chinatown. Many Chinese in large American cities live or work in such segregated districts, which take on the character of a sub-community. (George W. Gardner)

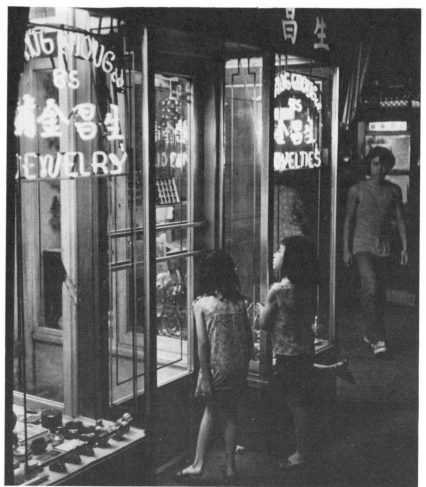

town provides services that are demanded or needed by the larger community, and in turn benefits by the economy of the metropolis. The Chinese hand laundry, in competition with steam laundries, can exist only in a city where there are enough people who want their clothing laundered by hand. Similarly, Chinese restaurants serving exotic foods under novel conditions can compete with standard restaurants and lunch counters only when there is sufficient demand for this kind of special service. The modern Chinatown has become something of a tourist attraction, featuring special foods, services, and works of Oriental craftsmanship. But it is more than a mere tourist mecca. In a real sense it is a community, a miniature society having a distinctive organization and style of living.

The nature of the interdependence between Chinese groups and the rest of the urban community may be changing. At least this is suggested by the tendency of the Chinese to move from Chinatowns to more dispersed locations in the city. It may be that, like other immigrant groups, as they become assimilated into American society they also become less concentrated residentially. Another reason is that the large Chinatowns, for all their exotic character, are slums, and many Chinese desire better housing. In 1940, 70 percent of San Francisco's Chinese lived in Chinatown, but by 1950 only 40 percent were living there.[14] Similarly, New York's Chinatown contained half of the city's Chinese in 1940 but not quite a third in 1950.

Residential Segregation of Blacks

In a classic study of race relations in the United States, Swedish sociologist Gunnar Myrdal observes that blacks were rather widely distributed in cities prior to the Civil War.[15] Many employed as domestic servants lived in back alleys or streets adjacent to their place of work; often they lived in servants' shacks behind the big house of their masters. Charleston, South Carolina, displayed this pattern. Frazier also states that small clusters of black servants were located "close to the houses of the whites in which the Negroes served,"[16] although he observed that with increasing industrialization this pattern is changing.

More recently Schnore and Evenson have provided evidence supporting the conclusions of other scholars.[17] Calculating indexes of residential segregation for southern cities as far back as census data were

---

[14] *Statistical Abstract of the United States* (1962), p. 29.

[15] Gunnar Myrdal, *An American Dilemma* (1944), vol. I, p. 621.

[16] E. Franklin Frazier, *The Negro in the United States*, 2d ed. (1957), p. 237.

[17] Leo F. Schnore and Philip C. Evenson, "Segregation in Southern Cities," *American Journal of Sociology*, 72 (July 1966), 58–67.

available, they concluded that the "backyard" pattern did indeed exist in earlier years and that it has survived in modified form to the present. But in newer southern cities, such as Tulsa, Houston, or Miami, the residential pattern is characterized by large concentrations of blacks in which most workers live some distance from their place of work.

There is some evidence, as the Taeubers indicate in their study, that the citywide picture of black segregation has recently shown a decline.[18] Such an apparent decrease may, however, be deceptive. It may actually mean that block-by-block segregation in cities is unchanged or even increasing while the overall picture of the same city may indicate a decline. This may be especially true of suburbs where the increase of a small black suburban population may not necessarily indicate extensive residential integration.

Certain institutional changes, however, function to reduce residential segregation of blacks. Antidiscrimination laws in respect to housing, especially public housing, have made it possible for many blacks to choose their residential locations, and upward occupational and income mobility has enabled large numbers of persons to afford residential locations heretofore too expensive for them. The decline of segregation in other spheres of life, notably schools, employment, and the armed services, plus organized pressures by blacks to eliminate discrimination in all aspects of the social order, may help to lower the barriers created by residential segregation. But however much institutional changes may affect the status of blacks, the "black belts" of American cities will not likely disappear soon.

There is a widely held notion that the black population in American cities will experience the same ecological history as other ethnic groups, namely, that with increasing gains and upward economic mobility they will, as in the case of cultural minorities, become assimilated and integrated into the social order and therefore be less segregated, both socially and ecologically. Empirical evidence does not support this idea. Indeed, blacks who have "arrived" by any measure of economic status are generally as segregated as those blacks who are less successful. They not only remain segregated from the nonblack population but also from the poor and destitute blacks.

Segregation and Decentralization

An important factor in residential segregation of blacks is the large-scale movement of the white population to the outlying areas of the metropolis. Usually these areas are not within the city limits but are separate towns, villages, or municipalities. White movement to suburbs, coupled with the heavy migration of blacks to the central cities of metropolitan

[18] Karl E. Taeuber and Alma F. Taeuber, *Negroes in Cities* (1969).

areas, has resulted in a spectacular rise in the proportion of blacks in the central city. This trend was general in the largest metropolitan areas of the United States. However, the easy generalization that black belts exist only in the central cities and that suburbs are solidly white does not square with the facts. Actually, there has been throughout the present century a considerable volume of black migrants to outlying or suburban districts. A few suburbs are occupied entirely, or at least mainly, by blacks. These include Kinloch, a suburb of St. Louis; Robbins, near Chicago; Lincoln Heights, in the metropolitan area of Cincinnati; and Richmond Heights, adjacent to Miami. Some of the older Chicago suburbs, such as Maywood, Harvey, and Chicago Heights, have experienced in recent years a heavy influx of blacks who have moved into dwellings vacated by whites.

Farley found that, between 1960 and 1968, the black population of suburban rings in northern and western cities increased, as a percentage, more rapidly than did the white population.[19] Only in the suburbs of southern cities did the white increase exceed that of blacks. The increasing proportion of black migrants to the suburbs does not, however, imply that the black suburban population is becoming decreasingly segregated. On the contrary, essentially the same patterns of spatial separation from whites continue to exist. But there is one difference: probably the majority of blacks moving from the central cities to the suburbs represent a higher economic and social position than those remaining behind.

Selected Studies of Segregation

A comprehensive study of residential segregation of urban blacks in the United States was done by the Taeubers, who based their analysis on census data.[20] The investigators employed a statistical device which they refer to as an "index of dissimilarity" (or segregation), the values of which range from 0 to 100. If, for example, blacks or whites were *evenly* distributed in all blocks of a given city in proportion to their representation in the total population of that city, no area would be all black or all white. In a city in which blacks represented 30 percent of the total population, each block would have 30 blacks and 70 whites for each 100 population. The index of dissimilarity (defined as the percentage of whites or blacks that would have to change their residential block to produce an unsegregated distribution) would be 0. None of them, that is, would have to change their residential location to maintain this balance.

[19] Reynolds Farley, "The Changing Distribution of Negroes within Metropolitan Areas: The Emergence of Black Suburbs," *American Journal of Sociology*, 75 (January 1970), 512–29.

[20] Taeuber and Taeuber, *op. cit.*, ch. 3. The index of dissimilarity was devised earlier by Otis Dudley Duncan and Beverly Duncan in *The Negro Population of Chicago* (1957).

If, on the other hand, all blocks were inhabited exclusively by blacks or whites, the index would be 100, representing maximum segregation. Thus, the higher the index the more segregated the population would be on the basis of race. The index for an entire city, as calculated by the Taeubers, would be the average of the indexes for all of the blocks included in the study. An index above 50 would indicate a high degree of segregation.

The Taeubers calculated the index of dissimilarity (segregation) in 207 cities of the United States. The range of the index was from 60.4 to 98.1, with a mean of 86.1. The overall distribution in percentages was as follows:

Over 90	38 percent
80 to 89.9	42 percent
70 to 79.9	16 percent
Under 70	4 percent

This procedure shows clearly that blacks are highly segregated in American cities, probably more than any other ethnic or racial group, and this condition applies to cities of all sizes and regions in the country. The black population in cities of the North and West was somewhat less segregated than in southern cities, the average indexes being 83 and 90.9, respectively. When indexes were calculated for Standard Metropolitan Statistical Areas, it was found that the overall index for 168 central cities was 86.8, and 82.3 for 30 suburbs. These indexes, of course, represent an overall picture of cities, and do not take into account individual variations. Galveston, a southern city, had a lower segregation index than Denver or Omaha. Suburban Richmond had a higher index than San Francisco, and the black population in Pasadena was more racially segregated than in nearby Los Angeles.

The Taeubers observed no straight-line trend between 1940 and 1960 in 109 cities for which comparable data were available. During the period from 1940 to 1950 the overall trend was in the direction of increased segregation, but in the period from 1950 to 1960 there was an overall decline.[21] Of these cities, 83 showed an increase in segregation during the first decade, and 45 during the second. Again, there were numerous deviations. Minneapolis, for example, showed a decrease for both periods; Birmingham showed an increase in segregation; while several cities showed a reversal, in the two census decades, of the upward or downward trend. Most of the cities had relatively small changes, but in a few the trend was quite striking. Charleston, South Carolina, had an increase in the segregation index of 8.3 in the first decade and 11.1 in the second, whereas Miami had a decreasing index of .1 in the first decade and an increase of .1 in the second. In general,

[21] *Ibid.*, pp. 39–40.

northern and western cities had moderate increases in the 1940–50 decade, while the increases in the South were considerably greater. In the following decade, cities of the North and West generally had a declining index, whereas most southern cities continued to increase. Using a similar yardstick, Cowgill compared the 1940 and 1950 indexes of residential segregation in 185 cities and found an increase in 129 cities, a decline in 52, and no change in 4.[22]

An early study by Lieberson was concerned with segregation, based on both race and national origin, of residents in ten major cities in the central and northeastern regions of the United States.[23] Trends in residential segregation were calculated for four census periods from 1910 to 1950, with data based on city wards in 1910 and 1920 and on census tracts in 1930 and 1950. When indexes of residential segregation were applied to native and foreign-born whites over the entire forty years, the trend was consistently toward decreasing segregation. And in none of the cities did the index exceed 50.

On the other hand, the indexes of segregation of blacks *from* both native whites and foreign-born whites were high. In all ten cities in 1950 it was even higher for the foreign-born than for the native whites. Furthermore, there was a consistent trend toward an increase in the index of segregation of blacks from both native and foreign-born whites.

The Necessity of Other Approaches

However valuable an empirical instrument may be for studying segregation quantitatively, it actually does not provide much insight into the social and psychological aspects of the phenomenon as an ongoing process. Segregated areas are ordinarily not static; the people who live in them are usually becoming *more or less* segregated. To understand the phenomenon of segregation, and particularly why segregation in any area may be increasing or decreasing, or even why it has occurred at all, we need to know a great deal about the status system of a society and about the values and behavior of people who are on different economic and social levels or who represent different cultural backgrounds. We can deal with people in the mass, as census data, and secure some understanding of the problem; but segregation is also an individual matter insofar as it is the person, not the mass, who is motivated (or not motivated) to reside in a particular area.

[22] Donald O. Cowgill, "Trends in Residential Segregation of Nonwhites in American Cities," *American Sociological Review*, 21 (February 1956), 43–46.

[23] Stanley Lieberson, *Ethnic Patterns in American Cities* (1963), p. 122. The cities included in the study were Boston, Buffalo, Chicago, Cincinnati, Cleveland, Columbus, Philadelphia, Pittsburgh, St. Louis, and Syracuse.

Segregation in Other
Countries

Brazil

In many cities of Brazil residential segregation exists as a carry-over from early days when the dominant Europeans settled in the most desirable areas and the Africans, either slaves or propertyless freedmen, in less attractive sections.[24] This pattern is quite extensive, but what appears to be strictly racial segregation is primarily segregation by socioeconomic status, since color and class tend to coincide, a condition as true for other parts of Latin America as it is for Brazil. An early study, at the University of Sao Paulo, of the racial situation in 36 small Brazilian cities, revealed that most colored people lived apart from the whites, but in no city did the blacks or mixed-bloods exclusively occupy a district. It appears to be the cost of housing and the location of work-place, not racial prejudice, that generally determines the residential location of the people in Brazilian cities. As Smith points out, "this gives rise to exclusive districts for the wealthy, residential areas occupied almost exclusively by families of middle-class status, working-class sections, slums, and various other types of residential districts."[25]

In one respect the Brazilian pattern of segregation differs conspicuously from the form that racial segregation usually assumes in cities of the United States. In Brazil, the outskirts of the cities as well as the valleys are populated mainly by blacks and darker mixed-bloods who are also low on the economic scale; in the United States, blacks and other racial minorities have tended to be centrally located.

Mexico

Segregation in Mexican cities is probably less related to race than to class distinctions and cultural characteristics of a population. There is, however, a fairly close relationship between race, on the one hand, and economic status, educational level, and life styles, on the other. Mexicans of European racial and cultural backgrounds generally reside in areas that separate them from the Indian population. This is true primarily because Europeanized Mexicans, as a category, have better incomes, more education, higher occupational status, and styles of life that distinguish them from most of the Indian population.

The traditional ecological pattern in Mexican and other Latin Ameri-

[24] Donald Pierson, *Negroes in Brazil: A Study of Race Contact in Bahia*, rev. ed. (1967); and Emilio Willems, "Race Attitudes in Brazil," *American Journal of Sociology*, 54 (March 1949), 402-9.

[25] T. Lynn Smith, *Brazil: People and Institutions*, rev. ed. (1972).

can cities was for the elite to cluster around or near a central plaza, on which was usually located a cathedral, government offices, and shops, including an open-air market. The middle classes, such as existed, lived somewhat farther removed from this central point, while the poor tended to congregate near the periphery where land was available and housing restrictions were minimal or nonexistent. This pattern has undergone considerable change over the years, especially in the larger cities. Technological improvements in transportation, for example, have made it possible for middle or upper class persons to reside further from the central plaza or other points of traditional concentration and to travel back and forth without serious inconvenience. Sometimes they are strung along arterial boulevards or clustered in fashionable districts in the city or adjacent suburbs.

Hayner indicates on a spot map the residential locations in Mexico City of persons listed in *Who's Who in Latin America*, probably a fair representation of the elite.[26] Only one residence is located near the

[26] Norman S. Hayner, *New Patterns in Old Mexico* (1966), p. 76.

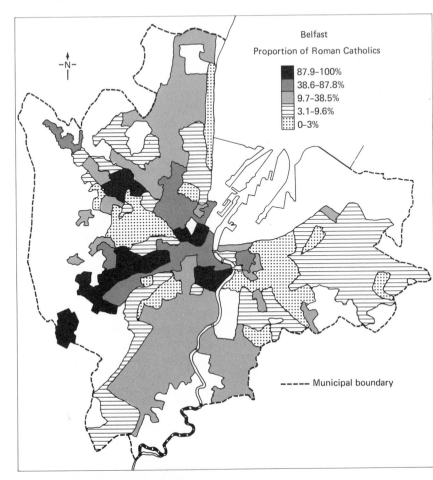

FIGURE 7.2 • Religious segregation in Belfast, Northern Ireland, reflects a long history of conflict between Roman Catholics and the numerically dominant Protestants who also mostly have higher incomes than the Roman Catholics. Source: Emrys Jones, "The Distribution and Segregation of Roman Catholics in Belfast," *Sociological Review,* Vol. 4, 1956.

Zòcalo, the central plaza; the remainder are scattered over a fairly wide sector of the city, extending from the point of highest land values in the central business district to the southern border of the metropolis, on or near the Paseo de la Reforma or the Avenida Insurgentes. The fashionable suburb of Jardines Pedregal, on the southwestern edge of the city, probably represents the most affluent of the city's population. Very few of the elite live on the eastern and northern sectors, which are mainly slums or blighted districts occupied by low-income residents. Recent urban renewal programs, however, have provided new housing for middle class families, thus introducing an element which changes somewhat the pattern of segregation by income or social class.

Guatemala

Like other Latin American cities, Guatemala City retains some of the characteristics of the classical configuration—a central plaza with the state capitol situated on one side, the national cathedral on another, and a major bazaar or market a block away. Many upper and middle class families, mainly *ladinos* of European ancestry, reside in the vicinity. The Indian population is distributed largely in areas removed from the plaza, their actual location being determined to a considerable degree by purchasing power. Impoverished and destitute residents tend to locate in certain sectors of the urban fringe. In recent years there has been a tendency for affluent, prestigious, or powerful families to reside a considerable distance from the center.

Puerto Rico

San Juan is perhaps the only large American city that retains the main elements of its Latin heritage. The rapid growth and industrialization of the city, together with the pervasive influence of the American mainland, have greatly altered the classical Latin American pattern. In a study of San Juan, Caplow concludes that race or ethnic background as such are relatively unimportant in the formation of segregated districts; rather, income, occupation, lineage, style of life, and education are the major conditions underlying the process of residential segregation.[27]

Caplow does note, however, that voluntary segregation by color or race does exist in small units such as neighborhoods or blocks. The relatively distinct residential boundaries that exist in North American cities are generally absent in San Juan. Dividing the city into six ecological zones, Caplow finds that most of the rich and well-to-do live separately from the poor or even those of moderate incomes. The median family income of

[27] Theodore Caplow, Sheldon Stryker, and Samuel E. Wallace, *The Urban Ambience* (1964), ch. 2.

the residents of the Beach Front, characterized by luxury hotels, guest houses for tourists, and high-rise apartments for the permanent residents, was over five times the median income of residents in the Slum Belt, and almost three times the income for the entire metropolitan area. But the Central District tends to be a hodge-podge of population types and institutions.

India

Segregation in Indian cities reflects differences in caste and occupation as well as in religion and economic status. Among the Hindus there is a strong tendency for members of the same caste to seek their own communal level in residential locations. One may find areas occupied mainly or exclusively by Brahmins, the highest caste; areas occupied solely by "untouchable" castes; or areas occupied by castes holding intermediate positions in the social hierarchy. Segregation on the basis of caste generally means segregation on the basis of religion to the extent that Hindus are segregated from other religious groups. Most of the larger Indian cities have fairly large Muslim populations that reside, for the most part, in distinct Muslim districts. Christians also manifest the same tendency.

But economic segregation tends to cut across caste and religious lines; hence, there is a tendency for wealthy or well-to-do families to live in fashionable high-income districts occupied by representatives of numerous castes or religions. Thus a wealthy Brahmin may live alongside a wealthy Parsee or Christian or Muslim; and because of similar occupational, political, intellectual, or social interests, they may have more in common with each other than with certain members of their own religious or caste group. Segregation in Indian cities is essentially voluntary; certainly it is not legally compulsory, although the dictates of custom are strong, prejudices do exist, and there is undoubtedly some discrimination. Since most untouchables[28] are impoverished, economic as well as social factors determine where they can reside.

A study by Gist of Bangalore revealed fairly distinct patterns of residential segregation based on religion and caste.[29] The percentage of population belonging to broad religious or caste categories was calculated for each of 55 areal units roughly comparable to census tracts in American cities. These units, however, were of unequal size and population density, and the categories of religion and caste in some instances included a number of subgroupings. Indian-Christians, for example,

---

[28] Untouchability was officially abolished by the Indian government in 1949 and various funds and job and scholarship quotas were established for the ex-untouchables. However, the social distinctions persist.

[29] Noel P. Gist, "The Ecology of Bangalore, India: An East-West Comparison," *Social Forces*, 35 (May 1957), 356–65.

included many specific denominations. Similarly, the untouchable caste category consisted of at least 100 specific castes or subcastes.

Brahmins, the "aristocracy" of the Hindu caste system, were concentrated most heavily on the northwestern and southwestern sectors of the city. Indian-Christians and Anglo-Indians, on the other hand, were located mainly on the eastern half. Muslims were probably the most segregated. The largest concentration of the depressed or untouchable castes was on the eastern sector. One predominantly Brahmin area on the southwestern side had less than one percent of its population Anglo-Indians, Indian-Christians, Muslims, or depressed caste members. Similarly, a Muslim area on the south side had less than one percent Anglo-Indians or Brahmins and only a slightly higher proportion of Indian-Christians. This ecological separateness, which reflects the social separateness that exists between various peoples in the city of Bangalore, is probably representative of other major Indian cities.

Some of the newer cities planned and built for specific purposes in India do not exhibit the traditional patterns of segregation by religion, caste, or national background. In Kharagpur, a railroad center and "company town," segregation tends to be mainly along economic lines. Brush comments that in Kharagpur "a Punjabi Sikh would be assigned quarters beside a Telugu Christian or a Marathi Hindu. The Muslims were mixed with Hindus."[30]

[30] John E. Brush, "The Morphology of Indian Cities," in Roy Turner, ed., *India's Urban Future* (1961), pp. 58–64.

FIGURE 7.3 • Capetown, South Africa, showing residential areas the government has allocated to five different racial and ethnic groups. Large-scale forced relocation of the population, especially the Coloreds, who are of mixed white and black African descent, has been undertaken to bring about these residential boundaries, reflecting governmental policies and power. Coloreds have been removed from areas within dotted and heavy lines, long their heartland. Source: © 1970 by The New York Times Company. Reprinted by permission.

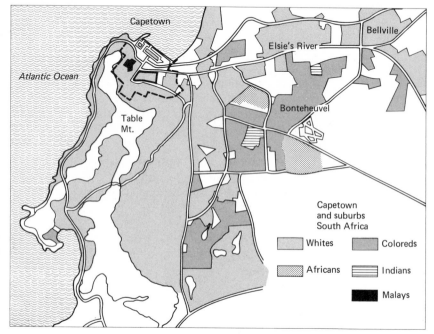

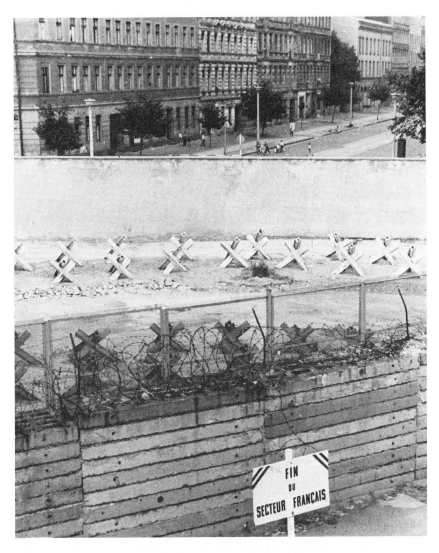

The Wall has forcibly segregated West Berlin from Communist East Berlin. A wall with mines and barbed wire separates the residents. Above are children playing on the East side. (Rhoda Sidney, Nancy Palmer)

While segregation in Indian cities on the basis of racial characteristics does exist, it is relatively unimportant as compared with social, cultural, and economic attributes. Bose describes in detail the segregation of population in Calcutta according to these characteristics.[31] Individuals and families often form residential clusters commonly made up of persons who speak the same language, have the same religion, belong to the same caste, come from the same village or district, follow the same or a similar occupation, or have comparable incomes and styles of life. Calcutta has sometimes been described as a metropolis made up of transplanted villages. Migrants to the city tend to gravitate to these segregated areas, where they hope to find the security and satisfaction of living among others of their own kind.

[31] N. K. Bose, "Calcutta: A Premature Metropolis," *Scientific American*, 222 (September 1965), 90–102.

South Africa

Racial segregation in the Union of South Africa is both *de facto* and *de jure*, voluntary and involuntary. As in American cities, the distinctions are not very clear in actual situations. But there is one important difference between the situation in South Africa and the United States: Nonwhites in South Africa are required by law to reside in specific areas. Nonwhites include not only Africans but also Indians and the Cape Coloured minority of dual (European and African) racial ancestry.

In a study of racial segregation in Durban, Kuper calculated indexes showing the degree of residential racial separation by census tracts in the 1951 census.[32] The range of segregation by this index was from 0, indicating an even distribution of the population in each precinct (no segregation), to 1.00, representing complete segregation, that is, 100 percent residential occupancy by a particular racial group. For the city as a whole, the average segregation index for the following combinations was found to be Europeans and Indians, 0.91; Europeans and Coloureds (African-European mixtures), 0.84; Indians and Africans, 0.81; and Europeans and Africans, 0.81.

The index for the European-African combination was comparatively low because at that time many African servants were permitted to reside in or near the homes of their European employers. Kuper observes that if these servants were excluded from the calculations, the index would be close to total segregation. Only the Coloureds and Indians, according to Kuper, reside in the same areas to any extent. The European-Indian segregation pattern, expressed differently, indicated that 40 percent of the Indians lived in the same areas as one percent of the Europeans, and that 60 percent of the Indians resided in the same districts as two percent of the European population.

Various laws formulated and enforced by the government, which is controlled by Europeans, prohibit nonwhite persons from moving into areas other than the ones to which they have been assigned, and likewise forbid property owners from selling their homes to persons of a different racial group. Thus the phenomenon of ecological invasion and succession that has been characteristic of American cities hardly exists in South Africa, except that the Europeans, being politically and economically dominant, can probably, if they choose, relocate other groups and take over their residential property. But since the non-European peoples are generally assigned to the least attractive locations in the city, even this form of invasion is not likely to occur on a large scale.

[32] Leo Kuper, *Durban: A Study in Racial Ecology* (1958), pp. 153–57.

The Implications of
Residential Segregation

Aside from the empirical facts relating to ecological segregation, it is even more important to recognize its significance. Certainly segregation tends to keep apart peoples differing in race, language, religion, economic position, or style of life rather than to bring them together. So long as it is voluntary, the residents of segregated areas may find life there satisfying. To reside with others of similar physical, cultural, or psychological attributes may afford a sense of belonging, of security. This is undoubtedly why human "birds of a feather flock together," in cities or elsewhere.

But life in a segregated area may become parochial. The spatial distances that separate peoples may have their counterpart in social and cultural distances. There may be limited communication with the "outside" world, a situation which minimizes understanding and maximizes the prospects of suspicion and alienation. Modern mass communication media have helped to lower the social and cultural isolation created by ecological segregation, but even these developments have not completely overcome it. Certainly ecological segregation has great significance for the exercise of citizenship in its communitywide or nationwide setting.

Summary

Cities are dynamic in nature, constantly undergoing change of one kind or another. This transformation is particularly apparent in the locational changes that occur when people and institutions move from one point to another. One of the end-products of these changes is ecological segregation or desegregation. In Chapter 8, we shall focus the discussion on the ecological processes of invasion and succession, which are dynamic aspects of spatial change. Invasion and succession are important because such spatial changes involve human relations, often conflict, between competing groups and individuals. Invasions occur not only when people move from one point within a city to another point but also when they move into a city from the outside. Institutional invasions are also characteristic of a dynamic city, although the personal reactions to such invasions may be less apparent than in the case of invasions of a district by people whose racial or cultural traits are different from those occupying the invaded area.

Selected Bibliography

BOOKS

Bradburn, Norman, Seymour Sudman, and Galen Gockel, with the assistance of Joseph Noel, *Side by Side: Integrated Neighborhoods in America*. Chicago: Quadrangle, 1971.

Darden, Joe T., *Afro-Americans in Pittsburgh: The Residential Segregation of a People*. Lexington, Mass.: Lexington Books, D. C. Heath, 1973.

Duncan, Otis Dudley, and Beverly Duncan. *The Negro Population of Chicago: A Study of Residential Succession*. Chicago: University of Chicago Press, 1957.

Firey, Walter. *Land Values in Central Boston*. Cambridge: Harvard University Press, 1949.

Glazer, Nathan, and Daniel Patrick Moynihan. *Beyond the Melting Pot: The Negroes, Puerto Ricans, Jews, Italians, and Irish of New York City*, 2d ed. Cambridge: M.I.T. Press and Harvard University Press, 1970.

Gottmann, Jean. *Megalopolis*. New York: Twentieth Century Fund, 1961.

Grebler, Leo, Joan W. Moore, and Ralph C. Guzman, *The Mexican-American People: The Nation's Second Largest Minority*. New York: The Free Press, 1970.

Hoover, Edgar, and Raymond Vernon. *Anatomy of a Metropolis*. Cambridge: Harvard University Press, 1959.

Laurenti, Luigi. *Property Values and Race*. Berkeley and Los Angeles: University of California Press, 1960.

Lieberson, Stanley. *Ethnic Patterns in American Cities*. Glencoe, Ill.: The Free Press, 1955.

Molotch, Harvey L., *Managed Integration: Dilemmas of Doing Good in the City*. Berkeley: University of California Press, 1972.

Moore, John W. and Frank G. Mittelbach, with the assistance of Ronald McDaniel. *Residential Segregation in the Urban Southwest; A Comparative Study*. Advance Report # 4 of the Mexican-American Study Project. Los Angeles; Graduate School of Business Administration, University of California, Los Angeles, 1966.

Nee, Victor G., and Brett de Bary Nee, *Longtime Californ': A Documentary History of an American Chinatown* (San Francisco). New York: Pantheon, 1973.

Patterson, S., *Dark Strangers*. Harmondsworth, Middlesex, England: Penguin Books, 1965.

Rossi, Peter. *Why Families Move*. Glencoe, Ill.: The Free Press, 1955.

Spear, Allan H., *Black Chicago: The Making of a Negro Ghetto, 1890–1920*. Chicago: University of Chicago Press, 1967.

Taeuber, Karl E., and Alma F. Taeuber. *Negroes in Cities: Residential Succession and Neighborhood Change*. New York: Atheneum, 1969.

Timms, D. W. G. *The Urban Mosaic: Toward a Theory of Residential Distribution*. Cambridge, England: Cambridge University Press, 1971.

Ward, David, *Cities and Immigrants: A Geography of Change in Nineteenth-Century America.* New York: Oxford University Press, 1971.

ARTICLES

Bose, N. K., "Calcutta: A Premature Metropolis," *Scientific American*, 222 (1965) 90–102.

Berry, Brian J. L., and Philip R. Rees, "The Factorial Ecology of Calcutta," *American Journal of Sociology*, 74 (March 1969), 445–92.

Caplow, Theodore, "The Social Ecology of Guatemala City," *Social Forces*, 28 (December 1949), 113–33.

Davison, R. "The Distribution of Immigrant Groups in London," *Race,* 5 (1963), 56–69.

Farley, Reynolds, "The Changing Distribution of Negroes within Metropolitan Areas," *American Journal of Sociology*, 75 (January 1970), 512–29.

Gist, Noel P. "The Ecology of Bangalore, India: An East-West Comparison," *Social Forces*, 35 (May 1957), 356–65.

Kantrowitz, Nathan, "Ethnic and Racial Segregation in the New York Metropolis," *American Journal of Sociology*, 74 (May 1969), 685.

Klaff, Vivian Z., "Ethnic Segregation in Urban Israel," *Demography*, 10 (May 1973), 161–84.

McElrath, D. C., "Social Areas of Rome: A Comparative Analysis," *American Sociological Review*, 27 (June 1962), 376–91.

Marston, Wilfred G., "Social-Economic Differentials within Negro Areas of American Cities," *Social Forces*, 48 (December 1969), 665–76.

Mehta, S. K., "Patterns of Residence in Poona, India," *American Journal of Sociology*, 93 (1968), 496–508.

Pinkerton, James R., "City-Suburban Residential Patterns by Social Class," *Urban Affairs Quarterly*, 4 (June 1969), 499–517.

Rhodes, A. L., "Residential Distribution and Occupational Stratification in Paris and Chicago," *Sociological Quarterly*, 10 (Winter 1969), 106–12.

Schnore, Leo F., and Philip C. Evenson, "Segregation in Southern Cities," *American Journal of Sociology* (July 1966), 58–67.

Sweetser, Frank, "Social Class and Single-Family Housing: Helsinki and Boston," in Sylvia F. Fava, ed., *Urbanism in World Perspective: A Reader.* New York: Thomas Y. Crowell, 1968, pp. 256–66.

8 • Ecological Change, Invasion, and Succession

 It should be obvious that the distribution in space of population in a dynamic, urbanized society is constantly changing. These changes may not be apparent from day to day, but over a longer period, say a decade or two, or even a century, they may be quite striking. The ecological patternings of cities in the industrial world were very different at the beginning of the twentieth century than they are today.

What may be less apparent than locational change is the relationship between ecological change and other social changes and structural characteristics. A society characterized by relatively high social mobility, indicative of changing social positions of individuals and groups, is also likely to experience extensive or even rapid changes in the ecological position of its members. As individuals or groups move up or down the social structure, they are likely to change their location. Change of position in space may precede or follow a change in social status, or the two may occur simultaneously. Change in both ecological and social position of individuals or groups, commonly families, reflects the highly competitive nature of modern urban society. Competition or conflict, either for status or survival, may lead to change in social and ecological position, although it would be an oversimplification to say that this invariably results.

Residential Desegregation

For a variety of reasons, groups that once tended to live together may disperse residentially and become scattered in localities occupied by people of different cultural or racial characteristics. Ecological desegregation is a countertendency to the segregative processes, thus preventing the formation of permanently frozen homogeneous "islands" within the city. Segregative and desegregative processes both lead to the constant forming and reforming of such island-areas based on ethnic, religious, occupational, or other traits.

Decentralization of Ethnic
and Racial Groups

The centrifugal shift of racial and ethnic groups in Chicago is revealed in an early study by Cressey.[1] By computing the median distance from the city's center of nine groups in 1898 and again in 1930, Cressey compared the extent of centrifugal movement of these people, taking the groups as a whole. For all nine groups there had been a centrifugal shift, but the ethnics from northwestern Europe—Swedes, Irish, and Germans—had moved farthest out, whereas the blacks and Italians still remained fairly close to the center of the city. However, in 1898 the Swedes, Irish, and Germans were already three or more miles from the central point of the city; hence, the distance moved over the thirty-two-year period was actually not much greater than the distance moved by some of the other groups. Since the ethnics from eastern and southern Europe arrived considerably later than those from northwestern Europe, and since they tended to settle first in central locations, it is not surprising that they were less widely diffused in 1930.

Using a similar technique, Ford followed up the Cressey study, bringing the data to 1940.[2] There was a continuation, he found, of the shifting that Cressey had earlier observed—a movement toward the periphery of the city or even beyond it.

A still more recent study than Ford's, by Duncan and Lieberson, shows that the decentralization of ethnic groups in Chicago has continued.[3] This trend has been particularly obvious among those foreign-born groups most centralized in the earlier years—the "new" immigrant groups from southern and eastern Europe (Poland, Czechoslovakia, Austria, the Soviet Union, Lithuania, and Italy). In 1950 these groups were much more decentralized than in 1930, although they were still not as decentralized as the "old" immigrant groups (those from England and Wales, Ireland, Sweden, and Germany). The outward movement of immigrant groups is a general phenomenon in American society. A study of nine cities in addition to Chicago—Boston, Buffalo, Cincinnati, Cleveland, Columbus, Philadelphia, Pittsburgh, St. Louis, and Syracuse—compared the degree of centralization of immigrant groups in 1930 and 1950.[4] In all of these cities the groups had become less centralized over

[1] Paul F. Cressey, "Population Succession in Chicago, 1898–1930," *American Journal of Sociology*, 44 (July 1938), 59–68.

[2] Richard G. Ford, "Population Succession in Chicago," *American Journal of Sociology*, 56 (September 1950), 156–60.

[3] Otis Dudley Duncan and Stanley Lieberson, "Ethnic Segregation and Assimilation," *American Journal of Sociology*, 64 (January 1959), 368–69. See also A. Hunter, "The Ecology of Chicago: Persistence and Change, 1930–1960," *American Journal of Sociology*, (November 1971), 425–45.

[4] Stanley Lieberson, *Ethnic Patterns in American Cities* (1963), pp. 101–8.

the twenty-year period. The tendency for immigrant groups from the southern and eastern European countries to remain somewhat more centralized than those from northern and western Europe was also generally found.

Studies of immigrant groups in American cities indicate that many ethnic communities established in the nineteenth century have tended to disintegrate, whereas communities established by later migrations are still fairly distinct. But time alone is not the only factor. Earlier immigrants—Scandinavians, Germans, English, Dutch, and Danes— actually set the cultural standards. Protestants for the most part, with strong addictions to cleanliness, godliness, and hard work, they arrived at a propitious time, just as industrial and commercial expansion was getting into full swing, and most of them prospered during this period of rapid growth.

After the turn of the century, many immigrants came from southern and eastern Europe—Poland, Italy, Greece, Bulgaria, Rumania, Czechoslovakia, Russia, Hungary. Predominantly Catholic or Greek Orthodox, they represented cultures often at considerable variance from the ones that had become firmly established. Arriving fairly late on the American scene, after most free agricultural land had been acquired by earlier immigrants and after industrial expansion was well under way, they crowded into the larger cities, establishing segregated cultural or ethnic islands in the midst of a polyethnic community. They were not only poor and uneducated, for the most part, but also they arrived too late to become established on the ground floor of the great American economic boom.

Dispersal of Italians in New Haven

In an analysis of the residential dispersal of Italians in New Haven, Connecticut, Myers has shown how ecological position and socioeconomic position are interrelated, that is, how changes in one may be associated with changes in the other.[5] Using a "quota fulfillment index" to indicate changes, Myers calculated the extent of underrepresentation and overrepresentation of Italians in each of six ecological areas and in each of six occupational groups, and also showed the changes that had occurred for six census decades. A quota fulfillment index of 100·signified that the proportion of Italians in a given area or occupational group was what would be expected if they were uniformly distributed. An index above or below 100 signified that the Italians were overrepresented or underrepresented in the area or occupational class.

[5] Jerome K. Myers, "Assimilation to the Ecological and Social Systems of a Community," *American Sociological Review*, 15 (June 1950), 367–72.

For the first three census periods (1890, 1900, and 1920), there were no Italians living in Area I, the fashionable residential district populated mainly by professionals and business executives. The quota fulfillment index was therefore 0. In 1920 the index was 3.39, and by 1940 had risen to 11.36. For Area II, occupied mainly by office workers and small-business proprietors, the index had changed from 0 in 1890 to 18.86 in 1940. Obviously the Italians were moving into the "better" residential districts, many of them coming from Area VI, the "poorest" residential district. In 1890 the index for Area VI was 181.46; it increased to 230.88 in 1920, dropped to 222.74 in 1930, and to 205.96 in 1940.

Using the same procedure, Myers found that the quota fulfillment index for unskilled workers showed a tendency to decline after 1920, whereas indexes for the higher occupational levels tended to increase. In 1890, for example, the index for professionals was 0, but by 1940 it was 43.90. Although Italians were still underrepresented among professionals, there nevertheless had been a pronounced movement by them into the professional occupations. On the other hand, the index for unskilled laborers in 1910 was 201.02, but by 1940 it had declined to 123.90. In all the occupational levels above that of unskilled workers there had been an increase in the representation of Italian personnel.

Movement up the occupational ladder was therefore associated with ecological dispersal of the New Haven Italians. Upward occupational mobility is often accompanied by residential movement from areas considered socially or physically undesirable. Insofar as upward occupational mobility means higher incomes, those who move to higher occupational levels are usually financially able to pay for better housing. Myers points out, interestingly enough, that some Italians remained in Area VI, even though they had moved up the occupational scale, preferring to remain in the area for sentimental or other reasons. Thus, there is no one-to-one relationship between occupational and ecological mobility, but only a high correlation.

The dispersal of the Italians in New Haven provides an almost classic case of the relationship between physical and social movement. On the basis of a number of ecological studies and of general knowledge of American cities, there has been rather widespread acceptance of the theory that ecological dispersal is associated with the assimilation of ethnic groups and that such dispersal tends to proceed from the center to the periphery of the city. However accurately this theory may apply to the ecological history of certain cultural groups, it does not fit the ecological facts of all.

There are exceptions to the linkage between decentralization, desegregation, and assimilation of ethnic groups. The Dutch in Chicago are an example of a group whose ecological position indicating decentralization is neither a result of movement from the center of the city nor associated with desegregation.[6] In the late nineteenth century, the Dutch settled heavily in an area about twelve miles from the center of Chicago where they were close to their jobs as farmers or railroad construction workers. Their high decentralization index is the result of the city's growing out to encapsulate their neighborhoods.

Other Social Aspects of Ecological Change

There are many areas in large cities where indexes of disorganization such as infant mortality rates, delinquency rates, public assistance, and the like have remained high for decades while successive groups of varying religion or nationality have inhabited the area. It would seem that as each group advanced economically, educationally, and otherwise, it left that area and was succeeded by a group having the same general socioeconomic status the preceding group had when it first settled in the area. We have long been familiar with this aspect of invasion-succession; at least this is suggested by the Duncans' study of racial succession in Chicago. At the various stages of the invasion-succession cycle, census tracts occupied by blacks tend to keep the same relative position in terms of housing characteristics and socioeconomic indicators compared with other census tracts, as when the areas were occupied by whites. In sum, middle class blacks tend to invade middle class white neighborhoods and lower class blacks, lower class white neighborhoods, so that the character of the neighborhoods remains roughly the same, although the race of the occupants changes.

The foregoing sections have been concerned with the dynamics by which population characteristics may change but an area may retain the same ecological function. But what of the situation where the area's ecological function changes; or where changes from one type of residential land use to another occur, as when apartment houses come to predominate over single-family homes in an area, or residential structures become obsolete ("walk-ups" compared with elevator buildings), or sparsely settled areas become fully built up with homes? When one type of residential use is succeeded by another, the area may become a less desirable place to live; it has taken a lower position in the hierarchy of residential areas. A change in residential land use does not inevitably mean downgrading, but in actuality cases of neighborhood deterioration far outweigh cases of improvement.

There are some instances of the later residential land use being on a higher level than the preceding one. Georgetown, in Washington, D.C., was a blighted district in the 1920's, but gradually private individuals restored the crumbling homes, many of them mansions from pre-Civil

---

[6] Duncan and Lieberson, *op. cit.*, p. 369.

War times, to their former splendor. Georgetown is now an expensive and attractive neighborhood in which many high government officials and business and professional leaders live.

Regardless of whether a neighborhood's attractiveness relative to other neighborhoods increases or decreases, the change in ecological position inevitably brings a change in the character of the population drawn to the neighborhood. As the row houses of the 1920's become obsolete, they attract a different group. As high-rise apartments in an area come to outnumber single-family homes, the kinds of people interested in living there change, too.

Ecological invasions probably occur in every country in which cities are growing rapidly in population and in which social and economic changes have accelerated in recent decades. But the invasions do not necessarily parallel those that have occurred in American cities. The technology that made possible urban "sprawl" in the United States has not figured so importantly in many countries, especially those of nonindustrial societies. Although growing cities in these countries have expanded the outer boundaries of settlement, this expansion has commonly been less rapid and extensive than in American cities whose peripheral extension has been facilitated by the mass use of the private automobile, and to a lesser extent by public transit facilities. Hence, the invasion of persons and institutions into unoccupied peripheral areas is on a much smaller scale. The high residential density of most nonindustrial cities, as compared with American or even European cities, reflects the limited peripheral expansion of the community. Without rapid transportation available to most residents of these cities, they tend to locate well within the city, even if it is necessary for them to live in congested neighborhoods. Nor have the central business districts expanded as in the United States, and few peripheral shopping centers have sprung up to displace residents or other institutions.

But peripheral invasions do occur, nevertheless. A recently developed area on the southwestern edge of Mexico City, for example, is now occupied by the financial and social elite, many of whom had moved from the inner city. Bangalore's southern "frontier" is being gradually pushed farther out as middle class residents occupy the vacant spaces. The peripheral settlement of Hong Kong's New Territory, actually on the mainland of China, is being expanded as some of the colony's population move into the unoccupied open spaces or already existing villages.

The Invasion-Succession Process

Ecological invasion and segregation are closely associated phenomena; indeed, they are often merely different aspects of the same general process. An area undergoing an ecological invasion may at the same time be undergoing segregation. As the invaders increase in numbers, they may, if they are homogeneous in respect to certain attributes, become a segregated group. If they displace residents who already occupy the area, the displacement may mean the gradual movement of the displaced group into another area, or the scattering of its members. Invasion, however, may merely represent movement into an unoccupied area; in this instance there is no displacement of residents, but the land may be put to a different use. Fringe areas of growing cities in the United States are constantly undergoing invasions of this type. Invasions into residentially unoccupied areas may or may not result in racial or ethnic segregation, but often such invaded areas manifest a certain degree of economic segregation in the sense that the settlers are fairly homogeneous as to income.

Ecological invasion may be viewed as a kind of barometer reflecting both the dynamics of a social order and the direction of certain social changes. In a society having little social or spatial mobility, invasion would probably not figure importantly in community life. It appears to be most characteristic of societies having an expanding economy, strong personal and institutional competitiveness, and widespread preoccupation of individuals with pecuniary and status objectives. Invasion should be considered in relative terms. Just as "one swallow does not a summer make," neither does the movement of one individual or family into an area ordinarily constitute an invasion of much sociological significance for the area unless the presence of the invading individual or family meets with resistance, creates a problem for the residents, or alters the existing pattern of neighborhood relationships.

In common usage the concept of invasion is applied to the movement of a considerable number of individuals or families into a particular area. The specific number is unimportant; what is important sociologically is the character of the invaders, the relationships between the invaders and the residents, and the effect on physical property, social relationships, and institutions. The movement of a half-dozen blacks into a white area of an American city may be of greater sociological significance than the movement of a hundred Polish-Americans into an Italian-American district. In the final analysis the sociological significance of ecological invasions into residential areas already occupied reflects the prevailing values both of the occupants and of the invaders.

Voluntary and Involuntary Invasion

As in the case of segregation, ecological invasions may be voluntary or involuntary, although most are probably voluntary. But there are numerous instances in which residential areas are themselves invaded by businesses or industry and the occupants forced to move; or instances in which families victimized by adversity are forced to shift to neighborhoods they would hardly choose under more auspicious circumstances. If their incomes are low, or if they are subject to racial or cultural discrimination, their choice of a new residential location is very likely narrowly limited. Often their move is merely from one deteriorated district to another, with no advantages, real or imagined, to be gained. Highway construction and urban renewal are other causes of involuntary residential relocation.

Voluntary residential invasions are usually a matter of infiltration by individuals or families motivated by a desire for more pleasant surroundings, occupational advantages, social prestige, or any number of things that rank high on their scale of interests. Ethnic or racial invasions are no exception. Except in cases of forced evacuation, residential movement —which is both movement away from an area and into a different area—is usually individualized behavior. While the movement may superficially assume the appearance of collective action, actually it is nothing more than shifts of individuals or families, each motivated by its own particular reasons. The appearance of collective action arises from the fact that the movements may be similar in direction and destination, and the people moving may be similarly motivated.

Institutional Invasion

Change in the character of land use may also result from institutional change. In an expanding, dynamic city there are frequent changes in the economy of an area as commercial, industrial, or other types of institutions invade a particular district, or as such buildings are removed to make way for an invasion of residents.

Institutional invasion may occur independently of population movement, it may precede or follow an invasion of population, or the two types of invasion may occur more or less concurrently. An invasion of an area by industry may be followed by a residential invasion of industrial workers who want to live close to the place of employment. An institutional invasion may also be the signal for an exodus of the residents of an invaded area because property values may be adversely affected or because the area becomes less suited to residential purposes.

The exodus of population from a residential area or the change in character of an area's population as a result of invasion may affect institutional functions. Sometimes churches are forced to move because members have left the area and the invaders are of a different religious persuasion. Church buildings often remain, but church organization may be shifted in the direction of relocated members. The invaders, on the other hand, may take over the church property and put it to a somewhat different use. Sometimes institutional invasion involves the

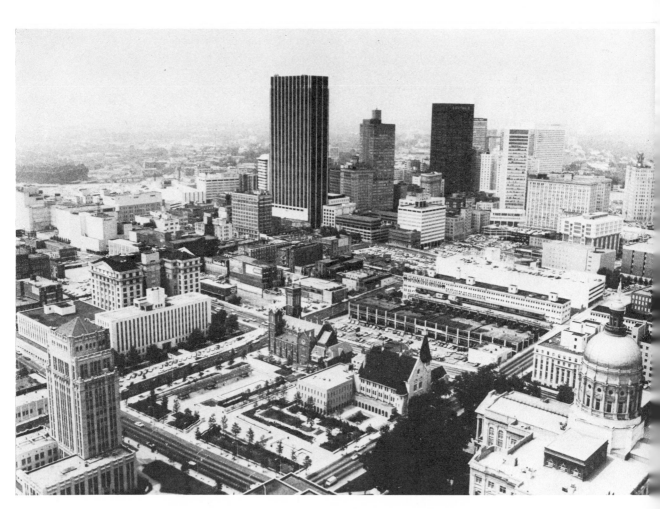

Institutional invasion in Atlanta. In the foreground, right, is an old church in an area that has been invaded by modern office buildings in the city's center. (Atlanta Chamber of Commerce)

movement of one type of establishment into an area occupied by another type. An expanding business district may result in the movement of commercial enterprises into areas already occupied by, say, light industry. Or commercial and industrial establishments may move into unoccupied areas, possibly replacing agricultural operations. The growth of various types of enterprises along main highways near cities is an example. Sometimes such commercial establishments form the nucleus for subsequent suburban or satellite settlements arising from the decentralization of population.

The central business districts of some American cities are no longer expanding, and the time will probably come when such districts in many cities will cease to grow. Extensive invasions by business or industry of adjoining areas will then cease. The blight that is already so conspicuous may continue to spread unless concerted efforts are made toward reconstruction of the area. This day seems to be hastened by the growth of outlying shopping centers and by the decentralization of residential population in metropolitan areas.

Invasion and Social
Mobility

Invasions in American cities are commonly associated with vertical social mobility, either upward or downward. Movement of an individual or family into a particular area is often a means to higher social or economic position or an indication that higher status has already been achieved. Individuals or families moving to a higher social position commonly expect to display the symbols appropriate to that position—a larger house, a more expensive car, a suitable residential location. The kind of neighborhood a family lives in is a fairly accurate criterion of its class status; to improve that status the family may seek a "nicer" area than the one it already occupies. We have already noted how the desegregation of ethnic groups in American cities is associated with the socioeconomic advancement of the immigrants.

This relation between ecological and social mobility in the United States appears to obtain when the social system is functioning normally and the avenues for social ascendancy are open. In times of economic distress, as in economic depressions, the channels for upward mobility are narrowed so far as the masses are concerned. It is in these periods of depression that the direction of ecological mobility tends to change considerably. As individuals move down the economic scale, as a result of loss of job or reduction in income, they may be forced to move into less expensive areas, regardless of their social aspirations. The march to attractive suburbs slows down, construction of new homes declines, and there is an invasion of the slums or blighted areas by families victimized by misfortune. Others, more fortunate but nevertheless troubled by insecurity, may lay aside their plans to move to a neighborhood symbolic of the status they would like.

Large-Scale Housing
and Invasion

Large housing projects are commonly associated with residential invasions. Sometimes the invaders are racial or ethnic groups; at other times they merely represent a movement into an area of persons who are higher or lower in economic status than the original occupants. Indeed, housing projects may be located in vacant areas, in which case the use of the land may be changed but there is no population displacement. In such instances land values generally rise sharply. Wholesale evacuation of residents from slum areas undergoing an urban renewal program usually occurs, but the people moving into the district may be on a higher income level, or they may actually be the evacuees or others of similar socioeconomic position who are admitted to the newly constructed houses. Recently large-scale housing projects have been undertaken on suburban or satellite land, and although these are mainly for middle-income families some are designed for people on the lower income levels.

Even though such housing projects may be racially and ethnically integrated, they often represent a form of economic or class segregation; this is especially true of public housing projects for low-income families.

Many high-rise office and apartment buildings in St. Louis have invaded the Mill Creek Valley area. This district has recently been cleared of old and deteriorated residential and business structures. (George W. Gardner)

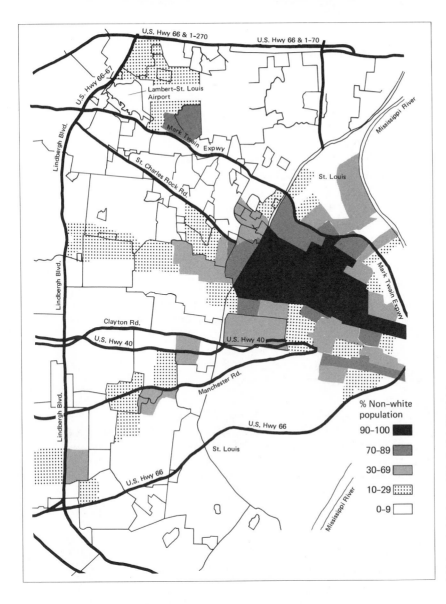

FIGURE 8.1 • Segregation of nonwhite population in St. Louis. Many of the black residents live in an area now undergoing extensive rehabilitation, as indicated by the opposite picture showing institutional invasion. Source: Thomas E. Baker and Rex R. Campbell, *Race and Residence in Missouri Cities*, Missouri Commission on Human Rights, 1971.

Stages of Invasion-Succession

Several efforts have been made to identify and conceptualize different stages in the invasion-succession cycle in American cities. Most of these studies have been concerned with the invasion of blacks into areas occupied by whites.

In their study of the processes of invasion and succession by blacks in Chicago, the Duncans viewed the process in terms of stages.[7] The initial stage, *penetration,* is usually characterized by the entry of a few blacks into an area occupied by whites. *Invasion* occurs when many blacks

[7] Otis Dudley Duncan and Beverly Duncan, *The Negro Population of Chicago* (1957), ch. 6.

217

follow the initial trail-blazers in substantial numbers. When a large number of blacks move into the invaded area and become the dominant group, numerically and even in terms of prevailing social patterns, the stage is referred to as *consolidation*. Finally, there is the stage of *piling up*, which occurs when population density in the invaded area becomes high and there is acute housing congestion.

The researchers insist that there is no immutable "law" specifying that ecological changes proceed through all these stages. Undoubtedly the process would vary from one American city to another. A fifth stage, *desegregation*, could also occur under certain circumstances. As the Duncans state, the rate of the invasion-succession process may be a variable, that the complete cycle may occur in a short period of time or over many years. This conceptual model would probably not apply very well to various ethnic or nationality groups in American or other cities, but it does seem most applicable to the black population in large cities of the United States.

Blacks and the Invasion-Succession Process

When large numbers of blacks move into an area occupied by whites, fears that the area is losing status often motivates whites to leave. This may be one of the factors underlying the "tipping" process, that is, the phenomenon of whites moving out of a neighborhood once the proportion of nonwhites exceeds the "tip point." The tip point varies from one city and one neighborhood to another. It is also revealing that several studies show that status considerations often override favorable attitudes toward blacks in the decision of liberal white families to leave racially changing neighborhoods.

Not all blacks in American cities tend to gravitate toward low-rent areas and to "pile up" in them, thus creating housing and areal congestion and other social problems. This does, of course, occur, and portions of black ghettoes in American cities are the consequences. But many blacks move *away from* rather than *into* ghetto slums. Generally this movement is centrifugal in direction, toward the city's boundaries or even beyond into the suburbs. The volume of such movement is limited, in the main, by the incomes of outward-bound blacks and the availability of housing. The latter may be determined by the extent and nature of discrimination against blacks seeking a more desirable location, or by the number of houses vacated by whites. Often these second-hand houses are in fact superior to those previously occupied by blacks. In some cities black areas extend from the central core of the city to peripheral areas, with distance from the core positively correlated with higher incomes of the residents.

Conflict and Accommodation
in the Invasion Process

White occupants of an area in the path of a black invasion may abandon the area in haste because of fears that they cannot live in peace with black neighbors, or that their physical safety, or that of their children, may be in jeopardy. Blacks having strong feelings of black nationalism may welcome the withdrawal of whites, since they often espouse a doctrine of separatism rather than integration. It is difficult for friendly neighborhood relations between blacks and whites to flourish in this kind of atmosphere.

But this situation is by no means universal. There are numerous instances in which blacks and whites live harmoniously together in the same neighborhood. The prospects for neighborly harmony would appear to be most favorable if the occupants, black and white, are relatively well educated and have a similar style of life. If there are marked educational and life-style differences, the prospects for amicable neighborly relations are less favorable.

Racial invasion without concerted resistance or violence occurs frequently in many American cities, especially in small or middle-sized communities. A midwestern university city, "Centertown," is an example. About 10 percent of Centertown's population is black, most of whom reside in a segregated district. The majority are on relatively low income levels, and many live in public housing. As the black population increased, the segregated district expanded in size, which occurred by a gradual invasion of an adjacent white district that was evacuated by many of the residents without organized resistance. At the same time several black professional and business families made deep penetrations into middle class districts, the reactions to which were varied. Some of the neighbors welcomed the black families and established friendly relations with them, but several groused about the situation, making it clear to the newcomers that they were not welcome. A few threatened to move away, but there was no mass exodus. Since the black families were widely scattered in preponderantly white neighborhoods, rather than being clustered in small segregated pockets, and since their style of life resembled that of the other residents, the invasion represented no serious threat to property values or to the physical attractiveness of the area.

Property Values
and Invasion

Resistance to residential invasion has often been defended on the grounds that otherwise property values would decline, a viewpoint that has been particularly strong with regard to the movement of blacks into white neighborhoods. Until recently, even the policy of federal agencies dealing with housing held that racial separation in housing protected property values. Despite widespread contention on this matter, there was little evidence to substantiate or refute it, until Laurenti made a careful study which provides some information to enable us to assess the relationship between property values and segregation.[8]

Laurenti obtained the sales prices for homes sold from 1943 to 1955 in twenty neighborhoods in San Francisco, Oakland, and Philadelphia that had formerly been all-white but had undergone some degree of nonwhite entry, ranging from less than two to over 29 percent. Home sale prices in each neighborhood were compared with a "control" area—a similar neighborhood in the same city except that it had remained all-white during the 1943–1945 period. Almost 10,000 individual home sales were involved in the study. It should be noted that while the neighborhoods represented a variety of home price categories, most were in single-family residential areas occupied by owner-occupants and were located outside the heart of the city.

The study did not support the idea that nonwhite occupancy necessarily lowered property values.

The major statistical finding of the present study is that during the time period and for the class studied the entry of nonwhites into previously all-white neighborhoods was much more often associated with price improvement or stability than with price weakening. A corollary and possibly more important finding is that no single or uniform pattern of nonwhite influence on property prices could be detected.[9]

Laurenti's findings suggest that home prices in the kinds of neighborhoods studied are not necessarily adversely affected by black entry. We might add that "panic" selling, if it occurs, may indeed lower home sale prices temporarily. This appears to be an instance of the "self-fulfilling prophecy." If white owners expect property values to fall when nonwhites move into the area, then many owners may put their homes on the market at once, thereby creating oversupply and bringing about the price decline they fear. There is debate over the facts of what happens in these instances of the self-fulfilling prophecy, particularly whether the process and the resulting behavior are irrational.[10] Certainly both Laurenti's results and the theory of the self-fulfilling prophecy make it clear that the relationship between property values and race should not be dismissed in stereotyped terms but merits further consideration.

[8] Luigi Laurenti, *Property Values and Race* (1960).
[9] *Ibid.*, p. 47.
[10] Eleanor Wolf, "The Invasion-Succession Sequence as a Self-Fulfilling Prophecy," *Journal of Social Issues*, 13 (1957), 421–36.

Resistance and Acceptance

The rate of displacement depends on a number of interrelated factors—economic, geographic, cultural, psychological. Each situation has unique features. An impending invasion of a white area by blacks may signal a wholesale exodus from the district, resulting in rapid displacement of white families by black families; or it may mean a last-ditch fight by whatever devices are available to prevent blacks from moving in. The reaction to an invasion by blacks in New York may be quite different from the reaction to such an invasion in Atlanta, San Antonio, or Johannesburg. Or the reaction in 1900 may have been different from the reaction in 1970, even in the same city.

The degree of resistance to invasion seems to be related to the following factors: (1) the socioeconomic status of the invading group, that is, groups regarded as equal or superior are rarely resisted; (2) the stand taken by leadership groups including the clergy, real estate men, citizen's associations, and the government; (3) the ability to secure equivalent housing elsewhere (If the housing market is tight, resistance is likely to stiffen.); (4) the meaning of housing to the individuals, particularly if it is primarily a status symbol; (5) length of residence in the area (Highly transient areas tend to have few individuals with an economic or sentimental stake in the community.); and (6) the stage of the family cycle (Families with young children are most apt to be concerned with the impact of the newcomers on educational or recreational facilities.).

THE MYERS CASE   The role of status considerations in the reaction to black residents is illustrated in the case study of Levittown, Pennsylvania.[11] Construction of this large suburban development began in 1951, and, by 1957, 15,500 families, about 60,000 people, lived there when William Myers, a thirty-four-year-old veteran, college educated and employed as a refrigeration engineer, purchased a four-year-old house and moved in with his wife and three young children. The Myers were the first blacks to live in Levittown. Pro- and anti-Myers factions quickly developed.

Myers' opponents were almost wholly recruited from the ranks of the relatively uneducated urban proletariat in the process of uncertain transit to the suburban middle class. . . . A high degree of ethnocentrism is a common phenomenon in the sub-college stratum, and as might as anticipated a goodly number of Levittowners had chosen to live in this community precisely because if offered an escape from "mixed" neighborhoods and those facing imminent desegregation. Moreover, these initial biases among industrial workers were

[11] Marvin Bressler, "The Myers Case: An Instance of Successful Racial Invasion," *Social Problems*, 8 (Fall 1960), 126–42.

frequently reinforced by status anxieties arising from their equivocal position in the class structure. . . . The appearance of a visible threat to the social status of the community in the persons of a Negro family could be expected to produce considerable apprehension among the inhabitants of a poorly defined no man's land on the margins between two classes.

· · · · ·

If Myers' fiercest antagonists exhibited an intense preoccupation with the social reputation of the local community his most vigorous defenders represented the cosmopolitan orientation. . . . College educated and career oriented, the cosmopolitan had not moved to Levittown in order to improve his social status. He had come for idiosyncratic reasons, out of economic compulsion, or because repeated references to a "planned" community had led him to indulge in the soon dispelled vague fantasy that he was being introduced to a sort of contemporary New Harmony. But whatever his motivations he was often embarrassed by his "Levittown address." Members of his occupational reference groups in Philadelphia sometimes behaved as if they regarded his tenure in Levittown as evidence of some unsuspected eccentricity and wondered when he intended to join his fellows in the more elegant western suburbs.

Moreover, the occupations of a significant proportion of the cosmopolitans inclined them to reject parochialism. Physicians, clergy, educators, and social workers, for example, are routinely accustomed to think and act according to universalistic norms. As recent graduates of American institutions of higher learning the majority of the cosmopolitans had been "broadened" in race relations courses and workshops. They had heard that decent men must forswear prejudice, that contact produces amity, that the UN was man's best hope, and one or two had even entertained foreign students.[12]

Harassment of the Myers family continued for several months until a court injunction forbade interference with their or any other black's rights of residence.

Some Empirical Studies of Invasion

New Orleans

In an analysis of the ecological history of New Orleans, Gilmore described the various invasions that have occurred during the nineteenth and twentieth centuries, relating these invasions to the topography of the city as well as to the segregation of ethnic and racial groups.[13] The earliest settlers were French, who came to be known as Creoles. To-

---

[12] *Ibid*, pp. 133, 137. Reprinted by permission.

[13] H. W. Gilmore, "The Old New Orleans and the New," *American Sociological Review*, 9 (August 1944), 385–94. This is one of the best ecological analyses of an American city because it brings into focus the historical, geographic, ethnic, economic, and technological factors involved.

gether with Spanish settlers later on, they developed a distinctive cultural life. Many of them prospered, their influence being based primarily on the plantation labor of slaves or the cheap labor of free blacks. Upper class families in New Orleans had a retinue of black servants.

With the expansion of the city's economy, an influx of migrants occurred, the first of whom were Americans whose money-making interests led them into business and industry. The area of first settlement was near the French quarter, in the central part of the city, an area to which large numbers of Irish immigrants were also attracted.

As the wealth of the Americans mounted and their numbers increased, they moved farther west on land adjacent to the Mississippi River, where they developed a pretentious residential district. The area they abandoned was filled up by Irish immigrants and came to be known as the

The French Quarter in New Orleans. This area, settled initially by the French, retains many aspects of French culture although it has been invaded by other ethnic peoples. (New Orleans Tourist Commission)

223

Irish Channel. The centrifugal movement of the Americans meant an invasion of the black residential fringe and their truck-gardening zone.

With the growth of the Creole population in the central area and the deterioration of their residential properties, many Creole families also moved outward, not in the direction of the Americans, but northward along one of the ridges, where they developed an attractive residential district.

In the early days the blacks lived on the premises of their masters or clustered in a horseshoe-shaped fringe around the Creole or American residential areas. When street cars later came into use, it was no longer necessary for the blacks to live in the immediate vicinity of their place of work. Since the outer black fringe had been invaded by the whites, displaced blacks turned toward the center of the city, moving into deteriorated areas or into the swamp zone between the districts occupied by whites.

Gilmore makes it clear that the topography of New Orleans, particularly the river and swamp areas, imposed limitations on the direction of invasions. But cultural differences and tensions between ethnic groups, especially between the Creoles and Americans, fostered segregation and operated to direct population movements toward different sections of the city.

A more recent study showed that ethnic relations continue as the most important determinants of change in the ecology of New Orleans.[14]

The Gilded Ghetto

A study in "North City," a midwestern metropolis, showed changes in the location and function of Jewish residential areas from one generation to another.[15] The first generation consisted of Jews who came to North City in the 1860's from Germany, Austria, and Hungary; in the 1900's they were joined by Jews from eastern Europe. Most of the first generation settled in an area called the North Side. In 1910, over 80 percent of all Jews in the city lived there. The second generation, that is, the native-born children of the immigrants, were less likely to live on the North Side. Many, particularly the financially successful descendants of the early German immigrants, moved to better neighborhoods on the South Side.

The authors call these areas "gilded ghettoes" because, although such areas were a far cry from the crowded slums of the North Side, the Jews resident in them still carried on their social life almost exclusively within their own group. Thus, the second generation had become assimilated in

---

[14] Forrest LaViolette, "The Negro in New Orleans," in Nathan Glazer and Davis McEntire, eds., *Studies in Housing and Minority Groups* (1960), pp. 110–34.

[15] Judith Kramer and Seymour Levantman, *Children of the Gilded Ghetto* (1961).

terms of standard of living but not in terms of social relationships. The third generation, native-born grandchildren of the original immigrants, definitely tended to settle away from the North Side. Indeed, by 1957 only 38 percent of the Jewish population still lived there. The third generation, for the most part "young marrieds" in white collar occupations, had moved to the southside suburbs, where they had many non-Jewish neighbors and friends. Jews of the third generation did not reject the heritage of their forefathers, but they appeared more interested in living in high-status communities than in the ghettoes—gilded or not—of the first and second generations.

This study and others showing the physical dispersion and upward mobility of ethnic groups raise the basic question of how assimilated the ethnic groups in American society are likely to become. There has been a noticeable decline in prejudice and discrimination against ethnic groups, in part due to the recognition of the contribution these groups have made to American life. For the members of many ethnic groups there is no longer any significant stigma attached to their ethnic origin. Therefore, for these groups, interest in and practice of the tradition of immigrant ancestral groups need not be rejected on account of connotations of social inferiority. Thus, under these circumstances ethnic segregation is likely to be voluntary rather than involuntary.

Boston

Changes in land use and type of occupants of Boston's Back Bay, once occupied almost exclusively by the city's elite, are illustrative of ecological transformations occurring in many American cities.[16] As invasions or changed land use in the twentieth century threatened the prestige of the area, the Back Bay's elite began their exodus, many of them moving to such fashionable suburbs as Newton, Milton, or Weston. Some of the brownstone mansions were demolished to make way for apartment buildings, or were transformed into kitchenette apartments or respectable middle class rooming houses to accommodate students, young professionals, and white collar workers. High rentals prevented an influx of low-income families. Although business houses encroached upon the area, there has been selective invasion, limited mainly to establishments featuring luxury items for women.

Beacon Hill, another of Boston's areas of fashionable occupance, has undergone a somewhat different ecological history. During the latter part of the nineteenth century, Beacon Hill families migrated from the area, possibly because of a threatened invasion of people without prestige. Some of the homes with halls were converted into rooming houses, several apartment houses were constructed, and such business

[16] Walter Firey, *Land Use in Central Boston* (1947), ch. 7.

establishments as tailor shops, stores, and clubs began moving into the district. But for many of the established families, particularly those with impressive pedigrees as well as the *nouveaux riches* in search of pedigrees, such incursions into sacred territory were resented and resisted. Firey interprets this as a refutation of ecological theories that view economic functions as the determinants of spatial phenomena. The preservation of the character of the area had cultural determinants running counter to the interests of those who might have made money by changing the residential amenities of Beacon Hill.

Kansas City

Another example of the invasion-succession process is the changing character of population in Quality Hill, a district in Kansas City, Missouri, which was once occupied almost exclusively by "quality folks," among them being the most prestigious and affluent families in the city. Quality Hill is located some ten blocks from the central retail and office district on an elevated promontory overlooking the confluence of the Kansas and Missouri Rivers. When the low-lying land near the rivers became industrialized, air pollution and the general unsightliness of the valley made the district less attractive for residential purposes than it had originally been. One by one the occupants abandoned the area, moving to locations on the south side of the city. Luxurious homes, once the symbol of affluence and power, were converted into apartments or rooming houses, whose occupants were often footloose and mobile. After World War II another invasion got underway, a reversal of the previous one. The construction of numerous high-rise apartments and luxury hotels again attracted well-to-do persons, married and unmarried, who apparently regarded a residential site near the center of downtown employment and shopping convenient for their needs. But many of the old homes, bypassed by the wrecker and bulldozer, remain as mute reminders of a gilded era.

Summary

The discussion of ecological segregation and invasion-succession logically leads us to a consideration of the spatial patterning of urban institutions. Even the most casual and unsophisticated observer must be aware of the varied distributive patterns in the location of institutions. In the following chapter, we shall consider the ways that institutions are distributed in the city. As in the case of urban people, institutions are likewise experiencing changes not only in their structures and functions but also in their locations. Indeed, the location may reflect the changing structures and functions of the institutions. As these structures and functions change from one year or decade to another, institutions are likely to move to locations that are considered to be more advantageous for their particular purposes. In the next chapter we shall observe the prevailing spatial patterns of various kinds of institutions and compare the patterns exhibited in urban-industrial societies with those of developing countries.

Selected Bibliography

BOOKS

Caplow, Theodore, Sheldon Stryker, and Samuel E. Wallace, *The Urban Ambience.* Totowa, N. J.: Bedminster Press, 1964.

Firey, Walter, *Land Use in Central Boston.* Cambridge: Harvard University Press, 1947.

Gans, Herbert, *The Urban Villagers.* New York: The Free Press, 1962.

Gottmann, Jean, *Megalopolis.* New York: Twentieth Century Fund, 1961.

Hoover, Edgar M., and Raymond Vernon, *Anatomy of a Metropolis.* Cambridge: Harvard University Press, 1959.

Kramer, Judith, *The American Minority Community.* New York: Thomas Y. Crowell, 1970.

Lieberson, Stanley, *Ethnic Patterns in American Cities.* New York: The Free Press, 1963.

Shevky, Eshref, and Marilyn Williams, *The Social Areas of Los Angeles.* Berkeley and Los Angeles: University of California Press, 1949.

Suttles, Gerald D., *The Social Order of the Slum.* Chicago: University of Chicago Press, 1968.

Taeuber, Karl E., and Alma F. Taeuber, *Negroes in Cities: Residential Segregation and Neighborhood Change.* New York: Atheneum, 1969.

Theodorson, George A., ed., *Studies in Human Ecology.* Evanston, Ill.: Row, Peterson, 1961.

Timms, D. W. G., *The Urban Mosaic: Towards a Theory of Residential Distribution.* Cambridge, England: Cambridge University Press. 1971.

ARTICLES

Bose, N. K., "Calcutta: A Premature Metropolis," *Scientific American,* 212 (1965), 95–102.

Berry, Brian J. L., and Philip H. Rees, The Factorial Ecology of Calcutta," *American Journal of Sociology*, 74 (March 1969), 445–92.

Caplow, Theodore, "The Ecology of Guatemala City," *Social Forces*, 28 (December 1949), 113–33.

———, "Urban Structure in France," *American Sociological Review*, 17 (October 1952), 544–49.

Dotson, Floyd, and Lillian Dotson, "Ecological Trends in Guadalajara," *Social Forces*, 32 (May 1954), 367–74.

Farley, Reynolds, "The Changing Distribution of Negroes in Metropolitan Areas: The Emergence of Black Suburbs," *American Journal of Sociology*, 75 (January 1970), 512–30.

Gilmore, Harlan W., "The Old New Orleans and the New," *American Sociological Review*, 9 (August 1944), 385–94.

Myers, Jerome K., "Assimilation to the Ecological and Social Systems of a Community, *American Sociological Review,* 15 (June 1950), 367–72.

Penalosa, Fernando, "Ecological Organization of the Transitional City: Some Mexican Evidence," *Social Forces*, 46 (December 1967), 221–29.

Preston, Richard E., "Zone in Transition: Urban Land Use Patterns," *Economic Geography*, 42 (July 1966), 236–60.

Wolf, Eleanor, "The Invasion-Succession Sequence as a Self-fullfilling Prophecy," *Journal of Social Issues*, 13 (1957), 421–36.

9 • Spatial Patterning of Urban Institutions

 If institutions in their physical aspects were located indiscriminately, without rhyme or reason, the ecological picture of cities would be a hodge-podge, a crazy-quilt mosaic, without much apparent orderliness in their spatial arrangement. But such is not the case. The locations of institutional establishments may not always appear rational, but generally there are rational judgments involved in the selection of sites. These judgments represent responses to, and evaluations of, various factors and conditions. In this chapter, we shall examine some of the factors in light of the urban ecological landscape, keeping in mind that they are by no means the same for all cities, and certainly not the same for cities with very different historical backgrounds and cultural settings. There is no universal ecological design for urban communities. If there is any universal aspect of urban ecology it is that change, planned or unplanned, slow or rapid, is constantly occurring, and that the ecological patterns of one decade or century or era are not the same as those that follow. Some of these changes are predictable, others not.

Our discussion will be essentially comparative in nature. We shall consider various "models" or ecological types, observing that large cities may differ from small ones, and, importantly, that the spatial configurations of cities vary from one society to another. What may be true of, say, New Orleans may not be characteristic of Boston or Bangkok or Bogotá.

Factors Associated with Institutional Location

Institutional establishments, especially commercial and industrial concerns in a system of private enterprise, compete for space as well as for customers, patrons, or clients—which, after all, amount to much the same thing. Land values are determined in considerable measure by such competition, the space with the highest actual or potential return being the most expensive. Such values may be artificially inflated, of course, not so much by their earning power as by speculation and high-pressure sales techniques. Aside from the fact that zoning regulations in many countries prohibit the indiscriminate location of factories or businesses in residential areas, competition forces many to locate or relocate where the costs of space are not prohibitive when assessed against the actual or anticipated returns on investment.

Technology has also been an important locational factor. The mass use of the automobile in North American cities has profoundly affected the location of business, industry, and various social or civic institutions. The early formula that business establishments locate at or near the intersection of main transit routes is no longer as applicable as it formerly was. The flexibility of automobile transportation has tended to detach many kinds of business operations from sites at the intersections of fixed transit routes and particularly at points where these routes converge. Such establishments are more likely to locate as close as possible to available parking facilities as well as at points easily accessible to automobile traffic. The development of outlying shopping centers near American and Canadian cities is illustrative of this situation.

Planning and Location

Cities in various parts of the world have developed around a planned central open space, usually square or rectangular in shape. The original plan of many American cities frequently centered around a "public square," which is sometimes used as a community park or a site for public buildings such as a courthouse or state capitol. Facing the square on one or more sides are stores, banks, restaurants, and other customer-oriented enterprises. If these cities or towns continue to grow and become more diversified, the focus of economic and social activities may shift to other streets or areas. Madison, Wisconsin, now a sizable metropolis, has grown up around a public square on which the state capitol is situated. The surrounding streets are lined with business firms or civic buildings, but the center of economic activity has shifted more and more to other streets, drawn especially to the university on the west and to the shifting of population in the same direction.

Once a plan is firmly established, especially in the early stage of development, there is considerable resistance to change. The ecological configuration of Washington, D.C., still bears the visible imprint of the original plan worked out in the eighteenth century by L'Enfant, the French planner. Plaza-centered cities of Latin America owe their distinctive character to their early plans. In the course of time, if the cities grow to large size, the initial plan generally becomes less important as population and institutions develop in directions hardly foreseen by the planners. Connaught Circle in New Delhi was planned as the central shopping center, with streets radiating outward from this point; and although the center has retained much of its original form, retail institutions are now located in various parts of the city.

The influence of early planning may also be observed in numerous European and Latin American cities. In Groningen, a medium-sized Dutch city, the central open space, a feature of the city's original medieval plan, accommodates a major civic structure. Part of the open space is used weekly as a temporary public market for the vending of fruits, vegetables, and other foodstuffs. On surrounding streets there are various retail stores and a major department store, and on the north side of the open center a thirteenth-century church and several municipal or civic buildings. The main shopping district, however, is on a street extending several blocks from the open center. In Bruges, Belgium, a city of comparable size, the open center follows the same design and function as that of Groningen. Similar in some respects is Constitution Place in Athens, a large plaza bounded by the parliament building on one side and such commercial establishments as hotels, specialty shops, and travel agencies on other sides. The ecological patterns of institutions in Latin American cities will be discussed later in this chapter.

Topography has also figured in the developing ecological configurations of institutions and population. Rio de Janeiro, for example, conforms in shape to the presence of mountains on one side of it and the sea on another. Stockholm had to adapt its street patterns and institutional sites to the protruding arms of the sea, and Amsterdam's distinctive configuration represents an adaptation to the network of canals developed on a site in what was initially a swamp several feet below sea level. Duluth, Minnesota, is located at the westernmost tip of Lake Superior, at a break in rail or truck and water transportation; but precipitous bluffs limit expansion of the city to a narrow strip near the shore line, with the result that the city is over twenty miles long and about a half-mile wide.

Continuity and Change:
The Central Business District

As we shall observe later, many changes have altered the traditional structure and functions of the central business district (CBD), commonly known as "downtown." Nevertheless, the area still retains some of its traditional features. It is the major center for the exercise of political and economic power. Here, in the large city, are located the captains of industry, merchant princes, publishers of metropolitan newspapers, leaders of labor, and high-placed bureaucrats and executives who find it expedient to be near the center of power. Here also are offices manned by personnel filling a multiplicity of roles: accountants, economists, and consulting engineers whose expertise is of value to those in positions of power; lawyers whose legal talents are purchasable by corporations engaged in varieties of operations; bookkeepers, stenographers, and private secretaries who perform endless paper work as a part of the system; salespeople, receptionists, and workers in the hotels and restaurants; and cadres of maintenance workers, from janitors and scrubwomen to skilled technicians. The diversity of occupational roles and institutional functions exceeds that of any other sector of the city.

The central business district is also a center of transmitted intelligence. The media of communication converge here where they are used most intensively. Financial institutions are peculiarly sensitized to news concerning political or economic conditions in the country or the world. The stock market, board of trade, or *bourse*, located in the center, is the focus of a complicated network of communications media—telephone, telegraph, radio, television—over which is transmitted information from or to the four corners of the globe, information that may influence the price of securities or commodities and therefore the economic climate of the city or country.

The Core Area and Images of the City

The persistent images that people hold of particular cities are generally the images of the central area more than of outlying sectors. Whatever changes are occurring in London, the core area remains relatively unchanged even though much business and industry have moved away. Here are the famous landmarks such as the Parliament building, the Tower of London, the royal palace, the concentration of government bureaus, historical churches and museums, as well as theaters, major hotels, office buildings, specialty shops, and department stores. It is the hub of the metropolis, the mecca for visitors from all parts of the world. The familiar cliché that if one stands very long in Piccadilly Circus at the center, one is almost sure to meet someone from his home town is only symbolically accurate, but not far from the literal truth.

It is the downtown area of Amsterdam, not its suburbs, that provides the prevailing image of that city, for here are the historic buildings, hotels and restaurants, department stores, canals, travel bureaus, and places of entertainment. In Paris the center is the locus of varied institutions and historic landmarks: the Louvre, the Arch of Triumph, the Eiffel Tower, Notre Dame cathedral, and the omnipresent hotels, restaurants, and theaters, as well as the business establishments, offices, and government buildings. The concentration of towering office buildings in "downtown" and "uptown" areas, the bright lights of Times Square, the theaters, department stores, specialty shops, and fashionable hotels—these are "New York" in the minds of countless persons.

Skyscrapers and Renewal

In some giant American cities there has been a "rebirth" of the central business district. In the 1930's, a depression decade, it appeared that skyscraper-building was approaching an end because numbers of such structures had become financially unprofitable. New York's Empire State building, for many years the world's tallest and most publicized skyscraper, was in serious financial trouble. Furthermore, the very existence of such structures created problems of traffic congestion by concentrating large numbers of workers in a small area. But the predictions were wrong, and the 1950's saw the beginning of a new era of skyscraper construction, an era that has continued into the 1970's. Outdistancing in height all existing skyscrapers are the John Hancock building and the Sears structure in the Loop district of Chicago. Other centrally located massive structures are the Prudential building in Boston, the Merchandise Mart in Chicago, the Pan American building on Park Avenue in New York, and the twin towers of the World Trade Center, also in New York. Hundreds of other tall buildings have been constructed in the downtown districts of American cities. Furthermore, skyscraper apartment buildings, such as the Marina Towers in Chicago's Loop, have been built in or near the central business districts of several cities. New high-rise hotels have also appeared in such cities as Atlanta; Kansas City, Missouri; San Francisco; Denver; Boston; and New York City.

As in American cities, the skyscraper has already modified the profiles of cities in many others parts of the world. London's familiar skyline has now been altered by the appearance of skyscraper office and apartment buildings in or near the city's center. Although there is considerable opposition, on sentimental or esthetic grounds, to the construction of skyscrapers in London, it seems likely that they are the architectural "wave of the future" in that city. An authority on city planning at the University of London remarked in 1964 that "it is fairly safe to prophesy that tall buildings will multiply rapidly in the next decade, and that London will change from a city with a moderately low skyline broken by silhouettes which have been carefully designed, to a city with single and clustered slabs and towers of uneven height. . . ."[1] In Dusseldorf, West Germany, a skyscraper twenty-five stories high has been built on a rehabilitated area at the edge of the central business district. Caracas, Rio de Janeiro, and Mexico City have office buildings exceeding thirty stories, also in or near the main business center. Hong Kong's waterfront is lined with tall office buildings and hotels, and in Tokyo skyscrapers

[1] William Holford, "The Changing Face of London," in Center for Urban Studies, *London: Aspects of Change* (1964), p. 152.

233

The view of Brussels (top) shows the seventeenth-century Grand Palace and Town Hall tower with modern buildings behind. Below, the skyline of Houston is altered by sky-scrapers clustering around the central business district. (Belgian Consulate General, N.Y.—top; Houston Chamber of Commerce—bottom)

tower over the Ginza and other parts of the downtown area. In large cities all over the world tall buildings, many of them scarcely in the skyscraper class, have been constructed since World War II. Aside from their economic functions (or dysfunctions), they become status symbols and landmarks for the communities in which they are located.

Diversity of City Types:
The Preindustrial and the Modern City

Earlier studies of cities tended in the main to be restricted to Western communities, mainly American, and the idea became widely held that urban phenomena were very similar regardless of geographical location. More recent research, however, has revealed an amazing diversity in structural and functional features, particularly in ecological patterning.

The most authoritative sociological study of preindustrial cities is Sjoberg's classic work, *The Preindustrial City* (1960), which we have dealt with at some length in the discussion of the historical development of cities in Chapters 2 and 6. In this study, encompassing a range of cities, including settlements of early historical periods as well as contemporary cities in developing societies, Sjoberg attempts to develop a typology or model of so-called preindustrial cities. But in so doing he understates the wide diversity of these communities, which are separated widely in both space and time. Yet the study does point up important differences between the preindustrial city and the modern industrial community.

The ecological patterns of preindustrial cities are primarily the products of societies having neither the technology nor the values which maximize economic production.[2] In the early cities people and goods moved by foot, horse carts, wagons, chariots, or similar vehicles, and to some extent this is true today in cities of the Third World. Early cities served mainly as political-administrative-religious centers and as forts. According to Sjoberg, the technology and values of the preindustrial city gave rise to three major ecological contrasts with the modern industrial city: (1) The central area, usually a plaza or square, was given over to public buildings and religious structures. The main market was located here. (2) The city was divided into rather self-sufficient quarters which were inhabited by distinct ethnic and class groups. Tradesmen and craftsmen typically worked in the houses they occupied. (3) Land use was not highly differentiated. Commercial, craft, and residential functions were scattered throughout the city and were often served by the same site. This theoretical model does not imply that variations in the

[2] Gideon Sjoberg, *The Preindustrial City* (1960), pp. 80–107. See also Chapters 2, 3, and 6 in this volume.

In Katmandu, capital of Nepal, goods are transported by human carriers. In contrast, technologically advanced industrial countries have vast networks of highways for transporting goods and people. (Noel P. Gist—top; Atlanta Chamber of Commerce—bottom)

pattern did not exist. Then, as now, each city was unique in numerous respects.

In today's world the model provided by Sjoberg does not always fit the actual situation. Some cities such as Aden in Yemen, Mecca in Saudi Arabia, or Katmandu in Nepal conform fairly closely to the historical model, but others in the developing world, a mixture of the traditional and the modern, have already been so influenced by modern technology and organization that they might properly be called *emergent* industrial centers. Cities like Madras and Ahmedabad in India have vast textile factories whose modern equipment and economic structure are comparable to those of industrial plants in Western manufacturing centers. In these cities, and many others of the developing world, much small-scale manufacturing is carried on in the home or in small structures widely scattered over the city's landscape. Some of the major cities have fairly large retail, centrally located establishments, but many business transactions in such cities as Singapore, Jakarta, or Bangkok commonly take place in the "shophouse," a structure combining residence and business activity, with shops on the ground floor and living quarters behind or above.[3]

Clustering and Scattering

Some institutions can compete more effectively if they are located near other institutions engaged in a similar function. Madison Avenue in New York is the locus of many advertising firms, and Wall Street, in the same city, represents a concentration of financial institutions. Large hotels are clustered in a small area in Miami Beach and along the ocean front of Atlantic City, all competing for customers with well-filled purses. Many fashionable or exotic restaurants have clustered in Soho, a small district in central London, and travel agencies cluster on a few central streets in Paris. A street in Bangalore, India, is lined for two or three blocks with shops displaying textiles, and close by is a street displaying various hardware items. Large department stores are located in the Ginza, the principal shopping district of Tokyo.

Many institutions also maintain a symbiotic relationship with institutions that are different in various respects. This functional interdependence represents a kind of linkage which can be best maintained, usually, if the institutions are spatially near. Hotels, restaurants, amusement places, and speciality shops are linked together because

[3] Norton S. Ginsburg, "The Great City of Southeast Asia," *American Journal of Sociology*, 60 (March 1955), 459. Compare Richard J. Coughlin, "The Chinese in Bangkok: A Commercial-Oriented Minority," *American Sociological Review*, 20 (June 1955), 315, and Richard J. Coughlin, *Double Identity* (1961).

The Ginza, a central business district in Tokyo. Here are located large department stores, fashionable cafes, office buildings, and recreational facilities such as night clubs. (Noel P. Gist)

customers of one establishment may likely patronize one or more of the others. Finance companies may function most effectively if they are near law or accounting firms. Major theaters in London's central area are conveniently close to hotels, travel bureaus, and retail shops, as well as near historic landmarks attracting tourists. The proliferation of outlying shopping centers in American cities is further evidence of this linkage in that the establishments in these centers usually include department stores, discount houses, restaurants, supermarkets, variety stores, and specialty shops, all of which can benefit from their proximity to each other.

These linkages may be weakened or strengthened, even broken, as a result of technological, economic, and social changes, or even changes in buying habits or recreational behavior. If the linkage is weakened or broken, the result may be bankruptcy, or the movement of establishments to new locations. Many business or industrial establishments have severed their ties with other institutions and moved to outlying locations where they may be able to compete more effectively.

Some institutions do not depend on proximity to other similar institutions, as has been particularly true of the school and church, which do not compete for space. Elementary schools are scattered widely over the urban landscape, each usually located within ten or fifteen minutes' walking or busing time from the homes of their students. Their location is determined by their accessibility to an area's school population. The same principle applies to high schools, although the distance between them may be considerably greater than between elementary schools. As the area of residential occupancy moves outward, so do the schools. Churches, likewise, are sensitive to the needs of their parishioners and therefore tend to locate at points of maximum accessibility for the people they serve. Of 48 churches in a medium-sized midwestern city in 1972, only 12 were in, or adjacent to, the downtown business district. Some downtown churches and synagogues, of course, remain in central areas, partly because they cannot afford the expense of moving to a different location, but also because they serve the daytime working population.

Centralization and Decentralization

Certain types of institutions tend to concentrate in the central area of a city. In ecological terminology this tendency or process is designated as *centralization*, although some writers refer to it as *nucleation*. Cities in which the central district is the only area of importance are termed *mononucleated*, while cities in which two or more areas are functionally important are considered *polynucleated*.

It is commonly known that many institutions can function more effectively if located away from the focal center. The tendency of them to so locate, or relocate, is usually referred to as *decentralization*. Traditionally, most cities have at one time been highly centralized in that most institutions developed within the inner zone. With the growth of communities, the expansion of the economy and technology, and the proliferation of organized economic and social activities, people and institutions became increasingly decentralized.

Institutional decentralization is undoubtedly more pronounced in the United States and Canada than in other countries, a development due in considerable measure to mass transportation by automobile. But decentralization of economic and social institutions has also occurred, especially since World War II, in metropolitan areas on every continent, varying in form and degree from one metropolis or country to another. Since technology is more developed in Europe than in, say, most African, Asian, or Middle Eastern countries, the decentralizing process and its ecological manifestations are more apparent in European cities than in the others.

Reasons for Decentralization

In seeking an explanation for the decentralization of industry and certain distributive facilities, one discovers that no single factor is responsible. Rather, changes in technology, economic organization, population distribution, and social standards usually influence the decentralizing process. To some extent, industrial relocation is partly a response to the changing distribution of population in the urban community because industry sometimes follows the labor force. However, the converse may be true: the work force may follow in the wake of a shifting industry, gravitating in that direction in order to be nearer the work site. One of the common complaints of industrial workers these days is that the decentralized plants are so remote from their residential locations that transportation to and from the work site is expensive, inconvenient, time-consuming, and physically wearing.

Certain technological developments have increased industrial flexibility. One is the changeover from machinery driven by water or steam to factories operated by electric power. In terms of available power, one site in a metropolitan area may be about as favorable as another. Second, the motor truck for transportation of materials, raw and finished, together with the passenger automobile for the journey to work, has increased the freedom of industry to operate profitably in locations far from sites on railroad lines or waterways. Third, only outside the central city can industrial or wholesale firms usually afford the large sites required for truck-loading areas and for the parking of workers' cars. Finally, production techniques in modern factories often require horizontal assembly-line methods, thus outmoding many of the multistory factories built in an earlier industrial era.

Special tax concessions, zoning provisions, or free land may be offered by cities or suburbs as attractions for industrial establishments, but often such communities favor light industries or research installations whose personnel are mainly skilled or professional workers in the upper-income brackets. The physical plants of such enterprises may have the appearance of a college campus or a modern civic building, and the industrial processes are not likely to clutter up and pollute the environment. For most communities an adjacent glue factory is not as welcome as a plant that manufactures precision instruments. Numerous communities have been opposed to the nearby location of such establishments as an atomic energy plant or an airport.

Downtown and Outertown

The downtown area, or central business district, in North American cities is a manifestation of the centralizing process. Although the central business district is usually viable institutionally, major spatial, structural, and functional changes in many cities are profoundly affecting the ecological patterns. Many institutions that once were found almost exclusively in the central business district have gravitated to outlying locations. By the 1970's some 10,000 shopping centers in American cities had been established at points removed from the downtown area. The shopping centers themselves vary in size from small neighborhood clusters for "convenience" shopping to large centers drawing customers from a considerable area, often the entire city.

The Ala Moana shopping center in Honolulu, the Northland center in Detroit, and the Northwest center in St. Louis are examples of giant institutional complexes that attract customers or clients from a wide area and that function in many respects as do the central business districts. Outlying department stores are often branches of a parent downtown store, but many are independent institutions newly established at locations remote from the downtown area. "Discount houses," a variation of the traditional department store, are usually located in an area where land values are lower than they are in the downtown area and where space is available for car-parking by both customers and employees.

Traditionally, the downtown areas of Western cities have been the locus of hotels, generally situated at points easily accessible to transportation facilities such as railway or steamship terminals. Although most of these hotels remain in the downtown areas, many of them catering to conventions or other major gatherings, in recent years new hotels have tended to become dispersed over the urban landscape. Motels serving the automobile-traveling public are found inside the city and on the outskirts. Some cities now provide parking facilities in peripheral locations for campers and other forms of touring vehicles.

Certain types of commercial recreation are no longer exclusively concentrated in or near the downtown section, but tend to locate at points farther out, sometimes on the urban fringe. Some of these facilities provide varied forms of recreation under a common roof such as bowling, skating, billiards, dancing, and concerts. Movie theaters are also widely dispersed. The peripheral drive-in theater is a post-World War II innovation, a product of the automobile age. The same decentralizing trend has also occurred in the location of offices, especially such enterprises as insurance companies, which are not directly dependent on pedestrian traffic or on other forms of economic activity. The John Hancock building in Kansas City and the Prudential buildings in Minneapolis and Houston are examples of major corporations with offices located a considerable distance from the central business district.

Is Downtown Becoming a Ghost Town?

The shifting of institutions from the center to the periphery of the city, as well as the competition afforded by gigantic merchandising corporations, has made it difficult for many centrally located institutions to carry out their intended functions. Customers or clients have tended to shift their patronage to establishments that are more accessible or conveniently located. The result has been, for many North American cities, economic strangulation of the central business district, although some institutions are more affected than others. One index of this change is the kind and number of establishments that have been forced to terminate their operations, among them older hotels unable to compete profitably with modern chain hotels and motels; downtown automobile display rooms requiring considerable space and parking facilities; small grocery stores and meat markets that are driven out of business by supermarkets; hardware, furniture, and drygoods stores that have lost business to department stores or discount houses carrying a wide range of products; and "mama and papa" hole-in-the-wall eating places unable to survive the competition with modernized restaurants. Within the central business district of many American cities are structures whose empty hulls are witness to the economic, technological, and ecological changes occurring in the community. The end-product of this process is urban blight and decay.[4]

"Old Town" and "New Town"

Many modern communities of ancient origin have literally outgrown the old city; in the course of their expansion new institutional centers have developed, commonly having the character of a modern city. Sometimes the new city has encircled and encapsulated the old city; in other instances the new city is a peripheral development. Benares, India, for example, claims that the original settlement, now surrounded by the modern city, is the oldest "living" city in existence, as well it may be. Life in the old city is undoubtedly similar to what it was hundreds of years ago. Here the streets, little more than narrow passageways between structures, are lined with tiny stalls displaying traditional goods for a traditional population. Almost cheek by jowl, however, is modern Benares, featuring luxury hotels, industrial firms, a major university, and shops displaying luxury items. Water Street in Hong Kong is the locale of Chinese people whose ways of life and institutions are traditional in the strictest sense of the word, but on the waterfront and across the narrow strait, in Kowloon, is the world of wealth, luxury, bright lights, and skyscrapers. The drab "old city" of Honolulu contrasts with Waikiki, which features glamorous hotels, fashionable restaurants, and other emporia catering to the tourist trade.

Often the traditional population and their institutions cluster in en-

---

[4] For a discussion of these changes, see James E. Vance, Jr., "Focus on Downtown," in Larry S. Bourne, ed., *Internal Structure of the City* (1971), pp. 112–20.

claves at various points in a city, contrasting with the people and institutions located elsewhere in the same community and representing a different way of life. Abu-Lughod presents this contrasting social and ecological picture of Cairo.[5] The traditional and the modern in Cairo are not restricted to a single locality but exist in several areas of the metropolis. Yet the "old" and the "new" are worlds apart in many respects.

Dual or Multiple Centers

Some cities in countries once dominated by Western colonial powers and subjected to prolonged Western influence have developed two commercial centers. A Western-style center of fashionable stores stocked with the latest American and European goods coexists with a traditional center of native stalls and merchandise. Such dual commercial centers, which may or may not be near each other, are a feature of many large cities in India, Southeast Asia, the Middle East, Africa, and Latin America. The retail structure of Manila, in the Philippines, combines many Eastern features with Western influences from Spain and the United States.[6]

In the cities of India, centralization of commerce is less apparent than in American cities. The main bazaar or market is centrally located but is not equivalent to the central business district of American cities. Also, this commercial function is widely diffused in the city because many other bazaars are located in neighborhoods and are somewhat comparable in function to the small shopping center in a Western city. These bazaars usually include a large number of small, privately owned or managed specialized shops which have for sale an endless variety of consumer goods—fruit and vegetables, cloth, articles for personal adornment, household appliances, luxury items, and so on. They are the traditional version of the modern department store.

The Varying Size of the Central Business District

The central business districts of most cities in developing countries are generally much smaller in area than those of cities comparable in size in industrialized societies. If one compares Chicago and Bombay, cities of similar size, the differences are impressive, and the same contrast holds

[5] Janet Abu-Lughod, *Cairo: 1001 Years of the City Victorious* (1971). See also her "Varieties of Urban Experience: Contrast, Coexistence, and Coalescence in Cairo," in Ira M. Lapidus, ed., *Middle Eastern Cities* (1969).

[6] Wallace E. McIntyre, "The Retail Pattern of Manila," *Geographic Review*, 45 (January 1955), 66–80.

when comparing Teheran or Cairo with London or Paris. In describing Calcutta's central business district, Kar writes: "The very small area of this zone, in comparison with any Western city of its magnitude . . . strongly contrasts with those of Western metropolises."[7] Our own study of Bangalore, whose population exceeds a million, confirms this generalization. Like many others, that city presents a polynucleated pattern of business, with a central business district only slightly similar to the downtown area of a Western city comparable in size. The comparative underdevelopment of the urban economy and technology in these countries probably accounts for the underdevelopment of the central business districts.

The Planned Shopping Center

Decentralized retail establishments, whether clustered at a focal point or located separately from other retail stores, are not an exclusive phenomenon of North American cities. This decentralizing trend is also apparent in European and Asian cities. But the *planned* shopping center, located in an outlying sector of a city, is more or less distinctive of cities in North America. Such centers are customarily planned by privately owned and managed land-development corporations, but subject to varying degrees of regulation by the municipality in which they are located. The usual procedure is for the corporation to acquire the land, erect the structures, and lease them to companies or individuals for business or related purposes. As we have noted, such centers are functional for the automobile age.

The Central Plaza in
Latin American Cities

The central plaza, or *plaza mayor*, in Latin American cities is an important ecological feature of the basic design of the Indian cities that existed before the Spanish conquest, as well as of the city plan the conquerors imposed upon the existing cities. Aztec cities, for example, were plaza-centered—Tenochtitlan, the forerunner of Mexico City, was so designed.[8] This pattern has persisted, although with the growth of population and the proliferation of institutions the form has undergone many changes.[9] The configuration has been variously described for such

[7] N. R. Kar, "Urban Characteristics of the City of Calcutta," *Indian Population Bulletin* (April 1960), p. 36.

[8] George C. Vaillant, *The Aztecs of Mexico* (1950), ch. 13, and Francis Violich, *Cities of Latin America* (1944), pp. 22–25.

[9] Leo F. Schnore, "On the Spatial Structure of Cities in the Two Americas," in Philip M. Hauser and Leo F. Schnore, eds., *The Study of Urbanization*, (1967), pp. 347–98.

cities as Sucre, Bolivia;[10] Guadalajara, Mexico;[11] Mexico City;[12] Guatemala City;[13] and La Paz, Bolivia, and Lima, Peru.[14]

The plaza design is characteristic of most cities, large and small, in Mexico, including the great metropolis, Mexico City, and medium-sized cities such as Puebla, Vera Cruz, and Mèrida. Often the plazas are the hub of various social activities, providing an appropriate setting for the evening's promenade and a place where friendly visiting can be carried on. Some of them take on the character of a small park, tree-lined and graced with flowers. Initially, the elite resided in the immediate vicinity of the plaza, but in recent times many of them have moved centrifugally to more fashionable or comfortable districts farther out.

The central plaza in Mexico City, generally referred to as the Zòcalo, is the historic hub of the city, but is now more important for its religious and political functions than for its economic role. On one side of the plaza are administrative and legislative buildings. Situated on its inner space is the national cathedral, and facing it on three sides, and on nearby side streets, are various retail stores and a major department store. With the rapid growth of the metropolis, commercial enterprises have tended to shift southward, lining major thoroughfares for several miles, as far as Chapultepec Park. Along or near the main thoroughfares that extend southward from the Zòcalo are the Palace of Fine Arts, fashionable hotels, apartments, restaurants, foreign embassies, specialty shops catering to the tourist traffic, travel agencies, banks, offices, and a major department store. One of the main markets, dealing with a wide variety of relatively inexpensive goods, is located several blocks east of the fashionable hotel and shopping streets, and to the north of the Zòcalo are clusters of small shops serving a low-income clientele.

Although the classical ecological pattern is still apparent in Latin America, it has been virtually obliterated in some major cities by the rapid increase of population and the expansion of business and industry. Nevertheless, the major commercial and financial establishments are generally located in or near the center of the city.[15] The decentralization of business has not occurred in these cities as it has in the United States;

[10] Harry B. Hawthorne and Audrey E. Hawthorne, "The Shape of a City," *Sociology and Social Research*, 33 (November 1948), 87–89.

[11] Floyd and Lillian Dotson, "Ecological Trends in the City of Guadalajara, Mexico," *Social Forces*, 32 (May 1954), 367–74; and Norman S. Hayner in collaboration with Una Middleton Hayner, *New Patterns in Old Mexico* (1966).

[12] Norman S. Hayner, "Mexico City: Its Growth and Configuration," *American Journal of Sociology*, 50 (January 1945), 295–304.

[13] Theodore Caplow, "The Social Ecology of Guatemala City," *Social Forces*, 28 (December 1949), 113–33.

[14] Walter D. Harris, Jr., *The Growth of Latin American Cities* (1971), pp. 253–54.

[15] *Ibid.*, pp. 257–58.

there are few shopping centers comparable to the thousands that have been developed in American cities. Doubtless one reason for this difference is that intracity transportation in Latin American cities consists mainly of public transit. In this respect Latin American cities resemble most European and Asian centers. However, small business enterprises are widely distributed throughout the residential districts. Caplow observed that in Guatemala City there is no sharp break between the commercial district and the residential zone; rather, the business area tapers off gradually, and with the exception of "foreign-type" suburbs to the south, there is no residential area completely without business or industrial establishments.[16] Food stores, textile factories, printing plants, churches, government buildings, barber shops, and dressmaking establishments are widely distributed over the city, most of them within walking distance of the homes of customers or employees.

But this pattern is not universal in Latin America. Caplow and his associates describe San Juan, Puerto Rico, as an "unnucleated" city, as distinguished from a mononucleated or polynucleated community. "In the unnucleated city," they write, "there is very little reason for a store or factory or government office to be one place rather than another. . . . Workshops, palaces, and hovels are likely to be found on the same street."[17] And in describing the central district they observe: "The mixture of functions is extraordinary. Expensive villas nestle between lumberyards. An automobile body shop faces an apartment house. A twelve-story steel and glass office building sprouts incongruously from a bed of semidetached wooden houses. A medical clinic is sandwiched between a warehouse and a driving school."[18]

The Institutional Ecology of Bangalore

In Bangalore, a South India metropolis, the major shopping center, known as Central Market, corresponds only roughly to the central business district in American cities. The market represents a focal point of retail activities concerned with such consumer goods as fruits, vegetables, flowers, household hardware, and inexpensive clothing. On nearby streets are located shops specializing in such merchandise as silk and cotton goods, silverware, drugs, and jewelry. Shops having the same type of merchandise tend to cluster together, sometimes creating specialized streets. The center for "big business," about a mile north of Central Market, includes major banking and insurance firms, film-distributing companies, a large transportation firm, numerous business

[16] Caplow, *op. cit.*
[17] Theodore Caplow, Sheldon Stryker, and Samuel E. Wallace, *The Urban Ambience* (1964), p. 22.
[18] *Ibid.*, p. 39.

offices, and large movie theaters. There are also several secondary commercial districts located in various parts of the city. Wholesale and retail functions are more closely identified in Bangalore than in an American city. Near Central Market, a cluster of wholesale establishments handles grain and vegetables and supplies the retailers in the market. Within the market area, wholesale and retail business are sometimes combined under the same roof. In this general area, near the railroad station, there are numerous small hotels and roominghouses, but the major hotels are dispersed in various parts of the city, mainly in or near high-income districts. Even municipal or government buildings such as the city hall, post office, and courts of law are some distance from the central business zone.

Decentralization of Wholesaling and Manufacturing

In his classic description of urban ecology in American cities, Burgess noted that wholesale houses tended to cluster adjacent to, although not necessarily within, the central retailing district of large cities; this was particularly true of Chicago. But this pattern has also undergone extensive change. The wholesale function has declined in recent years because many manufacturers are able to market their product directly to retail establishments or to an appropriate "middle man." In the case of perishable products, such as fruits and vegetables, the wholesaler is still located at a site near the central business district, from which the commodities can be distributed to retail outlets over the city or metropolitan region.

Light Industry in North America

Light manufacturing plants in North American cities were generally located on or near fixed transportation routes such as railways and waterways, and many were situated well within the inner city. The manufactured products could thus be shipped by rail or water, or distributed to various points within the city. Since light manufacturing may not require much ground space in the production process, and may even occur in multistoried buildings, as in the case of printing or the manufacture of garments or jewelry, such industrial enterprises accommodated fairly well to central-city location, near an ample labor supply in the inner city.

But technological, economic, and demographic changes have made it desirable, often necessary, that light manufacturing plants gravitate to more decentralized locations, as described above on pages 239–40. This by no means implies that all light manufacturing has moved to the suburbs or urban fringe. Indeed, there are instances in which plants have remained at or near their original locations in the inner core. The garment industry in New York, for example, clings closely to the retail and financial center, and near hotels, theaters, and restaurants for the convenience of out-of-town buyers. Many of the New York garment manufacturing plants are in multistoried buildings because they do not require large amounts of ground space. Communication-oriented industries also tend to be optimally located at points affording easy and direct contacts with consumers and with various agencies of mass communication. It is not an accident that daily newspapers are published (manufactured) in the downtown areas of cities. It should be noted, however, that the actual printing of books, magazines, and other literature may be done at locations somewhat remote from the central business district, while the editing, distribution, and financial transactions usually occur within the center. We remarked earlier that in many cities of Europe and the developing countries of Asia, Africa, and the Middle East, light manufacturing, such as the so-called cottage industries, or small shops featuring the products of skilled handicraftsmen, are widely distributed over the city.

Heavy Industry in North America

Until the late nineteenth century, heavy industry in the United States and Canada was generally located in the central core of cities, near wharves, docks, and railroad sidings, and close to the center of a labor supply. Early in the twentieth century, the process of decentralization began and has continued to the present. Because heavy manufacturing requires a great deal of ground space and produces or utilizes bulky materials, locations beyond the congested or built-up portions of the city became desirable or even necessary. This is especially true of plants producing automobiles, airplanes, petroleum products, farm machinery, steel, lumber, cement, or ships. The essential characteristics of heavy industry suggest the reasons for decentralization: (1) comparatively large size; (2) large ground area per worker required; (3) the presence of nuisance features such as odors, noise, and fire hazards; (4) the necessity of specialized buildings; (5) serious problems of waste disposal; (6) the requirement of large quantities of fuel or water; (7) and the availability of ample parking facilities for employees.

An important aspect of industrial decentralization is the planning and development of industrial "parks," usually located on the city's outskirts. Industrial parks are not remotely removed from cities or towns because accessibility is a primary condition in the choice of their sites. Therefore, most of them are within ten miles of a central city, nearly all are near or on major highways, and many are served by railroads.

Many heavy industries are located at points well beyond the downtown district, but not so far away as to be out of reach of the workers who reside in the central city. The gigantic automobile assembly plants in the vicinity of Detroit, airplane plants in Seattle and St. Louis, major electronics plants near Kansas City, steel furnaces near Chicago and Pittsburgh, shipbuilding facilities near various port cities, or oil refineries near Los Angeles and Houston are examples. It may be noted, however, that the most visible aspect of manufacturing such products as automobiles and airplanes is actually the assembly of parts that have been fabricated in many widely dispersed factories whose operations are carefully synchronized with the operations of the central assembly plant that turns out the finished product. McKenzie wrote of automotive plants in the Detroit area as gigantic assembly lines reaching to many remote places where the parts are actually manufactured and sent to the central assembly plant. "The transportation channels along which the different units are conveyed to the assemblying industry might also be considered as extension of that factory's assembly lines."[19]

In some instances industrial plants abandon entirely the city in which they are located and move to other areas or regions. This occurred in the case of the textile industry, which was initially centered in the cities of New England, which were far removed from the cotton fields of the South or the wool-growing ranches in other regions. In the course of time the textile plants gravitated to cities in the South, closer to the supply of cotton and with the advantages of lower production costs. The massive stockyards of Chicago, a city dubbed by the poet Carl Sandburg as "hog butcher of the world," were initially located on the city's outskirts; as the city expanded they eventually were encircled by the growing metropolis. But by 1972 they were almost completely abandoned, their functions being transferred to plants in other midwestern cities such as Omaha, Des Moines, or Oklahoma City. The manufacturing of shoes was once a major industry in St. Louis, but this function has been shifted to numerous small cities over the region where operating costs are lower.

Industrial Location
in Europe

Until the turn of the nineteenth century, most of the manufacturing in Europe was done inside the city. With the growth of metropolitan population and the expansion of the economy, factories requiring considerable space began to develop on the fringe of these communities. Although there are many small factories and workshops in such cities as Paris, Vienna, and Milan, heavy industries have either moved to outlying areas or, if newly established, have located initially in these areas. If the cities were encircled by protective walls during the Middle Ages or

[19] R. D. McKenzie, *The Metropolitan Community* (1933), p. 79.

before, the walls themselves were unable to contain the burgeoning population and institutions of modern times and therefore were often dismantled to make room for newer developments. Heavy industries in the metropolitan areas of such manufacturing centers as Rotterdam, Milan, Dusseldorf, and Paris are usually located some distance from the cities' boundaries.

In some European countries metropolitan and national planning has included the location or relocation of industries at points considered most appropriate for this kind of economic activity. Since World War II, the British government has taken the initiative in industrial planning, emphasizing the necessity of decentralization and offering inducements to industries to move to the countryside. The "new town" movement is an aspect of this trend. A score or more of new satellite cities have been developed in Britain, their purpose being to attract industry and people to the outlying areas and therefore relieve the internal pressures and congestion in such cities as London, Manchester, and Birmingham. The government of The Netherlands is undertaking a similar plan to induce industrial firms to locate, or relocate, in a newly planned community removed from the heavily populated urban centers on the western rim of the country—the *Randstad*, as this area is termed in Holland.

Industrial Location in
Developing Countries

The peripheral growth of industry is not confined to cities of the West. In Bangalore, India, for example, the trend is definitely toward the development of heavy industry on the outskirts of the city, or even well beyond the municipal boundary. On the east side of the city, some five or six miles from the municipal boundary, are located two large-scale industries manufacturing airplanes and telephones. On the northeast, at the edge of the city, is a large tobacco factory; and on the west, also in the fringe area, is a factory manufacturing electrical equipment. A large textile mill was established at the edge of the city early in the present century, but since that time the city has so expanded that the mill is now well within the municipal limits. An area on the western fringe has been set aside as an "industrial park." On the whole, however, decentralization of industry in Indian cities has been limited. Certain light industries, including the cottage industries, are widely distributed over the municipal area. Another factor unfavorable to industrial decentralization in developing countries is transportation; most workers are forced to walk to work or ride bicycles, although work trains are provided for employees in the airplane factory in Bangalore.

On the whole, however, most developing societies are not highly industrialized, except for small-scale industries in which the products are usually fabricated by human hands. Most large-scale industry is a

recent development. Cities that were administered by colonial governments were usually administrative centers, port cities whose principal
function was the shipment of raw materials to the colonial countries for
industrial processing, or commercial cities engaged in the distribution of
consumer goods to local residents. With the widespread adoption of
planning procedures, it seems probable that new and other large-scale
operations will be located either on the fringe of metropolitan centers or
near small cities. The peripheral location of numerous textile mills in
Coimbatore, a medium-sized city in South India, is an example of recent
industrial planning.

The Journey to Work

The most important development in urban transportation in Western
cities has been the mass use of the private automobile, which has made
it possible for workers and shoppers to move still farther from the place
of employment or business transactions. As industry and business have
become increasingly decentralized, the centripetal flow of traffic has
been reversed to a considerable degree: workers and shoppers travel
increasingly in a centrifugal direction to reach their destination. In
addition, there are cross-currents of travel in which workers or shoppers
move laterally as well as centrifugally or centripetally.

With the development of metropolitan regions, closely associated with
revolutionary changes in transportation technology, large numbers of
workers daily commute long distances to the work site, sometimes by
commuter trains or buses, but more often, in the United States and
Canada, by private automobile. Every large city in the West is now the
center of a network of motor car routes radiating out from the central
community and connecting subordinate hinterland settlements that lie
within the sphere of influence of a dominant metropolis. With modern
highways making possible rapid automobile travel, workers may travel
as far as fifty or seventy-five miles to the work site at no greater cost in
time than was true a half-century or so ago for a much shorter distance.
Traveling from one to two hours daily has become virtually a norm for
thousands of urban workers in almost every industrial country. Thus,
towns and villages and open-country communities that were once relatively isolated have been brought more closely within the economic and
cultural orbit of metropolitan centers. Even in countries where the
private automobile is not used extensively as a commuter vehicle,
electric or steam commuter trains daily transport cargoes of workers to
and from such great cities as Cairo, Bombay, and Manila.

The distance traveled and the time spent in the ebb and flow of persons
to and from the work site or market place varies, of course, with the size
of the city, the location of the residents, and the mode of travel. A study

of the journey to work in Pittsburgh indicated that work-trip distance for whites increased with the rise in occupational class, but that for blacks there was no consistent association between status and distance traveled to work.[20] Low-status white workers live closer to the place of employment than low-status blacks—2.57 miles compared with 3.38 miles. The explanation for these differences is that blacks are usually residentially segregated and are therefore not always free to live at the most convenient location for their journey to work. As industry became increasingly decentralized to locations well beyond the city proper, whites had more freedom than blacks in selecting home sites closer to their work sites. Thus, the higher cost of transportation to work bears more heavily on blacks than on whites, a difference that is especially important in light of the relatively low incomes of black workers. This situation apparently applies to many large cities in the United States.

Summary

In this chapter we have considered the ecological patterning of institutions in cities. At the outset we discussed the various factors associated with institutional location. We considered the various forms the central business district has taken, its characteristic institutions and the changes they are undergoing, and the ways in which it differs in the cities of industrial and developing societies. We also considered the phenomenon of clustering, that is, the tendency for institutions of like function to locate near each other, as well as the formation of linkages among institutions having different functional or structural features. Considerable attention was given to major ecological configurations of cities in Latin America, Asia, and Europe. The distribution of light and heavy industry and of wholesaling was considered, along with the changes that are occurring in the ecology of industrial institutions as a result of technological, organizational, and social developments. Finally, we related the character of the journey to work to industrial distribution, noting the effect of ecological change of the trip of the worker to his place of employment. From this discussion of ecological patterning of urban institutions we are led logically to a consideration of the inner city in its manifold aspects, the subject of Chapter 10.

[20] James O. Wheeler, "Work-Trip Length and the Ghetto," *Land Economics*, 44 (February 1968), 107–12. See also John F. Kain, "Urban Travel Behavior" in Leo F. Schnore and Henry Fagin, eds., *Urban Research and Policy Planning* (1967), pp. 161–92; and Donald R. Deskins, "Race, Residence, and Workplace in Detroit, 1880–1965," *Economic Geography*, 48 (January 1972), 79–94.

Selected Bibliography

BOOKS

Abu-Lughod, Janet L., *Cairo: 1001 Years of the City Victorious*. Princeton: Princeton University Press, 1971.

Birch, David L., *The Economic Future of City and Suburb*. New York: Committee for Economic Development, 1970.

Bourne, Larry S., ed., *Internal Structure of the City*. New York: Oxford University Press, 1971.

Caplow, Theodore, Sheldon Stryker, and Samuel E. Wallace, *The Urban Ambience*. Totowa, N. J.: Bedminster Press, 1964.

Dickinson, Robert E., *The City Region in Western Europe*. New York: Humanities Press, 1967.

Harris, Walter D. Jr., *The Growth of Latin American Cities*. Athens: Ohio University Press, 1971.

Hauser, Philip M., and Leo F. Schnore, eds., *The Study of Urbanization*. New York: Wiley, 1965.

Hawley, Amos H., *Urban Society*. New York: Ronald Press, 1971.

Liepmann, Kate, *The Journey to Work: Its Significance for Industry and Community Life*. New York: Oxford University Press, 1944.

Pahl, R. E., *Patterns of Urban Life*. New York: Humanities Press, 1970.

Vernon, Raymond, *The Changing Economic Function of the Central City*. New York: Committee for Economic Development, 1959.

ARTICLES

Berry, Brian J. L. and Philip R. Rees, "The Factorial Ecology of Calcutta," *American Journal of Sociology*, 74 (March 1969), 445–92.

Brush, John E., "The Morphology of Indian Cities," in Roy Turner, ed., *India's Urban Future*, pp. 57–70. Berkeley and Los Angeles: University of California Press, 1962.

———, "Spatial Patterns of Population in Indian Cities," *Geographical Review*, 58 (July 1968), 362–92.

Brody, S. A., "Urban Characteristics of Centralization," *Sociology and Social Research*, 46 (April 1962), 326–31.

Caplow, Theodore, "The Ecology of Guatemala City," *Social Forces*, 28 (December 1949), 113–33.

———, "Urban Structure in France," *American Sociological Review*, 17 (October 1952), 544–49.

Gist, Noel P., "The Ecology of Bangalore: An East-West Comparison," *Social Forces*, 35 (May 1957), 356–65.

Hauser, Francis L., "Ecological Patterns of Four European Cities," *Journal of American Institute of Planners*, 17 (1951), 111–29.

Penalosa, Fernando, "Ecological Organization of the Transitional City," *Social Forces*, 46 (December 1967), 221–29.

Preston, R. E. "Zone in Transition: Urban Land Use Patterns," *Economic Geography*, 42 (July 1966), 236–36.

10 • The Inner City

In this chapter and the following on the sub-urbs, we will discuss the ecological aspects of the two major segments of the metropolis. The inner city and suburb are two sides of the same coin, for they are inextricably linked as an economic and social entity, although not as a governmental one. Therefore we shall begin by describing the types of city-suburban interrela-tionships, moving on to examine the changing role of the inner city as the "heart" of the metropolis. The nature of city-suburban interrelationships and the changes they are undergoing raise basic questions about the direction in which American society is moving, particularly with regard to employment and housing opportuni-ties for the poor and minorities.

One might well ask "Whose inner city?"—the tourist's, the com-muter's, the runaway teenager's, the black ghetto resident's, or the high-rise luxury apartment house resident's? Although we have already explored the variety of inner-city areas in Chapter 7, we shall consider additional aspects here. One might also ask "Which inner city?", for there are definitional variations as to what constitutes the inner city.

The inner city is not only a place but also a state of mind, even an ideology. One's opinion of the inner city, whether based on factually true information or not, influences one's behavior. We will discuss some of these points of view and their programmatic consequences. Belief systems have an important ecological impact since they are reflected in migration patterns and in policies concerning the placement of sub-sidized housing, transportation routes, and financial grants.

The Ecology of City-Suburban Relationships

For over a decade, sociologist Leo F. Schnore has investigated city-suburban relationships to determine whether they conform to the

Burgess model of ecological distribution,[1] according to which the city expands from the center outward, resulting in the concentration in suburbs of higher socioeconomic groups who can afford the newer, more spacious housing there, as well as the increased transportation costs in getting them to and from work. City-suburban comparisons should therefore show that the city population is lower in socioecomomic status than the suburban population.

Schnore's testing of this proposition indicates that, while it is true in some degree, major variations occur which raise significant questions. Initially Schnore took as his data base the 200 Urbanized Areas of the 1960 census,[2] and defined the city as the municipally bounded central city of 50,000 or more and the remainder of the Urbanized Area as the suburbs. He then presented city-suburban comparisons of socioeconomic status using percentages of white collar workers, median family income, and percentage of those who had completed high school. On an aggregate basis the city population had lower socioeconomic status, but, as Schnore points out, a city-suburban generalization on that basis would be misleading.[3] Both size and age (measured as the decade when the central city first reached a population of 50,000) of the Urbanized Area are correlated with city-suburban status differentials. The older and larger Urbanized Areas manifest the Burgess pattern of low socio-economic status groups concentrated in the central city and high socio-economic status groups in the suburbs, but many of the smaller, "younger" Urbanized Areas do not display this contrast.

Types of City-Suburban
Contrast

More detailed study by Schnore revealed at least six types of city-suburban contrast.[4] Using educational attainment of the male population 25 years of age or over as the measure of socioeconomic status in the 200 Urbanized Areas, Schnore constructed an "index of suburbanization" for each of eight educational levels, indicating the extent to which a given level was represented among the residential population in proportion to the total male population 25 years of age or over. In this index, levels over 100 indicate overrepresentation in the city, and levels below 100 indicate overrepresentation in the suburbs. All but 12 of the 200 Urbanized Areas fell into one of six patterns. Table 10.1 shows the largest Urbanized Area manifesting each of the six patterns, along with

[1] A full description of Burgess' concentric zonal model is provided in Chapter 6, pp. 162–164.
[2] See chapter 3, p. 66 for the definition of Urbanized Area.
[3] Leo F. Schnore, "The Socioeconomic Status of Cities and Suburbs," *American Sociological Review*, 28 (February 1963), 76–86. Reprinted in his *The Urban Scene* (1965).
[4] Leo F. Schnore, "Urban Structure and Suburban Selectivity," *Demography*, 1, 1 (1964), 164–76.

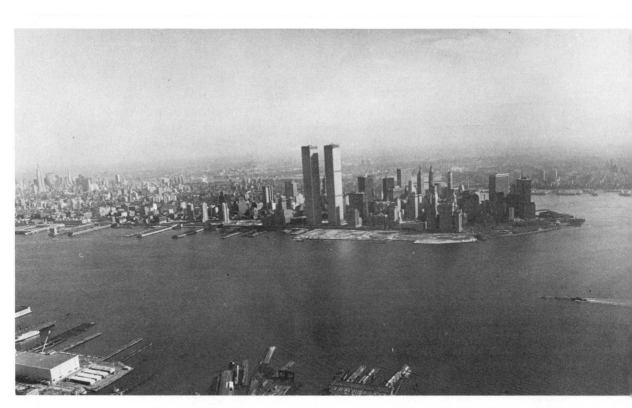

The traditional downtown area of Manhattan (left), dominated by the World Trade Center's 110-story twin towers, contrasts sharply with the more decentralized pattern evident in Century City (right), one of many commercial complexes in Los Angeles. Century City contains hotels, offices, and shopping facilities. (The Port of New York Authority—left; E. L. Pearson & Associates—right)

the "X" group, which shows no regular pattern. The six patterns may be briefly summarized as follows:

1. *Type "A,"* of which the Tucson Urbanized Area is the largest example, represents a complete reversal of the Burgess zonal pattern. The four educational groups with the least years of education are *underrepresented* in the central city, and those who have completed high school or attended college are *overrepresented* in the city. Consequently the suburbs of Tucson and the 13 other Urbanized Areas like it have an overrepresentation of those at the lower educational levels and an underrepresentation of those at the upper educational level. As Schnore notes, *"This is the exact reversal of the common image of suburbia."*[5]

2. *Type "B"* is similar to Type "A" except that there is a tendency toward a reversal of the pattern at the bottom of the educational ladder (those with no schooling at all).

[5] *Ibid.*, p. 169, italics in the original.

3. *Type "C"* contains 70 of the 200 Urbanized Areas, more than any other type. Los Angeles is the largest Urbanized Area to manifest the pattern in which males at both the top and bottom of the educational ladder are over-represented in the city, and those at the middle educational levels are overrepresented in the suburbs. This pattern, too, is a departure from that expected under the Burgess model.
4. *Type "D,"* with the Baltimore Urbanized Area as the largest example, shows an almost perfect conformity with the distribution expected under the Burgess model. Only at the top of the educational distribution is there a reversal, with somewhat fewer college graduates represented in the suburbs than the Burgess model would predict.
5. *Type "E"* includes 67 Urbanized Areas, the second largest number in the seven types, and has the New York Urbanized Area as its largest example.

This type represents the "classic" Burgess distribution, in which there is a systematic decline in index values as one reads down the column, indicating that "(a) the city is characterized by an overconcentration of persons with minimal education and (b) the suburbs are populated by a larger than expected proportion of persons with higher educational standing."[6]

6. *Type "F"* is similar to Type "E," except that those with no formal schooling are overrepresented in the suburbs, leaving only the intermediate educational groups overrepresented in the city.

7. *Type "X"* Urbanized Areas show no systematic variation in city-suburban residential distribution. In Memphis, for example, the index numbers for all eight educational groups are very close to 100, indicating that all educational groups are about proportionally distributed in the central city and the suburbs.

Using income data rather than education data, Schnore has replicated the finding that no one type of city-suburban socioeconomic differential describes all metropolitan areas.[7] He has also shown that the findings hold when SMSA's rather than Urbanized Areas are used to delineate the metropolitan community. City-suburban income contrasts indicate that the most frequent type is that in which the highest and lowest income groups are overrepresented in the central city and the middle-income range is overrepresented in the suburbs: this is the equivalent of Type "C" (Los Angeles) educational distribution. The Burgess distribution pattern, with the suburbanization of high-income groups and the concentration of low-income groups in the central city, is the next most frequent and is the equivalent of Type "E" (New York) educational distribution. The income equivalent of the Type "A" (Tucson) educational distribution, a reversal of the Burgess pattern, has high-income groups concentrated in the central city and low-income groups suburbanized. It is important to note that Schnore's findings in city-suburban status differentials are restricted to the white population. Nonwhite city-suburban status differentials vary significantly from those of the white population.[8]

In each of his studies Schnore found that the size and age of the metropolitan community were significantly related to the type of city-suburban differential. Only the older, larger metropolises displayed the Burgess pattern, that is, Type "E" or variations of it. Since most smaller, newer metropolitan areas are in the South and West, this means that the metropolitan areas departing from the Burgess model are concentrated in those two regions, while the metropolitan areas conforming to the

[6] *Ibid.*, p. 170.

[7] Leo F. Schnore, "Measuring City-Suburban Status Differentials," *Urban Affairs Quarterly*, 3 (September 1967), 95–108.

[8] J. John Palen and Leo F. Schnore, "Color Composition and City-Suburban Status Differences: A Replication and Extension," *Land Economics*, 41 (February 1965), 87–91. Reprinted in Schnore, *The Urban Scene.*

Table 10.1: Examples of Six Patterns of Residential Distribution of Educational Classes Based on Indexes of Suburbanization* for Selected Urbanized Areas: 1960

	Highest Educational Classes Are Over-represented in the City	Highest Educational Classes Are Over-represented in the City	Both Highest and Lowest Educational Classes Are Over-represented in the City	Lowest Educational Classes Are Over-represented in the City	Lowest Educational Classes Are Over-represented in the City	Intermediate Educational Classes Are Over-represented in the City	No Systematic Variation
Pattern label	(1) "A"	(2) "B"	(3) "C"	(4) "D"	(5) "E"	(6) "F"	(7) "X"
Name of area used in example	Tucson	Albuquerque	Los Angeles	Baltimore	New York	Miami	Memphis
School years completed							
None	90	85	131	128	129	83	98
Grade: 1–4	93	81	113	124	119	137	101
Grade: 5–6	96	88	110	117	111	136	101
Grade: 7–8	99	93	99	104	107	115	101
High school: 1–3	100	97	94	98	100	100	100
High school: 4	101	103	97	86	91	89	99
College: 1–3	102	106	102	86	87	81	100
College: 4+	103	110	106	87	84	81	100
Number of areas represented by example shown	14	10	70	23	67	4	12

SOURCE: Leo F. Schnore, "Urban Structure and Suburban Selectivity," *Demography* 1,1 (1964), 170.

*index of suburbanization: over 100 means educational class is overrepresented in city; under 100 means educational class is overrepresented in suburbs.

Burgess model are concentrated in the Northeast, thus introducing a regional element to the typology.

The Evolution of
Urban-Suburban Patterns

The association of size and age with metropolitan ecological patterns, and especially the finding that age is the most important variable, has prompted Schnore to suggest "that cities evolve in a predictable direction, for example, pattern "A" through pattern "E."[9] More specifically, he has suggested that

smaller and younger central cities in the United States tend to be occupied by the local elite, while their peripheral, suburban areas contain the lower strata. With growth and the passage of time, however, . . . (2) the central city comes to be the main residential area for both the highest and lowest strata, at least temporarily, while the broad middle classes are overrepresented in the suburbs. (3) A subsequent stage in this evolutionary process is achieved when the suburbs have become the semiprivate preserve of both the upper and middle strata, while the central city is largely given over to the lowest stratum. In a very rough fashion, of course, this last stage corresponds to the way in which the various social classes are arrayed in space according to the Burgess (1925) zonal hypothesis.[10]

Schnore also suggested, after examining studies of Latin American cities, that the evolution of the American city might be part of a more inclusive change from preindustrial to modern patterns.[11]

Schnore has attempted to test the applicability of the evolutionary hypothesis to American urban structure with equivocal results.[12] For one thing, the range and variety of data needed, both longitudinal and cross-sectional, are not readily available. A general review of the available literature by Pinkerton, a student of Schnore, indicates the fragmentary character of the information and suggests that "many of these hypotheses, rather than being contradictory, are actually applicable to different types of metropolitan areas during different periods."[13]

An extensive evaluation of Schnore's evolutionary scheme has been

---

[9] Schnore, "Urban Structure and Suburban Selectivity," p. 174.

[10] Leo F. Schnore and Joy K. O. Jones, "The Evolution of City-Suburban Types in the Course of a Decade," *Urban Affairs Quarterly*, 4 (June 1969), 421–22.

[11] Leo F. Schnore, "On the Spatial Structure of Cities in the Two Americas," in Philip M. Hauser and Leo F. Schnore, eds., *The Study of Urbanization* (1965). For additional discussion of this question, see Chapter 3, pp. 56–60, and Chapter 6, pp. 172–75, of this text.

[12] Schnore and Jones, *op cit.*

[13] James R. Pinkerton, "City-Suburban Residential Patterns by Social Class: A Review of the Literature," *Urban Affairs Quarterly*, 4 (June 1969), 516.

undertaken by Johnston,[14] who finds Schnore's model a very useful working hypothesis but suggests two major modifications. First, he sees the need to integrate the Burgess zonal model with the Hoyt sectoral model to take account of socioeconomic variations on a nonconcentric basis.[15] Second, he believes that the evidence does not support Schnore's evolutionary sequence of "a transition from 'Tucson' and 'Albuquerque' pattern (complete Burgess reversal), through 'Los Angeles' (centralization of highest- and lowest-status groups) to 'New York' and 'Baltimore' (the Burgess pattern)," which indicates that the middle class is the first to suburbanize.[16] Johnston argues instead that the sequence is (1) highest classes concentrated in the inner zone; (2) highest classes moving to the outer zone; and (3) middle classes moving beyond the highest-class areas. In this sequence upper classes suburbanize first.

Schnore's Contribution

At this point it may be useful to summarize Schnore's major contribution to the analysis of urban-suburban socioeconomic differentials. The most relevant point is *the necessity for disaggregating data.* Schnore's studies of the variety of urban-suburban contrasts make it clear that there is no single kind of central city or one kind of suburban ring; therefore, the aggregation of data for all central cities or for all suburban areas is bound to be misleading.[17]

Table 10.2 disaggregates some of the 1970 data along the lines of the typology suggested by Schnore in Table 10.1. It must be emphasized that this is a very limited application of Schnore's approach because the central-city data are compared to those for the whole metropolis rather than only to the suburbs, and all racial and ethnic groups are combined. Furthermore, education and income are represented by single measures for the central city and the metropolitan area rather than by indexes of degree of suburbanization.

Nevertheless, the tendency toward Burgess and reverse Burgess patterns in metropolitan socioeconomic distribution is clear. Thus, the Baltimore, New York, and Milwaukee central cities have lower median family income and less educational attainment than their metropolitan areas. In contrast, Tucson, Fort Smith, and Albuquerque present a reverse Burgess pattern, as central-city median family income and educational attainment tend to be *higher* than that for the whole metropolis, indicating a surrounding ring of relatively low-status suburbs. The "Los Angeles" pattern described by Schnore as the concentra-

---

[14] R. J. Johnston, *Urban Residential Patterns* (1971), pp. 141–96.

[15] The Hoyt model is described in Chapter 6, p. 164.

[16] Johnston, *op cit.*, pp. 140 and 184.

[17] This is particularly true because the older and larger metropolitan communities display the Burgess pattern and contain well over half of all the metropolitan population.

TABLE 10.2: Education and Income for Selected Central Cities, Urbanized Areas, and Standard Metropolitan Statistical Areas: 1970

Pattern of Residential Distribution[a]	Percent with High School or Some College Education (persons 25 Years or Older)			Median Family Income		
	Central City	Urbanized Area[b]	SMSA[c]	Central City	Urbanized Area[b]	SMSA[c]
Types "A" and "B"						
Tucson	63.0	62.5	63.1	$8,759	$8,725	$8,943
Fort Smith, Ark.	53.6	51.1	41.9	7,975	7,649	6,350
Albuquerque	70.7	66.7	66.2	9,641	9,053	9,031
Type "C"						
Los Angeles	62.0	62.8	62.0	10,535	11,142	10,972
Types "D" and "E"						
Baltimore	34.3	42.1	44.6	8,815	10,349	10,577
New York	46.9	52.0	51.8	9,682	11,142	10,870
Milwaukee	49.2	56.7	56.8	10,262	11,323	11,338

[a]See pp. 255–59 for detailed descriptions of types.
[b]See pp. 66–70 for census definitions.
[c]In SMSA's and Urbanized Areas with more than one central city, only the data for the largest central city are given.
SOURCE: *U.S. Census of Population: 1970. General Social and Economic Characteristics. United States Summary.* Final Report PC(1)–C1, Tables 183, 184, 185, 186, 187.

tion of both the highest and lowest socioeconomic groups in the central city and the suburbanization of the middle classes cannot be adequately measured by Table 10.2. The figures, which vary little between the Los Angeles central city and the total metropolitan community, are compatible with such a distribution, however, for we should expect the high- and low-status groups in the central city to "balance" one another to produce middle-level figures approximating those of middle-level suburbs.

In conclusion, the application of Schnore's typology, even in a preliminary fashion, enables us to discern some significant variations in the central-city and suburban distribution of social and economic characteristics. This approach is very important for raising major theoretical questions, as in the "evolution of the American city," but it also has major policy implications. Programs designed to "help the cities" should be clear about which kinds of cities in relation to what kinds of suburban hinterlands.

Jobs in the Inner City

As nineteenth-century American cities have become the central areas of metropolitan communities, their employment patterns have shifted, sometimes dramatically. The changes involve both numbers and types of jobs and have generated debates on such matters as municipal solvency, transportation subsidies, zoning, civil rights, home rule, and a whole host of political charges and countercharges. While our presentation will concentrate on describing employment changes, the most pressing policy issues will also be discussed. For our purposes, the inner city will be defined as the central city of a metropolitan area, but it must be understood that the bulk of jobs and economic activity in the central core is concentrated in the central business district, the "downtown" area.

The metropolitan economy is not simply a matter of direct negotiation between the producer of raw materials and the manufacturer, nor between the manufacturer and the consumer. The movement of a bushel of apples or a bale of cotton from the farm to its ultimate use as food or clothing involves a long series of facilitating moves by processors

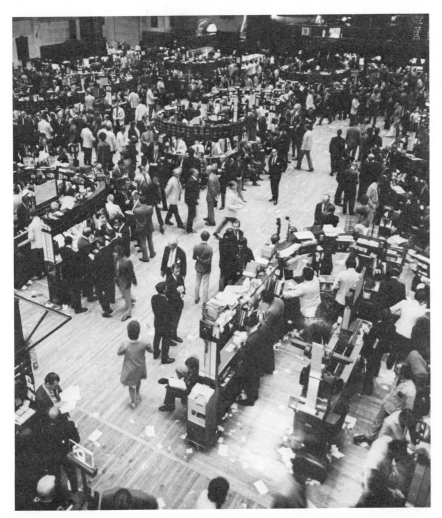

This scene on the floor of the New York Stock Exchange illustrates the organizational and managerial functions that remain concentrated in downtown areas, enabling them to coordinate far-flung activities. (The New York Stock Exchange)

and manufacturers, by legal and governmental agencies and inspectors, by advertising promotion, by wholesalers, and by large-scale retailers.

Under the influence of modern transportation systems and methods of communication, the location of these various specialized parts of the economy is characterized by great selectivity. No longer must the interrelated parts be centralized to be unified. Standardized, routine operations, whether in retailing, manufacturing, or management, desert the central business district for the lower costs, accessibility, and spaciousness of the metropolitan ring. Thus, retailing of everyday, medium-priced shoes becomes decentralized, but outlets for high-styled, high-priced, or specialty shoes (ballet, orthopedic, custom-made) remain highly concentrated in the core. Similarly, large-scale bulk printing of books and magazines is seldom found in the central business district, but "short-order" specialty plants serving newspapers or printing department-store handouts remain firmly attached to the downtown area.

The activities concentrated in the core are those that are predominantly unstandardized and hence require constant communication and revision; those requiring personal contact (judging the "mood" of Wall Street or the qualities of a prospective executive; planning legal, governmental, or industrial strategy); and those performed by small-scale producers who benefit from the "external economies" of the many downtown services (cafeterias, window cleaners, tax and accounting experts, and the like) they would not be able to maintain on their own in a suburban setting, or who require many small specialized suppliers and consumers in order to minimize the risk of the uncertainty of dependence on any one source.

Economist Raymond Vernon has summarized the emerging function of the central city, particularly the central business district, as involving activities which rely heavily on (1) face-to-face communication, (2) minimizing the risks of uncertainty, and (3) the external economies of scale.[18]

The Central City as a Service Center

The most fundamental change affecting central-city jobs is that the central city is no longer self-sufficient; rather, it is involved in an increasingly complex division of labor with the suburban portions of the metropolis, and, in some cases, serves the national and even international community. The central city has come to play the role of the coordinator or "switchboard" for the specialized activities distributed throughout the metropolitan area. In central cities there have been substantial gains in the employment categories represented by such

[18] Raymond Vernon, *The Changing Economic Function of the Central City* (1959).

TABLE 10.3: Change in Central-City Employment by Selected Categories, Distribution and Mean Annual Percentage Change for 8 Central Cities[a]: 1948–1967

Employment Category	Percent of Total Central-City Employment in 1963	Mean Annual Percentage Change	
		1948–1956	1956–1967
Finance	3.1	4.0	4.1
Insurance and real estate	3.9	1.8	−0.2
Government[b]	11.4	n.a.	2.0
Other services[c]	13.4	4.0	15.7

[a]Baltimore, Denver, New Orleans, New York, Philadelphia, St. Louis, San Francisco, and Washington, D.C.

[b]Data pertain to 1957–1962.

[c]Includes medical, legal, educational, and miscellaneous business services, as well as nonprofit membership organizations.

SOURCE: David L. Birch, *The Economic Future of City and Suburb* (New York: Committee for Economic Development, 1970), p. 8. Birch derived his data from National Planning Association, *Economic and Demographic Projections for Two Hundred and Twenty-Four Metropolitan Areas*, Regional Economic Projections Series, Report No. 67–R, Vols. I, II, and III; U. S. Bureau of the Census, *County Business Patterns* (1948, 1956, and 1958); and U. S. Bureau of the Census, *Census of Manufactures*, selected reports for various years, 1954–1963.

coordinating activities as financial institutions, insurance and real estate firms, government offices, and a host of "other services" in the fields of law, medicine, education, and business, as well as the activities of nonprofit membership organizations ranging from the Knights of Columbus to the Elks to CORE. Table 10.3 indicates these changes since 1948; by 1963 eight leading SMSA's had more than 31 percent of their jobs in these categories, which continue to expand. An indication of the central cities' specialization is that they accounted for the major share of employment in their SMSA's in these jobs classifications. Thus, in 1967 the eight central cities had 83 percent of their SMSA's jobs in finance, 80 percent in insurance and real estate, 60 percent in government, and 72 percent in "other services."[19]

In some cases the central cities "export" their coordinating activities far beyond their own regional boundaries. The proportion of office workers, another way of measuring the extent of service specialization, is 15.2 per 100 residents in metropolitan areas of at least a million in size but only 10.7 in the rest of the nation.[20] Among these largest metropolitan areas further specialization exists, as is evident in Figure 10.1. Those with the heaviest specialization in "the office industry" have from 15.6 to 20.4 office workers per 100 residents; they include New York, Los Angeles, San Francisco, Boston, Washington, D.C., Dallas, Seattle, and Minneapolis-St. Paul. The headquarters of giant corporations, the mass media, financial institutions, and government in these "national cities" are the policy-making and trend-setting centers of the United States. This is true to a lesser extent of the other large metropolitan areas

[19] David L. Birch, *The Economic Future of City and Suburb* (1970), p. 11.

[20] *The Office Industry: Patterns of Growth and Location* (1972), p. 24.

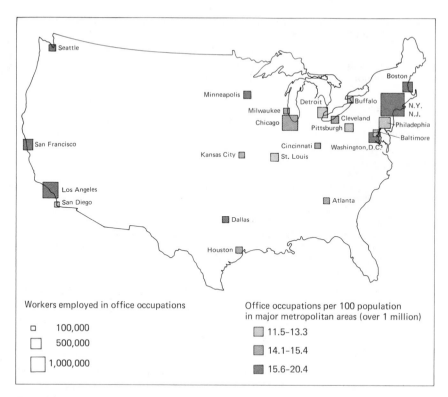

Workers employed in office occupations

☐   100,000
☐   500,000
☐   1,000,000

Office occupations per 100 population
in major metropolitan areas (over 1 million)

▨ 11.5–13.3
▨ 14.1–15.4
▨ 15.6–20.4

FIGURE 10.1 • Major metropolitan areas specialize in office occupations. Although metropolitan areas of over one million in size vary in the extent of their specialization, all of them have higher proportions of office workers than the 10.7 per 100 popula- tion prevailing in the rest of the Unit- ed States. Source: Regina Belz Arm- strong and Boris Pushkarev, *"The Office Industry:" Patterns of Growth and Location.* New York: Regional Plan Association, 1972.

in Figure 10.1, whose range of influence is sometimes restricted to a section of the nation or to a particular kind of service.

Although all of the SMSA's in Figure 10.1 are large and population size is related to specialization in office activities, it is not entirely determina- tive of the degree of specialization. Chicago, for example, is larger than Dallas, Seattle, or Minneapolis-St. Paul, but is not as specialized in office activity. Philadelphia, Detroit, and Pittsburgh are also somewhat less specialized in office activity than their size would suggest.

Job Decentralization

The specialization of the central city as an "elite service center"[21] is also evident in its relative decline as the locale of jobs in factory production

[21] Birch, *op cit.*, p. 10.

TABLE 10.4: Percentage Changes in Employment in 39 Metropolitan Areas, Cities, and Suburbs, by Selected Industrial Classification: 1948–1967

Year	Manufacturing		Retail Trade		Wholesale Trade		Selected Services*	
	City	Suburb	City	Suburb	City	Suburb	City	Suburb
1948–54	3.1	24.3	4.6	68.7	−4.7	34.2	54.6	86.9
1954–58	−9.3	3.1	3.6	−0.1	3.9	46.4	16.2	40.5
1958–63	−1.0	17.1	−10.2	10.0	−3.0	39.3	3.0	26.5
1963–67	7.3	25.9	2.2	22.5	3.7	29.1	3.0	19.2

*See footnote 22 for the occupations included in this category.
SOURCE: Neil N. Gold, "The Mismatch of Jobs and Low-Income People in Metropolitan Areas and Its Implications for the Central City Poor," in Commission on Population Growth and the American Future, *Population Distribution and Policy*, ed. Sara Mills Mazie. Vol. V of the Commission Research Reports (1972), p. 454.

and sales. The general reasons for the decentralizing trend were discussed in Chapter 9. Table 10.4 demonstrates that jobs in manufacturing, retail trade, wholesale trade, and "selected services"[22] have grown much more rapidly in the suburban rings than in the central cities of metropolitan areas. There have been two periods of absolute decline in central-city manufacturing jobs since 1948. The trend toward suburbanization in manufacturing is even more long-term, however, and is part of what in Chapter 3 we identified as the shift from the urban-industrial to the metropolitan community. In the earlier period the central cities contained the majority of the manufacturing jobs in their areas, often 80 percent or more, as shown in Table 10.5. By the midtwentieth century,

TABLE 10.5: Central Cities' Proportion of Manufacturing Production Workers in 10 Metropolitan Areas: 1899–1954

	1899	1929	1954
Baltimore	91.8	85.5	62.9
Buffalo	74.7	59.8	43.1
Chicago	88.0	73.6	65.2
Detroit	83.6	75.2	53.5
Los Angeles	83.4	66.6	42.3
New York City, Jersey City, Newark	69.9	69.8	63.0
Philadelphia	78.4	65.7	56.0
Pittsburgh	53.1	27.1	22.6
Saint Louis	80.6	69.9	63.9
San Francisco, Oakland	81.2	68.2	50.4

SOURCE: Raymond Vernon, *The Changing Economic Function of the Central City* (New York: Committee for Economic Development, 1959), pp. 74–75.

however, these same central cities contained as little as 22 percent of the manufacturing jobs in their metropolitan areas, and none of the central

---

[22] "Selected services" include such occupations as hairdressers, barbers, janitors, cooks, waiters, bartenders, firemen, policemen, guards, and elevator operators. It is *not* the same category as "other services" in Table 10.3.

cities contained more than two-thirds of the metropolitan manufacturing jobs, as shown in the figures for 1954 in Table 10.5.

Decentralization of retailing is also apparent in Table 10.4, with very marked differences in growth rates between central city and suburbs and some absolute central-city decline in retailing. To a large extent the suburbanization of retail sales represents the movement of stores closer to the growing suburban residential market. Although wholesale trade is not as closely tied to residential population, it also has risen in suburban areas, doubtless because rapid transportation and communication have given wholesalers, too, more freedom of locational choice. Once again the service category of jobs shows the least tendency to suburbanize, although Table 10.4 indicates that since 1958 there has been a greater disparity in central-city and suburban growth rates.

The net result of the geographic changes in the distribution of jobs in manufacturing, retail and wholesale trade, and selected services is that the central cities' share of total SMSA employment in these job categories declined from 70.6 percent in 1947 to 54.6 percent in 1968. In other words, central cities retain barely half the metropolitan-area jobs in these predominantly blue collar and lower-level white collar categories. Conversely the suburban share of total SMSA employment in these job categories increased from 29.4 percent in 1947 to 45.4 percent in 1968.[23]

Jobs and the Evolution of the City

The preceding analysis has indicated that the inner cities are becoming increasingly important as service centers, with a growing concentration of jobs that serve to direct, coordinate, and facilitate the operations of far-flung enterprises. Jobs that deal directly with raw materials or with the consumer, such as in factory production or in retail sales, are either leaving the central city or originally locating in suburban areas. However, when the data for metropolitan areas are disaggregated, significant variations appear, suggesting again that there are different types of metropolitan areas, in some ways reminiscent of Schnore's work discussed earlier.

While not drawing directly on Schnore's work, Birch examined trends in central-city employment in manufacturing, retail and wholesale trade, and selected services according to the same major variables Schnore used—the size and age of the metropolitan area, as shown in

[23] Neil N. Gold, "The Mismatch of Jobs and Low-Income People in Metropolitan Areas and Its Implications for the Central City Poor," in Commission on Population Growth and the American Future, *Population Distribution and Policy*, ed. Sara Mills Mazie, Vol. V of Commission Research Reports (1972), p. 450.

Table 10.6. The results indicate that both variables, but especially the age of the metropolitan area, are related to the growth or decline of various kinds of employment opportunities in the central city. The central cities of old metropolitan areas, that is, those SMSA's that would have qualified as SMSA's before 1900, are the central cities experiencing *declines* in retail employment and manufacturing. The young, smaller central cities are experiencing *gains* in manufacturing and retail trade jobs and, indeed, in all job categories noted.

Among the reasons for the across-the-board economic growth of these younger, smaller central cities are (1) their much lower densities and hence the availability of space for business growth and (2) the fact that, unlike the older cities, they are built around road networks rather than around railroads or water transportation. Birch suggests that the differences between the central cities of the older, larger SMSA's and those of the younger, smaller SMSA's indicate

a sequence whereby younger cities chew up low-density land at a good clip with manufacturing floor space, parking lots, and road networks. The other economic functions develop more slowly. As the city ages and becomes more densely populated, central-city land becomes more expensive, and manufacturing declines in significance, as does retail and wholesale trade. Services, in contrast, appear to thrive on concentration, . . . and, through a process of self-

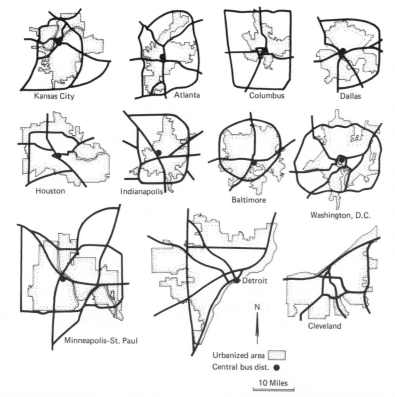

FIGURE 10.2 • The urban freeway systems in these 11 cities are typical of circumferential routes being built in American cities to handle movement generated by the decentralization of many activities. The earlier radial pattern of arteries leading to the city-center is also evident. Source: Adapted from Edgar Horwood and Ronald Boyce, *Studies of the Central Business District and Urban Freeway Development.* Seattle: University of Washington Press, 1959.

TABLE 10.6: Growth of Central-City Employment by Size and Age of SMSA (Percentage Change for 73 SMSA's by Major Industry Groups): 1948–1963 [a]

	Old SMSA's	Middle-Aged SMSA's	Young SMSA's	Average
RETAIL TRADE				
Large SMSA's	−11.1	19.8	73.5	4.2
Smaller SMSA's	−13.0	11.7	26.5	18.6
Average	−11.2	15.7	37.7	9.5
WHOLESALE TRADE				
Large SMSA's	4.1	43.9	111.6	23.6
Smaller SMSA's	17.0	26.5	54.2	42.2
Average	4.9	35.2	67.9	30.5
MANUFACTURING				
Large SMSA's	− 0.8	59.6	284.1	42.0
Smaller SMSA's	−10.9	52.6	89.8	69.9
Average	− 1.4	56.1	136.0	52.3
SELECTED SERVICES				
Large SMSA's	31.5	56.6	162.1	50.6
Smaller SMSA's	21.2	37.8	67.8	54.3
Average	30.9	47.2	90.2	52.0

[a] "Old" SMSA's qualified as SMSA's before 1900; "middle-aged," between 1900 and 1930; and "young," after 1930. "Smaller" SMSA's have a population of less than 500,000; "large" SMSA's contain over 500,000 people.
SOURCE: David L. Birch, *The Economic Future of City and Suburb* (New York: Committee for Economic Development, 1970), p. 12. Data were derived from the sources indicated in Table 10.3.

selection and survival, emerge as the dominant economic force in the older, larger cities. The tendency of central cities to become elite service centers appears, like rheumatism and decaying teeth, to be a strong function of age.[24]

The "life-cycle model," as Birch calls it, appears to be the employment-pattern counterpart of the evolutionary model proposed by Schnore for socioeconomic differences in central-city-suburban residential distribution. It is also useful to view the changes in central-city employment patterns against the broad change from urban-industrial to metropolitan urban forms we have described in Chapter 3.

Broad shifts in regional redistribution of economic activity are occurring and are likely to persist as a consequence of the life cycle of the city. Most of the young, growing metropolitan areas in the United States are in the South and West, and "whereas at present these younger areas account for only about 25 percent of total employment, over time their much greater growth rates will have given them an increasing share of the nation's gross national product. Conversely, the significance of the large northern metropolitan centers, which served as the nuclei of urban growth during the first half of this century, will decline in a relative

[24] Birch, *op cit.*, pp. 13–14.

TABLE 10.7: Employment Changes in 16 Central Cities and Suburbs for Selected Industrial Classifications: 1948–1967[a]

Increase		Decrease	
Anaheim-Santa Ana-			
Garden Grove	114,000	Baltimore	−22,000
Atlanta	59,000	Boston	−33,000
Dallas	150,000	Chicago	1,000
Houston	172,000	Cleveland	−58,000
Los Angeles	280,000	Newark	−38,000
Phoenix	88,000	New York	1,000
San Antonio	94,000	Philadelphia	−84,000
Seattle	39,000	St. Louis	−75,000

[a]Refers to manufacturing, retail and wholesale trade, and selected services.
SOURCE: Neil N. Gold, "The Mismatch of Jobs and Low-Income People in Metropolitan Areas and Its Implications for the Central City Poor," in Commission on Population Growth and the American Future, *Population Distribution and Policy,* ed. Sara Mills Mazie. Vol. V of Commission Research Reports (1972), p. 453.

sense."[25] This change is reflected in Table 10.7, which contrasts the increases in major southern and western metropolitan areas with the job decreases or stability of the larger northern areas. It is important to recognize that Table 10.7 gives data only for jobs in manufacturing, retail and wholesale trade, and selected services; it does *not* show employment in financial institutions, insurance and real estate, government, and other services, categories in which the large, old SMSA's of the North excel, a fact already reflected in Figure 10.1. The large centers of the North are changing their economic role, not shedding it, and will remain an indispensable part of national economic life.

The Mismatch of Jobs and People

In reviewing the data presented for city-suburban distributions in socio-economic status and in employment patterns, we note major lack of "fit" between the two distributions. The central cities of the older, larger metropolitan areas have steadily declined in factory production jobs and in entry-level white collar jobs such as in retailing, but the central-city populations in this type of metropolitan area include increasing proportions of lower socioeconomic groups that would be most qualified and interested in this kind of employment. The reverse mismatch occurs in the suburban areas where manufacturing jobs are expanding but where the higher socioeconomic groups are concentrated, necessitating considerable travel to the administrative, professional, and other "elite service" jobs expanding in the central city. In some of the newer metropolitan areas a mismatch occurs basically because the metropolis

[25] *Ibid*, p. 14.

is so large and so oriented to private automobile ownership that the poor are handicapped in holding jobs no matter where they are located. Thus, one of the sources of discontent in the Watts ghetto of Los Angeles was the cost, cumbersomeness, and inordinate time its residents consumed in getting to jobs other than by automobile. Still other geographic mismatches of people and jobs may occur in other types of metropolitan areas than the two described, but they have received little attention, probably because the metropolitan areas are smaller and the mismatch is easier to overcome.

The large-scale disparity within some metropolitan areas between the location of jobs and the residences of those equipped to fill them has generated a series of strategies designed to reduce the mismatch.[26] Extension of public transportation lines has been advocated to enable central-city residents to travel to suburban blue collar jobs. However, attempts to create such routes have had only limited success, partly because suburban factories and other installations are too dispersed to permit ready formation even of commercially viable bus routes. A broader strategy is the advocacy of much more "clustering" of jobs, stores, and other activities in suburbs, thereby permitting easier access, among other advantages. The difficulty with such an approach is its long-range and, indeed, utopian nature.

The most direct attack on the mismatch phenomenon is the movement to "open up" the suburbs by providing a broader range of prices and types of housing in suburbs, thus enabling low- and moderate-income workers to live closer to their job locations. It has been pointed out that between 1962 and 1967 nearly 80 percent of new public housing units were constructed in central cities although only one-third of new private housing units were built in central cities during that period. Although governmental efforts to build public housing in suburban areas have typically met vocal and effective local opposition, the approach is potentially effective. Attacks on "exclusionary zoning"—local zoning ordinances that prohibit small house lots or "look-alike" houses and that have the effect of excluding low- and moderate-income residents—have also been part of the drive to open up the suburbs. The Suburban Action Institute of White Plains, New York, has been a leading opponent of exclusionary zoning. Efforts to introduce less expensive housing to suburban areas have been complicated by the fact that many of the central-city persons who are potential residents in any low- and moderate-income suburban housing are nonwhite. Although the racial issue is seldom overtly raised, it is nevertheless important, considering the "lily-white" nature of much suburban housing.[27]

---

[26] See, for example, Gold, *op cit.*

[27] Data on the racial makeup of central-city and suburban populations are presented in Chapter 3, p. 90.

The problems caused by geographic mismatching are unlikely to just "go away." The vast majority—85 percent—of new jobs added in manufacturing, retail and wholesale sales, and selected services are being located in suburban areas according to data covering the period 1948 to 1967, leaving only 15 percent of the new jobs in these occupational categories locating in central cities. Continuation of these trends, without steps to alleviate mismatching, would lead to the permanent encapsulation of the poor and nonwhites in central-city areas where they have limited access to the expanding job market. One observer has summarized the problem as follows:

The geographical relationship between residences and work places in metropolitan areas is severely imbalanced at the present time. Semi-skilled and low-skilled jobs are rapidly suburbanizing out of reach of the central-city poor, particularly the minority poor. The resulting mismatch of jobs and low-income people has grave implications for central cities, for disadvantaged groups isolated in the urban core, and for the capacity of metropolitan areas to achieve equitable urban growth patterns.[28]

The Inner City— Myth and Reality

For many people the term "inner city" conjures up a picture of decaying slums inhabited by disorganized and even dangerous people who live relatively close to the downtown area's many commercial, cultural, and entertainment attractions. From this point of view the central city is a place to go *to* for a specific purpose or to go *through* in pursuit of physically and socially "greener pastures." To be sure most central cities contain areas that would be classified as blighted by any criteria, and there are manifestations of widespread commercial and residential abandonment of districts, causing them to resemble the "bombed out" sections of wartorn cities.[29]

But deterioration and decay are only part of the inner-city reality. The tendency to generalize these characteristics to the central city as a whole typifies the anticity bias discussed in Chapter 21. Here we will critically examine three of the specific assumptions underlying the negative view of the central city: (1) The assumption that the central-city population *as a whole* is invariably or even generally of lower socioeconomic status than that of suburban areas. Schnore's work, discussed earlier in this chapter, has already demonstrated the falseness of this assumption. (2)

[28] Gold, *op. cit,* p. 451.

[29] For data and discussion of the process of abandonment, which is not yet fully understood, see National Urban League, *The National Survey of Housing Abandonment* (1971), and George Sternlieb and Robert W. Burchell, *Residential Abandonment: The Tenement Landlord Revisited* (1973).

The assumption that, *within the central city*, there is a uniformity of residential areas and ways of life, an assumption belied both by the several ecological theories described in Chapter 6 and by the description of specific urban subareas and ecological change described in Chapters 7 and 8. However, we shall explore further the variety of central-city residential types. (3) The assumption that low socioeconomic status is associated with social disorganization, which we shall criticize in detail because of its important policy implications.

Ways of Life
in the City

A fruitful approach to the study of the city (or suburbs or rural areas) lies in viewing it as providing for a diversity of ways of life, rather than a single way of life. A recent analysis by Gans suggests there are at least five urban ways of life, based chiefly on social class and on stages of the family life-cycle.[30]

(1) Although the "cosmopolites" are of varying socioeconomic levels and may be at any stage of the life-cycle, they are alike in the high value they place on the "cultural" facilities the inner city offers. (2) The "unmarried" and "married and childless" vary by the permanency or transiency of these traits, but while they are unmarried, or married and childless, they actively participate in the city's varied activities. (3) The "ethnic villagers" are immigrant groups such as the Italians, Mexican-Americans, or migrant groups such as the Puerto Ricans, who carry on in urban enclaves the peasant life of their home communities. (4) The "deprived" are those whose handicaps of extreme poverty, emotional problems, and especially race prevent most of them from acquiring any but slum housing in the worst areas of the central city. (5) The "trapped" and "the downwardly mobile" are those for whom ownership of real estate, loss of social status, or other happenstance have resulted in their inability to move from crowded, deteriorated areas.

It is only the last two groups—the deprived and the trapped and downwardly mobile—whom we should expect to find concentrated in physically and socially disorganized inner-city areas, but even then there are numerous individual exceptions. The third group, the ethnic villagers, are concentrated in physically deteriorated but highly structured neighborhoods which do not merit the designation "slum," a point to which we shall return. The other two urban types, the cosmopolites and those not in the child-rearing stage of family life, live in a whole range of inner-city areas from anonymous luxury apartment houses and palatial

---

[30] The following discussion is based on Herbert Gans, "Urbanism and Suburbanism as Ways of Life: A Re-evaluation of Definitions," in Arnold Rose, ed., *Human Behavior and Social Process* (1962), pp. 625–48. See also Herbert Gans, *The Urban Villagers* (1962), for a participant-observation study of a particular urban way of life.

townhouse sections to "hippie," youth, and artistic colonies to undistinguished middle-income areas. The approach of the social area analysts, described in Chapter 6, is helpful in conceptualizing the variety of inner-city areas on the basis of socioeconomic status and family life-cycle.

Although Gans' analysis was based on American cities, his findings are provocative and reinforce impressionistic observations made in cities in underdeveloped countries. Cosmopolites probably make up an even smaller percentage of the urban population in these cities than in cities in the United States. Their interests and outlook are often international, and even if they do not have much income, as professionals and white collar workers their intellectual and social lives may be fairly broad and effectively detached from the traditional native life around them. "Villagers-in-the-city"—people who carry on their rural customs much as they have always done—make up a large part of the population of cities in underdeveloped areas. Among such people there may also be distinctive ways of life reflecting religious or tribal affiliations. In India, Muslims and Hindus, at least on the lower social levels, lead quite different life styles.

For cities in both developed and underdeveloped areas, there is no single urban pattern. Social status, family ties, ethnic affiliation, age, and other factors that modify urban environmental influences have to be studied in order to understand social life in the urban setting. Gans' analysis serves to emphasize the fact that the density, concentration, and variety of the inner city vary in significance and impact according to the characteristics, most importantly socioeconomic status and stage of family life-cycle, of the resident urbanites. The inner city might well be described as an interactive process rather than as a place with set features. The chapters on the urban family, urban work, and urban status systems present, in a nonecological context, some of the variety of urban ways of life, as do the chapters on leisure, formal and informal participation, and community power.

The Slum

"The term 'slum' is an evaluative, not an analytic, concept. . . . Current definitions of the term include two criteria—the social image of the area, and its physical condition"[31]—the latter of which we shall consider first.

The slum is typically composed of obsolete housing, small nondescript stores geared to the particular preferences of the local inhabitants,[32] and

---

[31] Gans, *The Urban Villagers*, p. 308.

[32] See, for example, Allan Pred, "Business Thoroughfares as Expressions of Urban Negro Culture," *Economic Geography*, 39 (July 1963), 217–33.

narrow cluttered streets. Whether a slum is interpreted in terms of the sector theory, the concentric zone theory, or social area analysis, its general location in most American cities is fairly conspicuous. Ordinarily it is situated around or near the central business district. In many metropolitan areas, slums lie beyond the municipal boundaries in sectors of the community that consist of converted summer homes, rural housing enveloped by urban growth, or aged suburbs.

Its physical deterioration alone makes the slum relatively unappealing as a residential area, at least to most persons. But one thing is in its favor: comparatively cheap rents, which means that it is populated largely by people who ordinarily cannot afford to live elsewhere. Poverty and physical deterioration thus go hand in hand. The slum area has been a port of entry for millions of impoverished and dispossessed migrants: Old World immigrants, blacks from the South, uprooted village and farm folk, Mexican laborers from across the border, and Puerto Ricans from the slums of San Juan.

The convenience of the area to downtown, coupled with its low rents, also attracts students, artists, "bohemians," and some intellectuals, as well as criminals and social deviants of various types who welcome the anonymity provided by the slum's density of population and by its lack of organized resistance to their residence. These various groups may live in separate sections of the slum or be intermingled to some extent.

The several typological approaches to the study of the slum deal mainly with the varieties of people who inhabit the physically deteriorated low-income areas that are all labeled slums. Often this human variety gives rise to distinct subareas within the slum, as in the contrast between Skid Row areas and racial or ethnic ghettoes. The distinction is made between "slums of hope," often inhabited by newcomers to the city looking for a better life, and "slums of despair," which mark the end of the line (or no beginning) for restricted minorities, for the aged, and social outcasts of every description.[33] A somewhat similar classification suggests two major dimensions of difference among slum residents— necessity and opportunity and permanence and change—which result in four types of slum dwellers.[34] The permanent "necessitarians" include the social outcasts and the long-term poverty population, while the temporary necessitarians include groups experiencing short-term poverty. The permanent "opportunists" are those whom the slum serves with opportunities they cannot find, or find only with difficulty, elsewhere —criminals, fugitives, and prostitutes—while the temporary opportunists include urban newcomers and purveyors of shady goods or services. The necessity of distinguishing among types of slum residents

[33] Charles Stokes, "A Theory of Slums," *Land Economics*, 48 (August 1962), 187–97.
[34] John R. Seeley, "The Slum: Its Nature, Use, and Users," *Journal of the American Institute of Planners*, 25 (February 1959), 7–14.

becomes clear when considering the alleged association between slums and social disorganization.

The Slum and Social Disorganization

The residential slum has commonly been interpreted as an area of social disorganization. So durable is this idea that periodically scholarly studies of slums achieve broad readership because they indicate, to the contrary, that human behavior in the slum is highly organized and social control quite effective.[35]

While the more well-known studies of slums have usually focused on ethnic groups, studies of other slum populations have also shown that they are tightly structured. The residents of Skid Row, for example, are typically stereotyped as alcoholics and "bums." While Skid Row does contain such a component, which is highly visible, most Skid Row residents are low-income unskilled workmen of middle age who are without families and are otherwise disaffiliated.[36] They work at day labor or are transient railroad workers, lumbermen, or seamen; the older of them often subsist on meager pensions. Most men of Skid Row do not conform to middle class standards of dress, propriety, or respectability, but they recognize a social code and hierarchy within their world. Skid Row provides them with the low-cost, male-oriented institutions and services they need—lodging houses, eating establishments, entertainment, barber "colleges," second-hand clothing stores, daily hiring halls, the social work and religious services of "rescue missions," and so on. It also provides opportunities for the sociability denied them by the rest of society. The social structure of Skid Row has come into sharper focus as Skid Rows, which are typically located just outside the central business district, face intrusions by other uses such as parking lots, expensive hotels, apartment houses, and office buildings. As sections are demolished, the difficulty of providing the dislocated men with equivalent

[35] The best-known examples of the last 30 years are William F. Whyte, *Street Corner Society* (1943); Herbert Gans, *The Urban Villagers* (1962); Elliot Liebow, *Tally's Corner* (1967); and Gerald Suttles, *The Social Order of the Slum* (1968). Chapter 13, pp. 370–72, details the structure of informal social participation described by Suttles, Gans, and Liebow for the respective slum groups they studied, while Chapter 14, pp. 394–6, summarizes the main characteristics of family life of the Italian-Americans Gans studied. The debunking of stereotypes of disorganization occurs with nonecological communities, too. For example, the "status community" of black New Orleans jazzmen, commonly believed to represent a "counterculture," has been shown in a recent study to have conventional family and other attitudes, to be highly stable residentially, and to participate actively in organizations. Jack V. Buerkle and Danny Barker, *Bourbon Street Black* (1973).

[36] Donald J. Bogue, *Skid Row in American Cities* (1963), and Howard Bahr, *Skid Row: An Introduction to Disaffiliation* (1973).

accommodations and services points up the meaningful cohesive milieu of Skid Row.[37]

The whole question of the relationship between slums and social disorganization has become more important as urban renewal and slum clearance have gained momentum. A study of turn-of-the-century housing reform points out that Americans have long had a simple faith that social betterment would inevitably result from the improvement of housing conditions.[38] To the contrary, an increasing number of professional and civic studies show that poor housing is not necessarily associated with social pathology; and even when such a correlation is indicated, improved housing will not necessarily guarantee improvement of the social pathology. The relationship between housing and social life is much more complex than that.[39]

As the wrecker's ball approaches ever more city slums, it becomes more urgent than ever to ask, "What is being destroyed?" Jane Jacobs, in her controversial book *The Death and Life of Great American Cities* (1961), contends that the mixed land use, density of population, and old buildings on small blocks, which usually lead to the labeling of an area as a slum, may not exemplify the slum in a social sense. She discusses Greenwich Village in New York City, among other cases, and urges reexamination of the haphazard destruction of so-called slums. After conducting a participant-observation study of the West End, an Italian neighborhood in Boston, prior to its replacement by luxury apartment buildings, Gans concluded that the West End was a low-rent area with a cohesive, stable social structure, albeit not organized around middle class standards of success.[40] Gans urges that a distinction be made between *low-rent* and *slum* districts. Although both have deteriorated housing, only in the slum is the deterioration associated with harmful effects on the individual or the larger society.

Ironically, social disorganization came to many former West Enders as a result of being forced to leave their neighborhood. The higher rents in other parts of the city strained their limited budgets, and separation from kin and friendship groups weakened the bases around which their social life was organized. Half a world away, in Nigeria on the West Coast of Africa, a slum clearance project in Lagos, the capital city, produced similar results and provoked similar criticism of redevelopment policies.[41]

[37] Ronald Vander Kooi, "The Main Stem: Skid Row Revisited," *Society* (formerly *Trans-Action*), 10 (September–October 1973), 65–71.

[38] Roy Lubove, *The Progressives and the Slums: Tenement House Reform in New York City, 1890–1917* (1963), pp. 245–56.

[39] Irving Rosow, "The Social Effects of the Physical Environment," *Journal of the American Institute of Planners*, 27 (May 1961), 127–33.

[40] Gans, *The Urban Villagers.*

[41] Peter Marris, *Family and Social Change in an African City: A Study of Rehousing in Lagos* (1962).

All of this should not blind us to the fact that there are areas of physical, social, and moral degradation that deserve to be called slums in the worst sense of the word and should be eliminated. We are calling attention here only to the uncritical assumption that physical blight and social disorganization necessarily go hand in hand.

The Slum and Race

In the past slums have been only a temporary abode for many of their residents. Immigrants, students, artists, and those temporarily "down on their luck" usually moved on when their economic position improved. Today, however, there is a danger that many slum residents, and their descendants, may become permanently trapped, primarily because so many of them are nonwhite. The large-scale movement of the white population to suburban areas and the replacement of immigration from abroad by internal migration from the rural South have dramatically increased the proportion of blacks in cities.[42] To a far greater extent than for the white immigrant groups that preceded them in the ghettoes, the nonwhite minorities have experienced discrimination primarily on the basis of the unchanging genetic characteristics of their skin color rather than on the relatively flexible cultural characteristics of distinctive dress, speech patterns, or customs of individual or group behavior.

In all but three of the 25 largest cities of the United States the black population has increased since 1960, sometimes very substantially as is shown in Table 10.8. Chicago, Detroit, Baltimore, Washington, D.C., Cleveland, and St. Louis each experienced increases of 10 percentage points or more in black population. By 1970 at least a third of the population of these cities was black, as was also true of Philadelphia, Memphis, and New Orleans. It has been predicted that by 1985 a continuation of recent trends would produce 11 additional major American cities (Washington, D.C., and Newark were already in that category) with black majorities: New Orleans, Richmond, Baltimore, Jacksonville, Gary, Cleveland, St. Louis, Detroit, Philadelphia, Oakland, and Chicago.[43] The 1970 census indicated that two more cities already had black majorities—Gary, Indiana, and Atlanta, Georgia, the latter city not even having been included among the 1968 predictions.

Once again in considering the inner city (and suburbs) it becomes important to disaggregate the data, as is done in Table 10.9, in which central cities are considered within the context of their metropolitan areas. When the metropolitan areas are arranged by size it is apparent

[42] See Chapters 3, 7, and 8 for details of black urban migration and segregation.

[43] *Report of the National Advisory Commission on Civil Disorders* (1968), p. 381. For a discussion of two "black cities," see Edward Greer, "The 'Liberation' of Gary, Indiana," *Society* (formerly *Trans-Action*), 8 (January 1971), 1–11; and "The Nation of Newark," *Society* (special issue), 9 (September–October 1972), 19–58.

TABLE 10.8: Percent of Population That Is Black in 25 Largest Cities of the United States: 1960 and 1970

1970 Rank	1960	1970
1. New York City	14.9	21.1
2. Chicago	22.9	32.7
3. Los Angeles	13.5	17.9
4. Philadelphia	26.4	33.6
5. Detroit	28.9	43.7
6. Houston	22.9	25.7
7. Baltimore	34.7	46.4
8. Dallas	19.0	24.9
9. Washington, D.C.	53.9	71.1
10. Cleveland	28.6	38.3
11. Indianapolis	20.6	18.0
12. Milwaukee	8.4	14.7
13. San Francisco	10.0	13.4
14. San Diego	6.0	7.6
15. San Antonio	7.1	7.6
16. Boston	9.1	16.3
17. Memphis	37.0	38.9
18. Saint Louis	28.6	40.9
19. New Orleans	37.2	45.0
20. Phoenix	4.8	4.8
21. Columbus, Ohio	16.4	18.5
22. Seattle	4.8	7.1
23. Jacksonville	23.2	22.3
24. Pittsburgh	16.7	20.2
25. Denver	6.1	9.1

SOURCE: *Statistical Abstract of the United States* (1972), Table 22, pp. 21–23.

that the white exodus from central cities is confined to the largest metropolises, those over 2 million, and that white population growth in other central cities is in inverse order of city size, with the central cities of the smallest metropolitan areas receiving the largest number of new white residents, 826,000. Black population growth in central cities shows the opposite pattern, the largest metropolises receiving the largest black increase, 1,755,000, and the central cities of successively smaller metropolitan areas receiving successively smaller numbers of blacks. The end result of these two patterns is the tendency for the black population to become concentrated in the central cities of the larger metropolises, sometimes as the numerical majority.

Racial discrimination acts doubly to isolate blacks in slums. Discrimination in education and employment places them in an economic position where few can afford any but low-rent housing. The 1970 census indicated the median income of white urban families was $10,629 while that of black urban families was only $6,581.[44] It is important to remember that poor urban whites outnumber poor non-

[44] *U.S. Census of Population: 1970. General Social and Economic Characteristics. United States Summary.* Final Report PC (1)-C1, Table 83.

TABLE 10.9: 1970 Population and 1960–1970 Change in Population for United States Metropolitan Areas by Size of Area and Race (in Millions)

Race and Size Class of SMSA*	1970 Population			Change, 1960–1970		
	Inside Central City	Outside Central City	Total	Inside Central City	Outside Central City	Total
TOTAL	63,824	75,549	139,374	3,194	16,598	19,793
2,000,000 or more	23,143	29,038	52,181	−424	6,013	5,590
1,000,000 to 1,999,999	11,668	16,764	28,433	1,034	4,931	5,966
500,000 to 999,999	10,871	11,563	22,434	748	2,683	3,431
250,000 to 499,999	8,670	10,592	19,261	783	1,901	2,664
Under 250,000	9,472	7,593	17,065	1,053	1,070	2,122
WHITE	49,450	71,061	120,512	−607	15,301	14,695
2,000,000 or more	16,025	27,260	43,285	−2,489	5,262	2,773
1,000,000 to 1,999,999	9,225	15,942	25,167	322	4,645	4,940
500,000 to 999,999	8,544	10,900	19,261	273	2,564	2,837
250,000 to 499,999	7,317	9,876	17,193	488	1,779	2,267
Under 250,000	8,338	7,084	15,422	826	1,051	1,877
BLACK	13,148	3,645	16,793	3,234	820	4,054
2,000,000 or more	6,536	1,475	8,011	1,755	547	2,302
1,000,000 to 1,999,999	2,270	663	2,934	637	182	820
500,000 to 999,999	2,016	444	2,460	417	33	451
250,000 to 499,999	1,256	607	1,864	238	69	307
Under 250,000	1,069	456	1,524	186	−11	174

*According to 1970 definition.
SOURCE: Office of the President, *Report on National Growth* (Washington, D.C.: Government Printing Office, 1972), p. 23.

whites by nearly two to one. However, poor whites amount to only eight percent of the urban white population while poor nonwhites constitute 25 percent of all urban nonwhites. Even more significantly, between 1959 and 1968 the proportion of nonwhites among the urban poor arose from 29 to 34 percent.[45]

Sometimes the slum does not even provide blacks with inexpensive housing. Because landlords realize that blacks have "nowhere else to go," apartments may be subdivided and each room rented to a family on a weekly basis, resulting in high rental costs. Or "furnished" apartments may be the basis for high rents for inferior facilities. Racial discrimination also operates to restrict the residential mobility even of those blacks who have the means and desire to move from the slums.

A broad range of programs and strategies has been suggested to break the vicious cycle of black ghettoization in slums. The policy choices were set forth by the so-called Kerner Commission which was called by the late President Johnson to investigate the race riots that occurred in

[45] Gold, *op. cit.*, pp. 448–49.

American cities in the mid-1960's.[46] (1) The "present policies choice" involves continuing the allocation of resources to the urban poor at the same or somewhat higher levels, as at present. "This course may well involve changes in many social and economic programs—but not enough to produce fundamental alterations in the key factors of Negro concentration, racial segregation, and the lack of sufficient enrichment to arrest the decay of deprived neighborhoods."[47] (2) The "enrichment choice" would go far beyond programs such as Model Cities, manpower training, and the War on Poverty in attempting to upgrade the quality of life in the ghetto. The investment and commitment would be sufficient to make a clear improvement in the black city ghettoes. For example, the programs initiated by the late Senator Robert F. Kennedy of New York for the Bedford-Stuyvesant area in Brooklyn were intended to "gild" that ghetto in order to reverse the cycle of deterioration, poverty, and dependency. The enrichment choice is not geared to preserving residential racial segregation, but rather to improving sufficiently education, housing, and economic opportunities for ghetto residents so that they can function in American society without handicaps. (3) The "integration choice" involves combining enrichment programs with massive efforts to integrate substantial numbers of blacks into residential areas outside the ghettoes. The report recommends this choice as the only strategy capable of halting the movement toward two separate Americas and that the commitment be made rapidly since "within two decades this division could be so deep that it would be almost impossible to unite: (1) a white society principally located in suburbs, in smaller central cities, and in the peripheral parts of larger central cities; and (2) a Negro society largely concentrated within large central cities."[48]

Is the Inner City Doomed?

The conjunction in inner cities of an economic base shifting from production of goods to production of services at the same time as the population base becomes increasingly low-income, nonfamily, or black raises far-reaching questions about the social and economic functions of the city. As our earlier analysis indicated, this conjunction occurs mainly in the older, larger central cities. Using Newark and St. Louis as their major examples, Sternlieb and Long recently provided some controversial responses to the question "Is the inner city doomed?"[49]

Sternlieb contends that *"the major problem of the core areas of our*

[46] *Report of the National Advisory Commission on Civil Disorders.* For a somewhat different version of the policy alternatives, written by the same person who wrote that section of the report, see Anthony Downs, "Alternative Futures for the American Ghetto," in his *Urban Problems and Prospects* (1970), pp. 27–75.

[47] *Report of the National Advisory Commission on Civil Disorders*, p. 396.

[48] *Ibid.*, p. 407.

[49] George Sternlieb, "The City as Sandbox," *The Public Interest*, 25 (Fall 1971), 14–21, and Norton E. Long, "The City as Reservation," *Ibid.*, 22–38.

cities is simply their lack of economic value."[50] Hence the cities can no longer function as agents of social transformation and upward mobility as they had during the period of heavy urban migration from abroad and from the rural areas of the United States. The problem, according to Sternlieb, is not racial, the racial composition of new urban population serving only to exacerbate the underlying economic issue. Instead of effective staging areas for newcomers the central cities are now functioning as "sandboxes."

A sandbox is a place where adults park their children in order to converse, play, or work with a minimum of interference. The adults, having found a distraction for the children, can get on with the serious things of life. There is some reward for the children in all this. The sandbox is given to them as their own turf. Occasionally fresh sand or toys are put in the sandbox, along with an implicit admonition that these things are furnished to minimize the level of noise and nuisance. . . .

That is what the city has become—a sandbox. Government programs in the core city have increasingly taken on this cast. A glance at [recent government programs] . . . is enough to make clear the lack of effective flow of much poverty money to its ostensible targets. Instead, the money has been used to create a growing bureaucracy which is sustained by the plight of the poor, the threat of the poor, the misery of the poor, but which yields little in the way of loaves and fishes to the poor. This is the height of sandboxism. When old programs begin to lose their credibility or become unfashionable, they are given new names—therefore they are new programs. The act of repackaging or re-labeling is equated with creativity.

This is not to belittle the importance of government programs. They do have trickle-down effects; they are creating, if not efficiently, then certainly in bulk, some measure of leadership, and this leadership is highly cynical about the nature of the faucet from whence all goodies flow and, possibly as a result, is increasingly effective. Perhaps most significantly, these programs have become forms of symbolic action. In their ritualistic aspects they are of particular value. They give psychic satisfaction to the patrons of the poor, convince outsiders—especially the media—that "something is being done," and indicate to the urban poor that someone up there really cares. In a word, these programs are placebos, and they often produce all the authentic, positive results which placebos can have in medical practice.[51]

Long's analysis is equally pessimistic, although differently focused. The services the central city provides, especially in education, fail to prepare deprived urban youth either technically or motivationally for the less skilled jobs still available in the city. More broadly, according to Long, the municipal bureaucracies and unions—whether in police work, sanitation, teaching, social service, or clerical and administrative work—are "milking" the city in terms of ever-higher wage and fringe benefits, but returning nothing in terms of increased efficiency. Consequently the city is becoming "an Indian reservation for the poor, for the

[50] *Ibid.*, p. 15.
[51] *Ibid.*, pp. 17–18.

deviant, and for those who make a business or career of managing them for the rest of society," an arrangement "economically dependent on transfer payments from the outside society made in consideration of custodial services rendered."[52] In sum, viewed as "sandbox" or as "reservation," the older central cities are irrelevant and parasitic to the ongoing concerns of the larger society.

An analysis by Ganz and O'Brien of 30 large cities in the United States, including all 24 of those with metropolitan-area populations of at least a million, has recently disputed both Sternlieb's and Long's conclusions.[53] Ganz and O'Brien conclude, on the basis of data for 1960 to 1968, that these cities have an expanding economic role as measured by the number of jobs, by the value of their output, and by worker productivity. For example, the 30 central cities accounted for 27.8 percent of the national increase in goods and services, while their suburbs accounted for 29.6 percent of the increase. This indicates, say Ganz and O'Brien, that the older larger cities are successfully making the transition from reliance on manufacturing and retail trade to service jobs and are, in fact, "dynamos" rather than "sandboxes" or "reservations."

The authors contend that the problems of these central cities are fiscal, not economic. Thus, the economic dynamos of these cities generated an additional $26 billion in federal and state revenues between 1960 and 1968, but the cities received only an additional $2.5 billion in direct payments from the federal and state governments. Consequently the cities are forced to rely heavily on the local real estate tax, which is inadequate to maintain the urban amenities, especially in view of the large proportion of disadvantaged population living in these cities. Sanitation, transportation, and other public services are often visibly deteriorating; they are not signs of economic decay, however, but of the central cities' failure to receive their fair share of return from the federal and state governments.

Ganz and O'Brien contend that, far from relegating the poor and nonwhites to sandbox and reservation status, the cities are performing their historic function of upgrading disadvantaged groups. To support their claim, the authors point to the results of recent studies showing that the number of low-income families was reduced from 35 million in 1959 to 20 million in 1970, that the median income of blacks rose from 52 percent of that of whites in 1959 to 64 percent in 1970, and that the percentage of blacks working in skilled occupations rose from 43 to 60 percent in the 1960–1970 decade.[54]

---

[52] Long, *op. cit.*, pp. 32–33.

[53] Alexander Ganz and Thomas O'Brien, "The City: Sandbox, Reservation, or Dynamo?" *Public Policy*, 21 (Winter 1973), 107–23.

[54] U.S. Bureau of the Census, *Consumer Income: Characteristics of Low-Income Population, 1970*, Series P-60, # 81 (November 1971), Table A; and U.S. Bureau of Labor Statistics, *Special Studies: The Social and Economic Status of Negroes in the United States, 1970*, Series P-23, #38 (July 1971), Tables 16, 46, 47, 66, 67, 68, 69.

There are other major debates concerning the future of the central city. A fundamental question in guiding urban social change is whether it is assumed that urban problems result from "individual deficiency" or from a "dysfunctional social structure."[55] Another major question is whether, and to what extent, government should play a role in bringing about change. One influential analysis holds that government programs to ameliorate inner-city problems only serve to increase them.[56] Another much-debated book contends both that the causes of urban problems are rooted in the individual and that the government should not and cannot intervene effectively to deal with those problems.[57] Although these issues cannot be explored in the compass of this chapter, the fact of their existence serves to point up, as we noted at the beginning of this chapter, that the "reality" of the inner city has an important subjective aspect.

Summary

Crucial to understanding the inner city is the recognition that there are several types of inner city. This is evident both from an examination of the socioeconomic characteristics of inner-city residents and from a study of inner-city job profiles. The data we have reviewed in this chapter indicate that only the older, larger central cities tend to have populations with relatively low socioeconomic status as compared to their suburbs. The newer, smaller central cities display several other types of central-city–suburban contrast, including that in which the central-city population is of higher socioeconomic status than the suburban population.

The age and size of the inner city are also related to the city's job profile. The older, larger cities are becoming elite service centers and have experienced large declines in manufacturing and retail trade jobs, which have relocated to the suburban rings. Consequently there is a "mismatch" in this type of metropolitan area between the location of low socioeconomic groups and the location of blue-collar and entry-level white-collar jobs. In the newer, smaller central cities, manufacturing and retail jobs are still concentrated in the core. The persistent association between the age and size of central cities and their population and economic characteristics indicate that orderly processes of change, possibly evolutionary in nature, are under way. These are one reflection of the broad social and economic changes occurring in a mature industrial society.

[55] For a penetrating analysis based on six different types of urban organizations in nine different cities, see Roland L. Warren, "The Sociology of Knowledge and the Problems of the Inner Cities," *Social Science Quarterly*, 52 (December 1971), 469–91.

[56] Jay Forrester, *Urban Dynamics* (1969).

[57] Edward C. Banfield, *The Unheavenly City* (1970).

The mythical element in discussions and descriptions of the inner city has long been evident in the widespread belief that there is only one way of life in the city and that it is somehow associated with disorganization. The evidence on the variety of urban ways of life and on the social complexity of slums belie these stereotyped approaches. The changes at work in present-day inner cities in the United States have increased the tendency for unsupported and emotionally based beliefs about the city to flourish. The resulting controversies are most evident in public debates about whether the economic changes in the central city mean that it is "doomed" and about the alternative outcomes of the increasing concentration of nonwhites in the older, larger central cities. In both instances these inner-city issues have profound implications for the entire society.

Selected Bibliography

BOOKS

Bahr, Howard, *Skid Row: An Introduction to Disaffiliation.* New York: Oxford University Press, 1973.

Banfield, Edward C., *The Unheavenly City.* Boston: Little, Brown, 1970.

Birch, David L. *The Economic Future of City and Suburbs.* New York: Committee for Economic Development, 1970.

Boykin, James H., *Industrial Potential of the Central City.* Washington, D. C.: Urban Land Institute, 1973.

Bogue, Donald J., *Skid Row in American Cities.* Chicago: University of Chicago Press, 1963.

Clark, Kenneth B., *Dark Ghetto.* New York: Harper and Row, 1965.

Clinard, Marshall B., *Slums and Community Development.* New York: The Free Press, 1968.

Forrester, Jay, *Urban Dynamics.* Cambridge: MIT Press, 1969.

Hunter, David R., *The Slums.* New York: The Free Press, 1964.

Lewis, Oscar, *La Vida.* New York: Random House, 1966.

Mangin, William, ed., *Peasants in Cities.* Boston: Houghton Mifflin, 1970.

Murphy, Raymond E., *The Central Business District.* Chicago: Aldine, 1972.

National Urban League, *The National Survey of Housing Abandonment.* Washington, D.C.: National Urban League, 1971.

New York Metropolitan Region Study. Vol. 1, Edgar M. Hoover and Raymond Vernon, *Anatomy of a Metropolis;* Vol. 3, Oscar Handlin, *The Newcomers;* Vol. 5, Sidney Robbins *et al., Money Metropolis;* Vol. 9, Raymond Vernon, *Metropolis 1985.* Cambridge: Harvard University Press, 1959–1960.

The Office Industry: Patterns of Growth and Location. A Report of the Regional Plan Association, prepared by Regina Belz Armstrong and edited by Boris Pushkarev. Cambridge: MIT Press, 1972.

Report of the National Advisory Commission on Civil Disorders. Washington, D.C.: Government Printing Office, 1968.

Rose, Harold M., *The Black Ghetto.* New York: McGraw-Hill, 1971.

Rubin, Israel, *Satmar: An Island in the City.* Chicago: Quadrangle, 1972.

Schnore, Leo F., *The Urban Scene,* New York: The Free Press, 1965.

Sternlieb, George, and Robert W. Burchell, *Residential Abandonment: The Tenement Landlord Revisited.* New Brunswick, N.J.: Center for Urban Policy Reserach, Rutgers University, 1973.

Suttles, Gerald, *The Social Order of the Slum.* Chicago: University of Chicago Press, 1968.

Urban America, Inc., and the Urban Coalition, *One Year Later: An Assessment of the Nation's Response to the Crisis Described by the National Advisory Commission on Civil Disorders.* New York: Praeger, 1969.

Valentine, Charles A., *Culture and Poverty.* Chicago: University of Chicago Press, 1968.

ARTICLES

Barrera, Mario, Carlos Munõz, and Charles Ornelas, "The Barrio as an Internal Colony," in Harlan Hahn, ed., *People and Politics in Urban Society,* pp. 465–98. Beverly Hills, Calif.: Sage, 1972.

Carey, George W., "Hippie Neighborhoods and Urban Spatial Systems," in Robert K. Yin, ed., *The City in the Seventies,* pp. 62–65. Itasca, Ill.: Peacock Publishers, 1972.

Deskins, Donald R., "Race, Residence and Workplace in Detroit, 1880–1965," *Economic Geography,* 48 (January 1972), 79–94.

Downs, Anthony, "Alternative Futures for the American Ghetto," in his *Urban Problems and Prospects,* pp. 27–75. Chicago: Markham, 1970.

Gans, Herbert, "Urbanism and Suburbanism as Ways of Life: A Re-evaluation of Definitions," in Arnold Rose, ed., *Human Behavior and Social Process,* pp. 625–48. Boston: Houghton Mifflin, 1962.

Ganz, Alexander, and Thomas O'Brien, "The City: Sandbox, Reservation, or Dynamo?" *Public Policy,* 21 (Winter 1973), 107–23.

Gold, Neil N., "The Mismatch of Jobs and Low-Income People in Metropolitan Areas and Its Implications for the Central City Poor," in Commission on Population Growth and the American Future, *Population Distribution and Policy,* ed. Sara Mills Mazie. Vol. V of the Commission Reports., pp. 441–87. Washington, D.C.: Government Printing Office, 1972.

Greer, Edward, "The 'Liberation' of Gary, Indiana," *Society* (formerly *Trans-Action*), 8 (January 1971), 1–11.

Long, Norton E., "The City as Reservation," *The Public Interest,* 25 (Fall 1971), 22–38.

Mera, K., "On the Urban Agglomeration and Economic Efficiency," *Economic Development and Cultural Change* (January 1973), 309–24.

Morrill, Richard, "The Negro Ghetto: Problems and Alternatives," *The Geographical Review,* 55 (July 1965), 339–61.

———, and O. Fred Donaldson, "Geographical Perspectives on the History of Black America," *Economic Geography,* 48 (January 1972), 1–23.

"The Nation of Newark," *Society* (formerly *Trans-Action*), 9 (September–October 1972) special issue, 19–58.

Pinkerton, James R., "City-Suburban Residential Patterns by Social Class: A Review of the Literature," *Urban Affairs Quarterly,* 4 (June 1969), 499–519.

Pinkerton, James, "The Changing Class Composition of Cities and Suburbs," *Land Economics,* 49 (November 1973), 462–69.

Pred, Allan, "Business Thoroughfares as Expressions of Urban Negro Culture," *Economic Geography,* 39 (July 1963), 217–33.

Schnore, Leo F., "Measuring City-Suburban Status Differentials," *Urban Affairs Quarterly,* 3 (September 1967), 95–108.

——, and Joy K. O. Jones, "The Evolution of City-Suburban Types in the Course of a Decade," *Urban Affairs Quarterly,* 4 (June 1969), 421–43.

Sternlieb, George, "The City as Sandbox," *The Public Interest,* 25 (Fall 1971), 14–22.

Vander Kooi, Ronald, "The Main Stem: Skid Row Revisited," *Society* (formerly *Trans-Action*), 10 (September–October 1973), 64–72.

Warren, Roland L., "The Sociology of Knowledge and the Problems of the Inner Cities," *Social Science Quarterly,* 52 (December 1971), 469–92.

11 • The Outer City—Suburbs

The economic and social changes for the inner city described in the previous chapter have their counterparts in the suburbs. The parts of the metropolis function as an ecological whole and must be understood in conjunction with one another. The decentralization of business and industry from the inner cities of the older larger metropolitan areas to their suburban rings has generated a "new look" in the suburbs. So, too, has the continued heavy suburbanward migration of population, which now includes a broad spectrum of classes and life styles. Although decentralization of core functions is not as pronounced in newer, smaller metropolitan areas, here, too, suburbs exhibit a variety of house types, social groups, and life styles. In short, just as our analysis indicated there is no single type of central city, so also there is no single type of suburb. An important fact is that suburbs present a greater array of types than ever before. A major point of discussion is whether the growth and variety of suburbs fall into an evolutionary sequence. Are the changes in the inner city paralleled by a process of invasion-succession in the suburbs?

In sum, change and diversity are the catchwords in understanding the contemporary suburban scene. Related questions dealt with in this chapter include the importance of socioeconomic class and other variables in forming the major types of suburbs, the impact of ideology in interpreting the meaning of suburbia, and the emergence in suburbs of "urban" problems.

Studying Suburbs

Suburbs are in many ways a residual category. Cities developed first and the tools for urban study were geared to them. For some time urban sociology has been "retooling" in an effort to analyze suburbs adequately. As we will discuss below the "retooling" has both definitional and theoretical aspects.

Types of Approach

Suburbs are much discussed but ill defined. One reason for the variety of definitions is that the census provides no criteria for suburban status. In the voluminous literature on suburbs there are, however, two general approaches to the problem of definition. The first relies on objective, relatively easily measurable characteristics, such as demographic characteristics of the population or the type of land use. The second emphasizes the social organization and values of suburbanites. The two approaches are not mutually exclusive, but nevertheless it is useful to make a distinction between the two. The following are examples of the first type of definition.

A. An inclusive definition which has the virtues of simplicity and comparability defines as suburban all the territory within the census Standard Metropolitan Statistical Area but outside the central cities. On this basis, almost 40 million Americans were suburbanites in 1950, almost 59 million in 1960, and over 76 million in 1970.

B. A more refined definition of suburbs is based on the census delineation of Urbanized Areas. The suburban population may be defined as that within the Urbanized Area but outside the central cities. On this basis about 21 million Americans were suburbanites in 1950, almost 38 million in 1960, and over 54 million in 1970.

Whichever of these or similar definitions is used, suburbs are clearly a major and growing aspect of the American landscape.[1] Using the SMSA approach to the definition of suburban population, a recent census projection of present trends indicates that nearly half of the American people will be living in the suburban portion of metropolitan areas by 1985.[2] In a numerical sense the United States is already a nation of suburbanites, as shown in Figure 11.1. In 1970 the 76 million suburbanites (SMSA definition) represented 37.6 percent of the total United States population of 203 million, a greater percentage than either the 63 million who lived in the central cities of metropolitan areas (31.4 percent) or the additional 63 million who did not live in metropolitan areas (31.0 percent). The more restricted Urbanized Area definition indicated the 54 million Urbanized Area "fringe" residents represented 26.8 percent of the total United States population.

The interest in suburbs arises from far more than numbers and characteristics that can be readily quantified. A basic question is the study of the social significance of the new spatial distribution. This is the second major way of studying suburbs. When examined in terms of

---

[1] See pp. 65–70, Chapter 3, for explanations of the SMSA and the Urbanized Area census definitions.

[2] Social and Economic Statistics Administration, Bureau of the Census, *Our Cities and Suburbs*, We the Americans, Report # 7 (May 1973), p. 14.

social structure, suburban characteristics have been said to include neighboring, emphasis on family values, status-seeking, and conformity. However these conclusions are under dispute, particularly in light of recent suburban development. Suburbs have also been contrasted to the city in terms of religiosity, formal and informal social participation, political behavior, use of leisure time and "philosophy of life." Obviously such items are difficult to measure with precision, although techniques of measurement do exist. Later in this chapter we shall discuss the evidence for a suburban way of life.

The theories applied to the study of suburban social organization have been for the most part extensions of concepts developed to study the city. While this may indeed be the most appropriate way to understand suburbs, it is also important to recognize that no significant new dimensions have been added to urban theory to encompass suburbs. Thus, Schnore's major studies of city-suburban relationships[3] are cast in the framework of the Park-Burgess concentric zonal theory. Louis Wirth's classic urban theory, expressed in "Urbanism as a Way of Life,"[4]

[3] These are described at length on pp. 254–62, Chapter 10.

[4] *American Journal of Sociology*, 44 (July 1938), 3–24.

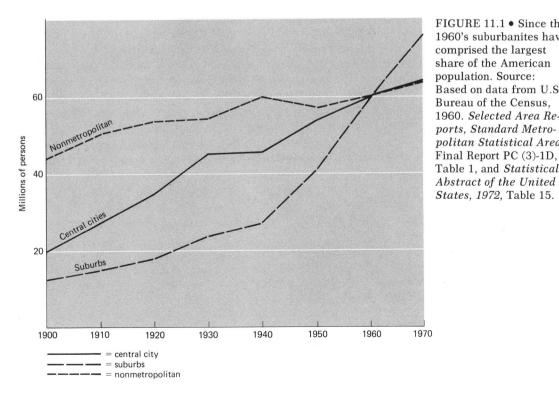

FIGURE 11.1 • Since the 1960's suburbanites have comprised the largest share of the American population. Source: Based on data from U.S. Bureau of the Census, 1960. *Selected Area Reports, Standard Metropolitan Statistical Areas.* Final Report PC (3)-1D, Table 1, and *Statistical Abstract of the United States, 1972,* Table 15.

——————— = central city
— · — · — = suburbs
- - - - - - = nonmetropolitan

has also been revised to encompass suburbs.[5] The urban theories represented by Park, Burgess, and Wirth were predicated on a concentrated city, expanding from a single center, to which the diverse population groups were oriented, as were all the major economic, social, and cultural affairs of the city. Whatever suburbs may be, they are not merely the city "thinned out"; yet urban theory has not advanced very far toward incorporating the significant features of suburban development. "Today's urban systems appear to be multinodal, multiconnected social systems in action, in which the traditional centralization of the population into metropolitan areas has been counterbalanced by a multifaceted reverse thrust of decentralization. The situation is very different from the period at the end of the nineteenth century from which we derive the concept of urbanization. Decentralization and an outward urge have replaced centralization and core orientation; differentiation and segregation substitute for the integrative role of the melting pot."[6]

One need not choose between defining suburbs in objective geographic terms or as a distinctive type of social organization. Both definitions are necessary and the real difficulty lies in relating the two types. Do the demographic and locational characteristics of suburbs produce the social characteristics; or do certain social traits produce suburban settlement patterns; or is there some combination of these types of causation? These are basic ecological questions in suburban dress, and the full answers have not yet been provided by current research and theory. It is the point of view of this book that both types of causation operate in the ecological process generally and will be found to do so in the suburban situation, too. However as pointed out above, a comprehensive approach to understanding suburbs has not yet been formulated.

The Suburban Mystique

The study of suburbs is complicated by ideology and belief.[7] Just as there are images of the city that are value judgments rather than statements of fact, so there are images of suburbia. The images are diverse.

---

[5] See, for example, Sylvia F. Fava, "Suburbanism as a Way of Life," *American Sociological Review*, 21 (February 1956), 34–37; Herbert J. Gans, "Urbanism and Suburbanism as Ways of Life: A Re-Evaluation of Definitions," in Arnold Rose, ed., *Human Behavior and Social Processes* (1962), pp. 625–48; and Janet Abu-Lughod, "The City is Dead—Long Live the City: Some Thoughts on Urbanity," in Sylvia F. Fava, ed., *Urbanism in World Perspective* (1968), pp. 154–65.

[6] Brian J. L. Berry and J. S. Cohen, "Decentralization of Commerce and Industry: The Restructuring of Metropolitan America," in Louis Masotti and Jeffrey K. Hadden, eds., *The Urbanization of the Suburbs* (1973), p. 453.

[7] This topic is developed more fully in Chapter 21, pp. 590–93.

To some people suburbia represents the fulfillment of the American middle-class dream; it is identified with the continued possibility of upward mobility, with expanding opportunities in middle-class occupations, with rising standards of living and real incomes, and the gadgeted good life as it is represented in the full-color ads in the mass-circulation magazines. To less sanguine senses, for example, those of some architects, city planners, estheticians, and designers, suburbia represents a dreary blight on the American landscape, the epitome of American standardization and vulgarization, with its row upon monotonous row of mass-produced cheerfulness masquerading as homes, whole agglomerations or "scatterations" of them masquerading as communities. To these eyes, the new tract suburbs of today are the urban slums of tomorrow. There is a third group to whom the myth of suburbia is also important; I mean sociologists and other students of contemporary social and cultural trends. . . . (They tend) to see in suburbia the convergence of some of the apparently major social and cultural trends of our time (other-direction, social mobility, neoconservatism, status anxiety, and the like), thus making of suburbia a microcosm in which the processes at work in the larger society can conveniently be studied. Finally, the vocabularies of some recent left-wing critics of American society seem to have substituted the terms "suburb" and "suburban" for the now embarrassingly obsolete term "bourgeois" as a packaged rebuke to the whole tenor of American life. What used to be condemned as "bourgeois values," "bourgeois style," and "bourgeois hypocrisy" are now simply designated as "suburban."[8]

Most images of suburbia are critical. Berger suggests that the critique of suburbia is part of the criticism of "chrome idols" and mass culture.

To some suburbia represents a flight from urban ills and evils and a search for idealized rural values, a retreat from urban reality to a green cocoon. In noting that "the rural ideal is clearly invoked by the very labels given to suburban development—'Country Village,' 'Woodbury Knolls,' 'The Ridge,' 'Pinewood,'" Dobriner suggests that these names seem to promise the city dweller uncorrupted nature and a sense of community.

The names of suburbia say, "Come back!" Come back to the *real* things—the green mansions, the sylvan hollows, and sun-sprayed meadows, the private, small and uncorrupted little green places. Come back to the permanent, immutable, and trusted forms of nature. . . . Return to the "Country Village" and Colonial America. No great heaving city this, no paranoid bureaucracy, just a simple untroubled rural village where there is a family and "roots" and friends. Everything is in order, and a man can see all the forces which shape his life.[9]

If these promises pull people to suburbs the promises may often be unfulfilled. Over-building and lack of planning frequently negate the outdoor attractions and, as Dobriner points out elsewhere in his book, cleavages of social class and ethnicity often prevent suburban com-

[8] Bennett M. Berger, *Working-Class Suburb* (1960), pp. 99–100.
[9] William M. Dobriner, *Class in Suburbia* (1963), p. 73.

munity harmony and integration. The important issue, however, is not so much whether suburbanites find allegedly rural virtues in the suburbs, but whether they went there in search of them.

The suburban myth is complex and sometimes conflicting. Needless to say, it is a projection of wishes and assumptions rather than a reflection of suburban reality. At most, various components of the myth reflect some portions of suburbia at a given time. Nevertheless the myth is "real" insofar as it forms part of people's perceptions and it influences their actions. The suburban myth is also real in that is is a social product and can be subjected to sociological analysis and understandings, a process now underway.[10] Finally, the suburban myth is important because the student must be aware of these "symbolic locales and associated sentiments"[11] as he examines the rapidly mounting volume of pronouncements and reports on suburbia.

Suburbs Yesterday and Today

Suburbs are by no means a new feature on the urban landscape. They have existed around the larger American cities for well over a hundred years. For most of this period, however, they were only "a footnote to urban civilization."[12] Not until well into the twentieth century, particularly after World War II, did suburbs come to dominate American life, heralding a new era whose consequences are still only partially understood. The emergence, change, and spread of suburbs are part of the transformation of American society reflected in the community forms characteristic of particular periods of American history. Three major periods of American urban development, and an emergent fourth, have already been described extensively in Chapter Three. The stages of suburban growth described below parallel those broader periods, although by the nature of the approximate categorization of any "periods," there is no perfect fit. In ecological terms, the change in the extent and character of the suburbs is an aspect of change in the total urban system of which suburbs are a part.

Stages of Suburban Growth

Viewing decentralization as a long-time trend, the social historian Frederick Lewis Allen has identified five stages of suburban develop-

---

[10] Scott Donaldson, *The Suburban Myth* (1969); and Sylvia F. Fava, "The Pop Sociology of Suburbs and New Towns," *American Studies*, 14 (Spring 1973), 121–33.

[11] Anselm Strauss, "The Changing Imagery of American City and Suburb," *The Sociological Quarterly*, 1 (January 1960), p. 24.

[12] Harlan Paul Douglass, *The Suburban Trend* (1925) p. 25.

ment in the United States.[13] These periods, by no means clearly distinct but tending to overlap, are especially applicable to great metropolitan areas.

The first stage, the horse-and-buggy period, began in the latter years of the nineteenth century and lasted until about the close of World War I. During the nineteenth century many well-to-do people had maintained country homes, which they occupied part of the year, but late in the century some of them adopted the practice of year-round living in their rural or semirural homes, commuting to work by train or trolley. As the advantages of outlying residence gained wider appeal, numerous persons moved to the rim, settling in clusters within walking distance of railroad or interurban stations. "Streetcar suburbs" and "mainline suburbs" were characteristic of this era of dependence on "fixed track" transportation.

In this period, particularly in some cities on the Eastern seaboard, the suburbanization process had already proceeded extensively. Warner describes the vast proliferation of "streetcar suburbs" around Boston between 1870 and 1900, resulting in an estimated half of metropolitan Boston living in such locations by the turn of the century.[14]

The second period, according to Allen, covered approximately the 1920's, a period of revolution in transportation when the number of

View of Fountain Square, Evanston, Illinois, in 1894 illustrates an early stage of suburban growth with dependence on street cars and local railroads for commuting to Chicago. Evanston's population of 4,400 in 1880 grew to 19,000 by 1900. (Courtesy Evanston Historical Society)

[13] Frederick Lewis Allen, "The Big Change in Suburbia," Part I, *Harper's Magazine*, 208 (June 1954), 21–28.

[14] Sam Bass Warner, Jr., *Streetcar Suburbs: The Process of Growth in Boston, 1870–1900* (1962).

Park Forest, Illinois, shown in a 1952 view, is an example of the postwar mass-produced suburb. Built on an open-country site of 2,400 acres about 30 miles south of Chicago, Park Forest was designed for 30,000 residents. (Courtesy Chicago Historical Society)

automobiles increased from 9 million in 1920 to 26 million in 1930. Open cars were replaced by all-weather closed cars, and road-building was undertaken on an unprecedented scale. Although the number of persons carried by railroad and interurban lines increased, the number carried by private cars increased by leaps and bounds. Streets criss-crossed undeveloped tracts on the outskirts of cities to reach the suburban developments needed to accommodate the thousands of families bent on moving to the country.

The third period, from 1930 to 1945, covered the Great Depression and World War II. When the depression, which started in 1929, began to stifle the nation's economy, the headlong flight to the suburbs was stopped. Real estate developments that had been blithely undertaken on a shoestring collapsed, partly because families that had purchased property on an equally slender shoestring were unable to keep up their payments, partly because uncommitted families would not risk their savings in suburban property. As the country regained its economic health in the late 1930's, there was a resumption of suburban developments but on a modest scale. Much of it was what Allen calls "filling in the chinks" around the edge of cities, between cities and nearby suburbs, or along radial thoroughfares. Heavy government expenditures in peripheral areas for parkways, bridges, cloverleaf intersections, and express highways laid the stage for another flight to the suburbs. But building and transportation restrictions imposed by the war prevented the flight from occurring. During the whole of this third period, population growth in the suburbs was about the same as for the country as a whole.

The years following World War II, in Allen's view, represent the fourth and fifth stages. The fourth stage featured the mass-produced suburb built for war veterans and other young families with limited means. Unlike many suburban developments, that grew mainly by slow accretion as new houses were gradually added one by one, the mass-produced suburbs around the great cities were constructed as large-scale engineering enterprises. Levittown near New York, Drexelbrook in the Philadelphia area, Park Forest outside Chicago, Parkmerced near San Francisco, and Lakewood outside Los Angeles are examples of entire communities being constructed on the assembly-line principle. As Allen put it these suburbs were built for an intensely domestic generation of young people who wanted babies and who took parental duties seriously; who could not afford servants and would not know what to do with them if they had them; who enjoyed sharing the work in and about the house; who fully subscribed to the do-it-yourself credo of a generation of household tinkerers; and who subscribed equally fully to the cult

Willowbrook Mall, at the junction of major highways in Wayne County, New Jersey, illustrates the current suburban period, "the discovery of the suburbs by business." The Mall contains several department stores, numerous small shops, a movie house, and a legitimate theater. (Willowbrook Mall Merchants Association)

of informality, getting into slacks or shorts as soon as they reached the suburbs and continuing to wear them until they left for town.[15]

By no means all of suburban growth during the postwar period took the form of large-scale enterprises. Wealthy or well-to-do families, as well as many families of limited incomes, built private homes according to individual tastes and interests. Nevertheless, even in the vicinity of small and medium-sized cities much of suburban growth was of the development type but on a small scale.

Allen's fifth period is what he calls the "discovery of the suburbs by business." This trend was discussed in Chapter 10 dealing with decentralization of business and industry from the inner city. Although in past decades movement of business to the suburbs had been considerable, it reached an unprecedented scale in the postwar period.

Suburbs Today— The Outer City

The decentralization of industry, commerce, and other activities to suburban areas has now proceeded so far that suburbs have become citified in many ways. In the 1970's they have begun to be called the "outer city."[16]

The urbanization of the suburbs[17] includes the emergence of suburbs as major employment centers. The 1970 census reports that nearly 60 percent of the workers living in the suburbs of metropolitan areas also worked in the suburbs, thus relegating to history the picture of the typical suburbanite as one who commuted to the city to earn his living. A special study by the *New York Times* indicates that in the 15 largest metropolitan areas the proportion of suburbanites who both live and work in the suburbs is even higher—72 percent.[18] The highest percentages were Los Angeles–Long Beach, 78.6; Philadelphia, 77.8; New York, 77.7; Detroit, 76.3; Pittsburgh and Houston, both 76.2.

THE SUBURBAN ECONOMY.   The increasingly broad suburban economic base stems not only from the decentralization of retailing and manufacturing, although as indicated in Chapter 10 these are basic shifts. Charles Haar, who headed a major Presidential commission on suburbs, has noted that 32 percent of suburban communities are now industrial

---

[15] Allen, *op. cit.*, pp. 25–28.

[16] The term appears to have been used first in a widely cited and reprinted series of five articles in *The New York Times*, "The Outer City: U.S. in Suburban Turmoil," (May 30–June 3, 1971).

[17] Louis Masotti and Jeffrey K. Hadden's reader, *The Urbanization of the Suburbs* (1973) is an important example of the recognition and description of this new era of suburbia.

[18] Jack Rosenthal, "Large Suburbs Overtaking Cities in Number of Jobs They Provide," *New York Times*, October 15, 1972), pp. 1, 58.

and many of the others have become commercial.[19] A wide variety of goods and facilities ranging from French couture to major sports events are increasingly available in suburban locations. Suburban shopping centers have often become more truly centers, offering not only department stores and convenience shopping, but a broad array of specialized goods and services. The Monroeville Mall, twelve miles east of midtown Pittsburgh, offers 129 attractions, including boutiques, restaurants, snack shops, department stores, professional offices, a reference library, a night club, a Roman Catholic chapel, and a personal counseling service headed by a Protestant minister. Banks, ballet schools, art galleries, discotheques, and movie theaters are located in many shopping centers, while art shows, youth and musical festivals, auto shows, and jazz concerts have been held on the malls. By 1970 there were nearly 13,000 large scale shopping centers in the United States, most of them built in the 1960's; 500 of these are enclosed malls.[20]

View of the interior of the mall in Los Cerritos Center, Los Angeles, shows some of the many facilities for shopping and entertainment. (Bruce Barnum, Photographer)

[19] Charles Haar, ed., *The End of Innocence: A Suburban Reader* (1972), Preface, no pagination.

[20] Seth S. King, "Supermarkets Hub of Suburbs," *New York Times* (Sunday, February 7, 1971); and Rose De Wolf, "Main Street Goes Private," *The Nation* (December 18, 1972), p. 626.

In the suburbs one can now find major sports events and facilities. The Detroit Lions, for example, are now based in suburban Pontiac. The newly constructed Nassau Coliseum, serving Nassau County, a major suburban area of New York City, features top-ranked athletic teams and sports events. On a site near Independence, Missouri, two stadia and a large sports complex have just been completed to house the Kansas City Chiefs football team, the Kansas City Royals baseball team, the Kansas City Kings basketball team, as well as hockey teams, track meets, auto racing, livestock and horse shows. All these facilities have gargantuan parking lots whose only link with public transportation is buses.

A new dimension has been added to suburbia in the emergence of a broader spectrum of health, cultural, and convention facilities. A new level of suburban hospital has appeared, usually serving a regional population and including the most sophisticated and expensive equipment and staffed by specialists and research teams. These complexes are capable of treating rare and unusual diseases and of performing complicated team surgery. Formerly such hospitals were found only in large cities. They are not yet standard in suburban regions, but their appearance is another indication of the wider and wider variety of services available in suburbs. Cultural facilities such as museums, theaters, symphony orchestras, and even opera companies have also been established in some suburbs, although as yet in limited numbers. More frequent are convention centers built around meeting rooms and living arrangements but also offering some on-site recreation and shopping. Most of these centers are located en route from airports or near major highway interchanges. Typically they can accommodate groups of limited size; conventions numbering thousands of participants must still use the inner city hotels, ballrooms, and lecture halls. Yet the emergence of these mini-centers for business and professional meetings is a straw blowing in the same decentralized direction as other phenomena.

Suburban newspapers, reflecting the fact of increasing suburban population, buying power, and voting power, have become more numerous and less exclusively local in coverage. While many inner city newspapers are dead or dying from loss of advertising and decreased circulation, suburban newspapers are doing very well. A prime example is *Newsday*, which serves Nassau and Suffolk, two suburban counties of Long Island, New York, whose combined population in 1970 was over two and a half million.

OFFICE DECENTRALIZATION   The crucial question regarding the suburban (and inner city) economy is whether offices, especially corporate headquarters, have or are likely to locate significantly in suburbs. Offices do locate in suburban areas, of course, but an early study indicated decentralization of offices to such areas is limited and highly selective. At least this is suggested by an investigation in the San

Francisco metropolitan area of the location of new offices and the relocation of established ones.[21] From 1948 to 1954, the proportion of top administrative offices concentrated in downtown San Francisco dropped from 61 percent of all San Francisco metropolitan area top administrative offices to 49 percent of such offices. However, further analysis disclosed that almost all of the suburban offices relocated or initially established in this period were attached to nonoffice facilities, such as manufacturing plants, warehouses, or transportation terminals. Less than one percent of the relocation of new offices in the suburbs was of detached headquarters offices. The supremacy of the central business district in attracting new offices and holding existing ones is clear. Total downtown office space in San Francisco grew from 10.2 million square feet in 1946 to 13.2 million in 1956.

A more recent study of the New York metropolitan region[22] indicates that in 1963 Manhattan's central business district contained 138 of the headquarters of *Fortune's* 500, a list of the nation's largest corporations; by 1969 the number had fallen to 122, not allowing for several firms that had merged in the interim. Virtually all of the headquarters that had moved, relocated in New York City suburbs, especially in western Fairfield county, Connecticut. Suburban Greenwich, Connecticut, has emerged as a prestige office location in the New York region and has counterparts in Clayton, Missouri, and Southfield, Michigan, which have absorbed office relocation from St. Louis and Detroit, respectively.

The New York study also indicates, as did the San Francisco study, the selective nature of office decentralization.[23] Offices directly related to the population they serve or to production—that is, offices in transportation, government, construction, and retailing—are more likely to suburbanize, while offices related to finance and business services are least likely to suburbanize. Such a pattern is expected in terms of the coordinating function of the central city, and especially of the central business district, in the modern metropolis.

If there were a clear trend toward the suburbanization of the offices performing the "switchboard" and elite service functions described in Chapter 10, it would signify a radical change in the nature of metropolitan structure. Utilizing census data from 157 SMSA's, Kasarda tested the assumption that central cities perform functions of economic coordination and integration for their suburban rings.[24] His empirical

[21] Donald L. Foley, *The Suburbanization of Administrative Offices in the San Francisco Bay Region* (1957).

[22] *The Office Industry: Patterns of Growth and Location*, A Report of the Regional Plan Association, prepared by Regina Belz Armstrong and edited by Boris Pushkarev (1972) p. 60ff.

[23] *Ibid.*, p. 94ff.

[24] John Kasarda, "The Theory of Ecological Expansion: An Empirical Test," *Social Forces*, 51 (December 1972), 165–75.

study concluded that the central cities do indeed perform such functions and, in fact, that the organizational development of the central city increases in direct proportion as the size of the suburban ring expands. This suggests that large-scale suburbanization of offices and head-quarters is not on the horizon and may never come to pass.

THE SUBURBAN POPULATION   Suburbs house more people and more varied people than ever before. By 1970 almost six out of ten metro-politan residents were suburbanites and included groups who had hitherto been underrepresented in suburbs. The aged, the divorced, single adults, and childless couples are found with increasing frequency in suburbs, contrasting with the earlier predominance of families with young children. Suburban heterogeneity is the population counterpart to the decentralization of economic activities and jobs.

As heterogeneity increases in the suburbs and especially "as the proportion of childless residents without house maintenance respon-sibilities becomes significant, other indicators of an increasing life-style mix emerge: singles bars, nightclubs, more and better restaurants, first-run movies, and adult recreational facilities. Suburbia is clearly no longer just a 'family place.' Regardless of marital status, age or stage in life cycle, there is, or soon will be, a residential option with a reasonably good sociocultural support structure. Another indicator of 'urbs in sub-urbs.'"[25] The addition of sizable groups of nonfamily population to suburbs is visibly reflected in new housing types. Apartment houses, both the garden type and high rise, are spreading in suburbia, as are attached row houses. In suburban areas multiunit housing structures almost doubled in the 1960–70 decade, while single-family homes rose by only 17 percent.[26] Sometimes the building of multifamily housing is resisted by particular suburbs as aesthetically disruptive and intruding an allegedly more transient, less locally committed population; in other suburbs the new housing types are welcomed because they attract a population that has few school-age children and makes few other costly service demands, thereby strengthening the local tax base.

The poor are another group increasingly represented in suburbia. Over a fifth (22 percent) of the nation's poor families (family income of less than $4,140 a year in 1969) lived in suburbs in 1970.[27] Central cities have more of the poor, housing about a third (32 percent) of the nation's poor families, but the suburban percentage is substantial and con-tradicts the image of the affluent middle-class composition of suburbs.

[25] Louis Masotti, "Prologue: Suburbia Reconsidered—Myth and Counter-Myth," in Masotti and Hadden, *op. cit.*, p. 19.

[26] Census of Population and Housing, 1970. *General Demographic Trends for Metropolitan Areas, 1960 to 1970.* Final Report PHC (2)-1 (1971), p. 15.

[27] Social and Economic Statistics Administration, *Our Cities and Suburbs, op. cit.*, p. 12.

During the 1960's blacks, too, began a suburban migration, albeit on a small scale. During the 1960–70 decade, blacks increased as a proportion of the suburban population in every region except the South. Nevertheless the black population remained highly concentrated in central cities: of all the black population living in SMSA's, only 15.1 percent lived in the suburban portion in 1960 and this figure rose to only 16.2 percent by 1970.[28] The nature and significance of the black suburban migration are vitally important to the future of suburbs as well as the central city and American society as a whole and will be discussed in a later section of this chapter.

Despite the increasing heterogeneity of suburban population, homogeneity is still the rule within most individual suburbs. The "suburbanization of everyone" has not resulted in suburban integration of economic groups, social classes, and races. Instead it has resulted in a wider array of suburbs. Joining the well-known and often stereotyped picture of the upper middle class and child-rearing suburbs are blue-collar suburbs, suburban slums, retirement "villages," black suburbs, "gilded" ethnic ghettos, and other emerging suburban community types.

In concluding this review of the widening spectrum of economic and population decentralization which has made the suburbs "where the people, the power, and the problems are moving,"[29] it may be well to ask whether the suburbs are still suburban. In one basic way suburbs continue to contrast markedly with the city. "The major difference is that cities have a single governmental system with the real potential for authoritative control and regulation of the functions within its jurisdiction. Suburbia lacks a comparable control system and operates, willy-nilly, on the basis of intersuburban competition for scarce resources, like industrial, commercial, retail, and residential developments with low public service costs and high tax production."[30] The governmental fragmentation of suburbia sets it apart from the city and raises some fundamental questions about the economic and political ability of suburbs to cope with the growing variety of demands and problems that urbanization is bringing in its train.

Profile of Suburbia

Despite the many changes that have occurred in suburbia in the post-World War II period there are still major overall contrasts in economic and social characteristics between the central cities and suburbs of metropolitan areas. The contrasts reflect the superior ameni-

[28] William W. Pendleton, "Blacks in Suburbs," in Masotti and Hadden, *op. cit.*, p. 173.
[29] Gail Miller and Donald Canty, "The Suburbs: Frontier of the 70's," *City*, 5 (January/February 1971), p. 13.
[30] Masotti, *op. cit.*, in Masotti and Hadden, *op. cit.*, p. 17.

ties of the suburban environment, such as spaciousness and new housing, and the drawing power of such amenities for the population able to afford them. The growing diversity of suburbs is scarcely reflected in overall city-suburban contrasts, partly because such statistics do not lend themselves to display variation. Also, the trend toward suburban social and economic diversity should not lead us to expect an ironing out of accumulated differences, especially as long as the black and other disadvantaged minorities remain concentrated in the central cities.

City-Suburban Population Contrasts

Defining as suburban the metropolitan (SMSA) population living outside the central cities, we find that the suburbanites have higher income, more education, higher status jobs, and are more likely to consist of families with children. According to the 1970 census, as shown in Figure 11.2, the median yearly income of all suburban families was $11,210 as compared with $9,510 for central city residents. Higher suburban incomes also prevailed for the black and Spanish heritage populations.

The favorable income position of suburbia is underscored by the fact that in 1970 all of the 30 wealthiest counties in the United States were suburban, as listed in Table 11.1. None were central city counties and none were in nonmetropolitan areas. Furthermore, 53 percent of the

TABLE 11.1: 30 Wealthiest Counties, 1970*

County	Median Family Income	County	Median Family Income
1. Montgomery, Md.	$16,708	16. San Mateo, Cal.	$13,218
2. Fairfax, Va.	15,697	17. Macomb, Mich.	13,108
3. Nassau, N.Y.	14,625	18. Fairfield, Conn.	13,074
4. Du Page, Ill.	14,457	19. Lake, Ill.	12,998
5. Marin, Cal.	13,931	20. Waukesha, Wisc.	12,792
6. Oakland, Mich.	13,823	21. Norfolk, Mass.	12,747
7. Westchester, N.Y.	13,774	22. Montgomery, Pa.	12,743
8. Rockland, N.Y.	13,751	23. Ozaukee, Wisc.	12,620
9. Arlington, Va.	13,740	24. Union, N.J.	12,590
10. Bergen, N.J.	13,591	25. Santa Clara, Cal.	12,453
11. Anchorage, Alaska	13,590	26. Prince Georges, Md.	12,445
12. Howard, Md.	13,461	27. Contra Costa, Cal.	12,422
13. Somerset, N.J.	13,432	28. Monroe, N.Y.	12,420
14. Morris, N.J.	13,420	29. Geauga, Ohio	12,411
15. Johnson, Kans.	13,382	30. St. Louis, Mo.	12,375

*Only counties with population of at least 50,000 are included.
SOURCE: Compiled from U.S. Bureau of the Census, *County and City Data Book*, 1972, U.S. Government Printing Office, Table 2.

nation's 2.4 million families with incomes of $25,000 or more live in suburbia; not quite a third (31 percent) live in the central cities of metropolitan areas. The remaining 16 percent of families in this income bracket live in nonmetropolitan portions of the United States.[31]

Educationally the suburban population led the cities, six of every ten suburban adults (59.2 percent) having at least a high school education, compared to only five out of ten central city adults (50.8 percent). The educational contrast was in the same direction for the Spanish heritage population, but not for the black residents. The occupational distribution of the suburban population, shown in Table 11.2, is to be expected in view of suburban income and educational characteristics. Compared to urbanites the suburban labor force has higher representation in the professional, managerial, and sales categories. The fact that the percentage of residents employed as draftsmen or foremen is higher in

[31] Social and Economic Statistics Administration, *Our Cities and Suburbs, op. cit.*, p. 7.

TABLE 11.2: Types of Jobs by Area of Residence

	CENTRAL CITIES	SUBURBS
Total employed 16 or older	**25.2 million**	**28.9 million**
Professional, Technical	15.2%	16.8%
Managers and Administrators	7.6	9.4
Sales workers	7.3	8.0
Clerical workers	21.6	18.7
Craftsmen, Foremen	12.1	14.9
*Operatives, non-transport	12.9	12.2
Transport equipment operatives	3.8	3.6
Farmers, Farm managers	0.1	0.8
Farm laborers	0.2	0.8
Nonfarm laborers	4.5	3.8
Service workers, nonhousehold	12.9	9.9
Private household workers	1.7	1.0

*Operate machines or do similar work.
SOURCE: Social and Economic Statistics Administration. Bureau of the Census. *Our Cities and Suburbs.* We the Americans. Report #7. U.S. Government Printing Office. May 1973, p. 8.

the suburbs than in the central cities, is due to the long-term trend toward the suburbanization of industry, whose top-paid workers are able to afford suburban living.

Suburbia still contains a somewhat higher proportion of "normal" family groups than cities. As Figure 11-2 shows, almost nine out of ten suburban families have both husband and wife present, while only eight out of ten central city families are in this category. The remainder of the families are headed by divorced, widowed, or single parents. A higher proportion of husband-wife families in the suburbs is also evident among the black and Spanish heritage populations. Among the total suburban population and also among black and Spanish heritage suburbanites, a higher proportion of children under 18 live with both parents than in the central city population.

Types of Suburbs

Overall comparisons between *the* suburbs and *the* central city obscure as much as they reveal, however. Just as city areas range from the "bright lights" of downtown to the "bombed out" areas of deteriorated and abandoned homes and stores to the "gold coasts" of luxury dwellings, so, too, do suburban sub-areas vary in land use and in the characteristics of the residents. Schnore's early study, originally published in 1957, distinguished between "satellites," suburban subcenters devoted to employment and "suburbs," subcenters devoted to residence;[32] but as suburban residential population and economic functions have become more diverse it has become increasingly important to distinguish more precisely among types of suburbs.

Constructing typologies requires assumptions about the significant dimensions of variation among suburbs. The resultant typologies will therefore differ somewhat from one another. Table 11.3 presents two broadly applicable typologies that include four different variables only one of which, the socioeconomic status of the residents, is common to both typologies. The Harris survey includes, in addition, whether or not the suburb is still expanding or already appears to have reached its peak. By implication the Harris typology is restricted to residential suburbs. Thorns' typology includes as a variable whether the suburb is residential (more people commute out of the suburb for jobs than work within it) or industrial (more people commute into the suburb for employment than commute out). Additionally, Thorns classifies the suburbs according to whether they are planned or "just grew." The Harris typology was derived from a survey of over 1,600 suburban Americans in 100 different communities located in the noncentral city portions of SMSA's. Thorns' typology derived from examining case studies of suburbs in the United States and the United Kingdom.

[32] Leo F. Schnore, "Satellites and Suburbs," in his *The Urban Scene* (1965), 137–51.

TABLE 11.3:   Two Suburban Typologies

Harris*	Thorns**
A. Affluent Bedroom	1. Middle-Class Planned Residential
B. Affluent Settled	2. Working-Class Planned Residential
C. Low-Income Growing	3. Middle-Class Unplanned Residential
D. Low-Income Stagnant	4. Working-Class Planned Industrial
	5. Working-Class Unplanned Residential
	6. Middle-Class Planned Industrial
	7. Middle-Class Unplanned Industrial
	8. Working-Class Unplanned Industrial

*2 variables: SES and growth
**3 variables: SES, planning, dominant activity
SOURCE: Louis Harris survey conducted for *Time* and reported in "Suburbia: The New American Plurality," *Time* (March 15, 1971), 14–20; and David C. Thorns, *Suburbia*, London: MacGibbon and Kee, 1972, pp. 77–92.

Only two of the twelve suburban types delineated by Harris and Thorns resemble the archetype of suburbia on which so much of the suburban mystique is based. Residents of the Harris survey's Affluent Bedroom are in the top ranks of income and home ownership; they have

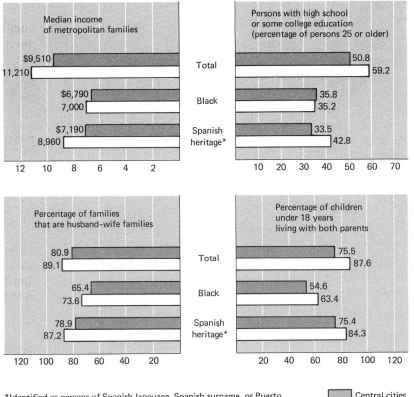

FIGURE 11.2 ● On an overall basis suburban residents have higher socioeconomic status and more of them live in complete families than do central city residents. Source: Social and Economic Statistics Administration. Bureau of the Census. *Our Cities and Suburbs.* We the Americans. Report #7. U.S. Government Printing Office, May 1973, pp. 5, 7, 11.

*Identified as persons of Spanish language, Spanish surname, or Puerto Rican birth or parentage, and may include persons of any race.

 Central cities
☐ Suburbs

high proportions working in the professions or as executives and more of them commute to work in the central city than in other suburbs. Most of the residents are white, Protestant, and Republican.[33] New Canaan, Connecticut, Winnetka, Illinois, Atherton, California, and Leawood, Kansas are examples of this type of "classic" suburb. Thorns' Middle-Class Planned Residential suburb includes such habitats of "the organization man" as Park Forest, Illinois, Levittown, Long Island, and Crestwood Heights, Canada.[34] These large developments, constructed after World War II on largely vacant land, often by a single developer who also installed stores and recreational facilities, typically attracted young married couples owning their first home and raising young children. Their efforts to establish social institutions in this setting gave rise to the social critics' often parodying descriptions of frantic togetherness, shallow roots, and "cracks in the picture window." The resemblance of these suburbs to Allen's fourth stage of suburban growth, described earlier, is obvious.

In comparison to the Affluent Bedroom type, the Harris Affluent Settled type represents suburbs that are not growing as rapidly, are more self-sufficient in terms of employment opportunities and shopping, and whose populations are somewhat more varied in terms of income, religion, and political affiliation. Fairfield, Connecticut, Huntington, Long Island, Arlington, Virginia, and Evanston, Illinois are examples.

Thorns' typology includes three additional middle-class types. Two of these, the Middle-Class Planned Industrial and the Middle-Class Unplanned Industrial are logical suburban types but as yet no specific cases have been studied. In any event they are likely to be infrequent types because of the nonmanual nature of middle class jobs. Thorns' remaining middle class type, the Middle-Class Unplanned Residential suburb is both frequent and important. Often these originated as rural villages and may have a long, even historic, past, but have now been caught up in the outer reaches of suburban expansion. Conflict between the "old settlers," accustomed to running the community, and the newcomers, whose life styles and spending patterns often differ considerably from those of the established residents, is always a possibility in suburbs of this type. William Dobriner describes a "reluctant suburb" on eastern Long Island in which dissension focused on the educational system, with the newcomers wanting the latest innovations in educational technology and methods—and willing to pay for them—while the more conservative original inhabitants opposed both the innovations and the taxes.[35]

The several low-income and working-class types of suburbs delineated by the Harris survey and by Thorns are variations on the theme of

[33] Louis Harris survey conducted for *Time* and reported in "Suburbia: the New American Plurality," *Time* (March 15, 1971), 14–20.
[34] David C. Thorns, *Suburbia* (1972), pp. 77–92.
[35] Dobriner, *op. cit.*, pp. 127–40.

blue-collar suburbs. Low-Income Growing suburbs differ from the Low-Income Stagnant not only in their economic vitality but, perhaps because of this, the former attract an upwardly mobile blue-collar population living close to their suburban jobs, while the latter contain less mobile groups. Sylvania, Ohio, Billerica, Massachusetts, and El Monte, California are examples of Low-Income Growing suburbs according to the Harris survey; while Cambridge, Massachusetts, McKeesport, Pennsylvania, Joliet, Illinois, and Bell Gardens, California, and such black suburbs as East Orange, New Jersey, and Compton, California, are examples of Low-Income Stagnant suburbs.

The planned working-class suburb, whether residential or industrial (Thorns' types 2 and 4), is more common in the United Kingdom, where the national government has considerable power over industrial location and residential building, than in the United States. Occasionally a large manufacturing plant will establish itself in suburbia and private developers will build nearby moderate-income housing for the workers, as in the move of a Ford plant to Milpitas, California.[36] In the more usual American case, suburbs are more likely to welcome the industrial plant but resist the building of housing for the workers and their families. Thorns' unplanned suburbs (types 5 and 8) are the more frequent working-class suburban types in the United States and, in fact, overlap with the low-income suburbs described by the Harris survey. The unplanned nature of most American working-class suburbs is underscored by the fact that they have often deteriorated from higher status use, a point elaborated on below.

Evolution of Suburbs?

The variety of suburbs can be viewed in a time perspective as well as in the cross-sectional approach used in the typologies described above. Classifying the broad suburban rings from a time perspective led to the distinction between "suburbs," located relatively close to the central city and hence developed first in the wave of expansion, and the "rural-urban fringe," located further out and displaying the mixed characteristics of areas still in transition from agricultural to nonagricultural use.

SUBURBS AND FRINGE The "suburbs" have a consistent nonfarm residential pattern of land use, the population works at urban jobs, and at least some services such as water supply, sewage disposal, cooking gas piped in from street mains, and a full-time paid fire department, are provided by a local government. In contrast the "fringe" exhibits an amazing variety of people and land use, both of which are not neatly separated into clusters but intermingled without much rhyme or reason.

[36] This community is analyzed in Bennett M. Berger, *Working Class Suburb* (1960).

One study found that the fringe differed from suburbs precisely in that homogeneous communities on various levels of income, occupation, and so on, were characteristic of suburbs but not of the fringe.[37] Also the fringe residents rely on individual artesian wells, septic tanks, bottled cooking gas, and volunteer fire fighters.

Some of the fringe residents are strictly agricultural by occupation; some are part-time farmers for whom the urban job is a major source of income; others are rural by residence only—persons whose interests, values, occupation, and style of life are those of the city or the metropolis. There are wealthy business or professional people whose spacious estates are exhibits of conspicuous consumption; middle class folk whose land holdings range from small plots to large farms operated by tenants or members of the family; working-class families who perform the dual role of part-time farmer and urban worker. Within the fringe are residential community developments of varying size, density, and character; areas in which families are sparsely and unevenly distributed in the open country; areas in which residence and business establishments are strung in monotonous rows along the main radial thoroughfares.

There is no neat formula that describes what the fringe or its people are like. In this zone one may find, often side by side, junk yards, trailer courts, roadhouses, hot dog stands, golf courses, truck gardens, tourist courts, oil depots, commercial farms, factories, cemeteries, airports, middle class homes, fashionable estates, and residential slums, not to mention vacant spaces that are too expensive for agricultural use and undesirable for residential occupancy.

THE AGING SUBURB   A time perspective presupposes change. As applied to "suburbs" and "fringe" this suggests that the fringe becomes suburban in that the former agricultural hinterland becomes clearly suburban in land use, density, and occupational orientation. But what of the closer-in suburbs that developed earlier? By the late 1960's the vast suburban expansion after World War II was over 20 years old and signs of change, including incipient and actual deterioration and decay, were apparent in some post-World War II suburbs as well as in still older suburban areas. The changes indicate a "maturing" process of suburbia including the turnover of housing stock to groups lower on the socio-economic ladder, as the earlier higher-ranking groups move to the current mode of modern home, often located further out.

Dobriner noted an early instance of this process, akin to invasion-succession, in Levittown, Long Island, where 62 percent of the male residents were in white collar jobs in 1950–51, but by 1961 only 50 percent were so classified.[38] During the same period the proportion of

---

[37] Leslie Kish, "Differentiation in Metropolitan Areas," *American Sociological Review*, 19 (August 1954), 388–98.

[38] Dobriner, *op. cit.*, pp. 98–108.

blue collar residents rose from 38 to 45 percent. Dobriner describes
differences in outlook and activities between the middle class and
working class groups which had led to friction within local neighborhoods in Levittown. The middle class values are privacy, initiative, and
upward mobility; the working class places less emphasis on privacy or
appearances and is more concerned with living for the moment than
planning for the future. In leisure-time pursuits the middle class emphasizes reading more than television, while the reverse is true of the
working class. Middle class Levittowners are less concerned with maintaining traditional sex roles in home and child-rearing than are working
class Levittowners. The middle class group appears to do more entertaining and visiting with business associates and non-Levittown
friends and less entertaining of relatives than does the working class
group.

In East Cleveland, a close-in Cleveland suburb, with housing built
mainly in the 1920's, the transition during the 1960's has been from
white blue-collar to black blue-collar residents.[39] In 1960, 2.4 percent of
the suburb's population was black but by 1967 the black population had
grown to 44.6 percent of the total.

Many of the suburbs classified as low income by Harris or as unplanned working class suburbs by Thorns arrived at that SES level
through a cycle of change. The following description of East Orange,
New Jersey, is indicative:

East Orange has many faces: the tree-lined streets and substantial houses of
the well-heeled First Ward, the old, rundown frame houses of the Fifth Ward,
the modern apartment buildings that tower over both. The citizens of East
Orange lead parallel but unlinked lives. Some 55 percent to 60 percent of them
are black, and black-white contacts are guarded. . . . The lines also divide the
have from have-not, black middle class from black working class. . . .

For many of the blacks, East Orange has been the first step out from the city,
from Newark or New York, a reach for a suburban hinterland of open space
and green grass and fresh air. Once it was that for wealthy whites. Long before
World War II, it was a gracious, self-contained suburb with some mansions
that verged on the palatial, imposing apartment buildings, a Baptist seminary
and Upsala College.

Most of that changed after the war. Black families moved in, looking for
better housing and better schools. Whites drifted away toward the shore or to
the mountains, either because they felt uncomfortable among the newcomers
or because their houses were now too large to manage. . . . The white middle
class thinned out. . . .

Once, branches of elegant New York City stores lined Central Avenue; now
East Orange has little to offer its residents commercially. It has no shopping

[39] Paul Delaney, "The Outer City: Negroes Find Few Tangible Gains," *The New York Times*
(Tuesday, June 1, 1971), pp. 1, 28; Arthur D. Little, Inc., *East Cleveland: Response to
Urban Change* (1969); and Roldo Bartimole, "Cleveland," in "The Suburbs: Frontier of the
'70's," *City* (special issue), 5 (January–February 1971), 43–45.

center of its own. The people of East Orange do their business either in New York or Newark, or at the shopping malls and plazas that have sprung up in the other suburbs. Central Avenue is not dead, but it is decaying. . . .

East Orange used to be middle-to-upper-class, staunchly Republican, pre-dominantly white; now it is middle-to-lower class, Democratic, predominantly black.[40]

Sternlieb and Beaton applied the term Zone of Emergence to the older suburbs in which relatively good quality housing is available at moderate prices to minority group members moving from the inner cities. They contend that these suburbs "are increasingly becoming staging grounds for the upwardly mobile blacks and Puerto Ricans who are following in the footsteps of earlier groups on the way toward a middle class orientation and setting."[41] Plainfield, New Jersey, an example of this type of suburb, according to Sternlieb and Beaton, was studied in detail. Plainfield originated as a substantial railroad commuter town in conjunction with the development of the Jersey Central Railroad, but in time lost or downgraded most of its major retail and industrial base in the competition with highway-oriented facilities, an indication of the same loss of economic function in the older suburbs as had earlier affected the city centers, say Sternlieb and Beaton.[42] By the 1970's Plainfield had a population of almost 47,000, of whom almost 19,000 were black, representing an increase of 90 percent in the black population since 1960.[43]

Sternlieb and Beaton's survey of a sample of the Plainfield population in 1970 indicated that 61 percent of the whites own their own homes compared with 54 percent of the nonwhites and that while whites have higher educational and income levels and higher status occupations than blacks, the black population of Plainfield had higher levels of these characteristics than the black population of Newark or of New Jersey as a whole.[44] These data support Sternlieb and Beaton's contention that Plainfield represents a Zone of Emergence.

Revealingly, in the largest United States metropolitan area, suburban expansion has reached the point where the Regional Plan Association, a major nonprofit organization concerned with planning issues in the New York metropolitan region, has delineated three suburban rings in the metropolis, based on a thirty-one-county metropolitan region which is far larger than the official census definition of the New York metropolis.[45] *The Inner Ring* includes all or part of six counties. About 1960 these

[40] Harris survey, *op. cit.*, p. 19.

[41] George S. Sternlieb and W. Patrick Beaton, *The Zone of Emergence: A Case Study of Plainfield, New Jersey* (1972), p. 1.

[42] Sternlieb's economic view of the central city is presented on p. 283 Chapter 10.

[43] Bureau of the Census, *City and County Data Book, 1972* (1973), p. 726.

[44] Sternlieb and Beaton, *op. cit.*, pp. 15–35.

[45] *The Office Industry, op. cit.*, p. 57.

counties housed 25 percent of the New York metropolitan region's population at a developed land density of 7,600 per square mile, and they contained 19 percent of the region's employment. The studies of East Orange, Bergen County, and Plainfield, Union County, were carried out with no reference to the Regional Plan Association's division into suburban zones, yet both these communities are included in Inner Ring counties. Another sign of developing change in Inner Ring counties is the Census Bureau's announcement that in the two years following the 1970 census both Nassau and Bergen counties declined in population.[46] It must be noted that most Inner Ring suburbs are quite wealthy and show no signs of deterioration or population decrease. We are presenting straws in the wind that presages ecological trends in the older portions of suburbia.

The Intermediate Ring is further out than the Inner Ring, housed 21 percent of the New York region's population at a developed land density of 3,500 per square mile, and contained 17 percent of the region's jobs, all lower levels than in the Inner Ring. However, the Intermediate Ring is now the most rapidly growing suburban belt, attracting a broad mix of population and economic activities. *The Outer Ring* is comparable to the "fringe" designation noted earlier. It consists largely of rural land and contains only 6 percent of the region's population and only 5 percent of its jobs.

The cycle of growth and decline of communities successively further from the city center is expected in urban ecological theory, at least in the well-known Burgess formulation described in Chapters 6 and 10. Using data for 20 Urbanized Areas for 1950–1970, Norval Glenn had indicated how the registered declines of central city population and the socioeconomic status distribution of suburban population can be explained by the expansion of the "natural city," that is, the metropolitan area rather than the legally-bounded city.[47] In Burgess's terms this means progressively higher socioeconomic status is found as distance from the central city increases. As the metropolitan area continues to expand, some areas experiencing influxes of lower SES population may be in suburban zones. Glenn's data generally support Schnore's suggestion that some American metropolitan areas have evolved in accordance with the Burgess distribution.[48] Both Glenn and Schnore stress that a Burgess-type evolution of cities and suburbs is most evident in the older metro-

[46] "U.S. Reports First Drop in Population of Nassau," *The New York Times*, October 29, 1973), p. 37.

[47] Norval D. Glenn, "Suburbanization in the United States since World War II," in Masotti and Hadden, *op. cit.*, pp. 51–78.

[48] See Chapter 10 for presentation of Schnore's evolutionary hypothesis; see also Schnore's, "Suburbanization in the Sixties: A Preliminary Analysis," *Land Economics* XLVIII (February 1972), 23–33, and Vivian Z. Klaff and Schnore, "The Applicability of the Burgess Zonal Hypothesis to 75 Cities in the U.S.," Center for Demography and Ecology, The University of Wisconsin, Madison, Working Paper 72–28, November 1972.

politan areas, that not all metropolitan areas display this distribution, and that there is no necessity for the future growth of metropolitan areas to follow the same course.

Suburban Life Styles

In "the swampy science of suburbia,"[49] one fact is clear: there is no one suburban way of life. The search for knowledge of how people live in suburbs, whether they behave differently than urbanites, and why any differences exist, is complicated by several factors, described below.

Problems in Studying Life Styles

1. Types of suburbs differ in life styles. For example, findings about weak kinship ties in suburbs catering to middle level management personnel who are continually transferred from city to city as they climb the corporate ladder may not apply to working class suburbs. Similarly, the homogeneity of a large planned tract development does not apply to suburbs that have grown slowly by accretion or to older suburbs that are pock-marked with decay. Generalizations based on findings about suburban ways of life are limited by time and place. As yet the typology of suburbia is insufficiently advanced to permit adequate assessment of the application of generalizations about suburbs. In fact, "a definitive study of suburban life in the United States will have to provide a representative sample of communities as well as populations. . . . Our data strongly suggest that an adequate typology of communities can make a major contribution in explaining the development of divergent life-styles."[50] Implicit in this statement is the need also for comparative norms for urban and rural types of communities.

2. Ideology colors the movement to suburbs and studies of suburbs. Earlier in this chapter we pointed out that the question of suburban social organization has brought forth a flood of opinions, critiques, and value-judgments. The ideological roots of suburbia for the middle class in the United States have been traced to the prorural bias and the emphasis on private family life, leading to the suburb as "an ideal urban life style."[51] Thus, despite the commentators who, as Dobriner notes, are

---

[49] The phrase is from Richard L. Stauber, "The Swampy Science of Suburbia: A Case for the Sociology of Knowledge," *Kansas Journal of Sociology*, 1 (Summer 1965), 137–54.

[50] Irving Tallman and Ramona Morgner, "Life Style Differences among Urban and Suburban Blue-Collar Families," *Social Forces*, 48 (March 1970), 346.

[51] Jeffrey K. Hadden and Josef J. Barton, "An Image That Will Not Die: Some Thoughts on the History of Anti-Urban Ideology," in Masotti and Hadden, *op. cit.*, p. 109.

almost unanimously opposed to suburbs, regarding them as "homogenized" communities where "social and personal differences are submerged beneath a great wet blanket of conformity,"[52] people continue to flock to suburbs. The negative views of the commentators regarding suburbia are, of course, another instance of ideology.

3. Differences in research approach and theoretical orientation influence the study of suburban life styles. Most fundamentally, the question is the extent to which suburban life styles are determined by factors within the suburban setting as opposed to factors such as social class or ethnic heritage, which suburbanites bring with them.[53] Obviously several combinations and modifications of these two emphases are possible.

Social Consequences of Suburban Location and Population

Several observers have noted that the demographic and structural characteristics of suburbs have fairly predictable social consequences. Thus, Fava has pointed out the relatively small size, low density, and greater homogeneity of population in suburbs are conditions favorable to informal neighborhood contacts.[54] Her later study in the New York metropolitan area confirmed that higher levels of neighboring were indeed more characteristic of suburbs than of central city areas.[55]

Martin has pointed out that in addition to relatively low community size and density of population, such characteristics of suburbs as outlying location and commuting to work in the central city may be important in determining the type and frequency of social interaction.[56] Thus, a daily trip to a work place separated from home by long distance, social differences, and, perhaps, political jurisdiction may produce a division of suburbanites' participation and interests. Daily commuting prolongs the absence of men from their place of residence and may therefore also result in more important roles for women in suburban

[52] Dobriner, *op. cit.*, p. 5.

[53] An alternative classification scheme, compatible with that above, is presented in Harvey Marshall, "Suburban Life Styles: A Contribution to the Debate," in Masotti and Hadden, *op. cit.*, p. 123–48.

[54] Sylvia F. Fava, "Suburbanism as a Way of Life," *American Sociological Review*, 21 (February 1956), 34–37.

[55] Sylvia F. Fava, "Contrasts in Neighboring: New York City and a Suburban County," in William Dobriner, ed., *The Suburban Community* (1958). Additional evidence for the suburban application of the Wirth thesis, from which the variables of size, density, and homogeneity are derived, is reviewed in Claude S. Fischer, "'Urbanism as a Way of Life': A Review and an Agenda," *Sociological Methods and Research*, 1 (November 1972), 224–5.

[56] Walter Martin, "The Structuring of Social Relationships Engendered by Suburban Residence," *American Sociological Review*, 21 (August 1956), 446–53.

activities. Both Fava and Martin stress that migration to suburbs has been selective of white, native-born, middle class couples who are rearing families. The resulting homogeneity may produce a high degree of community involvement. These hypotheses require further testing, but are suggestive of the possible social consequences of objective suburban characteristics. Obviously, if in time the external characteristics of suburbs change—for example, suburbs become larger, more densely populated, and more heterogeneous in population composition, and if more suburbanites have nearby jobs than commute to the central city—then there will be related social changes also.

Values and Suburban
Social Organization

Suburban and urban social organization may differ, not only as a consequence of socially relevant external characteristics of population and location, but also as a consequence of differences in values, standards, beliefs, and preferences. There is some evidence that the dominant values of suburbanites emphasize familism, the local group, and direct participation to a greater extent than do the values of urban residents.

A study in several suburbs in metropolitan Chicago disclosed a greater emphasis on familistic values, defined as the orientation of life goals and activities around the home and children, than on alternative value systems centered on career aspirations or enjoyable consumption.[57] The three values and related life styles—familism, career, and consumership—are to some degree antithetical, often forcing the individual to make a choice. For example, devotion of time and money to the family may interfere with upward occupational mobility and with achieving as high a standard of living as possible. Familism was measured by asking the suburbanites why they had moved from the city. Eighty-three percent gave responses classified as familistic—"more healthy for children," "nicer children for playmates," "better schools," "home ownership provides greater security for children than living in an apartment." Only 10 percent gave responses involving upward social mobility, and only 43 percent gave responses classified as consumership. Since many suburbanites gave more than one type of reason, the percentages total more than 100.

In another phase of the study, suburban and urban residents were forced to make a choice between familistic, career, and consumership responses on a questionnaire. Table 11.4 shows that, although familism obtained more first choices than either career or consumership in each of

[57] Wendell Bell, "Social Choice, Life Styles and Suburban Residence," in William Dobriner, *The Suburban Community, op. cit.*

TABLE 11.4: Percentage Distribution of First Choices in Each of Three Life Styles, by Suburban or City Residence and Neighborhood Economic Status

	CITY		SUBURBAN	
Life Style	Jackson Blvd. (Low Econ.)	Near North Side (High Econ.)	Bellwood (Low Econ.)	Kenilworth (High Econ.)
Familism	55%	45%	75%	61%
Career	18	27	17	17
Consumership	27	28	8	22
	100%	100%	100%	100%

SOURCE: Wendell Bell, "Social Choice, Life Styles and Suburban Residence," in W. Dobriner, ed., *The Suburban Community* (New York: Putnam's, 1958), p. 241.

the suburban and urban communities, the predominance of familistic responses was greater in the suburban communities. The table also shows that familism varies by economic status as well as by city or suburban location, but that suburbs have a higher proportion of familistic choices than economically equivalent urban areas. Thus, suburban Kenilworth residents gave familistic responses 61 percent of their first choices, compared with 45 percent of the residents of the urban Near North Side.

There is no evidence that there are any uniquely suburban values. Bell's study is typical in showing that there are concentrations of people with familistic values and preferences in suburbs. Lesser concentrations of people live in accordance with those same values in the city. This suggests that suburban location itself does not determine the values. As suburban facilities and amenities change, particularly in contrast with the central city, the relative drawing power of suburban locales for other than familistic value orientations may also change.

Social Class and Suburban Life Styles

It is becoming increasingly clear that residential location is only one of the many factors influencing suburban life styles. Suburbanites come from many backgrounds and, as indicated earlier, the heterogeneity of suburban population is increasing. Groups and individuals retain many of their former activities and allegiances in the suburbs. For example, urban Democrats appear to continue to vote for that party after they move to suburbs, rather than joining the Republican majority found in many suburbs.[58] Church attendance among Protestants and Catholics is as frequent among urban as among suburban residents, contrary to the belief that religious participation is more frequent among sub-

[58] Bernard Lazerwitz, "Suburban Voting Trends, 1948–59," *Social Forces*, 39 (October 1960), 29–36.

urbanites.[59] Patterns of ethnic segregation also persist in suburbs. A study of ten large metropolitan areas disclosed that "first- and second-generation groups have patterns of segregation from each other and from native-white populations that are frequently similar to those of their central-city members."[60]

Herbert Gans is one of the strongest advocates of the view that suburban location per se has relatively little influence in producing a suburban way of life. He contends that the most powerful determinants of suburban—and urban—ways of life are social class and family-cycle stage.[61]

Gans' participant-observation study of Levittown, New Jersey, showed that this largely lower-middle-class child-raising population experienced few changes in way of life as a result of their move to suburbia. Some changes did occur but they were mainly *intended* changes, often representing the fuller acting-out of their class and family-cycle attributes.[62] Thus, comparison of interviews with the Levittowners immediately after the move and two years later showed that major changes were new satisfaction due to home ownership and increased family morale resulting from the availability of space. The Levittowners also participated more in social activities with their neighbors and friends and in formal organizations than they had in their previous residences. For most these increased activities were one of the things they had looked forward to in the new community or else they had had a high level of participation previously.

Gans notes that there were also *unintended* effects of the move to Levittown and some of these represent the influence of suburban location: meeting neighbors of different ethnic and religious backgrounds, separation from relatives, long commuting trips, tax increases. These are few in number and have minor impact on suburbanites compared with their class and family-stage characteristics, according to Gans.

Comparison of two case studies reveals that basic differences in life styles are maintained in the suburbs. On the basis of a field study of 100 working class families living in a suburb of the San Francisco Bay area,

[59] Bernard Lazerwitz, "National Data on Participation Rates among Residential Belts in the United States," *American Sociological Review*, 27 (October 1962), 691–96. A recent study of Catholics in Montreal indicates that public religious involvement is higher for suburban Catholics, but is often only nominal; see Serge Carlos, "Religious Participation and the Urban-Suburban Continuum," *American Journal of Sociology*, 75 (March 1970), 742–59.

[60] Stanley Lieberson, "Suburbs and Ethnic Residential Patterns," *American Journal of Sociology*, 67 (May 1962), 773–81.

[61] Herbert J. Gans, "Urbanism and Suburbanism as Ways of Life: A Re-Evaluation of Definitions," in Rose, *op. cit.* Gans' five major ways of life are described in Chapter 10, p. 274.

[62] Herbert J. Gans, *The Levittowners* (1967); and Gans, "The Effect of a Community on Its Residents," in his *People and Plans* (1968), 12–24.

Berger pointed out that there is no reason to believe that what is characteristic of "organization men" or of middle class suburban groups is also characteristic of working class suburbs.[63] Most of the men of the families Berger studied were employed in blue collar jobs in a nearby Ford plant. He found that the families lived for the most part as they had before they moved to the suburb, rarely participating in formal associations or engaging in mutual visiting with suburban neighbors. They continued to vote for Democratic party candidates and their church participation remained low. Berger also found "little evidence of pronounced striving, status anxiety, or orientation to the future." Life in this suburb contrasted markedly with that of middle class groups in Crestwood Heights.

The upper middle class life style of Crestwood Heights, a suburb of Toronto, includes many elements of the life style erroneously regarded as typically suburban.[64] The larger kinship group is relatively unimportant and the "family" consisting of parents with children living at home, highly valued its privacy and relied on specialized agencies for leisure, educational, and other services. The family orientation is toward status and upward mobility, as manifested by the use of the home to display a variety of artifacts having not only utilitarian and esthetic functions but also symbolic relevance for the status of the occupants.

Participation in formal voluntary organizations is high in Crestwood Heights for both men and women and is used primarily as a vehicle for upward social mobility. Leisure, too, is linked to social mobility. It consists of scheduled activities such as learning and displaying appropriate skills (golf, bridge) rather than just "loafing." Children are trained strictly although usually with a "velvet glove" so that they may assume their places as adults in this upper middle class world.

"Does Suburbia Make a Difference?"

A provocatively entitled article by Zelan suggests the complexity of the causes of suburban life styles.[65] Zelan examined the assertion that suburban residence fosters anti-intellectual attitudes. His data included questionnaire responses from over 33,000 college seniors graduating in 1961 from 135 colleges in the United States. Zelan's initial comparison

---

[63] Bennett M. Berger, *Working-Class Suburb* (1960). A recent comparison of blue collar families in urban and suburban locations suggests that Berger's analysis of working class suburbs may be overdrawn and can be generalized in only a limited way. In the new study, suburban working class families were found to be more likely than their urban counterparts to adopt aspects of middle class life style. See Tallman and Morgner, *op. cit.*

[64] John R. Seeley, R. Alexander Sim, and E. W. Loosley, *Crestwood Heights* (1956).

[65] Joseph Zelan, "Does Suburbia Make a Difference: An Exercise in Secondary Analysis," in Sylvia F. Fava, ed., *Urbanism in World Perspective* (1968), pp. 401–8.

showed no significant differences in intellectual attitudes between those college seniors who had been raised in cities and those who had been raised in suburbs. Further analysis showed that there *is* a relationship between suburban residence and anti-intellectualism but it is more complex than commonly supposed. When the items measuring anti-intellectualism were cross-tabulated with the kind of communities students said they *wished* to live in rather than by the communities they had grown up in, then the suburb-oriented students differed significantly from the urban-oriented students in anti-intellectualism. That is, those "who indicated a *desire* to live in the suburbs were less likely to be concerned with access to cultural activities and less likely to think of themselves as intellectuals."

The final analysis of Zelan's study suggests that anti-intellectualism in suburbia is partly a result of family-cycle (more married students prefer suburbs and they are likely to have less time for intellectual activities), partly a result of selectivity (the students expressing a preference for suburban living are more anti-intellectual), and partly a result of the influence of community of origin (regardless of their marital status and intellectual attitudes, students who were brought up in suburbs more often expressed a desire to live in suburbs than those who had been raised in the city). Extrapolation from these students' preferences about suburbs should be limited. However, the results provide a specific illustration of the relative contribution of life cycle, values and ideology, and the long-lasting, if largely unexplained, effects of childhood residence.

Black Suburbs

The overall picture of metropolitan residential segregation in the United States is of black population concentrated in central cities and white

FIGURE 11.3 • In 1950–1960 both white and black populations grew in the central cities and suburbs, but in 1960–1970, white population rose only in the suburbs. Source: U. S. Bureau of the Census, *Statistical Abstract of the United States, 1972,* p.4.

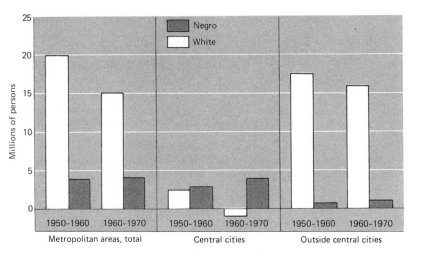

population concentrated in suburbs. As Figure 11.3 shows, from 1960 to 1970 all of the metropolitan increase in white population was in suburbs, the white population of central cities having declined during the decade. In contrast the bulk of the black metropolitan population increase was in the central cities. Within this general trend an important, but as yet minor, countertrend had emerged by the end of the 1960's, namely an increase in the black suburban population.

At this point the absolute numbers of blacks involved in suburbanization are small and most black suburbanization is occurring in the rings of the largest cities, especially Chicago, Los Angeles, New York, Cleveland, Newark, and Washington, D.C. For example, the number of blacks in the Los Angeles suburbs doubled between 1960 and 1970 with an increase of 124,000; around Washington, D.C., blacks doubled in number with an increase of only 84,000; and in the New York City suburban areas an increase of 77,000 blacks represented a gain of 55 percent in the total black suburban population.[66]

In terms of life styles a crucial question is whether the black suburbanites differ from those who do not suburbanize. It has been shown that within metropolitan ghettos black groups are residentially segregated from one another by income and, to a lesser extent, by stage in the family cycle, in a manner analagous to the white population.[67] These objective characteristics provide, as with the white population, a useful index to life styles although, of course, there are also other determinants. Analysis of the 1970 census data shows that, for the first time, the socioeconomic status of black suburbanites exceeds that of central city blacks.[68] This reverses the historic trend for suburban blacks to be of lower SES than central city blacks and means that since 1960 city-suburban socioeconomic differences among blacks resemble those observed among whites.[69]

The implication of this change for racial integration, busing, political

---

[66] Philip Hauser, "The Census of 1970," *Scientific American*, 225 (July 1971), p. 21; and Harold X. Connolly, "Black Movement into the Suburbs," *Urban Affairs Quarterly*, 9 (September 1973), p. 95. For additional discussion of black and white residential distribution in cities and suburbs, see Chapter 3, p. 90.

[67] Ozzie L. Edwards, "Patterns of Residential Segregation within a Metropolitan Ghetto," *Demography*, 7 (May 1970), 185–93.

[68] Reynolds Farley, "The Changing Distribution of Negroes within Metropolitan Areas: The Emergence of Black Suburbs," *American Journal of Sociology*, 75 (January 1970), 512–29; Connolly, *op. cit.*; and Eunice Grier, *Black Suburbanization in Metropolitan Washington*. Report #1, Characteristics of Black Suburbanites. The Washington Center for Metropolitan Studies (October 1973); and Peter C. Labovitz, "Racial Change Comes to the Suburbs," *Planning 1970* (American Society of Planning Officials), pp. 145–52.

[69] It should be noted that although the SES of suburban blacks is higher than that of central city blacks, it is not as high as that of suburban whites. Changes in the magnitude and direction of these several comparisons will be important reflections of the relative position of suburban blacks.

power, and job opportunities are beginning to be widely discussed, although it is still too early for a clear assessment.[70] One interpretation is that blacks are following the historic route of American immigrant groups by moving out from the central city as they move up to middle class status. However, black suburbanization, at least at this stage, apparently does not involve residential desegregation, differing in this respect from the decentralization of American immigrant groups.[71] Blacks who move to the suburbs live for the most part in heavily black areas.

Problems of Suburbia

The traditional view of suburbia as a bucolic haven free of city problems has been shattered by the mounting evidence of suburban problems. The suburbs always had problems as do all communities, but there is no doubt that the increase in suburban population size and variety and the decentralization of so many economic activities have brought in their train a set of concerns unprecedented for suburbia. These range from traffic congestion to poverty and include rising crime rates, vandalism and loitering in shopping centers, drug problems, air pollution, despoilation of the physical environment, race tension, housing obsolescence, and financial crises.

Two indicators of deep-seated difficulties in suburban areas are substantial increases in poverty and crime rates. Although 30 percent of the American poor now live in the central cities, which is more than the 21 percent living in the suburbs of these metropolitan areas, the suburban poverty population is growing faster. According to the Census Bureau the suburban poor rose by 650,000 between 1959 and 1969, reaching a total of 5.2 million, while the central city poor rose by only 400,000, to a total of 8.2 million.[72] Similarly, suburban crime rates are still below those of the central city but the gap is narrowing. McCausland notes that the increases can be attributed in part to the spread to the suburbs of big city conditions associated with high crime rates—slums and commercial and industrial development. He also notes, however, that "even in the traditional suburban environment (middle class, white, residential), crime of various sorts is becoming a major problem, all the way from

[70] See, for example, Bernard J. Frieden, "Blacks in Suburbia: The Myth of Better Opportunities," pp. 31–49 in Resources for the Future, Inc., ed., *Minority Perspectives* (1972); and Albert J. Hermalin and Reynolds Farley "The Potential for Residential Integration in Cities and Suburbs: Implications for the Busing Controversy," *American Sociological Review*, 38 (October 1973), 595–610.

[71] Farley, *op. cit.*, pp. 426–7; Connolly, *op. cit.*, pp. 99–100.

[72] "Poverty Growing in Suburbs," *HUD Newsletter* (Department of Housing and Urban Development) 3 (January 10, 1972), p. 4.

vandalism, drug offenses, and larceny of delinquents to robbery of branch banks and organized crime. In part, this can be attributed to the increased mobility automobiles have given criminals from the city. In part, it is due to changes in the suburban population itself."[73]

What resources does suburbia have to meet its problems? This is itself a problem, as the marshalling of resources in suburbia runs headlong into the fragmented political jurisdictions of the suburbs and the sacred principle of home rule. As a result the suburban response to problems is often totally inadequate, sometimes consisting of attempts to protect its own enclave by sending the problems elsewhere. ("We'll take the tax-paying plant, *you* take the low-income workers.")

Examples of the consequences of political fragmentation abound. A drive to install a traffic light on a street between a library and a school was stymied in one suburban county (Nassau County, N.Y.) because there are three townships, 64 incorporated villages, and 280 special districts for such functions as police, fire, school, sewers, lighting, and water, and it could not be determined into which jurisdiction this traffic light would fall; after more than a year the light still had not been installed.[74]

On a more important level the difficulty in marshalling suburban resources is noted in the nonexistence or minimal number of county employees in housing and urban renewal activities. In 1970, when housing deterioration was already evident and increasing rapidly in the suburbs of large metropolitan areas, four of the six suburban counties of Washington, D.C. had no employees in housing and urban renewal; the most populous county of the Washington, D.C. SMSA—Prince Georges County, Maryland—had only four such employees. In the Indianapolis SMSA there were no housing employees in the seven suburban counties. Suburban counties around such large central cities as New York City, Detroit, San Francisco, Philadelphia, and Chicago also show very low employment in housing and urban renewal activities, contrasting markedly with the central cities. The Department of Housing and Urban Development comments that "these figures point up the fact that suburban governments are not yet providing the organizational structures necessary to establish programs of low and moderate income housing."[75] Others have pointed out that suburban governmental fragmentation places undue fiscal burdens on older suburbs where many of the new low and moderate income suburban residents are settling.[76]

Perhaps the clearest indication of the gravity of emerging suburban

[73] John L. McCausland, "Crime in the Suburbs," in Haar, *op. cit.*, p. 62.
[74] Samuel Kaplan, "The Balkanization of Suburbia," *Harper's Magazine*, 243 (October 1971), 72–74.
[75] "Housing and Urban Renewal Employment, City vs. Suburb," *HUD Challenge*, 11 (August 1971), p. 31.
[76] Sternlieb and Beaton, *op. cit.*

problems was their official recognition in 1967 when President Lyndon Johnson appointed a task force, headed by Charles Haar, to prepare a report on suburban problems. The six-volume report was completed the following year and though the entire document has not been released, some studies and the overall summary and recommendations are available. Their searching study led the Task Force to conclude that it "believes that the suburban problem is with us now. We must act now to prevent the problem from becoming a crisis."[77]

Summary

The chief points about suburbs may be briefly noted as follows:

1. As suburban living has been taken up by more and more Americans, a greater variety of suburbs and suburban life styles has developed than the simple, middle class, child-rearing suburb of the past. Decentralization of a broader range of economic activities has also contributed to suburban heterogeneity.

2. There are still many urban-suburban differences, but they co-exist with ethnic, religious, and, especially, social class differences within suburban communities.

3. Further changes and problems are underway in suburbia as some areas "age," potentially initiating a new phase of invasion-succession.

Selected Bibliography

BOOKS

Anderson, Robert, and Barbara Gallatin Anderson, *Bus-Stop for Paris*. Garden City, N.J.: Doubleday, 1965.

Clark, S.D., *The Suburban Society*. Toronto: University of Toronto Press, 1966.

Berger, Bennett M., *Working-Class Suburb*. Berkeley and Los Angeles: University of California Press, 1960.

Dobriner, William M., *Class in Suburbia*. Englewood Cliffs, N.J.: Prentice-Hall, 1963.

———, ed., *The Suburban Community*. New York: Putnam's, 1958.

Donaldson, Scott, *The Suburban Myth*. New York: Columbia University Press, 1969.

Downs, Anthony, *Opening Up the Suburbs: An Urban Strategy for America*. New Haven, Conn.: Yale University Press, 1973.

[77] "Report of the President's Task Force," in Haar, *op.cit.*, p. 270.

Gans, Herbert J., *The Levittowners.* New York: Pantheon, 1967.

Greer, Scott, *The Urbane View.* New York: Oxford University Press, 1972.

Gruen, Nina, and C. Gruen, *Low and Moderate Income Housing in the Suburbs: An Analysis of the Dayton, Ohio Region.* New York: Praeger, 1972.

Haar, Charles, ed., *The End of Innocence: A Suburban Reader.* Glenview, Ill.: Scott, Foresman, 1972.

Kramer, John, ed., *North America Suburbs: Politics, Diversity, and Change.* Berkeley, Calif.: Glendessary Press, 1972.

Masotti, Louis, and Jeffrey K. Hadden, eds., *Suburbia in Transition.* Chicago: Quadrangle Books, 1974.

———, *The Urbanization of the Suburbs.* Beverly Hills, Calif.: Sage Publications, 1973.

Orr, John B., and F. Patrick Michelson, *The Radical Suburb: Soundings in Changing American Character.* Philadelphia: The Westminster Press, 1970.

Schnore, Leo F., *Class and Race in Cities and Suburbs.* Chicago: Markham, 1972.

Seeley, John R., R. Alexander Sim, E.W. Loosley, *Crestwood Heights.* New York: Basic Books, 1956.

Sobin, Dennis P., *The Future of the American Suburbs.* Port Washington, N.Y.: National University Publications, 1971.

Sternlieb, George S., and W. Patrick Beaton, *The Zone of Emergence: A Case Study of Plainfield, New Jersey.* New Brunswick, N.J.: Transaction Books, 1972.

Sternlieb, George S., Robert W. Burchell, and Lynne B. Sagalyn, *The Affluent Suburb: Princeton, New Jersey.* New Brunswick, N.J.: Transaction Books, 1971.

Thorns, David C., *Suburbia.* London: MacGibbon and Kee, 1972.

U.S. Bureau of the Census, *Current Population Reports.* Series P-23, # 33, "Trends in Social and Economic Conditions in Metropolitan and Nonmetropolitan Areas." Washington, D.C.: U.S. Government Printing Office, 1970.

U.S. Bureau of the Census, Census of Population and Housing 1970, *General Demographic Trends for Metropolitan Areas, 1960 to 1970.* Final Report PHC (2)-1 U.S. Washington, D.C.: U.S. Government Printing Office, 1971.

Vogel, Ezra, *Japan's New Middle Class: The Salary Man and his Family in a Tokyo Suburb.* Berkeley, Calif.: University of California Press, 1963.

Warner, Sam Bass, *Streetcar Suburbs: The Process of Growth in Boston, 1879–1900.* Cambridge, Mass.: Harvard University and the MIT Press, 1962.

Wirt, Frederick M., *et al., The City's Rim: Politics and Policy in Suburbia.* Lexington, Mass: Heath, 1972.

Wood, Robert C., *Suburbia—Its People and Their Politics.* Boston: Houghton Mifflin, 1958.

ARTICLES

Bell, Wendell, "The City, The Suburb, and a Theory of Social Choice," pp. 132–68 in Scott Greer, Dennis L. McElrath, David W. Minar, and Peter Orleans, eds., *The New Urbanization.* New York: St. Martin's Press, 1968.

Carlos, Serge, "Religious Participation and the Urban-Suburban Continuum," *American Journal of Sociology*, 75 (March 1970), 742–59.

Connolly, Harold X., "Black Movement into the Suburbs," *Urban Affairs Quarterly*, 9 (September 1973), 91–111.

Davidoff, Linda, Paul Davidoff, and Neil N. Gold, "The Suburbs Have to Open Their Gates," *The New York Sunday Times Magazine* (November 7, 1971), 40–44.

Edwards, Ozzie L., "Patterns of Residential Segregation within a Metropolitan Ghetto," *Demography*, 7 (May 1970), 185–94.

Farley, Reynolds, "The Changing Distribution of Negroes within Metropolitan Areas: The Emergence of Black Suburbs," *American Journal of Sociology*, 75 (January 1970), Part I, 512–29.

Fava, Sylvia F., "The Pop Sociology of Suburbs and New Towns," *American Studies*, 14 (Spring 1973), 121–33.

Fine, John, Norval D. Glenn, and J. Kenneth Monts, "The Residential Segregation of Occupational Groups in Central Cities and Suburbs," *Demography*, 8 (February 1971), 91–101.

Frieden, Bernard J., "Blacks in Suburbia: The Myth of Better Opportunities," pp. 31–50 in Resources for the Future, Inc., ed., *Minority Perspectives*. Baltimore: The Johns Hopkins Press, 1972.

Gans, Herbert J., "Effects of the Move from City to Suburb," pp. 184–201 in Leonard Duhl, ed., *The Urban Condition*. New York: Basic Books, 1963.

Goodwin, L. "How Suburban Families View the Work Orientation of the Welfare Poor," *Social Problems* 19 (Winter 1972), 337–48.

Kasarda, John, "The Impact of Suburban Population Growth on Central City Service Functions," *American Journal of Sociology* 77 (May 1972), 1111-1125.

Labovitz, Peter C., "Racial Change Comes to the Suburbs," pp. 145–53 in *Planning 1970*. Chicago: American Society of Planning Officials, 1970.

McIntosh, James R., "The Urban Fringe: Social Life, Social Change and the Urban Voyeur," pp. 303–13 in John Walton and Donald Carns, eds., *Cities in Change*. Boston: Allyn and Bacon, 1972.

Phares, Donald, "Racial Change and Housing Values: Transition in an Inner Suburb," *Social Science Quarterly* 52 (December 1971), 56–73.

"Suburbia: A Myth Challenged," *Time* (March 15, 1971), 14–20.

Rose, Harold, "The All Black Town: Suburban Prototype or Rural Slum?" pp. 397–433 in Harlan Hahn, ed., *People and Politics in Urban Society*. Beverly Hills, Calif.: Sage Publications, 1972.

Tallman, Irving, and Ramona Morgner, "Life Style Differences among Urban and Suburban Blue-Collar Families," *Social Forces* 48 (March 1970), 334–48.

"The Outer City: U.S. in Suburban Turmoil," *The New York Times,* series of five articles (May 30–June 3, 1971).

"The Suburbs: Frontier of the 70's," *City* 5 (January/February 1971), 13–95.

Walter, Benjamin, and Frederick M. Wirt, "The Political Consequences of Suburban Variety," *Social Science Quarterly* 52 (December 1971), 746–69.

Warren, Donald L., "Suburban Isolation and Race Tension: The Detroit Case," *Social Problems* 17 (Winter 1970), 324–40.

THE ORGANIZATION OF URBAN LIFE

12 • Urban Status Systems

Social stratification, or the status system, will be the main focus of this chapter. Here we shall answer such questions as the following: What is the nature of the status system in cities, and what is the significance of urbanism and the development of urban communities to the forms and processes of stratification? What changes in the stratification system are occurring as a result of economic, technological, and other developments? What is the effect on the class structure of migrations to cities, especially when the migrants are people whose ethnic, racial, educational, and occupational backgrounds and style of life differentiate them from others? Who are the top dogs, the underdogs, and the middle dogs, and what if any are their distinguishing characteristics?

Perspectives of Social Stratification

Social stratification in any society is a complex social system which may vary in character from one society or community to another. In every society it undergoes change with the passage of time, although the change may be slow or rapid. It has many social, cultural, psychological, economic, technological, and political components, each bearing on the others in one way or another. As societies or communities evolve into more or less integrated social systems, the people within the systems come to occupy social positions which entitle them to rewards that are differentiated by levels of prestige or status, degrees of power or influence, incomes and amounts of wealth, and life styles that vary in many ways.

The Weberian Perspective

German sociologist Max Weber developed a theoretical approach to social stratification which has been useful in obtaining a meaningful perspective of a social system, at least in industrialized societies. Although Weber was quite aware that all the component elements of a social system are interdependent and interlocking in varying degrees, in his theoretical analysis he developed a stratification model having three distinct, but overlapping, levels of inequality. These he stipulated as *prestige* classes (inequality of status), *economic* classes (inequality of income and wealth), and *political* classes (inequality of power).

The prestige classes are determined by varying forms or degrees of status conferred on people in a given society or community. These statuses include such matters as family or ethnic lineage, amount and kind of education, occupation, membership in various groups, the kind of residential house or neighborhood lived in, leisure-time activities, or personal attributes such as racial traits, manners, speech, appearance, attire, food behavior, and the like. In an urban-industrial society the numbers and variety of statuses are endless. Economic classes are determined by the amount and source of income an individual or family receives, and also by the amount and kind of wealth or property possessed. Political classes, as Weber defined them, refer to the levels of power, whether economic, political, or military.

While there is clearly an interdependence and overlapping of these three dimensions, they are by no means coterminous. Persons who have great power are not necessarily wealthy, or vice versa; but power may be translated into wealth, or wealth into power, and both power and wealth may entitle the individual to deference and other symbols of prestige. These levels of inequality, or "social classes," provide a frame of reference for the study of many aspects of the social order. Viewed from this perspective, a wide range of phenomena may be examined and analyzed—the life styles and behavior of people, levels of aspiration and achievement, the distribution and exercise of power, attitudes and values, the "life chances" of people for obtaining basic physical or social needs, and so on.

Economic Differentials

One may focus on the various economic levels as indicated by the amount and source of income received by individuals or families, and the amount or kinds of wealth, whether money, land, or industrial-commercial establishments. Income is probably the simplest criterion of economic stratification in urban-industrial societies, and this is usually highly correlated with a prestige hierarchy of occupations. In some societies the possession of land is the most important economic criterion of social position.

An examination of the distribution of income in the American population shows glaring differences. Nonfarm families with incomes under $3968 in 1971 were defined and specified by the United States Census

Bureau as "poor," that is, unable to adequately provide food, clothing, shelter, education, health care, and other essentials for themselves.[1] Yet 8.2 percent of white families and 29.7 percent of nonwhites (mainly blacks) had incomes that year under the minimum figures.[2] Even more striking was the fact that 1.5 percent of all American families, involving over a million persons, had incomes under $1000, scarcely sufficient for luxurious living! At the other end of the spectrum, over one-half of the white families and 30 percent of the nonwhites had incomes in excess of $10,000 in 1971.

Status Polarization and Equalization

The economic spread between the top and bottom strata of society is greater in agrarian than in urban-industrial societies, although in all countries there is a considerable spread between the polar extremes. In 1962, there were 59,572 persons in the United States who possessed wealth of one million dollars or over, yet there were many thousands who owned no property other than their clothes or other personal belongings. In some developing societies such as the Philippines or Brazil the upper stratum has monopolized wealth, power, and privilege, making it extremely difficult for the destitute masses at or near the bottom to improve their way of life.

After examining a considerable body of evidence, Lenski concludes that the top one or two percent of the population in nonindustrial societies, as a whole, usually receives not less than half of the total income of the country.[3] Urban-industrial countries exhibit a much narrower spread. For example, the top two percent of the population in Great Britain received 8.5 percent of the total income after taxes in 1954; and in Sweden, with a highly socialized economy, the upper 1.8 percent of the population received approximately 10 percent of the national income before taxes.

In most urban-industrial societies there has been a long-time trend toward equalization of rights and privileges for all classes in which the power of the elite has been reduced, their monopoly of wealth broken, and a gradual extension of civil, economic, and political rights to all classes of people. Almost every industrial country and many developing societies have extended voting rights to adults on all social levels,

---

[1] This figure is only an average and is not applicable to every family. The needs of families vary considerably according to the number of persons in the household, whether their place of residence is rural or urban, and so on. Generally, the incomes of urban residents are higher than those of rural persons, but the costs of living in the city are also higher than living costs in the country.

[2] *Statistical Abstract of the United States,* (1973), p. 328.

[3] Gerhard Lenski, *Power and Privilege* (1966), p. 309.

minimum-wage laws to improve the economic position of the working classes, and graduated income taxes utilized as a share-the-wealth principle. Numerous other institutional devices to equalize opportunities and provide protection for the people have been adopted, including social security for the unemployed, children, the physically handicapped and ill, and retired persons; education for the masses; free public recreational facilities; and a judicial system to protect the rights of individuals whatever their position in the social structure may be.[4] This is not to say that these provisions always function effectively and without prejudice in any country. They do not. But conditions of life and work in urban-industrial societies have made their adoption imperative, whereas in nonindustrial societies such protective facilities for the masses may be even more inadequate. Yet the concentration of economic and political power in most urban-industrial countries is still formidable.

Components Criss-Crossing the Social Structure

Cutting across the various levels of a class structure are such components as race, ethnicity, and religion, each adding to the complexity of the system. In American cities, racially visible minorities are distributed throughout the entire social structure, but most are concentrated on the lower levels. This is especially true of the black population, but it also applies to other minorities such as Mexican-Americans, American Indians, and Puerto Ricans. Although black and other racial minorities have generally moved up considerably in the economic structure in recent years, their *relative* positional change in the social system has been small or even nonexistent. Hence, the social and economic gap between them and the white majority has not been reduced very much if any at all because the whites have also moved upward in the economic system. Most urban blacks have been viewed by whites as "lower class," partly because of their low incomes, limited possessions, and life style; partly because they are people against whom white prejudices are often directed; and partly because the white majority is reluctant to relinquish its position of privilege and prestige.

Status Systems in Cities and Towns

The foregoing discussion has compared the societal stratification systems of urban-industrial and nonindustrial countries, but there is another perspective: the status systems of specific communities, urban or rural, metropolitan or small-city. Social scientists have conducted nu-

---

[4] See especially T. H. Marshall, *Class and Citizenship* (1965), ch. 5. Compare Lenski, *op. cit.*, chs. 8–12.

merous studies of the social structure of communities. Some of these studies have attempted to provide an overall picture of the entire community class system; others have focused on particular facets of the system such as the power structure, the life styles of people on different levels, or class-induced attitudes. But from all of the studies one valid generalization can be drawn: the class structure of a great metropolis is different from the system of a small city or a rural community. It is one thing to speak of the upper class of, say, an agricultural trading center, but quite another to speak of an upper class in megalopolis. When Warner asserted that "to study Jonesville (a small midwestern town) is to study America,"[5] he made assumptions not supported by the facts.

Contrasts in housing are striking in Latin America. This upper class residence in Mexico City reflects a very different social class and life style of the occupants from the housing shown in the photographs of Caracas in chapters 20 and 22. (Noel P. Gist)

Achievement and Ascription

Western urban-industrial countries have sometimes been called "achieving" societies because so many of the statuses and roles of individuals or families are achieved through competitive effort— keeping up with the Joneses, or surpassing them, in various affairs of

[5] W. Lloyd Warner and Associates, *Democracy in Jonesville* (1949), p. xv.

life. In nonindustrial countries individual or family status and role are likely to be ascribed by tradition and custom.[6] These differences between the urban-industrial and nonindustrial societies are, of course, relative; many statuses and roles in the former type are indeed a matter of cultural inheritance, while status by competitive achievement is fairly common in nonindustrial societies, and becoming more so as these countries become urbanized and modernized and as the educational level of the masses is raised. Even within an urban-industrial society there are differences, in this respect, between urban and rural communities.

Changing Status Systems in Industrial Societies

Among the changes accruing from urbanization and industrialization has been the alteration in systems of stratification and power. Viewed from the standpoint of the Weberian approach, these factors stand out:

1. Urbanism and industrialism, both associated with great changes in science and technology, have profoundly altered the economic basis of stratification. Owing to technological and economic changes, many countries, especially those in the West, have experienced an abundance of manufactured materials and a general improvement of income for the masses, both urban and rural. Technological and organizational changes have also altered the worker's actual relation to the productive processes. Through mechanization and automation he has been relieved of much drudgery, and at the same time his productivity has increased. Thus, he (or his children) has been given an opportunity to engage in other occupational pursuits, or time to spend his increased earnings and thereby alter his life style.

2. In urban-industrial societies there has been a proliferation of groups or associations which often have a function of conferring prestige on their members. The number of such groups is legion, and, while commonly performing utilitarian functions (sometimes as a mask), they become important features of the status system. In the course of time they assume a kind of hierarchical arrangement in terms of the prestige they may confer, so that certain groups become identified with a particular social class. Since the actual existence of such groups and the activities necessary to maintain them depend in considerable measure on the amount of wealth and leisure possessed by their members, the activities themselves have considerable status significance. Thus, membership in status groups and participation in their activities are symbolically significant for the status system.

[6] Gideon Sjoberg, *The Pre-Industrial City* (1960).

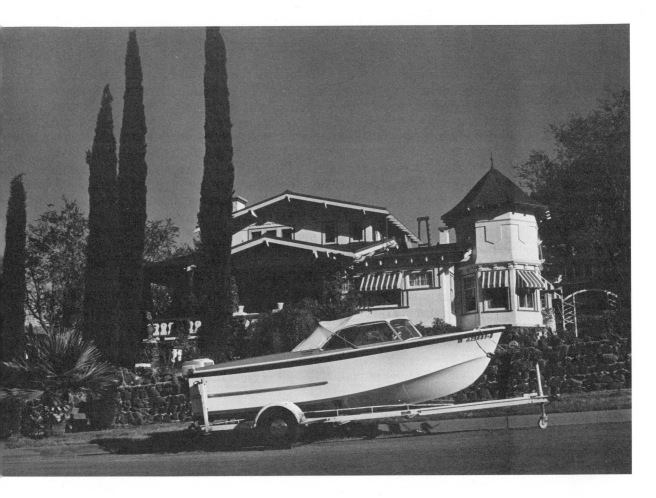

The plethora of manufactured goods in urbanized societies has served to focus interest on consumption. Not only do consumer goods have symbolic value for status, but the actual behavior involved in their consumption likewise has symbolic significance. In urban-industrial countries there is considerable preoccupation with both *what* and *how* to consume, and under what circumstances. Economist Thorstein Veblen, one of the first theorists to deal systematically with this matter, coined the phrase "conspicuous consumption" to describe the lengths to which the "leisure class" often goes in a frantic effort to gain prestige through wasteful and excessive consumption of both goods and leisure time.[7]

3. The rise of hierarchically structured bureaucracies in modern urban society has had a direct bearing both on the distribution and character of power and on the status system itself. While there are bureaucracies in agrarian as well as urbanized societies, it is in the latter particularly that the great economic, governmental, and military

Aside from housing there are other symbols of status. The occupants of this residence, in an Arizona suburb, display a boat, a familiar status symbol even of middle class families. (George W. Gardner)

[7] Thorstein Veblen, *The Theory of the Leisure Class* (1899). See also David M. Potter, *People of Plenty* (1954); John Galbraith, *The Affluent Society* (1958); and Percival Goodman and Paul Goodman, *Communitas* (1947).

335

bureaucracies provide a mechanism for the concentration and exercise of power. Often members of the power elite are themselves drawn from the upper levels of the status system, but not entirely.

Change in the American Class System

Large-scale changes in the major patterns of stratification in the United States have been associated with the rise of urbanism in the nation. As Mayer points out, the earlier expansion of the economy as related to industrialism and the growth of cities had the effect of producing a large urban working class.[8] Until well into the twentieth century, this urban proletariat was generally underpaid and overworked, and the life style imposed upon it by adverse conditions reflected its underprivileged position in the economy.

During the past few decades, however, a substantial portion of the urban working class has adopted a middle class style of life. The basic change making this possible has been the rise of incomes and the shorter work week. With higher incomes and more leisure time, opportunities are provided for workers to have and do those things which were possible in the past for only members of the privileged middle or upper classes. Many have acquired the consumer "needs" of the middle classes such as modern homes and household equipment, annual vacations and travel, leisure-time activities, and so on.

Change in the British Class System

One of the world's most urbanized and industrialized countries, Great Britain, has also undergone radical changes in its class structure.[9] A century or so ago, the country's class structure was made up of an impressive and influential upper class consisting mainly of wealthy and powerful merchants and industrialists, landed gentry, and titled nobility; a relatively small middle class consisting of shopkeepers, professionals, and clerical workers; and a large body of manual workers employed extensively in manufacturing and shipping, who were underpaid and overworked and who lived under miserable slum conditions. The middle of the twentieth century presents a very different picture. The nobility and landed gentry still exist but with declining significance and influence except for snob appeal; there are still wealthy industrial or business magnates, but their power and influence have been reduced by

[8] Kurt Mayer, "Changes in the Class Structure of the United States," *Transactions of the Third World Congress of Sociology* (1956).
[9] G. D. H. Cole, *Studies in Class Structure* (1955).

the socialization of parts of the economy and the rise of trade unionism; the middle classes have greatly expanded as white collar occupations have attracted an increasingly large proportion of employed persons; and, finally, the working classes, while declining in relative numbers, have experienced a great improvement in incomes and working conditions, often making it possible for them to have a standard of living and a life style comparable to those of the middle classes.

Changing Status Systems in Developing Societies

It is almost axiomatic that the status systems of developing countries generally change at a slower pace than those in industrialized countries—barring, of course, great social upheavals such as revolutions or destructive wars. In countries that are predominantly agricultural, social change in general has not been, at least until recently, pervasively affected by technology or the emergence of an ideological cult favorable to change in the social, economic, and political systems. Class and caste lines and other status distinctions were hardened by centuries of observance. But with the introduction and application of modern forms of technology and economic organization, together with the diffusion of ideologies favorable to social change, the traditionally rigid status system has been undermined, although not necessarily abandoned. Much of this change has occurred in cities, not in rural villages, but the values and life styles associated with a more flexible status system have filtered into the rural sectors, planting the seeds of a "revolution of rising expectations." No better illustration is the changing caste system of India, which has existed in its pristinely rigid form in the villages more than in the cities. Although the system is still intact as a going concern, its function, and to some extent its structure, has changed considerably in recent decades. No longer is it the tyrant that determines the status and life chances of the individual Hindu. Rather, the society has moved more in the direction of an open-class system with emphasis on achievement rather than ascription.[10]

---

[10] See especially David G. Mandelbaum, *Society in India: Continuity and Change* (1970); and M. N. Srinivas, *Social Change in Modern India* (1966).

Profiles of Community Class Systems

Yankee City

One of the early studies of status systems was made by W. L. Warner and his associates of a small New England city ("Yankee City").[11] In this study the researchers attempted to describe the social system in its entirety, not merely a segment of it. Warner devised four criteria of status and from them constructed a scale he called the Index of Status Characteristics. Four variables were employed—reputation of the residential neighborhood, quality of housing, occupation, and source of income. In addition, individuals interviewed were asked to place themselves and other persons they knew at a point in the status hierarchy of the community. Other information was obtained about the social life of the residents.

The approach Warner employed resulted in the identification of six social strata or "classes." Although he insisted that the strata so designated were indeed discrete entities, many scholars regard his delineation of class boundaries as unduly arbitrary, that the classes were instead conceptual artifacts arrived at by his particular methodology. Warner was especially concerned with what Weber considered "prestige" classes, and much of his research involved a description of the characteristics of these classes, particularly the ethnic composition of the people on the various levels, their occupations, formal and informal associations, family organization and relationships, life styles, and class attitudes and symbols. The six social strata were designated as upper upper (1.4 percent), lower upper (1.6 percent), upper middle (10 percent), lower middle (28 percent), upper lower (33 percent), and lower lower (25 percent). The Yankee City study is cited here because its methodology was a pioneer effort in this field and because of its great influence on stratification research.

Kansas City

Following a modified Warner approach, Coleman and Neugarten more recently undertook a study of the status system in metropolitan Kansas City.[12] Because of its sophisticated methodology, and especially because it is the only study of its type made of a major city in the United States, a profile of the status system in that metropolis is presented here, based on

---

[11] W. L. Warner and Paul S. Lunt, *The Social Life of a Modern Community* (1941). The actual city was Newburyport, Mass., with a population at that time of about 17,000. Four volumes based on this research were published.

[12] Richard P. Coleman and Bernice L. Neugarten, *Social Status in the City* (1971). The field work for this research was done in the 1950's.

the findings of the researchers. Whereas Warner interviewed all adults in Yankee City, the Kansas City study employed a statistical sample of individuals and families, presumably representative of the entire city. And whereas Warner made use of four variables in his initial study, the Kansas City analysis was based on several status variables, which included the character and reputation of the residential neighborhood or district, types of housing, income and occupation of the respondents, membership and participation in social clubs or other organizations of varying prestige, religious affiliation, and educational background such as the amount of formal schooling and types of schools or colleges attended. Each of the variables was ranked on a seven-point scale from low to high prestige. Individuals or families interviewed were located at some point in the social structure as indicated by a single scale based on rankings in each of the variables. A body of nonstatistical information was also amassed concerning the style of life, attitudes, and other relevant data obtained from personal interviews and observations.

On the basis of data amassed in the Kansas City study the researchers designated five social "classes" and thirteen substrata, as follows:

upper class:
    "capital society" (the pinnacle people)
    "noncapital society" (high status but with lesser symbols of lineage, wealth,
       power, or achievement)
upper middle class: elite; core; marginal
lower middle class: elite; core; marginal
working class: elite; core; marginal
lower class: poor but reputable; slum dwellers and disreputables

The researchers emphasized that no precise placement in the social structure could be made of an individual or family because the various statuses were often incongruous. A high-income plumber, for example, might live in a rundown neighborhood and belong to a prestigious church, or a wealthy gambler with no formal education might reside in a splendid house in the "gold coast" but be barred from fashionable clubs and shunned by his neighbors. Thus, some persons might qualify for a particular stratum on one variable but not on another. For this reason the class delineations are imprecise and the placements overlapping.

THE UPPER CLASS Kansas Citians at the very summit of the status pyramid represented a small minority, only about twenty families. For the most part they were inheritors of great fortunes and descendants of prominent families. The men were generally directors or executives of major commercial or industrial companies, and some served as trustees of educational or cultural institutions. They belonged to the most prestigious clubs and were usually members of Episcopal or Presbyterian churches. All of the men had attended college or professional schools, usually such institutions as Harvard or Princeton, and Wellesley or

Vassar if a woman. Their precollege education was mainly in fashion-able and expensive private schools. Some, but not all, lived in impressive mansions because the size and value of residence, unlike earlier days, were not the major criteria of prestige.

Included in the upper class, but somewhat below the pinnacle of prestige, were some two thousand adults whose claims to elite status were less impressive, at least to the people at the summit. They included professionals or executives who were outstandingly successful in terms of achievement or income—corporation lawyers, for example. Yet they were hardly recognized as top-level elitists because they lacked the necessary credentials of family lineage, education, social polish, or life style, although some were in positions of considerable power or in-fluence.

THE UPPER MIDDLE CLASS Within the broad spectrum of the upper middle class the researchers identified three strata. On the higher level were the "elite," the semiexecutives whose managerial or proprietorial positions carried less power, income, or prestige than the big-time executive or administrative positions at the top. Many professionals were independent or "fee" lawyers, doctors, dentists, or engineers. Most of the men and women had attended a "good" but not distinguished college or professional school.

Next below this level were the "core" people—the middle middle class—mainly minor managers, small business proprietors, and profes-sionals who were only moderately successful by accepted criteria. Specifically, they included such occupations as personnel and sales managers, accountants, middle-range government officials, and salaried professionals such as engineers, ministers, or lawyers.

On the bottom layer were "the marginals," families who lived in modest homes, some near the outskirts of the city or in newer mass-built suburbs. Less successful than those on higher levels, they were mainly small-shop proprietors, supervisors, minor government functionaries, or such professionals as teachers or ministers of middle class congrega-tions. About half of the men and women had attended college, mainly public or minor private institutions, and were comparable in education to the core group but less successful occupationally and financially. About one-fourth of the wives were gainfully employed.

THE LOWER MIDDLE CLASS On the status levels within the lower middle class the differences were largely determined by the prestige ratings on the several variables. The most prestigious adults were employed mainly in office or sales jobs, or as teachers, social workers, or ministers of small churches. Many were also blue collar or uniformed workers such as chief electricians or transcontinental bus drivers who received substantial incomes. Somewhat lower in status were the "marginals"—barbers,

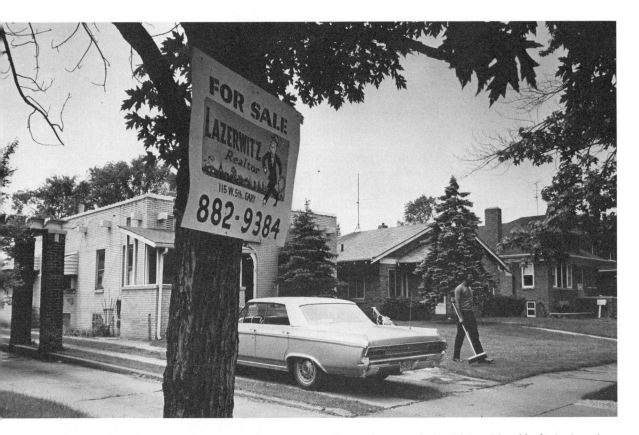

female hairdressers, firemen, policemen, mail carriers, and the like. None of the marginals had a college degree, although about one-fifth had attended college or vocational school. Most of the lower middle class lived in modest homes in "respectable" neighborhoods. Family life of the lower middle class was relatively stable, with little family disorganization in terms of divorce or separation.

THE WORKING CLASS Most of the adult men in the working class were blue collar personnel, skilled and semiskilled. Socially, they ranked below the white collar people in the lower middle class, but their incomes were generally higher. A large portion of this class, at least those on the most prestigious level, were craftsmen, foremen, plumbing contractors, and the like, but many were semiskilled operatives in factories, bus drivers, shipping clerks, or warehouse workers. Some of the families in this class were blacks or ethnics of recent European origin. Typically the working class lived in the older sections of the city, in homes whose exteriors exhibited signs of hard use and often neglect. Except for the highly skilled workers, there was limited job security. Most of the older persons had advanced no further than the eighth grade in school, but the younger adults had generally attended high school. None of the working class in the sample had a college degree. Most of the families had experienced a considerable upward mobility in income, but their extra

Most blacks in American cities live in districts that are often congested and deteriorated. This is a working class residential area in Gary, Indiana, an industrial suburb of Chicago. (George W. Gardner)

342   The Organization of Urban Life

earnings were spent mostly for material objects such as household furnishings, cars, or television sets but without much basic change in their overall life style.

THE LOWER CLASS Of the adults in the lower class, about 45 percent were blacks, 12 percent so-called hillbillies, seven percent American Indians, six percent Mexican-Americans, five percent eastern Europeans, four percent Italian-Americans, and two percent Asians. The remaining 19 percent were of northern European stock, mostly whites born in the Middle West.

Two social levels were identified in this class: the "respectable" poor and the "disreputable" poor. About half of the lower class families lived in abject slums, but subsequent to the date the research was done many of the slum residents moved to new public housing quarters. Lower class neighborhoods were scattered throughout the metropolitan area, some of them in small pockets, and many of the families were assisted by welfare agencies or other charitable organizations. The average number of children born to each adult woman in this class was 4.8, compared with 2.6 for the working class, 1.9 for the lower middle class, 1.7 for the upper middle class, and 2.1 for the upper class. Family life was less stable than in the higher social strata—one in five adults was living alone, either single, widowed, or separated from spouse.

Over half of the men were common laborers, working as janitors, garbage collectors, floor sweepers, porters, members of construction or maintanance gangs, and the like; and the working females were generally in domestic service or employed as hotel maids, laundry workers, scrub women, or operatives on assembly lines. About one of five had attended high school, many of them having been school dropouts. Social life in the lower class was highly restricted to informal relations with kin

TABLE 12.1 Kansas City Class Hierarchy

	Upper	Upper Middle	Lower Middle	Working	Lower
Median family income (1954)	$34,000	$11,900	$6,300	$4,300	$2,600
Self-employed	74%	34%	16%	10%	0%
College degree	66	41	6	0	0
Church affiliation or preference					
Protestant	74	72	78	77	62
Catholic*	13	15	18	22	38
Jewish*	13	13	4	1	0

*Catholics constituted 20 percent of the white population of Kansas City, while Jews represented only 3 percent of the total population.
SOURCE: Adapted from Richard P. Coleman and Bernice L. Neugarten, *Social Status in the City* (1971), Table 2.

and neighbors, or with persons belonging to the same ethnic, racial, or religious group. For the most part, the people on this level were outside the mainstream of the city's social, political, economic, and cultural life.

SOME STATUSES IN SUMMARY   Table 12.1 shows a summarized statistical picture of some of the status differentials discussed in the preceding description of Kansas City. The figures shown below the family incomes are percentages.

Other Urban Class Studies

A few notable researches have been conducted on specific strata of metropolitan communities, one of which is a study of the elite in Philadelphia, made by Baltzell in the 1950's.[13] Another is really two studies, by Lewis, who worked with small samples of families on the bottom class in Mexico City and San Juan, Puerto Rico.[14]

Philadelphia Gentlemen

In his study of the Philadelphia elite, Baltzell actually considers two categories of elite: the "social aristocracy" occupying the topmost prestige level, mainly those listed in the *Social Register* of that city; and the "achieving elite," those listed in *Who's Who in America* because of their reputed accomplishments in the various affairs of society. Most of Baltzell's research was concerned with the social elite whose members were entrenched at the peak of the prestige structure, but he also found numerous achieving elite at the apex of the prestige pyramid. The *Social Register* in 1940 listed 5,150 families, while 770 persons in that city were in *Who's Who*. Of the achieving elite, only 29 percent were in the *Social Register*. Clearly, Philadelphia residents known for their achievements were not always awarded the highest status as members of the social aristocracy.

   Philadelphia "gentlemen" and their ladies often had close ties with the elites of other metropolitan areas such as New York or Boston, and were considered among the elite of the entire nation. Family lineage, inherited wealth, and a prestigious occupation were among the criteria for membership in this class. Some of the "old families" proudly proclaimed descent from illustrious, or at least well-known, ancestors. Many of the families were large kinship groups having strong bonds of clan solidar-

---

[13] E. Digby Baltzell, *Philadelphia Gentlemen*: The *Making of a National Upper Class* (1958).

[14] Oscar Lewis, *La Vida* (1965); *Five Families* (1959); and *Children of Sanchez* (1961). Compare his theoretical discussion in *A Study of a Slum Culture* (1968).

ity. Intermarriage generally occurred between elite families, a fact that added to the castelike character of this class. Marriage into a lower class was not viewed with favor, although it occasionally did occur.

There was no uniformity of life styles among the members of this class, but certain aspects of their *modus vivendi* did provide the basis for considerable class solidarity. Many belonged to prestigious clubs and therefore associated socially with others of their own kind. These associational activities afforded a common ground for sharing ideas and experiences which often isolated them from persons on lower social levels. Most of the adults formerly attended fashionable private schools, and later studied at such prestigious universities as Pennsylvania, Harvard, Yale, or Princeton.

Residentially, the Philadelphia elite were mostly located in fashionable suburbs or areas within the city. In the summers many lived in luxurious resorts, where they fraternized with each other and with the elites from other cities. By religion, they were mainly Episcopalians or Presbyterians. Occupationally, they were business and finance executives, or professionals in the more lucrative and prestigious fields such as medicine, law, or engineering. Of the 32 bankers listed in *Who's Who*, three-fourths were in the *Social Register*; but of the 178 educators listed as eminent "achievers," only 16 percent were among the recognized social elite. Most of the social elite were of Anglo-Saxon ancestry; a few Jews and southern Europeans were included, but there were no blacks.

The Culture of Poverty

The "culture of poverty" is the focus of Lewis's research in Mexico City and San Juan. Although these cities differ in certain respects, particularly in their ethnic composition (there are no Indians or Indian culture in San Juan) and in the historical circumstances of their development, they do have in common a "mother tongue" and religion. Lewis also found striking similarities in the life styles of the people in the class underbelly of both cities.

A common pattern for the lower lower stratum was the relentless struggle for survival, with perhaps a little money available at times for nonessentials. The specter of hunger, exposure, or illness was never far away, and was often a reality. Economic security was a mirage.

Instead of conventional marriage and family relations, marriages were mainly free unions whose tenuous bonds were easily and frequently broken. The sexual adventures of husbands and wives, before and after marriage, prolonged absences of husbands from their families, or irresponsible spending of limited earnings tended to create an atmosphere of mutual distrust.

Packed into small living quarters, the families ate, slept, and performed other bodily functions under crowded conditions that made harmonious living difficult. Family bickering was frequent and physical violence common. The adults were either illiterate or, as former drop-outs, had received only a few years of schooling. From the viewpoint of middle class values, their spoken language was vividly expressive—shocking to many conventional persons.

The families were nominally Catholic, but church attendance was limited mainly to the females, and religion played a limited role in their lives, except as they commonly gave lip-service to religious beliefs or myths. They made little or no use of such institutional facilities as banks, libraries, art galleries, or museums, but were frequent movie-goers and often found relaxation in drinking at local bars. They belonged to no clubs or other leisure-time associations, nor were they affiliated with a labor union or any other power-oriented organization. Illegitimacy and prostitution were common and, although not approved, tended to have a different meaning in this cultural setting than among conventional people on higher social strata. Most of them had impaired health even though they did have access to clinics or hospitals in case of serious health problems.

Who Are the Underdogs?

Who, then, are the people on the bottom stratum of most cities? Some are "skidders" who have seen better days but who have descended the social ladder only to land in the slum or on skid row. Some are newcomers who have entered the city at the bottom level and who lack the education, occupational skills, motivation, opportunities, or abilities to achieve a higher social position. Some have inherited, both biologically and social-ly, their lower lower position, having been born or reared at the bottom and socialized into the culture of that stratum. The cards are stacked against them, especially if they are blacks or ethnics who are objects of racial or cultural prejudice.

It is on this level that unemployment and unemployability are usually widespread. Especially in an industrial society, in which much work is done by the machine, adults on this level are expendable and often surplus—the last to be hired and the first to be fired. Many of the families or individuals rely on public welfare for their support; they usually have no savings, no bank account, no credit, no property beyond meager personal possessions or house furnishings.

In sheer numbers, middle class persons in urban-industrial societies are far more numerous than upper class and lower class persons. But this generalization would not necessarily hold for other societies. In cities of developing countries, say, Latin America, the Middle East, or South Asia, there is a relatively small middle class and a very large lower class. Yet relatively few systematic studies have been made of middle class sectors.

If it is sociologically acceptable to describe the life styles of people on the lowest rung of the social structure as the "culture of poverty," it should also be appropriate to identify the way of life at the top as the "culture of affluence." And if, as Lewis insists, the culture of poverty is a way of life passed on from generation to generation, with the children of each oncoming generation being socialized into this culture, one may also conclude that a culture of affluence is transmitted from one generation to another through the socialization of the children, as among the elite of Philadelphia. Indeed, one may view the life styles and values of the in-between strata (the middle classes) as cultural systems, or subsystems, that overlap but do not duplicate the subsystems on higher or lower levels.

Viewing the class structure of a city in strictly economic terms gives a distorted picture of the system. As Valentine suggests, there is a difference between a *condition* of poverty and a *culture* of poverty.[15] Poor people may subscribe to a middle class value system and strive to achieve a middle class way of life, at least for their children. By the same token, there is a difference between a *condition* of affluence and a *culture* of affluence (Philadelphia elite style). Wealthy people often reject the values and behavior of the elite, preferring a life style more characteristic of the middle or lower classes. The culture of poverty, as Lewis describes it, may be different in a Western metropolis than in a communist community or a city organized along caste lines.

Any conceptual profile of a social class should be viewed with a critical eye. There is no clear-cut line of demarcation separating the various strata; rather, there is considerable overlapping in the economic, behavioral, psychological, and cultural assets of people on different conceptual levels. In cities of industrial countries the various statuses of an individual may be inconsistent or incongruous, whereas in a village or folk community in nonindustrial societies the statuses tend to be relatively consistent and the strata clearly identifiable.

Urbanism and Social Mobility

Urbanized and industrialized societies afford greater prospects for social mobility than nonindustrial societies. Highly urbanized societies, or even those moving in this direction, commonly have expanding economies, which means increasing job opportunities and rising incomes. Growing cities, and particularly large cities, have a complex division of labor which involves the creation of new occupations or more jobs, and a need for personnel to fill these positions. Thus, there are opportunities

[15] Charles A. Valentine, *Culture and Poverty: Critique and Counterproposals* (1968), pp. 114–20.

for upward occupational mobility—or prospects for downward mobility. Urbanized societies tend, then, to be "achievement" societies. Such urbanized countries as the United States and those of western Europe are more favorable to upward social mobility than such traditional societies as those of the Middle East, Latin America, or parts of Asia.

Forms of Vertical Mobility

There are many forms and criteria of vertical mobility, and different perspectives from which to view it. One may distinguish status mobility from class mobility. An individual may have many statuses and may rise or fall in any or all of them. Status mobility may be readily observed and perhaps easily measured. It is quite another matter to determine when or what kinds of status changes add up to changes in an individual's class position. This is so because the elements of class position are numerous and varied, making it difficult to delineate class boundaries except in an arbitrary manner. Social scientists do not always agree on the number or criteria of social classes, yet all agree that class mobility within the system does occur.

Before the scientific and technological revolution, which began in the Western world, villages and folk communities experienced relatively little change from one generation to another. There were few channels for upward mobility of the individual or his family, and even they were ordinarily so constricted that not many could rise to a higher social or economic position, although broad disruptive social changes such as war or revolution did bring about considerable vertical or spatial shifting of many people. But with the multiplication and growth of cities, commonly associated with technological developments, mobility channels were widened, prospects for improving one's social and economic position were increased, more wealth was created and distributed, and bonds that kept individuals or families in their traditional statuses and roles were loosened. As the urban-industrial type of society emerged and expanded, countless numbers of persons were able to move from the lower levels of the social structure to more favorable positions. In many parts of the world, developing countries are in the early stages of urban-industrial expansion.

In nonindustrial countries, "vacancies" in the socioeconomic structure above the lowest stratum are less numerous. Even if they do exist, the number of persons qualified to fill them may be limited. When the Congo (now Zaire) became an independent country in the 1960's, there were only a few college or university graduates in the whole land, and only a handful of doctors, nurses, engineers, teachers, or qualified administrators available to fill the positions so crucial to a functioning social system.

The Distance, Direction, and
Velocity of Mobility

If there are more opportunities for upward mobility, or chances for downward movement, in cities than in rural or folk communities, it is also true that the urban person can move farther in either direction than the rural dweller because the social distance from the apex to the bottom of the social structure is greater in the city, especially in the metropolis. Popular literature is replete with examples of the poor city boy who became immensely rich or powerful—the rags-to-riches legend. The spectacular rise of a few individuals always attracts wide interest and contributes to the Horatio Alger myth that every deserving person can do the same if he applies himself. It is usually true, of course, that the farm or village boy (or girl) who is strongly motivated to succeed in terms of occupation, education, wealth, or power may find it expedient to move to a city where the mobility channels are wider and longer and the rewards greater than in rural regions.

But for every person who makes a spectacular ascent, the great majority of people either remain relatively stationary or move only a short distance on the social escalator, which incidentally moves in both directions, upward and downward. Even for those who have moved upward a long distance in the course of a lifetime, the moves have usually been a series of short steps, a notch or two at a time. Similarly, those who move downward ordinarily make the descent rather slowly.

The majority of in-migrants to American cities have entered the social structure at or near the bottom, whether they are immigrants from abroad or migrants from the rural hinterlands. Excluding those with high racial or cultural visibility, who may be handicapped in various ways, most in-migrants, or at least their children, have moved to higher social and economic levels. Many became assimilated into the dominant culture and integrated into the organized social system. Even some of the racially visible peoples or their children have moved fairly rapidly (over a generation or so) into higher social strata.

The situation in Honolulu is an example of the changing class positions of racially visible Orientals, who came to Hawaii originally as contract laborers or impoverished immigrants and found employment on the plantations.[16] In the course of time most of them, especially the Chinese and Japanese, moved to the city, acquired an education, entered business, the professions, or public services, and rode the mobility escalator to higher economic and social levels. Today, some of the most affluent, powerful, and otherwise distinguished residents of that city are descendants of Asians who entered the system at the lowest level. But at

---

[16] Andrew W. Lind, *Hawaii's People* (1967), and Romanzo Adams, *The People of Hawaii* (1923).

or near the bottom are other Asians, notably the Filipinos, who arrived later than the Japanese or Chinese.

Conditions Facilitating or
Obstructing Social Mobility

The value system which holds that upward mobility is desirable is almost universal; in Western urban-industrial societies it is an article of faith held by most persons, who believe that upward mobility leads to the good life and is within reach of those who will strive for this goal. Yet the high road to such a goal is often blocked by conditions that make upward mobility difficult or even impossible. Prejudice may become a barrier preventing individuals of a particular race or ethnic group from rising higher in the system. A roadblock to upward mobility is created when the elite monopolize wealth or power or both, thereby preventing individuals from moving upward into the top stratum. In his study of stratification in two Latin American cities (Queretaro, Mexico, and Popayan, Colombia), Whiteford found that class lines were tightly drawn, that movement into the elite class was almost impossible because power and wealth were virtually monopolized by those at the top and because possible aspirants needed such credentials as a university education, illustrious family lineage, and a prestigious occupation, all of which were out of reach of the masses, especially those of Indian ancestry.[17] Evers observed in Bangkok, Thailand, that a fairly high rate of upward mobility occurred in the early stages of urbanization and industrialization, but that this rate has declined as a result of the monopolization of power and wealth by the bureaucratic elite who had "arrived."[18]

The chances for upward or downward mobility vary greatly according to various situations or the prevalence of particular attitudes. Coleman and Neugarten, in their Kansas City study, found that blacks were not as upwardly mobile as whites, that in two samples 40 percent of the adult blacks but only five percent of the whites had been born in the lower class and remained there throughout their lives.[19] When vertical mobility of the white population in Kansas City was considered, it was evident that in the upper middle, lower middle, and working classes most of the persons on these levels had moved upward from lower strata, suggesting that any of these three levels are within reach of white persons from lower levels. But the upper class was an exception; few persons had hurdled the upper class barriers.

[17] Andrew H. Whiteford, *Two Cities of Latin America*, (1960).

[18] Hans-Dieter Evers, "Formation of a Social Class Structure: Urbanization, Bureaucratization, and Social Mobility in Thailand," *American Sociological Review*, 31 (August 1966), 480–88.

[19] *Op. cit.*, p. 224.

On the Skids

Relatively little empirical research has been done on downward mobility and its social and personal effects. A survey of men residing on the "skid rows" of several American cities revealed a varied pattern of upward and downward mobility.[20] Almost half of the men had experienced an early rise in mobility, followed by a continuously downward movement. About one-fifth had been downwardly mobile only, presumably from some socioeconomic level occupied by their parental families. At any rate, alcoholism appeared to be related to their downward mobility, although it may have been a symptom rather than a cause. About one in five was rated as neurotic or psychotic, and an additional third had some "odd" personality traits. Almost all of them appeared to have been poorly adjusted before they landed on skid row, but whether such disabilities contributed to their fall is not clear.

Summary

In our discussion of urban status systems in this chapter, we have observed that patterns of social stratification vary from one city, region, or country to another, and that life is organized to a considerable extent in accordance with the existing status system. It is logical that we now turn to one of the ways in which urban society is organized and the forms of social participation which occur. The focus of the following chapter will be on voluntary associations, their structure and functions, and the nature of participation in such groups. Although all the evidence points to the remarkable proliferation of formally organized associations in the cities of industrialized countries, it should be emphasized that the formation of such groups is not solely a development peculiar to urban communities. Actually, such organizations also exist in rural communities, but the conditions of rural society are not such as to make possible the multiplication of associations comparable to the conditions of an urban environment. It will be noted in the discussion to follow that formal voluntary associations tend to be synchronized to the status system, that one of the functions of the association is the conferral of status on the members, and that another function is to provide an escalator for vertical social mobility.

[20] Donald J. Bogue, *Skid Row in American Cities* (1963), chs. 14, 17, and 18.

Selected Bibliography

BOOKS

Baltzell, E. Digby, *Philadelphia Gentlemen: The Making of a National Upper Class.* New York: The Free Press, 1958.

Bendix, Reinhard, and Seymour Martin Lipset, *Social Mobility in Industrial Society.* Berkeley and Los Angeles: University of California Press, 1960.

———, ———, *Class, Status, and Power.* New York: The Free Press, 1966.

Berger, Bennett M., *Working Class Suburb.* Berkeley and Los Angeles: University of California Press, 1960.

Chudacoff, Howard, *Mobile Americans: Residential and Social Mobility in Omaha, 1880–1920.* New York: Oxford University Press, 1972.

Cole, G. D. H., *Studies in Class Structure.* London: Routledge and Kegan Paul, 1955.

Coleman, Richard P., and Bernice L. Neugarten, *Social Status in the City.* San Francisco: Jossey-Bass, 1971.

van Heek, F., *et al., Sociale Stijging en Daling in Nederland* (Social Ascent and Descent in the Netherlands). Leiden: Institute for Social Research, 1958.

Kinlock, G. C., M. E. Close, and B. Wright, *Urbanization and the Plural Life: A Case Study of Flatlife in South Africa.* Durban: Logans Academic Press, 1970.

Laumann, Edward O., *Social Stratification Research for the 1970's.* Indianapolis: Bobbs-Merrill, 1970.

Lenski, Gerhard, *Power and Privilege.* New York: McGraw-Hill, 1966.

Schnore, Leo F., *Class and Race in City and Suburb.* Chicago: Markham, 1972.

Shostak, Arthur B., *Blue-Collar Life.* New York: Random House, 1969.

Smelser, Neil J., and Seymour Martin Lipset, eds., *Social Structure and Mobility in Economic Development.* Chicago: Aldine, 1966.

Suttles, Gerald D., *The Social Order of the Slum.* Chicago: University of Chicago Press, 1970.

Vogel, Ezra, *Japan's New Middle Class.* Berkeley and Los Angeles: University of California Press, 1963.

Whiteford, Andrew H., *Two Cities of Latin America.* Beloit, Wis.: Logan Museum of Anthropology, Beloit College, 1960.

ARTICLES

Bennett, William S., Jr., and Noel P. Gist, "Class and Family Influences on Student Aspirations" (Kansas City), *Social Forces*, 43 (December 1964), 167–73.

Curtis, R. F., "Differential Association and the Stratification of the Urban Community," *Social Forces*, 42 (October 1963), 68–77.

Desu, A. R., "Urbanization and Social Stratification," *Sociological Bulletin*, 9 (December 1960), 7–15.

Evers, H. D., "Social Class Structure: Urbanization and Social Mobility in Thailand," *American Sociological Review*, 31 (August 1966), 480–89.

Greer, Scott, "Social Structure and Political Process in Suburbia," *Rural Sociology*, 27 (December 1962), 438–60.

Haller, A. O., D. Holsinger, and H. U. Saraiva, "Variations in Occupational Prestige Hierarchies: Brazilian Data," *American Journal of Sociology*, 77 (March 1972), 941–56.

Handel, Gerald, and Lee Rainwater, "Persistence and Change in Working Class Life Style," *Sociology and Social Research*, 48 (April 1964), 281–89.

Land, A., "Occupational Mobility in Six Cities," *American Sociological Review*, 33 (October 1968), 740–50.

Laumann, Edward O., and James S. House, "Living Room Styles and Social Attributes: The Patterning of Material Artifacts in a Modern Urban Community," in Edward O. Laumann, Paul Siegel, and Robert W. Hodge, eds., *The Logic of Social Hierarchies*, pp. 189–204. Chicago; Markham, 1970.

Lewis, David M., and A. O. Haller, "Rural-Urban Differences in Preindustrial and Industrial Evaluations of Occupations by Japanese Adolescent Boys," *Rural Sociology*, 29 (September 1964), 324–29.

Lipset, Seymour Martin, "Social Mobility and Urbanization," *Rural Sociology*, 20 (September–December 1955), 220–28.

Reissman, Leonard, "Readiness to Succeed: Mobility Aspirations among the Poor" (New Orleans), *Urban Affairs Quarterly*, 4 (March 1969), 379–97.

Sewell, William H., A. O. Haller, and George Ohlendorf, "The Educational and Early Occupational Status Attainment Process: Replication and Revision," *American Sociological Review*, 35 (December 1970), 1014–27.

Williamson, R. C., "Social Class and Change in Bogotá," *Social Forces*, 46 (March 1968), 317–28.

———, "Some Variables of Middle Class and Lower Class in Two Central American Cities," *Social Forces*, 41 (December 1962), 195–207.

Vorwaller, D. J., "Social Mobility and Membership in Voluntary Associations," *American Journal of Sociology*, 75 (January 1970), 481–86.

Wolf, Eleanor P., and Charles Lebeaux, "Class and Race in the Changing City," in Leo F. Schnore, ed., *Social Science and the City*. New York: Praeger, 1968.

13 • Social Participation and City Life

Social participation is a process through which a society, community, or group coheres to perform expected or needed functions; it is also a process through which the human personality is shaped and conditioned for group life. The process involves human interaction on various levels and with varied degrees of frequency and intensity of feeling. It occurs within the framework of formal structures, as well as in social situations that are loosely structured or even unstructured. It is as much a feature of rural as of urban community life, of traditional as well as urban-industrial societies. Social participation occurs in many forms and at many levels. Aside from universal participation in family, neighborhood, and friendship groups, there are other forms that may indicate, albeit in a crude way, the integration of individuals in society or community life. Organized voluntary associations providing the structural framework for social participation appear to proliferate under conditions of urban or metropolitan life, particularly in urban-industrial societies having a comparatively large middle class. Voting and activities in political organizations are indexes of civic participation, just as membership in religiously oriented groups is an index of religiosity, and participation in complex economic organizations usually involves an occupational role. Social participation becomes more than mere involvement with others in social groups and situations; it is also a *modus vivendi*, a life style that has social, cultural, and psychological ramifications.

The principal focus of this chapter will be on participation both in formal associations and in intimate, informal groups and neighborhoods in urban-industrial society.

New Forms of Organization
in the City

The rise of urban-industrial societies has created conditions limiting the functions and influence of such ascriptive institutions as the family, tribe, caste, or village community, which traditionally provided the ties that held the larger society together and made it functionally viable.[1] As a society becomes increasingly urbanized, it also becomes increasingly heterogeneous and internally differentiated, creating an infinite variety of values and life styles which are not always supportive of ascriptive institutions and groups. To provide integrative functions for the societies undergoing such changes, as well as supplying the personal needs of people in these societies, formal organizations emerge and proliferate to perform a multitude of specific functions.

Such organizations have multiplied and flourished more particularly in democratic rather than totalitarian societies because in the latter the monopoly and exercise of power by the state leaves little room for voluntary associations that might be incompatible with the expressed objectives and political processes of a dictatorial regime.

As societies become more urbanized, traditional forms of organization are often unable to carry out expected functions or to perform other functions necessitated by the changing of community life. Such a transition was observed by Anderson and Anderson in their study of the associational structure of a Danish island community that had been transformed, over a half-century, from an isolated fishing town to an urban annex of Copenhagen.[2] During this period, the traditional forms of organization had declined and were replaced by new associations around which the life of the town tended to be mobilized. The complexities and demands of urban life are such that traditional institutions cannot, by themselves, satisfy all human needs and provide the mechanisms for effective participation. To meet these needs, however defined by the persons involved, various forms of participatory mechanisms have emerged, although the development of such mechanisms has not been uniform from one society or community to another, or even from one social class or ethnic group to another in the same society.

Where family and neighborhood are the hubs around which a social system revolves, as in the village life of traditional societies, the social and cultural needs of the people may be effectively met by these mechanisms. But when people from such a milieu, or others like them, move to a city and are confronted there by situations that are new and

---

[1] See especially David Horton Smith, "The Importance of Formal Voluntary Organizations for Society," *Sociology and Social Research*, 50 (July 1966), 483–94.

[2] Robert T. Anderson and Gallatin Anderson, "Voluntary Associations and Urbanization: A Diachronic Analysis," *American Journal of Sociology*, 55 (November 1959), 267–73.

strange and perhaps baffling, some other mechanism may be needed to facilitate their participation in community life. Under such conditions various groups emerge, performing a variety of functions that the traditional primary groups cannot perform effectively under urban conditions—or even in rural settings of urban-industrial societies.

Associations in Urbanized Societies

In the dynamic, democratic societies of the West, urbanization has found expression in the proliferation of voluntary associations, although even here the numbers and character of such organizations have varied considerably. The high incidence of residential change, separation of the home from place of work or of recreation, and occupational mobility—all have tended to detach the individual from his traditional moorings and create needs, psychological and otherwise, which existing structures have often been unable to satisfy. Given a competitive social system in which much of the effort of individuals is directed toward the achievement or defense of status, it is not surprising that so many associations function toward enabling their members to achieve these ends.

As Western societies have become increasingly urbanized, there has been a corresponding tendency for urban types of associations to spread beyond the boundaries of cities and become adopted in nonurban communities as well. This diffusion of formal associations has been an important aspect of the "urban impact."

Urbanization has tended to produce mass societies that are exceedingly complex, and it is this complexity, together with the rapid changes that occur in the social order, that is difficult, even impossible, for individuals to comprehend to the fullest extent. They may feel powerless, buffeted about by forces that are mystifying and threatening. The voluntary association may provide the individual with a basis for personal security and a meaningful group identity. Ordinarily such a group is small enough in size, simple enough in structure, and specific enough in its functions to be comprehended and appreciated by its members, who may share with each other a sense of loyalty to the group and satisfying experiences from their collective activities.

Mass Transportation, Communication, and Social Participation

In technologically oriented societies facilities for mass transportation and communication have become a feature of the urbanizing process. As individuals move with comparative ease from one location and social situation to another, as in the case of migration of rural folk to cities or from one city to another, they often need to participate in collective activities to achieve the security, companionship, or social roles they desire. Commonly this means identifying with one or more associations. Modern mass media have likewise expanded the horizons and experiences of almost everyone in urban-industrial societies. For one, they facilitate the wide dissemination of information about associations and their functions. This, of course, does not discount the importance of face-to-face communication.

A large proportion of formal associations are patterned after organizations already in existence. Often these organizations are linked to others to form a coalition or federation of associations belonging to the same "family," performing the same or similar functions and having similar structures. This patterning process is exemplified by the tendency of local groups such as labor unions, lodges, churches, and professional or business organizations (the number is legion) to become formally affiliated with other similar associations.

Communication is commonly maintained between such organizations and a centralized headquarters usually located in a major city. Through the channels of communication between the associations and the headquarters, relevant information may be disseminated, controls exercised, and guidance provided for the local groups belonging to the same family. Of some 17,000 nationally or regionally organized associations in the United States, as listed in a compendium in 1972, some one-third were headquartered in the New York metropolitan area; and when Chicago and Washington are added, the three metropolitan centers account for three-fifths of the national or regional headquarters.[3] About one-third of the headquarters were located in other metropolitan areas, but less than 10 percent were in nonmetropolitan cities.[4]

How Associations
Are Formed

Voluntary associations arise when there is a "felt need" for them by two or more persons, although such a need is not automatically translated into organized functioning groups. Often associations are organized after changes in an established way of life present a social crisis which may be met through collective action within the framework of an organization, either formal or informal. One example of the emergence of voluntary associations is described by Gans in a study of Levittown, a middle class mass-produced suburb in New Jersey.[5] Some 12,000 fam-

[3] *Encyclopedia of Associations*, 8th ed. (1972), vol. 1, p. 7. See also Stanley Lieberson and Irving L. Allen, Jr., "Location of National Headquarters of Voluntary Associations," *Administrative Science Quarterly*, 8 (1963), 320–37.

[4] See also Arthur J. Vidich and Joseph Bensman, *Small Town in Mass Society* (1958).

[5] Herbert J. Gans, *The Levittowners: Ways of Life and Politics in a New Suburban Community* (1967), ch. 3.

ilies moved into the community when it was opened for occupancy in 1958. Of the 77 associations (excluding churches and church-related groups) that had been established during the first four or five years of Levittown's existence, most of them were organized in the first two years. About one-third were organized by outsiders such as officers or representatives of national or regional organizations. The Levittowners themselves established many branch organizations. However, almost half were independently organized in response to some felt community or personal need, often by a number of persons who discovered a common set of interests or recognized a common need.

Studies in Britain (Coventry, Luton, Sheffield, Oxford, and London) tend to confirm the observations made by Gans that in the early period of newly developed housing projects voluntary associations proliferate and flourish.[6] The residents were mostly working class families that had been resettled en masse in planned housing "estates." As they faced new and different situations, there was at first a flurry of activity when various associations were formed to deal with immediate problems such as providing necessary amenities. But when these objectives were

Urbanization of India has been associated with marked increases in travel within and between cities. Transit facilities are often overcrowded, as shown by these railway coaches at Delhi. (United Press International Photo)

357

[6] R. E. Pahl, *Patterns of Urban Life* (1970).

achieved the enthusiasm of many residents waned, factional disputes sometimes occurred, and many families fell back on the familiar pattern of indifference to collective action and participation.

Somewhat different results were obtained in a study by Berger of automotive workers who had moved to Milpitas, a semirural suburban community near San Jose, California, when the factory was shifted from Richmond. At the time of the study, 70 percent of the respondents belonged to no club or other organization and only eight percent were members of more than one association.[7] Actually, 20 percent of the respondents belonged to fewer organizations than they had before they moved. Berger concluded that mere movement to a suburb did not necessarily mean a change from a working class to a middle class way of life or value system.

Participation in Voluntary Associations

Functionally, associations are of two kinds. Some are *instrumental* in the sense that they are organized explicitly for the purpose of achieving certain goals or objectives through the collective efforts of the members or others of similar interests. *Expressive* associations are those whose primary function is to afford satisfaction for the participants in informal fellowship among like-minded persons. These have often been referred to as cliques or friendship groups. Obviously, both types may be found in cities and in villages or open-country communities, and, furthermore, an instrumental association may also have an expressive function.

The conditions of modern urban-industrial society have been particularly favorable to the growth of instrumental associations. Generally they have a formal structure in order to facilitate the achievement of designated goals, whereas expressive groups usually have a simple structure, or perhaps no formal structure at all. Instrumental associations may be large or small, whereas expressive associations, by their nature and functions, almost always have a small number of members or adherents.

Integrative Functions

There are many associations, characteristically urban, which are integrative in both their manifest and latent functions. Occupational or trade associations are, in the main, cooperative organizations in which members of the same occupation combine to further their own interests

---

[7] Bennett M. Berger, *Working-Class Suburb: A Study of Auto Workers in Suburbia* (1960), p. 59.

and objectives, which may or may not parallel the objectives of other groups or the community as a whole. Community teachers' associations or chambers of commerce ostensibly represent the interests of both their members and of the community at large. Federations such as local ministerial alliances, councils of social agencies, or federations of labor unions have the manifest function of integrating certain groups within a given area; these are the organizations' intended and recognized functions. Such civic organizations as the League of Women Voters or the Red Cross Board are integrative in the sense that they represent the larger community or society rather than special-interest groups. In addition to their manifest functions, organizations may have latent functions such as good fellowship or status striving, functions that are neither overtly intended or recognized by the members.

It has been said that voluntary associations are the cement that holds together the structure of an urbanized society. Although perhaps only a half-truth, it does have some basis in fact, for example, the widespread tendency of many urban dwellers to identify with more than one formal organization, thus providing a linkage between several groups with disparate manifest functions. An individual may, for example, be affiliated with a religious denomination, a political party, an occupational association, a civil rights group, a social welfare organization, a cultural association, a social club, and the like; and if he is active in them, he forms channels of communication among them.

Divisive Functions

Voluntary associations may be divisive as well as integrative. Whatever social cleavages exist within a community or society, whether along economic, racial, ethnic, or religious lines, associations tend to reflect these social boundaries and reinforce the cleavages that are already present. The very heterogeneity of an urban population, especially a metropolis, creates cleavages of one kind or another.

Differentiation of associations by race, nationality, religion, and status is demonstrated in a study by Minnis of women's organizations in New Haven, Connecticut,[8] in which she found that the most rigid distinction was racial, with at least 90 percent of New Haven's organizations being racially exclusive. Those with racially mixed memberships were mainly church auxiliaries, veterans' organizations, and associations providing community services supervised by administrative officers. Three-fourths of the organizations were denominationally exclusive, revealing a cleavage among Protestants, Catholics, and Jews. More than half of the organizations were structured along ethnic lines. Some groups restricted

[8] Mhyra S. Minnis, "Cleavage in Women's Organizations," *American Sociological Review*, 18 (February 1953), 47–53.

membership along three lines—race, religion, and ethnicity; for example, a Catholic group that admitted only Italians of Caucasian ancestry. Some black groups admitted only Protestants. Many groups represented a particular social stratum; there were Protestant Junior Leagues, Catholic Leagues, Negro Leagues, Jewish Leagues, Swedish Leagues, Italian Leagues, and Polish Leagues, all of which occupied different positions in New Haven's status hierarchy. Inasmuch as cities, especially metropolitan communities, are generally more heterogeneous than the village or open-country community, it is almost inevitable that these organizational microcosms reflect the differentials and cleavages in the macrocosms of city or society.

Social Mobility
as a Function

Providing an "escalator" for socially mobile individuals is one of the functions of voluntary associations. In urban-industrial societies of the West, the urban dweller is faced with numerous opportunities for membership in such groups, and if he desires to do so he may join one or more of them to enhance his status. Membership may thus bring him in contact with persons who may be helpful in furthering his aspirations, and may even open doors to opportunities for a better job, more power, or the satisfaction of associating with persons on the status level to which he aspires. Thus he may join a social club, a political organization, a church or church-related group, or an occupational association.

Selected Studies of Participation
in Urbanized Societies

Data on voluntary associations by sample surveys in six countries suggest that the rate of membership of adults is influenced by several factors, including the extent of urbanization and industrialization, cultural values and practices, and educational and income levels.[9] Four of the countries (the United States, Canada, Britain, Germany) are highly industrialized and urbanized, one (Italy) only moderately developed in this respect, and one (Mexico) predominantly agricultural and relatively underdeveloped industrially. Average incomes in Italy and Mexico were much lower than in the other four countries. The percentages of population affiliated with one or more voluntary associations, including labor unions, are indicated in the table below. Percentages of persons belonging to two or more organizations are in parentheses.

[9] The data on Canada is reported in James Curtis, "Voluntary Association Joining: A Cross-National Comparative Note," *American Sociolgical Review*, 36 (October 1971), 872–80. For the other five countries, data were assembled by Gabriel A. Almond and Sidney Verba, *The Civic Culture* (1963), ch. 11.

TABLE 13.1   Percentage of Population Affiliated with Voluntary Associations

	Total	Males	Females
Canada	64 (36)	73	56
United States	57 (32)	68	47
Great Britain	47 (16)	66	30
Germany	44 (12)	66	24
Italy	29 (6)	41	19
Mexico	25 (2)	43	15

One striking difference is the comparatively low percentage of memberships in Italy and Mexico as compared with the four other countries. Although Canada and the United States are similar to Britain and Germany in the extent of urbanization and industrialization, in the North American countries there is a tradition of individualism combined with a strong drive for success leading to upward mobility. Also, Canada and the United States, being similar in economy and culture, tend to encourage participatory roles of women in social and civic affairs.

The differences in associational affiliations of women are especially marked between Italy and Mexico and the four other countries: 19 and 15 percent, respectively, as compared, for example, with 56 and 47 percent, respectively, in Canada and the United States. However, there were certain similarities in all six countries: Persons on higher educational and economic levels were more likely to be members of voluntary associations than those on lower levels. Also, there was no consistent relationship in all countries between associational membership and the size of the community of residence.

Two reports on voluntary associations in France are in only partial agreement on the extent of membership in voluntary associations in that urban-industrial nation. Rose assembled data from three surveys which indicated that about 41 percent of French adults belong to some kind of formal association.[10] After interviewing a number of informed persons, Rose concluded that many of the associations were "paper" organizations that were neither viable nor influential. In his opinion, the French-Catholic tradition of encompassing the individual within the church, and of encouraging priests rather than laymen to participate in local welfare and improvement activities, tended to deter the formation of associations for civic purposes. A study by Gallagher in a French provincial city of 50,000 suggested, however, that voluntary associations were more numerous and important than Rose had concluded.[11]

[10] Arnold Rose, "Voluntary Associations in France," in Arnold Rose, ed., *Theory and Method in the Social Sciences* (1954), ch. 4.

[11] Orvoell R. Gallagher, "Voluntary Associations in France," *Social Forces*, 36 (December 1957), 153–60.

The United States

One of the early studies of associations in the United States was made by Warner and his associates in Yankee City, a small New England city. The investigators identified and analyzed 357 associations, and the persons interviewed had an average of about two memberships.[12] A study in Detroit revealed that two-thirds of the persons in the sample belonged to one or more organizations other than a church, and that 17 percent were members of a church.[13] A survey of voluntary associations in Minnesota in 1957 indicated that the number of reported memberships was nearly 3 million, more than the entire population of the state, that some 400 were statewide in scope, and that the headquarters of the larger organizations were mainly in the Minneapolis-St. Paul metropolitan area.[14]

The impressive network of formal associations to be found in American cities has tended to create a false stereotype of all urban dwellers as joiners. Various studies indicate that a sizable proportion of the adult urban population is without any formal affiliations. In New York City, Komarovsky found that over half (52 percent) had no organized group affiliations, except for church membership.[15]

Membership and participation rates in voluntary associations and other organized activities are generally lower for blacks than for whites in American society. However, when socioeconomic status is controlled so that comparisons can be made between blacks and whites of comparable strata, these differences sometimes disappear. In a citywide sample of adults in Indianapolis taken in 1968, Olsen found that the membership and social participation of blacks in voluntary associations was somewhat greater than for whites of corresponding socioeconomic strata.[16] In fact, when comparisons were made for other forms of social participation, as in political organizations, churches, and voting, a similar pattern was observed. An earlier study in Detroit in which a similar procedure was followed yielded roughly comparable results.[17] Two studies, of course, do not provide enough data for broad generalizations, but it seems evident that race per se is not the most important variable in social participation.

[12] W. L. Warner and Paul S. Lunt, *The Social Life of a Modern Community* (1941), p. 313.

[13] Morris Axelrod, "Urban Structure and Social Participation," *American Sociological Review*, 21 (February 1956), 13–18.

[14] William C. Rogers, "Voluntary Associations and Urban Community Development," *International Review of Community Development*, No. 7 (1961), 140–41.

[15] Mirra Komarovsky, "The Voluntary Associations of Urban Dwellers," *American Sociological Review*, 11 (December 1946), 686–98.

[16] Marvin E. Olsen, "Social and Political Participation of Blacks," *American Sociological Review*, 35 (August 1970), 682–97.

[17] Conducted in 1957 by the Institute for Social Research at the University of Michigan.

Are Americans becoming more or less participative in voluntary associations? There is no ready answer to the question because such data are not abundant. Hyman and Wright compared the results of two national surveys made by the National Opinion Research Center, one in 1955 and another in 1962;[18] from the surveys, which employed comparable methods, they noted a "small but noteworthy" increase in association memberships during the period the surveys were taken. The increase was not confined to the upper income strata but occurred on all levels, especially among those of low economic status, and it applied to both blacks and whites. That the 1950's and 1960's was a period of increasing metropolitanization and suburbanization, and of rising incomes and educational levels, may have accounted to some extent for this increase. But it was also a period in which blacks, especially those living in urban centers, were becoming more politically conscious and active in civil rights organizations, which may have accounted partly for their increased participation.

Available studies generally indicate a tendency for people with high incomes and high-status occupations to participate more extensively in formal associations than individuals on lower socioeconomic levels. In Detroit, Axelrod found that four-fifths of the respondents in the upper-income brackets belonged to one or more associations, compared with two-fifths of those on the low-income levels.[19] Middle-income persons were about as active as those having high incomes. Furthermore, three-fifths of the professionals, managers, and proprietors taken together belonged to one or more associations, compared with two-fifths of the skilled and semiskilled manual workers taken together.

In her study of New York City, Komarovsky found that about two-fifths of the male manual workers, half of the white collar employees, two-thirds of the businessmen, and four-fifths of the professionals were affiliated with associations.[20] Among the women, about one-tenth of the working class women, one-third of the white collar females, half of those engaged in business, and five-sixths of the professionals held memberships in one or more associations. In a sample of fifty working class families in New Haven, Dotson found that three-fifths of the men and four-fifths of the women had no affiliations with formal associations, and even the affiliates of labor unions and fraternal societies were not ordinarily active participants.[21]

[18] Herbert H. Hyman and Charles R. Wright, "Trends in Voluntary Associations of American Adults," *American Sociological Review*, 36 (April 1971), 191–206.

[19] Axelrod, *Op. cit.*, p. 13.

[20] Komarovsky, *op. cit.*, p. 688.

[21] Floyd Dotson, "Patterns of Voluntary Associations Among Working Class Families," *American Sociological Review*, 16 (October 1951), 687–93.

Kansas City Associations
in a Class Setting

A survey of the status system of an entire metropolis, Kansas City, revealed the class orientation of formal organizations.[22] Five major classes and eight substrata were delineated in the survey. Most of the groups had a membership that cut across one or two class boundaries, but about one-fifth were identified with only one of the five major classes, and these were mainly in the upper and middle class levels.

On the highest status level there were the exclusive social clubs in which members were usually admitted by invitation. Persons on this level were commonly associated with various civic, charitable, cultural, or business organizations and with such prestigious religious denominations as the Episcopal church. Organizations associated with the upper middle class were likewise symbolic of status, but on a somewhat lower level. There were the class-oriented country clubs, art leagues, bridge clubs, golf clubs, and such organizations as the Masonic Lodge, Rotary Club, and the Methodist or Congregational churches. Women in this class tended to support such organizations as PTA, Camp Fire Girls, and church-affiliated groups. On both the upper and upper middle levels, the members were often active in civic, cultural, and business associations.

Persons in the lower middle class also participated in organizational activities, but their groups tended to be symbolic of a lower status order. Men were inclined to join such organizations as the American Legion, the Elks or Woodmen lodges, and middle class churches; but generally they were less active than the residents on higher social levels. Aside from labor unions, lodges, and churches, they did not participate extensively in the organized social life of the community. Women on this level were mostly active in church-related groups.

The working class "elite" (mainly skilled workers) generally were inactive in organizations except labor unions. More than three-fourths held union membership, compared with one-fourth of the lower middle class and none of the upper middle class. About one-fourth of the women on this level belonged to church guilds and related groups, compared with only five percent of the men. Church membership was mainly in fundamentalist sects or in working class congregations affiliated with major denominations.

About the only organized activities of the men in the lower class were in labor unions, of which about half were union members; only a few women belonged to church-related groups. Otherwise, the people in this class lived pretty much isolated from the mainstream of the community's organized group life. This did not mean that they had no social life; as numerous other studies indicate, many were socially involved with neighbors, friends, or relatives, but in an informal manner.

[22] Richard P. Coleman and Bernice L. Neugarten, *Social Status in the City* (1971), ch. 6.

Table 13.2 relates the organizational activities of the respondents to the five income classes.

TABLE 13.2 Percentage Distribution of Adult Respondents, Classified by Income Class and Organizational Activity

	Upper	Upper Middle	Lower Middle	Working	Lower
Median Family Income 1954	$34,000	$11,900	$6,300	$4,300	$2,600
Active in Church Groups					
Men	25%	34%	18%	5%	0%
Women	62	73	40	26	3
Active in Civic Groups					
Men	56	32	12	4	0
Women	80	51	16	5	0
Exclusive Social or Country Clubs					
Men	80	23	0	0	0
Women	85	21	0	0	0
Fraternal Orders					
Men	16	42	22	8	0
Women	0	25	18	4	0

SOURCE: Adapted from Richard P. Coleman and Bernice L. Neugarten, *Social Status in the City* (1971), Table 2, p. 75.

Clubdom in Philadelphia

In a study of the social elite in Philadelphia,[23] Baltzell reported that among upper class persons in the *Social Register* some nine-tenths belonged to one or more prestigious clubs, membership in which is by invitation, generally meaning that those invited to join must qualify in terms of status, lineage, wealth, power, and other attributes of the top social class.

These clubs constitute a kind of miniature social world in which the members and their wives meet informally with others from the same social class. Furthermore, the clubs have a kind of interlocking membership that allows members of a prestigious Philadelphia club to enjoy the facilities and hospitality of other prestige clubs in, say, New York, Boston, or Chicago. Thus, the social aristocracy of Philadelphia, as well as other large cities, tend to associate socially with their own kind through the structures of their clubs. Such associations provide a common ground for persons of high status, and at the same time insulate their members from less prestigious or influential persons on lower class levels.

[23] E. Digby Baltzell, *Philadelphia Gentlemen: The Making of a National Upper Class* (1958), ch. 13.

Associations in Developing Countries

Asian Cities

Many associations in South Asian cities are importations from the West, although in recent years, since the independence of several countries and with increasing industrialization and urbanization, associational life has tended to become more important. A survey conducted in the Indian city of Kolhapur, with a population of about 80,000, revealed only sixty-three voluntary associations, which included Western-style clubs.[24] Almost any American city of comparable size would have many times that number. Sovani concluded that less than four percent of the population of Kolhapur had any direct involvement with formal associations, compared with about half of the adults of most American or Canadian cities.

Coughlin's study of the Chinese minority in Bangkok, Thailand, revealed that the formal associational structure was highly developed by this ethnic group, which consisted of a half-million residents.[25] Formal associations flourished more luxuriantly in the Chinese culture than among the native Thai people, whose society tended to be loosely structured so far as organizational life was concerned. One possible explanation is that the Thai government did not provide extensively for the welfare of the Chinese community so that its members had to depend heavily on their own mutual-aid organizations. Also, the Chinese in Bangkok had higher levels of income and education than the Thai, most of whom clung to their village life style.

African Cities

Associations in West African cities are varied as to structural and functional features. A review by Little of associations in Accra, Lagos, Abidjan, Freetown, and several smaller centers identified and described two major types of associations: tribal or cultist and modern.[26] The tribal

[24] N. V. Sovani, *Social Survey of Kolhapur City* (1952).
[25] Richard J. Coughlin, *Double Identity* (1960).
[26] Kenneth Little, *West African Urbanization* (1965), chs. 2, 4. See also Robert Bogdan, "Youth Clubs in a West African City," in Paul Meadows and Ephrim H. Mizruchi, eds., *Urbanism, Urbanization, and Change: Comparative Perspectives* (1969), pp. 223–41.

Urban community centers are usually multi-functional, providing facilities or services to meet recreational, educational, health, or other needs of local residents. In the photos are (top) a community center in Harlem, New York City, an area occupied by blacks and Puerto Ricans, and (bottom) a civic center in Accra, a city in Ghana. (Louise E. Jefferson)

or cultist organizations were aspects of the traditional or indigenous culture of the people, mostly uneducated, who had migrated to the city and settled there. These organizations functioned to provide their members with mutual assistance, tribal companionship, and recreation. The modern associations, among them organized church societies such as the YMCA or the Methodist Womens' Fellowship, cultural associations such as debating or literary clubs, fraternal lodges, sports clubs, and dining clubs, reflected the cultural influence of the West. Most of the members of such associations belonged to the educated elite, some of whom were Europeans living in West Africa.

In the rapidly growing cities of West Africa the majority of residents have at one time or another migrated from the village countryside. Many of the associations, whether traditional or modern, symbolize and facilitate a transition from tribal and kinship groups to a highly differentiated social system emphasizing achieved rather than ascribed status. Through the mechanisms of these associations, urban ideas, behavior, and technical skills, as well as new forms of social relationships, are transmitted to the members, many of whom have recent village backgrounds. For many, such associations become a surrogate for the extended family or the tribe, affording an opportunity for social participation and companionship on the basis of common interests and status. They represent a bridge from the traditional society to the cosmopolitan metropolis, from the traditional village to a heterogeneous community.

In those countries of Africa that have achieved independence during the past three or four decades, there has been an apparent upsurge of participation in voluntary associations. Although undoubtedly in part the result of increasing urbanization, it is also due to the greater freedom of action of the people that has created a need for collective participation of one kind or another. La Fontaine brings this point out in his study of Kinshasa (formerly Leopoldville), the burgeoning capital of Zaire (formerly the Congo).[27] Many of the associations still in existence had been established by the Europeans, who kept a tight rein on activities of all kinds; but after they left, voluntary associations of many types proliferated among the indigenous population. Trade unions, for example, which were prohibited during the colonial era, have emerged, as have other organizations concerned with political and economic activities.

Informal Associations

Some informal groups have a structure sufficient only to identify them as a social entity. They may have no name, no rules, no formal agreements,

[27] J. S. La Fontaine, *City Politics: A Study of Leopoldville, 1962–63* (1970), ch. 16.

no designated purpose; social ties binding the members together are based essentially upon mutual attraction of personalities or upon emotional or intellectual satisfactions afforded by intimate associations. Old cronies who gravitate fairly regularly to a convenient loafing place in a park; habitués of a tavern or saloon among whom a "we" feeling has evolved into a sense of group-belonging; street-corner hangers-on who drift regularly to the same spot to fraternize with "the boys"; coteries of housewives who regularly hold their midmorning kaffeeklatsches to the exclusion of other neighbors; small clusters of workers who regularly eat together at lunch time, away from other workers in the same plant or store—all are representative informal groups characteristic of urban society. Sometimes members of such groups meet together at a designated time and place; other times they meet irregularly to suit their fancy or convenience. Slightly further up the organizational scale are informal groups distinguishable by a name and even by a specified central purpose or activity. Often their names are indicative of their functions or intragroup relationships; for example, the Sewing Susies or Happy Hot Rodders.

Scope and Character

Earlier writers on urban life often gave the impression that the residents of ghettoes were socially isolated and therefore had relatively few intimates and friends.[28] There is, of course, evidence that personal isolation and alienation are features of rooming-house districts and "hobohemias," but these districts are probably atypical. Numerous studies of neighborhood and friendship relations in the ghetto indicate that a network of intimate personal contacts does indeed exist, although this interaction tends to be confined to persons who are similar in race, ethnicity, religion, and age. Feagin found that among black residents of a low-income area in Boston only three percent reported no friends, about two-thirds said they had from one to three friends, one-fifth reported four or five friends, and about one in twelve had six or more friends.[29] Friendship "intensity" scores indicated that most of the respondents had frequent contacts with their friends.

Various other studies indicate clearly that informal associations or "cliques" are an important part of the urban social landscape, no less a feature of cities than of villages or open-country communities. Warner's early study of Yankee City revealed some 22,000 clique memberships— many persons were members of two or more cliques.[30] Warner did not

[28] A well-known example of such a perspective is Harvey Zorbaugh's *The Gold Coast and the Slum* (1929).

[29] Joe R. Feagin, "A Note on the Friendship Ties of Black Urbanites," *Social Forces*, 49 (December 1970), 305–6.

[30] Warner and Lunt, *op. cit.*, pp. 350–55.

"discover" the cliques—their existence was generally known to almost everybody—but he did emphasize their social significance in maintaining the class structure, providing a means of social mobility, and affording a group identity for the members. In a study of adolescent group life in Elmtown, a small town near Chicago, Hollingshead identified 259 cliques.[31]

Tally's Corner

A vivid account of street-corner cliques in a low-income black district in the District of Columbia is provided by Liebow, who assumed the role of participant-observer in a study of interpersonal relationships among the residents.[32] Liebow views these cliques as a "personal community," a "web-like arrangement of man-man and man-woman relationships." At the core of such friendship groups are persons, not necessarily kinsmen or neighbors, who are "walking buddies," best friends, or girl friends who spend much of their nonworking time together, "drinking, dancing, engaging in sex, playing the fool or wise man, talking about nothing or everything." They are the people who are turned to for aid in case of emergency, who provide assistance or counsel or friendship, and who in turn expect to receive the same favors from their close associates in the friendship network.

These associates may be relatives, neighbors, fellow workers on the job, or any other person who has similar interests and who wishes to share these interests with others in an informal relationship extending beyond the immediate family. Some of the groups have a pseudo-kin relationship in which two or more persons simulate a brother-brother or brother-sister relationship—"going for brothers," as they say, a special case of unusually close friendship ties. These groups, in general, differ from the majority of formal organizations in that the participants, as a collectivity, are not concerned about self-improvement, the job, community activities, cultural or religious life, or politics—the distinguishing features of an instrumental type of group.

Peer Groups in Little Italy

In an analysis of the social system of an Italian working class neighborhood in the West End of Boston, Gans concluded that social life outside the place of work tended to revolve around the "peer group," which consisted of both compatible kinsmen and congenial friends of similar age, economic level, and cultural interests.[33] These groups were not

[31] A. B. Hollingshead, *Elmtown's Youth* (1949), ch. 9.
[32] Elliot Liebow, *Tally's Corner* (1967), ch. 6.
[33] Herbert J. Gans, *The Urban Villagers* (1962), chs. 2 and 4.

formally structured; rather, they were informal collectivities that, in their totality, constituted a network of associations for the district.

The peer groups meet more or less regularly in the kitchens and living rooms of the residents. There are, Gans observes, no formal notices of meetings and no invitations; members drop in for the evening, usually after dinner, and the talk goes on, commonly until after midnight. Usually the conversation centers around such topics as weddings and celebrations, recollections of earlier days, local anecdotes, deviant behavior, neighborhood activities, and, for the women, child-rearing and housekeeping. There is little interest in politics or other developments that do not touch their lives more or less directly. Nor is there much interest in formal organizations, with the exception of church-related groups, a labor union, and a few informal clubs that meet in halls or vacant rooms. The West Enders, says Gans, "live within the group; they do not like to be alone." Privacy, so often cherished by the middle classes, has little appeal. From childhood on they have been socialized to belong to a peer group; to be apart from it brings anxieties and discomfort.

Peer Group Life in a Chicago Ghetto

A major study affording an intimate picture of the dynamics of ghetto groups—both of interaction among the members and of their relations with other groups—is provided by Suttles, who lived and worked for three years in a ghetto district of Chicago's Near West Side,[34] an area occupied mainly by blacks, Italians, Puerto Ricans, and Mexicans.

The main focus of the study was on voluntary associations of the local residents, including adults, teenagers, and even younger children, in a district noted for high delinquency rates and intergroup conflict. The groups tend, for the most part, to restrict membership along racial or ethnic lines, but they are also structured according to age, sex, and residential location within the district. Many of the associations have an identifying name, but some tend to be informal and nameless cliques that gather at hangouts for which territorial rights are claimed. Although the "name" groups have recognized leaders and often exercise considerable power, they are usually not formally organized with elected officers and an explicit set of rules and regulations. Rather, they operate by implicit expectations of individual roles and of collective action by the group.

The main concern of Chicago's ghetto groups, according to Suttles, is to afford companionship and a sense of "belonging" for the members having a similarity of interests, racial or ethnic identity, and neighbor-

[34] Gerald D. Suttles, *The Social Order of the Slum* (1971).

hood location. Each of the youth groups is a personalized microcosm in which the members may be rewarded for their personal qualities and behavior such as toughness, fighting ability, and loyalty. Authority and leadership in the group are based on the individual's force of character. Formal associations do exist in the district, such as groups dominated or sponsored by the "Y," churches, or labor unions, but Suttles observed that most of the young people derive little satisfaction from membership in groups having definite individual role assignments and explicit functions, preferring informally structured groups of their own making.

Neighboring and City Life

By the very nature of village life in traditional societies, intimate neighborhood relations are virtually mandatory. "In the small rural village with long-established traditions, a common way of life, an intertwining of work, family, and social relations, neighboring is a by-product of life itself," writes Keller.[35] But with the vast changes in life styles and work patterns associated with urbanism and industrialism, the individual is far less dependent on neighborhood contacts for the fulfillment of his needs. This is true not only of city dwellers but also of most villagers and farm folk in an urban-industrial society. One may say, then, that the neighborhood in its traditional role has declined, relatively, with a society's urbanization.

Several reasons account for the decline of neighborhood interaction. One is the proliferation of organizations, both public and private, that cushion the individual against adversity, help him to meet his personal and family crises, and afford him an opportunity for contacts and entertainment outside his immediate neighborhood. Another reason is the wider range of choices the city offers, far greater than the options available in the traditional village or farm community in almost every sphere of life. Still another reason is that physical and social mobility in Western cities in recent years has been accelerated for the masses, and both forms of mobility have tended to remove the individual from his locality and neighborhood moorings. The latent function of social control through neighborhood gossip and rumor becomes less effective in the urban setting because social controls tend to become institutionalized and imposed by the larger community or society. Finally, the mass media in modern urban societies have for many persons become the principal source of information and ideas, supplanting to some extent the neighborhood personal communicator or, in some instances, reinforcing person-to-person communication.

Physical and technological changes also have affected neighborhood

[35] Suzanne Keller, *The Urban Neighborhood* (1968), p. 48.

life. A considerable portion of city dwellers, especially those residing in large cities, live in multifamily dwellings which, by their structural characteristics, often isolate individuals and families residing in the same neighborhoods. But many persons prefer the privacy apartment life affords. Under such living arrangements backyard visiting generally disappears. Although neighbors may live in physical proximity, they are less visible to each other, less likely to become acquainted, less likely to "pop in" unannounced for a friendly visit, less likely to sit on a front porch or stoop and exchange small talk with their friends or neighbors passing by. Also, for those employed outside the home, the daily journey to and from work may take time that might be used in a different setting for visiting friends or neighbors.

The foregoing is not intended to imply that the neighborhood and neighboring have disappeared from the urban scene. Neighboring persists as an important feature of urban life, although there are neighborhoods in which the residents are merely "nigh-dwellers," as well as neighborhoods in which intimate and friendly interaction is a central feature of social life. This is particularly true of migrants with rural backgrounds who have, in a sense, created a replica of village or farm neighborhood life in an urban setting. It is particularly true of racial, ethnic, or religious minorities that have settled down in neighborhoods occupied by others having similar interests and backgrounds.

Park Forest

Whyte's classic study of Park Forest, a mass-produced, middle class suburb of Chicago, revealed a network of friendly relations among neighbors, especially among the housewives who had more time for neighborly visiting than their commuting husbands.[36] The daily neighborhood kaffeeklatsch was a well-established group activity. Whyte observed that the spatial layout of the suburb had an important bearing on the informal social life of the neighborhoods. A principal feature of the design was the superblock, which was subdivided into "courts." Social groups generally included people along and across streets, but seldom residents on the other side of the backyards. Thus, the design of the residential arrangements provided an "imaginary line" beyond which other residents were not usually included in the informal groups and person-to-person visiting.

[36] William H. Whyte, *The Organization Man* (1956).

Urban and Suburban Neighboring

Comparisons with regard to neighboring are commonly made of suburban and central-city residents, and, as might be expected, the results of such studies are by no means uniform. For one, the character of suburbs and central cities may vary from one locality to another, depending on the demographic characteristics and economic structures of the communities involved. But there is another reason for the invalidity of such comparisons, namely, that the core of the central city generally includes the ghetto or slum districts whose residents may differ economically, ethnically, and socially from the people who live farther out but within the central-city boundaries. To lump all the central-city population together, as well as all suburbanites, is unrealistic; thus, the results of urban-suburban comparisons are fictive at best.

An attempt at a more realistic assessment of this problem was made by Tomeh in a study of informal social participation in Detroit.[37] The metropolitan area of the city was divided into three parts: the inner city, extending six miles from the center of the business district; the outer city, beyond the six-mile zone but within Detroit's city limits; and the suburban belt outside the city limits. The respondents, matched by age, sex, education, race, religion, and migrant status, were classified as (1) neighbors, (2) relatives (not in same household), (3) coworkers, and (4) other friends. There was a high frequency of contacts with relatives, with no significant differences between the three zones. A similar pattern prevailed for interaction with coworkers, although with a much lower frequency in all zones. However, in the case of neighboring and contacts with friends, there was a higher frequency among suburbanites than among residents in the other zones.

A study by Fava which compared neighboring activities in the New York metropolitan area showed a similar pattern.[38] In a field survey the incidence of neighbor interaction in the inner city (Manhattan), outer city (Queens), and a suburb (Nassau) tended to increase with each degree of removal from the inner core. The three samples were controlled for age, sex, marital status, length of residence, nativity, and size of community of childhood. Using the Wallin neighboring scale designed to measure informal contacts and associations with geographic neighbors, Fava found that suburban residents had the highest neighboring scores and those of Manhattan the lowest, while Queens fell about midway between the central city and the suburbs.

---

[37] Aida K. Tomeh, "Informal Group Participation and Residential Patterns," *American Journal of Sociology*, 70 (July 1964), 28–35.

[38] Sylvia Fava, "Contrasts in Neighboring: New York City and a Suburban County," in William Dobriner, ed., *The Suburban Community* (1958), pp. 122–31.

A somewhat similar urban-suburban study of informal participation, but limited to blue collar residents, was undertaken by Tallman and Morgner in the Minneapolis-St. Paul metropolitan area.[39] It was quite clear that neighboring, for example, was more frequent in the suburban district than in the central city, and this held for both men and women. Among the men, for example, 69 percent of the suburbanites and 39 percent of the urban residents visited immediate neighbors at least once a month, while 52 percent of the suburban women and 44 percent of the city residents visited regularly with their neighbors. Similarly, a higher percentage of men and women living in the suburbs, compared with the city residents, knew more than one neighbor well enough to visit regularly.

Summary

As we have observed in this chapter, social participation may take many forms, but we have been concerned primarily with participation in formal and informal voluntary associations. At the outset we related the proliferation of voluntary associations to the conditions of city life created by urbanization. Some of the factors associated with the emergence of voluntary associations have been emphasized, as well as the functions these associations perform in an urban society. Associations are not evenly distributed over the social landscape; rather, they vary greatly according to socioeconomic class and other aspects of the social order. Various studies indicate that the conditions that exist in cities in industrial countries tend to be more conducive to the formation of voluntary associations than is true of traditional societies, in which familism, tribalism, and an authoritarian social system play important roles. We have also considered the nature and function of informal associations, and of changing neighborhood life in cities in industrial countries. In the chapter that follows we shall discuss urban family life in various settings, comparing the family system in cities of both industrial and traditional societies, as well as in racial and class sectors of those societies.

[39] Irving Tallman and Romona Morgner, "Life Style Differences among Urban and Suburban Blue Collar Families," *Social Forces*, 48 (March 1970), 334–48.

Selected Bibliography

BOOKS

Babchuk, Nicholas, and C. Wayne Gordon, *The Voluntary Association in the Slum.* Lincoln: University of Nebraska Press, 1962.

Baltzell, E. Digby, *Philadelphia Gentlemen: The Making of a National Upper Class.* New York: The Free Press, 1958.

Berger, Bennett M., *Working Class Suburb: A Study of Auto Workers in Suburbia.* Berkeley and Los Angeles: University of California Press, 1960.

Booth, Alan, and John Edwards, eds., *Social Participation in Urban Society.* Morristown, N. J.: Schenkman, distributed by General Learning Press, 1972.

Coleman, Richard P., and Bernice L. Neugarten, *Social Status in the City.* San Francisco: Jossey-Bass, 1971.

Dore, R. P., *City Life in Japan: A Study of a Tokyo Ward.* Berkeley and Los Angeles: University of California Press, 1958.

Duncan, Otis Dudley, Howard Schuman, and Beverly Duncan, *Social Change in a Metropolitan Community* (Detroit). New York: Russell Sage Foundation, 1973.

Gans, Herbert J., *The Urban Villagers.* NewYork: The Free Press, 1962.

———, *The Levittowners: Ways of Life and Politics in a New Suburban Community.* New York: Pantheon, 1967.

Keller, Suzanne, *The Urban Neighborhood.* New York: Random House, 1968.

Kinlock, G. C., M. E. Close, and B. Wright, *Urbanization and the Plural Society: A Case Study of Flatlife in South Africa.* Durban, South Africa: Longman Academic Press, 1970.

Laumann, Edward O., *Bonds of Pluralism: The Form and Substance of Urban Social Networks.* New York: Wiley, 1973.

Liebow, Elliot, *Tally's Corner.* Boston: Little, Brown, 1967.

Little, Kenneth, *West African Urbanization.* Cambridge, England: Cambridge University Press, 1966.

Mitchell, J. Clyde, ed., *Social Networks in Urban Situations: Personal Relationships in Central African Towns.* Manchester, England: Manchester University Press, 1969.

Smith, Constance, and Anne Freedman, *Voluntary Association.* Cambridge: Harvard University Press, 1972.

Suttles, Gerald D., *The Social Order of the Slum.* Chicago: University of Chicago Press, 1971.

Whyte, William F., *Street Corner Society*, rev. ed., Chicago: University of Chicago Press, 1955.

ARTICLES

Anderson, Robert T., "Voluntary Associations in History," *American Anthropologist*, 73 (1971), 209–22.

———, and Gallatin Anderson, "Voluntary Associations and Urbanization," *American Journal of Sociology*, 55 (November 1959), 263–73.

Babchuk, Nicholas, and Alan Booth, "Voluntary Association Membership: A Longitudinal Analysis," *American Sociological Review*, 34 (February 1969), 31–45.

Banton, Michael, "Voluntary Associations," in David L. Sills, ed., *International Encyclopedia of the Social Sciences*, vol. 16, pp. 357–62. New York: Macmillan Company and The Free Press, 1968.

Curtis, James, "Voluntary Association Joining: A Cross-National Note," *American Sociological Review*, 36 (October 1971), 872–80.

Feagin, Joe R., "A Note on Friendship Ties of Black Urbanites," *Social Forces*, 49 (December 1970), 305–6.

Hyman, Herbert H., and Charles R. Wright, "Trends in Voluntary Associations of American Adults," *American Sociological Review*, 36 (April 1971), 191–206.

Key, William H., "Urbanism and Neighboring," *Sociological Quarterly*, 6 (Autumn 1965), 379–85.

Little, Kenneth, "The Role of Associations in West African Urbanization," *American Anthropologist*, 59 (1957), 570–96.

Litwak, Eugene, "Voluntary Associations and Neighborhood Cohesion," *American Sociological Review*, 26 (April 1961), 258–71.

————, and Ivan Szelenyi, "Primary Group Structures and Their Functions: Kin, Neighbors, and Friends," *American Sociological Review*, 34 (August 1969), 465–81.

Mangin, William P. "The Role of Regional Associations in the Adaptation of Rural Migrants to Cities in Peru," in Dwight B. Heath and Richard N. Adams, eds., *Contemporary Cultures and Societies of Latin America*. New York: Random House, 1965.

Marshall, Dale, "Who Participates in What? A Bibliographic Essay on Individual Participation in Urban Areas," *Urban Affairs Quarterly*, 4 (December 1968), 201–23.

Rose, Arnold, "Voluntary Associations in France," in Arnold Rose, ed., *Theory and Method in the Social Sciences*, ch. 4. Minneapolis: University of Minnesota Press, 1954.

Smith, David Horton, "A Psychological Model of Individual Participation in Formal Voluntary Associations: Chilean Data," *American Journal of Sociology*, 72 (February 1969), 31–45.

————, "The Importance of Formal Voluntary Associations for Society," *Sociology and Social Research*, 50 (July 1966), 483–94.

Tomeh, Aida K., "Informal Group Participation and Residential Patterns," *American Journal of Sociology*, 70 (July 1964), 28–35.

Vornwaller, Darrel J., "Social Mobility and Membership in Voluntary Associations," *American Journal of Sociology*, 75 (January 1970), 481–95.

14 • Urban Family Life in Transition

This chapter makes no prentensions at being a systematic treatise on the urban family system; within the necessary limitations of space it would be impossible to achieve such an objective. Rather, our focus will be mainly on the changing structures, functions, and internal relationships of the family system in cities of urban-industrial societies, particularly those of the United States, and also in a selected sample of cities in developing societies. Thus, by enabling the reader to compare the family systems of industrial and nonindustrial societies he may derive a cross-cultural perspective of family systems as they exist in cities and as they react to the impact of urbanization.

In almost every major city, a multiplicity of family patterns exists: families representing various ethnic, racial, or religious groups that differ in marriage customs and kinship organization; families organized along authoritarian principles and others emphasizing equalitarian ideals; families that are loosely structured companionate liaisons between childless couples and large kinship groups living under the same roof. The conditions under which families live are diverse, and the broader social system of which they are a part varies from one country or region to another. For example, the structure and functions of upper class families and interactional patterns among their members are quite different from the corresponding characteristics of lower class family groups in the same community or society. Or family life on any level in Buenos Aires may be different in many respects from life in Bombay or Boston. In all societies there may be differences between family life in cities and life in villages or on farms. Family organization in urban-industrial countries may differ in various respects from the dominant form of organization in agrarian or peasant societies. The patterns are quite varied.

Family Organizational Models

All of the three family or kinship models that will be briefly described here may exist simultaneously in the same society or even the same city, but most societies manifest a particular dominant form of kinship organization.

1. The classical joint or *extended family* is the dominant form of family organization in most traditional societies, for example, the Hindu family system of India. As Gore describes it, the joint family, in its ideal-typical form, consists of a male "head" and his wife, their adult sons and their wives and children, unmarried sons and daughters, and brothers of the family head and their wives and children.[1] There are, of course, many variations of this pattern. Imbedded in the structure of such a kinship group is the small nuclear family unit, consisting usually of husband, wife, and children, which is subordinate in almost all respects to the larger kinship group, the basic unit. In its ideal-typical

The extended family system prevails in most developing countries, even in the cities. Normally extended families represent three generations. This Chinese family is headed by Shih Chen-yu, shown with some of his grandchildren at their home, a commune near Peking. (Arthur W. Galston)

[1] M. S. Gore, *Urbanization and Family Change* (1968), ch. 1.

form the kinship group's various members live in the same household and hold their property jointly, although the conditions of life and work in cities often dictate changes in such an arrangement.

2. *The modified-extended family*, which is predominant in the Western world, consists of family units related by blood or marriage (or adoption) who recognize and maintain a variety of interpersonal relations with kin outside the household. The component element of this family model is the nuclear household normally consisting of parents and children who are enmeshed, in varying ways and degrees, with a larger kinship network, which is not an organized entity. Although the nuclear family unit generally resides in an independent or separate household, the network of interpersonal connections between the basic unit and its relatives, as in the joint-family system, serves both expressive and instrumental functions—expressive in the satisfaction of certain social and emotional needs, instrumental in the form of mutual assistance.

3. *The isolated nuclear family*, in its most characteristic form, consists of parents and children who maintain no functional ties with other persons related to them by blood or marriage. Their connections, if any, are with nonkin of similar interests or residential location, not with kinsmen beyond the immediate family unit. Nonkin ties tend to be with neighbors, fellow members of voluntary associations, or associates at the place of work. The conditions conducive to family isolation are legion, but among the most significant are changes in social and spatial location which cause a family to become detached from its larger kinship moorings by social or geographic mobility.

In Western urban-industrial countries the small family group, which commonly forms the nucleus of a modified-extended kinship circle, is the dominant pattern, although there is historical evidence that this structural pattern is not necessarily the product of either urbanization or industrialism. The American conjugal family system is an import from western Europe, where it existed before the Industrial Revolution. That is to say, the predominant American family system is not solely the product either of technology or an urban environment, although technology and economic developments associated with urbanization have certainly had an impact on the structure and functions of the family.[2]

It seems fairly evident that with the urbanization of any society the trend of family organization is toward the conjugal or nuclear type of family unit, either the modified-extended system or the isolated nuclear family, even though the specific characteristics of the family unit will vary from one country, community, or class to another. Goode has concluded, however, that an isolated nuclear family *system* could not

[2] Sidney M. Greenfield, "Industrialization and the Family in Sociological Theory," *American Journal of Sociology*, 67 (November 1961), 312–22.

logically predominate, separate and apart from larger kinship networks, even in highly urbanized societies.[3]

The Kinship Network

Even within the same society, the kinship network may vary according to the ethnicity or class position of a family group. Goode holds, for example, that the upper classes in Western society tend to be more favorably disposed to extensive kinship networks and interaction among kin than is generally true of lower class families.[4] This is apparently borne out by Baltzell's description of upper class families in Philadelphia,[5] and by Warner's early study of Yankee City.[6] A study by Winch, Greer, and Blumberg of extended familism in an upper middle class suburb of Chicago indicated that Jews interacted more with their kin, and did so more frequently, than did Catholics or Protestants, although the economic status of all three groups was fairly similar.[7] A study of Jewish welfare clients in New York City also indicated a comparatively large kinship circle. Ethnic and religious ties are clearly factors in the formation of kinship networks, but they are by no means the only factors.

Some form of the modified-extended family is predominant in both the black and white population. But it is one thing to recognize, assist, or communicate with other members of the kinship group, quite another to have close personal ties with kinsmen beyond the immediate family unit. It would appear that the nature of a kin network is closely associated with conditions of life, particularly with economic status and personal needs. In a study of married black couples in a midwestern city, individuals in the sample were found to be highly selective of the kinsmen whom they considered "very close" to them.[8] Of 74 couples (148 respondents), the average number of kinsmen with whom close primary relationships were maintained was 4.3 for the wives and 3.8 for the husbands. Of the wives, 70 percent said they were "very close" to their *own* kin, while of the husbands, 72 percent felt "very close" to their *own* relatives. This study is cited because it does suggest an important consideration in the study of extended family relations, even in the city: the fact that husbands and wives alike generally have closer ties to their

---

[3] William J. Goode, *World Revolution and Family Patterns* (1963), p. 70.

[4] William J. Goode, *The Family* (1965), pp. 80–85.

[5] E. Digby Baltzell, *Philadelphia Gentlemen* (1959).

[6] W. Lloyd Warner, *The Social Life of a Modern Community* (1941).

[7] Robert F. Winch, Scott Greer, and Rae Lesser Blumberg, "Ethnicity and Extended Familism in an Upper-Middle-Class Suburb," *American Sociological Review*, 32 (April 1967), 265–72.

[8] Nicholas Babchuk and John Ballweg, "Primary Extended Kin Relations of Negro Couples," *The Sociological Quarterly*, 12 (Winter 1971), 69–76.

own kin than to the relatives of their spouses. Close ties between kinsmen may be central to social life for many persons, rural or urban, black or white.

Other researchers also indicate the existence of kinship networks beyond the boundaries of the nuclear family. A study in Detroit revealed that 67 percent of the adults interviewed had personal contacts with their relatives once a week, 20 percent once to several times a week, and 13 percent a few times a year or less. None of the interviewees said that they never had contacts with a relative.[9] Interviews with young married adults, all of whom were white, in Greensboro, North Carolina (with a population of about 150,000), revealed similar kinship relations.[10]

Continuity and Change in Kinship Solidarity

Studies of numerous countries indicate that extensive kinship solidarity persists. For example, the kinship network of French-Canadians in Montreal, a highly industrialized metropolis, has retained much of its vitality, and "the collected evidence," writes Garigue, "indicates no trend toward the transformation of the present French-Canadian urban kinship system into the more restricted system reported for the United States."[11]

This is not to say, however, that kinship systems in an urban mileu are not affected in various ways by the experiences of living and working in a city. The diversity of roles performed by individual members of the family tends to affect interpersonal relations. It is commonplace in the city for a family's adult members to hold jobs that separate them during working hours from other members of the family group. In contrast to farm families, which usually function as an economic unit whose members work at closely related tasks, children in urban families sometimes know little or nothing about the work their parents perform. Children or youth in cities usually engage in occupational, educational, or leisure-time activities that separate them from the family during the day or even at night. This diversification of roles is, of course, not peculiar to life in the city; it is only more pronounced there than in rural communities. But with modern transportation facilities available to ruralites and urbanites alike, even rural youth in the United States spends considerable time away from the family hearth.

In the early stages of urbanization and industrialization the kinship unit, reinforced by tribal, clan, religious, or caste systems, is generally

---

[9] *A Social Profile of Detroit* (1955), p. 26.

[10] Bert N. Adams, *Kinship in an Urban Setting* (1968), pp. 19, 27.

[11] Philip Garigue, "French-Canadian Kinship and Urban Life," *American Anthropologist*, 58 (December 1956), 1098–99.

more resistant to social change than is the case in modernized urban-industrial societies. But even in technologically advanced countries, ethnic or religious ties tend to strengthen kinship or family unity. "Family institutions everywhere are subject to the pressure of disruptive forces," writes Comhaire, "but extended family relationships in many countries have displayed much more vitality than in . . . Western societies."[12]

There is reason to believe that the larger kinship network has a stabilizing influence on the nuclear family or its individual members, although in particular instances it may have the opposite effect, as in the case of relatives meddling in family affairs. Functionally, the kinship network is of special importance for migrant families or individuals settling in a new community, for example, from a rural to an urban setting. Migrants on arriving in cities commonly turn to their relatives, if any are present, for assistance. A study of migrants from a poor Appalachian region revealed that they retained the conjugal form of family organization but also developed a network of extended kinship groups in the same city.[13] In fact, the presence of kin in a particular city often attracts relatives from the outside to the city, thus enabling them to retain their connections with the "folks back home."

The Joint or Extended Family and Urban Residence

It is often stated that the classical model of the joint or extended family is structurally unsuited for an urban environment. In some respects this assessment has considerable validity, but it is not inevitable that the joint family disintegrates when its members move to the city. Although some atomization of the family structure actually occurs, especially if newly married couples establish separate households, such changes do not necessarily mean that the joint-family system is no longer functional. Indeed, kinship ties and obligations may remain firm, even though the members do not live in the same household or hold their property jointly.

Families that have migrated from a traditional type of society and settled in a city in an urban-industrial country usually find it necessary to change certain accustomed rules and roles of behavior and in various respects adopt a different life style. These changes are therefore both structural and functional, but they do not necessarily mean family disintegration, although that may occur if family unity cannot be maintained in the face of powerful centrifugal forces. Parental authority may be weakened as the generation gap widens and individuals pursue

---

[12] Jean L. Comhaire, "Economic and Change and the Extended Family, *Annals*, 305 (1956), 126.

[13] Cited in C. C. Harris, *The Family* (1969), p. 139.

their own interests without reference to their family. Kinship ties may be replaced by loyalties to groups beyond the family circle. Increased dependence on institutional structures may undermine some of the functions of the kinship network. The history of immigration to American cities is replete with instances in which individualized behavior has replaced the traditional cohesiveness of the family group, with the result that the second- or third-generation of descendants became alienated from their parents and other kin.

Changing Family Functions and Institutional Changes

Whether families adhere to equalitarian or authoritarian principles, whether they conform to any of the models we discussed earlier, whether they reside in a traditional or an urban-industrial society, the idealized image of family life does not always fit the reality—what people want the family to be as opposed to what it actually is. If a family unit afforded its various members a full measure of satisfaction, a fulfillment of their psychological needs for security, affection, and companionship, that unit might well conform to its idealized image. But families cannot or do not always function effectively to satisfy these needs, and conditions of city life in particular appear to increase the difficulties of families in performing such functions. Tensions and conflicts within the family often occur; individualization of behavior tends to have an atomizing effect on family life; generation gaps may widen as parents and children hold conflicting views of appropriate roles and behavior for each other; multiplication of different life styles and values in an urban environment tends to exert a centrifugal influence on family relationships. But even in an environment in which varied urban values and ways of life predominate, most families manage to serve the psychological function with varying degrees of effectiveness, as indicated by the fact that most family groups continue to "hang together" and retain some semblance of family unity.

The Replacement of Family Functions by Institutional Functions

From the cradle to the grave, "from womb to tomb," the urbanite is served by a vast array of organizations that supplement or replace the self-service function of the Western rural family. The city dweller is usually entitled to the services of a municipal health clinic or hospital, to an education in the city's schools, to recreation in the city's parks, playgrounds, and amusement emporia, even to a place in correctional institutions if he misbehaves. Specialized or semispecialized functionaries cater to his needs: clinicians, social workers, teachers, playground directors, police, turnkeys in the local jail, mostly at public expense. This is not to imply that everyone is served equally well; class and racial distinctions do make a difference. The affluent can, of course, provide these services at their own expense if they prefer, and many do. But the long-time trend in Western industrial society is toward an extension of the "rights of citizenship" in social, political, legal, and economic matters.[14]

The foregoing sketch of changing family functions in Western industrial society does not necessarily fit the facts of family life in traditional societies, although comparable changes have occurred in those regions to some extent, particularly among the rich and powerful. But most families in cities of the nonindustrialized world are less reliant on certain types of outside organizations and services, partly because such facilities are not available, or because they cannot afford or do not need them. Some self-help services are provided by members of the traditional joint family or kinship group. In these countries most urban families (or their servants) do their own cooking, washing, sewing, and preserving of foods; they seldom patronize restaurants or hotels, although inexpensive guest houses for travellers are often available. They look after the needs of their dependents, whether the young or the old. A behavior clinic for children or a home for the aged is exceptional. Yet even in such cities there has been an expansion of both public and private facilities to provide various services such as housing, medicine, social welfare, and recreation.

The Changing Economic
Roles of Women

The trend in many countries, especially urban-industrial societies, has been for an increasing proportion of the labor force to be made up females, married or unmarried. One of the striking features of this trend in the United States is the sharp increase in the employment of married women over three decades, from about 17 percent of the female population in 1940 to 41 percent in 1971.[15] Over the same period the percentage of *all* women (single, married, widowed, and divorced) in the labor force increased from 27 to 43. This period in American history was one of an expanding economy in which jobs were relatively plentiful, and in some fields there was an actual shortage of workers. It was also a period of rapid urbanization and rising standards of living so that in order to maintain the desired life style, or an approximation of it, many married women entered the labor market, in addition to those forced by necessity to work outside the home.

[14] See especially T. H. Marshall, *Citizenship and Social Class*, (1965), ch. 4.
[15] *Statistical Abstract of the United States* (1972), p. 219.

Economic independence has increasingly placed women in a competitive position with men in the occupational world, a trend that has been reflected in greater equality within the household, especially so among the urban middle classes. Many occupational roles are interchangeable so far as sex is concerned, and interchangeability of roles can be translated into greater equality in both the home and the place of work. The husband may no longer be essential as a family breadwinner; indeed, he may even be dispensable. It might reasonably be expected that the trend toward husband-wife equalitarianism would likewise have an effect on parent-child relationships toward more democratic principles of child-rearing. To give an economic interpretation to these trends, however, would be misleading. Other institutional and ideological changes have also been a factor.

Demographic Factors Bearing on Urban Family Life

As noted in an earlier chapter, mass migration to cities has occurred in almost every country. This migration is highly selective of age, sex, and other attributes such as race or nationality. Young adults are attracted to cities in disproportionate numbers, commonly at an age when they are entering, or expecting to enter, the labor market. Probably the majority of adult female migrants in an urban-industrial society are single persons expecting to marry and establish a family after they have obtained employment or educational training. In some traditional societies married men often travel to cities without their families, either returning periodically to visit their wives and children and other kin or arranging to have their families join them in the city. In South African cities native workers employed in heavy industries are commonly required by the government or employers to leave their families in their home villages and to live in special compounds occupied exclusively by males.

Sex Ratios and Migration

One is often struck by the preponderance of males in many large cities of Asia, Africa, and the Middle East, the result of selective migrations. Among the residents of Cairo, for example, the number of males born outside that city is considerably greater than that of females. Calcutta, Bombay, and Bangalore had a similar preponderance of males around the middle of the present century, but as in Cairo, sex ratios in the Indian cities have been declining in recent years.

The greater selectivity of male migrants as compared to females in many countries may be explained both in economic terms and in terms

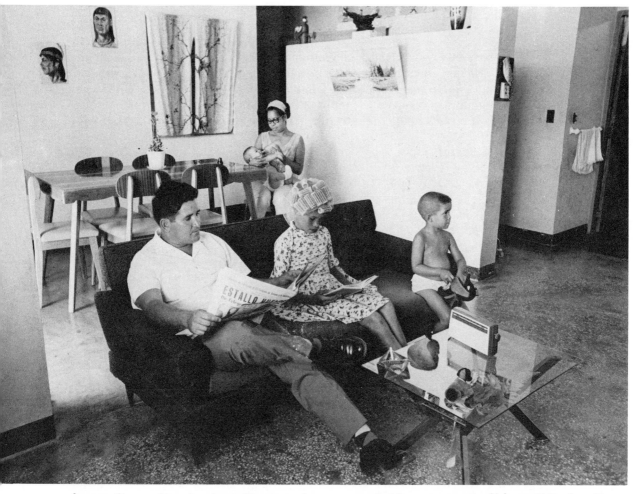

of prevailing cultural values. For one, there are probably more oppor-tunities for employment open to men than women in most cities, and finding a job is probably the prime reason so many forsake the country-side for an urban community. But traditional mores do not generally approve the migration to cities of single women; those who do migrate usually are accompanied by adults who are members of their own family. Similarly, in Mexico, the migration of unmarried Mixtec women from the state of Oaxaca to Mexico City is "virtually unknown," accord-ing to Butterworth.[16] Whereas young women in Western urban-industrial societies often leave their rural homes alone to seek a career, an education, or a husband in the city, such behavior is not condoned by conventional standards in many traditional societies. Some districts of major cities in such countries as India, Pakistan, Burma, and Egypt are overwhelmingly occupied by males whose lives are devoid of familiar

Urban middle class Vene-zuelans generally are members of a nuclear family consisting of two generations. Here is a middle class family in the city of Santo Tome de Guayana, Venezuela. (United Nations)

[16] Douglas S. Butterworth, "The Urbanization Process Among Mixtec Migrants from Te-lantonigo in Mexico City," *America Indigina*, 22 (1962), 257–74.

family relationships. In consequence, they associate mainly with other males, often in groups composed of persons from their own village or caste. In some of the larger Indian cities a surrogate or simulated family may be organized by groups of unattached men having similar problems and background, an arrangement known colloquially as "messing."

Social Aspects of Uneven Sex Ratios

The fairly even sex ratio of males and females in American cities often conceals the fact that unattached men and women live under conditions of social isolation from the opposite sex. Every metropolis has its homeless and often jobless males who live in barren rooms and eke out a bare existence on Skid Row. These "hobohemias" have attracted the *deracines*, the uprooted, who are unable or unwilling to participate in a "normal" family life. Higher in the social and economic scale is a veritable army of unattached men and women residing in rooming houses, bachelor apartments, or residential hotels. Some of them eventually marry; others go it alone, whether by necessity or choice. Such districts are in sharp contrast to most suburbs whose residents usually are attached to a family group; hence, sex ratios there are fairly even.

Any tilting of the sex ratio, whether toward males or females, may have far-reaching effects on family life, as indeed it may affect a wide range of social relationships. If the tilting is slight, the effects may be correspondingly slight; if there is a heavy preponderance of either sex, the consequences may be considerable. In European cities after World War II, there was a preponderance of females as a result, in the main, of the heavy loss of men during the war. Most of these women had no choice other than widowhood or spinsterhood, no opportunity to marry and have a normal family life. Single-sex districts or neighborhoods, as exist in many cities, afford a setting favorable to socially deviant behavior such as prostitution and homosexuality.

Families against the City

The structure and function of a family are determined, in part, by the reactions of the family members to their social environment. One is not justified in concluding, as some sociologists do, that the nuclear family is better adapted to the conditions of an urban-industrial society, or to metropolitan life, than is the case of joint or extended families. Probably this questionable interpretation reflects to some extent the failure of many analysts of family life to view the structural and functional features of families from both a historical and a contemporary perspective.

In a notable study of family life in Union Park, a Near West Side community in Chicago, Sennett examines in detail the census records for several decades in the late nineteenth century and from them derives certain generalizations about family life in that part of the city.[17] Within this relatively small area are delineated two "types" of families—the nuclear or "intensive" family unit, mainly middle class, and the more complex extended family group, mainly working class. The interpersonal relationships within these two family types, Sennett found, were quite different, and the forms of adjustments they made to a similar urban setting were likewise not parallel.

Sennett portrays the intensive family of the late nineteenth century as a relatively small self-contained unit that functioned as a refuge from the external city environment with all its disorders, conflicts, and instability. At the end of the day or week the family head, the principal breadwinner, could retreat from the stressful world of work into the warm confines of the family group whose members were preoccupied with interpersonal relations within this microcosm. If the outside world represented a threat to those adults who ventured into that world, the intensive family provided security in the insecure world of an industrial metropolis. The adult sons remained unmarried until they had obtained a job that would enable them to support a wife, residing in the paternal household until they could offer a prospective spouse some degree of economic security. Young women looked with considerable disfavor on marriage until their husbands could assure them of an appropriate life style. The sons and daughters were thus socialized into a family group which provided an escape from the outside world; within the intimate circle of this family microcosm their experiences did not qualify them to meet successfully the demands of the outside world. In such a microcosm the father became an unadmired occupational model for the sons; and one of the consequences, according to Sennett, was weak motivation for upward social mobility among both father and sons. For these and other reasons, Sennett argues, from historical data, that the intensive family of this inner-city district during a period of rapid change did not effectively qualify its members for life in a modern industrial metropolis at that particular time and place.

The extended families, mainly working class, which resided in the same area were more successful in coping with the stresses and strains of a pluralistic and rapidly changing metropolis. These families were fairly large and represented a working collateral kin of varying ages. In contrast to the intensive families, the extended-family groups were work-oriented, and the working members shared with each other their experiences in the outside world. Fathers tended to be motivated toward occupational success goals and therefore were likely to be upwardly mobile. They thus became acceptable models for emulation by their

[17] Richard Sennett, *Families against the City* (1970).

sons, who in turn aspired to be upwardly mobile. In these families the sons looked to their fathers for guidance, whereas sons in the intensive families received limited guidance from this source. Hence the generation breaks in the extended families occurred more smoothly than in the intensive groups, with less tension between fathers and sons. Members of the extended families were socialized not only into the family system but also into the world of work. "What," inquires Sennett, "was the impact of this presence of work on children in such families? They heard a great deal about work from the perspective of more than one worker's job experience; and the facts of work, the comparisons between the different kinds of jobs, were something they would immediately know through dinner-table discussion or casual talk."[18]

One is not justified in formulating broad generalizations about the "fit" of particular types of families; Sennett's research was limited to a small inner-city district of an expanding industrial metropolis. But within the limits of our present knowledge of urban families in different societies and community settings, it seems a plausible hypothesis that no particular family type is predestined to fit better than other types in the varied kinds of urban community situations that do exist.

The Urban Black Family in the United States

Black families in the United States probably differ among themselves as much as white families do in terms of structural, functional, and internal relationships. There are differences based on rural and urban residence, differences reflecting social-class positions, and differences arising from residential locations within a city. However, whatever may be the characteristics and life styles of black families, they are subjected to restrictions and socially imposed handicaps not ordinarily experienced by white families, whether in choice of residential location, access to the labor market, or opportunities to participate in community life and activities. These restrictions, both past and present, have left their mark on black family life.

Historically, the black population was overwhelmingly rural, mainly employed as workers on southern plantations or as domestics or day laborers in the small towns of the South. All of this has now changed. Beginning with heavy migrations to cities about a half-century ago, the majority of blacks now reside in urban centers, mostly metropolitan centers in both the North and South. In fact, this rural-urban imbalance is even more pronounced than in the case of white families. Furthermore, the majority of blacks reside in the central cities, commonly in

[18] *Ibid.*, p. 210.

congested slums, and their residential segregation from whites appears to be increasing as more whites move to the suburbs.

Black families on different socioeconomic levels exhibit both differences and similarities in life styles and values, as do white families. Indeed, the *modus vivendi* of lower class black families may resemble in many respects the life style and organization of white families on the same or similar economic level and living under comparable conditions in the same city. By the same token, middle class black and white families have much in common in terms of organization and behavior patterns. But whereas middle class black families represent a small percentage of the total black population, middle class whites constitute the greater percentage of the total white population.

The Impact of the Urban Slum on Black Families

The urban slum environment appears to have an impact on families, whether black or white. But the impact of ghetto living on black families is probably more severe than for whites because the majority of blacks are fairly recent migrants who are forced by circumstances to live in slums, a kind of experience they are unprepared for. It is not so much poverty per se that accounts for the instability of many ghetto black families, but the fact that they are subjected to influences and stresses for which they have neither the education nor occupational skills to provide a protective armor against adversity or discrimination.

The high proportion of urban black families broken by separation, divorce, or widowhood is often related to the difficulties of one or both parents to earn a livelihood or support other members of the family unit. These difficulties arise from a variety of situations: lack of occupational skills or education, discrimination in the labor market, unemployability because of psychological or character defects, and so on. Because of these or other handicaps, many black males are reluctant or unable to assume the responsibilities of family breadwinner and parenthood. At any rate, responsibility for supporting the family and rearing the children often rests on the mother, who may be married, single, separated, or widowed. If she is employed outside the home, the children are denied the advantage of family life with both parents present, unless the grandparents or other kin assume some of this responsibility, which is often the case. Poverty, crowding in homes, the prevalence of neighborhood crime and delinquency, the lack of work opportunities or recreational facilities, plus a sense of frustration at being trapped in a ghetto with little prospect of getting out of it, of achieving the "good life" when others have attained it, often by escaping to the suburbs—these are generally the conditions of black family life in the city.

Children Born Out of Wedlock

It is generally known that a higher illegitimate birth rate exists among blacks than among whites, even when allowing for differences in economic position and living conditions. For the population as a whole in the United States, the number of illegitimate live births per thousand in the white population increased from 40 in 1940 to 155 in 1968, while for the black population, over the same period, the increase was from 49 to 184.[19] This was a period of extensive urbanization and high geographic mobility. Rates reported for major cities were notably high, and generally increasing. For sixteen cities the ratios of illegitimate births to all live births increased in the black population between 1950 and 1962. In Chicago, for example, the ratio for blacks increased from 223 to 290, representing a percentage increase of 30; in Minneapolis, the ratio increased from 165 to 294, or 78 percent; in Philadelphia, the increase was from 224 to 233, or only four percent.[20] The ratios of illegitimate births for whites in these cities increased correspondingly during this period.

Although mother-centeredness is somewhat more characteristic of black than of white families, even when allowance is made for residential location and income, it should be noted that even in the low-income urban population over half of the families are headed by two parents, and on the middle- or upper-income levels more than 90 percent are two-parent families. The percentage of mother-headed families of both races is also higher for urban than for rural residents, and the difference between blacks and whites is not very large when the variables of residence and income are considered.

The preceding profile of the black family applies particularly to the central city, but not all ghetto residents fit this picture, nor does it apply to the majority of middle class families. Although families on the middle- or upper-income levels may be forced to live in deteriorated slum neighborhoods, the family as a group is generally as stable as white families on a similar economic level. The adults are relatively well educated, and often have occupational skills that make upward mobility possible. There is more supervision of the children and more emphasis on education; parents are more conservative in behavior and moral values and more active in organized social and religious life, especially organizations relating to the black community and its problems.

[19] *Statistical Abstract of the United States* (1972), p. 57.

[20] U. S. Department of Health, Education, and Welfare, *Vital Statistics of the United States*, annual reports.

The Puerto Rican Family
in New York

The experience of the Puerto Rican family in New York is indicative of social change that has occurred in the family organization of migrants.[21] Although the basic family unit in New York, as in Puerto Rico, is the nuclear family, there is a larger unit known as the "united family" (*familia unida*), consisting of a number of nuclear families whose members bear a special relationship to their kinsmen such as brothers and sisters, uncles and aunts, cousins, and grandparents. Acknowledged members of a united (modified-extended) family are relatives who can be relied upon in times of trouble or crises, or on occasions when a helping hand from relatives may be a convenience. There are also special occasions, such as birthdays, weddings, christenings, and celebrations of holidays, when the members get together to express their feelings of affection or respect. In major crises, members of two or more of the related nuclear families may gather and remain in one of the households until the uncertainties have passed. The very existence of these united families implies a strong sense of obligation to kinsmen— though not necessarily to all kinsmen, for there are some who are indifferent to these responsibilities or to united family activities.

But, as Padilla points out,[22] the united family is changing as the nuclear families and their members are assimilated into the prevailing culture and integrated into New York's metropolitan life. This has been especially true of Puerto Ricans who have been in New York for several years. Their geographic dispersal has often made it difficult for members of the united family to get together. And as social differentiation has occurred among the members, as values and interests have been modified, and particularly as the nuclear family unit—parents and children—has become more and more the principal focal point of interest, the united family has declined in importance. Nevertheless, it still functions effectively among the recent migrants who are often in need of the assistance and companionship that only relatives or close friends can give. So long as the heavy stream of migration from Puerto Rico continues, the united family system will probably be supported by the recent arrivals. Migration from Puerto Rico has always fluctuated in response to both mainland and island economic conditions. Since the midsixties, conditions have been such that in some years more Puerto Ricans return to the island than remain on the mainland.

It should be emphasized that there is no "typical" Puerto Rican family in New York. Of the approximately one million persons of Puerto Rican heritage in New York City, there are differences among them in income, educational level, family structure, and color, all of which have an

---

[21] Elena Padilla, *Up from Puerto Rico* (1958).
[22] *Ibid.*, 133–34.

important bearing on family life, residential location, and intergroup relations. Glazer and Moynihan point out that a frequent pattern of migration from Puerto Rico is for the father to migrate alone, reside for a while with friends or relatives, and when established bring the rest of the family to New York.[23] Another form of migration is for a mother, having been separated from her husband, or perhaps an unmarried mother, to move with her children to New York, hoping to find life easier there. Many unattached childless persons also move to the city.

The Italian Family in Boston

The family system of the Italian community in Boston, as observed by Gans, shares some of the characteristics of both the modified-extended family and the classical extended family.[24] The "households" are made up of nuclear or conjugal family units, but over and beyond this are the "family circles" consisting of two or more nuclear families whose members are related by blood or marriage. Those included in the family circle are persons who are, or can be, mutally helpful, enjoy intimate association with other kin, and whose social life generally involves frequent visiting with kinsmen. Friends and neighbors, also usually Italian, may be included in the family circle, which serves numerous functions such as providing mutual assistance in time of need, providing and reinforcing a sense of identity, and affording an opportunity for pleasurable leisure-time association such as visiting. Nevertheless, adaptations to an urban way of life have been necessary, and these adaptations have sometimes involved structural changes in the family unit and kinship circle. As Gans observes, "What matters most . . . is that there be a family circle which is wider than the nuclear family, and that all of the opportunities, temptations, and pressures of the larger society be evaluated in terms of how they affect the ongoing way of life that has been built around this circle."[25]

Three Generational Changes in Italian Families in the United States

Campisi has analyzed the changes that have occurred in the Italian family in the United States from the initial immigrant family through the first- and second-generation family groups.[26] Most of the Italian immigrants included in his analysis came from villages in southern

[23] Nathan Glazer and Daniel Patrick Moynihan, *Beyond the Melting Pot*, 2d. ed. (1970), pp. 122–28; and Oscar Lewis, *La Vida* (1968).

[24] Herbert J. Gans, *The Urban Villagers* (1962), p. 45.

[25] *Ibid.*, p. 245.

[26] Paul J. Campisi, "Ethnic Family Patterns: The Italian Family in the United States," *American Journal of Sociology*, 53 (April 1948), 443–49.

Italy, settling for the most part in major American cities. As villagers or peasants their family life was closely orchestrated to religious institutions, the seasonal planting and harvesting of crops, and traditional ceremonies. The first-generation family (the children of the immigrants) was in a state of transition, although striving against formidable odds to preserve the traditional way of life and values, with considerable internal conflict and disorganization occurring, especially between the parents and their children. By the time the second generation (grandchildren) had established households, the family system and its members had become extensively acculturated and oriented to the predominantly American style of life, although the larger kinship circle continued to exist and most of the members preferred to reside in an Italian neighborhood. Some of the specific changes recorded by Campisi are mentioned here, with only the immigrant family and the second-generation groups included to indicate the main trends.

It must be emphasized that the foregoing changes are a kind of "profile" of trends; numerous individual variations from these currents of change undoubtedly occur. Since Campisi did his study, fourth-

TABLE 14.1 Italian Families in Italy and U.S.

Peasant Family in South Italy	Second-Generation Italian Family in the United States
Emphasis on sacred and traditional values and behavior	Emphasis on secular values and behavior
Many family celebrations of feasts and holidays	Christmas only family affair; sometimes Thanksgiving
Father has highest status and authority	Father shares status with wife and children, and with limited authority
Individual subordinate to the family	Family subordinate to the individual
Women educated for marriage and family duties only	Emphasis on general education rather than marriage
Selection of mate by parents	Selection of mate by individual
Must marry someone from same village and religion	Many marriages outside nationality and religion
Dowry rights customary	No dowry rights
Primogeniture, that is, eldest son has high status and special rights	No primogeniture: all children equal in status and rights
Mother center of domestic life; must not work for wages	Mother has domestic responsibilities, but reserves time for social life and may work for wages

generation Italian families have appeared, and it seems probable that the trends he identified in the third generation have continued in the same direction for the fourth.

Urban Family Life in India

In reviewing the literature concerning the effects of urban life on the Indian family, Mandelbaum concludes that city residence per se does not necessarily bring about profound changes in family organization. Villagers who take up residence in a city commonly live close together in a kinship circle "which serves them as a refuge against the anonymity of city life and as a source of protection against urban dangers."[27] Urban influences on the family seem to be less a matter of residence in a city than of interacting factors such as changes in occupational careers, increased formal education of family members, awareness of various ideologies and behavior patterns through the mass media and personal contacts, necessary restructuring of social roles of parents and children, appeals of voluntary associations with resulting fragmentation of interests and loyalties, and so on. But kinship ties in the city are sometimes strengthened, as Mandelbaum points out.

Some Effects of City Life in India

In most Asian countries some variant of the joint-family system predominates, and changes in the family must be viewed from this perspective. Actually, the changes may be more apparent than real in many instances. Members of nuclear-family units in the city commonly retain their connections with kinsmen and identify with the larger group. Srinivas concludes from his research in South India that the urban household, even a nuclear-family group, is often merely "a satellite of a kin group in a village or town several hundred miles away."[28] He also reports that the greatest changes are occurring in families of the new elite—well-educated, well-to-do, and upwardly mobile persons who have left the village for the anticipated advantages of city life.

In India, male villagers, whether married or unmarried, often leave the family circle and migrate individually to the city, expecting to gain employment and perhaps later to be joined by their families. But village and kinship ties are normally strong, and even if the men remain in the

[27] David G. Mandelbaum, *Society in India: Continuity and Change* (1970), vol. 2, pp. 650–51.
[28] M. N. Srinivas, *Social Change in Modern India* (1966), p. 138.

city they generally return periodically to visit their families in the home town. Probably most migrant men or women hope to return eventually to the village scene in their old age to live out their remaining years amidst relatives and friends. But not all of them retain strong identities and loyalties with the ancestral village. The anonymity of city life, the appeal of the exotic and the romantic, and the opportunities for individualized behavior have weakened for many their sense of village loyalty, or even induced them to sever their village and family ties. Nor have women who go to the city to live been unaffected. Gainful employment of females has been of particular importance since it has taken them out of the home, reducing the influence they normally exert in the village family, or the controls that the family has over their behavior.

Most Indians belong to an extended three-generation family. The women shown here are part of 7 related families, 60 persons, who together migrated to the Terai area of India where they cooperatively farm 160 acres. (United Nations)

The Changing Japanese Family

The rapid urbanization and industrialization of Japan has been associated with numerous changes in the structure and functions of the Japanese family. Few societies have experienced as many societal changes in so short a time; yet certain traditional values and structures have been retained in family life. Often the traditional clashes with modernized forms of behavior. One trend is the increasing emphasis on individual choice in the selection of a mate, with more young persons than old ones, and more urban than rural residents, preferring this kind of arrangement to the traditional mate selection by parents.[29] During the present century a consistent rise in the average age of marriage has occurred, which is also true of several Western countries in the early stages of industrialization. Husband-wife relationships are more equalitarian than in the traditional system; decisions directly affecting the family are often jointly made, and husbands commonly assist in household work. Children are less influenced by the traditional concepts of filial piety and obedience; yet family ties and intimate relationships between members of the family group are still strong, and an awareness among children that they are loved and wanted continues to reinforce a sense of security. Sentimental and expressive relations with the larger kinship circle are still important in their lives. The illegitimate birth rate has consistently declined since 1890, which may mean widespread use of contraceptives by young persons rather than a change in sexual mores. Similarly, concubinage has declined, probably because the new civil code put into effect at the end of the nineteenth century in Japan did not include a formal position for the concubine in the household. It may be that the concubine has become a "mistress" in the Western sense, without formal recognition by the man's family.

In his study of a predominantly middle class district of Tokyo, Dore describes some of the changes that have occurred in Japanese family organization.[30] The traditional family of rural Japan is generally known as the "stem" family, consisting of husband and wife, the man's unmarried brothers and sisters, his eldest son and his wife and children, and unmarried sons and daughters. (The stem family is obviously a variant of the classical joint family system described earlier.) As soon as the younger sons reach maturity and marry, they establish a "branch" family, at the beginning a nuclear-family unit but subsequently evolving into another stem family. On marriage the daughters leave their own family and enter the stem family if their husband is the eldest son, or otherwise become part of a conjugal husband-wife unit. Traditionally,

[29] William J. Goode, *World Revolution and Family Patterns* (1963), ch. 7. This section draws heavily from Goode's study.

[30] R. P. Dore, *City Life in Japan: A Study of a Tokyo Ward* (1958), chs. 8–11.

loyalty of the members has been to the stem family as a unit, not solely to individuals in that unit. It is a tightly structured system.

With mass migrations of villagers to Tokyo in recent years family patterns have changed, not abruptly but gradually, as branch families have become separated geographically from stem families. Interpersonal ties and responsibilities to the stem family have declined in Tokyo; family units are smaller; and children spend considerable time in school and are therefore not in close constant contact with grandparents and other relatives. Many of the traditional family symbols and rites lose their importance; economic interdependence between branch and stem families is lessened; more time is spent outside the family group than was the case in the rural stem family, or even the urban stem family; women have achieved considerable economic independence by gainful employment and are not under the domination of the mother-in-law if they are married; and participation in occupational organizations or leisure-time groups outside the family unit is commonplace. Individualization of behavior, Western style, is a major trend.

All these trends point to the fact that continuity between generations, maintained under the old system, is weakened. This is not to imply, however, that traditionalism in thought or action has disappeared altogether, or that the family unit is seriously threatened. Structural and functional changes have occurred as adjustments are made to the conditions of city life. But as Dore points out, the idealized image of the family held by the Japanese people is not the same as the *real* urban family in the metropolis—with due allowances made for social class differences.

Urban Family Life in Africa

The urbanization of Africa south of the Sahara has had a profound effect on the family life of the indigenous peoples. Because family patterns vary a great deal from one city or country to another in Africa, and also because they are continually changing, generalizations should be made with caution. Generally speaking, indigenous families of Africans residing in villages are joint or extended and are closely articulated with the tribal system. Under preurban conditions the kinship-tribal system successfully carried out the various functions of family life. Roles were clearly defined and synchronized, authority vested in family heads or tribal chiefs was respected and usually observed, and conformity to accepted norms of conduct was expected and enforced.

But conditions associated with industrialism and urbanism have brought about many changes in family life, both for families living in the cities and for those remaining in the village.[31] African men, and even some African women, often journey in large numbers to industrial centers where they may find employment in the mines and mills and other establishments. Removed from the village setting, they are no longer subjected to the authority imposed by tribal and kinship groups. Deviant behavior in the form of crime and vice often results, and even among those whose behavior remains fairly conventional there tends to be lessened respect for authority and the established norms when they do return to their village homes.

In the village a man's social and economic status depends on his having a wife, and a woman's security is enhanced through marriage. But in the cities a woman does not necessarily add to a man's prestige, and she may be viewed as a costly luxury. Sexual satisfactions for both sexes are easily obtained in the city, without the responsibilities of family life. Consequently, illicit sexual behavior in some groups is common, and a considerable proportion of children are born out of wedlock. Women in the city, in contrast to village life, find gainful employment which enables them to enjoy luxuries and a degree of economic independence beyond the dreams of tribal women.

Summary

Changes in the structure and functions of the urban family give rise to many problems and at the same time are influenced by situations that exist beyond the bounds of a family group. In many respects, the family is profoundly influenced by the work roles its members perform. In traditional nonurbanized societies, mainly agricultural, work is closely integrated with other facets of family and community life. But in urban-industrial societies work tends to become highly specialized; in the city particularly it becomes a function that commonly separates the employed worker from family and neighborhood. In an agricultural society members of a family usually share work roles; in an industrial society work roles are not performed within the context of a family group but rather as separate individual functions. The specialization of work roles in an urbanized society invariably leads to diversification of occupations. Such a setting rather resembles a gigantic cafeteria in which the individual has a wide range of occupational choices, in contrast to the resident of a village or farm community, whose range of choices is limited. Furthermore, the various occupational roles may serve as a mobility elevator which the worker may ride in either

[31] Much of the information relating to the urban impact on African families is obtained from the conference held at Abidjan under the auspices of UNESCO and the International African Institute. Reports of the conference were published as *Social Implications of Industrialization and Urbanization in Africa South of the Sahara* (1956).

direction, upward or downward; but often the elevator stalls and the worker goes nowhere. These and other aspects of the urban world of work will be discussed in the following chapter.

Selected Bibliography

BOOKS

Adams, Bert N., *Kinship in an Urban Setting.* Chicago: Markham, 1968.

Billingsley, Andrew, *Black Families in White America.* Englewood Cliffs, N.J.: Prentice-Hall, 1968.

Edwards, John N., ed., *The Family and Social Change.* New York: Knopf, 1969.

Goode, William J., *World Revolution and Family Patterns.* New York: The Free Press, 1963.

Gore, M. S., *Urbanization and Family Change.* Bombay: Popular Frakashan, 1968.

Laslett, Peter, and R. Wall, eds., *Household and Family in Past Time.* New York: Cambridge University Press, 1972.

Marris, Peter, *Family and Social Change in an African City.* London: Routledge and Kegan Paul, 1961.

Rainwater, Lee, and William L. Yancey, eds., *The Moynihan Report and the Politics of Controversy* (including the text of Daniel Patrick Moynihan's study, *The Negro Family: The Case for National Action*). Cambridge: Massachusetts Institute of Technology, 1967.

Rosenberg, George, and Donald F. Ansbach, *Working-Class Kinship.* Lexington, Mass.: Lexington Books, D. C. Heath, 1973.

Ross, Aileen D., *The Hindu Family in Its Urban Setting.* Toronto: University of Toronto Press, 1961.

Sennett, Richard, *Families against the City.* Cambridge: Harvard University Press, 1970.

Willie, Charles V., ed., *The Family Life of Black People.* Columbus, Ohio: Merrill, 1970.

Willmott, Peter, and Michael Young, *Family and Class in a London Suburb.* London: Routledge and Kegan Paul, 1960.

Winch, R. F., and Louis Wolf Goodman, eds., *Selected Studies in Marriage and the Family*, 3d ed. New York: Holt, Rinehart and Winston, 1968.

ARTICLES

Aldous, Joan, "Urbanization, the Extended Family, and Kinship Ties in West Africa," *Social Forces*, 41 (October 1962), 6–12.

Babchuk, Nicholas, and John Ballweg, "Primary Extended Kin Relations of Negro Couples," *Sociological Quarterly*, 12 (Winter 1971), 69–76.

Blood, Robert O., Jr., and Donald M. Wolfe, "Negro-White Differences in Blue-Collar Marriages in a Northern Metropolis," *Social Forces*, 48 (September 1969), 59–64.

Blood, Robert O., Jr., "Impact of Urbanization on American Family Structure and Functioning," *Sociology and Social Research*, 49 (October 1964), 5–17.

Bott, Elizabeth, "Urban Families: The Norms of Conjugal Roles," *Human Relations*, 9 (1956), 325–42.

Coombs, Lolagene C., *et al.*, "Premarital Pregnancy and Status Before and After Marriage," *American Journal of Sociology*, 75 (March 1970), 800–20.

Erickson, William, "The Social Organization of an Urban Commune," *Urban Life and Culture,* 2 (July 1973), 231–56.

Key, William H., "Rural-Urban Differences and the Family," *Sociological Quarterly*, 2 (January 1961), 49–57.

Levine, Robert A., Nancy H. Klein, and Constance R. Owen, "Father-Child Relationships and Changing Life Styles in Ibadan, Nigeria," in Horace Miner, ed., *The City in Modern Africa,* pp.215–56. New York: Praeger, 1967.

Rainwater, Lee, "Crucible of Identity: The Negro Lower Class Family," *Daedalus*, 95 (1965), 172–216.

Rosen, Bernard C., and Anita La Raia, "Modernity in Women: An Index of Social Change in Brazil," *Journal of Marriage and the Family*, 34 (May 1972), 353–60.

Tallman, Irving, and Ramona Morgner, "Life Style Differences among Urban and Suburban Blue-Collar Families," *Social Forces*, 48 (March 1970), 334–48.

Winch, Robert F., *et al.*, "Urbanism, Ethnicity, and Extended Familism," *Journal of Marriage and the Family*, 30 (February 1968), 40–45.

Winch, Robert F., "Permanence and Change in the History of the American Family and Some Speculations about Its Future," *Journal of Marriage and the Family*, 32 (February 1970), 6–15.

15 • The Urban World of Work

 In any country the urban occupational system is merely a part of a general occupational structure which includes farm and village work roles as well as those of city people. Numerous occupations are distinctively urban, and some of them are found only in large cities. Even countries whose economies are predominantly agrarian have cities, often very large cities, in which the occupational structure may resemble that of cities in industrial societies.

Cities with a diversified economy tend to attract workers more varied in their skills and training than cities having a narrow economy.[1] Big cities generally afford a wider range of occupational choices than small cities, indicating that a worker may be in a favorable position to find a job commensurate with his ability, education, and interests. The great metropolises of the world have, generally, become highly diversified occupationally, which is one reason that they are so attractive to all kinds of persons interested in employment or advancement. The one-industry city is usually relatively small, and if any serious disruption occurs in the economy of such a city the effects on the labor force can be catastrophic.

Throughout this volume we have attempted to present, wherever appropriate or possible, a cross-national perspective with a particular focus on industrial and nonindustrial or traditional societies. It is important to note that almost every country, whether industrial or nonindustrial, places a high value on industrialization because industrialism is commonly associated with a desired standard of living. Consequently, even in nonindustrial or developing countries, there is a strong drive to industrialize as extensively and as rapidly as possible. And since industrialization usually occurs in an urban setting, cities become the principal focus of industrial development.

But industrialization involves far more than just technological change

---

[1] Angela Lane, "Occupational Mobility in Six Cities," *American Sociological Review*, 33 (October 1968), 740–49.

and capital investment. It also involves new forms of economic organization, often away from small family owned and managed enterprises to large and complex bureaucracies, as well as a proliferation of specialized occupational roles and the skills or knowledge to perform these roles. It requires new work habits that must conform to the demands of the clock or the calendar, or at least to the demands of those having managerial authority. It involves, for many, a set of values and a way of life different from those deeply imbedded in the traditional system. Certainly it means, for many, urban rather than rural residence. It is not surprising that the industrialization of traditional societies has proceeded slowly, with many stops and starts. But as it develops it invariably means increasing urbanization—in some instances over-urbanization and the acceleration of societal change.

The Specialization and Professionalization of Work

A distinctive feature of work in an urban-industrial society, or in a city, is the proliferation of specialized work roles. The trend in such societies is definitely toward increasing emphasis on expertise in role performance, and such expertise is manifest on various levels. On one level there is the "expert" whose limited skill or knowledge can be achieved fairly easily, or at least without prolonged training and study: the mechanic or the factory operative, for example. On another level is the sophisticated expertise of the architect or electrical engineer, for example, which generally necessitates specialized training or experience because of the difficulty in achieving competence. In an urban-industrial society the expert, by and large, is unexpendable, that is, he or she cannot be easily replaced, while the nonexpert is easily replaceable. An urban society could scarcely exist, and certainly not function very effectively, without vast numbers of workers on various levels of expertise, but the unskilled worker whose expertise is rudimentary at best is in limited demand.

The person on the assembly line is, of course, a kind of specialist and may have considerable skill in performing his work role. Similarly, the programmer working with an electronic computer, or the electrician, may be highly specialized and skilled in the performance of a technically difficult work role. In a dynamic urban-industrial society the occupational system is constantly undergoing change. The processes of change are manifest in various ways as occupations rise or decline in prestige, or even remain stable for a considerable time, as their functions are altered and they gain or lose in power or influence.

The occupational expertise and specialization associated with urbanization have usually been accompanied by professionalization of work. There are, of course, no clear-cut distinctions between professions and

other occupations; indeed, there are the established and fully recognized professions, the semiprofessions, and other occupations whose claim to professional status is recognized by only the claimants. In an urban-industrial society, and even in cities of predominantly agrarian countries, there is a strain toward professionalism that runs through much of the occupational structure, a process which undoubtedly reflects the emphasis on specialized expertise and the tendency of specialists to strive collectively for status, security, privilege, and even power.

One of the steps in the attempted professionalization or upgrading of an occupation is a change of its name, usually to create a more favorable image of the vocation. Thus, junk dealers become salvage consultants, undertakers become funeral directors, newspaper reporters become journalists, secretaries become administrative assistants, traveling salesmen become sales engineers, laboratory technicians become medical technologists, and so on. Another step any vocational group striving to upgrade its own occupation commonly engages in is propaganda or political activities to enhance its prestige in the eyes of the public or to defend its interests by supporting or opposing particular proposals. Through organization the group may attempt to keep out allegedly

Semi-skilled operatives were necessary in mass production industries at the turn of the century, as shown by this photo of a textile mill in 1913. At present such machinery is automated. (Merrimack Valley Textile Museum)

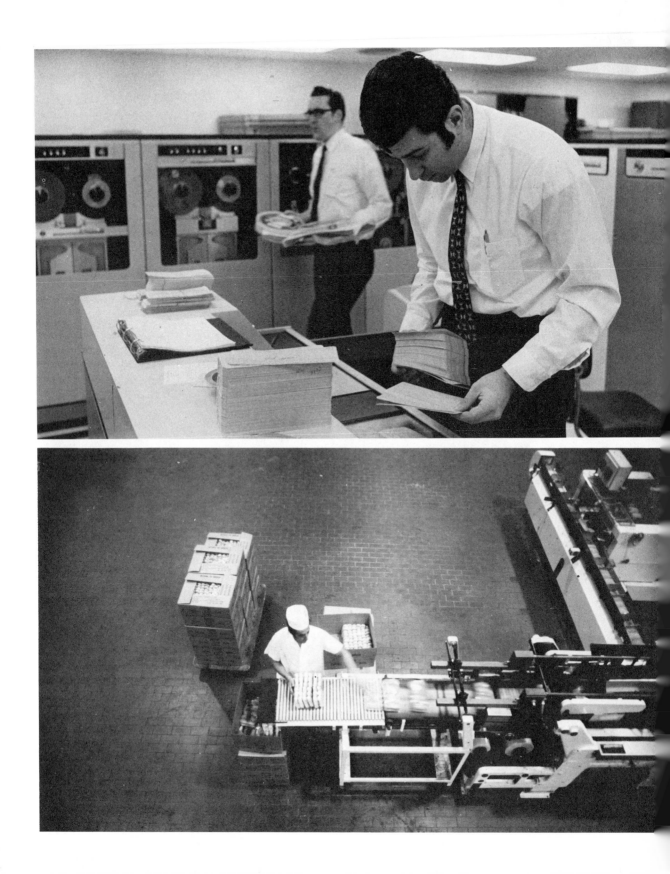

Electronic computers are used in the bank (above) and semi-automated machinery (below) packs and wraps buns in a bakery. In both blue and white collar work, many jobs have been automated. (Jan Jachniewicz, Chase Manhattan Bank—top; John Zoiner, AMF Incorporated—below)

disqualified or otherwise undesirable persons, or in some cases competitors, by erecting membership barriers making admission of new members very difficult—commonly in the guise of service to "society" but quite as much to protect or improve the status of the occupation and the rewards that accrue to it.

Wilensky has illustrated the process of professionalization by indicating some of the levels of professional achievement.[2] There are, for example, the firmly established professions such as law, medicine, dentistry, or architecture. Some occupations, such as social work, journalism, or librarianship, are marginal professions. There are new semiprofessions such as city management, city planning, computer programming, and hospital administration. Then there are the aspiring occupations that have doubtful professional status, such as advertising or funeral directing. At all of these levels there is a strain toward professionalization and a concerted effort to maintain the status already achieved.

Within the most prestigious professions, or, as Hughes has expressed it, the "proud" occupations,[3] there exist levels of prestige both within a specific occupation and between occupations in the professional category. In medicine, for example, there are the elitist practitioners such as surgeons or neurologists and the rank-and-file generalists, whose prestige is lower than that of the specialists. Then there are status gaps between doctors whose professional standing has been legitimated by law and tradition and peripheral groups, such as podiatrists or chiropractors, who strive for professional acceptance but are either rejected by the "fundamentalists" or excluded from the inner circles of the elite. A somewhat comparable situation exists within the law profession—between the big-time corporation lawyer or the high-court judge, on the one hand, and the lawyer who receives a modest salary and little prestige for his tedious work in a law office or government bureau, on the other. Or, in education, the chasm that separates the professor in a distinguished university from the teacher in a junior college or high school.

[2] Harold L. Wilensky, "The Professionalization of Everyone?" *American Journal of Sociology*, 60 (September 1964), 143.

[3] Everett C. Hughes, "The Humble and the Proud," *Sociological Quarterly*, 11 (Spring 1970), 151.

The Organization of Work

The more urbanized and industrialized a society becomes, the more numerous are the organizations within it relating to specialized work roles. Almost every established vocation directly involving a considerable number of persons is represented by some form of organization which may have one or more functions to perform in behalf of its members. The 1960 census listed some 2,500 business and labor organizations in the United States, and similar organizations have come into existence in other urban-industrial societies. Even the larger cities of developing nations have work organizations, although they are less numerous than in cities of industrial societies.

Most work organizations have headquarters in cities, although some of the members may be employed in nonurban communities. Some examples of such organizations in the United States are the Association of Consulting Engineers, the Brotherhood of Railway Trainmen, the American Association of University Professors, the United Shoe Workers of America, and so on. Often such organizations represent a broad spectrum of occupations. For example, the AFL-CIO is a coalition of more than one hundred labor unions, each of which is organized by and for the benefit of its members, and the National Association of Manufacturers is a coalition of organizations of industrialists. Many organizations represent highly specialized occupations. In the United States, for instance, six national organizations are concerned with the manufacture and distribution of buttons, nine are related to the mining, processing, transportation, and distribution of coal, and seventeen are concerned with cotton. There are even two that deal exclusively with diapers!

The Functions of Work Organizations

The modern occupational association is likely to be multifunctional, but the nature and variety of its functions depend on the size of its membership, the social, economic, and political setting in which it exists, the kinds of work roles its members perform, and so on. Some associations are structured to exert political and economic power in behalf of their members. And although the power they are permitted to exert is limited by governmental authority, they probably have greater latitude in democratic than in authoritarian societies. Certainly the right to conduct a strike is more widely accepted in modern societies having a democratic system of government than in others.

Organizational functions are commonly specified to serve various interests, needs, and rights: the rights of individual members and of the occupational group as a whole; the rights of the people who are served by the workers or employers; the need for an institutional mechanism to define relations with employees, employers, or the public at large; the need to formulate specific rules of work performance and remuneration for the performance of work tasks; the need of the organized group to maintain a high level of morale among its members; and the need for favorable environmental conditions in the work settings. Many organizations have a complex of rules that specify the recruitment of new members and determine their eligibility for membership, or that formulate codes of ethics for the members in the performance of their respective roles.

Work as a Way of Life

For some occupations, work is more than economic behavior; it is a way of life, the central focus of interests and behavior, a career and not merely a job. This is particularly true of the professions or other occupations that make heavy demands on the individual's skill, knowledge, and ingenuity. Work for such persons tends to become an end in itself, not merely a means to some unrelated end. They do not make a sharp separation between work and nonwork. For the professional or executive, work does not necessarily begin at nine in the morning and end at five in the afternoon.

A study of professional nurses revealed that about four-fifths of the respondents specified that their central life interest was in work and only one-fifth in nonwork.[4] Dubin found just the reverse in a study of urban-industrial workers, of whom one-fourth were primarily interested in work and three-fourths in nonwork activities.[5] Two-thirds of the nurses found satisfaction in their work, as compared with only 15 percent of the industrial workers. In this respect lower white collar personnel—typists or office machine operators, for example—have much in common with industrial manual workers. At the end of the day or week their interests shift to other matters—family, amusement, religion, hobbies, and so on.

Work Symbols and Stereotypes

The work role itself is symbolic of status, but there are also ancillary symbols which serve to establish identity, facilitate work performance, or indicate status—or all three. In the city, which is often characterized by anonymity and impersonality, visible identity is important in defining interpersonal and intergroup relations. The uniform is one means of

[4] Louis H. Orzack, "Work as a Central Life Interest of Professionals," *Social Problems*, 7 (Fall 1959), 117.
[5] Robert Dubin, "Industrial Workers' Worlds: A Study of the Central Life Interests of Industrial Workers," *Social Problems*, 3 (January 1956), 131–42.

establishing the occupational identity of the person in a work role and of indicating the status of that role. By and large, persons in occupations having a service function—domestic servant, policeman, priest, waitress, porter, soldier, railway conductor, airline hostess or pilot, mail carrier, or nurse—may be expected or required to wear a uniform for identification and for defining the relationship between them and those they serve. Dress other than a uniform may also be symbolic of the status and function of particular work roles: the rough clothing of the workingman or the formal attire of the professional man on the job. Honorary or deferential occupational titles—doctor, judge, professor, colonel, governor—serve a similar symbolic purpose.

The proliferation of specialized occupations in an urban-industrial society, and especially in large cities, makes it impossible for any individual to know much about other existing vocations. By contrast, in a village or open-country community, where there are few occupations, most persons know a great deal about the nature of work in each occupation and generally have some knowledge of the persons in these work roles. But in the city one must depend, to a considerable degree, on symbols and stereotypical images of many occupations and the people so occupied.

In American society, for example, the popular image of the surgeon is that of a trim, tall, handsome white man with graying hair, whose very demeanor suggests a person of high intelligence and skill who miraculously performs surgical feats for the benefit of mankind—at a price. Women, blacks, Orientals, hunchbacks, or fat men do not fit this image. The stereotype of the business executive is that of a middle-aged white man, Protestant, with an English surname, who is formally and neatly attired, expressive of self-confidence, and whose views on many or all aspects of modern life are often considered authoritative. Or the female school teacher is often depicted as a "school marm," a spinster, who is plain in physical appearance, old-fashioned in dress, puritanical in behavior, and dedicated to her occupation even though it is not accorded high status. Obviously, some stereotypes are favorable, others unfavorable.

Occupational stereotypes are, of course, grossly inaccurate. They are also subject to change as the values of a society undergo change, and such changes are more extensive and pervasive in the urban environment. Occupational roles are now being assumed by persons whose sex, racial or ethnic identity, or other physical or behavioral characteristics do not fit the traditional stereotypes. Opposition to changing occupational roles, and defense of traditional stereotypes, is rationalized by such expressed values as "woman's place is in the home," "black people are not responsible or smart enough" to perform nontraditional roles, and the like. Resistance to these changes has signalled a collectively organized reaction such as the Women's Liberation Movement or the civil rights legislation for the admission of persons, irrespective of sex, race, or cultural background, to jobs previously closed to them. The urban environment is the breeding ground for such movements.

Main Currents of Occupational Shifts

Associated with the phenomenal growth of cities in the Western world since World War II has been the unprecedented expansion of such fields as aeronautics, space exploration, electronics, nuclear power, retail merchandising, scientific training and research, engineering, and organized recreation. Expansion of these activities has been accompanied in many instances by the proliferation of specialized occupations and the contraction of others. Striking increases have occurred in the number of airplane pilots, office-machine operators, radio and television personnel, space engineers and scientists, automobile mechanics, newspaper and magazine writers, social workers, teachers, and librarians. But the wheel of fortune has often turned in the other direction. Sharp declines have occurred among such workers as telegraphers, bill collectors, street-car and railway conductors, coal miners, and paperhangers.

The Change and Stability of Occupations

Many urban occupations, more particularly the established professions, provide considerable stability and continuity of employment, short of drastic changes in the economy or technology. Those trained for a professional career may function in a specified role for a long period of time, probably through their working lives. One who has spent much time and money preparing for a career in the "proud professions" will be reluctant to abandon his specialized role for a different kind of job, unless the rewards are substantially higher.

But jobs for which little or no preparation is necessary are usually unstable, lacking in continuity, and offer meager rewards in terms of income or security. Changes in the economy or new developments in technology may easily disrupt the employment pattern, eliminating some work roles and creating others. Workers on this level may flit from one job or occupation to another without ever becoming emotionally committed to any particular role. Not surprisingly, studies of worker morale generally indicate that the highest level of satisfaction is found in stable occupations and that workers on the low-prestige and low-income levels are more likely to be dissatisfied with their jobs or occupations.

These conditions apply particularly to the situation in urban America. In a different cultural setting the reactions may be different. In urban

Japan, for example, corporate managers generally have a paternalistic concern about the welfare and security of their salaried employees, who in turn have a strong sense of loyalty to the organization and expect to remain with it indefinitely.

THE WORK ROLES OF WOMEN   The increasing percentage of persons living in cities is usually accompanied by a rising proportion of women in the labor force. This has been particularly true in communist societies, where women have been drawn more extensively into gainful employment than in noncommunist countries. One of the striking aspects of this general trend has been the recent marked increase in the number of married women who are employed. These trends in the United States are shown in Table 15.1.

TABLE 15.1: Distribution of Women Over 14 Years of Age in the Civilian Labor Force, by Marital Status and Percentage of Female Population, 1940–1971

Years	Single	Married
1940	48.1	16.7
1950	50.5	24.8
1960	44.1	31.7
1971	52.7	41.4

SOURCE: *Statistical Abstract of the United States* (1972), p. 219.

That the increasing employment of women is predominantly an urban phenomenon is evidenced by the fact that about four-fifths of the female workers in the United States live in cities, although only about 70 percent of the total population are urban residents.

The Psychosocial Aspects of Work

The Prestige Hierarchy

In every society or city there is an occupational prestige hierarchy. Even when individuals know very little about a particular occupation, they may be sufficiently familiar with certain aspects of that occupation to have a general idea of its prestige in relation to their assessments of other occupations. In a village community with perhaps not more than a score of occupational specialities such an assessment is fairly simple, but in a city, especially a metropolis, with its multitude of specialized occupations, an accurate image of the occupational prestige hierarchy is impossible for any individual, although he may accumulate a smattering of information about a considerable range of work roles through formal education, hearsay, and the mass media. Even if little or nothing is known about specific work roles, one may have some notion of the prestige of an occupation if it is seen in a larger frame of reference such as a professional, business executive, or skilled manual worker.

Prestige Ranking and Changes

Several notable attempts have been made to construct and apply an empirical scale to measure the prestige of occupations. Perhaps the best-known scale, developed in 1947 by North and Hatt, was based on a national sample.[6] Respondents were asked to evaluate each of 90 occupations, and from these evaluations a prestige score was calculated and expressed as an average of all the individual ratings. The range in prestige ranking was from one to 90. This study was replicated in 1963 to determine what changes, if any, had taken place during the sixteen-year interim, a period of rapid urbanization.[7]

The replicated study indicated that only minor changes had occurred in the prestige ratings of most occupations; some had increased in prestige, others declined. When the specific occupations were placed in 11 occupational classes, eight increased in prestige and three declined. Of the 90 occupations taken as a whole, there was a prestige rank gain of 1.7 percent.

International Comparisons

Cross-cultural studies indicate that the prestige hierarchy of occupations is strikingly similar in various countries. Inkeles and Rossi found, in a study of six urban industrial societies (Germany, Great Britain, Japan, New Zealand, the Soviet Union, and the United States), that the prestige ratings of occupations among them were similar,[8] and a study in another urbanized country, The Netherlands, provided a similar picture of the occupational prestige system there.[9] That these similarities are not confined to urban-industrial states but are also characteristic of pre-industrial societies is indicated in studies conducted in the Philippines[10] and in Indonesia.[11] These cross-national similarities strongly suggest

[6] C. C. North and Paul K. Hatt, "Jobs and Occupations: A Popular Evaluation," *Opinion News*, September 1, 1947. Reprinted in Reinhard Bendix and Seymour Martin Lipset, eds., *Class, Status, and Power* (1953), pp. 411–26.

[7] Robert W. Hodge, Paul M. Siegel, and Peter H. Rossi, "Occupational Prestige in the United States," *American Journal of Sociology*, 70 (November 1964), 286–302. An expanded version of this report is included in Reinhard Bendix and Seymour Martin Lipset, eds., *Class, Status, and Power*, 2d ed. (1966), pp. 322–47.

[8] Alex Inkeles and Peter H. Rossi, "National Comparisons of Occupational Prestige," *American Journal of Sociology*, 61 (January 1956), 329–39.

[9] F. van Heek *et. al.*, *Sociale Stijging en Daling in Nederland* (1958), pp. 25–26.

[10] Edward A. Tiryakian, "The Prestige Evaluation of Occupations in an Underdeveloped Country: The Philippines," *American Journal of Sociology*, 63 (January 1958), 390–99.

[11] E. Murray Thomas, "Reinspecting a Structural Position on Occupational Prestige," *American Journal of Sociology*, 67 (March 1962), 561–65.

that occupations considered most essential and commonly involving considerable ability and training are accorded the greatest rewards and therefore the most prestige. Such occupations appear to be much the same for all societies. One must allow, however, for the fact that the upgrading of specific occupations may be easier and more widespread in urbanized societies than in predominantly agricultural countries.

Minorities and the Occupational Structure

Most ethnic and racial minorities in the United States are concentrated heavily in cities and in particular classes of occupations. Historically, the Jews have engaged in trading or intellectual activities. Italians and Greeks in American cities have been oriented toward the preparation and serving of foods, although many have also gone into unskilled or semiskilled manual occupations. Poles have been attracted in great numbers to heavy industries, especially mining, smelting, and manufacturing, and the Chinese in American cities have been associated with restaurants and laundries. Porter observes a rather similar ethnic occupational distribution in Canada.[12] There, in 1961, the Jewish community had by far the highest proportion of employed persons (16 percent) in the top occupational brackets—business and the professions—while only 3.4 percent of the Canadian workers of Italian origin and 1.1 percent of the Indian aborigines were in the high-prestige occupations. Only one percent of the Jews were unskilled workers, but about one-fifth of the Italians and almost half of the Indians were so classified.

The Changing Occupational Roles of Black Americans

It is common knowledge that the black population of the United States, as a whole, is concentrated on the lower levels of the occupational structure. Historically, the job ceiling for blacks has been imposed at a low level, and even though the ceiling is being slowly raised it continues to be difficult for a black man or woman to rise to middle or top positions in the occupational structure. The result is that blacks are still forced into low-paying, low-prestige jobs. Yet during and since World War II, the barriers have been lowered, civil rights legislation, unionization of black workers, and better educational training, among other things, accounting for some of the changes that have occurred. Still, a wide occupational differential between the white and nonwhite populations exists, as is indicated in Table 15.2.

[12] John Porter, *The Vertical Mosaic* (1966), pp. 562–65.

TABLE 15.2: Percentage Distribution of Employed Persons in Major Occupational Classes in the United States, 1957 and 1971, by Race

	White		Nonwhite	
	1957	1971	1957	1971
White collar	44.3	50.6	12.7	29.1
Blue collar	38.2	33.7	41.8	39.9
Service occupations*	9.1	11.8	32.0	27.6
Farming and farm labor	8.4	3.9	13.5	3.4

*Includes domestic servants, cooks, waiters, security personnel, and the like.
SOURCE: *Statistical Abstract of the United States* (1972), p. 231.

Several facts are strikingly apparent in the table, one of which is the difference in the occupational distribution of whites and nonwhites. A much larger concentration of whites than of blacks is in the white collar occupations for both 1957 and 1971. Conversely, a higher proportion of blacks than of whites remains in blue collar jobs and service occupations. Both racial categories have experienced proportional declines in agriculture—down to about four percent of the total labor force.

A second fact is that white workers in the nonmanual occupations increased by about six percentage points, from 44 percent to approximately half, while for nonwhites the percentage of nonmanual workers more than doubled, from 12.7 to 29.1. A slight decline occurred in the proportions of whites in blue collar jobs, and the percentage of nonwhites on this level decreased slightly. In the service occupations the percentage of whites increased slightly but the proportion of nonwhites declined. Since almost three-fourths of the population resides in cities, the data, except for farmers, provide a fairly clear picture of the main configuration of the urban occupational structure.

The sharp decline of nonwhite farm workers in recent years has probably contributed to the increase in the proportions of unskilled or semiskilled manual workers in cities because most rural migrants enter the urban occupational structure at or near the bottom. The proportion of whites employed as factory operatives has been declining in recent years, but nonwhites in those occupations have increased proportionally. Blacks are still heavily represented in the service occupations, mostly as domestic servants or other workers engaged in menial tasks, but proportionally they have decreased substantially.

A notable change in the occupational distribution of whites and nonwhites has occurred in the professional and technical occupations. White personnel in this category increased from 11 to 15 percent while nonwhites increased from four to eight percent. The proportion of white skilled craftsmen declined slightly from 1957 to 1971; nonwhites in this category increased from 5.7 to 8.5 percent.

The Occupational Distribution
of Blacks

A different perspective on black representation in the American occupational structure is revealed by the calculation of ratios for two periods, 1948 and 1969. The percentage of blacks in the entire labor force in 1969 was 9.6. Thus, if the black working population were evenly distributed in all of the occupational classes, it would account for 9.6 percent of the workers in each class. But blacks in fact are underrepresented in many occupations and overrepresented in others, as is indicated by the ratios in Table 15.3, which are calculated by dividing the percentage of blacks in each occupational class by the percentage of blacks in the total population.

TABLE 15.3: Distribution of Male Nonwhites in Major Occupational Classes, 1948 and 1969, by Percentages and Ratios

	Percentage in 1969	Ratios		Direction of Change
		1948	1969	
Nonwhites in the total labor force	9.6			
Occupational classes				
Professional and technical	3.5	.33	.40	Increase
Managers, officials, proprietors	2.0	.20	.21	Increase
Clerks	6.8	.24	.71	Increase
Salesworkers	2.1	.17	.22	Increase
Craftsmen, foremen (skilled)	4.9	.36	.51	Increase
Operatives (semiskilled)	11.1	1.00	1.16	Increase
Service workers	21.5	2.30	2.24	Decrease
Farm laborers and operators	24.0	2.82	2.50	Decrease
Laborers (except farm)	26.1	2.92	2.72	Decrease

SOURCE: *Statistical Abstract of the United States* (1961), p. 216; (1970), p. 223.

If blacks had been evenly distributed in the occupational classes in 1969, the ratio in each class would be 1.00, but such was not the case. The proportion of blacks in the professional and technical category, for example, was only two-fifths of what it would be on the basis of chance distribution—a ratio of .40. But the ratio of laborers was almost three times as large as might be expected on the basis of random distribution—a ratio of 2.72. At both dates, 1948 and 1969, five occupational classes were underrepresented (less than 1.00) and four were overrepresented. Among nonfarm laborers and service workers the ratios declined. Doubtless the decrease in unskilled labor was due in considerable measure to the application of "labor-saving" technology, which reduced the manpower needed in that area. Although the ratios do indicate a widespread upgrading of blacks in the occupational hierarchy, the changes over the two decades were small. Only in the clerical category was there a significant increase.

When ratios are calculated for female black workers, the pattern of over- and underrepresentation is even more pronounced. For private household workers the ratio in 1969 was 4.26, for example, or four times the distribution on the basis of chance, whereas for clerical workers it was only .28, or only one-fourth what it would be by random distribution.

Lest the data in Tables 15.2 and 15.3 be interpreted that blacks are being rapidly upgraded and therefore catching up with whites, it should be emphasized that white workers as a whole have also been upgraded, so that the white-black status gap remains about as wide as ever. The increase of blacks in the professional class has been largely in the ministry, teaching, social work, and entertainment, not medicine and law.

The Vicious Circle

As has been noted, there are actually more occupational choices in the city than in rural areas, and urban residents are probably more aware of these potential choices. Yet most black persons in the United States experience occupational handicaps at almost every stage of life. Initially, they are usually handicapped by conditions of poverty; they generally receive an education inferior than that of whites; they are commonly socialized into a ghetto culture not conducive to personal stability or intellectual growth; their initial employment is usually of a low order whether judged by status, income, or job security; and throughout their occupational careers most are considered expendable, the last to be hired and the first to be fired.[13] Faced with this accumulation of handicaps it is not surprising that black men and women in the United States have continued to be concentrated in the lower echelons of the occupational structure and are slow to move upward from that level.

Such occupational handicaps as experienced by blacks are also evident in varying degrees and forms in other racial or ethnic communities, such as Mexican-American, Puerto Rican, American Indian, and Asian, many of whose members reside in ghettoes and are concentrated heavily in low-status and low-income jobs, if indeed they have a job at all. Yet breaking the occupational barrier has been more difficult for blacks than for other minorities.

[13] For a discussion of the "vicious circle," see Peter M. Blau and Otis Dudley Duncan, *The American Occupational Structure* (1967), pp. 199–205.

Occupational Mobility

The Velocity and Forms of Mobility

There is reason to believe that an urban-industrial society is more conducive to occupational mobility than an agrarian society, and, similarly, that conditions of city life are more conducive to mobility than conditions in the village or countryside. In addition, a large city is generally more favorable to vertical mobility than a small city, if for no other reason than that a fairly large proportion of the working population is engaged in nonmanual work for which recruits may be attracted from the manual working classes.[14] The rapid growth of large cities in most countries during the present century has resulted in the multiplication of high-level positions available to qualified persons. Furthermore, the dynamics of an urban economy tends to accelerate the velocity of mobility, at least during periods of economic expansion. But conditions of city life may also impede mobility: It could hardly be said that an urban ghetto provides an effective springboard for upward mobility for its residents.

There are numerous ways of measuring or viewing occupational mobility. Mobility may be *intergenerational*, involving changes in the occupational position between, say, fathers and sons; or it may be viewed as *career*, with reference to the occupational or job changes an individual makes during his working life. Occupational mobility may also be interpreted as the changes that occur in the occupational position of an entire group, or even a stratum of society, over a period of time. For example, certain European and Asian immigrants who came to the United States as peasant or unskilled workers have moved extensively into middle class, or even upper class, occupations. Changes in the social and economic structure may either restrict or expand opportunities for employment on any or all levels. If the status-bearing occupations are expanding, opportunities for upward mobility from low-status positions may increase correspondingly.

In every country, even in the most dynamically urbanized societies, many persons continue, by choice, custom, or necessity, to follow in the vocational footsteps of their parents. The nature and extent of occupational "inheritance" varies from one country to another, and certainly

---

[14] See especially Seymour Martin Lipset and Reinhard Bendix, *Social Mobility in Industrial Society* (1959), pp. 216–19.

Occupational mobility is restricted in many traditional societies. Washing clothes in Bombay shown above is an ascribed occupation. In contrast the American girl below who operates a computer, has chosen her job. (Noel P. Gist—top; George W. Gardner—bottom).

from one stratum of society or community to another in the same country. It is generally believed that occupational inheritance is less a feature of urban-industrial societies than of agrarian countries. Yet even in the traditional societies now experiencing industrialization and urbanization, occupational inheritance is less pronounced than it once was, especially in the cities.

A cross-cultural study by Cutright leads to the conclusion that the level of occupational inheritance is relatively low in urban-industrial societies having a highly developed technology, a small agricultural labor force, a prevalence of small nuclear families, and a system of rewards to talented individuals.[15] This conclusion suggests that in predominantly agricultural societies the level of occupational inheritance is high and the velocity of occupational mobility low. In countries in which land, minerals, and industrial establishments are owned and controlled by a small minority in positions of superior economic and political power, the roadblocks to upward mobility are often insuperable, especially for persons born into families at or near the bottom of the occupational pyramid. This is notably true of most Latin American countries.

The Direction of Mobility Trends

A considerable number of studies indicate that the predominant trend of intergenerational mobility has been upward since World War II,[16] a period of great economic and technological expansion and rapid urbanization. It has also been a period during which the white collar and professional classes have expanded, thus creating vacancies into which the sons and daughters of manual workers and farmers have been able to move.

But the mobility "escalator" runs in three directions—upward, downward, and horizontally—and for some it does not run at all. It would be premature to conclude that the trend of upward mobility in the United States during and after World War II will continue indefinitely. In periods of major societal disruptions, such as depressions or revolutions, downward mobility may exceed upward mobility in volume or even velocity. Similarly, technological or economic changes may force many persons unable to find employment at their job level to reluctantly take positions lower in income or prestige. Many city denizens of Skid Row

---

[15] Phillips Cutright, "Occupational Inheritance: A Cross-National Analysis," *American Journal of Sociology*, 73 (January 1968), 400–16.

[16] Elton F. Jackson and Harry J. Crockett, Jr., "Occupational Mobility in the United States," *American Sociological Review*, 29 (February 1964), 5–15; and Otis Dudley Duncan, "The Trend of Occupational Mobility in the United States," *American Sociological Review*, 30 (August 1965), 491–98.

have been skidders from jobs that at one time afforded them a comfortable living and recognized status in the community.

Education and Mobility

There is general consensus that, in urban-industrial societies, education is the most important path to upward occupational mobility, although certainly not the only one. Blau and Duncan conclude from their investigation that "the proportion of men who experience some upward mobility increases steadily with education from a low of 12 percent for those reporting no schooling to a high of 76 percent for those who have gone beyond college."[17] Almost half of the men in their sample having less than five years of schooling remained on the same occupational level as their fathers. This positive relationship between upward mobility and the amount of formal education does not hold as consistently in the case of downward mobility. Although laborers usually have limited education, they do not experience much downward mobility because they are already at the bottom and have no direction in which to move except "up" or "out."

By the 1970's the amount of formal education of skilled workmen in the United States approached that of clerical and sales personnel. "As this assimilation of life styles proceeds," in the opinion of Mayer, "the traditional social distinction between white collar and manual occupations, never as sharp in the United States as in Europe, is becoming increasingly blurred. . . . If these trends continue, and there is no reason to assume otherwise at the present time, the class structure of American society will once again become predominantly middle class in the near future."[18]

Conditions of Mobility

The real test of vertical occupational mobility is the permanence of the shift. In a study of career mobility in Oakland, California, Lipset and Bendix found that the greatest amount of shifting from manual to nonmanual work was to self-employment as owner of a business, although there was also some shifting into lower white collar and sales positions.[19] But such movement did not necessarily mean that the individual was permanently changing either his specific job or occupational class. Likewise, Chinoy found in a study of automobile workers in a large manufacturing city that many who became disenchanted by the

[17] Blau and Duncan, *op. cit.*, pp. 157–58.

[18] Kurt Mayer, "Changes in the Class Structure of the United States," *Transactions of the Third World Congress of Sociology* (1956).

[19] Lipset and Bendix, *op. cit.*

grim realities of the automotive plant left their jobs to try their hand at being their own boss as a small-business entrepreneur. However, most of them failed and returned to the assembly line.[20]

Occupational Aspirations and Mobility: The Kansas City Study

The occupational aspirations of younger persons have a direct relationship to their actual mobility in later years, although their aspirations do not necessarily coincide with their achievements. In a study by Gist and Bennett of high school students in Kansas City, about evenly divided between blacks and whites, levels of aspiration of the two groups were compared.[21] The method employed was to ascertain the level of aspiration of the students in relation to the occupational level of their fathers. A revised North-Hatt occupational prestige scale, representing 90 occupations, was used. This scale was divided into nine prestige levels. The occupation of each father and the aspired-to occupation of each student were placed in appropriate prestige categories. By this procedure a comparison was made of the aspiration level of the student with the actual occupation of his father. These comparisons are indicated in Table 15.4.

It is clear that the majority of students, both black and white, aspired to occupations above the prestige level of their fathers' work. Some three-fourths desired more prestigious jobs than those held by their fathers, but only 13 percent preferred jobs of lesser prestige, and about the same percentage wished to stay on the same level. There was no significant difference in this respect between blacks and whites. Surprisingly, the students' levels of actual *expectations* were strikingly similar to the distribution of their *aspirations*.

In the study, *social distance* was interpreted as the difference in prestige level of the father's occupation and the son's desired occupational level. If, for example, the son of a janitor (low-prestige score) aspired to become a lawyer (high-prestige score), the distance of mobility aspiration would be considerably greater than the distance if the son of a high school teacher aspired to become a lawyer. When the nine prestige levels were compressed into two levels, "low-moderate" and "high" mobility aspirations, the black students of both sexes exceeded the white students in the distance of occupational aspiration. This was, of course, partly because most of the black fathers themselves were in low-prestige occupations.

Whether the students, both black and white, were sufficiently motivated to actually rise above their fathers' occupational levels, or whether

[20] Ely Chinoy, *Automobile Workers and the American* Dream (1955).

[21] Noel P. Gist and William S. Bennett, Jr., "Aspirations of Negro and White Students," *Social Forces*, 42 (October 1963), 40–48.

TABLE 15.4: Percentage Distribution of 202 Negro and 250 White Male Students, by Occupational Aspiration Levels in Relation to Occupations of Fathers*

	Percent	
Level Aspired to	Black	White
Above prestige rank of father		
Six	6	4
Five	11	9
Four	15	8
Three	21	20
Two	12	18
One	9	13
Same rank as father	14	15
Below prestige rank of father		
One	7	9
Two	6	4

*About half of the students were female, but for this discussion only males are included. Father-daughter comparisons were rather similar to those of males.

their aspirations were fantasy, or at least unrealistic, cannot be ascertained until they have been actually placed occupationally. On the basis of available evidence, though, it seems likely that the level of aspiration of many young persons will not be realized, and this holds true especially for disadvantaged persons such as the blacks. The evidence derived from this study, however, does not square with conclusions from various other studies, which indicate that the level of aspiration is lower for children of disadvantaged and low-income families than for those in families on the middle and upper class levels. But for the most part the other studies employ a different research method.[22]

Intergenerational Mobility

Inheritance and Mobility in the United States

In their comprehensive study of occupational mobility, Blau and Duncan[23] obtained a sample of some 20,700 male respondents from 20 to 64 years of age in the American labor force in 1962. The respondents were classified in 17 occupational categories, similar to the major census

[22] See especially William H. Sewell, A. O. Haller, and Murray A. Strauss, "Social Status and Educational and Occupational Aspirations," *American Sociological Review*, 22 (February 1957), 67–73.
[23] Blau and Duncan, *op. cit.*

classification, except for additional subcategories.[24] Data were obtained on the occupations of the fathers when the respondents were 16 years old, and on the occupations of the respondents at the time of the interview. Relevant data were also obtained on education, race, national origins, migrations, family life, and so on. From the data it was possible for Blau and Duncan to calculate the flow of manpower, both into and away from occupational groups, and also to determine the extent of occupational inheritance. Table 15.5, showing the upward and downward mobility for seven of the 17 occupational classes, is adapted from more detailed tabulations of the Blau and Duncan study.

TABLE 15.5: Intergenerational Mobility from Fathers' Occupational Class to Sons' Class, 1962, for Males 25-64, by Percentages*

Fathers' Occupational Class	Sons' Occupational Class						
	1	2	6	8	11	14	16
1 Professional (self-employed)	**14.5**	3.9	0.8	0.3	0.3	0.2	0.5
2 Professional (salaried)	7.0	**9.5**	3.8	1.6	2.1	1.4	0.3
6 Clerical	4.9	7.3	**4.5**	2.9	1.2	1.5	0.0
8 Craftsmen (manufacturing)	3.8	8.3	5.7	**12.0**	6.2	4.5	0.5
11 Operatives (manufacturing)	5.2	6.4	7.5	12.9	**13.7**	14.5	1.2
14 Laborers (manufacturing)	0.0	1.0	1.3	2.6	3.2	**5.9**	0.6
16 Farmers (except laborers)	11.2	10.8	18.3	20.1	26.6	29.5	**82.0**

*The 10 other occupational classes were omitted in this table for reasons of space. If all 17 occupational classes were included, here, the total percentages in each column would be 100.
SOURCE: Adapted from Peter M. Blau and Otis Dudley Duncan, *The American Occupational Structure* (1967), Table 2.8, p. 39.

One striking aspect of the data is the relatively large percentage of sons recruited from the farming class—over 10 percent of these in each of the other six occupations. The percentages from farm origins increased, however, from 11.2 in the professional class to 29.5 in the laborers-in-manufacturing group. The massive outflow from farm background into predominantly urban occupations is in contrast to the mere trickle from nonfarm occupations into farming. Indeed, over four-fifths of those engaged in farming were sons of farmers (Column 16).

The bold face figures, running diagonally across the table from upper left to lower right, indicate the percentage of sons at the time of the study who were in the same occupational class as their fathers. Figures above the diagonal indicate the percentage of sons in each class who had moved downward in the occupational hierarchy from their fathers'

[24] The categories were arranged in what might be considered a prestige hierarchy.

class. Percentages below the diagonal indicate those who were upwardly mobile from the class of origin. Data for the entire table suggest that the overall trend toward upward intergenerational mobility exceeds downward mobility.

Of the 17 occupational classes in the Blau and Duncan survey, the percentage of occupied persons who had moved upward from the class of origin was greater in 12 of the occupational categories, while the proportion who had moved downward from the parental occupation and into their present class was lower in five. The five classes in which the downward flow, from parental to present occupation, was greater than the upward flow were the service occupations, laborers in manufacturing, other laborers, farmers, and farm laborers. Of course, there was no upward movement into the farm labor category because this occupation itself was at the bottom of the occupational structure. Moreover, the upward flow into the farmer class was small because the only recruitment from a lower income class was from farm labor. In the service occupations, however, over half of the occupied persons had moved downward as compared with about one-third who had moved upward, with eight percent remaining in the occupational class of origin. On the other hand, over four-fifths of the self-employed professionals had moved into this class from lower levels, with only one-seventh following in the vocational footsteps of their fathers.

Occupational Inheritance and Mobility in Great Britain

A study made in Great Britain by Glass and his associates provides a picture of intergenerational occupational inheritance and mobility that may be compared with mobility patterns in the United States. It must be noted, however, that the occupational categories in the two studies are not strictly comparable, although the occupational classes are so arranged as to suggest a status hierarchy.

In the British sample, for example, three-fourths of the unskilled laborers had moved downward from the parental class, while one-fourth remained in the same class of origin. What appears here to be very high downward mobility stems partly from the absence of upward mobility into the unskilled class because that class is already at the bottom of the structure. In the case of semiskilled workers, three-fourths had moved down to this level from the class of origin, about one-seventh had moved up, and one-fourth were in the same class as their fathers. Among the skilled workers, one-half were in the parental class, about one-fifth had moved down from a higher level, and almost one-third were recruited from the occupational class (semiskilled and unskilled) of the fathers. For each of the four classes on the middle and higher levels, however, the proportion that had moved upward from levels below their class of

TABLE 15.6: Percentage Distribution of 3,497 British Sons by Occupational Status in Relation to the Occupational Class of Their Fathers

Fathers' Occupational Class*	Sons' Occupational Class						
	1	2	3	4	5	6	7
1 Professional and high administrative	**48.5**	11.9	7.9	1.7	1.3	1.0	0.5
2 Managerial and executive	15.5	**25.2**	10.3	3.9	2.2	1.4	0.7
3 Nonmanual (higher grade)	11.7	22.0	**19.7**	14.4	18.6	3.9	5.0
4 Nonmanual (lower grade)	10.7	12.6	17.6	**24.0**	15.6	10.8	7.5
5 Skilled and routine nonmanual	13.6	22.6	34.5	40.3	**50.0**	43.5	44.6
6 Semiskilled manual	0.0	3.8	5.8	8.7	12.5	**24.1**	16.7
7 Unskilled manual	0.0	1.9	4.2	7.0	9.8	15.3	**25.0**
	100%	100%	100%	100%	100%	100%	100%
	(103)	(159)	(330)	(459)	(1429)	(593)	(424)

SOURCE: D. V. Glass and J. R. Hall, "Social Mobility in Great Britain: A Study of Inter-Generation Changes in Status," in D. V. Glass et al., Social Mobility in Britain (1954), Table 2, p. 183.

origin exceeded 50 percent in all instances. Possibly this is because the middle classes are more strongly motivated to move upward in the occupational structure, or even because there may be more opportunities for them to obtain jobs higher up.

American and British Mobility Compared

A comparison of American and British occupational mobility can only be very general because of differences in the size of the samples, dates when the surveys were conducted, and, most importantly, the different occupational categories constructed by the researchers. For example, when only seven categories are used, as in the case of the British study, a higher percentage of workers would be in the same occupational class as their fathers than was true of the American sample in which 17 classes were constructed. Also, the hierarchical arrangement in the American survey was based on median income and educational level in each of the 17 categories in 1962, whereas the ranking in the British study was based on status or prestige assessments by a panel of judges. With these differences in mind, we will compare the British and American intergenerational mobility patterns. Some of the American data we shall refer to may be found only in the detailed table in the Blau and Duncan analysis.

One striking similarity between the American and British data is the strong pattern of upward intergenerational mobility in both countries.

And in both, the occupational elevator also runs downward, and this movement is particularly pronounced in the lower levels of the occupational structure. In both countries there is a sizable inflow to present occupations from both directions, from above and below the level of origin.

As in the American situation, the flow from the lowest to the highest occupational classes in the British study is very limited. Actually, none of the British personnel in the elitist professional and high administrative class were drawn from the unskilled or semiskilled classes of origin, and only about six percent in Class 2, managerial and executive, had unskilled or semiskilled fathers. Similarly, less than one percent of the sons in the unskilled and semiskilled occupations had fathers on the top level, and only about two percent were from families on the managerial and executive level. Clearly, there is almost no mobility, upward or downward, between the top and bottom levels of the occupational structure in Great Britain.

The situation in the United States is similar, although there appears to be slightly more mobility between the top and bottom levels. There were no persons in the self-employed professional class whose fathers were factory laborers, only three-tenths of one percent of the self-employed professionals had fathers who were farm laborers, and one percent were from other unskilled parents. In fact, each of the four highest income classes (self-employed professionals, salaried professionals, managers, and salesmen) drew less than one percent of their personnel from the farm labor class. Similarly, less than one percent of the unskilled sons were drawn from each of the four highest occupational status classes. The distance from top to bottom, so far as mobility is concerned, flies in the face of the great American myth that "everybody has a chance to be President."

In the British study, about half of the professional and high administrative persons had moved into this category from lower levels as compared with over four-fifths of the self-employed American professionals. Or, viewing the data from another angle, almost half of the British on the top level were in the same occupational category as their fathers, compared with about one-seventh of the self-employed Americans. Although the British and American occupational categories are not strictly comparable, the data do suggest, but do not prove, that upward mobility into the top levels is greater in the United States than in Great Britain. Likewise, the data also suggest, but do not prove, that occupational inheritance, the tendency for sons to remain on the same occupational level as their fathers, is more pronounced in Great Britain than in the United States.

Summary

In this chapter we have considered various features of an occupational system and of the changes that have been influenced by urbanization and industrialization. Among these features are the trend toward specialization and professionalization of occupations, the organization of work, the psychosocial aspects of occupations, some of the main currents or trends in occupational systems, the changing occupational roles of women and minority peoples, and occupational mobility in industrial societies. It is self-evident that the occupational system—work—figures importantly in every society, whether urban or rural, industrial or nonindustrial, even though there are innumerable variations of work patterns. But people do not live by bread alone, nor are their lives normally committed entirely to obtaining that bread. We now turn to a consideration of the other side of people's lives—their leisure time and how they spend it. The phenomenon of leisure provides a measure of the character of a civilization. The pervasive changes associated with urbanization and industrialization have had profound social and psychological ramifications for people everywhere.

Selected Bibliography

BOOKS

Becker, Howard S. *et. al.*, *Boys in White*. Chicago: University of Chicago Press, 1961.

Blau, Peter M., and Otis Dudley Duncan, *The American Occupational Structure*. New York: Wiley, 1967.

Caplow, Theodore, *The Sociology of Work*. Minneapolis: University of Minnesota Press, 1954.

Chinoy, Ely, *Automobile Workers and the American Dream*. Garden City, N. Y.: Doubleday, 1955.

Cole, Robert E., *Japanese Blue Collar: The Changing Tradition*. Berkeley and Los Angeles: University of California Press, 1971.

Geertz, Clifford, *Peddlers and Princes: Social Change and Economic Modernization in Two Indonesian Towns*. Chicago: University of Chicago Press, 1963.

Hall, Richard H., *Occupations and the Social Structure*. Englewood Cliffs, N.J.: Prentice-Hall, 1969.

Hughes, Everett C., *Men and Their Work*. New York: The Free Press, 1959.

Lipset, Seymour Martin, and Reinhard Bendix, *Social Mobility in Industrial Society*. Berkeley and Los Angeles: University of California Press, 1960.

Mills, C. Wright, *White Collar*. New York: Oxford University Press, 1956.

Simon, Yves, *Work, Society, and Culture*. New York: Fordham University Press, 1971.

Stern, James L., and David B. Johnson, *Blue to White Collar Mobility*. Madison: University of Wisconsin Press, 1968.

Taylor, Lee, *Occupational Sociology*. New York: Oxford University Press, 1968.

Udy, Stanley, *Work in Traditional and Modern Society*. Englewood Cliffs, N.J.: Prentice-Hall, 1970.

Vollmer, Howard M., and Donald L. Mills, eds., *Professionalization*. Englewood Cliffs, N.J.: Prentice-Hall, 1966.

Whyte, William H., Jr., *The Organization Man*. New York: Simon and Schuster, 1956.

Work in America. Report of a Special Task Force to the Secretary of Health, Education, and Welfare prepared under the auspices of the W. E. Upjohn Institute for Employment Research. Cambridge: MIT Press, 1973.

ARTICLES

Adams, Stuart, "Origins of American Occupational Elites," *American Journal of Sociology*, 62 (January 1957), 360–69.

Broom, Leonard, and F. L. Jones, "Career Mobility in Three Societies: Italy, Australia, and the United States," *American Sociological Review*, 34 (October 1969), 650–58.

Campbell, J. T., and L. H. Belcher, "Changes in Non-White Employment, 1960–1966," *Phylon*, 28 (Winter 1967), 325–37.

Cutright, Phillips, "Occupational Inheritance: A Cross-National Analysis," *American Journal of Sociology*, 73 (January 1968), 400–16.

Duncan, Otis Dudley, "The Trend of Occupational Mobility in the United States," *American Sociological Review*, 30 (August 1965), 491–98.

Hughes, Everett C., "The Humble and the Proud: Comparative Study of Occupations," *Sociological Quarterly*, 11 (Spring 1970), 147–56.

Jackson, Elton F., and Harry J. Crockett, "Occupational Mobility in the United States," *American Sociological Review*, 29 (February 1964), 1–15.

Lieberson, Stanley, and Glenn V. Fuguitt, "Negro-White Occupational Differences in the Absence of Discrimination," *American Journal of Sociology*, 73 (September 1967), 188–201.

Porter, John, "The Future of Occupational Mobility," *American Sociological Review*, 33 (February 1968), 5–19.

Perucci, C. C., "Social Origins, Education, and Career Mobility," *American Sociological Review*, 35 (June 1970), 451–63.

Rhodes, A. L., "Residential Distribution and Occupational Stratification in Paris and Chicago," *Sociological Quarterly*, 10 (Winter 1969), 106–12.

Thielbar, G., and S. D. Feldman, "Occupational Stereotypes and Prestige," *Social Forces*, (September 1969), 64–72.

Wilensky, Harold L., The Professionalization of Everyone," *American Journal of Sociology*, 70 (September 1964), 137–59.

16 • Work, Leisure, and Life Style

Work as a means to survival has been a central activity of mankind throughout history, and such is still the lot of the great masses of the world's people. Yet all peoples at all times have devoted part of their time to activities or interests that are not directly a means to survival or occupational achievement. The amount of time given to such activities or interests will vary from one individual, community, or society to another. In some societies an elite minority may be relieved of the necessity to work, riding on the shoulders, as it were, of the masses who must labor to support themselves as well as the leisured classes. But with the urban-industrial revolution, a fairly recent phenomenon, the pressures of work have been eased for many persons wherever these revolutionary changes have occurred. This is especially apparent in the urbanized countries of the world; in agrarian societies the survival demands of work have been only slightly altered for the toiling masses, although even these countries usually support an elitist minority that has the choice of working or not working for a livelihood.

In this chapter we shall discuss leisure mainly within the context of an urbanized society. Some comparisons with nonindustrial societies will be presented, and at times references will be made to historical developments of the culture of leisure. We have not intended a global treatment, but material will be used wherever it is relevant to leisure in countries other than the United States. In this respect, it should be noted, major leisure trends in urban-industrial societies are paralleled in predominantly agrarian societies, especially in the major cities.

The Nature of Leisure

Leisure as we define it here is the time an individual is free from work or other duties so that he may use such time for relaxation, diversion, social achievement, or personal development. Like many other definitions, this one does not clearly demarcate leisure from nonleisure, or leisure activity from activity that is obligatory; indeed, what is often considered leisure-time behavior may be, in part, a response to social pressures or powerful inner drives, and may not, therefore, be a preferred form of behavior.

An individual's behavior as a wage earner, for example, is clearly not a leisure-time activity, even though it may afford relaxation and other satisfactions. But these satisfactions are by-products of his work, not ends in themselves. If an individual returns from his place of employment at the end of the day to toil in his garden or workshop, this could be defined as leisure activity in terms of the motives involved. If his purpose is primarily the augmentation of his income by producing vegetables or making some product to sell, such activity could hardly be considered leisure; but if he undertakes it primarily for enjoyment, either by himself or with his family, then it is a leisure activity. Even so, a clear-cut distinction is hardly possible since complex motives may be involved in the same activity.

Some activities outside the sphere of work may be mandatory and therefore marginal to leisure. Church attendance or participation in civic affairs may be obligatory; hence the time so devoted is not, strictly speaking, a leisure activity, although the personal responses may be the same as those in voluntary participation. If such participation carries no reward other than personal gratification, and if such participation is voluntary, then it may be considered a leisure-time "pursuit."

Leisure-time activities assume a multiplicity of forms. Some are home-centered, others are community-centered. Some are individual activities, others are group-oriented. Some are undertaken under the auspices of government organizations, others are strictly private, either commercial or noncommercial. Some are built into existing institutions, such as schools or churches, others are completely detached from any institutional moorings. Some are spectator-oriented, others are participant-centered. Many are age-graded, or sex-linked, or characteristic of a particular social stratum. Viewed in perspective, leisure-time activities represent a complex of organizations, behavior patterns, and material equipment.

Work, Play, and Clock Time

The concept of time has been revolutionized by the invention and application of the mechanical "timepiece." Before its invention, time was perceived mainly by the changes from day to night or vice versa, by seasonal changes, or by changes in weather and temperature. Doubtless this is true today of many people living in simple folk communities or on farms removed from urban influences. But the invention of the mechanical clock made possible a more precise calculation of time, and as the device became widely used for various purposes it profoundly altered the ways of life of the people who became dependent upon it.

In modern urban society "work time" for the vast majority of persons (except possibly farmers, independent professionals, and proprietors) is tightly geared to the clock. The synchronization of work time and activity in the modern bureaucracy is possible only when most of the workers begin and end their work day or week at a signal from the clock. Punching a time clock and being checked with a stop watch are a daily rite in many work places. The mass-production factory system in which human activities and machines are orchestrated according to a specific time schedule concretely illustrates the way modern society is geared to the functioning of the mechanical timepiece.

By the same token, much "free time" is dominated by "clock time." One must be at a movie, or a club meeting, or church services, or a luncheon or dinner, or at the doctor's office, or catch a bus to work at a specified time. Failure to obey the dictates of the clock may mean trouble, or at least inconvenience. The number of clock demands is endless, both in nonwork and in work, the price exacted by an urban community. As de Grazia comments: "Clock time first governs work time (one sees the same happening today in countries moving toward industrialization), while social life holds to the old pattern. Later the clock's hands sweep over life outside of work too. . . . Free time takes its bow, like work decked out in clock time."[1]

Differentials of Leisure
Activities and Interests

One of the revolutionary changes in urban-industrial society has been the emergence of a mass culture whose components represent an infinite variety of leisure activities in which people may participate in ways of their own choosing. And in these societies it is the cities that have provided most of the opportunities, facilities, and resources for mass leisure and the mass consumption of symbolic objects related to leisure.

Another revolutionary change in urban-industrial society is the transformation of values concerning leisure. That is, the pleasures accruing from leisure-time activities become legitimate objectives in life and not merely a means to another objective, in contrast to the earlier Protestant ethic in which free time was supposed to be used for rest and recuperation in preparation for the work tasks ahead. Thus, leisure has tended to become relatively autonomous, detached in many ways, and for many people, from work roles.[2] Whereas earlier Western society was work-

[1] Sebastian de Grazia, *Of Time, Work, and Leisure* (1962), pp. 305–6.
[2] See especially Kenneth Roberts, *Leisure* (1970), ch. 6.

centered, today's urban-industrial society has become increasingly leisure-centered, at least for workers who find more personal fulfillment in leisure-time activity than in their jobs. For such persons leisure becomes the dominant life style.

Scene at a Paris street cafe illustrates a leisure-time activity widespread in Europe. Patrons may linger for hours over simple refreshments without harassment from the proprietor. (Michel Cosson)

Leisure Publics

In virtually all societies there are special leisure publics. In traditional agrarian societies the number or variety may be small, but in modern urban-industrial societies the differentiation of leisure interests and activities has created many leisure publics, some of which are very large. Contemporary popular culture in, say, music has attracted vast numbers of devotees, predominantly young adults. The throngs that attended pop music festivals such as Woodstock and Watkins Glen attest to the magnitude of the pop music public. Pop religious revivals featuring such folk heroes as Billy Graham and Oral Roberts have a comparable appeal. But tastes differ, and in some kinds of leisure the publics represent a minority, even within the segment of society in which the

433

Mass recreation is an important leisure activity in urban-industrial societies and a source of jobs and income. Miami's municipal bandshell (top) and Disneyworld, Florida (bottom). (Miami News Bureau—top; George W. Gardner—bottom)

members of a public tend to be concentrated. A survey by the British Broadcasting Corporation in England reported, for example, that 16 percent of the respondents claimed to be interested in motor-car racing, 22 percent in classical music, 17 percent in church attendance, 16 percent in tennis, 13 percent in ballet, and so on.[3]

The Rhythm of Leisure and Its Democratization

With the rise of urban-industrial society various changes have occurred in the place of leisure in the lives of people. In all societies the use of free time has tended to be synchronized with various patterns of life resulting from rhythms of work, seasonal changes, daytime and nighttime, and the like. But the specific use of leisure time, and of the values associated with it, has undergone many changes, while retaining its rhythmic character. For the urban worker the rhythm of leisure is closely synchronized with the rhythm of work as well as the rhythm of daylight and darkness.

One conspicuous trend in the urban-industrial context is the democratization of leisure in the sense that most persons have access to almost every form of leisure regardless of their station in life, providing, of course, they are not financially or physically handicapped. This trend is a counterpart of the democratization of citizenship, education, and political participation. By contrast, in medieval England and other countries of that era, hunting and jousting were exclusively upper class activities which the lower classes were prohibited from participating in. The various social strata each had their own designated free-time activities.[4] Even in traditional societies today, recreation may be more closely linked to the individual's station in life than it is in urban-industrial societies.

Leisure and Institutions

As leisure has become more differentiated and institutionalized it has continued to maintain a close relationship with other institutions and organizations. Leisure is, of course, the counterpart of work, and it becomes meaningless when not viewed in that context. But it has, in many ways, an independent existence. Although the kind of work one does, and the time and place spent on the job, may affect the way the worker spends his leisure time, it does not necessarily follow that one's

[3] W. A. Belson, *The Impact of Television: Methods and Findings in Program Research* (1967).

[4] Roberts, *op. cit.*, p. 91.

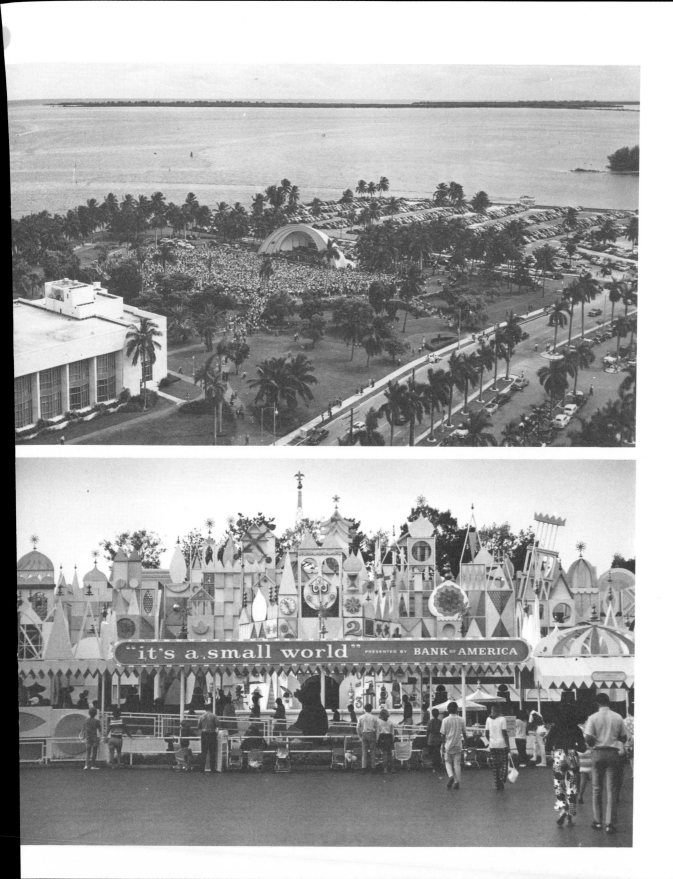

occupation determines his leisure activities and interests. Indeed, a worker's leisure interests may influence his choice of an occupation or his work performance. The success of labor unions in obtaining shorter work hours and time for vacations undoubtedly stems in part from the desire of workers to have more free time to use as they prefer.

This leisure ethos has been influential in bringing about other institutional changes. Many urban religious denominations have so expanded their programs that the church has become a recreational center quite as much as a place of collective worship. The school is no longer an institution limited to formal learning but is, in addition, a center of leisure activities. An important function of modern government—whether municipal, state, or national—is the provision of facilities for leisure and the regulation or supervision of the activities that take place at such facilities. The provision and maintenance of public parks and playgrounds is an important governmental function at all levels. Even the work establishment commonly maintains facilities for the leisure-time activities of its employees. These expanding institutional structures and functions have occurred because leisure interests rival interests in work, worship, and formal learning.

Leisure has also become institutionalized and differentiated in its own right, giving rise to a proliferation of specialized occupations concerned with the management and planning of leisure activities and the training of performers. Innumerable organizations such as social clubs exist exclusively or primarily to serve the leisure interests of their members. Many occupations directly concerned with entertainment such as talent and booking agencies are organized for the benefit of musicians, actors, and lecturers. Other organizations exist to serve the diverse leisure interests of people who themselves may be differentiated by age, sex, or social class—persons interested in tennis, golf, hobbies, bowling, boating, scouting, stamp-collecting, fishing, camping, and so on. This trend is present in many urbanized countries like England, Germany, Canada, Japan, and Scandinavia, and even in semi-industrialized countries like Mexico or Argentina.

The Decline of Work Time and Increasing Leisure Time—An Illusion?

During the past century the amount of time spent at work has declined sharply in urban-industrial societies, particularly among certain segments of the urban population. A century or so ago the average work week was about 70 hours long. Before the end of the nineteenth century a decline in work time had begun; today, in many countries the urban labor force generally works, on the average, about 40 hours a week. The eight-hour day and five-day week have become widely accepted in the non-agricultural sector of urban-industrial countries, and even in many cities of predominantly agrarian societies.[5]

The relatively short work week is an *average* which does not apply to all occupational groups. In the 1960's some 15 million employed persons, or about 20 percent of the total, were working 48 or more hours weekly.[6] These included three categories of persons employed for extended work weeks: (1) those who are genuinely dedicated to their work, preferring to stay on the job than having more free time; (2) those who have heavy job responsibilities and are required to work long hours; and (3) those who are seriously in need of more income, commonly young married males in low-paying occupations. The first two categories mainly consist of professional or managerial personnel. In the third category long work weeks are often the result of overtime work. A report in the 1960's indicated that almost 30 percent of the nonagricultural employees in the United States work overtime on a single job.[7]

Many persons hold two or more jobs—"moonlighting" as it is called. De Grazia estimates that in 1959 some 3 million workers, or about 5 percent of the labor force, in the United States moonlighted an average of 12 hours a week during weekends, in evenings after the regular work day, in the daytime if their regular jobs involved night work, or during holidays or vacation periods.[8] Probably the number of moonlighters is underenumerated since this practice may be either illegal, in the case of public employees, or discouraged by employers.[9] Most moonlighters are employed primarily in white collar occupations, and their secondary or tertiary jobs often are in such work as tutoring, selling insurance or real estate, or sales-clerking in evenings or on weekends. Whatever the nature of the extended work week, whether by overtime or moonlighting, the fact remains that the additional income often makes possible more leisure than otherwise would be within financial reach, although it clearly reduces the amount of time available for purely leisure activities.

The increase in "spare" time has been due in part to increased efficiency in the system of production whereby workers can increase their output while reducing their work-hours. This technological efficiency means that fewer employees in a factory or on a farm can produce all that is required by those who have the money to buy the

[5] For a detailed discussion of trends in work and free time on the international scene, see Archibald A. Evans, "Work and Leisure, 1919–1969," *International Labor Review*, 99 (January 1969), 35–59.

[6] Peter Henle, "Leisure and the Long Work Week," *Monthly Labor Review*, 89 (July 1966), 721–27.

[7] James Wetzel, "Overtime Hours and Premium Pay," *Monthly Labor Review*, 90 (May 1967), 41–45.

[8] de Grazia, *op. cit.*, pp. 70–71.

[9] Reginald Carter, "The Myth of Increasing Non-Work vs. Work Activities," *Social Problems*, 18 (Summer 1970), 62–64.

products. For several decades, however, there has been an increasing proportion of workers in white collar occupations—clerical workers, sales people, professionals, technicians, and the like—who, by the very nature of their work, cannot increase their output as much as factory workers, miners, or farm hands. It may well be that the amount of free time—freedom from the job—cannot be reduced significantly in the foreseeable future for most employed workers.[10]

Obligatory Nonwork

Much free time is taken up with obligatory activities not directly associated with a regular occupation. There may be chores to do around the house or apartment—mowing the lawn, repairing household equipment, running errands, shopping for food and other essentials, taking care of children, and the like. For the employed woman, managing a household usually takes considerable time and effort beyond the hours spent on a regular job. Beyond these obligatory activities there are various demands and pressures to support and participate in civic, social, political, religious, or occupational organizations. Even the journey to and from work in a large city commonly takes a block of time estimated at from 10 to 20 percent of the hours worked.

In his vivid description of life styles characterizing the "exurbanites," residents of an upper middle class commuting suburb near New York, Spectorsky noted that the long weekends, free from work obligations, are a continuing round of parties and other enervating activities which are virtually mandatory for social acceptance in the prevailing status system.[11] If travel-to-work time is counted as a phase of work activity, the free time for employed exurbanites is strictly limited during the week. And although their wives may have ample money to afford servants and modern household appliances, as well as large homes, most of their time is taken up with a variety of demanding tasks such as managing a household in a manner appropriate to status-striving families, driving the husband to the commuting train in the morning and meeting him in the evening, transporting small children to and from school or social gatherings, attending meetings of the PTA and other organizations, taking part in various financial drives or in local political activities, and so on. For them, leisure is something of an illusion.

Similar patterns of leisure-time usage prevail in Crestwood Heights, an upper middle class suburb of Toronto, where both leisure and work are geared to a fairly fixed time schedule. Unscheduled "loafing" is not considered an appropriate way to spend leisure time.

[10] See especially Gilbert Burck, "There'll be Less Leisure Than You Think," *Fortune*, 81 (March 1970), 86–89.

[11] A. C. Spectorsky, *The Exurbanites* (1955).

Crestwooders nevertheless agree that the man works to have "time off," and that when he leaves his male environment of harsh exacting deadlines to return to his home and family, he expects and is expected to relax. Family life, however, is not entirely oriented around the father's work and leisure. His wife has her own activities outside the home which are carefully scheduled; and both have, as well, joint social engagements which bear on his career. The children have their school—which demands punctuality—scheduled appointments with dentist and dancing teacher, and numerous social activities. Home life is indeed often hectic, although there is for many a measure of quiet and relaxation in performing simple family duties and acts of mutual aid.[12]

Obligatory nonwork, like regular work, may afford satisfaction to the individual who performs the assigned or chosen roles, providing relaxation and emotional or intellectual gratification in full measure. On the other hand, he may view it as drudgery, a waste of time. For those who are enmeshed in the network of obligatory nonwork activities there may be a mix of satisfaction and dissatisfaction. Free time nonactivity, or sheer idleness, for many, is preferable to activity. But the ethos of Western society, at least the United States, sets a high value on activity rather than idleness. Continued idleness, unless it is enforced by circumstance, is therefore more a sin than a virtue. The frenetic search of many for "happiness," for "fun," for "thrills" seems to support this conclusion. In recent years the ethic of hard work has had little appeal for many persons, especially young adults who are disillusioned with the existing system, and who have adopted a different life style and system of values.

The amount of free time to be spent as the individual chooses appears, then, to be less than the popular notion would have us believe, especially in the urban middle and upper classes. Yet with all the restrictions on the use of free time, most urban dwellers undoubtedly have more leisure time than previous generations had. The institutionalization of leisure activities has at least afforded forms of leisure and time to enjoy them unknown to their ancestors. In most countries, even in the cities of nonindustrial societies, the short work week and the annual vacation of two or more weeks are a part of the work-leisure calendar.

The Uneven Occupational
Distribution of Leisure

The farm owner-operator may himself decide how much free time he can take and when it can be used, subject, of course, to the dictates of the seasons and the weather. But the urban worker in a factory or office usually has such decisions made for him by institutional managers. If he is a salaried or wage-earning employee, the amount of free time for vacations, holidays, or weekends is decided by established policy. Fur-

[12] John R. Seeley, R. Alexander Sim, and E. W. Loosley, *Crestwood Heights* (1956), pp. 64–65.

thermore, the termination of one's work career by formal retirement may impose upon him months or years of enforced free time for which he may be unprepared psychologically and economically, a problem today for millions of retired workers. For most of them, meaningful gainful employment is out of the question, and they may have no psychological or cultural resources, or physical strength, to make satisfactory use of their new-found leisure. Just waiting to die is not very rewarding. Many are, as Wilensky puts it, leisure-stricken as well as poverty-stricken.[13] Inasmuch as the age of mandatory retirement for most urban employees is between ages 60 and 70, the average life span means 10 or 15 years of free time for many elderly persons.

But farm operators, small-business proprietors, and independent professionals do not ordinarily face a cutoff date for retirement. They may work as long as they wish, or until failing health or waning strength make work withdrawal necessary. Even when they do retire their disengagement from work may be gradual rather than abrupt, and adjustment to increased free-time circumstances may therefore be relatively easy. Another source of enforced free time is unemployment, which weighs heavily on manual and low-level white collar workers, and even salaried professionals.

The chief beneficiaries of free time in urban-industrial society are salaried white collar workers and wage-earners, especially organized blue collar workers. Manual or clerical workers in the city may close their minds as well as the door on the job at day's end, and have considerable free time to do other things. But the professional or executive may have less of this freedom; he is likely to work longer hours and "take the job home with him in a brief case" at the end of the day. "It seems likely," writes Wilensky, "that we are headed toward an organization of work in which a small group of executives, merchants, professional experts, and politicians labor hard and long to control and service the masses, who in turn are 'taking it easy' on a progressively shorter work week, in jobs that deemphasize brawn and native shrewdness and play up discipline, reliability, and training."[14] However, the professionals or administrators ordinarily do not punch a time-clock or are not required to maintain a pace set by a machine, and their vacation periods, when they do take them, may be considerably longer than those of clerical or blue collar employees.

[13] Harold L. Wilensky, "The Uneven Distribution of Leisure," *Social Problems*, 9 (Summer 1961), 55–56.
[14] Harold L. Wilensky, "Work, Careers, and Social Integration," *International Social Science Journal*, 12 (1960), 558.

Work and Leisure:
Integration or Polarization?

In traditional or folk societies leisure activities are closely integrated with work. Ceremonial dancing, singing, and feasting are often symbolically related to the tasks of planting, harvesting, hunting, or herding. Wax comments on the fusion of work and leisure in an African tribe: "I do not believe that any Bushman could tell us—or would be interested in telling us—which part of his activity was work and which was play."[15] And, as Parker observes, in many tribal or folk societies work and leisure are not differentiated; such economic activities as hunting or market-going also have a recreational function, and often work tasks are done conjointly as the participants engage in singing or story-telling while at work.[16] In these societies recreational activities such as feasting or ceremonial dances are held on special days and are often related to the dominant work patterns such as the harvesting of crops. In rural America of an earlier day neighboring farmers often made a social occasion out of a collective work undertaking.

This work-play relationship also exists among modern urban workers and manifests itself in various ways. Participating in social activities with colleagues in a labor union or trade association is a common leisure activity, and the same applies to leisure time spent with work colleagues in which the major topic of conversation is the work situation. In some occupations there is a convergence of work and free time to the extent that the workers form a sociological community in which there is a sharing of both work and leisure activities. This is more likely to be true of the professions or other occupations in which the working personnel are closely identified with their vocation.[17]

In a middle class suburb of Tokyo, as Vogel notes, businessmen and physicians have long working days, but their shops or offices are near or in their own homes so that they are able to find rest and relaxation during periods between waiting on customers or seeing patients.[18] Furthermore, professional or business colleagues in Tokyo may engage in a range of leisure-time activities such as drinking parties, group games, and trips. Such colleagueship is also common among manual workers who may have favorite hangouts such as bars or coffeehouses which they frequent together on their way home from work.[19] The "coffee break" in offices or

---

[15] R. H. Wax, "Free Time in Other Cultures," in W. Donahue *et al.*, eds., *Free Time: Challenge to Later Maturity* (1958), p. 4.

[16] Stanley Parker, *The Future of Work and Leisure* (1971), p. 39.

[17] See especially the study of London architects and Cambridge railway workers by Graeme Salaman, "Two Occupational Communities: Examples of a Remarkable Convergence of Work and Nonwork," *Sociological Review*, 19 (August 1971), 389–407.

[18] Ezra Vogel, *Japan's New Middle Class* (1965), pp. 27–28.

[19] *Ibid.*, p. 104.

shops, customary in many cities of the West, provides an opportunity for work associates to find brief respite from their daily tasks. Proprietors or managers of modern industrial and commercial establishments commonly provide recreational facilities for their employees, presumably as a means of strengthening morale among the workers and thereby improving labor-management relations and increasing work efficiency.

But just as the place of residence in American cities is usually separated geographically from the place of work, a situation commonly different from that existing in agricultural communities or societies, so has the locus of leisure-time activities tended to become separated from the work site—separated not only in terms of space but also in terms of social values, interests, and interpersonal relations. Polarization of work and recreation has thus occurred in both spatial and behavioral terms.

Job Alienation and Leisure Time

Mounting evidence exists that many workers in urban-industrial societies are alienated from both their jobs and their employers. The sources of their estrangement are varied: pressure to keep up with the pace set by a machine, monotony of work, atomization of work tasks, unfavorable working conditions, tensions between management and workers, and disenchantment with the prospects of the future. The never-ending monotony of assembly-line work, the deadening repetition of simple tasks performed hour after hour, day after day, these and other situations have created a compelling desire among many to escape from the incessant grind. Sometimes the escape is merely fantasy in which the worker creates a dream world to his liking; often it is characterized by excessive absenteeism and collective protests; more often, perhaps, the worker finds surcease in free-time activities that afford relaxation, diversion, amusement, or excitement. Since a permanent escape may be difficult or impossible, temporary escapes over weekends, after-work evenings, holidays, or vacations may afford some relief from the pressures of the market place.

As Mills so graphically expressed it, "Each day men sell little pieces of their lives in order to buy them back each night and each weekend with the coin of 'fun.' With amusement, with love, with movies, with vicarious intimacy, they pull themselves into a sort of whole again, so that they are different men."[20] Their aim is to keep work and leisure as far apart as possible, to isolate themselves from the world of work until they return to it at the beginning of the next day or week or month. As we noted previously, earlier generations embracing the Protestant ethic viewed work and frugality as ends in themselves, with free time as an

---

[20] C. Wright Mills, *White Collar* (1951), p. 237.

Workers in industrial or other establishments in Chinese cities are expected to participate, as a group, in physical exercises, a feature of health programs imposed by the government. (Arthur W. Galston)

opportunity for rest and regeneration in preparation for another day or week of work. For many, the present-day ethic is the reverse: they view free time as an end in itself, and work as a means to that end.

What we have reported so far about alienation applies more particularly to those whose work is monotonous, grueling, and unrewarding. Studies indicate that work dissatisfaction and alienation are found less often in the professions and managerial occupations. A survey by Blauner, for example, supports this generalization.[21] When a national sample of respondents was asked what their course of action would be if they were to inherit enough money to live comfortably without working, 68 percent of the professionals said they would continue in their present work as compared with only 16 percent of the unskilled manual employees. Comparative studies, by Orzack and Dubin, of professional nurses and industrial workers revealed that, proportionally, four times as many nurses as workers gave work as their central life interest.[22]

[21] Robert Blauner, "Work Satisfaction and Industrial Trends in Modern Society," in Reinhard Bendix and Seymour Martin Lipset, eds., *Class, Status, and Power* (1966), p. 476.

[22] Louis Orzack, "Work as a 'Central Life Interest' of Professionals," *Social Problems*, (Fall 1959), 125–32; and Robert Dubin, "Industrial Workers' Worlds: A study of the Central Life Interests of Industrial Workers," *Urban Social Problems*, 3 (January 1956), 131–42.

Professionals and managers tend to view their work as a *career*, semiskilled or unskilled manual workers as a *job*.

The generalization about alienation from work and escapism into leisure-time activities by no means implies that this is the only, or necessarily the most important, source of alienation in urban society. Some persons are alienated from the church, others from their own families, still others from existing political institutions and processes, and perhaps even more from friends and associates. Some appear to be alienated from the whole of society, of which estrangement from work is only a part. Certainly the impersonal character of a bureaucratic system as it exists in the modern urban community commonly induces a sense of alienation among those who live or work in such a system.

Class Interests and Leisure Interests

Leisure time and its use have been defined, directed, and limited by technological developments, particularly in mass communication and transportation, but also in social organization. It is for this reason that leisure in modern urban-industrial society is strikingly different from leisure in a folk or peasant society, or even in some rural communities in industrial societies, although the pervasive influence of technology has altered even the leisure life style in the rural backwaters. Furthermore, mass communication and transportation have had a leveling effect within an urban-industrial society in the use of leisure time. The observations of French sociologist Georges Friedmann seem applicable to all countries of the Western world:

> Young workers, coming out of their factories at Paris, Frankfurt, or Milan, are likely to see the same cinema and television programs, hear on the radio the same variety shows, songs, and jazz records, and look at the same magazines as the sons (or daughters) of their foreman, engineer, or overseer, and middle-class adolescents in general. Workers are to be found more and more often, during their holidays with pay, frequenting the same organized holiday clubs, sunbathing on the same beaches as the middle classes.[23]

There are limits, of course, in this leveling process. While persons on different social-class and educational levels may have equal access to the "culture of leisure," and to a considerable extent share in it, they also manifest differences in tastes, interests, and values. The nature and extent of their participation in voluntary associations or in political activities, the kinds of entertainment they prefer or the literature they read, the extent to which they use libraries or museums, the kinds of

[23] Georges Friedmann, "Leisure and Technological Civilization," *International Social Science Journal*, 12 (1960), 517.

games or sports that interest them, the patterns of informal social life—all bear the imprint of class influence.

We have observed in Chapter 13 that middle and upper class persons are more inclined to participate in voluntary associations than working class persons, but that the latter spend proportionately more of their leisure time in informal visiting with relatives or neighbors.

In Chicago, for example, a study of leisure patterns revealed that the neighborhood tavern tended to be the workingman's recreational center, whereas the cocktail lounge, generally located in or near a commercial district, attracted patrons mainly from the middle or upper classes.[24] Similarly, a study of taverns in Queens and Nassau counties in metropolitan New York indicated that the patrons were mainly white collar or skilled manual workers, and that such professionals as teachers, lawyers, physicians, or ministers were conspicuously absent.[25] In Kansas City, Coleman and Neugarten observed that the various nonwork organizations such as social clubs, fraternal orders, and churches were structured in accordance with the interests and financial resources of people on different class levels.[26]

In a study of social-class differences in the use of leisure time in the Cleveland area, White observed that upper middle class adults engaged in more activities during a designated week than did those on the lower social levels.[27] But perhaps even more striking were the differences between the classes in the kinds of activities in which they participated. In the use of parks and playgrounds the rate per 100 was 1.6 for the upper middle class, 7.0 for the lower middle class, 12.2 for the upper lower class, and 23 for the lower lower class. This pattern was reversed for the use of libraries, participation in ethnic-racial organizations, and attendance at lecture-study groups. With respect to the use of commercial amusements the upper middle class had the lowest rate. White also found that time spent in activities related to television, radio, movies, and sports was almost twice as great for the upper lower class as for the upper middle category.

In a similar study of a metropolitan sample in Columbus, Ohio, Clarke found important class differences in the use made of leisure time.[28] Locating the respondents in five occupational categories ranked according to prestige, Clarke found that those in prestigious Category 1 participated most frequently in such activities as attending plays, concerts, and

[24] David Gottlieb, "The Neighborhood Tavern and Cocktail Lounge," *American Journal of Sociology*, 62 (May 1957), 559–62.

[25] Cara E. Richards, "City Taverns," *Human Organization*, 22 (Winter 1963–64), 262.

[26] Richard P. Coleman and Bernice L. Neugarten, *Social Status in the City* (1971).

[27] R. Clyde White, "Social Class Differences in the Use of Leisure," *American Journal of Sociology*, 61 (September 1955), 145–50.

[28] Alfred C. Clarke, "Leisure and Occupational Prestige," *American Sociological Review*, 21 (June 1956), 301–7.

lectures, visiting museums or art galleries, reading for pleasure, attending movies, entertaining at home, and playing bridge. On the lowest
prestige level, Category 5, leisure time was spent most frequently in
watching television, fishing, playing card games other than bridge,
attending outdoor movies and baseball games, driving or riding in a car
for pleasure, spending time at a tavern, and visiting a zoo.

On the basis of his research in Kansas City, Havighurst concluded that
the place of residence, whether in the central city or in a suburb, in a
single-family residence or an apartment, did not appreciably affect to
any great extent the leisure life style of persons in the same social class
and age bracket in that city.

An upper-middle-class man in his forties spends his leisure as follows: he
attends a luncheon club once a week; he plays golf in season and perhaps
handball; he spends a good deal of time on weekends looking after his lawn
and caring for his flowers. The upper-lower-class man of the same age goes
fishing on week-ends, and on vacation; he works around the house a good deal,
redecorating it and adding a new room at the back; he watches television
several hours each evening and on week-ends when he is not doing something
else.[29]

Working Class Leisure
in Suburbia

In his study of a working class suburb near San Francisco, Berger
challenges the stereotypical image of suburbia as a community occupied
exclusively by white collar workers or by professionals adhering to a
middle class life style, or that working class persons change their life
style when they move from city to suburb.[30] The residents included in
Berger's study were automobile factory workers who had moved there
from Richmond when the factory was shifted to a suburban location. But
there was little evidence that they desired to adopt a middle class style of
leisure, although they may do so with the passage of time. Mutual
visiting between friends and neighbors was infrequent, except for the
women, but participation in family activities and visiting relatives
occurred often. Some of the women participated in daytime kaffee-
klatching with neighbors, but the men seldom spent the evenings with
"the boys." On weekends the family might go to a drive-in movie, attend
the auto races, or stop for a drink at a local tavern. They rarely belonged
to clubs or other organizations that afforded leisure activities, but spent
considerable time watching television.

Somewhat different findings were reported by Gans from his study of
Levittown, a mass-produced single-family suburb in New Jersey about

---

[29] Robert J. Havighurst, "The Leisure Activities of the Middle-Aged," *American Journal of
Sociology*, 63 (September 1957), 152–62.
[30] Bennett M. Berger, *Working-Class Suburb* (1960).

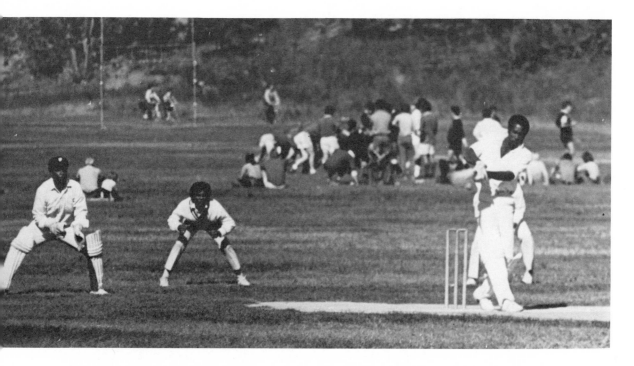

seventeen miles from Philadelphia.[31] When the suburb was opened for occupancy in the late 1950's it was settled mainly by lower middle class families but also by numerous families having upper middle and working class backgrounds. A few years after the first arrivals, almost three-fourths of the respondents reported a change in their kinds of leisure activities, and about half said they had less spare time than they enjoyed before moving. Since most of the families had been tenants in apartment buildings before coming to Levittown, the shift to single-family homes made possible a change in the use of spare time, especially outdoor activities such as over-the-fence visiting with neighbors, back-yard cookouts, or swimming in a neighborhood pool. Although the residents were involved in both community-centered and home-centered activities, Gans concluded that they spent most of their free time in the home.

Ethnic patterns persist in urban leisure. In Van Cortlandt Park, New York City, three different groups are playing soccer, cricket, and rugby (Roland J. Chenard)

Inner-City Leisure

There are, of course, many variations in working class patterns of leisure-time activity. Suttles observed in his study of a Chicago slum that a firmly established activity pattern by adolescents and young adults was "hanging out" in small groups or gangs at a designated meeting place in the neighborhood, or participating in athletics at their social clubs.[32] Whyte observed much the same style of leisure activity in an earlier

[31] Herbert Gans, *The Levittowners* (1967), pp. 267–70.
[32] Gerald D. Suttles, *The Social Order of the Slum: Ethnicity and Territory in the Inner City* (1968).

study of an Italian district in Boston.[33] In a working class district of Boston, Gans observed that neighborly visiting was a major leisure pattern among the Italian adult residents.[34] An intensive study of a sample of factory workers in a small Massachusetts city likewise revealed a marked similarity of leisure-time activities with the patterns observed in other researches.[35]

The "Leisure Industry" and the Consumer

An overall picture of the economics of leisure reveals a vast amount of wealth that urbanites in the United States and Europe spend each year for goods and services related to leisure, while only a small minority in nonindustrial societies have the time and financial resources to spend freely for leisure purposes.

The editors of *Fortune* magazine estimated, in 1955, that the American people were spending about 30.6 billion dollars annually for leisure activities and goods, or about one and one-half times the amount they paid for clothing and shelter, although some of the latter expenditures were undoubtedly related to leisure.[36] A decade later Seligman estimated that about five times as much was spent on leisure as on medical care, and his estimates did not include the costs of transportation involved in leisure activities.[37] A later estimate, in 1969, indicated that leisure spending was about 83 billion dollars, almost three times the expenditures reported for 1955.[38] Major items purchased were boats, camping vehicles, color television sets, motor bikes, bicycles, snowmobiles, musical instruments and phonograph records, do-it-yourself tools, and athletic, hunting, or fishing equipment. Automobiles used partly or entirely for leisure were not included in these estimates. Some 35 billion dollars were spent for vacations and recreational trips in the United States, and another 5 billion dollars for travel abroad. Money expended for such things as golfing fees, clubs dues, or admission to sports events ran into the billions.

In a society geared to the dictates of the clock and calendar, the problem, to be decided individually or collectively, of how to spend time is on a par with that of how to spend money. Indeed, the two issues are

[33] William Foote Whyte, *Street Corner Society* (1961).

[34] Herbert J. Gans, *The Urban Villagers* (1962).

[35] Milton M. Gordon and Charles H. Anderson, "The Blue-Collar Worker at Leisure," in Arthur B. Shostak and William Gomberg, eds., *Blue-Collar World* (1964).

[36] Editors of *Fortune*, "The Changing American Market" (1955).

[37] Ben B. Seligman, "On Work, Alienation, and Leisure," *American Journal of Economics and Sociology*, 24 (October 1965), 337–60.

[38] *U. S. News and World Report*, 67 (September 15, 1969), 58–61.

not necessarily inseparable because spending leisure time commonly means spending money and vice versa. In urban-industrial societies most city people appear to be more interested in matters relating to consumption than to production, farmers and other primary producers being possible exceptions. Much of this concern and interest centers around activities and objects relating to leisure. In this respect the consumption of time is about as important as the consumption of objects or symbols relating to leisure usage.

In the urbanized societies of the West, and in such Eastern countries as Japan, consumerism has become a way of life, a means of acquiring status or improving it, a basis for social interaction, and a formula for obtaining physical or psychological pleasures. Much of the conversation between individuals is concerned with the consumption of goods and services, the proper way, as well as the proper time and place, to consume them.

Gambling and Card-Playing

Gambling in some form is probably universal, and its origins undoubtedly go far back in the annals of history. Ordinarily it takes place when individuals have some time free from the immediate demands of work. Historically, gambling was largely an activity of a leisured minority that had time and resources to spare. In urban-industrial societies, however, as increasing amounts of free time and surplus wealth have become available to the masses, gambling has become not merely a "sport of kings" but also an activity in which participants are numbered in the millions. Sometimes gambling occurs under institutional auspices in which the rules of the game, often competitive, are established both for the active participants and the gamblers.

Most large cities maintain institutional facilities for games or sports that are highly competitive and therefore afford opportunities for betting. In the United States, parimutuel and off-track betting at horse races, betting at cockfights and dog races, or wagering on prizefights, wrestling matches, and football, basketball, and baseball games account for large sums of money that change hands each year. In England, a recent estimate indicated that nearly 5 billion dollars are spent in gambling in a single year, including betting on races, elections, football games, casino gambling, lotteries, and bingo.[39] It is estimated that almost half of the adult males in England place bets in some form, although the total spent on gambling in America is several times higher than in England. Betting on horse races in the large cities of India is a popular pastime, as is true of betting on bullfighting in the cities of Spain and Latin America. Institutional facilities for gambling are big business.

[39] J. K. Glassman, "Gambling in Britain," *Atlantic*, 228 (September 1971), 23–24.

Las Vegas in Nevada, Cannes in France, and Monte Carlo in Monaco are famed as centers of the gambling business, which attract thousands of persons hoping to "win big" at the gaming tables. Scattered over the world's cities are gambling facilities for the masses—slot machines, lotteries, bingo, policy or numbers games, bookmaking shops, and the like.

Some 50 million decks of playing cards are purchased annually in the United States, an indication of the popularity of card games. Card-playing may or may not involve betting. There are professionals who play the game for large stakes, but most amateurs probably bet small sums, if any at all. Two surveys indicate that slightly over half of adult Americans play cards either regularly or occasionally.[40]

Sports

The large number of sports arenas and outdoor stadia in the world's cities attests to the popularity of competitive athletic contests in providing leisure activity for the masses. Interest in spectator sports became especially intensified after World War II, with the result that a vast organizational complex developed to satisfy the mounting leisure interests of people. Cities as well as colleges and universities pooled their financial and other resources to provide facilities and personnel necessary to stage sports spectaculars. The mass media have been an important influence in popularizing spectator sports, as is indicated by the extensive coverage of athletic events and performers by radio, television, and the press and the considerable time spent by fans as consumers of sports news. This intense spectator interest has naturally led to professionalism in that many activities are conducted for profit as business enterprises, with the players and other functionaries serving the enterpreneurs and promoters as salaried employees.

Leisure and the Mass Media

It is commonplace that television-viewing has become a major form of leisure for many of the world's peoples, more particularly those who reside in urban-industrial societies. Robinson estimates that in the United States 28 percent of all leisure time is spent in watching television, a figure that is somewhat higher for men (32 percent) than for employed women and housewives (25 percent for both).[41] Furthermore,

[40] American Institute of Public Opinion, *Public Opinion Quarterly*, 12 (Spring 1948), 48; and Irving Crespi, "The Social Significance of Card Playing as a Leisure-Time Activity," *American Sociological Review*, 21 (December 1956), 717–22.

[41] John P. Robinson, "Television and Leisure Time: Yesterday, Today, and (Maybe) Tomorrow," *Public Opinion Quarterly*, 33 (Summer 1969), 213.

twice as much time is spent in television-watching as on all other forms of mass media combined (books, newspapers, magazines, radio, and movies). Over 90 percent of American families own one or more television sets, and much the same situation exists in other highly urbanized societies such as Japan and England. But some countries low in the scale of urbanization and industrialization—India, Saudi Arabia, Bangladesh, for example—either do not have television facilities or provide television programs on a restricted basis. In such countries, predominantly agricultural, the inexpensive transistor radio set is the counterpart of the television set in highly urbanized societies.

An international cooperative survey of time budgets recently completed provides a basis for comparing time spent in television-viewing, as well as in other forms of nonwork activities.[42] The data were obtained from samples of adults in selected small and medium-sized cities (30,000 to 280,000 population) of ten countries, including in several instances villages in the vicinity of the cities. Some 30,000 persons interviewed were asked to keep a detailed diary for one complete day in which all of their work and nonwork activities were recorded and the time spent in each activity designated. As one might expect, residents of the highly urbanized and relatively affluent countries spent more time viewing television than was the case of countries on a low level of urbanization.

Fads and Foibles in Leisure Behavior

The continual round of faddish behavior is a conspicuous feature of leisure-time activity in Western societies. Such are the dance crazes that suddenly, as if out of nowhere, become popular only to disappear about as suddenly, giving way to other crazes; or the song hits, popular overnight, that provide mass entertainment until they shortly outlive their appeal; or the new books or films that create a sensation, but are virtually forgotten by the end of the year; or the fashions in sports, such as boating, skiing, surfing, or jogging, which may have a short-lived appeal, to be replaced by other ephemeral activities. If these and other forms of leisure culture reflect the dynamics of the society in which they occur, they also are the creation of the mass media, of advertisers and promoters who find in them lucrative sources of income, especially when they involve the consumption of salable goods or services.

In the decades following World War II, much leisure behavior assumed the form of collective faddism. For many this behavior undoubtedly provided respite from the unpleasant or unrewarding realities of life and

[42] Alexander Szalai, "The Multinational Comparative Time Budget Research Project," *American Behavioral Scientist,* 10 (December 1966), pp. 1–31.

work; for others it afforded fun, excitement, or spiritual rebirth, at least for a brief time. In the 1960's discotheques became popular places where night-club patrons could dance in packed and noisy ballrooms. Mass rock festivals attract youthful fans, from throughout the United States, by the tens of thousands. (In the summer of 1973, the number of persons gathered at such a festival was estimated to be about 500,000!) College spring vacations witness mass migrations of students to the sunbathed beaches of Florida or California—a latter-day Children's Crusade, except that the objective is fun and frivolity. Exponents of mod culture congregate in places like Haight Street in San Francisco, Soho in London, or the Left Bank in Paris. Mystical revivals of occultism have developed and spread rapidly over the country as thousands of persons explore esoteric beliefs and practices such as astrology, witchcraft, and parapsychology.[43] Waves of religious interest and fervor such as the Jesus Movement occur. Participation in mass revivalist meetings sometimes take on the character of an emotional orgy. More restrained and introspective are the devotees of Zen Buddhism and other Eastern religions—a movement which apparently may have reached its peak in the 1960's. All these, and others, involve consumption of time as well as consumption of symbolic objects.

Lowenthal has observed that the "star," the popular idol in the world of entertainment, has replaced the businessman and the scientist as the folk hero in contemporary urban society,[44] and there is a mass-consumer market for his "products"—theater, films, newspaper and radio commentary, and the like. Created particularly by the mass media, the star, the celebrity, exerts a profound influence on leisure interests and activities. The meteoric ascendancy of stars in the world of music, drama, or sports has provided diversion, excitement, and role models for mass audiences who are always on the lookout for the novel and unusual. Popular idols usually make a spectacular appearance, only to be replaced shortly by new stars that offer a different mass appeal. The life expectancy of stardom is almost invariably short. "Within less than one year from the time a Cockney girlchild nicknamed Twiggy took her first modelling job," writes Toffler, "millions of human beings around the globe stored mental images of her in their brain. A dewy-eyed blond with minimal mammaries and pipestem legs, Twiggy exploded into celebrityhood in 1967."[45] Her face and figure were pictured in news-

[43] Marcello Truzzi, "The Occult Revival as Popular Culture," *Sociological Quarterly*, 13 (Winter 1972), 16–36. Truzzi reports that 364 hardback books on occultism were published in 1969. One publisher turned out 49 horoscope publications in 1969, and sold some 8 million horoscope "dope sheets" in the same year.

[44] Leo Lowenthal, "Biographies in Popular Magazines: From Production Leaders to Consumption Idols," in Amitai Etzioni and Eva Etzioni, eds., *Social Change: Sources, Patterns, and Consequences* (1964).

[45] Alvin Toffler, *Future Shock* (1971), p. 152.

papers, magazines, and on television screens the world over, but within five years she had virtually disappeared from public view. So it is with other luminaries, females with massive mammaries and curvaceous legs or males exhibiting maximum machismo, who are adored but whose popularity fades when their admirers find other, more appealing models. The folk heroes who appear and disappear in rapid succession provide a major focus of leisure-time interests of countless persons who read about them in the press, watch them on television or the movie screen, crowd into public places to see or hear them perform "in the flesh," even strive ecstatically to contact them physically. The mass media find it profitable to create or "discover" such potential celebrities.

Summary

The urbanization and industrialization of society have had a profound effect upon the way people make use of their spare time. In this chapter we have considered the nature of leisure, noting particularly its relationship to work, since each is a facet of much the same phenomenon. One of the most significant trends in highly urbanized societies has been the shortening of the work day or week, thus allowing workers more free time. However, this trend has not applied uniformly to all employed persons, especially to professionals and executives who do not punch a time clock or leave their jobs at the end of a forty-hour week.

Alienation of the individual from his work situation has become widespread in industrial societies. In early days, free time was regarded as a means of preparation for the work tasks that lay ahead; now, many consider work a means toward the end of leisure time. We have also observed the class differences in the use of leisure time and the institutionalization of leisure in the modern world.

In the next chapter we turn to another aspect of urbanization, namely, the community power structure and political participation.

Selected Bibliography

BOOKS

Anderson, Nels, *Work and Leisure*. London: Routledge and Kegan Paul, 1961.
Dumazedier, J., *Toward a Society of Leisure*. New York: Macmillan, 1967.
de Grazia, Sebastian, *Of Time, Work, and Leisure*. New York: Twentieth Century Fund, 1962.
Friedmann, Georges, *The Anatomy of Work*: New York: The Free Press, 1961.
Jacobs, Norman, ed., *Culture for the Millions*. Boston: Beacon Press, 1964.
Kaplan, Max, *Leisure in America*. New York: Wiley, 1960.

Miller, P. Norman, and Duane M. Robinson, *The Leisure Age*. Belmont, Calif.: Wadsworth, 1963.

Parker, Stanley, *The Future of Work and Leisure*. New York: Praeger Publishers, 1971.

Roberts, Kenneth, *Leisure*. London: Longman Group Ltd., 1970.

Smith, C. Ray, *The American Endless Weekend*. Washington, D.C.: American Institute of Architects, 1973.

Spectorsky, A. C., *The Exurbanites*. Lippincott, 1955.

Stone, Gregory P., ed., *Games, Sport, and Power*. New Brunswick, N. J.: Transaction Books, 1972.

ARTICLES

Craig, William, "Recreational Patterns in a Small Negro Urban Community: The Role of the Cultural Base," *Economic Geography*, 48 (January 1972), 107–15.

Crespi, Irving, "The Social Significance of Card Playing as a Leisure-Time Activity," *American Sociological Review*, 21 (December 1956), 717–22.

Friedmann, Georges, "Leisure and Technological Civilization," *International Social Science Journal*, 12 (1960), 509–21.

Gerstl, J. E., "Leisure Taste and Occupational Milieu," *Social Problems*, 9 (Summer 1961), 56–69.

Glassman, J. K., "Gambling in Britain," *Atlantic*, 228 (September 1971), 23–33.

Havighurst, Robert J., "The Leisure Activities of the Middle-Aged," *American Journal of Sociology*, 63 (September 1957), 152–63.

Irwin, John, "Surfing: The Natural History of an Urban Scene," *Urban Life and Culture*, 2 (July 1973), 131–60.

Meyerson, Rolf, "Television Viewing and the Rest of Leisure," *Public Opinion Quarterly*, 32 (Spring 1968), 102–12.

Reissman, Leonard, "Class, Leisure, and Social Participation," *American Sociological Review*, 19 (February 1954), 76–84.

Robinson, John P., "Television and Leisure Time: Yesterday, Today and (Maybe) Tommorrow," *Public Opinion Quarterly*, 33 (Summer 1969), 210–22.

Seligman, Ben B., "On Work, Alienation, and Leisure," *American Journal of Economics and Sociology*, 24 (October 1965), 337–60.

Social Problems, 9 (Summer 1961), entire issue.

Szalai, Alexander, "The Multinational Comparative Time Budget Research Project," *American Behavioral Scientist*, 10 (December 1966), entire issue.

Truzzi, Marcello, "The Occult Revival as Popular Culture," *Sociological Quarterly*, 13 (Winter 1972), 16–36.

White, R. Clyde, "Social Class Differences and the Use of Leisure," *American Journal of Sociology*, 61 (September 1955), 145–50.

17 • Community Power, Organization, and Political Participation

The concept of *power* as we shall use it in this chapter refers to the capacity or authority of an individual or group to command or influence the behavior of others. Central to the phenomenon of power is the way it is achieved or exercised. Power vested in persons who are selected or appointed by a socially approved procedure is considered *legitimate.* Such power is sometimes referred to as *authority.* But persons "without portfolio" may also achieve and hold power by persuasion or even physical force.

Two crucial aspects of power are the processes of policy formulation and decision-making. Those in positions of power are given, or assume, the right to make decisions that affect others, and that right usually gives them the authority to enforce or carry out these decisions, which may apply to an entire community or to any of its parts. Thus, the importance or scope of the decisions is one measure of power. Power is an essential element in community life, for without it a community, or even an entire society, would be unable to "hang together" to carry out the functions necessary to make it a viable enterprise. In our discussion we shall focus on community power systems in the democratic societies of the Western world, mainly in American communities.

The Community Setting

Whatever forms of power and governance exist in cities, the rapid tempo of events in recent decades has profoundly altered the American urban system and social processes. Issues in the 1970's are by no means the same as those of the 1920's or earlier. The growth of suburban communities has added a new dimension to metropolitan life as the flight of population to the new communities has created a different set of economic, political, and social issues such as taxation, annexation, and "invasions" of racial minorities. Suburbanites who work in the central city are usually resistant to taxes imposed by the center and opposed to annexation. The movement of middle and upper class persons to the suburbs has drained the central city of its major sources of tax revenue to support its institutions, which are also used by suburban residents. Another major change, related to the proliferation of the suburbs, is the increasing concentration of racial minorities in the central city—mainly blacks but also Puerto Ricans and Chicanos—whose political perceptions and stands on issues are quite different from those of the city's "old families" or of suburbanites. To some extent this cleavage is between the "haves" and the "have nots."

One might expect that the "one-industry" city or a "company town" would have, other things being reasonably equal, a power system different from the city with a highly diversified economy. In most suburban communities the power structure tends to be different from that of the adjacent central city. Cities having a diversity of racial or ethnic groups, each deeply concerned about its own status and rights, tend to have a diversified power structure, with each group practicing pressure politics in its own interest. A city in which labor is highly organized and influential suggests a power structure different from cities that are mainly middle class and have few or no labor unions. Resort cities like Atlantic City, retirement centers like St. Petersburg, Florida, or educational centers like Ann Arbor tend to attract a population that differs in age, sex composition, and life style from most cities.

No system of community power remains static. New methods of making decisions and carrying them out; the replacement of one set of leaders by another, or one bloc of voters by another; alterations in the political structure such as the replacement of a strong-mayor with a city-manager form of government; changes in the economy such as the growth of a large industry; changes in voting patterns reflecting shifts in the political climate; new mechanisms for achieving, maintaining, exercising, or restricting power; the intrusion of state or national governmental policies into the local scene—all of these factors and more, or any combination thereof, are the kinds of changes that alter the power structure.[1]

Two Concepts of Power

The Monolithic or Elitist Power Structure

A widely current image of municipal governance is that of a monolithic or elitist structure in which major decisions are made by an omnipotent

[1] See especially Robert E. Agger, Daniel Goldrich, and Bert E. Swanson, *The Rulers and the Ruled: Political Power and Impotence in American Communities* (1964), pp. 80–82.

political boss or official, or a small coterie of influential persons often operating behind the scenes. This image had some validity in earlier years when astute political bosses held the reins of power in a number of American cities, among them such well-known personalities as Tom Pendergast of Kansas City, Abe Reuf of San Francisco, Mayor James Curley of Boston, Big Bill Thompson of Chicago, Mayor Crump of Memphis, William Vare of Philadelphia, and numerous other political titans. More recently Mayor Richard Daley has dominated the political scene in Chicago.[2] Popular literature about these men of great power has often given the impression that their power was virtually absolute. Yet such literature overlooks the fact that their authority was actually limited, that they had to walk a tight political rope, so to speak, appeasing this group or that, distributing favors to constituents, making compromises, or pitting one group against another in order to survive politically. Nor does such literature, focused as it is on personalities and machine politics, provide a very realistic picture of the way the system of governance functions in most communities.

It may be historically instructive to describe briefly how Pendergast of Kansas City maintained and exercised power in that city. The only political office he ever actually held was that of justice of the peace, but as head of the local Democratic "machine" he exercised control of City Hall, the center of municipal government. To finance the operations of the political machine, all appointive officeholders were required to make a contribution to the party, and legitimate businesses were also expected to contribute or suffer the consequences. If apartment-house landlords, for example, declined to make a contribution their business license could be revoked at City Hall on such a pretext as their maintaining a building "unfit for human habitation." Minor functionaries in the political machine, for instance, precinct captains, had direct contact with the people in their respective districts, conferring favors such as providing assistance in times of personal or family crises or distributing food to needy families. The real payoff for Pendergast was the lucrative benefits he received as proprietor of three businesses. As head of a ready-mix cement company he was consistently awarded choice contracts in municipal construction projects; as head of a wholesale liquor business he "invited" retail liquor dealers to handle his product, or otherwise have their licenses revoked; and as head of a private garbage-collection firm he regularly was awarded the city's contract for his service.

Thus, Pendergast's political machine was well-oiled financially, he was generally supported at the polls on election day by the people who had received favors from the organization, and he personally accumulated considerable wealth from the businesses under the protective umbrella of his party machine. Some of the money collected seeped

---

[2] See especially Mike Royko, *The Boss* (1971), a readable but probably overdrawn account of Mayor Daley's methods of achieving and exercising power in Chicago.

down to lower functionaries in the political machine, such as precinct workers or ward committeemen, thus making the organization a profitable activity for many persons.

The swashbuckling empire-builders in the classic mold have, for the most part, vanished from the municipal political scene. Party organizations may still have a virtual monopoly in the operation of public affairs, but generally the power of the party boss to dictate governmental policy has been greatly reduced. There are various reasons for the decline of bossism, but a preeminent factor is the increasing influence in local community affairs of federal and state officials, who often dictate policies that in earlier days were the prerogative of a party boss or his cronies in municipal office. Another reason is that technical or administrative expertise has become increasingly vital if modern municipal government is to function effectively; hence the selection of personnel through a merit system rather than a system of patronage is now a widely accepted procedure. However, patronage is still a factor in machine politics: Mayor Daley of Chicago, who has weathered several political storms, controls an estimated 25,000 jobs that he fills with his political supporters.

The Company Town: An Elitist System

"An estimated 5 million Americans live in company towns where checks and balances vital to democracy have been overwhelmed by the economic power of one corporate employer," write Schuck and Wellford about a small city in Georgia dominated by a paper mill that employs most of the city's working population.[3] Such companies undoubtedly vary considerably in the influence they exert on the local community by virtue of their economic power to hire and fire and to provide support for friendly influentials. Since the industrial plant in the Georgia town has virtually a monopoly on the job market, the workers have little opportunity to find another job in the community. The firm is a client of a local attorney who for a number of years was the elected county representative in the state legislature, and in this role he has sponsored legislation favorable to the company but at the expense of the community. He is also city and county attorney. The town's mayor is a company employee, as are the city tax assessors and members of the school board. The local newspaper is owned by a brother of the firm's attorney and is "little more than a company newsletter," providing support for the company in local matters. Within the community there is little countervailing power such as might be provided by strong labor unions. The payoff for the company, of course, is low tax assessments and similar advantages without any

[3] Peter Schuck and Harrison Wellford, "Democracy and the Good Life in a Company Town," *Harper's*, 244 (May 1972), 55–66. This city has a population of about 5,000.

effective restriction on operating methods, which results in a serious air and water pollution problem.

Pluralistic Power Systems

The concept of pluralistic community power holds that power is diversified and diffused within communities in a democratic society. While it accepts the fact of power concentration in formal government or in other community institutions, it rejects the notion that a few influential men in the community "rule even though they do not reign," or that this group, sometimes operating outside the open political arena, formulates all major policies or makes proposals that are carried out by lesser men in the power hierarchy. The concept of pluralistic power recognizes the importance of special-interest groups and of public opinion in making decisions either of communitywide or segmental application, that these groups may cancel each other out in their influence, and that they usually act as a curb on those in official or unofficial positions of power. The proponents of the pluralistic concept do recognize, however, that a small minority in every community actually makes the decisions, but emphasize that this minority, whether consisting of public officials or

Some cities are dominated almost completely by a single institution. Eindhoven, The Netherlands, is an example. Here is shown one of the plants of the giant Philips Electric Works. (Aerophoto Nederland, Zestienhoven-Rotterdam)

459

others, is influenced by public opinion and the prospects of rejection at election time. If the general public does not in fact formulate policies or make the actual decisions in problem-issues, it at least has "veto power," as David Riesman has called it.

Power and Social Organization

Power has two facets: organization and function. First, power is usually anchored in the social structure (organization), which may be viewed as a relatively stable, though changing, pattern of relationships between individuals and groups. Second, the way in which power is achieved or exercised is its functional facet. Any form of social organization is likely to embody a system of power in that certain individuals are given or assume the right to formulate policies and make decisions for the group or community, whether municipal government, large-scale organizations, or smaller voluntary associations. But that right is ordinarily not absolute: it must depend on the consent of others, at least in a democratic society, and it may be challenged or curtailed.

Power in Large-Scale Organizations

Complex organizations are often characterized by a hierarchical power structure in which policies are formulated and decisions made or carried out by persons on different levels of authority. Such power is legitimate in that the decision-makers and those designated to implement the decisions are formally authorized to perform these roles. The authorization may be the collective expression of voter opinion in elections, or it may issue from other legitimated bodies such as city councils or policy-making boards.

Such organizations are not solely a feature of urban-industrial societies, but the process of urbanization and industrialization has fostered the growth of giant bureaucracies which have made possible the concentration of immense economic or political power. Government has expanded its structure and multiplied its functions, sometimes becoming a virtual power monopoly. Economic institutions have likewise expanded in size and functions. These gigantic systems of power tend to be centered in major cities, but they extend their influence, in a variety of ways, far beyond a city's boundaries. Through mergers and coalitions they have become so large and powerful that they affect other organizations as well as the lives of innumerable persons. The emergence in recent decades of great conglomerates or coalitions of organizations exemplifies this trend. The International Telephone and Telegraph

Company, headquartered in New York but functioning in many cities, is a case in point. The company's name belies its structural and functional characteristics; actually, it is a conglomerate consisting of more than a hundred companies having many functions, but all of which are under direction of the parent corporation. With its increasing size and complexity its power potential has grown accordingly.

One of the important developments in the sphere of power in recent decades has been the growth of an influential occupational group: the professional manager, ordinarily associated with a bureaucratic organization. Professional managers occupy key positions in the institutional structures of communities and entire societies; for example, city managers, whose number in the United States has increased rapidly. Large-scale public and private enterprises are likely to be administered by specialized managerial personnel such as hospital administrators, corporate executives, administrators of school systems, and the like. While such personnel have considerable power, within certain limits, the principal power base is often located elsewhere—in a board of directors, or a city council, or even in the voting public.

External Power and Local Community

Although we are here concerned primarily with the system of power within the local community, in urban-industrial societies decisions made outside the local community may have great effect on that community. Institutional power centered in state or national governments, or in the national headquarters of giant industrial, commercial, or labor bureaucracies, may affect local community life in many ways. Such power structures may provide various services for local communities, or control the conditions under which these services are provided.[4]

Subgovernments in a Local Power System

In every major city there are many governmental structures, not just a single one. As Banfield remarks in his study of political influence in Chicago, "The Chicago area, from a purely formal standpoint, can hardly be said to have a government at all. There are hundreds, perhaps thousands, of bodies, each of which has a measure of legal authority and none of which has enough of it to carry out a course of action which other bodies oppose."[5] Among these subgovernments are school districts;

---

[4] See especially Arthur Vidich and Joseph Bensman, *Small Town in Mass Society* (1958), for an excellent analysis of this situation in a small community in upstate New York.

[5] Edward C. Banfield, *Political Influence* (1961), p. 235.

special districts dealing specifically with such matters as sewage disposal, fire protection, water supply, and flood control; separate municipalities, many of which are satellite communities; counties; and towns or townships. In the 243 SMSA's in the United States in 1970, there were literally thousands of governments, each of which had a power structure in which decisions were made and carried out.[6] Obviously, the number of decisions, both major and minor, made in the course of a year in any metropolitan community is very large indeed. Often these decisions are segmental in that they apply to only one aspect of community life.

In addition to these subgovernments there are quasigovernmental organizations that represent power structures of varying dimensions and that are involved in the decision-making process. Some are strictly local; others are extensions of state or national organizations superimposed on the local community. Often they are functionally related to the local governmental structure. Among such organizations are public housing authorities, social security administrative organizations, associations for the administration of public health or recreational activities on the community level, city-planning organizations, and so on.

Decision-makers in large corporate structures do not necessarily exert a powerful influence beyond their own institutional system. Although the merger of economic and political power seems to have occurred in many American cities, especially in company towns, the trend has been toward political decision-making for the community by politicians or by professional personnel with special expertise in community affairs. In a study of the power system in two medium-sized cities in the Middle West, for example, Clelland and Form concluded that "the formal political and economic power structures have tended to become bifurcated over time."[7] One possible explanation for this separation is that top influentials in the corporate structures, commonly organized on a national or international basis, tend to restrict their decision-making activities to economic matters and to avoid extensive participation in local civic affairs, except when their own institution is directly affected by local events. This trend is apparently more characteristic of major cities than of small towns in which the economic dominants are likely to be local business proprietors who have deeply rooted interests in the community.

Special-Interest Groups

In both medium-sized and large cities, where the population is usually diversified by economic interests and roles, by racial or ethnic character-

[6] See U.S. Bureau of the Census, Census of Governments, 1971.
[7] Donald A. Clelland and William H. Form, "Economic Dominants and Community Power: A Comparative Analysis," *American Journal of Sociology*, 69 (March 1964), 521.

istics, by religion, and the like, each group seeks a voice in the decisions of primary concern to its members, and often collectively expresses its views through its leaders, especially those who are influential in local politics. In many American cities such minorities as blacks, Chicanos, Indians, Italians, or Puerto Ricans generally support their leaders who represent the group's interests most persuasively. In recent years the power systems of racial and ethnic minorities have changed as a "new" leadership has emerged.[8] Inasmuch as ethnic or racial minorities in

[8] See especially Lewis M. Killian and Charles U. Smith, "Negro Protest Leaders in a Southern Community," *Social Forces*, 38 (March 1960), 253–57.

The 110-story twin towers of the World Trade Center, built by the New York Port Authority in Manhattan, symbolize the power of quasi-governmental organizations. (The Port of New York Authority)

American cities tend to cluster in districts that may be coterminous with political wards or precincts, their collective voting patterns can represent a political force of considerable strength.

The political influence of such groups, or any other, varies according to the political skills and mass appeals of local leaders, the control exercised by executives over major economic institutions, the extent of voter participation and turnout at the polls, the role of the mass media in local issues, and so on. Those in top political positions of community power, or others seeking such power, generally heed the advice of leaders of local groups whose support may be helpful in the consolidation or attainment of power. Party leaders generally seek and accept political support from any source, but those individuals or groups whose support is considered politically minimal may be ignored in the political decision-making procedures later on. This competitiveness of political leaders and the groups represented in the body politic creates situations conducive to corruption—both "honest graft" and "dishonest graft," as Boss Plunkett of Tammany Hall in New York once expressed it.

Decentralization of Power

Interest groups within a community may represent centers of power, the extent and effectiveness of which depends partly on the way a group is organized. It is an empirical fact that power in most major American cities is diffused to a considerable degree. Mott cites the factors or conditions that favor an increase in the number of local centers of power: "the number of centers of power is to increase as (1) the population (of the community) increases, (2) the ethnic composition becomes more heterogeneous, (3) functional specialization increases, (4) the number of self-conscious social classes increases, and (5) as in-migration increases."[9] An exception is the company town, which we discussed earlier.

Voluntary Associations and Social Movements

Leaders, whether endowed with legitimate power or not, may speak effectively when their voice is the voice of the people they represent. Almost every city is the setting for social movements designed to effect certain changes or to obstruct changes that the people and their leaders do not want. Sometimes these movements are strictly local, in other instances they are a part of a larger movement extending beyond the community. It is in such a situation that voluntary associations com-

[9] Paul E. Mott, "Configurations of Power," in Michael Aiken and Paul E. Mott, eds., *The Structure of Community Power* (1970), pp. 85–86.

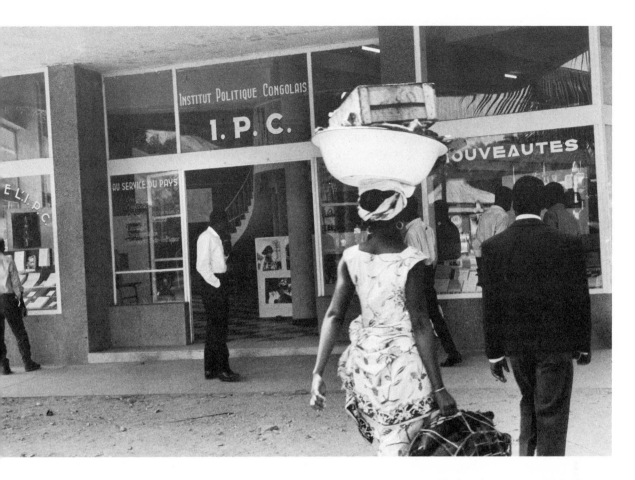

monly play a role in which the resources of the group are assembled and orchestrated in support of a movement's objectives. Many instrumental associations not only support a movement but actually spearhead it through their leaders. Among such associations are the League of Women Voters, labor unions, real estate boards, parent-teacher associations, the National Association for the Advancement of Colored People, the American Civil Liberties Union, the National Conference of Christians and Jews, and so on.

Political leaders recognize voluntary associations as a source of strength. Power so derived tends to be segmentalized according to the special interests of the members and is centered mainly in the middle and upper strata of the community because of the disinclination of working class people to join such groups, except labor unions and churches. There is considerable evidence that residents of a community who participate in voluntary associations tend to be more interested in broader problem-issues and more likely to vote at elections than is true of nonparticipants. Such experiences, it seems, help to prepare the individual participant for the responsibilities of self-government. Furthermore, as Rose remarks, organizations acting as pressure groups "are

Urbanization in developing countries has apparently stimulated political awareness among the people. Here is a political information office in Kinshasa, Zaïre (formerly The Congo). (Louise E. Jefferson)

465

prime examples of voluntary associations functioning to distribute power."[10] Such groups become agents of social change.

Leaders of voluntary associations may exert economic pressures on existing institutions, or so organize their followers to use the ballot box at election time to achieve desired ends. Although relatively few labor leaders achieve power by election or appointment to governmental posts, their indirect power in local government or the economy can be considerable. Highly organized denominational groups such as the Catholic church have a well-defined power structure that may function as a pressure group in support of, or opposition to, particular policies. When the blacks of Birmingham, Alabama, were organized by Martin Luther King to boycott local bus lines in protest against discrimination, the impact of this boycott on the local Establishment was effective in terminating discrimination in transportation. Under the leadership of Saul Alinsky the residents of a blighted district in Chicago were organized effectively to bring pressures on local government leaders to improve living and working conditions in the area.[11]

Associations that serve as a base of operations for power leaders do not always function independently; on public issues there may be coalitions of groups that have similar interests and objectives, with the leaders of such groups cooperating to plan tactics and strategies. Thus labor union leaders will coordinate their forces with the leaders of, say, social welfare organizations to strengthen social security legislation. Or leaders of the local medical association will ally with the local real estate board and chamber of commerce in opposing legislation for public housing or "socialized" medicine. Many public issues involve opposing coalitions consisting of numerous associations, each of which may be a source of power in influencing public opinion.[12]

Pressure Tactics of a Real Estate Board: A Case Study

The functions of the local real estate board of "Grand Valley," a medium-sized midwestern city described by Bouma, are probably representative of the role of certain groups in the power system of a local community.[13] The board was made up of 425 members associated with 125 of the city's real estate firms. On such issues as public housing or taxation the board generally took a firm stand, often opposed by the local

[10] Arnold Rose, *The Structure of Power* (1967), p. 248.

[11] Saul D. Alinsky, *Reveille for Radicals* (1946).

[12] See especially Robert Perrucci and Marc Pilisuk, "Leaders and Ruling Elites: The Interorganizational Bases of Community Power," *American Sociological Review*, 35 (December 1970), 1040–57.

[13] Donald H. Bouma, "Analysis of the Social Power Position of a Real Estate Board," *Social Problems*, 10 (Fall 1962), 121–32.

council of churches, labor unions, social welfare organizations, and the press, but supported by the chamber of commerce. One source of the board's strength was the discipline it imposed on member firms or their personnel. Since no departure from the decisions made by the board was permitted, a "united front" was possible. A "war chest" was maintained to meet the expenses of a propaganda campaign to get public support in a campaign for or against a proposal. Such funds were used to distribute literature in support of the board's position, and to buy space or time in the local mass media. If the board decided that petitions signed by city residents were to be used as a pressure technique in a particular situation, each real estate firm was ordered to obtain a specified number of signers. The board or its directors formulated policies, usually in line with policies followed by the national association of real estate boards. On such matters as bond issues the board was able to muster heavy popular support for its position at election time. Furthermore, in the election of public officials, including city councilmen and state representatives, the board gave its support to favored candidates, themselves realtors or otherwise persons in sympathy with the board's economic philosophy. Thus, as measured by its repeated successes it became an impressive wielder of power and influence in the city.

The Public Speaks—
or Does It?

Political power in cities of the Western democracies depends in considerable measure on the support of voters at the polls. Realizing that most persons who participate in political activities vote according to their self-interests, which include job security, income, education for their children, law and order, civil rights, a decent place to live—bread-and-butter issues—local political leaders emphasize these matters in their appeals for support. "Whatever the controlling clique in the local political system," write Bollens and Schmandt, "its members are conscious of the fact that they or their surrogates can best retain the trappings of power by offending no group and by disturbing the status quo as little as possible."[14]

Civic Indifference

Although most politicians or civic reformers strive to persuade the voters to vote at election time, in most elections held in American cities they have had limited success. In the early days the well-oiled political machine could consistently "deliver" the vote of the party faithful, but,

[14] John C. Bollens and Henry J. Schmandt, *The Metropolis* (1965), p. 241.

with the diffusion of power, this has become increasingly difficult to do. However, voter participation in local elections, or even state or national contests, tends to be characterized more by indifference and apathy than by civic alertness and involvement. On local issues, the turnout of voters is generally less than half the number eligible by age or residence to vote. Actually, the average turnout of voters over the years in local elections usually does not exceed one-fourth of the total number eligible, except in elections personalized by well-known political leaders or when the issues elicit marked emotional reactions. Studies conducted in St. Louis and Dayton, for example, indicate that around one-fourth of the citizens eligible to vote in those cities had never cast a ballot.[15] Those who do vote often register a protest rather than support of a candidate or policy.

Various explanations have been advanced for nonparticipation of voters in the political process. The relatively high physical mobility of the urban population, the frequent moves from here to there, either in the same city or between communities, may afford little time or opportunity to become involved in community affairs. Of the millions of migrants to cities, some from the rural hinterlands, others from abroad, many find the political system baffling and therefore may not vote unless some tangible rewards are dangled before them by party politicians. In the early days of boss rule the immigrant population residing in cities were the major source of political strength for the party organization and were exploited by the political bosses. Another factor positively related to voting behavior is home ownership; home owners are more likely to be involved in community affairs than nonowners, since they have a stake in the community, or at least feel they do.

But psychological factors also have a direct bearing on nonparticipation in the political process. Many persons experience a sense of alienation, a feeling of powerlessness in the face of forces that appear formidable, a conviction that those in positions of power have little or no concern for the "common people." Problem-issues are often complex and baffling, especially for persons with limited education and experience. The feeling is widespread among nonparticipants that "my vote wouldn't make any difference anyway." As Riesman states the matter, "This feeling of futility tends to cause a withdrawal by the individual from political participation and a retreat into the little world of his own immediate and personal problems."[16]

Whatever may be the method employed in the study of community power, all of the research findings so far have clearly indicated that a very small proportion of the people participate directly in the formulation of policies concerning major local issues. A great many persons and

[15] See especially John C. Bollens, ed., *Exploring the Metropolitan Community* (1962), p. 182.

[16] David Riesman, *The Lonely Crowd* (1950). See also Morris Rosenberg, "Some Determinants of Political Apathy," *Public Opinion Quarterly*, 18 (Winter 1954), 349–56.

voluntary associations may be involved indirectly, and bring their influence to bear on the actual decision-makers, but when the chips are down, it is a small minority that makes the major decisions concerning communitywide affairs. Such a conclusion, however, by no means supports a monolithic conception of power, although in some communities this actually may be the case.

Methods of Studying
Community Power

Although researchers have employed several methods to identify the power elite of a community and to study the procedures used in achieving, maintaining, and exercising power, they usually make use of one of the following three:

a. The *positional* method by which the power elite are identified as the major administrative personnel in the principal institutions of a community.
b. The *reputational* method by which a panel of local citizens are asked to identify the power elite, that is, the leaders and decision-makers in issues pertaining to a community.
c. The *decisional* method by which the power-wielders are identified on the basis of their participation in the decision-making process involving a community's affairs.

Of the three approaches, the first two are similar in that both focus on identifying the major wielders of power and give some attention to the methods by which their power is exercised. They are dissimilar in that in the positional method the researchers themselves identify the power elite, basing their judgments on available evidence and their own observation, whereas in the reputational method the identifications are made by a panel of judges who are presumably representative of the community. In the study of power by the decisional method, which has recently been emphasized, the procedure is to focus on the major issues that have arisen in the community and to identify the persons making the decisions designed to resolve the issues. The results of these studies generally indicate (1) that the decision-makers are not necessarily persons with reputations as wielders of power or individuals in high executive positions in the institutional structure, (2) that the decision-makers may exercise power in a single sector of community life but not in the entire community, and (3) that many persons may be involved, directly or indirectly, in the decision-making process.

The reputational and positional approaches tend to support a monolithic or elitist theory of power in which a few high-placed persons exercise power to their own advantage, or to the advantage of others in comparable positions. The "second string team" supporting the major power-wielders consists of persons of limited influence who may be used, however, to further the interests of the top-level power elite. The decisional approach tends to support a pluralistic theory of power, according to which there may be numerous decision-makers representing different, and sometimes competitive, sectors of community life, who may have the effect of cancelling each other out. The power of such decision-makers often rests on a consensus of large numbers of persons active in voluntary associations or in local movements who may express their opinions in either supportive or veto acts. Those who hold to the pluralistic interpretation of community power acknowledge that the situation varies from one community to another, that in some there is a monopoly of power by a few, but that the concept of a monolithic system has been exaggerated.

Investigating the Community Power Structure

A number of empirical studies of power in cities exist, conducted mainly by sociologists and political scientists. Most of these researches have been carried out in American cities. Whether in a local community or the larger society, several salient questions, such as the following, are foremost in the study of power systems:

a. Is there a single, monolithic power structure in a community, or are there different power structures which represent a dispersal of power?
b. Who are the power elite, how are they selected, what groups or organizations do they represent, and how do they exercise power in terms of decision-making or control of institutional functions?
c. To what extent are there interlocking power positions which include authority derived from political, economic, and social organizations?
d. In what ways is a community power system interlaced with a regional or national power system?
e. Is there an "invisible" government which functions behind the visible political stage; if so, who are the practitioners of power on this level and how do they operate?
f. What is the role of popular leadership and public opinion as a supportive or veto force in the power system?

Middletown

The influential research conducted in the 1930's by the Lynds, which illustrates the positional approach,[17] was of a small community (actually Muncie, Indiana) that was selected for study because it was considered fairly representative of small cities in the United States. The Lynds

[17] Robert S. Lynd and Helen M. Lynd, *Middletown in Transition* (1937).

identified Middletown's power elite as a kinship group which they referred to as the "X family" (actually three brothers and their respective conjugal families). The power structure, as they described it, was monolithic, with the X family entrenched in power by their domination of existing economic institutions such as banks, loan companies, factories, a department store, and a railroad. Members of the family were also members of the boards of control of other institutions. The power of these persons lay in corporate ownership and control, and particularly in their control of employment and credit facilities. Members of the family were also actively involved in philanthropic, educational, and civic affairs, giving substantial sums to local institutions, and therefore having a strong voice in the formulation of local policies, both political and nonpolitical.

Regional City

An influential systematic study undertaken in an American city—a pioneering research in this field—was Hunter's research of community power in Regional City (actually Atlanta, Georgia),[18] in which he employed the reputational method of identifying the persons who formulated major policies or made the decisions affecting all or a considerable part of the community. Closely linked to the power elite, but lower in the policy-making structure, were persons who carried out policies formulated on the higher echelons. Hunter sought, first, to identify the major persons of power and, second, to describe the actual processes of power formulation and execution. In identifying the power elite he used a panel of citizens familiar with the local community, and through this method finally selected 40 persons who figured prominently in local issues. Most of them were executives of local economic institutions, but included a few governmental officials, labor leaders, professionals (mainly lawyers), and leaders of social and civic organizations. Hunter also undertook to identify the power-wielders in the black subcommunity, using much the same procedure as he had for the white community.

An important feature of the system, as Hunter interpreted it, was that the policy-makers tended to associate together in private cliques or committees, or in organizations having a restricted membership. Rarely were policies formulated in an open forum, though the forum did play an important part in the execution of policies. Hunter makes it clear that the formulation and execution of power in Regional City was not a conspiracy of malevolent men; rather, it was action by conservative leaders who probably interpreted their roles and policies as being in the public interest.

[18] Floyd Hunter, *Community Power Structure* (1953).

New Haven

Polsby conducted a study in New Haven, Connecticut, in which he identified community leaders who had been participants in three public issues involving the entire community—urban redevelopment, political nominations, and public education.[19] On the issue of urban redevelopment, 428 persons were actively involved in one way or another; on political nominations, the number involved was 497; and on public education, 131 were identified as participants.

The second step in the research was to conduct lengthy interviews with the participants in order to identify, first, the key decisions that had been made on each of the issues, and, second, the persons who were involved in the decisions and the roles they played. Polsby found little evidence of a monolithic power structure in the community. There was, indeed, little overlapping of "leadership pools" representing the three issues. The leaders, or decision-makers, were more or less specialized in their interests and activities.

The investigator then attempted to determine how two elites—economic and status—participated in the decisions relative to the issues.[20] Although there was some overlapping, he found that it was not extensive. Of the 239 members of the economic elite, 48 were involved in the urban redevelopment program, but most of them were appointed by the mayor and did nothing more than sit passively on one of the committees. Only six of the economic elite were involved in political nominations, and none at all in the issues centering around public education. Of the 231 members of the social elite, 28 were participants in the urban redevelopment program, two in political nominations, and two in public education. Polsby sees no evidence from the New Haven study to support the idea of an elitist power system such as Hunter reported in Regional City and the Lynds in Middletown. There is no "crowd" that makes the big decisions for New Haven and transmits these decisions down to individuals in the lower echelons for collective action. It is, rather, a pluralistic system of community power.

Support for a pluralistic interpretation is likewise expressed by Dahl,[21] whose own analysis of power in New Haven parallels the findings of Polsby. Dahl traced in great detail the decision-making and strategy-mapping processes in the three "issue areas" considered by Polsby, and found that, for this city, at least, the theories of monolithic power did not apply.

---

[19] Nelson W. Polsby, "Three Problems in the Analysis of Community Power," *American Sociological Review*, 24 (December 1959), 769–803.

[20] The economic elite were identified as executives of major corporations or banks, directors of corporate institutions, employers of 25 or more workers, or wealthy persons. The status elite were persons who belonged to a fashionable set and subscribed to the *New Haven Cotillion*.

[21] Robert A. Dahl, *Who Governs?* (1961).

Edgewood and Riverview

In a notable study in which both the decisional and reputational methods were employed, Presthus investigated the power structure of two small cities in upstate New York—Edgewood and Riverview.[22] These cities differed considerably in certain respects: the population of Edgewood was largely of northern European background, whereas various ethnic groups from eastern and southern Europe comprise Riverview's population. Residents of Edgewood had a higher average income and more formal education than those living in Riverview. Occupationally, Edgewood had a higher proportion of professionals and white collar persons than Riverview, many of whose residents were factory employees.

To identify the decision-makers the investigator selected five major issues in each of the cities, concerning school bonds, new industries, hospital programs, flood control, public housing, and a new community center. The first four issues occurred in both cities, and public housing was an issue only in Riverview. Those nominated by the reputational method were designated "influentials"; positional leaders as heads of major organizations were designated "organizational leaders"; and persons participating actively in the major decisions in these issues were "decision-makers." These categories were then subclassified as political, economic, and specialist—the latter including a residual category that contained professionals or others usually concerned with education, welfare, or similar matters.

From the evidence assembled Presthus concluded that two decision-making systems existed, one political and the other economic. The political power system was based mainly on public support at the polls and support from federal or state agencies, all of which were dependent in considerable measure on the tactics of politicians, mostly elected officials in the local government. The economic decision-makers were mainly in high positions in industry, finance, and business who also enjoyed superior status in the class system. Whereas the decision-makers in the political system were primarily concerned with "public" issues, such as those involving the use of public funds, the economic leaders were mainly concerned with "private" issues, such as the use of private funds in institutional operations. The specialists, while having considerable prestige in the community because of their professional status or superior education, had very limited power even though they were active in community issues and were therefore highly visible.

Decisions made by the political leaders did not occur in a vacuum of public opinion; on the contrary, citizens did exert both direct and indirect influence on the decision-makers—through the ballot, public meetings, and participation in and financial support of particular programs or opposition to them. Overall citizen participation in Edgewood was

[22] Robert Presthus, *Men at the Top* (1964).

considerably higher than in Riverview, although on most issues the proportion of citizens actively participating was very low in both communities.

There was, of course, some overlapping in decision-making by the three categories of leaders, more than Dahl found in New Haven.[23] In both Riverview and Edgewood there was considerable congruence between those designated by the reputational method and the leaders who were actively involved in decisions concerning the issues, but the overlapping varied considerably between the two communities: about two-thirds of the decision-makers in Riverview were designated reputationally as leaders, compared to slightly over two-fifths in Edgewood. Some of the persons reputed to be top leaders actually did not participate in any decisions concerning the issues.

Presthus believes that the results of his research support the pluralistic theory of community power, as opposed to an elitist theory. However, he concludes that "over the long run" economic leaders exert more power than political leaders, primarily because their tenure in positions of power is usually longer than that of the elected or appointed officeholders.

Syracuse

In view of the considerable disagreement among social scientists concerning the methods for identifying community leaders and assessing their roles in community affairs, Freeman and his associates employed four approaches in a study of the power structure in Syracuse, New York.[24] They used the decision-making, reputational, and positional methods, but added another approach which emphasized activities in various voluntary associations. From a list of about 250 community issues that had appeared in Syracuse between 1955 and 1960, 39 were selected according to certain specified criteria. Information was obtained concerning the identity of participants in community affairs, and of these 506 were finally selected as respondents for the study.

The study indicated that the top leaders according to one approach or method were not necessarily the same as those of another method. The major leaders identified by the reputational procedure appeared to derive their reputed power from position rather than from actual participation in decision-making. Those identified by reputation were generally the top executives of the major industrial, business, governmental, labor, educational, or religious organizations, but they were not necessarily the

---

[23] Dahl, *op. cit.*, pp. 180–83.

[24] Linton C. Freeman *et al.*, *Patterns of Local Community Leadership* (1960). See also Linton C. Freeman *et al.*, "Locating Leaders in Local Communities," *American Sociological Review*, 28 (October 1963), 791–99.

most active participants in community affairs. The active participants—decision-makers—were considerably removed from the pinnacles of economic power, being, for the most part, government and professional personnel or employees of the larger corporations. Below them in the power system were the activists who lacked a substantial power base except insofar as they were members of various associations and clubs. Deeply involved in local issues, they brought considerable influence to bear on the major decision-makers. One of the major conclusions of this research, so far as Syracuse was concerned, was that differing approaches or methods tend to reveal a different set of leaders or people of power. The researchers also concluded that individuals present when major decisions were made did not necessarily have a strong voice in that decision, thus contradicting the idea that the heads of organizations invariably call the shots in the major decisions concerning community affairs.

Chicago

In Chicago, Banfield investigated the procedures leading to the resolution of seven major local issues.[25] These issues centered around a proposal to enlarge the county hospital by establishing a branch medical center, merging the welfare facilities and therefore eliminating duplication of services, improving rapid transit facilities, rehabilitating a blighted area in the city, establishing a branch of the University of Illinois, and the construction of a municipal exhibition hall. All seven of the proposals were highly controversial and many persons were actively involved either in support of or opposition to them. Banfield's study concentrated on the decisions that were made and the kinds of influence that were brought to bear in attempts to resolve the issues.

In considering power and influence in Chicago, Banfield rejects the notion that a small coterie of powerful or prestigious business leaders get together behind the scenes and make decisions affecting the entire community. One reason that the reputed men of power do not perform in such a manner is that there is often a conflict of interest among them, that they may be found on different sides of important issues. If they are able to agree, of course, they might present a formidable influence, but such an elitist conception of power, in the opinion of Banfield, is more myth than reality. Another reason is that many of the powerful corporate managers exercise power only at the discretion and direction of boards of directors. They are hired hands, not proprietors or owners.

[25] Banfield, *op. cit.*

International Comparisons

Community Power in the United States and England

Using the reputational method, Miller conducted a comparative study of power and leadership in two cities, one in the United States (Pacific City) and the other in England (English City),[26] each of which had a population of about a half-million. When the results of Miller's study were compared with Hunter's study of Regional City, some rather striking differences appeared. Over half (58 percent) of the major decision-makers in Regional City were identified as representatives of business, finance, or industry, but were only one-third of the key influentials in the other two cities. In Regional City, only 15 percent were from the combined occupations representing labor, education, and government, but in Pacific City this occupational combination accounted for 48 percent of the major decision-makers and in English City for 46 percent. In the latter city, one-fifth of the reputed power elite represented labor alone, higher than for either of the American cities. That this may fairly accurately reflect the position of labor in the power structure of English City is further indicated by the composition of its city council in 1955: 35 percent were trade union members, mainly manual workers; 30 percent represented the business community; and 37 percent included professionals, housewives, retired persons, and "others."

El Paso, C. Juarez, and Tijuana

A comparative study by Form and D'Antonio in El Paso, Texas, and C. Juarez, Mexico, was concerned with the problem of whether the power elites in the two cities represented an integrated, cohesive unity that could, and did, act in concert on matters of community interest.[27] They found a considerable degree of integration and cohesion in both cities, but definitely more in El Paso than in C. Juarez, whose institutional boundaries, especially between business and government, were fairly sharply delineated. In neither city was there evidence of a single, monolithic power system in which decision-making was the monopoly of a coterie of "strong men."

Klapp and Padgett came to similar conclusions based on their study of

[26] Delbert C. Miller, "Industry and Community Power Structure: A Comparative Study of an American and an English City," *American Sociological Review*, 23 (February 1958), 9–15. See also Delbert C. Miller and William H. Form, *Industry, Labor, and Community* (1960).

[27] William H. Form and William V. D'Antonio, "Integration and Cleavage among Community Influentials in Two Border Cities," *American Sociological Review*, 24 (December 1959), 804–14.

Tijuana, Mexico, in which the reputational method was used.[28] Of the top 30 influentials identified by a panel of judges, 21 were businessmen. An "important clique" of high-ranking businessmen was observed, and there was evidence of a "loosely knit and poorly defined—though identifiable—group of leaders who recently became wealthy, drawn largely from business and the professions." Most of their social life centered around Rotary, Lions, and the country club.

Summary

This discussion of theory and method concerning the structure of community power does not point with certainty to the most valid procedure in local power analysis. However, the evidence tends to support the pluralistic as opposed to the elitist or monolithic power system in most American cities, and perhaps also in other cities of the Western democracies, at least in the middle of the twentieth century. But even in these cities there may be many patterns of power, ranging from a high concentration of power in such communities as company towns to a wide diversity of power groups each acting as a check on the power of others. One thing does seem fairly certain: the method of community-power research tends to influence the interpretations of the system. Thus the practitioners of the reputational method generally "discover" an elitist system, whereas the emphasis on decision-making as an index of power usually "reveals" a pluralistic system of power.

With the overview of community power, organization, and political participation presented in this chapter, we shall move on to consider various additional aspects of urban society. It should be emphasized that political power, however organized and manifest, is a universal feature of community life, whether urban or rural. Urban power systems are generally more complex, more closely related to large-scale organizations than is the case of rural communities. Power in whatever form tends to influence almost all aspects of community life, and community power systems may extend their influence far beyond the boundaries of the city in which they exist. An urban power system, then, may be viewed as an aspect of the urban impact, which we shall observe in the following chapter. It is also related to other social and behavioral influences of the city, including deviant behavior, social conflict, and either the unification or disruption of social groups and institutions.

---

[28] Orrin E. Klapp and L. Vincent Padgett, "Power Structure and Decision-Making in a Mexican Border City," *American Journal of Sociology*, 65 (January 1960), 400–6.

Selected Bibliography

BOOKS

Agger, Robert E., Daniel Goldrich, and Bert E. Swanson, *The Rulers and the Ruled: Political Power and Impotence in American Communities.* New York: Wiley, 1964.

Aiken, Michael, and Paul E. Mott, *The Structure of Community Power.* New York: Random House, 1970.

Banfield, Edward C., *Political Influence.* New York: The Free Press, 1961.

Bollens, John C., and Henry J. Schmandt, *The Metropolis.* New York: Harper and Row, 1965.

Bonjean, Charles M., Terry M. Clark, and Robert L. Lineberry, *Community Politics: A Behavioral Approach.* New York: The Free Press, 1971.

Clark, Terry N., ed., *Community Structure and Decision-Making.* San Francisco: Chandler, 1968.

Dahl, Robert A., *Who Governs?* New Haven: Yale University Press, 1961.

Gilbert, Claire, *Community Power Structure: Propositional Inventory, Tests, and Theory.* Gainesville: University of Florida Press, 1972.

Greenstone, J. David, and Paul E. Peterson, *Race and Authority in Urban Politics.* New York: Russell Sage Foundation, 1973.

Greer, Scott, *Metropolitics: A Study of Political Culture.* New York: Wiley, 1963.

——, *The Urbane View: Life and Politics in Metropolitan America.* New York: Oxford University Press, 1972.

Hahn, Harlan, ed., *People and Politics in Urban Society.* Beverly Hills, Calif.: Sage Publications, 1973.

Hawley, Willis D., and Frederick M. Wirt, eds., *The Search for Community Power.* Englewood Cliffs, N. J.: Prentice-Hall, 1968.

Hayes, Edward C., *Power Structure and Urban Policy: Who Rules in Oakland?* New York: McGraw-Hill, 1972.

Janowitz, Morris, ed., *Community Political Systems.* New York: The Free Press, 1961.

Presthus, Robert, *Men at the Top.* New York: Oxford University Press, 1964.

Rose, Arnold. *The Power Structure.* New York: Oxford University Press, 1967.

ARTICLES

Clark, Terry N., "Power and Community Structure," *Sociological Quarterly*, 8 (Summer 1967), 291–316.

Clelland, Donald A., and W. H. Form, "Economic Dominants and Community Power," *American Journal of Sociology*, 69 (March 1964), 511–21.

Danziger, M. Herbert, "Community Power Structures: Problems and Continuity," *American Sociological Review*, 29 (October 1964), 707–17.

D'Antonio, William V., "Review of Nelson Polsby's *Community Power and Political Theory,*" *Social Forces*, 42 (March 1964), 375–76.

——, Howard J. Ehrlich, and Eugene C. Erickson, "Further Notes on the Study of Community Power," *American Sociological Review,* 27 (December 1962), 848–854.

Friesema, H. P., "The Metropolis and the Maze of Local Government," *Urban Affairs Quarterly*, 2 (December 1966), 68–90.

Gilbert, Claire, " The Study of Community Power," in Scott Greer *et al.*, eds., *The New Urbanization,* pp. 222–45. New York: St. Martin's Press, 1968.

Miller, Delbert C., "Design Strategies for Comparative International Studies of Community Power," *Social Forces*, 51 (March 1973), 261–74.

Perrucci, Robert, and Marc Pilisuk, "Leaders and Ruling Elites: The Interorganizational Bases of Community Power," *American Sociological Review,* 35 (December 1970), 1040–57.

Spinrad, William, "Power in Local Communities," *Social Problems* 12 (Winter 1965), 335–56.

Walton, John, "Differential Patterns of Community Power Structure," *Sociological Quarterly*, 9 (Winter 1968), 3–18.

Wolfinger, Raymond E., "Reputation and Reality in the Study of Community Power," *American Sociological Review*, 25 (October 1960), 636–44.

THE SOCIAL PSYCHOLOGY
OF URBAN LIFE

18 • Urbanization: Impact and Process

The concept of urbanization has a dual meaning. In one aspect, it is demographic, referring to the increasing proportion of population in a country or region who reside in cities. In another aspect, it has reference to the process whereby people are influenced by the values, behavior, institutions, and material things that are identified as urban in origin and use. It is well to keep this dual meaning in mind; yet the two meanings are invariably related. As a country or region becomes more urbanized in the demographic or ecological sense, the people, rural and urban alike, are increasingly influenced by the process.

In this chapter we shall consider various aspects of urbanization, emphasizing its social and cultural consequences, but against the background of demographic factors. We shall also discuss the interaction and reciprocal influences between cities and their hinterlands. As we have noted earlier, Europe and North America started early on the road to urbanism and industrialism, and the forces set in motion by these developments have literally penetrated all parts of the globe, to the extent that this phenomenon is often referred to as "Westernization." National as well as regional and municipal boundaries are easily hurdled in the transmigration of culture and ideas born of urban-industrial developments in the Western world. Perhaps not a single non-Western society remains unaffected, even the traditional or developing societies. But urbanization also continues apace in the very societies that generated the trend.

Stages of Urban Development and Selected Indicators

Any consideration of the impact of urbanism must take into account many variables: the behavior and values of persons who may be affected by urban influences; the geographic location of persons, whether residing in cities or the hinterlands; the effects on the political, economic, and occupational organization of the cities or the hinterlands; the health, education, and general welfare of individuals involved; and so on. It must also be kept in mind that the social and cultural systems of societies differ and that these differences invariably have a bearing on the interaction between a city and its hinterland.

The extent of demographic urbanization provides a crude barometer of urbanization in the social and cultural sense. For certain indexes the differences between highly industrialized and urbanized societies, on the one hand, and countries with a small percentage of the population living in cities, on the other, are often considerable. These differences for countries in various stages of demographic urbanization are indicated in Table 18.1. National Group I represents highly urbanized countries (6); Group II, countries with 25 or more percent urban in 1920 (3); Group III, other countries that had reached 25 percent urban between 1920 and 1960 (10); and Group IV, countries that had not reached 25 percent urban by 1960 (29).[1]

TABLE 18.1: Averages of Social Indicators for Countries Classified According to Extent of Urbanization

	Group I	Group II	Group III	Group IV
Percent urban[a]	52	56	32	11
Infant mortality[b]	20	71	62	103
Life expectancy[c]	71	64	58	45
Literacy rate[d]	98	88	53	26
Daily newspaper circulation[e]	369	162	68	11
Physician ratio[f]	990	977	2,492	12,395
Mail circulation[g]	176	30	22	9
Income per capita[h]	$1066	$320	$292	$137

[a]Cities of 20,000 or over.
[b]Deaths of children under one year, per 1,000 live births.
[c]Expectancy of life at birth, both sexes.
[d]Percentage of males and females 15 years or older able to read and write.
[e]Number of copies of newspaper per 1,000 inhabitants.
[f]Number of inhabitants for each registered physician.
[g]Number of pieces of mail received or sent yearly for each inhabitant.
[h]Dollar equivalent.
SOURCE: United Nations, Department of Economic Affairs, *Urbanization: Development Policies and Planning* (1968), pp. 22–23.

The brief list of indicators in Table 18.1 is by no means complete; many other variables or criteria would probably vary according to the stage of urban development, among them the incidence and velocity of vertical mobility, social and economic differentiation, the institutionalization of education, the number and kinds of organizations, and so on.

---

[1] United Nations, Department of Economic Affairs, *Urbanization: Development Policies and Planning* (1968), pp. 22–23.

For example, as societies become increasingly urbanized, social emphasis is placed on achievement rather than ascription.

It would be misleading to interpret the differences in indicators solely in terms of a cause-and-effect relationship with urban growth, since there are various unrelated factors that may account for such differences. What one may observe, however, is the existence of significantly high statistical correlations between the level or stage of urbanization and several social indicators. In 1960, for example, there was a positive coefficient of correlation of .69 between percent of population urban and newspaper circulation, a correlation of .65 with literacy, and a correlation of .72 with life expectancy. On the other hand, there was a negative correlation of $-.52$ with infant mortality.[2] Although the process is complex, the effects of urbanism are quite clear; therefore, we shall frequently mention urban or metropolitan influence in the following discussion.

Institutional Networks
Relating City and Hinterland

Because every community in an urban-industrial society is involved in an institutional network, it is therefore misleading to regard a community as a separate entity apart from the larger society. This trend appears to have gone far in technologically advanced countries. Even in developing societies such as exist in Asia, Africa, and the Middle East the small community is part of a larger organizational and cultural network, which may, of course, differ in complexity and functions from networks in urban-industrial societies.

Springdale

In their study of this small town in New York State, Vidich and Bensman have described the organizational network that connects the villagers with urban mass society.[3] These organizations have provided the mechanism through which outside mass culture has been funneled into the local community, largely because they are national or international in scope. Among them are 4-H Clubs, Future Farmers of America, Boy and Girl Scouts, the American Legion, Masonic and Odd Fellows lodges, the National Grange, a Parent-Teacher Association, and religious denominations. State and national governments involve Springdale through such agencies as the Social Security Administration, agricultural marketing organizations, university extension, the state recreation

[2] *Ibid.*, p. 27.

[3] Arthur J. Vidich and Joseph Bensman, *Small Town in Mass Society* (1958), see page 493 for a description of the economic impact of mass society on Springdale.

commission, and the state department of education. Representatives of these organizations, as leaders or experts, through their personal contacts with the local community, are important carriers of culture from the outside.

Plainville

Much the same picture is presented by Gallaher in a study of a small town in Missouri.[4] The establishment of federal agencies relating to agriculture was, in Gallaher's opinion, a significant factor in effecting changes through the diffusion of technology and techniques, which have greatly altered the traditional style of work and life. By the same token, connections with private or cooperative organizations have also brought the town into a greater dependency relationship with the larger society. Since Plainville, like many other communities, is confronted with problems too complex to be settled by local action alone, the community is forced to accept external authority and assistance through the various organizations that link the town to the wider urban world. Thus, the people of Plainville, through the mass media and through organizational ties with the outside, have been brought into the mainstream of urban America. Gallaher concluded:

> And so it goes—the community of Plainville has opened up more to the socioeconomic impact and cultural influences of urban American society since 1939–40 than in all its previous history. As urban values steadily penetrate the Plainville subculture, it is little wonder that the people increasingly depend upon external sources of authority for innovations and assistance. They, and similar rural communities, are caught in a complex web of the mass society which now impinges in some form or another upon most institutionalized areas of their behavior.[5]

All of these changes have a bearing on status systems. Gallaher has placed considerable emphasis on these changes in Plainville, noting that imported agricultural machinery and techniques provide an important basis for enhancing the prestige of farmers. "Thus, a farm family derives greater or lesser prestige through ownership of technological equipment which now becomes an end in itself, a symbol of economic achievement. Those who invest heavily in machinery gain, among other things, considerable prestige satisfaction, whereas those who do not are judged as 'backward,' 'behind the times,' and 'tight.'"[6] Gallaher is of the opinion that change in Plainville's status system is a kind of secondary effect derived from possession of agricultural techniques and technology which further economic achievement and therefore symbolize social prestige.

[4] Art Gallaher, *Plainville Fifteen Years Later* (1961).
[5] *Ibid.*, p. 247.
[6] *Ibid.*, p. 207.

Urban Influences in
Nonindustrial Countries

The foregoing discussion applies particularly to urban-industrial countries of the West, but the same process of regional formation and urban dominance is emerging in developing countries in which the bulk of the population resides in villages and small towns. Almost all of these countries have large and medium-sized cities which may be political capitals or other centers that dominate culturally and economically, in varying degrees, their regional hinterlands. Yet this domination is less pervasive than that of cities in urban-industrial countries, largely because technology applied to industry, transportation, and communication is relatively undeveloped. Whereas rural people in North America, western Europe, and Australia or New Zealand are highly urbanized in the cultural sense, the rural populations of developing countries, except those residing close to cities, have not experienced the impact of urban culture as have Western people.

India

A study of India by Ellefsen demonstrates some differences between metropolitan regions in that nation and those of the United States that probably typify the differences between developed and underdeveloped countries.[7] The study examined the nature and extent of the hinterlands of Bombay, Delhi, Madras, Hyderabad, and Baroda, all very large cities of metropolitan stature. Many measures used to delineate the boundaries of metropolitan influence in Western countries are unsuitable in India. For example, rates of metropolitan newspaper circulation as a regional index are of limited value when most of the population is illiterate.

Data from the Indian census were used to measure the degree to which the territory adjacent to the built-up areas of the cities exhibited traits that resembled the city rather than the rural villages. Such characteristics as population density, the proportion of the labor force employed in nonagricultural pursuits, and literacy were shown to decline with distance from the city, the usual gradient pattern of metropolitan influence. The pattern of metropolitan hinterlands in India does not extend evenly around the cities but radiates along the sectors which are most accessible to them, thus underscoring the importance of transportation and communication systems in determining the extent of metropolitan influence. Beyond that, the rural landscape and way of life are typically those of the traditional village.

---

[7] Richard A. Ellefsen, "City-Hinterland Relationships in India," in Roy Turner, ed., *India's Urban Future* (1962), pp. 94–114.

In India there is a sharp rural-urban contrast, both socially and physically, whereas in the United States and western Europe metropolitan influence extends further, and differences between city and country are often only matters of degree. Radio, telephone, television, and the mass circulation of newspapers and magazines expose Americans and Europeans, whether in city or country, to a wide diversity of ideas and standards. Relatively high farm incomes allow farmers to buy the same goods as city dwellers and widespread transportation systems enable them to visit cities frequently. None of these things pertain to India, except for people living close to an urban center.

The Diffusion Process and Content

Urban or metropolitan impact may occur at different parts of a region or subregion, and in many different ways, as urban culture becomes diffused beyond a city's political boundary. The cultural content may be disseminated by human carriers who transmit their ideas, techniques, skills, and modes of behavior through interpersonal contacts, or by mass transportation and communication. A villager who has lived or worked in a city and who returns to his rural home is a carrier capable of transmitting to his village kin or friends some of the culture he has acquired through urban residence.

This process of diffusion is reversed through the flow of culture into the city from the outside. Indeed, much of the discussion in Chapter 20 on the adjustment of migrants in the city is concerned with urbanization as a socializing, acculturative, and diffusion process. As a rural hinterland becomes urbanized in a cultural and social sense, so do urban communities become ruralized, partly by the presence in the city of rural or village folk who take with them their values and behavior patterns when they visit or take up residence in an urban community. But the outflow of urban culture is generally greater in volume and the impact more penetrating, at least more dramatic and apparent, than the impact of rural culture on urban people and their social life. Even so, the process remains a reciprocal one.

In the interaction between a city and its hinterland there are many ways in which the city itself is influenced by the hinterland. Let us take migration as an example. For every incoming migrant certain facilities must be provided, and often at considerable cost. These include health-care facilities, housing, schools, and the like. If the adult in-migrant is well educated or highly skilled the community must provide him with a place of employment. Drucker estimates that an average community investment, in public or private funds, of $20,000 is needed for each "knowledgeable" worker.[8] For teachers, there must be schools; for

---

[8] Peter F. Drucker, "The Surprising Seventies," *Harpers Magazine*, 243 (July 1971), 38.

physicians, hospitals and laboratories; for specialists in public recreation, recreational facilities; for ministers, churches; for architects or city planners, facilities for carrying out their occupational specialty. To be sure, these people may be needed, and the community may be compensated by the services they provide. They are economic and social assets. In-migrants with lesser education and skills may also be assets, but such persons have become increasingly dispensable because of mechanization and automation, and are often more an economic liability than an asset to the city, at least in the short run.

Organized Diffusion

Of special relevance is urbanization through planned cultural diffusion, most notably the many organized efforts to disseminate Western urban culture to underdeveloped areas in recent decades. Among the most important of these are the community development programs now being carried on in the rural sections of various countries, often with the assistance of the United Nations or of particular industrialized coun-

A community development worker gives a cooking lesson for residents of La Cruz de la Paloma, a Venezuelan City. The government maintains a center for training in community development. (United Nations)

tries. Through the introduction of modern techniques of agriculture, medicine, and education (mainly Western), it is expected that the level of physical, social, and economic well-being of the villagers will be improved. A more comprehensively planned cultural diffusion is embodied in government-sponsored programs, or those sponsored by philanthropic foundations, which include such agents as technical experts, educators, artists, industrialists, editors, and so on.

In the United States, diffusion is commonly organized as when agricultural extension services headquartered in universities convey, directly or indirectly, to the rural dweller many kinds of skills and techniques, including information that may be applied to various aspects of his way of life. The mass media also play significant roles in diffusing new knowledge, organization, and techniques.

Once an element of urban culture is accepted and incorporated into the values and institutional system, its effects become cumulative. Often the secondary or tertiary effects may be unanticipated and thus problems arise. An agricultural implement invented and manufactured in an industrial city and adopted in a farming community will very likely improve production, raise the farmer's income, and probably elevate his social status and that of his family. But it may also modify some of the traditional roles and life styles and therefore alter interpersonal relationships. In addition, it may undermine some of the folk beliefs concerning agriculture, and by increasing agricultural efficiency it may reduce the need for farm workers, who may then head for the city to find jobs. Many other familiar technological, scientific, and organizational innovations conceived and developed in an urban milieu have had effects, a chain reaction, that were completely unanticipated at the time they were introduced.

Some Specific Aspects of Urbanization

The application of modern technology has destroyed some occupations while strengthening others or creating new ones. Rural craftsmen have often been unable to compete with mass-production factories. The village smithy was a familiar figure on the American rural scene until well into the twentieth century, but his role has been assumed by the automobile or tractor mechanic. Similarly, the village miller has been rendered obsolete by grain-processing plants in urban centers. Even artistic craftsmen have turned to machine production to provide cheap consumer goods for the tourist market. In North African cities, according to LeTourneau, artisans with their age-old techniques have been unable to compete with the flood of factory-made goods produced in the United States, Europe, and Japan.[9]

One of the important distinctions between urban and peasant or rural society lies in the conception and observance of time. In the city, work and life in general are subject to the tyranny of the clock or the calendar. City people become acutely conscious of time because many phases of their existence are regulated according to a specific schedule reduced to hours and minutes. As rural communities come under the influence of the city, particularly through the mass media, their awareness of time is heightened and behavior patterns are altered to meet its demands.

The Effect of Cities on Small Communities

Urbanism's influence on rural life in urban-industrial societies has resulted in profound alterations in the size and functions of many small communities. In the United States, thousands of hamlets and crossroads villages are "drying up" as motorized farmers bypass them to shop, attend church, go to the movies, visit friends, obtain medical treatment, or work at jobs in larger centers. Throughout rural America there are ghost towns that once provided jobs, services, and recreation for local residents. Now the people are gone, except perhaps for a few aging pensioners.

Although many villages still provide certain basic institutional functions such as schools, churches, and facilities for "convenience" shopping, major purchases are usually made in larger centers. Often the population in such rural places has remained fairly stable, with the number of out-migrants balancing the natural demographic increase.[10] Many rural communities have become commuter towns in which working residents shuttle back and forth daily between city and village or farm. Although the economies of these communities cannot provide jobs for all of the people who live there, many residents nevertheless maintain their rural residence and travel a considerable distance to an urban work place.

Consumer Behavior

The availability of factory-made goods in urban-industrial countries has modified changes in consumer behavior and values. The preoccupation is not only with *what* to consume but also with *how* to consume

[9] Roger LeTourneau, "Social Change in the Muslim Cities of North Africa," *American Journal of Sociology*, 60 (May 1955), 31–32.

[10] Glenn V. Fuguitt, "The City and Countryside," *Rural Sociology*, 28 (September 1963), 246–61.

according to socially approved standards. Much social conversation is concerned with matters relating to consumption. Food culture, for example, has radically changed in both rural and urban areas in the United States. Villagers and farmers live out of factorymade containers, though not to the same extent as urban dwellers. Rural clothing styles are urban styles, dictated by designers in the great cities, advertised and described in the urban-centered mass media, and distributed, often ready-made, to rural and urban purchasers alike. Residents of Small-town are not easily distinguishable in their attire from those who live in Megalopolis.

The same trend in consumer behavior and values may be observed in nonindustrial countries, although the influence of cities in this respect is undoubtedly less than in urban-industrial societies for fairly clear reasons: fewer factory-made goods are available; most people have limited purchasing power, which is often directed by necessity to "survival" goods; the mass media carrying information about consumer goods or behavior reach only a limited percentage of the population; and transportation facilities are such as to restrict direct contacts between urban and rural folk, especially those living in remote districts. Yet in one way or another, awareness of consumer goods is increasing as information concerning them penetrates the hinterlands.

Social Organization

Long-time trends in the increasing variety and complexity of organizations have been characteristic of cities in urban-industrial societies, and to a lesser extent in nonindustrial countries. One of the "exports" of cities to rural hinterlands has been forms of organization, bearing the imprint of urban origin, that sometimes provide a channel of communication between rural or small-town people and urban residents. A considerable number of organizations that are national in scope, with membership drawn from all kinds and sizes of communities, originated in cities. These include such diverse groups as veterans' organizations, book clubs, religious groups, civic associations, and the like. The Rotary Club, for example, was organized in Chicago in 1905, but within 30 years about two-fifths of all local Rotary clubs were in towns of less than 5,000.[11]

Agricultural marketing associations may have their headquarters in cities, but their members are mainly rural people engaged in agriculture. As the differentiation of economic functions so characteristic of the city has spread to rural environs, agriculture particularly has become increasingly specialized. And by the same token, the trend toward large-scale organization has also occurred in the rural sectors, as is evidenced

[11] Lewis Atherton, *Main Street on the Middle Border* (1954), pp. 290–93.

by farming carried on as a corporate enterprise, a far cry from the traditional family farm. The increasing number of gigantic farms, some thousands of acres in area, are owned and managed through corporations headquartered in cities. They are veritable "factories in the fields."[12]

Changes in Agriculture

Various measures of land use indicate the pervasive nature of metropolitan influence in the United States as it spreads even to far-removed farm areas and villages. The so-called milk-shed is an apt illustration. Because milk is a highly perishable commodity, its delivery to city consumers must be done rapidly and with regularity. Owing to improved means of transportation and to efficient methods of production and processing, the milk shed around major cities has come to encompass an increasingly larger area. Milk trucks range over the rural hinterland many miles from a metropolis, delivering milk to the central dairies for processing and redistribution. In general, the larger the city the greater is the milk region.

Springdale, a town of about 2,500 in upstate New York, illustrates the impact of widening milk supply areas.[13] With the advent of the milk truck, the production of butter and cheese, buckwheat, maple syrup, hay, and sheep was gradually superseded in Springdale by the production of fluid milk for daily delivery to urban markets. The mechanized accessories of milk processing outmoded the large farm family, many of whose members migrated elsewhere. Thus, mechanization and increased contact with the outside world transformed the social and economic life of Springdale.

Gottmann observed a similar trend among farmers in three Pennsylvania counties not far from the metropolitan concentrations on the Atlantic seaboard.[14] Here the farmers are more or less specialized, producing fluid milk to be picked up and delivered daily to the city by milk trucks or raising and marketing animals and their by-products for urban consumption. As farming in the area has become specialized, the farmer's dependence on city markets has correspondingly increased. Urban "middle men" set the prices he will receive for his commodities, and he must conform to certain state, federal, and local laws pertaining to the production and marketing of his products. Thus, the vaunted independence of the farmer is rapidly becoming a tradition of the past in American society.

One of the changes in agriculture associated with urban developments

---

[12] See especially Peter Barnes, "The Great American Land Grab," *New Republic*, 164 (June 5, 1971), 19–23.

[13] Vidich and Bensman, *op. cit.,* pp. 10–11.

[14] Jean Gottmann, *Megalopolis* (1961), pp. 225–32.

in the United States has been part-time farming within the commuting zone of cities. Rural dwellers who commute to work in nearby cities often reside on farms operated by one or more members of the family who are not employed at urban jobs, or by the urban worker himself in the evening, or on weekends and holidays. Such farms vary in size, depending on the nature of the agricultural operation and the amount of manpower needed. The raising and grazing of livestock on pasture land, for example, is suitable for part-time farming because manpower needs are commonly minimal. Often urban workers who operate small tracts on a part-time basis produce farm products for home consumption or even for sale to supplement family incomes. Since many urban-employed workers commute fifty miles or more to work, part-time farming in an urban region may develop fairly extensively in large areas.

Urbanization in Africa

The African family in an urban environment is often shorn of its religious, educational, and economic functions,[15] which, as in all urban communities, have been taken over by other groups or agencies. But the changes have been so rapid in recent years that serious dislocations have occurred. The lack of a stable community having norms of behavior recognized and supported by a general consensus has made itself acutely felt in parent-child relationships. Parental authority is undermined by the influence of gangs, movies, and street life in general. As opportunities for gainful employment have increased the independence and prestige of African women, they no longer are automatically held in a position of subordination. But their new independence has contributed to marital instability, which in turn has been associated with such deviant behavior as illicit sex relations.

New forms of social stratification, reflecting occupational and income differentials, are emerging in African cities. Those on the higher levels of the emergent social structure are manifesting many characteristics of Westernization—in food habits, dress, etiquette, formal education, recreation, house furnishings, and the like—and diversification of interests has found expression through varied types of voluntary associations, some of which are fashioned after Western models. Breakdowns, stresses, and tensions associated with urbanization have not yet been counterbalanced by new norms of conduct appropriate to city life.

Writing of the new societies in Africa, Hunter observes: "There is a constant coming and going, from town (city) to village and village to town, of labor migration, for education, to visit relations, to trade. Towns

[15] UNESCO, *Social Implications of Industrialization and Urbanization in Africa South of the Sahara* (1956).

in themselves, in any part of Africa, force new ideas upon the visitor."[16]

The Urban Impact on African Village Life

In certain respects the urban impact in Africa is felt as keenly in rural tribal communities as it is in the cities. The migration of males to the cities for employment may increase family incomes, but when mainly women and children are left behind the peasant economy is undermined, even if only temporarily, because no one is left to cultivate the village's holdings. Factory-made objects have come to be valued for their status symbolism as well as for their utility; hence, there is considerable inducement to spend money for luxuries instead of food and other physical necessities. The skills the migrants learn in the city may have little functional value in the tribal community when they return. Wage earners returning from the city with well-filled pockets and esoteric notions of behavior are inclined to flout the traditional system of authority and repudiate those responsible for its maintenance.

The increase in village incomes through outside earnings has added an important element to the prestige system in emphasizing status by achievement rather than by tribal or kinship ascription. Marriageable girls accord preferential treatment to men who have returned with glamorous accounts of life in the city; hence, individualization of mate selection is encouraged in contrast to the traditional system of selection by families.

These and other influences affecting family organization result in an increase of broken homes and various forms of individualized deviant behavior. Since family and tribe are integrated into the same social system, the disruptive effects have manifest themselves in what has been called "detribalization." A basic factor in this disruption is the decline in ascribed kinship and tribal authority as urban equalitarian values associated with pecuniary achievement have become widespread. Clearly the villages are going through some kind of transition which may presage the emergence of a different social and economic system.

Urbanization in Asia

In Asia, as in Africa, the urbanizing process has affected the functions and structure of the family, whether rural or urban. In parts of Asia, though not in all, the joint family, or larger kinship group, which

[16] Guy Hunter, *The New Societies of Tropical Africa* (1962), p. 90.

functions as a unit, has tended to give way in the cities to the nuclear family consisting of parents and children.[17] Occupational differentiation in urban centers has made possible the gainful employment outside the home of married and unmarried women. These role changes have invariably altered the social status of women and affected interpersonal relationships both within and outside the home. The migration to cities of large numbers of males who leave their families in the native villages has likewise created problems of deviant behavior, since the men are removed, at least temporarily, from the immediate influences of their own families.

Another striking aspect of urbanization in Asia is the alteration of economic behavior in both rural and urban communities. Consumer habits have been modified and "needs" created in peasant communities as factory-made goods are made available at prices many can afford. Although cities all along have had a money economy, this system has spread to their rural hinterlands, partially replacing the system of barter and introducing various kinds of credit and financial facilities. Monetization and its associated attitudes afford precise pecuniary evaluations of work and goods, greater freedom of action than has been traditionally the case, and greater flexibility in social relationships. It has also made possible the extensive diffusion of factory-made goods and therefore new patterns of consumer behavior and new consumer interests.

The Urbanization of
Two Indian Villages

SHAMIRPET In the urbanizing process the diffusion of technology or skills generally occurs fairly rapidly, but changes in social organization or patterns of thought usually occur more slowly, a disparity Dube pointed out in his study of Shamirpet, an Indian village near the city of Hyderabad. Continuous interaction between the village and city familiarized the villagers with many aspects of the metropolis—and Western culture as well. Dube noted that the contacts of the Shamirpet villagers with Hyderabad were varied and numerous. They frequently visited their relatives and friends in the city, and the city dwellers often returned to the village to visit their friends or relatives. There were occasional excursions to the city for shopping or to attend a movie or a ceremony, and urban-employed workers shuttled back and forth between the city of employment and the village they regarded as home.

---

[17] S. C. Dube, *Indian Village* (1967), pp. 212–35. This change, however, may be more apparent than real. Often the nuclear family remains an integral part of a joint or extended family, although residing in separate locations and functioning as a family unit within the context of the larger kinship group, which is also organized as a unit. For further discussion of related points, see Chapter 12 on urban status systems and Chapter 14 on urban family life.

In Shamirpet, mill-made clothing and shoes of Western design partly replaced indigenous attire. Articles having considerable prestige symbolism such as factory-made bangles, sunglasses, fountain pens, watches, and safety razors were in demand. Factories in Hyderabad turned out cheap cigarettes, replacing the hand-made cigarettes produced in the village, and various beverages produced in the city were consumed in quantity. Craftsmen like blacksmiths, carpenters, and tailors were using factory-made tools and instruments. Modern clinical medicine had become competitive with folk medicine, and many families purchased cheap patent medicines in Hyderabad or at the local dispensary. At the time of the study there was one phonograph in the village, and one crystal radio set, located in the tea shop. In keeping with his exalted position, the village headman had acquired an antiquated automobile, the only one in town. Recreationally, some of the young men played volley ball and cricket, both Western importations, and many patronized the cinema in the city.

Many social and psychological changes were also fairly evident in Shamirpet. Dube noted rather widespread dissatisfaction of the younger people with village life. Those with some education tended to idealize

The traditional and the modern. The contrasting attire of a mother and daughter in downtown Tokyo symbolizes the social-cultural changes associated with Japan's rapid urbanization. (Noel P. Gist)

497

city life and had considerable contempt for the rustic ways of village folk, thus often creating disharmony within family groups and raising serious questions concerning the principles which, by custom, accorded special priorities and privileges to persons on the basis of age and kinship status. Not only had family solidarity declined, in Dube's opinion, but there had also been a decline in sentimental attachments for the village community. Many caste rules such as prohibitions against interdining were relaxed, and new manifestations of political consciousness and interest, including voting behavior, were beginning to appear. "In a small rural community such as Shamirpet, which is situated near a big and modern city and is in everyday contact with it, the prevailing climate of opinion in social, economic, and political matters in the city is bound to influence its general outlook and ways, for apart from their practical value city-ways are gradually coming to be regarded as more 'respectable' and 'progressive'."[18]

Yet there was also evidence in Shamirpet of complete or partial rejection of certain aspects of urban culture. This was manifest in competition between sentiments and loyalties directed toward city culture or the greater social order, and those in support of the regional or local culture with its own customs and values. Many idealized the traditional and familiar, yet tended to follow the lead of the urbanized and powerful elite. The caste and kinship system, though weakened by the impact of urbanism, was still a "going concern," fairly intact so far as structural features were concerned. Independence of action had increased, but parents still selected mates for their marriageable children and defined their intrafamily relationships in many respects. Although secularization had occurred, most of the people in the village retained their religious ideologies and practiced the ancient ceremonies of the Hindu faith. Western conceptions of equalitarianism and achievement were finding acceptance, but adherence to nonequalitarian principles of a rigidly hierarchical social system had not changed very much, and ascribed statuses in all aspects of of life were widely observed. Shamirpet was truly a community in transition.

NAMHALLI Reporting on a study of Namhalli, an Indian village not far from the metropolis of Bangalore, Beals described in considerable detail the changes associated with modernization or urbanization of the community from around the turn of the century until the 1950's.[19] During the early part of this period, families began to develop a "need" for machine-made goods. Villagers finding employment in Bangalore, and farmers and artisans marketing their wares in the same city, were reimbursed in cash. This transition to a money economy enabled the

[18] *Ibid.*, p. 228.

[19] Alan R. Beals, "Interplay among Factors of Change in a Mysore Village," in McKim Marriott, ed., *Village India* (1955), pp. 78–101.

visitors to purchase such things as factory-made cloth, iron plows, roofing tile, bicycles, and the like. Western manners and mannerisms were imitated, and European styles of clothing and haircuts for men became the vogue. Village ceremonials were continued, however, but on a reduced scale, since urban forms of entertainment, either in Bangalore or Namhalli, became increasingly competitive. These included the movies, radio, horse-racing, and recreation in the city's coffee shops. Urban-style courts of justice, introduced in the 1920's, tended to replace the village councils (*panchayats*) in the settlement of disputes. These courts have had far-reaching effects because they have provided new interpretations and definitions of such matters as property rights and interpersonal relations.

Beals pointed out that Namhalli was only one of many villages that have experienced modernization or urbanization through the influence of Bangalore, as well as influence coming from the larger society. "Buses, motor trucks, and railroads carry thousands of villagers to Bangalore every day. Many of them leave with urban gimcracks in their shopping bags and new ideas in their heads."[20]

Permanence and Change
in Indian Villages

In reviewing the literature on social change in Indian villages, Lambert concludes that the urban impact has often been exaggerated, that village social systems have been remarkably stable.[21] Social changes have occurred, of course, but Lambert believes that many of them have been relatively superficial. He cites, for example, the case of the village of Bhadkad, located two miles from a railway line that connects with the metropolis of Bombay. Two studies of Bhadkad were conducted, one in 1913, the other in 1955, during which changes in food habits, attire, living conditions, work patterns, and so on were recorded. But the pattern of caste had not changed appreciably, nor had customs and ceremonials regulating marriage and family life. The general picture of the village was one of stability, and the changes that occurred, in Lambert's judgment, "seem not to be linked to urban centers, but to reflect changes in the whole society."[22]

Lambert believes that among the most effective agents of social change were former villagers who returned from the city to their home community and brought to the village "not just an urbanized but a Westernized life style."[23] If they had considerable wealth—retired pen-

---

[20] *Ibid.*, p. 78.
[21] Richard D. Lambert, "The Impact of Urban Society upon Village Life," in Roy Turner, ed., *India's Urban Future* (1962), ch. 6.
[22] *Ibid.*, p. 124.
[23] *Ibid.*, p. 126.

sioners, for example—they were accorded prestige and, through emulation by the villagers, became agents of change. It was also Lambert's opinion that the diffusion into the villages of new functions of cities resulted in serious rural dislocations.

In his study of Rampur, an Indian village near Delhi, Lewis was impressed with the stability of the community, its local life and institutions, "despite the many urban influences to which it has been subject."[24] He found that the agricultural economy had not changed much, that the caste system and kinship organization remained strong and dominated the life of the villagers. It was definitely a *gemeinschaft* type of community, less formally organized than Tepoztlan, the Mexican town studied by Lewis. Although located near a major metropolis, it nevertheless showed evidence of considerable cultural and social isolation. Lewis concluded that the familiar theoretical models of folk and peasant villages can easily become stereotypes, that there are marked variations in their internal structures, relationships, and forms of social change.

Urbanization in the Middle East

In an analysis of the urbanizing and Westernizing process of social change in the Middle East,[25] the authors employed the concept of "modernization" in somewhat the same sense that we have used "urbanization." In the modernizing process, cities are the primary variable[26] because they provide the physical and psychosocial conditions that set in motion the need for modernization and the facilities for bringing it about. A second variable is literacy, which the authors consider both an index and an agent. Cities in the modern world invariably require a large literate population in order to function properly. A third related variable, going hand in hand with literacy, is media participation—the use made of the media of communication, or the consumption of its contents. A fourth variable is political participation as indicated by interest in public issues and the expression of this interest in discussion and voting behavior.

These four variables are positively correlated, that is, city growth and the other variables tend to occur together. After a certain proportion of the population residing in cities is reached, however, the further growth of cities becomes less important because the modernizing forces have already been set in motion.

[24] Oscar Lewis, *Village Life in Northern India* (1958), pp. 322–27.
[25] Daniel Lerner and Lucille W. Plevsner, *The Passing of Traditional Society* (1958).
[26] *Ibid.*, pp. 61–65.

Modernization, as the authors see it, then, is the transition toward a Westernized and urbanized society whose characteristic members are literate, consumers of the mass media, capable of imagining themselves in varieties of situations beyond their immediate boundaries, and willing to formulate opinions and make judgments (voting) relative to public issues. Such a society they designate as "modernized," and its ideal-typical members are Modern Men. At the other pole of this typology is the society in which the characteristic members are nonliterate, nonpartici-pants in the mass media, commonly incapable of imaginatively project-ing themselves beyond their immediate milieu, and lacking in interest or opinions concerning problems of a community or societal character. Such persons, in this typology, are Traditional Men. In between these two types, and having characteristics of both, are the Transitionals. By means of a scaling procedure the authors developed a three-category typology based on quantitative data and used in their analysis of Middle Eastern cultures.

With this conceptual approach, they explored the modernization (or urbanization) of several Middle Eastern countries: Turkey, Lebanon, Egypt, Syria, Jordan, and Iran. Through extensive personal interviews, both in rural and urban communities, they obtained a great deal of data on the nature and process of modernization and on the persons who had or had not been influenced by contacts with urban culture. Some of these persons were cosmopolitan in outlook, urbane, intellectually sophisticat-ed, curious about the world around them and the world beyond their own milieu.

But others were Traditional Men without either sophistication or curiosity. "My God! How can you say such a thing?" said a shepherd in Turkey when asked to imagine himself as head of the Turkish govern-ment and to state what he would do if he were the head. Such questions when put to the Traditionals were often "baffling, disturbing, and even impious," but when asked of the Moderns they were more likely to be considered interesting and stimulating. The Traditionals characteristi-cally thought public issues beyond their comprehension and actually none of their business; the Moderns commonly had knowledge of the issues and held opinions about them. Table 18.2 highlights some of the differences that distinguish the three types.

Other distinctive differences were observed by Lerner and Plevsner. The urbanized Moderns are motivated to achieve higher status and to re-evaluate their roles, while the Traditionals are more likely to accept the roles and statuses assigned to them. Moderns are more secularized in the sense that their mosque or church attendance tends to decline, while the Traditionals retain their loyalty to religion, family, and village. Moderns join clubs and other voluntary associations, but these groups have little influence in the lives of the Traditionals. Familiarity with urban culture, and particularly with the content of the mass media,

TABLE 18.2: Percentage Distribution of Turkish Moderns, Transitionals, and Traditionals According to Designated Attributes

	Modern	Transitional	Traditional
Residents of cities over 50,000	81	61	35
Clerical, professional, and business occupations	85	68	43
Education above elementary level	70	46	8
Literacy	98	71	19
Source of last news received:			
Newspapers	54	46	8
Radio	39	26	10
Word of mouth	6	26	78
Attend movies	88	63	27
Ability to imagine being Turkish president	86	63	35
Know what United Nations is	82	55	10
N =	(105)	(105)	(49)

SOURCE: Daniel Lerner and Lucille W. Plevsner, *The Passing of Traditional Society* (1958); adapted from Tables 1, 2, 4, and 8, pp. 137–44. Reprinted with permission of the publisher. Copyright 1958 by The Free Press, A Corporation.

affords prestige. "When my son comes from the city," said an illiterate Lebanese mother, "he feels like a lord among the neighbors because he reads the newspaper in the city, and he always has many new things to tell the people in the village around."[27]

The Urbanization of a Canadian Village

The impact of urban culture on St. Denis, an isolated French-Canadian community, was studied by Miner, who compared the changes that had occurred there between 1936–1937 and 1949.[28] Although this was not a long period of time, many changes were nevertheless apparent, both in material and nonmaterial cultural forms. The introduction of farm machinery altered in numbers of ways the traditional mode of life. Store-bought goods such as bakery bread, overstuffed furniture, manufactured soap, and ice cream were introduced into the households during the period, and many houses were supplied with running water and indoor toilets. Homespun clothes were replaced by manufactured attire purchased from a local store or mail-order houses. "Both men and women," says Miner, "want to dress like city people." Judging from the increased circulation of newspapers during the period, the habit of

[27] *Ibid.*, p. 189.

[28] Horace Miner, "A New Epoch in Rural Quebec," *American Journal of Sociology*, 51 (July 1950), 1–10. See also his *St. Denis: A French-Canadian Parish* (1963).

reading had become more widespread. Folk medicine, although still practiced, was being replaced by modern medical techniques introduced by doctors moving into the locality. An immediate effect of the change in medical practice was the decline of infant mortality. The rise of money incomes during the war period made it possible for the people of St. Denis to acquire the symbols of urbanism as manifest in technology, clothing styles, food, and amusements.

The Urbanization of a French Village

In their study of a small village in France (population 2,000), the Andersons undertook to trace the basic changes from the recorded origin of the community to the present, a period of some 870 years.[29] By combining the historical and anthropological approaches, the researchers obtained data, from records and their own observations, that provide a perspective of the processes that have culminated in contemporary village life. The community selected for the analysis was Wissous, a rural-suburban town some ten miles from Paris. During the long period of recorded history, including present-day conditions, the town changed from a *Gemeinschaft* to an emergent *Gesellschaft* type of community; that is, it changed from a form of community in which social groups and institutions were governed by custom and tradition and grew by accretion to a community in which legal-rational forms of organization emerged and became increasingly important in the lives of the villagers. These changes in Wissous were the by-product of the pervasive influence of urbanization and industrialization, not merely the influence of nearby Paris but of the entire nation. At the time of the study (1957–59) Wissous represented a blending of two groups—those that had evolved without formal organization or specified objectives and those that were legal-rational and crescive, that is, rationally and deliberately created and structured for designated functions.

The Andersons view the French Revolution of 1789 as an event of lasting influence involving basic changes in the entire political and economic system of France. But the influence of the Revolution on Wissous was indirect. For centuries the people of Wissous lived an existence self-sufficient from the rest of the nation, and especially from Paris. The immediate force that has left an indelible imprint on the community was what the researchers termed the "silent revolution," the technological and economic evolution associated with urbanism and

[29] Robert T. Anderson and Barbara Gallatin Anderson, *Bus Stop for Paris*, 1965. Cf. Laurence Wylie, *Village in the Vaucluse*, 1957, ch. 18, for a discussion of changes that occurred in another French village during the 1950's.

industrialism. For the most part, these revolutionary changes have occurred during the present century, although the foundation was laid earlier. With the development and application of technology to transportation, communication, and factory production, the people of Wissous late in the nineteenth century became increasingly influenced by the urban-industrial processes that were molding a different social order.

Technological changes, such as manufacturing, which developed initially in Paris and elsewhere, began to have an impact on Wissous around the turn of the century when factory-made goods were introduced to the community. The direct effects of industrialism were felt in the 1930's when several small firms were established in the town, to be followed by larger factories as metropolitan Paris spread to the environs of Wissous. The products of industry, and also the employment provided by the factories, had the effect of altering the economic and social system of the villages and the life styles and thought patterns of the people. The legal-rational forms of social organization that emerged represented an accommodation to the intrusion of technology and scientific innovations.

New forms of energy made possible many changes in transportation and communication, which in turn affected everyday life styles of the villagers. The introduction of electricity in the village in the early years of the present century made life easier for the people. Radio, introduced in the 1930's, brought the villagers into contact with the outside world, mainly Paris, and the advent of newspapers in this period likewise broadened the cultural and intellectual horizon of the people. A considerable number of families abandoned Paris for residence in the hinterlands, and the counterpart of this trend was the increasing frequency of travel of villagers to the nearby metropolis. Thus the residents became involved in an expanding network of social contacts. To accommodate to these changes public schools replaced the traditional and limited educational facilities of earlier years. Youth especially responded to these changes, becoming more urbane and less parochial, thus breaking with the traditions and life styles of the older generations. Even family ties, traditionally considered sacred and unbreakable, could now be severed, although the number of divorces did not increase very dramatically.

The researchers placed considerable emphasis on the emergence and proliferation of formal voluntary associations as evidence of the shift toward a legal-rational social order. These associations, for the most part, represented an attempted adjustment to a predominantly legal-rational society brought into existence by the forces of urbanism and

Institution building is a feature of urbanism. The structure in the top photograph is the all-India broadcasting headquarters in Delhi. Below are buildings in a major medical complex in Mexico City. (Noel P. Gist)

industrialism. The voluntary associations were a late arrival on the scene; only four existed prior to the twentieth century. By the late 1950's, some forty associations had emerged. These included community-wide associations such as those related to education, organizations of youth and sports, an organization for neighborhood development, church-related associations for laymen, organizations for the protection and support of families, and various economic organizations such as those meeting the needs of merchants, farmers, and industrialists. These voluntary associations did not replace the established institutions of family, church, or state; rather, they generally supported these traditional institutions, but were governed by rational judgments instead of custom. Structured formally and supported legally, they served to integrate the community with the larger society, often functioning as affiliates of national or regional associations. Thus Wissous was in the process of becoming an urban suburb, and its people were becoming an urban population.

Summary

The urban impact is a central issue in the sociology of the city. In the twentieth-century world, few people are completely removed from the influence of cities, even though they may live remote from the actual centers of city life. But in industrial societies this impact is felt in a multiplicity of ways and with observable effects—ecological, cultural, psychological, and demographic. If one views the urban impact from the perspective of history it seems evident that the influence of the city on people's lives is increasing, a trend that technology and modern forms of organization make virtually inevitable.

In the following chapters we will examine some of the institutional, cultural, and behavioral aspects of the urban impact. As one acquires an understanding of the very nature of city life it is not surprising that deviant behavior in its many forms becomes a feature of the urban scene. Generally it is more prevalent in the city than in rural communities, whether in industrial or developing countries. The worldwide migration of peoples to the city may likewise be viewed as a by-product of the urban impact; and the adjustments the migrants make to the urban situation is an aspect of the influence exerted on the conditions of life and work in nonurban settings. Since cities are culturally, socially, and economically heterogeneous, the diversity of human values and life styles often leads to conflict, either on an individual or collective level. Finally, the city tends to generate images and stereotypes of what the city is really like, which are also an aspect of the urban impact.

Selected Bibliography

BOOKS

Anderson, Robert T., and Barbara G. Anderson, *Bus Stop for Paris: The Transformation of a French Village.* Garden City, N.Y.: Doubleday, 1965.

Dube, S. C., *Indian Village.* New York: Harper and Row, 1967.

Duncan, Otis Dudley, Howard Schuman, and Beverly Duncan, *Social Change in a Metropolitan Community* (Detroit). New York: Russell Sage Foundation, 1973.

Foster, George M., *Traditional Cultures and the Impact of Technological Change.* New York: Harper, 1962.

Galliher, Art, *Plainville Fifteen Years Later.* New York: Columbia University Press, 1961.

Germani, Gino, ed., *Modernization, Urbanization, and the Urban Crisis.* Boston: Little, Brown, 1973.

Hunter, Guy, *Modernizing Peasant Societies.* London and New York: Oxford University Press, 1969.

Lerner, Daniel, and Lucille W. Plevsner, *The Passing of Traditional Society.* New York: The Free Press, 1958.

Lewis, Oscar, *Life in Mexican Village: Tepoztlan Restudied.* Urbana: University of Illinois Press, 1951.

McGee, Reece, *The Urbanization Process in the Third World.* London: Bell, 1971.

Miner, Horace, *St. Denis: A French-Canadian Parish.* Chicago: University of Chicago Press, 1963.

Srinivas, M. N., *Social Change in Modern India.* Berkeley: University of California Press, 1966.

Vidich, Arthur J., and Joseph Bensman, *Small Town in Mass Society.* Princeton, N.J.: Princeton University Press, 1958.

Wiser, William, and Charlotte Wiser, *Behind Mud Walls, 1930–1960.* Berkeley: University of California Press, 1963.

ARTICLES

Abu-Lughod Janet L., "Urbanization, Technology, and the Division of Labor: Present State and Future Prospects," *Economic Development and Cultural Change*, 13 (April 1965), 313–43.

Beals, Ralph, "Urbanism, Urbanization, and Acculturation," *American Anthropologist*, 53 (January–March 1952), 1–10.

Carroll, Robert L., and R. H. Wheller, "Metropolitan Influence on the Rural Nonfarm Population," *Rural Sociology*, 31 (March 1966), 64–73.

Cornelius, W. A., "Urbanization as an Agent in Latin American Political Instability," *American Political Science Review*, 63 (September 1969), 833–57.

Ellefsen, Richard A., "City-Hinterland Relationships in India," in Roy Turner, ed., *India's Urban Future*, Berkeley: University of California Press, 1962.

Epstein, A. R., "Urbanization and Social Change in Africa," *Current Anthropology*, 8 (October 1967), 275–95.

Goldsmith, Harold, and James Copp, "Metropolitan Dominance and Agriculture," *Rural Sociology*, 29 (December 1964), 385–95.

Grindstaff, C. F., "The Negro, Urbanization, and Relative Deprivation in the Deep South," *Social Problems*, 15 (Winter 1968), 342–52.

Gutkind, C. W., "African Urbanism, Social Mobility, and the Social Network," *International Journal of Comparative Sociology*, 6 (March 1965), 48–60.

Halpern, J., "Peasant Culture and Urbanization in Jugoslavia," *Human Organization*, 24 (Summer 1965), 162–67.

Hauser, Philip M., "On the Impact of Urbanism on Social Organization, Human Nature, and the Political Order," *Confluence*, 7 (Spring 1958), 27–30.

Lambert, Richard D., "The Impact of Urban Society on Village Life," in Roy Turner, ed., *India's Urban Future*. Berkeley: University of California Press, 1961.

LeTourneau, Roger, "Social Change in the Muslim Cities of North Africa," *American Journal of Sociology*, 60 (May 1955), 31–36.

Micklin, Michael, "Urbanization, Technology, and Traditional Values in Guatemala," *Social Forces*, 47 (June 1969), 438–46.

Payne, Raymond, "Leadership and Perception of Change in a Village Confronted with Urbanism," *Social Forces*, 41 (March 1963), 264–70.

Portes, A., "The Factorial Structure of Modernity: Empirical Replications and a Critique," *American Journal of Sociology*, 79 (July 1973), 15–44.

Reissman, Leonard, and Thomas Ktsanes, eds., "Urbanization and Social Change in the South," *Journal of Social Issues*, 22 (January 1966), entire issue.

Smith, Wilford E., "The Urban Threat to Mormon Norms," *Rural Sociology*, 24 (December 1959), 355–61.

Weinryb, B. D., "Impact of Urbanization in Israel," *Middle East Journal* (Winter 1957), 23–26.

Whitney, Vincent H., "Urban Impact on a Rural Township," in Marvin B. Sussman, ed., *Community Structure and Analysis*. New York: Thomas Y. Crowell, 1959.

19 • Deviance and Urban Life

 The study of deviant behavior in the city is a major way of examining the relationship between the person and his community. Does the city person behave differently than his counterpart in other kinds of communities? Is there something about the urban milieu that is conducive to personal disorganization and social problems? Can social control be effective in cities? Many questions can be raised concerning urban deviance, a large subject that cannot be covered in depth in a chapter. In order to arrive at some overall assessment of the disorganizing effect of the city we will focus on three comparisons: (1) deviance in urban-industrial and developing societies, with an assessment of the social-psychological impact of various levels of urbanization as well as the degree of industrialization; (2) deviance in rural and urban communities within a society; and (3) variations in deviance within the city. Our presentation will focus on mental health and on crime, although there are many types of deviant behavior that could be included, such as suicide, alcoholism, riots and uprisings, and sexual aberrations.

In view of the long-standing antiurban bias and the consequent tendency to associate city life with personal disorganization and social disorder, our presentation will concentrate on empirical treatments.[1] Finally we will deal briefly with the thesis that mass violence and civil disorder are more frequent in the city.

Deviance in Urban-Industrial and Developing Countries

Recognizing the difficulties that beset attempts at empirical tests of such slippery phenomena as mental health and crime, we nevertheless find it

---

[1] See Chapter 21 for discussion of the antiurban bias.

useful to compare their occurrence in modern urban societies and developing societies and, if data exist, in nonurban societies. Such comparisons should help determine the dynamics of any differences found among these societies.

Impressions of Urban Personality

First, we present the "conventional wisdom" regarding urban personality and mental health. These generalizations are for the most part the result of logical deductions from a set of postulates about urban life.[2] Since these postulates are often rooted in incomplete, stereotyped, or antiurban views of the city, the resulting deductions about urban people have unduly emphasized the disorganizing features while the integrative aspects of urban personality have often been overlooked.

What features of urban social life affect human personality? What direction do these changes take? The deductive analyses have stressed the complexity and impersonality of city life with the consequent expectation that city people would be more "nervous" and insensitive; the compensating advantages of anonymity and variety are supposed to give urbanites increased freedom of thought and action. The four psychological traits most often pointed out as characteristic of city people are *anxiety*, stemming from instabilities of status and the highly differentiated set of social roles to be performed; *emotional deprivation*, resulting from personal isolation and from the impersonal contacts of city life; the process of *externalization* and superficiality imposed by large-scale organizations and mass society; *nervous enervation*, that is, blasé attitudes and other protective psychological devices developed against the multiplicity of urban stimuli.

All deductive analyses of urban personality have hinged on the fact that the urbanite is involved in a specialized division of labor. He is necessarily involved, therefore, in a ramifying set of roles whose total structure he usually perceives dimly, if at all. It has been said that because the urbanite is just "a cog in a machine" he feels helpless and inadequate. Specialized roles are most obvious in the field of work, whether on the factory assembly line or the office bureaucracy; but

[2] The well-known analyses of Wirth and Simmel are examples of this deductive, rather than empirical, approach. Georg Simmel, "The Metropolis and Mental Life," in *The Sociology of Georg Simmel,* translated, edited, and with an introduction by Kurt H. Wolff, (1950), pp. 409-24. Louis Wirth, "Urbanism as a Way of Life," *American Journal of Sociology,* 44 (July 1938), 1-24. Wirth, an American sociologist, was a professor at the University of Chicago during the period when its Department of Sociology, under Robert Park and Ernest Burgess, was the most important center of urban studies in the United States. Wirth died in 1952 at the age of 55. Simmel (1858-1918) was a brilliant German theoretician, whose work influenced Park and Burgess.

specialization permeates virtually all aspects of urban life. Even one's recreational activities are likely to be commercialized, thus becoming another aspect of someone else's work role. For example, major league baseball, the urban spectator's pastime, is serious business for the players and the rest of the baseball industry.

Specialization in the city is accentuated by rapid change; new roles are constantly being added and current roles become outmoded or their content changed. Witness the job categories added by the advent of television and space flight. Meanwhile, the blacksmith has become a rarity and the coal miner and the railroad fireman promise to become so as machines take over many of their functions. Most recent management-labor disputes have arisen over the loss of jobs through automation. In the nonoccupational field, the "teenager" is a newly-developed role. The term "teenager" itself was rarely used before World War II, but the role has now expanded so rapidly that many commercial markets cater to this new subculture (for example, special magazines, much popular music), while learned volumes dissect it. In an earlier day, "career girl" and "working wife" were new roles. Role specialization and change are not confined to cities, but they are more characteristic of the city and tend to originate there. In rural areas, the orientation to farming provides a central core of common occupational interest and sets limits to other role specialization.

The diversity and change built into the urbanite's roles may result in a weakening of the individual's psychological roots. Insecurity can result from the world of work—will one have a job or can one meet its demands? Even more importantly, at least so runs the argument, the urban individual is cut off from a stable chain of cultural transmission and support. For example, while the farmer or the villager is usually able to pass on his work skills to his son, the urban father seldom has the opportunity for such transmission. Urban occupations remove the individual from his family not only for training and for work activity itself but often in social interests as well, thereby loosening the bonds of tradition and conformity. The father engaged in professional work, for example, often finds that his occupation leaves little time for his family or kin, and that even when they are together his work is too technical for mutual interest and discussion.

In addition, the fluidity of urban role structure has been conducive to the expectation and, often, the realization of vertical social mobility, a factor that allegedly increases the isolation of many urbanites. Communication and understanding between the generations of a family or between relatives who have moved into different levels of the class structure may be difficult. The individual finds he is not committed to the past way of life, and he may not have a clear idea of the future standards he will follow.

From this formalistic analysis one would expect that stability and a sense of meaning in life would be difficult for the urbanite to achieve on the shifting sands of urban social structure. However, empirical analysis indicates that the urban reality is much more complex.

SEEMAN'S STUDY OF URBAN ALIENATION   Seeman has pointed out that many of our ideas about the social and psychological characteristics of modern urban life are based on the "sacred" idea of urban alienation and suggests that "there is something here about which an empirical demonstration has to be made—the critical, evocative, and even romantic spirit that has infused the literature on alienation, whatever its very valid uses in some respects, being no substitute for clarity and rigor."[3] Alienation refers to the feeling people have when they cannot relate to large areas of the complex world around them.

Seeman's analysis of detailed questionnaire surveys in the United States, France, and Sweden suggests that urban alienation is a complex and multiple concept. The questions measured four aspects of alienation: (1) estrangement from work, that is, engaging in labor that is not intrinsically rewarding; (2) feelings of powerlessness in the political sphere; (3) social isolation, supposedly resulting from lack of local community contacts; and (4) cultural estrangement, that is, the breakdown of commonly held values.

Contrary to deductive theories about urban alienation Seeman found that urbanites varied greatly in their degrees of alienation and, most importantly, that their scores on the four types of alienation were not highly related to one another. For example, in all three countries he studied, Seeman found that the factory workers who indicated work alienation did not also feel powerless. He concluded that the thesis of "urban alienations" represented a "one-dimensional pessimism" and "on empirical grounds, I think that this image of a tight bundle of urban alienations is too pessimistic and too 'totalitarian' by far. I refer to the image of a general and encompassing metropolitan malaise that combines the sense of alienation in work, powerlessness in politics, dislocation from common values, generalized distrust, and the like."[4] Although his empirical evidence is limited to modern urban societies, Seeman regards both the one-dimensional view of alienated urban man and the romantic view of the well-adjusted people of the preindustrial world as equally stereotyped. We shall therefore next examine the evidence on preindustrial societies.

REDFIELD'S AND LEWIS'S FIELD REPORTS   The communities most different from cities are folk societies—small, isolated, nonliterate, and self-

---

[3] Melvin Seeman, "The Urban Alienations: Some Dubious Theses from Marx to Marcuse," *Journal of Personality and Social Psychology*, 19 (August 1971), p. 135.
[4] *Ibid.*, p.139.

sufficient. Examples of these would be tribal and village societies. In such societies, technology is simple, there is little specialization, almost all contacts are primary, and the family is paramount. These social conditions, so very different from the city and seemingly more integrated, were supposed to be especially suited to the adjustment of personality. The findings, however, suggest that personality adjustment in folk societies has been overrated.

We have an opportunity to examine personal adjustment in folk society by comparing the reports of two anthropologists, Robert Redfield and Oscar Lewis, who studied the same community. Redfield, who developed the concept of folk society, studied a number of Maya Indian communities on the Yucatan peninsula of southeastern Mexico. And, in 1926, he studied Tepoztlan, a small Mexican agricultural village about 50 miles south of Mexico City. Oscar Lewis did field work in the same community, Tepoztlan, seventeen years later, in 1943.[5] Redfield described the village as harmonious and the people as well-adjusted and content, but Lewis found considerable evidence of violence, cruelty, and suffering, and of strife both within the village and in its relations with other villages.

The reasons for such divergent reports on personality in folk society as Lewis's and Redfield's appear to lie in methodology and in attitudes. The methodology of the social sciences is inadequate to deal with measures of disorganization and personal adjustment; our antiurban bias unconsciously predisposes us toward finding "sweetness and light" among folk populations. Other studies have indicated that Lewis's view of folk personal relationships is more accurate than Redfield's.[6] We have failed to realize that a precarious living off the land and an inescapable closeness to others may be as productive of anxiety and personal problems as urban specialization and impersonality.

MENTAL ILLNESS IN FOLK SOCIETY The incidence of serious mental disorder in folk societies provides another way of comparing folk-urban personalities. Precise studies are few but indications are that simplicity of social structure has not "immunized" people against psychoses. A review of data on the extent of schizophrenia among primitive people, including some living in preliterate and tribal societies, suggests that the illness is neither absent nor rare. Similarly, a survey of a wide variety of

[5] Robert Redfield, *Tepoztlan—A Mexican Village* (1930); Oscar Lewis, *Life in a Mexican Village: Tepoztlan Re-Studied* (1951). Tepoztlan is discussed further in Chapter 2, pp. 33-5.

[6] George Foster, "Interpersonal Relations in Peasant Society," *Human Organization,* 19 (Winter 1960-61), 174-84; Joseph Lopreato, "Interpersonal Relations in Peasant Society: The Peasant's Point of View," *Human Organization,* 21 (Spring 1962), 21-24. It should be noted that Tepoztlan is an example of peasant-folk society rather than the simpler tribal-folk society.

non-Western cultures, many of the folk type, shows the various psychoses are prevalent in such societies.[7]

One of the most thorough studies of the incidence of mental illness in a closely-knit nonindustrial community is Eaton and Weil's study of the Hutterites.[8] The Hutterites are an Anabaptist religious sect located in the Middle West, particularly in eastern South Dakota. They are farmers and have a very cohesive social structure based on their religious principles. Because their communities provide the individual Hutterite with such a high degree of support, it might be expected that mental illness would be rare. Eaton and Weil's study uncovered 199 cases (including 53 diagnosed as psychotic) of past or present mental illness among the 8,542 Hutterites. Thus, one in every 43 Hutterites either had active symptoms of mental disorder or had recovered from such a disorder. One clear finding emerges from the Hutterite study; it demolished the stereotyped notion that people living in stable, self-contained communities necessarily have a negligible amount of mental illness.

GOLDHAMER AND MARSHALL'S STUDY OF HISTORIC TRENDS   The opposite kind of community process in mental illness has been studied by Goldhamer and Marshall, who used an historic series of mental illness rates to determine whether urban populations are especially prone to mental illness.[9] They reasoned that if urban life is inherently disorganizing for the individual, then mental illness rates should rise as more and more of the population live in cities. Their outstanding historic study established that accurate statistics were available for Massachusetts for several periods going back to the early nineteenth century. Goldhamer and Marshall also established the fact that mental hospitals were as available to the Massachusetts population then as they are now and that the diagnoses of doctors then were similar to those today, although the terminology differed.

Goldhamer and Marshall computed that the rates for admission for psychosis in Massachusetts were 41 per 100,000 in 1840-45; 58 in 1880-84; and 85 in 1941, assuming in each case that the age structure of the population was that of 1840. This suggests that as urbanization proceeded so did mental illness. But Goldhamer and Marshall turned up a surprising and significant fact: when the over-all rates of admission were broken down by age groups, it was found that for those between ages 20 and 50 the admission rates were the same in the nineteenth century as in the twentieth! It was the age group over 50 that showed

[7] N.J. Demerath, "Schizophrenia among Primitives," in Arnold Rose, ed., *Mental Health and Mental Disorder* (1955), pp.215-22; Tsung-Yi Lin, "Effects of Urbanization on Mental Health," *International Social Science Journal,* 11 (1959), 24-33.

[8] J. Eaton and R. Weil, *Culture and Mental Disorders* (1955).

[9] Herbert Goldhamer and A. Marshall, *Psychosis and Civilization* (1953).

much higher admission rates in 1940. In other words, the fact that there are indeed proportionately more people in mental hospitals today than in the nineteenth century may result from an increasing tendency to hospitalize older people for mental disorders. This does not necessarily mean that old people have higher rates of mental illness today. Farm chores and country living make it easier to care for senile oldsters than do city apartments and jobs that keep the family away all day.

Goldhamer and Marshall's findings have raised much speculation. The fact remains that adults, aged 20 to 50, were hospitalized as often for mental illness in the nineteenth century as in the twentieth. This fact does not support the notion that mental illness has increased as our civilization has become more urban.

REVIEW   The evidence from the studies by Seeman, Redfield, Lewis, Eaton and Weil, Goldhamer and Marshall is, of course, fragmentary and subject to methodological criticism. Nevertheless it is sufficient to establish the falseness of viewing urban society as inherently disorganizing, even in contrast to much simpler social settings, including folk and village societies. Undoubtedly the community and total society influence the individual psyche but in multiple ways that are not reflected in the cardboard contrast between the allegedly disorganizing city and the wholesome effects of smaller, simpler milieus.

Industrialization and Crime

The emergence of industrial economics in developing countries has been linked with rising crime rates. The following have all been pointed to as possible causative factors: dislocation of vast numbers of people who move to the slum areas of the burgeoning cities; the weakening of family and kinship ties as women enter the labor market and relatives disperse; widespread poverty; the stimulation of new wants and new ideas by the mass media; the heterogeneity and variety of urban people; and the inability, and perhaps unwillingness, of the governments of many developing countries to meet the rising expectations of their citizens.

Clinard and Abbott have completed a comprehensive survey of data on crime in developing countries, indicating that "despite the variation in the adequacy of statistics and the criticism justly leveled at official crime reports, data concerning the extent and serious nature of the crime problem almost unanimously substantiate the generalization that criminality is rapidly increasing in the less developed countries."[10] Armed robbery and other property offenses are increasing especially rapidly as people attempt to steal items such as bicycles and wristwatches, which

[10] Marshall Clinard and Daniel Abbott, *Crime in Developing Countries* (1973), p. 11. The following discussion is based on pp. 35-69.

are useful and also marks of prestige and modernization. However, such property offenses as auto theft and vandalism of schools are uncommon in developing countries, where automobiles are rare and schools are held in high respect. Crimes that are common in developing countries but that might be expected to decline as development progresses include the use of juveniles by adults to beg, steal, or smuggle; theft by servants; theft by postal employees of uncancelled stamps from letters; adulteration of food; sorcery and witchcraft; and riding public transport without payment. Corruption among civil servants and public officials, ranging from "gifts" for the most minor bureaucratic function to filling one's own pockets from the public till, is widespread in developing societies where change has been so rapid that a sense of disinterested service and loyalty to the nation have not superseded loyalty to one's own kin, caste, village, ethnic or linguistic group.

CLINARD AND ABBOTT'S STUDY OF CRIME IN UGANDA   As part of their world survey, Clinard and Abbott undertook an in-depth study of crime in Uganda, particularly in Kampala, the capital city. Despite the fact that Uganda is still an overwhelmingly rural country, 95 percent of its labor force being involved in agriculture and only 3 percent of the population living in cities of 20,000 or more, economic development is proceeding rapidly. As indicated in Figure 19.1 various development indicators are rising more rapidly than the general population, but the cumulative increase in reported crime is increasing faster than any other variable considered. In Uganda, as in other developing countries, juvenile delinquency and crime are concentrated in the cities and are committed mainly by young males. Kampala had reached a population of 330,000 in 1969, an increase of 110 percent over the 1959 figure; the 1969 crime rate per 100,000 population in Kampala was 4,187 for property offenses and 1,803 for offenses against the person, a total crime rate seven and a half times the national Ugandan rate.

Clinard and Abbott's study of a random sample of males over 18 in two slum areas in Kampala, one (Kisenyi) with a high crime rate and the other (Namuwongo) with a low one, illuminates the causal processes.[11] A crucial difference between Kisenyi and Namuwongo, as derived from interviews with the residents, was the higher degree of internal integration in Namuwongo, as measured by the greater tendency to restrict friendship to members of one's own locally resident tribe, to visit often in the local community, and to participate frequently in local community organizations. The greater prevalence of this locally oriented behavior in Namuwongo apparently allowed the elders of the community to maintain more of their traditional authority and control over the behavior of youth. This was true despite the fact that on objective indicators, such as

[11] *Ibid.*, pp. 132-88.

medical services, water supply, and physical surroundings, and in terms of the socioeconomic status of young men, Namuwongo ranked lower than Kisenyi, and deprivation was thus more pressing in Namuwongo. According to Clinard and Abbott poverty in itself is not the key to explaining crime in developing nations; rather it is the extent to which an individual's immediate enviroment provides the "opportunity structure" for acquiring the values and learning the techniques to use illegal means.

INTERNATIONAL COMPARISONS OF CRIMES AGAINST THE PERSON   Crimes against the person—such as murder, assault, and rape—are much less frequent in all countries, developed and developing, than property offenses. Furthermore there is no clear association between industrialization and increases in offenses against the person. Table 19.1 indicates that while such highly industrial countries as the United States have high murder rates, other industrial nations such as Sweden and England and Wales have very low rates. Similarly, economically underdeveloped nations are found at both the high and low ends of the homicide scale.

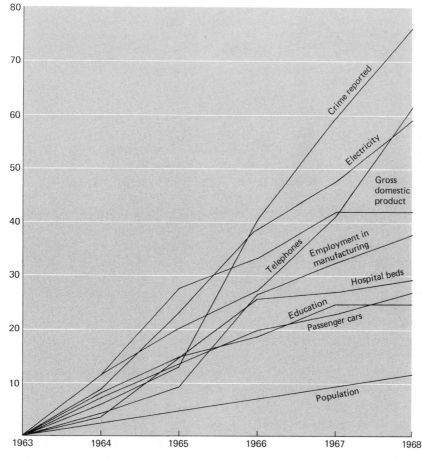

Figure 19.1. Uganda: A Case of Rapid Increase in Crime. Cumulative percent increase of development indicators and total reported crime, Uganda, 1963–68. Source: Marshall Clinard and Daniel Abbott, *Crime in Developing Countries.* New York: Wiley-Interscience (1973), p. 15.

TABLE 19.1 International Murder Rates, Per 100,000 Inhabitants*

Country	Rate	Country	Rate
Ceylon	14.0	Japan	2.2
Kuwait	8.1	Scotland	1.9
UNITED STATES	7.2	Malawi	1.9
Luxembourg	6.8	Australia	1.8
Singapore	5.2	Hong Kong	1.7
Libyan Arab Republic	4.9	Korea (Republic of)	1.5
The Netherlands	3.9	Finland	1.2
Germany (Fed. Republic of)	3.3	Cyprus	1.2
Ivory Coast	3.2	Portugal	1.1
Fiji	3.0	Sweden	0.6
Israel	2.6	Malaysia	0.5
Austria	2.5	England and Wales	0.4
		Norway	0.2

*Comparing the murder rates of different countries must be approached cautiously. The rates shown represent the number of persons per 100,000 inhabitants identified by the police as having committed or attempted willful murder (except for the United States, where the figure represents the number of willful killings per 100,000 inhabitants; attempts to kill are classified as aggravated assaults, not as murder). These rates reflect only detected offenders and crimes. The actual number of murders may remain undisclosed because of unreported offenses, which can vary greatly depending on a country's political situation and its national law enforcement levels. Figures are based on 1969 data—the latest available.

SOURCE: Data from Interpol (International Criminal Police Organization) and the Federal Bureau of Investigation's *Uniform Crime Reports* and table published in *The Official Associated Press Almanac 1973*, p. 147.

Crimes involving physical aggression against others probably derive from a rather different set of causes than crimes against property.[12] Specifically, crimes against the person seem to result in part from established subcultures of violence, found in both developed and developing countries. In many parts of the world carrying weapons, such as knives and machetes, is expected and culturally sanctioned, and in certain situations, such as gambling, family or personal disputes, aggressive reactions are culturally defined. In Latin America and Arab countries the male role is defined to include *machismo* and the aggressive defense of "honor." The tendency to settle disputes by violence is apparently not linked with industrialization or urbanization.

High rates of criminal offenses against persons are often found in rural areas and in villages. In Colombia the large-scale violence, *Violencia Colombiana,* originated in 1948 in the countryside and spread to the cities. The close personal contacts in villages and tightly-knit traditional communities may lead to high rates of criminal homicide, as in Ceylon. Clinard and Abbott's study of Kisenyi and Namuwongo indicated that in

[12] *Ibid.,* pp. 17-18, 57-62.

the latter, a more traditional area, the rate of crimes against the person was fairly high, although crimes against property were low.

CRIME TRENDS IN ENGLAND, THE UNITED STATES, AND FRANCE   There is accumulating evidence that the increases in crime, especially property crime, experienced by developing countries may be a transitional phenomenon with crime rates declining as economic development proceeds. In nineteenth century England, as in the contemporary developing countries, the increased urban crime rate has been attributed to the large proportion of young, unskilled migrant males of whom only a minority could be absorbed into the fledgling industrial economy. Reviewing historical documents, Tobias notes also that neither housing nor educational facilities kept pace with the influx of population to cities, nor were parents working long hours able to give children adequate supervision.[13] Tobias concluded that "if we are to look for a parallel in the field of crime with the England of the first sixty years of the nineteenth century, it is not to the England of the twentieth century that we should look, but to those countries that are today undergoing the experience of industrialization and urbanization."[14]

The downward trend in crime in Boston in a century lends substance to the thesis that the cities of established urban-industrial societies have lower crime rates, contrary to the popular belief that crime is growing worse every year. Ferdinand examined the annual arrest reports of Boston for 1849-1951 for seven major crimes: murder, manslaughter, forcible rape, robbery, assault, burglary, and larceny.[15] Collectively these crimes show a clear downward trend, as illustrated in Figure 19.2.

The seven types of crime vary in their pattern of change, however. Murder, larceny, and assault display a clear decline. Burglary and robbery show a general decline with intermittent peaks associated with particular national events, such as wars and severe depressions. Thus, the highest burglary rates in 100 years were reached during the depression years of 1873-78 and 1937-39. Manslaughter deaths rose from the early twentieth century until 1934-36, when they began to decline; the twentieth century increase is explained by deaths in automobile accidents, and the more recent decline may result from improved highways and regulation of drivers. Only forcible rape has shown a consistent increase in rate over the 100 year period, a fact largely unexplained, although changes in the status of women and greater readiness to report such crimes may be factors.

Ferdinand attributes the general decline in the crime rate to several

---

[13] J.J. Tobias, *Urban Crime in Victorian England* (1972), pp. 244-55.

[14] *Ibid.*, p. 49.

[15] Theodore N. Ferdinand, "The Criminal Pattern of Boston since 1849," *American Journal of Sociology,* 73 (July 1967), 84-99.

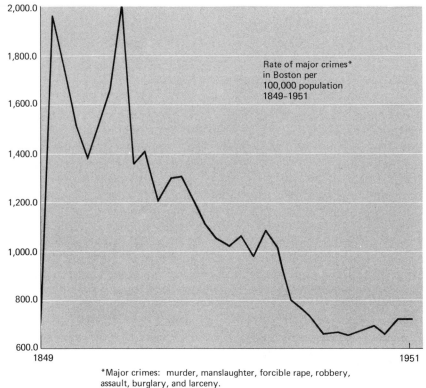

2,000.0

1,800.0

Rate of major crimes*
in Boston per
100,000 population
1849-1951

1,600.0

1,400.0

1,200.0

1,000.0

800.0

600.0
1849   1951

*Major crimes: murder, manslaughter, forcible rape, robbery,
assault, burglary, and larceny.

FIGURE 19.2 • The rate of major crimes in Boston over a century shows a clear downward trend, contrary to popular beliefs. Source: Theodore N. Ferdinand, "The Criminal Patterns of Boston since 1849," *American Journal of Sociology* 73 (July 1967), p. 87.

factors symptomatic of advanced modernization: an expanding middle class, the assimilation of the Irish and Italian immigrants who earlier made up a large proportion of Boston's population, and the gradual rise in the standard of living. These changes alleviated the social dislocation and economic distress that had contributed to high crime rates.

Somewhat similarly Lodhi and Tilly concluded from an examination of arrests for crime in rapidly urbanizing France over the century 1831-1931 that crimes against property declined steadily during this period and crimes against persons fluctuated in a narrow range and without trend, indicating that increasing urbanization is not the cause of either type of crime.[16] There is some indication of rural-urban differentials in crime rates, however; detailed statistical analysis for 1841-1851 shows that property crimes were very much more frequent in cities, presumably because of the "accessibility of wealth and the ease of escaping detection."[17] If these differentials are shown to persist over the total century they would imply that the tension allegedly produced by rapid urbanization is not the cause of urban crime, but rather that the urban setting itself is conducive to property crime, although the levels of urban property crime do decline significantly over time.

[16] A.Q. Lodhi and Charles Tilly, "Urbanization, Crime, and Collective Violence in 19th Century France," *American Journal of Sociology*, 79 (September 1973), 296-318.

[17] *Ibid.*, p. 305.

Deviance in Rural and
Urban Settings

Studies of rural-urban differences in deviance are much more numerous
than folk-urban comparisons or those between developing and developed
countries. Rural-urban comparisons within one society also have the
advantage of holding constant general cultural background, thus affording greater focus on the urban setting *per se.* We shall find that in terms
of mental health, there is no clear indication of rural superiority, or even
that the personalites of urbanites and ruralites differ very much. Criminal behavior does show higher urban levels, at least for some types of
crime, suggesting the nature of the criminogenic process.

Rural-Urban Comparisons
in Personal Adjustment and
Mental Illness

Few questions in urban sociology have generated more interest among
both professionals and laymen as that of whether personality differences
exist between rural and urban dwellers. And if differences exist, what
are they?

Recent rural-urban comparisons based on empirical studies of mental
health have not brought out any striking differences. The absence of
clear-cut contrasts may be explained in various ways. (1) Major differences may have existed but have declined as specialization broke down
the self-sufficiency of rural areas, and modern transportation and communication reduced their isolation. (2) The sampling methods and
definitions of rural and urban vary from one study to another so the units
cannot really be compared. (3) The instruments used to measure attitudes and personality are inadequate. (4) Age, sex, education, income,
occupation, and other factors also affect values and psychological
outlook and, on the whole, are more important than differences based on
place of residence. (5) Rural-urban comparisons are often obscured by
the fact that many adults live in areas different from the ones they grew
up in. All of these factors undoubtedly have some influence, but which
factors are most important has not yet been established.

One of the most thorough surveys of personal adjustment was carried
out in the United States as part of the Mental Health Study Act of 1955.[18]
Researchers from the University of Michigan Survey Research Center
interviewed 2,460 Americans over 21 years of age who were representative of the total population in terms of age, sex, education, income,
occupation, and place of residence. Individuals in prisons, hospitals, and

---

[18] Gerald Gurin, Joseph Veroff, and Sheila Feld, *Americans View Their Mental Health*
(1960), pp. xxv, 228-30.

other institutions were excluded. This sample of the presumably normal adult population of the United States was questioned at length about its satisfaction in various areas of life. Nearly one in four of these adults at some time in life had felt sufficiently troubled to need help, mainly in the areas of marriage, parenthood, the job, and psychological problems. One in seven had actually sought help from religious, private, or public sources.

Dissatisfaction was apparently fairly widespread among Americans. Differences in feelings of satisfaction showed no consistent relationship to place of residence. Thus, people in metropolitan areas expressed more worrying and less happiness than other residential groups; but in marital adjustment, metropolitanites reported greater happiness and fewer feelings of inadequacy. Most important was the fact that differences in level of gratification by place of residence were overshadowed by differences based on sex, age, education, and income. A young educated male farmer is perhaps more like a young educated male New Yorker than either of them is like his own father. Differences in place of residence are not crucial in feelings of personal satisfaction.

MENTAL HEALTH AND CHOICE OF RESIDENCE   An analysis by Srole of tests on a national probability sample of 6,672 American adults suggests the startling conclusion that urban residents may have superior mental health to those living in smaller sized communities.[19] The tests consisted of ten self-reported psychosomatic symptoms and two questions asking whether the individual had ever experienced a nervous breakdown or felt one impending. The communities of residence were divided into six categories, so that fine-grain comparisons could be made. The results, for white women and men, show that the higher scores—that is, more psychosomatic symptoms and nervous breakdowns—occur in the smaller communities. For both men and women the same contrast is apparent—those living in the three largest community sizes (metropolitan areas of various sizes) have lower scores than those living in the three smallest sized communities (nonmetropolitan urban places, rural nonfarm and rural farm communities). The major differences between the sexes are that women generally have higher scores and for women the degree of difference among the various sized communities is greater.

These data must be interpreted cautiously since they have not been adjusted for differences in socioeconomic status and age among the community groups. A more fundamental problem is that the study classifies people only by their present residence. Since Americans are very mobile this is a serious deficiency. Srole suggests that the current community of residence of American adults is of limited relevance in

[19] Leo Strole, "Urbanization and Mental Health: Some Reformulations," *American Scientist,* 60 (September/October 1972) 576-83.

analyzing their mental health. In view of the freedom to choose one's community and the multiple community histories of most Americans, he suggests that "the prime research question is no longer: what effects do community differences exert on the mental health of their inhabitants? Rather, the relevant issue is, in mental health terms, what kinds of people differentially stay in or are drawn to various kinds of community milieus? This represents, of course, a very considerable turn-about in the formulation of a very old scientific question."[20]

Viewed in the light of selective migration the better mental health of large city dwellers might be interpreted as follows. (1) The "cream" of the young people of smaller communities move to large cities where their superior abilities have appropriate scope. Srole's study of residents in "mid-Manhattan," a local area of New York City, found that higher status migrants have few adjustment problems.[21] The mental health ratings of those migrants of middle and upper class background who had moved to New York City were in fact superior to those of similar status who had lived in New York City all their lives. (2) A second stream of migrants to cities are those whose attitudes, tastes, or behavior make it difficult for them to adjust to the restrictions of a small community; in the large city they are more likely to find others of similar views who give them emotional support and prevent or contain the psychological problems that might have developed in smaller communities. For both these groups the city environment is psychologically therapeutic, although there are, of course, other urban groups. Srole contends that poverty, which is found in both urban and rural settings, is a major cause of psychological distress. Srole concludes by submitting the thesis that

... up to a point a mobile society on balance is psychologically eugenic, whereas an immobile, static society, holding its members as "local captives," is more often pathogenic. If that is so, it would follow that the main unfinished business of American society is to redress the institutional rigidities and resistances that deprive people, whatever their present mental health status, of the options to move in the economic structure and in social space. Although it still has far to go in these directions, the metropolis, for all of its failings within and beyond its control, is here hypothesized as offering a greater range of opportunities for self-fulfilling movement than all other kinds of places on the present community spectrum.[22]

THE LIBERATING EFFECTS OF URBAN LIFE The potentially liberating and beneficial effects of urban life have been stressed in a somewhat different way by Sennett, who holds that "affluence and the structures of a dense, disorganized city could encourage men to become more sensitive to each other . . ."[23] The necessity for some kind of adjustment to the

[20] *Ibid.*, p. 582.

[21] Leo Srole *et al.*, *Mental Health in the Metropolis: The Midtown Manhattan Study* (1962), p. 266-68.

[22] Srole, "Urbanization and Mental Health: Some Reformulations," *op.cit.*, p. 583.

[23] Richard Sennett, *The Uses of Disorder: Personal Identity and City Life* (1971), p. 189.

contending interests and groups of the city works against rigidity, isolation, fear of being different, "shame about status and helplessness in the face of large bureaucracies." Conflict, says Sennett, can humanize the large-scale urban institutions, making them more responsive to the felt needs of the individual urbanite, thereby maximizing his development.

A short statement cannot do justice to the provocative and many-faceted exposition of Sennett, but it is important to take note of his philosophical position, which has freed itself of the assumption that the disordered city is necessarily disordering in its personal impact. Others have been led by a very different route to a rather similar conclusion about the impact of the city. Fischer, for example, has systematically reviewed the evidence bearing on the allegedly disorganizing effects of urban size, density, and heterogeneity, concluding that Wirth's classic model has logical flaws and is not well-supported by research. Fischer concludes that alternative models must be developed.[24]

Urban and Rural Crime Rates

On the basis of the incidence of crimes known to the police it may be inferred that crime is more prevalent in urban than in rural communities. Yet these differences may be partly a matter of definition; they may also reflect differences in the efficiency and honesty of law enforcement personnel, differences in the accuracy and completeness of records, or differences in social and economic conditions. These differences are accentuated by the fact that submitting reports to the FBI for preparation of the Uniform Crime Reports is voluntary. Coverage is much more complete for urban areas than for rural areas; and the rural communities that do not contribute reports may be those with higher crime rates. In 1972, 98 percent of the Standard Metropolitan Statistical Areas reported their crime data to the FBI, as did 91 percent of other urban areas; but only 75 percent of the rural jurisdictions reported their data.[25]

From the data in Table 19.2, it appears that as a whole there are fewer criminal offenses in small and middle-sized cities and in rural areas than in large metropolitan centers. Even when generous allowance is made for inaccurate or incomplete data, the differences are impressive. Comparisons in other countries show a similar progression.[26] The table shows that rural and urban areas differ less in rates of certain offenses against

---

[24] Claude S. Fischer, "Urbanism as a Way of Life: A Review and an Agenda," *Sociological Methods and Research,* 1 (November 1972), 187-242.

[25] Federal Bureau of Investigation, *Uniform Crime Reports* (1972), p. 61.

[26] See, for example, male crime rates in Denmark reported in Karl C. Christiansen, "Industrialization and Urbanization in Relation to Crime and Juvenile Delinquency," in Daniel Glaser, ed., *Crime in the City* (1970), p. 51.

TABLE 19.2: Offenses Known to Police, and the Rate per 100,000 by Class of City, 1972

	CLASS OF CITY		
Offense	Metropolitan Areas	Other Cities	Rural
Murder and non-negligent manslaughter	9.9	5.1	7.4
Forcible rape	26.9	11.0	11.2
Robbery	243.5	38.7	16.1
Aggravated assault	211.9	150.7	109.0
Burglary	1,340.7	754.3	507.5
Larceny	1,027.6	789.4	363.0
Auto theft	552.4	168.3	69.7

SOURCE: Federal Bureau of Investigation, *Uniform Crime Reports* (1972), p. 61.

the person than they do in offenses against property (larceny, burglary, auto theft). Probably this is because there is more property in the city and more opportunity to steal it. Rural and urban areas differ most in their rates of robbery, classified by the FBI as a crime against the person since it involves taking property under threat of force; despite this classification robbery is clearly a crime with a property component.

Crime rates rise consistently with city size as shown in a study by Wolfgang. Data were compared for United States cities grouped in six classes by size ranging from 250,000 in population to those under 10,000.[27] For each of the seven major offenses the crime rates increased regularly with city size resulting in the following dramatic contrasts between the largest cities and the smallest: robbery rates per 100,000 population were 16 times greater in the cities of 250,000 or over than in cities of 10,000 or less; auto theft rates were five times higher; while burglary, larceny, murder and non-negligent manslaughter each occurred at twice as high a rate in the largest cities as in the smallest. Narcotic drug law violations, gambling, prostitution, and commercialized vice are among the crimes most highly concentrated in the largest cities. According to Wolfgang, the regularity and consistency of these data suggest criminogenic forces in the city.

Very large cities nevertheless vary in their crime rates, suggesting that other factors than population size are important in influencing crime rates. Among United States cities of 250,000 or more, Miami (Florida), San Francisco, Los Angeles, New York, and Detroit have major crime rates over 5,200 per 100,000 inhabitants, while Boston, St. Louis, Houston, Minneapolis, Memphis, and Cleveland have rates below 3,600.[28]

[27] Marvin E. Wolfgang, "Urban Crime," in James Q. Wilson, ed., *The Metropolitan Enigma,* (1967), vol. 2, p. 238-41.

[28] *Associated Press Almanac 1973,* p. 147.

CLINARD'S STUDIES OF RURAL AND URBAN CRIMINALS A comparative study of criminals with rural and urban backgrounds may cast more light on the problem of crime in rural and urban areas than a comparison of crime rates. Three related studies have examined the characteristics of rural and urban criminals. Clinard studied 200 property offenders in Iowa who were classified by farm, village, or urban residence before imprisonment.[29] A similar study was repeated in Iowa about ten years later by Eastman.[30] Recently, Clinard repeated his original study with criminals of rural and urban background in Sweden.[31] The conclusions of the three studies with respect to the influence of rural and urban background on criminals convicted of offenses against property differ somewhat, but they agree on the importance of the community factor.

According to the original Clinard study, offenders with urban backgrounds tended to conform to criminal social patterns; that is, they conceived of themselves as criminals, made use of established techniques, spoke a criminal argot, frequently looked upon crime as a way of life or vocation, considered themselves enemies of the police and the courts, and associated with prostitutes, pimps, and racketeers. Village offenders manifested in a slight way some of the characteristic features of the criminal social pattern, but the prisoners with farm backgrounds showed few of these criminal traits. The same progression was evident in the Eastman and Swedish studies, but they did not disclose as clear-cut a criminal social type in cities as had the original study.

The significant findings of the three studies may be summarized as follows: (1) The urban environment is more conducive to crimes against property than are rural or village environments. These differences reflect differences in values and organization of rural and urban community life. The relative compactness of the rural community and the effective operation of such primary controls as gossip make it difficult for a criminal culture to exist. In the metropolis, however, high mobility, anonymous relationships, and the prevalence of pecuniary values are conducive to crime and the development of criminal personalities. (2) However, differences between urban and rural environments are declining as rural and village areas become less isolated and urban values and behavior patterns are transmitted to them. Thus, the two later studies show gang behavior among rural and village youth has increased. (3) Perhaps of most importance is the finding of the two later studies that the degree to which the urban environment produces a definite criminal social type may have been overstated.

[29] Marshall B. Clinard, "The Process of Urbanization and Criminal Behavior," *American Journal of Sociology,* 48 (September 1942), 202-13.

[30] Harold D. Eastman, "The Process of Urbanization and Criminal Behavior: A Restudy of Culture Conflict," unpublished Ph.D. dissertation, University of Iowa, 1954.

[31] Marshall B. Clinard, "A Cross-Cultural Replication of the Relation of Urbanism to Criminal Behavior," *American Sociological Review,* 25 (April 1960), 253-57.

YOUTH AND VIOLENT CRIME   A persistent belief has been that juvenile delinquency has increased with urbanization and has become increasingly violent. Wolfgang indicates that both these propositions are dubious.[32] He indicates that the *recording* of juvenile delinquency has increased, not necessarily the incidence of juvenile delinquency. Furthermore, most offenses committed by juveniles are property offenses. Persons under 18 account for about two thirds of all those arrested for auto theft and one-half of all arrests for burglaries and robberies, but only about eight percent of those arrested for criminal homicide and about 18 percent of forcible rape arrests.

Wolfgang points out that in computing delinquency or crime rates, data on the age composition of the population must be included, if any validity is to be attached to the rates. This has seldom been done and is particularly important in computing rates for juveniles since the relevant age span is brief and much affected by short-term birth rate bulges and the like. Wolfgang's age-specific computations, presented in Table 19.3, of juvenile arrests for violent crimes in urban areas show, he believes, that of the five types of violent crime only the assault categories show cause for concern, but even these require further confirmation.

TABLE 19.3: Urban Arrest Rates for Crimes of Violence, 1958–1964: Persons Arrested Aged 10–17, for Cities with Population 2,500 or more

	1958	1959	1960	1961	1962	1963	1964
Criminal homicide: Murder and non-negligent manslaughter	1.9	2.3	3.0	3.2	2.9	2.9	3.1
Negligent manslaughter	1.15	0.98	1.10	0.96	0.79	1.00	0.87
Forcible rape	10.0	9.8	10.9	11.4	11.2	10.3	10.0
Aggravated assault	34.4	35.5	53.2	60.1	61.6	63.0	74.5
Other assaults	95.9	118.0	118.7	126.0	139.2	153.7	163.6

SOURCE: Marvin Wolfgang, "Urban Crime," in James Q. Wilson, ed., *The Metropolitan Enigma.* Washington, D.C.: United States Chamber of Commerce, 1967, volume 2, p. 249.

In conclusion Wolfgang points out that "an alarmist attitude does not appear justified" with regard to juvenile crime. The *absolute* amount of juvenile delinquency can be expected to increase because of the increase in the number of juveniles in the population, but age-specific rates indicate "there is no basis for assuming that *rates* of juvenile violence will increase."[33]

The consideration of juvenile delinquency highlights the importance of considering the composition of populations in analyzing rural and urban delinquency and crime rates. If rural and urban populations differ

[32] Wolfgang, *op. cit.*, pp. 246-52.
[33] *Ibid.*, p. 251.

substantially in age or sex composition the crime rates are likely to differ for reasons having little to do with inherent community characteristics. Glaser has noted the estimates that one-third of the increase in violent urban crime in the 1960s was due to the "bulge" of young men in their twenties resulting from the "baby boom" immediately after World War II.[34] The proportion of the urban population living in "subcultures of violence" coupled with deprivation and poverty is also important as "we have had a southern rural and Latin American subculture of violence transplanted to the slum areas of our northern and western cities."[35]

ARE SUBURBS LIKE CITIES?   As ever larger proportions of the American people live in suburbs it becomes increasingly important to ask whether suburbs are more like cities or like rural areas in their crime patterns. Defining suburbs as those portions of metropolitan areas outside the central cities, we find that suburban crime rates are lower than central city rates, but have risen in recent years, probably as a result of the changing economic pattern and population composition of the suburbs.[36]

Research conducted in 1968 with an area probability sample of adults living in the central cities, suburbs, and small towns and rural areas of Missouri yielded suggestive findings on the nature of neighborhood controls operating in these three types of communities.[37] Central city residents were significantly more likely than suburban or rural residents to expect serious personal or property crime to occur in their neighborhoods. Rather surprisingly, rural residents had somewhat higher expectations of local crime than suburban residents. If crime did occur, the majority of respondents from all three areas believed that neighbors seeing the action would call the police, although only 84 percent of the central city residents believed this, a statistically smaller percentage than the 92 percent of both suburban and rural residents.

The majority of the residents of all three types of area also believed that their own particular neighborhood was safe, although, again fewer urban than suburban or rural residents believed this. In exploring the reasons for this belief in neighborhood safety, the rural residents relied significantly more frequently than either the suburban or urban residents on the general character of the larger community; both suburban and urban residents relied more on formal controls, especially the police, to keep their neighborhoods safe.[38] These findings are in keeping with

---

[34] Daniel Glaser, "Violence and the City," in Daniel Glaser, ed., *Crime in the City* (1970), p. 201.

[35] *Ibid.,* pp. 202-3.

[36] See Chapter 11, pp. 302-3.

[37] Sarah L. Boggs, "Formal and Informal Crime Control: An Exploratory Study of Urban, Suburban, and Rural Orientations," *Sociological Quarterly,* 12 (Summer 1971), 319-27.

[38] There is an apparent contradiction between the rural beliefs in informal controls and the findings noted above that rural residents expected more crime than suburban dwellers. Probably the explanation lies in the variety of rural communities.

the greater population density and impersonality of the suburban and urban areas as contrasted with rural areas.

Additional findings showed that only in central city areas was there a significant number of residents who felt their neighborhoods were unsafe, who expected serious crime in their own locality, and who took special precautions for safety. These beliefs were more pronounced among urban blacks than whites; urban blacks also felt more dependent on formal controls, especially police, but were less satisfied with the quality of police protection.

This study dealt with only one state and at only one point in time and so its results cannot be generalized broadly. However, it is hardly unexpected to find that suburbs, if not midway between rural and urban areas in terms of residents' expectations of crime and methods for dealing with it, are a hybrid with characteristics related to both other types of areas.[39]

Variations in Deviance Within the City

The variations in personality adjustment within the city are in most cases greater than any variations revealed in rural-urban comparisons. The city is not one environment but many.

Density, Juvenile Delinquency, and Mental Illness

For example, a recent study of New York City concluded that income and ethnic factors were the most relevant factors in explaining variations in juvenile delinquency and in mental illness rates within the city.[40] Data on juvenile offenses and on psychiatric patients were analyzed according to the New York City Health Area in which the individual lived. Measures for each Health Area were also obtained on population density, median income, percentage white, median years of education, percentage of the population under 18 years of age and over 65, substandard housing, unemployment, and change of residence. Density, income, and percentage nonwhite were the variables correlated with both juvenile delinquency and mental illness.

However, the three variables were highly interrelated with each other and a more sophisticated statistical analysis (stepwise multiple regres-

[39] On other characteristics suburbs may clearly be closer to urban or rural norms. See, for example, Claude S. Fischer, "On Urban Alienations and Anomie: Powerlessness and Social Isolation," *American Sociological Review*, 38 (June 1973), 311-26.

[40] Jonathan L. Freedman, "Population Density, Juvenile Delinquency, and Mental Ilness in New York City," in Commission on Population Growth and the American Future, *Research Reports*, Vol. V. *Population Distribution and Policy*, Sara Mills Mazie, ed., (1972), 512-23.

sion) was performed to determine which were causative. This analysis showed that population density, whether measured as density per acre or density per room, explained virtually none of the variation in juvenile delinquency among the Health Areas and only a small portion of the areal variation in mental illness. This suggests that "those who blame all of the ills of the cities on population density are greatly overstating the case."[41] Juvenile delinquency and mental illness are concentrated in the most densely settled parts of the city not because density caused delinquency and mental illness but because these are the areas where the poor and the nonwhites are concentrated. Low income and ethnic status are major determinants of delinquency and mental illness, although in recognizing this we should not commit the opposite error and assume that poverty areas and ghetto sections of the city are characterized only by social pathology and personal disorganization.[42]

THE ECOLOGY OF MENTAL DISORDERS   Some parts of the city have a higher incidence of mental and nervous disorders than other parts. The classic study of the ecology of mental disorders in Chicago, by Faris and Dunham, revealed that the incidence of schizophrenia, alcoholic psychoses, drug addiction, and general paresis was much higher in the slum area, and that the rates tended to decline from the Loop district in the center of the city to the peripheral areas.[43] There was one exception: manic-depressive psychoses showed no such pattern but were about as frequent in one section as another, although there was some tendency for manic-depressives to be on a higher socioeconomic level than the other psychotics. Suicide and crime rates also show variations from one section of the city to another. Illegitimacy, prostitution, and other forms of sexual deviation tend to be concentrated in particular areas of the city, though no section is entirely free of them. Later research by Dunham in Detroit and by Levy and Rowitz in Chicago has modified specific findings but confirmed the systematic variation of mental illness rates in subareas of the city.[44]

[41] *Ibid.*, p. 522.

[42] For discussions of the social and personal strengths of these areas, see David C. Perry and Joe R. Feagin, "Stereotyping in Black and White," in Harlan Hahn, ed., *People and Politics in Urban Society* (1972), pp. 433-63; Robert A. Wilson, "Anomie and the Ghetto: A Study of Neighborhood Type, Race, and Anomie," *American Journal of Sociology*, 77 (July 1971), 66-88.

[43] R.E.L. Faris and H. Warren Dunham, *Mental Disorders in Urban Areas* (1939).

[44] H. Warren Dunham, *Community and Schizophrenia* (1965); and Leo Levy and Louis Rowitz, *The Ecology of Mental Disorder* (1973).

Social Class and Personality in the City

Social class appears to be one of the most important factors related to variations in personal adjustment. Since people of a given social class tend to live in the same neighborhood, this helps account for the variations in personality adjustment found among different sections of the city.

THE MIDTOWN MANHATTAN STUDY   A study in a densely settled section of Manhattan, at the heart of metropolitan New York City, demonstrates the relationship of social class to personality adjustment.[45] Semistructured interviews were conducted at home with a representative sample of white adults, aged 20 to 59. The responses were rated independently by two psychiatrists in terms of the number and severity of psychological symptoms. The "well" group had no significant symptoms. The "mild" and "moderate" groups carried on their adult activities successfully despite psychological difficulties. The "impaired" group had symptoms of a neurotic or psychotic nature severe enough to handicap them considerably, sometimes completely, in everyday life. Table 19.4 below

TABLE 19.4: Mental Health Levels of Highest and Lowest Socioeconomic Strata in Midtown Manhattan Study

	Highest Socioeconomic Stratum	**Lowest Socioeconomic Stratum**
Well	30.0%	4.6%
Mild symptom formation	37.5	25.0
Moderate symptom formation	20.0	23.1
Impaired	12.5	47.3

SOURCE: Leo Srole, *et al., Mental Health in the Metropolis: The Midtown Manhattan Study* (1962), I, 230. Copyright 1962, McGraw-Hill Book Company, Blakiston Division. Used by permission.

contrasts the mental health ratings for the topmost and bottommost socioeconomic levels.[46] Clearly the highest socioeconomic stratum has proportionately few individuals with poor personal adjustment and proportionately many with good personal adjustment. The picture is just the reverse for the lowest socioeconomic stratum.

THE NEW HAVEN STUDY   Serious mental illness, that is, psychosis, shows the same kind of relationship to social class as does general

---

[45] Leo Srole, et al., *Mental Health in the Metropolis: The Midtown Manhattan Study* (1962), vol. I.

[46] It should be noted that the psychiatrists made their first mental health ratings "blind," that is, without knowledge of information that might identify the socioeconomic class of the individual. Thus, knowledge of the individual's class could not influence the psychiatrist's mental health rating. *Ibid.*, p. 413.

TABLE 19.5: Social Class and Rate of Treated Mental Illnesses, New Haven Study

Social Class	Rate per 100,000
I-II (highest)	556
III	538
IV	642
V (lowest)	1,659

SOURCE: A. B. Hollingshead and F. Redlich, *Social Class and Mental Illness* (1958), p. 210.

personality adjustment. The relationship is inverse, that is, the higher one variable the lower the associated variable. In this case, the higher the social class the lower the prevalence of mental illness. Hollingshead and Redlich's survey of treated psychiatric patients in New Haven gave the results shown in Table 19.5. The lowest social class, V, had a rate of treated mental illness, 1659 per 100,000 population, more than three times as great as that of the two top classes, 556. A follow-up study of the patients also revealed differences by social class in methods of treatment and in ultimate outcome.[47]

Crime in Urban Subareas

The early study of Shaw and McKay showed that within cities delinquency and crime vary widely among different neighborhoods.[48] They found the following : (1) rates of delinquency and adult crime declined with distance from the center of the city; (2) areas with the highest rates of crime and delinquency were also characterized by physical deterioration, declining population, high density, economic insecurity, poor housing, family disintegration, transiency, conflicting social norms, and an absence of constructive positive agencies; (3) areas having the highest rates of crime and delinquency in 1900 also had the highest rates in 1930 despite the fact that the ethnic composition in the areas had undergone virtually complete change. The crime and delinquency rates in areas nearest "downtown" remained high.

These findings have generated a large volume of later research by Shaw and McKay and by others, both in Chicago and in other American cities, on the whole confirming Shaw and McKay's findings. Thus, in Baltimore, Detroit, and Indianapolis high delinquency rates were found in central areas and associated with overcrowded housing, low education and income, and a high percentage of households containing unrelated individuals. The association of delinquency with foreign-born population appears to have lost its significance over time, however, as

[47] Jerome K. Myers and Lee L. Bean, *A Decade Later: A Follow Up of "Social Class and Mental Illness,"* (1973).

[48] Clifford R. Shaw and Henry D. McKay, *Juvenile Delinquency and Urban Areas* (1942), (1969, revised edition, with an Introduction by James F. Short), page references are to the revised edition.

immigrant groups have become assimilated into the mainstream of American life.

Additional light on the association of ethnic status with delinquency is presented by McKay's data presenting trends in recorded delinquency in 74 subareas of Chicago for 1927-61.[49] He found that four of the five communities with the most pronounced *upward trends* and four of the five communities with the most pronounced *downward trends* were black communities. Short comments that

The most significant difference between these communities appears to be the fact that the upward-trending communities have begun and completed the familiar cycle of Negro invasion, disruption of institutional life, and succession of the population to a Negro majority most *recently* in the series, while the downward-trending communities have constituted the heart of the Negro community in Chicago . . . for more than thirty years . . . .

. . . a more general formulation of the processes at work. The impact of rapid residential shift from an invading socially and economically disadvantaged population is such as to decrease the capacity for social control of the community . . . Time and stability are required for the establishment of traditions and institutions. For the American Negro, time and tradition have been disruptive of stability and conventionality. But there is evidence of great change—of emerging political leadership, more stable and affluent economic institutions, more stable family patterns, . . . such as have developed among other ethnic communities.[50]

These results point to the importance of local community dynamics rather than ethnic characteristics themselves as explanations of areal variations in delinquency.

The Urban Confrontation

Thus far we have dealt with deviance on the individual level. There are, however, group phenomena that can also be regarded as forms of deviance, including civil disorders, mass violence, riots and rebellion, and movements of social protest. Traditionally the city has been viewed as providing fertile soil for large-scale disorder and dissent. We shall examine this view and also an alternative view, that these signs of "deviance" are signs of the freedom of urban life. Our discussion of this many-faceted topic will be limited to the competition and conflict arising from intergroup relationships and to civil disorder in industrial cities.

A look at some of the world's great cities attests to their diversity. Possibly every race and nationality is represented in New York City. In this great metropolis there are as many Jews as in Israel; as many

[49] *Ibid.*, (revised edition) chapters 14 and 15.
[50] *Ibid.*, Introduction by Short, pp xxix-xxx.

persons of German descent as there are residents of Darmstadt; as many blacks as there are in Kinshasa, capital of the African nation of Zaire; as many Italians as there are citizens of Genoa; and several times as many Protestants as live in Belfast. Perhaps equally heterogeneous is Chicago, the great crossroads of the Middle West, and for decades a mecca for Old World immigrants and dispossessed blacks from the American South. San Francisco is a meeting place of peoples and cultures from the East and West. Around the world we find the same phenomenon, varying only in degree of heterogeneity and in the character of social patterns. Bombay, Singapore, Manila, Johannesburg, and Algiers, to name a few, are cities of great cultural, social, religious and linguistic diversity.

As people of different races and cultures jostle each other in the metropolis, stresses and strains occur, and the traditional forms of interaction are often weakened as old racial and cultural boundaries are crossed. New forms of social organization may arise, some reflecting cleavages along racial and cultural lines, others reflecting cooperative arrangements between individuals and groups. Cultural interests and loyalties may fade as members of certain groups are rapidly integrated into the larger society, while other groups, especially those of high racial visibility, remain in comparative isolation. If the city is a melting pot, as the playwright Israel Zangwill once said, it often boils over and sometimes explodes when human passions run high. And if it "melts," as no doubt it does, the blending process, whether biological or social, by no means occurs evenly for all people and cultures.

Intergroup Competition

"City air" says the proverb, "makes men free." Taken symbolically, the proverb may mean freedom of competition, both for individuals and for groups. When individuals in a community do not differ appreciably in appearance or behavior, competition tends to be viewed mainly as an individual relationship. Even if a racial or ethnic minority is represented in a community by a very few persons, competition between them and others is highly individualized, and if conflicts arise from competitive situations they are largely personal in nature.

But if a minority group becomes so large or powerful that it appears to threaten the status of other groups, competition tends to assume more the character of intergroup than of interpersonal relations. Hostilities, if they arise, are generally directed primarily toward the collectivity rather than its individual members. When immigrants from abroad were relatively few in American cities, their presence was hardly noticed and their competition, if felt at all, was mainly an individual matter. But when their numbers increased to the point that they were considered a threat to the social or economic positions of numbers of the people, whether long-time residents or other newcomers, competitive conscious-

ness shifted to a group basis: they were judged opprobriously and categorically as Jews, Polacks, Wops, Hunkies, Japs, and so on. Such has been the case for blacks. As long as blacks in northern cities represented a small and unobtrusive minority the reactions to them tended to be individualized; but when their numbers increased as a result of heavy in-migrations, competition shifted to a group basis. It was out of such a competitive situation that bitter conflicts sometimes emerged.

French students demonstrate in Paris. Although 25,000 took part there was no violence. In cities large numbers and diverse populations provide conditions for large-scale confrontations. (United Press International Photo)

Wherever peoples of differing race, religion, nationality, or culture live and work together competitively in the same community, there is always a possibility that intergroup tensions will occur and will result in some form of discrimination. Whether the tensions so generated will culminate in overt conflict depends on the circumstances. In American cities almost every minority or majority group—racial, religious, or ethnic— has at one time or another been the object of hostility and sometimes discrimination.

For example, until 1948, through a quasi-legal device known as a "protective covenant," property owners and realtors in many American cities agreed not to rent or sell property to persons of a designated race or religion. In 1948, the United States Supreme Court unanimously ruled that judicial enforcement of racially restrictive covenants was unconstitutional. Hence, while restrictive real estate covenants based on exclusion of racial, religious, or ethnic groups are still used, they are not legally binding. Since that time there has been a spreading movement by state and local governments to enact legislation prohibiting racial and religious discrimination in various parts of the housing market. In the early stages, the trend was to ban discrimination in housing that received government aid, such as public housing or housing covered by federal government mortgages. In recent years, however, the trend has been to extend the prohibitions to the general housing market, that is, to homes that are privately financed. The passage of the 1968 civil rights bill by the federal government prohibited discrimination in the sale or rental of about 80 percent of all housing. Nevertheless discrimination in housing continues, via such devices as the "private club" or corporation to which an individual must be admitted before he can purchase property in a given area. The resort to such devices to circumvent the law attests to the strength of group prejudice in cities (and rural areas).

INTERGROUP CONFLICT   Conflict between racial or cultural groups may assume a variety of forms, depending upon historical and situational circumstances and other specific factors. Janowitz's recent analysis indicates that there have been three dominant forms of collective urban racial violence: (1) "communal" race riots from World War I to World War II; (2) "commodity" race riots dating from World War II; and (3) terrorist violence, particularly evident since the late 1960's.[51]

The "communal" riots were interracial clashes over urban territory, typically taking place on the boundaries of expanding black neighborhoods. "Commodity" riots, so called because looting is a characteristic feature, typically take place within the black ghettos and involve clashes between the local blacks and the law enforcement agencies. These riots are being replaced by "a new form of racial violence, a more selective, terroristic use of force with political overtones, again mainly against whites, by small organized groups of blacks."[52] These destructive outbursts, whether "communal," "commodity," or terrorist can be understood, Janowitz points out, "in a symbolic sense, . . . as expressions of energies to participate in and transform the larger society. In all phases of life, the Negro is not merely reacting [against his subordinate status] but acting."[53]

For many years the cities of North Africa, especially Algiers and Oran, seethed with unrest as tensions between the French colonial overlords

[51] Morris Janowitz, "Patterns of Collective Racial Violence," in Hugh D. Graham and Ted. R. Gurr, eds., *Violence in America: Historical and Comparative Perspectives* (1969), vol. II, pp. 317-39.

[52] *Ibid.*, p. 318.

[53] *Ibid.*, p. 337.

and the indigenous peoples assumed much of the character of a civil war, or at least a war for national independence—until independence was actually achieved in 1962. But it was also a struggle between peoples who differed in religion and way of life. More recently the continued warfare between Protestants and Roman Catholics in Belfast, Northern Ireland, has been the focal point of long-standing conflict representing not only different religious orientations but also demands for equal access to jobs and housing, and the right to political self-determination.

In 1958 black residents of London were subjected to a series of violent attacks by British citizens who resented the presence and competition of "foreigners." For years, people from the commonwealth countries had

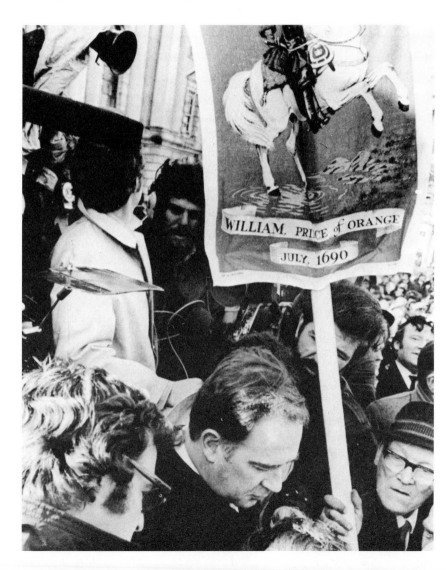

In current religious struggles, a militant Protestant group in Belfast, Northern Ireland, carries a standard marking the victory of King William, Prince of Orange, over the Catholic monarch, King James, in 1690. (United Press International Photo)

migrated to British cities. Many came from Africa and the West Indies and were racially distinct from the Europeans. But with jobs, housing, and the necessary amenities of life in short supply, these outsiders were viewed by many as a serious threat to their own economic and social status. Competition in interpersonal relationships was exemplified in the associations of black men and white girls, a situation resented by many white men. Having high racial visibility and distinctive habits, the black persons were easily identified and thus became easy targets for many Britishers who resented their presence, or at least their competition, and who directed their hostilities against the black men, either by economic or social discrimination or by physical assault. Swift action on the part of London officialdom, however, avoided the destructiveness often resulting from unbridled rioting.

URBAN MINORITY MOVEMENTS   Demands for change by no means always take the form of violent protest. The city has also become the locus for organized social movements: movements reflecting the aspirations of minority peoples for freedom and equality, or movements by the majority to maintain a superior position in a system of inequality. The ill-fated Garvey movement among American blacks, for example, was centered in New York; the Black Muslims also have major centers in New York and Chicago. Indeed, organized efforts of blacks throughout the United States to break the shackles of discrimination generally originate in a metropolis. In South Africa, Negroes and Asians in such cities as Durban and Johannesburg have organized to protect themselves against the increasing discrimination of whites and to gain at least a measure of the freedom that has been denied them.

The sharing of interests, convictions, and anxieties by members of racial or ethnic groups is commonly manifest in formal organizations through which some form of collective action may be carried out. If ethnic or racial groups represent a minority against which there is discrimination, it is all the more likely that organizations will be established for defensive or offensive purposes.

Such organizations have become an important feature of American urban society. Sometimes these organizations are local; more often, however, they are links in a larger chain of national or internation scope. Frequently they include members from other racial or cultural groups. Organizations to protect and advance the rights of blacks and Jews have long been a familiar feature of American cities and have come to include some that pursue a militant strategy. The 1960's and 1970's have seen a proliferation of groups representing the interests of other ethnic groups such as the Mexican-Americans, Italian-Americans, Americans of Oriental background, as well as non-ethnic interest groups—women, the aged, and homosexuals. Despite their sometimes bizarre and disruptive tactics such groups have legitimate grievances and points of view. It

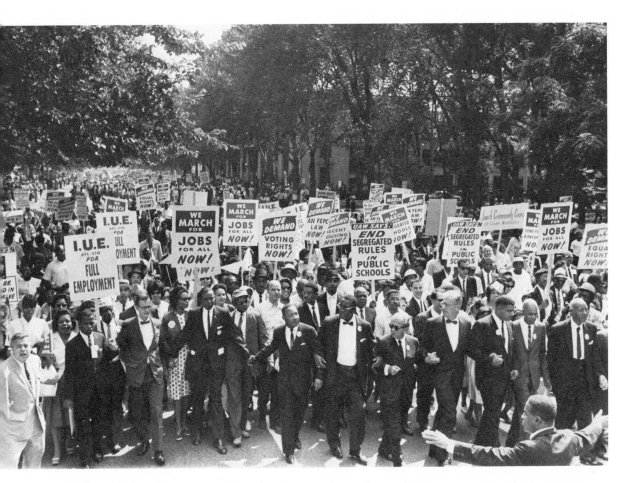

speaks well for the urban milieu that it provides a forum for listening and action.

The March on Washington, 1963, a massive nonviolent demonstration for racial equality and civil rights. (United Press International Photo)

The Industrial City and Collective Disorder

The "cataclysmic theories of urbanization," to borrow Tilly's phrase,[54] hold that the city is a destructive force. Industrialization, one of the allegedly destructive components, has been critically reviewed by Blumer in relation to social disorder.[55]

In his evaluation Blumer contends that there is no constant relationship between the coming of industrialization and social disorganization, especially if one views the impact at the local level. Scholars may have been misled because of unwittingly biased observation of the highly visible, attention-getting instances of social disorganization. He notes

[54] Charles Tilly, "The Chaos of the Living City," in Herbert Hirsch and David Perry, eds., *Violence and Politics: A Collection of Original Essays* (1972), p. 34.

[55] Herbert Blumer, "Industrialization and Problems of Social Disorder," *Studies in Comparative International Development,* V (1969-70), 47-58.

also that other factors, apart from industrialization, may produce the socially disruptive consequences attributed to industrialization. For example, a society undergoing industrialization is typically widely exposed to new goods, ideas, and people from other countries and areas.

Blumer's most important criticism is that there is great variation in what industrialization itself actually consists of, particularly in terms of specific conditions of work in the factory. Similarly there is great variation among the societies and groups experiencing industrialization. The crucial question then becomes the way in which a given society, group, or community reacts to the specific instance of industrialization. The result may or may not be social disorder. Blumer sums it up as follows:

To seek or to see disorganization in the changes which take place or in the problems which take place or in the problems which arise is to move in the wrong direction. Instead, disorganization should be sought and perceived in the state of the social machinery which exists for concerted action and control. A society may become disorganized in the face of few problems or minor crises; contrariwise, a society faced with many problems and major crises may escape disorganization by virtue of being able to act concertedly and decisively with regard to those problems. Thus, in the case of early industrialization, disorganization does not exist in the removal of productive functions from the family, or in the separation of the nuclear family from the extended family, or in migration to congested urban areas, or in unsatisfactory conditions of work, or in severing individuals from a paternalistic or feudal system, or in the rise of new sets of wishes and aspirations. These may set occasions for disorganization but are not its substance. Instead, whether or not disorganization occurs depends on how the family deals with the removal of its productive functions, how the nuclear family mobilizes itself when removed from the extended family, how migrants work out adjustments to urban living, how workers organize themselves in the face of unsatisfactory working conditions, how individuals address the opportunities for greater freedom as well as the loss of support from others, how the local and central governments attack the new social problems which face them. In each of these instances the *how* is not given by the particular situation which sets the need for action. Its explanation must be sought elsewhere, predominantly in the state of the resources which allow for the mobilization of action. Scholars concerned with disorganization under early industrialization will be misled by preoccupation with the changes, problems and crises which may arise. Of more crucial importance are the facilities, the means, and the will to deal with changes, problems, and crises.[56]

THE URBAN POOR IN DEVELOPING COUNTRIES   A study of countries currently undergoing rapid urban development has focused on the part played by recent migrants to the city and by the urban poor in collective violence.[57] In these Third World cities Nelson found that these groups

[56] *Ibid.,* p. 54-5.

[57] Joan Nelson, "The Urban Poor: Disruption or Political Integration in Third World Cities?" *World Politics,* 22 (April 1970), 393-414.

did not exert a destabilizing influence, yet according to the traditional view it is precisely among these groups that one would expect most cause for unrest. For migrants the alleged "shock" of adjustment to the city was cushioned, Nelson found, by the fact that many had help from their kin, friends, or organizations of their tribe or caste in finding housing and jobs and that many migrated to large cities from smaller urban places rather than directly from rural areas. Although most migrants had an economically marginal position in the city most also felt they were better off than they had been previously, hardly a condition impelling them to riot and disorder.

With respect to the already established urban poor the traditional theory holds that continued exploitation turns them into "radical marginals." Nelson's careful sifting of the available data lends little support to this view. However, she believes that certain current conditions may lead to higher levels of political activism among the poor: local organizing, prevalent among urban squatters; spreading of expectations and information by mass media, such as the radio; and a generally greater interest in and responsiveness to the poor among political groups. Nelson concludes, however, that even if there is greater collective action among new migrants and the urban poor "the challenge . . . is not the containment of extremist or anarchic outbursts, but the evolution of means to respond to concerns and usually moderate demands without the sacrifice of other development objectives."[58]

Summary

This chapter has sought to challenge the uncritical assumption that the city is a spawning ground for unprecedented rates of deviance. In reviewing the available evidence we have pursued three main types of comparisons: (1) urban-industrial with developing countries; (2) rural vs. urban; (3) variations within the city. Urban personality and crime were examined in depth and in neither case does the city itself appear to cause these forms of deviance, except in the case of crimes against property. Even in this instance there is some evidence that urban rates of property offenses are declining over the long run, although the rural-urban differential of higher urban rates persists.

The findings of the studies reviewed raise as many questions as they answer. If the city is not the prime cause of most forms of deviance, what then are the dynamics? Poverty, differential opportunity, and political oppression are probably causes, as indicated particularly in the examination of variations in deviance within the city, although the actual network of cause and effect is far from established.

[58] *Ibid.,* p. 414.

Finally we have viewed deviance as a mass phenomenon in the form of the "confrontation" among contending urban groups. Intergroup competition is no doubt heightened in cities, but with some beneficial effects. Collective disorder, especially by the urban underclass, seems not to be linked to industrialization and urbanization per se.

In conclusion we must sound a recurring theme: urban deviance, whether in personal attributes or mass protest, is not necessarily a sign of disintegration and decay but of life, of individual and group striving for fulfillment and change, "the chaos of the living city."[59]

Selected Bibliography

BOOKS

Berube, Maurice, and Marilyn Gittell, eds., *Confrontation at Ocean Hill-Brownsville.* New York: Praeger, 1969.

Clark, Peter, and Paul Slack, eds. *Crisis and Order in English Towns, 1500-1700.* London: Routledge and Kegan Paul, 1972.

Clinard, Marshall, and Daniel Abbott, *Crime in Developing Countries.* New York: Wiley, 1973.

Crain, Robert L, Elihu Katz, and Donald Rosenthal, *The Politics of Community Conflict: The Fluoridation Decision.* Indianapolis: Bobbs Merrill, 1969.

Daly, Charles, ed., *Urban Violence.* Chicago: University of Chicago Center for Policy Study, 1969.

Glaser, Daniel, ed., *Crime in the City.* New York: Harper and Row, 1970.

Graham, Hugh, and Ted R. Gurr, eds., *Violence in America: Historical and Comparative Perspectives,* two volumes. Washington, D.C.: A Report to the National Commission on the Causes and Prevention of Violence, 1969.

Kaplan, Berton H., *Psychiatric Disorder and the Urban Environment: Report of the Cornell Social Science Seminar.* New York: Behavioral Publications, 1971.

Levy, Leo, and Louis Rowitz, *The Ecology of Mental Disorder.* New York: Behavioral Publications, 1973.

Masotti, Louis, and Don Bowen, eds. *Riots and Rebellion: Civil Violence in the Urban Community.* Beverly Hills, Calif.: Sage, 1968.

McGee, T.G., *The Urbanization Process in the Third World.* London: Bell, 1971.

Myers, Jerome K., and Lee L. Bean, *A Decade Later: A Follow Up of "Social Class and Mental Illness,"* New York: Wiley, 1973.

Oppenheimer, Martin, *The Urban Guerilla.* Chicago, Quadrangle, 1969.

Powell, Elwin H., *The Design of Discord, Studies of Anomie: Suicide, Urban Society, War.* New York: Oxford University Press, 1970.

Sennett, Richard, *The Uses of Disorder.* New York: Vintage, Random House, 1970.

Shaw, Clifford R., and Henry McKay, *Juvenile Delinquency and Urban Areas.*

---

[59] The phrase is from Tilly, *op. cit.,* as translated from Beaudelaire.

Chicago: University of Chicago Press, 1969, revised edition with an Introduction by James Short. (originally published 1942).

Suttles, Gerald D., *The Social Construction of Communities.* Chicago: University of Chicago Press, 1972.

Tobias, J.J., *Urban Crime in Victorian England.* New York: Schocken, 1972.

ARTICLES

Boggs, Sarah, "Formal and Informal Crime Control: An Exploratory Study of Urban, Suburban, and Rural Orientations," *Sociological Quarterly,* 12 (Summer 1971), 319-27.

Clinard, Marshall, "The Relation of Urbanization and Urbanism to Criminal Behavior," in Ernest Burgess and Don Bogue, eds., *Contributions to Urban Sociology.* Chicago: University of Chicago Press, 1964, pp. 541–59.

Ferdinand, Theodore N., "The Criminal Pattern of Boston since 1849," *American Journal of Sociology,* 73 (July 1967), 84–99.

Fischer, Claude S., "On Urban Alienations and Anomie: Powerlessness and Social Isolation," *American Sociological Review,* 38 (June 1973), 311–27.

_____, "Urbanism as a Way of Life: A Review and an Agenda," *Sociological Methods and Research,* 1 (November 1972), 187–242.

Freedman, Jonathan L., "Population Density, Juvenile Delinquency and Mental Illness in New York City," in Commission on Population Growth and the American Future, *Research Reports,* volume V, *Population Distribution and Policy,* Sara Mills Mazie, ed. Washington, D.C.: Government Printing Office, 1972, pp. 511-23.

Gordon, R.A., "Issues in the Ecological Study of Delinquency," *American Sociological Review,* 32 (December 1967), 927–44.

Lodhi, A.Q., and Charles Tilly, "Urbanization, Crime, and Collective Violence in Nineteenth Century France," *American Journal of Sociology,* 79 (September 1973), 296–318.

Masotti, Louis, ed., "Urban Violence and Disorder," special issue *American Behavioral Scientist,* 2 (March-April 1968), 1–55.

Nelson, Joan, "The Urban Poor: Disruption or Political Integration in Third World Cities?" *World Politics,* 22 (April 1970), 393–414.

Perry, David C., and Joe R. Feagin, "Stereotyping in Black and White," in Harlan Hahn, ed., *People and Politics in Urban Society.* Beverley Hills, Calif.: Sage, 1972, pp. 433–63.

Seeman, Melvin, "The Urban Alienations: Some Dubious Theses from Marx to Marcuse," *Journal of Personality and Social Psychology,* 19 (August 1971), 135–43.

Srole, Leo, "Urbanization and Mental Health: Some Reformulations," *American Scientist,* 65 (September/October 1972), 576–83.

Tilly, Charles, "The Chaos of the Living City," in Herbert Hirsch and David C. Perry, eds., *Violence and Politics: A Collection of Original Essays.* New York: Harper and Row, 1972, pp. 2–42.

Wilson, Robert A., "Anomie in the Ghetto: A Study of Neighborhood Type, Race, and Anomie," *American Journal of Sociology,* 77 (July 1971), 66–89.

Wolfgang, Marvin, "Urban Crime," in James Q. Wilson, ed., *The Metropolitan Enigma.* Washington, D.C.: United States Chamber of Commerce, 1967, volume II, 237–68.

20 • Urban Migrants and Their Adjustments

As long as cities have existed they have attracted peoples from the outside, whether from their hinterlands or from other cultures or countries. A considerable portion of population growth in most cities has thus been the result of in-migrations. As long as a region or country has rural open spaces capable of maintaining a population engaged in primary production, many persons settle there and follow an agrarian way of life. This was true of the early migrations to the United States from Europe and elsewhere, as well as of the movements of people to Canada and parts of Latin America.

But many of the world's agricultural regions no longer afford vocational opportunities for internal migrants or immigrants from abroad. Such areas may be overpopulated in terms of land resources, or economic and technological changes have made them economically unattractive to people on the move. Hence, the major currents of migration during the twentieth century have been in the direction of cities, especially large cities, a trend that seems to be as true of predominantly agrarian countries as of industrialized countries, although it began somewhat later in the former than the latter regions.

The population growth of cities is the result of both a natural increase (the number of births minus the number of deaths) and net migration (the number of in-migrants minus the number of out-migrants). Of 77 metropolitan areas in the United States, the total estimated increase between 1960 and 1969 was 14,565,000 persons, of whom almost 5 million represented net in-migration.

In Europe, since the end of World War II, large numbers of workers have migrated to cities in England, Germany, Holland, France, and Scandinavia to find employment. England alone has received over a million persons from the Commonwealth countries, mainly India, Pakistan, the West Indies, and parts of Africa. In 1972, after some 50,000 Asians, mainly Indians and Pakistanis, were forcibly expelled from Uganda, most of them settled permanently in cities of the United Kingdom. Literally millions of persons have entered the United States from other countries. In the early years of immigration most of them, especially those from northern Europe, headed for the open spaces; but later arrivals, largely from southern and eastern Europe (Italy, Greece, Poland, Russia, and Hungary), settled in cities that afforded opportunities for advancement. Although immigration to American cities has declined during the twentieth century, nevertheless 3 million persons were admitted to the United States during the decade of the 1960's, about half of them from Europe, and most of them going to cities.

In Argentina, most of the immigrants in recent years have also come from Europe; half were from Italy, a third from Spain, a fifth from Poland, followed in numerical order by Russians, French, and Germans.[1] Over two-thirds of the foreign-born population in Argentina in 1960 lived in large cities, mainly metropolitan Buenos Aires. Israeli cities—mainly Tel Aviv and Jerusalem—have drawn Jews from all parts of the world, most of them expecting to settle there permanently.

The flow of population into cities has become a veritable flood in many other countries. Abu-Lughod reports that over one-third of the permanent residents of Cairo were born outside that city, most of them migrants from the rural hinterlands.[2] Of the 60 million residents of Indian cities in 1961, some 7 million were in-migrants over 10 years of age, or about 12 percent of the total urban population.[3] Doubtless that proportion has increased since then. Madras, for example, received 490,000 migrants between 1941 and 1951, and almost half the population of Calcutta are migrants.[4] In the United States the mass migrations to cities of blacks from the rural South and whites from the worn-out farms of Appalachia and the Ozarks have had profound social and economic effects.

The Causes of Migration

"Push" and "Pull" Factors

In some situations migration to cities is a matter of economic survival. For example, the mechanization of agriculture in the American South forced millions of black laborers or tenant farmers to abandon that region and move to cities. Farm families in the "dust bowl" region of the

[1] Gino Germani, "Mass Immigration and Modernization in Argentina," in Irving L. Horowitz, ed., *Masses in Latin America* (1970), p. 293. With restrictive legislation these proportions have recently changed. Very few immigrants now arrive from the communist countries.

[2] Janet Abu-Lughod, "Migrant Adjustment to City Life: The Egyptian Case," *American Journal of Sociology*, 67 (July 1961), 23.

[3] Donald J. Bogue and K. C. Zachariah, "Urbanization and Migration in India," in Roy Turner, ed., *India's Urban Future* (1962), pp. 31, 41.

[4] S. C. Sen, *The City of Calcutta: A Socio-Economic Survey* (1960).

1930's had no choice but to leave the land and head for other places, often cities on the West Coast. The pressure of population on the land and resources of India and Pakistan has almost literally forced millions of persons to migrate, mainly to metropolitan communities. These are examples of the "push" interpretation of migration. Probably an even greater number of rural persons have moved to cities not out of necessity but to achieve certain educational, social, or occupational goals beyond their reach in the rural community. It is for these persons that the "pull" explanation of migration has been formulated. Actually, for most migrants, a combination of both push and pull factors account for their movement; it is not an either-or situation but one of degree.

Probably the majority of urbanbound migrants, whether internal or from other countries, now head for metropolitan cities because that is where they expect to find favorable economic or social opportunities. Some remain permanently in the city of destination, but others become "floaters," moving from one city to another, or from city back to rural community and back again to city. A study in Delhi, India, revealed that more than half of a sample of in-migrants had tried their luck in numerous cities before reaching the capital city.[5] Seasonal migrations account for some of the in-and-out movements in cities, the direction of the move being determined mainly by job opportunities such as the harvesting of fruit and vegetables. Workers in the construction industry are often required to move from one city to another, remaining in each locality only as long as the job holds out. Urban residents may abandon the city for rural communities, but in general they are older persons, and the volume of such movement is a trickle compared with the heavy flow of younger persons into cities.

In recent times, war and revolution have uprooted millions of persons. The 1970 World Refugee Report specifies that at least 17 million persons, displaced by manmade disasters, are wandering the earth or festering away in refugee camps. The 2 million refugees from mainland China that have swarmed into Hong Kong after the communist takeover in 1949 now represent half the population of that city. Refugees from the wartorn areas of South Vietnam have sought protection in Saigon, swelling the population of the capital city to three times its prewar size. Over a half-million persons left Cuba after the communist revolution in 1959, most of them taking up residence in nearby Miami or other cities in the United States. Millions of residents of Bangladesh abandoned their homes in 1972 in the face of a military invasion by West Pakistan, many seeking refuge in Indian cities. In the Middle East, 2 million refugees, victims of the ongoing Arab-Israeli conflict, live in refugee camps, mainly in or near the cities of that region. Major natural disasters such

[5] M. B. Deshmukh, "Delhi: A Study of Floating Migration," in UNESCO, *The Social Implications of Industrialization and Urbanization* (1956), pp. 143–226.

as droughts or floods force people to seek protection elsewhere, sometimes permanently in cities.

The Migrants' "Port of Entry"

The majority of migrants to cities enter the community at or near the bottom of the economic structure. This is especially true of migrants from rural hinterlands or other countries who do not possess the skills, education, or experience that would qualify them for jobs that offer attractive rewards in income or security. Black migrants from the American South, as well as the floods of immigrants who came to American cities from the Old World, have been handicapped in this way. However, world events, as well as selective legislation relating to the admission of immigrants, have affected changes in the educational or occupational qualifications of incoming peoples. Some, such as professionals, have occupational skills that are in demand in the host city or country.

Many Cuban refugees settling in American cities after the communist revolution were middle- or upper-class persons. Of the thousands of people who escaped from the Nazi fury in Germany in the 1930's and settled in cities in various countries, most were well educated. Most Asian immigrants once almost categorically excluded from the United States, but now admitted in larger numbers, have acceptable records of education or occupational training and experience. The problems of adjustment of such people are undoubtedly quite different from those of unskilled, unlettered, and unsophisticated migrants, many of whom are destined to experience serious deprivation in the urban setting.

Selective Migration

Migrations of population to cities, whether from the rural hinterlands or from other countries, is selective in one way or another, but the specific nature of selection and its social or personal implications are not always clear. Indeed, such selectivity may vary from one region or country to another.

In some developing societies male migrants to cities greatly outnumber females, a situation particularly true of cities in India and Pakistan. The sex ratio in Calcutta, India's largest metropolis, is about 60–40, that is, 60 males for each 40 females. This sex imbalance has far-reaching implications for the host community as well as for the migrants themselves. The Calcutta Planning Board estimated in 1963 that at least half of the "households" in the city were either single-member families or "messing families," the latter referring to groups of males who live together in a household, preserving some semblance of family life, but without females or children. This sort of imbalance was also true of American cities in the early stages of immigration from other lands, but the ratio was radically changed as females, married or unmarried, were attracted in increasing numbers to urban centers. In fact, the sex ratio in many American cities is now slightly tilted in favor of females. Some demographers believe that a similar change of sex ratios will probably occur in later stages of urbanization in developing societies.

Age selection in migrations to cities is probably universal, and young adults generally outnumber the very young or the very old. They arrive at or near the beginning of their working career, the most productive period of their lives. This means that the social and economic costs of their upbringing and education have been assumed by their families or home communities, only for them to leave at the stage of life when "repayments" for these costs might be made. In many respects, the city gains by this form of selection.

In American cities at least, in-migrants heading for the suburbs are, by and large, on higher educational and occupational levels than those moving into the central cities. Suburbs are thus populated mainly by persons moving away from the central city and by individuals moving in from the outside; in both instances they are generally middle or upper class persons, or at least persons who can afford to live in suburban communities and are not prevented from doing so by racial or other forms of discrimination. Whether this tendency exists in other urban-industrial societies we do not know, but there is considerable evidence, as indicated in an earlier chapter, that urban in-migrants in non-industrial countries often locate in peripheral settlements and there construct shantytowns, for the reason that they cannot afford to buy or rent homes in the built-up areas of the central city.

The Adjustment of Migrants

For internal migrants or foreign immigrants coming from a village or farm background, settlement in a city commonly represents a sharp break with the past in many spheres of life. Work roles and working conditions are different; consumer behavior may vary sharply from the earlier mode of life; housing conditions may make normal family life difficult; and demands by the community or larger society are often confusing to the newcomer. Indeed, the very complexities of city life, the extremes of poverty and wealth, the rapid tempo of events, contrasting with the rural community, are often bewildering, especially if there are difficulties of adjustment due to language or other cultural differences that become a barrier to social interaction. For these and other reasons the migrants are marginal people who live, at least for a time, on the edge of the established social order.

But for most migrants in Western cities, except those who are highly visible racially and the objects of discrimination, marginality decreases with the passing of time. Unless they return to their native habitat, as some do, they usually become integrated, in varying degrees, into the economy, participate in political and civic activities, learn the prevailing folkways pertaining to consumer behavior and appearance, and internalize many of the values and meanings of city life where they are located.

Two sisters in East London, South Africa—a study in contrasts. Although the sister at left is a domestic in town and has adopted a European way of life, the other sister follows traditional Xhosa tribal practices. Around the world many urban migrants have retained some of their ethnic heritage. (Reproduced by permission of the Institute of Social and Economic Research, Rhodes University, from Philip Mayer, *Townsmen or Tribesmen,* Oxford University Press, 1961.)

Levels of Adjustment

It is possible to view the adjustment of migrants to cities from the perspective of three levels,[6] each of which represents a theoretical continuum from "imperfect" to "perfect" adjustment. Adjustment on the *organizational* level may be of two dimensions: One is the degree and nature of integration into the institutional system of the city, including the assumption of occupational roles which the migrant is able or permitted to perform. He may be excluded from any or all roles, for various reasons, or he may be accepted for the roles which he can perform and which he finds satisfactory. In modern urban society many of these roles are a salient feature of bureaucratic structures. The other dimension of organizational adjustment involves participation in voluntary associations, civic or welfare organizations, political or religious groups, informal friendship groups, and so on. Sometimes this form of adjustment occurs when the migrant joins or participates in an organization whose membership includes nonmigrants as well as migrants. In other instances the organization may be established by migrants for their own collective or individual interests, such as the Hispanic Confederation, which we shall describe briefly later in this chapter.

The state of the urban economy and the level of technology have an important bearing on the adjustments the migrant is able to make. Those whose occupational skills are appropriate to a rural or agricultural economy may be at a disadvantage when confronted with a highly complex and specialized occupational system such as exists in the metropolis. Earlier immigrants from Old World backgrounds, or those from the rural hinterlands, came at a time when the need for factory hands was at its peak in American cities. Now, technological advances, especially automation, have decreased the demand for unskilled workers. The poorly educated, unskilled migrant or immigrant, whether white or black, enters a metropolitan job market with shrinking requirements for untrained muscle power. He also finds increased hazards in self-employment of the neighborhood type of private business. Urban industrial societies are becoming so bureaucratically structured that the vast majority of workers, on every level, are institutional employees, which means that the migrant must possess the skills appropriate to the needs of the institution.

On the organizational level the most crucial adjustment of immigrants or internal migrants is an occupational role which provides economic support and an opportunity to obtain a more satisfactory life style. Probably the majority of in-migrants in cities of the Western world have,

[6] For a similar point of view, see especially S. N. Eisenstadt, *The Absorption of Immigrants* (1954), ch. 1.

sooner or later, found jobs and been able to ascend the status ladder, if only for a few steps. The history of immigration to American cities supports this generalization. Even the blacks who have migrated to urban centers, especially those from rural backgrounds, have generally improved their income and occupational status, even though the majority have remained at or near the bottom of the occupational structure.[7]

Culturally the migrant's adjustment may be conceptualized as acculturation in which he acquires or becomes familiar with the material and nonmaterial features of the host society or community. An individual may thus acquire such traits as attire, dietary habits, or various behavioral patterns of the prevailing life style—or he may reject or ignore these things. As a part of his acculturation he may learn the language of the host society, acquire certain occupational skills and appropriate manners, and learn its traditions.

The level of assimilation is concerned with the psychological aspects of adjustment—acquiring the values, meanings, sentiments, prejudices, or ideologies held by others of the host society or community. It is essentially a matter of learning and internalizing, through experience, intimate association with others, formal teaching, observation, or indoctrination, the meanings embedded in the dominant culture.

Related to assimilation is the satisfaction or dissatisfaction of the migrant in the community of destination. The migrant's reaction to the new community setting or its component parts may run the gamut from high satisfaction to extreme dissatisfaction. The reactions may be generalized with reference to the total community situation, or they may have as specific reference points such matters as the work situation, housing, neighborhood of residence, interpersonal relations, recreational facilities, and so on. Undoubtedly these reactions are related, in one way or another, to the adjustments on the organizational and cultural levels, but few researches have been undertaken to construct a comprehensive picture of adjustments taking into account the many variables that are involved. Furthermore, the adjustment of migrants arriving in a city for the first time may be quite different from that of return migrants who are arriving at the original city of departure about which they already have some familiarity.

The three levels of adjustment—organizational, cultural, and psychological—are interrelated. Integration into the institutional structure invariably involves a certain degree of acculturation, often a minimal degree. An immigrant may obtain a job, but aside from his associates in the work situation or market place he may acquire little of the prevailing culture of the host community, although in the course of time the acculturative process continues. Acculturation of the migrant or im-

---

[7] Peter M. Blau and Otis Dudley Duncan, *The American Occupational Structure* (1967), pp. 259–71.

migrant may occur even when organizational integration is limited, but the acculturative and integrative processes tend to reinforce each other. Finally, the assimilative process, while not always occurring at an equal rate with the other processes, is nevertheless influenced by what takes place on the organizational and cultural levels.

Adjustment on any or all of these levels commonly involves considerable internal stress for the individual, which may manifest itself in anxiety syndromes, overt deviant behavior, or conflict of one kind or another. The reactions of migrants or immigrants to the many facets of an urban social environment depend on a number of things. Some migrants under certain conditions, and subject to certain influences, become rapidly integrated into the organizational system, acculturated, and assimilated, while others do not.

Eventually most migrants or their progeny become involved in a variety of ways in established social institutions, and the extent and nature of these involvements are a fairly reliable gauge of adjustments on the level of organizational integration. Children attend school and come in contact with a considerable range of ideas and behavior patterns, associating with other persons from different social and cultural backgrounds. Adults and children may identify with religious institutions and through participation in them extend their range of social contacts. The migrant or immigrant may apply for some kind of institutional assistance and therefore become familiar with the structural and functional aspects of organizations dispensing aid. Some join labor unions or other power-oriented organizations. Adjustments through institutional integration, however, does not necessarily apply to all migrants or immigrants.

Trial and Error, Success or Failure

For most migrants, adjustment to city life probably occurs on a trial-and-error basis, and success or failure is usually a matter of degree. Generally speaking, the larger the city the wider the range of possible choices the migrant is able to make, in contrast to the village or small town. The city in this respect may be likened to an enormous "cafeteria" in which a wide variety of things to choose from are on display; but it differs from a cafeteria in that the migrant may not be free or qualified to make certain choices, or indeed may not be aware of the many possible choices he could make. And this inability to make choices in terms of roles or the possession of objects may engender in him a sense of frustration and deprivation.

There is no single criterion for evaluating the migrant's adjustment. It may be either an internal or external matter—how the individual reacts subjectively to a situation or how he behaves overtly. He may obtain employment and earn a comfortable income, but may detest the system, yearn to return to his native heath, or feel isolated, alienated, and rebellious. On the other hand, the jobless migrant may be content with his lot, preferring the bright lights of a city to the humdrum life of a small town or farming community. There are many yardsticks of adjustment.

City-to-City Migrants

Several studies provide evidence that urban-to-urban migrants, as a whole, are more successful in their adjustments to city life than rural-to-urban migrants.[8] This is hardly surprising since the urban migrant who has lived or worked in another city has had the benefit of experiences which may give him an advantage over migrants from rural communities. Generally, urban migrants from other cities are better educated and possess more usable occupational skills than migrants from rural backgrounds. Yet there are intervening variables, and for such a generalization to have much validity the comparison should be more selective than is provided by a mere rural-urban dichotomy. It should, for example, compare black migrants who have moved from another city with black migrants from rural communities; and even this comparison should be refined by comparing blacks of a similar age or educational level.

One reason that city-to-city migrants apparently tend to make a more successful adjustment than rural-to-urban migrants is that they are less dependent on their kinship or friendship primary groups than those who come from rural environs.[9] Because rural migrants generally enter the urban social structure at or near the bottom, at least lower than the majority of city-to-city migrants, they are compelled to rely more on their relatives or friends for guidance and support rather than meeting directly and more independently the challenge of city life and coming to terms with it.

Group Identity and Support

For migrants who are conspicuously different in race, religion, culture, language, and life style from the host community, reliance on friends or relatives provides them with a sense of security and the warmth of being with others of their own kind, in what may be an unfamiliar and sometimes forbidding situation. This tendency to seek out and associate closely with others with whom they have in common many things may

[8] Arnold M. Rose and Leon Warshay, "The Adjustment of Migrants to Cities," *Social Forces*, 36 (October 1957), 72–76.

[9] Charles Tilly, *Migration to an American City*, Agricultural Experiment Station and Division of Urban Affairs, University of Delaware, 1965.

be observed among migrants in cities all over the world. If this tendency retards the adjustment process it at least provides the individual with a cushion against the unfamiliar and adverse, as well as emotionally satisfying experiences. Group support is an important element in the adjustment of migrants in cities, especially if they are set apart from the majority in the host community. In the course of time, the primary-group support may be extended to include formal mutual-aid associations that provide a variety of benefits. The number and character of mutual-aid associations set up in American cities by migrants from abroad during the great migrations are impressive indeed.

The Conflict of Roles and Values

Various forms of cultural conflict, or conflicting values, may impede the adjustment of migrants. One of the difficulties that certain tribal peoples or villagers have in adjusting to urban demands is the unfamiliar conceptions and expectations of work roles. Work in a tribal or village community is not usually performed according to a fixed time schedule, or with specified results, as may be the case in a city. The pace or schedule of agricultural work may be defined by custom or socially approved personal inclinations, but in the city the work schedule, dictated by formal contractual agreement, specifies the work routine and tasks, including the beginning and end of work day or week and the amount of time spent in the performance of one's work roles. Interdependence of such roles and of workers usually makes these specifications necessary in the city. If the worker ignores them he may be fired or otherwise penalized.

Conflicting values such as these have been observed in the case of American Indians, whose *modus vivendi* on reservations or in other tribal communities does not usually harmonize with the roles and expectations of city life when they migrate to urban communities. The employer may view their behavior as irresponsible, while the workers may conclude that the employer's demands are unreasonable. These and other reactions of many migrants on entering the city whose culture and social system are unfamiliar might be described as "culture shock."

A heavy influx of immigrants or internal migrants differing greatly in social and cultural backgrounds usually creates stresses and strains in the host community. An appropriate illustration is the varied cultures and regions represented among the immigrants settling in Israel.[10]

---

[10] Eisenstadt, *op. cit.*, pp. 118ff. See also J. Isaac, "Israel—A New Melting Pot?" in W. D. Borrie, ed., *The Cultural Integration of Immigrants* (1959), ch. 11; and Yoram Ben-Porath, "On East-West Differences in Occupational Structure in Israel," in M. Curtis and M. Chertoff, eds., *Israel: Social Structure and Change* (1973), pp. 215–37.

Among the immigrants entering Israel from over fifty different countries some are Westernized Jews from Europe and the Americas, while others arrive from such barren regions as Yemen or Saudi Arabia. They speak a variety of languages, follow different life styles, and have different educational backgrounds. Some have fled to escape persecution, others are motivated by an altruistic spirit. Some are impoverished, others well-to-do professional or business people. But they have one thing in common: the Jewish religion, which provides the bond that forms the basis of community life, although the adjustments are not always easily achieved by the newcomers.

Adjustment Problems
Yesterday and Today

Present-day conditions affecting the adjustment of migrants in the host community differ from the situations experienced by earlier migrants in American cities, a distinction Padilla discusses in her study of the adjustment problems of Puerto Ricans living in New York.[11] The great migrations of Europeans to American cities occurred at a time when the economy, technology, and city life were very different from what they have been in recent years. Most European and Asian migrants came at a time when labor at all levels in all sectors of the economy was in short supply. By contrast, the in-flow of Puerto Ricans coincided with the development of automation and the extension of electric power, with the result that the jobs available to them were largely in the marginal sectors of the economy. In this respect their migrations paralleled the heavy urbanward flow of blacks.

In the early days migrants to American cities were left largely to their own devices in solving their problems with the help of their kinsmen and friends. But since World War II a veritable network of laws and both public and private organizations have provided a cushion against adversity for migrants and others in need, applying especially to problems of housing, health, education, and jobs. But even these protective devices are not always adequate to provide security and opportunities for the newcomers or their children. Although having the advantage of many facilities and institutional supports unknown in earlier periods, present-day migrants commonly experience strong feelings of deprivation. One does not necessarily suffer psychologically from poverty when everyone else around him is poor, but poverty in the midst of riches, as is the case in most cities, may create feelings of acute deprivation.

Glazer and Moynihan, after reviewing the evidence concerning the acculturation and assimilation of blacks, Puerto Ricans, Jews, Italians, and Irish in New York City, conclude that the "melting pot" concept is

[11] Elena Padilla, *Up from Puerto Rico* (1958), pp. 83–86.

misleading, that these minorities, most of whom are migrants or descendants of migrants, have retained a strong sense of ethnic or racial identity even though they have changed their life styles and conform in various respects to the prevailing *modus vivendi* of that metropolis.[12]

Some of the early ethnic immigrants settling in American cities, however, have become so thoroughly integrated, acculturated, and assimilated into the prevailing culture and social system that they have only a superficial sense of identity with their traditional ethnic group. This would apply particularly to the English, Germans, Scandinavians, Dutch, Austrians, or Swiss whose ethnic identity usually plays a small part in their lives. Most of them have been almost completely absorbed into the dominant culture and social system. Some flaunt their ethnic identity on special occasions—wearing a green necktie on St. Patrick's Day, for example—but that is about the extent of their ethnic consciousness.

Five groups migrating from rural areas to cities within the United States—blacks, white southerners, Puerto Ricans, American Indians, and Mexican-Americans—differ from many earlier immigrants in that they are American citizens and, except for some Puerto Ricans, Mexican-Americans, and Indians, English is their native language. But, like the bulk of earlier immigrants, they must make the transition from the comparative simplicity of a rural *gemeinschaft* community to the complexities of a *gesellschaft* society.

Most white rural migrants now occupy the social and economic position in American cities that the immigrants of a previous generation occupied—and they suffer, as did the bulk of the earlier immigrants, from the dual burdens of poverty and urban inexperience. This situation is well illustrated by comparing the experience of rural migrants with other migrants. A study of migrants to Chicago reported that those from rural-farm areas, especially in the South, showed the low occupational status, high unemployment rate, and low educational level of "problem" migrants.[13] In contrast, migrants from rural nonfarm areas, and those migrating from another city to Chicago, had equal or higher socioeconomic status, on the average, than the resident Chicago population.

Black Migrants in American Cities

Black migrants in American cities have several strikes against them from the moment they arrive. To begin with, they are the objects of racial prejudice often manifest in overt or covert discrimination in many spheres of life—housing, education, jobs. And if their education and

[12] Nathan Glazer and Daniel Patrick Moynihan, *Beyond the Melting Pot*, 2d ed. (1970).
[13] Ronald Freedman, *Recent Migration to Chicago* (1950), pp. 30ff.

financial resources are limited, which is often the case, their choice of a residential neighborhood is usually restricted to a segregated district, commonly a congested slum. Finally, most of them have no occupational skills that are in demand above the level of unskilled labor, or for those who do have such skills few suitable jobs may be available.

Given this set of circumstances it is not surprising that the black community exhibits a high incidence of deviant behavior and emotional problems, although it is likely that some forms of deviant behavior are attempts at adjustments which conventional society disapproves of. Many blacks feel trapped in a situation that holds no prospects for a satisfactory way of life, and in their frustrations they resort to various forms of behavior that bring them into conflict with the institutional system of the larger community.

Except for blacks, most immigrant and migrant groups have had a proud ethnic identity apart from their American identity that served the function of sustaining them in the early period of residence in the United States and in later years marked them as a respected ethnic community. None of this was possible for American blacks, since slavery abruptly cut them off from their African heritage. Their only meaningful identity was as Americans or as blacks, but the position given them was so low as to constitute almost a nonidentity. The high rates of crime, delinquency, illegitimacy and other indexes of social disorganization among black-American migrants in cities are a product of the marginal participation they have been limited to in American society.

Puerto Rican Migrants in an American City

A study by Rogler describes in detail the efforts of Puerto Rican migrants in a medium-sized New England city to effect a better adjustment to existing conditions by developing an organization designed to function in the interest of the ethnic minority.[14] The city's Puerto Ricans were concentrated in an ethnic ghetto and were located in the social structure mainly in low-skilled and low-income occupations. Most were Spanish-speaking, with a limited knowledge of English. Although their incomes in the American city were generally higher than they had been in Puerto Rico, the community lacked the political and economic skills and experience to deal collectively with such problems as unemployment, illness, and deviant behavior. Moreover, the Puerto Ricans had no organization through which they could communicate their needs and grievances to the power elite in the larger community.

From Rogler's participant-observer research over a period of nearly four years there emerged a "life history" of the Hispanic Confederation's

[14] Lloyd H. Rogler, *Migrant in the City: The Life of a Puerto Rican Action Group* (1972).

representation of the Puerto Rican community's attempts to obtain a voice in local affairs and, thereby, the cooperation of city officials. The development of the Confederation was characterized by many starts and stops: periods of enthusiastic cooperation and expressions of solidarity among the members were followed by periods of apathy or hostile interpersonal relations; effective demonstrations of leadership were followed, or preceded, by ineptness on the part of the leaders, by opposition from city officials or power-hungry fellow ethnics; and, finally, official support was achieved. Through the agonizing and frustrating efforts of the leaders there emerged an organization with a considerable degree of effectiveness in the Puerto Rican community.

White Migrants from Rural Backlands and Backwoods

The disadvantaged from rural areas, notably Appalachia and the Ozarks region, differ in certain respects from many migrants settling in American cities. Most are Protestant in religion, English-speaking, native-white descendants of early Americans, and of Anglo-Saxon stock. Thus they have no racial or religious characteristics that would differentiate them from many other peoples in the host community. Thus, their adjustment problems are of a different order. Many of them have settled, at least temporarily, in cities of the Middle West and North, where adjustment to metropolitan life has not been easy for them.

A study of rural migrants as workers in a factory near Chicago revealed that their background had not prepared them for the highly formal, circumscribed behavior required by the extensive division of labor of industrial society.[15] Because specialized jobs must be coordinated, each worker's behavior must be dependable and predictable. The migrants, accustomed to individual work on farms or in hunting and fishing, carried over into the factory the habit of working at their own pace which, as a consequence, disrupted productivity. Even such a minor requirement as punching a time card was novel to them.

The industrial work adjustment of southern whites, as with other migrants from rural areas, is complicated by the fact that many are "sojourners"; that is, they are not yet fully committed to the city in terms of allegiance or permanent residence. Often having family farms and rural kin to depend on, they frequently quit their jobs or take long weekends to go "home" for family occasions, because urban jobs or life are not to their liking. Some even limit their city "sojourn" to the winter when chores on their farms are less demanding.

Because absenteeism and unreliability lead to low seniority and little advancement, the migrant worker may develop no stake in his industrial

---

[15] See especially James S. Slotkin, *From Field to Factory* (1960).

job. This is also reflected in his lack of interest in unions or social security; thus, he may develop few ties or common interests with fellow-workers apart from those of his own background. In sum, his lack of ties to urban occupations is likely to make him marginal from the point of view of both his employer and fellow-workers.

Italian Migrants in American Cities

In his study of the Italian minority in Boston, Gans observed a strong sense of identity with the ethnic community.[16] Personal relationships are mainly limited to other Italians, and the sense of kinship is strong. Marriage outside the ethnic group is generally disapproved. Even so, the acculturative process has extensively eroded the indigenous Italian culture. By the third generation the Italian language has become a foreign language to many. Although Italian foods are served, dietary habits for the second and third generations have been "Americanized." The community's younger members adopt prevailing fashions and fads, whether in attire, in esthetic interests, or recreational patterns. Names are commonly anglicized, Giuseppe becoming Joseph, for example. These forms of adjustment and change do not apply uniformly to all persons, but rather vary as to such factors as age, occupation, social class, and education.

The family as a social unit usually plays an important part in the adjustment process of its individual members. Italian immigrants generally adhere to a family-centered ethnocentrism that is deeply rooted in the culture of rural or village Italy. In a study of Italian immigrants and their children in New York City, Covello observed that moral behavior is primarily applicable to one's own family.[17]

A dominant motif of American culture is *self*-advancement, but the central motif in the society of Italian immigrants is *family*-advancement. It would be difficult to imagine an Italian peasant contributing to the Red Cross, writes Covello; his contribution, if any, would go to his relatives. Here, then, is a conflict of cultural values, a conflict that affects the adjustment of Italian immigrants. Nevertheless, the strong sense of family identity provides a social anchorage for the individual and affords him a sense of security that he otherwise might not have.

---

[16] Herbert Gans, *The Urban Villagers* (1962), pp. 34–35.

[17] Leonard Covello, *The Social Background of the Italo-American School Child*, Doctoral dissertation, Yale University, 1944, p. 276.

Migrants in Urban England

In her study of migrants from the West Indies residing in London, Patterson records the difficulties—social, cultural, and psychological—many have in adjusting to British urban life, especially in the work situation and living conditions.[18] Often they come with romanticized expectations of life in London, only to undergo considerable disillusionment when these expectations do not materialize—the pot of gold at the base of the rainbow turns out to be a mirage. Work roles, if the migrants are fortunate enough to obtain employment, are exacting, unrewarding, and confining. Assembly-line work is completely alien to their original experience.

If they reside in neighborhoods with other persons of similar cultural backgrounds and life styles they may be crowded into unsightly tenement structures, in contrast to the more spacious areas of residence they occupied "back home." They may encounter color prejudice among British or other workers, which is often expressed as discrimination in housing and jobs, and their different sexual mores and marital behavior tend to isolate them from the conventional Anglo-Saxon population. A large percentage of the migrants' children are born out of formal wedlock, and marital union commonly occurs without benefit of religious or official recognition. They bring to the city few skills appropriate for an industrial economy and are therefore handicapped in obtaining the employment that leads to security and a higher standard of living. Some return to the West Indies, disenchanted and embittered, but most remain if for no other reason than that living in London, with all of its disadvantages, at least offers a better standard of living than their homeland.

Of the migrants from India who have settled in cities of the United Kingdom, the Anglo-Indians have apparently made an easier adjustment than many others from the same country. This is so because their cultural orientation is Western: their mother tongue is English, their religion Christian, and their life style essentially European, whereas most of the other migrants are non-Western in culture, religion, language, and life style. But in spite of the cultural similarities of the British and the Anglo-Indians (who are of dual racial ancestry, European and Indian), the race or color prejudice of the British has often resulted in the migrants' social isolation and alienation, although most of them have found employment and earn incomes far higher than they received in India before leaving there. Actually, social barriers now apply less to the children and young adults, who commonly mingle freely and select British spouses. In another generation or two, it seems probable that the Anglo-Indians will have become so well integrated and assimilated into

[18] Sheila Patterson, *Dark Strangers* (1963).

the social system that they will almost cease to exist as a socially distinct community.

Rural Migrants
in Yugoslavia

The processes and problems of adjustment of rural-to-urban migrants is similar in semiindustrial and developing societies, although the situations from one country to another are not always exactly parallel. In his study of rural migrants in Belgrade, the capital city of Yugoslavia, Simić observes that the transplanted villager does not face a serious language problem on arrival in the city, which is often not the case in other countries.[19] But there are certain cultural and behavioral patterns in the city which may be alien to his rural experience. As in most countries, the immediate problem of obtaining housing is a serious one, since in Yugoslavia living quarters are in short supply.

Incoming migrants to Belgrade seldom experience a complete break with their village pasts; most maintain a reciprocal relationship with kin remaining in the village. From their earnings they commonly send money to their kin, or during the summer months return to the homesite to assist in the annual harvest, taking with them store-bought presents for their family members. On their return to the city they may take a supply of home-grown and processed foodstuffs. This is the economic side of the reciprocal relationship; the other side pertains to the affective satisfactions derived from these visits.

If any members of the kinship group are already in the city when the migrant arrives, or even others from the same village, he generally receives from them assistance in such matters as locating a job or finding housing. These kinship ties and reciprocities persist, and Simić found few families, regardless of their length of residence in Belgrade, that had completely severed their ties to their kin, either those in the village or in the city. Nevertheless, the process of adjustment involves the extension of ties to a widening circle of friends in the city, mainly to persons of similar cultural and geographic backgrounds, while the intensity of kinship bonds tends to decline and is gradually replaced or supplemented by new ties relevant to the urban setting. Thus the migrant comes to live within the context of two social worlds: the world of the kinship group and the world of the social network of the city involving persons having comparable occupational or social interests.

Simić points out that one of the first steps in the acculturation of the migrants, and perhaps the easiest one, is the adoption of urban forms of dress, although younger migrants make this adjustment more easily than older ones. They must also make an adjustment to life in a strictly

---

[19] Andrei Simić, *The Peasant Urbanites* (1973).

cash economy and its application to a wide variety of consumer goods and services, in contrast to the village situation with its limited variety of purchasable goods and available activities, especially leisure-time pursuits. One adjustment for many is the urban use of time, a problem, as we noted earlier, also experienced by migrants to cities in Western countries. Simić gives the example of an orthodontist who had a serious scheduling problem with clients, parents who seldom, if ever, brought their children to the clinic on schedule for dental care.

The Returned Migrant

Migrants who had migrated to a city but returned to the community of original settlement are confronted by the problem of adjustment to what was earlier a familiar setting. Little empirical research has been done on the adjustment of returned migrants, in spite of the fact that return has become a widespread pattern of population movement. Often the point of origin of migrants is a rural community, but in the United States, at least, the migration pattern is increasingly a city-to-city movement rather than a rural-to-urban one. In the case of black Americans the dominant pattern of migration has for many years been from southern communities to northern cities. While this pattern probably continues to prevail, there has been increasingly a reversal of the direction; many black Americans who left the South for northern cities are now returning to communities in the southern region. We do not know, however, if the returnees have made a more successful adjustment than they made in the northern cities.

A recent study, rather limited in scope, compared the adjustment of 101 returned migrants in Birmingham, Alabama, with a control group of 55 persons, matched approximately as to age, sex, educational level, incomes, and occupational class.[20] Among the findings that emerged from the research was that the control group as a whole seemed to be better satisfied with life in Birmingham than the returned migrants, and that the returnees on the lower socioeconomic levels were better adjusted, by the criterion of satisfactory adjustment, than those with higher status.

The Adjustment of Migrants in Developing Countries

The floodtide of migrants to cities in developing societies, a fairly recent phenomenon, has often created problems of a magnitude and character

---

[20] Daniel Johnson, "The Adjustment of Returned Migrants," Doctoral dissertation, University of Missouri, 1973.

beyond the capacity of the community to cope with them. Most of the cities in these countries have not experienced an expansion of the economy commensurate with the vast numbers of migrants who have arrived in search of jobs or other economic benefits. Furthermore, the cities have not had the financial capacity to meet the educational, health care, social welfare, transportation, and housing needs of migrants, as well as other amenities. Nor are the future prospects favorable, since the flow of migrants to the large cities shows no signs of abating, especially in the heavily populated countries where rural people are commonly "pushed" off the land.

In the nonindustrial countries, migrants in the cities often become marginal urbanites in both a physical and a social sense. That they are in the city but not of the city is evident in the following ways: (1) Urban growth often stems from problems in rural areas rather than from opportunities in the cities. (2) The magnitude of city growth has reached "flood" proportions, presenting almost unmanageable physical problems. (3) The dual physical structure of the cities—a small modern core ringed by shantytowns—mirrors the cultural clash between the wealthy Westernized elite and the traditional ways and subsistence economy of peasants or tribesmen. (4) The ultimate social effects of migration to cities in the underdeveloped regions are not yet clear, although it seems safe to predict that the effects will not parallel those in the Western industrial nations. There is much disorganization, social and personal, but there are signs of readjustment in the development of stable "urban villages," in the vitality of family and kin relationships, and in the expansion of formal self-help organizations.

Migrants in Cairo

In a study of migrants in Cairo, Abu-Lughod points up the levels of adjustment we have considered in this chapter.[21] First of all, she notes that the migrants differ in backgrounds and in their adjustments to city life. One migrant type represents the village "have nots" who have been pushed off the land; the other consists mainly of younger persons "pulled" to the city as they set out in search of education and economic opportunity. Migrants in the first category generally attempt to reconstruct within Cairo a village culture to serve as a protective haven and a cushion against adversity; those in the second category have the motivation for rapid assimilation and integration into Cairo's culture and social system.

A profile of the migrant of the first type "is a young man whose first contact in the city is often with a friend or relative from his original village, with whom he may even spend the first few nights. Later more

---

[21] *Op. cit.*, pp. 22–23.

permanent lodgings are found, usually in the same neighborhood. This process, in the aggregate, results in a concentration of migrants from particular villages within small subsections of the city, far beyond what would be expected by chance. It would take a keen observer indeed to distinguish between a 'village' in Cairo and one located miles beyond its boundaries.[22]

Egyptian culture, according to Abu-Lughod, places a high value on intimate personal relationships even at the expense of personal privacy.[23] Hence the dependence on informal associational life. The coffee shop provides an opportunity for males to conduct much of their social life and business activities. Since few of the migrants belong to a labor union, civic association, or political group, the coffee shop becomes an important institution serving to facilitate an adjustment to city life, at least for males, for it is there that they can share with fellow-migrants their problems and interests. But there are also formal associations that facilitate adjustment. One such form of organization is the benevolent association, numbering more than a hundred in Cairo, which provides assistance to members in need of various services.

Occupationally, a change of work roles represents an important adjustment for Egyptian migrants. The traditional rhythm of agricultural work involves periods of intense seasonal activity, followed by periods of leisurely work interspersed with social activities; work days are also long or short, depending on the stage of the seasonal work cycle. No such rhythmic work cycle exists in Cairo, where the work days are of uniform length and there are no major seasonal variations. The work schedule is regulated more by the clock than by the calendar or the season. If the migrant is employed as a factory worker or laborer, he comes in contact with others of different backgrounds; in the village, much of the work is communal within the extended family or the village.

Migrants in African Cities

Migrants from villages to African cities also retain social ties with their home communities. Gugler has noted that throughout Sub-Saharan Africa (except South Africa), urban residents who have migrated to the

---

[22] *Ibid.*, p. 25. See Chapter 6, pp. 176–8, for an ecological perspective on these transplanted villagers in Cairo.

[23] *Ibid.*, p. 31.

Town and country in Southern Rhodesia. General view of Salisbury (below), the capital city, which grew from 117,000 in 1955 to 435,000 in 1970. Many migrants have come there from Rhodesian agricultural villages like that of Ziyambe (above). (United Nations)

city and live there, at least temporarily, generally visit their ancestral village, maintain land rights, present gifts to their relatives or friends, help support their kinsmen if they can afford to do so, marry local women, and expect to retire sooner or later to the home community.[24] They may also cherish the prestige accorded a city man by the villagers, especially if he has been successful. In a sense, these persons live in a dual community system, the city and the village, and have a marginal or segmental relationship in each.

In his study of tribal migrants in Freetown, a West African city, Banton observes that adjustment is a dual process of personal accommodation to city life and group alignment.[25] He believes that migrants are attracted to the city for varied reasons; urban squalor in particular is preferable to the humdrum life of the village. The change involved in work and residence in the city does not necessarily constitute a critical problem of adjustment for most migrants in this cultural context. The process by which the migrant is drawn into membership of a local group of persons of the same tribal or village unit provides an identity and a satisfying sense of security.

Migrants in South American Cities

Several studies of the adjustment of migrants in cities of South America have been conducted. Germani observed that recent migrants living in working class districts in Buenos Aires participated much less in social life outside the family group than was true of city-born residents.[26] Their contacts were mainly with members of their own kinship group or persons from the same locality, except for the casual contacts they had with fellow-workers. In this respect they were not as well integrated into community life as city-born people. Germani also found a higher incidence of truancy among the children and youth of the recent migrants than was true of those whose families had lived in the city for a long time. The young found social outlets in gangs that often engaged in disruptive behavior, indicating limited controls exerted by their families, which were often disorganized.

Pearse likewise found that the kinship group in Rio de Janeiro was the principle source of stability for the in-migrants in the *favelas* (slums) of

[24] Josef Gugler, "The Theory of Rural-Urban Migration: The Case of Sub-Saharan Africa," in J. A. Jackson, ed., *Migration* (1969), ch. 6.

[25] Michael Banton, "Social Alignment and Identity in a West African City," in Hilda Kuper, ed., *Urbanization and Migration in West Africa* (1965), pp. 146–47.

[26] Gino Germani, "An Inquiry into the Social Effects of Urbanization in a Working-Class Sector of Greater Buenos Aires," in Philip Hauser, ed., *Urbanization in Latin America*, (1961), pp. 206–32.

that city.[27] The Brazilian family, essentially authoritarian, emphasized the principle of mutual aid within the kinship group, in which each member was expected to contribute according to his or her competence. The broad network of social relations that developed when individual family members married provided considerable security for the slum dwellers.

Another investigator has emphasized the problems of adjustment of migrants to the work situation in São Paulo.[28] In terms of adjustment, a distinction was observed between the migrants from the state of São Paulo, whose culture and economy are similar in many respects to that of the metropolis, and those from the isolated underdeveloped areas of

[27] Andrew Pearse, "Some Characteristics of Urbanization in Rio de Janeiro," in Hauser, *op. cit.*, pp. 191–206.

[28] Juarez Rubens Brandao Lopes, "Aspects of the Adjustment of Rural Migrants to Urban-Industrial Conditions in São Paulo, Brazil," in Hauser, *op. cit.*, pp. 234–248.

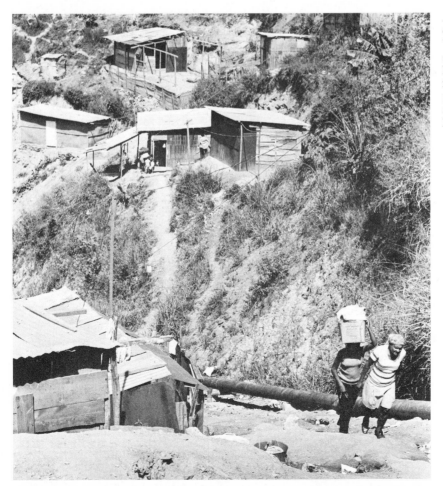

A migrant barrio on the outskirts of Caracas, Venezuela. Photograph shows some stages of house construction. Residents are trying to have government install sewers and running water. (Mary D. Howard)

northern Brazil. It was the latter group that encountered the greatest difficulties in adjustment to the conditions of work. For the most part, the former, the *Paulistas*, came as a family group with the intention of remaining, whereas the others were more likely to arrive alone and with no intention of becoming permanent residents of the city. The members of the migrant families pooled their resources and thus made a fairly easy adjustment to city life and work. On the other hand, the migrant individual required a much longer length of time before finally settling down, often moving from the city to the home community and back again several times before finally remaining in one place or the other. Often the individual migrant remained in São Paulo only because he was unable to make enough money to achieve his objectives at his original community. One source of satisfaction the author mentions is the prestige that the migrant achieves in the eyes of his fellows in the home community, thus sometimes motivating him to return to the city once again if only to earn the admiration of his bucolic friends or kin when he eventually reappears in the home town.

Some Effects of
In-Migration

Generalizations concerning the effects of in-migration must be made in terms of specific "impacts" on the individual or on a particular group or community. The inflow of migrants with varied racial, cultural, or social backgrounds tends to increase the heterogeneity of the host city's population. The metropolis especially is a magnet attracting people from all parts of the globe, from rural and urban communities, from all strata of society—people who are diverse in almost every respect, differing both from each other and from the established residents of the host community. Any empirical measure would probably indicate an increase of heterogeneity from small cities to large ones. The metropolis becomes a meeting place of peoples and cultures. There is a saying that if one stands very long in Piccadilly Circus in the center of London he is sure to meet some one from his home town or country.

"Second-Generation" Migrants

Some authorities have contended that the burden of adjustment falls more heavily on the second generation—the native-born sons and daughters of foreign-born immigrants.[29] The argument holds that the immigrants in American cities are protected from the worst effects of disorganization by having grown up in a traditional culture whose

[29] See, for example, Will Herberg, *Protestant–Catholic–Jew* (1955).

values still guide their behavior as adults, even though they have moved to another community setting. Their children, however, are said to be caught between the conflicting demands of their parents' standards and those of American society transmitted to them by education and the mass media. Herberg argues, for example, that the second generation tends to reject religious participation because the religious customs their parents attempt to pass on to them are often considered "inferior" or "odd" by American society. Others have noted that culture conflict may lead to high crime rates in the second generation. What has been said about the second generation of immigrants appears to be at least partly valid for the children or grandchildren of in-migrants from the rural hinterlands, especially if they are destined for urban ghettoes. These observations concerning the effects on in-migrants are based mainly on evidence obtained from American cities. Whether such generalizations are valid for other countries is an open question. But even in the United States certainly not all in-migrants, or their children, become personally disorganized or mentally ill.

"Migrations" within the City

Residential movements within a community represent, in a sense, a form of migration in that adjustments may be made, or at least attempted, by members of families that move. There is some reason to believe that intracity residential changes are more frequent in American cities than in other countries, although comparative data are not easy to obtain. Of the 130 million residents of metropolitan areas in 1970, a total of 23 million, or almost 18 percent of the population over one year of age, had moved by 1971, but most, some 15.5 million, moved into another house *within the same county*. About one-half of the within-county movers were central-city residents, the other half residing in the outer areas of the metropolis. Among those 7.5 million who moved to a different county, not necessarily within the metropolitan area, suburban residents were most numerous.[30] Census reports do not indicate the direction of the moves—from central city to suburb or the reverse, for example—nor do they specify the reasons for this form of mobility. However, a number of studies in American cities indicate that about three-fifths of the residential moves within communities are efforts to find more satisfactory housing.[31]

We are not aware of any studies of intracommunity moves that distinguish migrants from nonmigrants. A survey over the 1962–1967

[30] *Statistical Abstract of the United States* (1972), p. 36, Table 44.

[31] Nelson N. Foote *et al.*, *Housing Choices and Housing Constraints* (1969), ch. 6. See also Peter H. Rossi, *Why Families Move* (1955).

period, however, suggests some of the factors involved in moving.[32] About half of the rental housing had a change of occupancy each year, compared with only 7 percent of the owner-occupied residences. In low-value residences, in both black and white districts, 38 percent of the houses had a change of occupancy each year, whereas in medium-value houses 20 percent changed occupancy, and in high-value homes only 10 percent changed.

Many reasons other than unsatisfactory housing conditions account for changing residential location: to reside in a district symbolic of higher status, to escape from unpleasant neighborhood surroundings, or to be close to schools or place of work. Inasmuch as many in-migrants are of low economic and social status, it obviously follows that their choice of residence is restricted. If the move is mandatory, as in the case of low-income families transplanted from slum neighborhoods to public housing projects or evicted by landlords, the change may generate emotional stresses and interpersonal tensions, especially if the move is resisted. Often the move necessitates a different life style, which may not be desired.

Summary

The present chapter opens with a discussion of the scope and magnitude of migrations to cities in selected countries. Following this discussion there is an analysis of the conditions that dispose people to migrate and of the selective character of movements to cities. The main thrust of this chapter, however, is the adjustment of migrants or immigrants after arrival in a city. The various forms of adjustment are analyzed, with some consideration given to the levels of adjustment and to the factors that affect, favorably or unfavorably, the adjustment process. Finally, there is an account of selected empirical researches of migrant adjustment in cities in various countries of the world.

It is apparent, from this chapter, that the adjustment process often involves conflict between persons or groups differing in race, culture, language, economic status, or life style. But there are many other aspects of conflict in the city, also.

[32] Ronald R. Boyce, "Residential Mobility and Its Implications for Urban Spatial Change," *Proceedings of the Association of American Geographers*, 1 (1969), 22–26.

Selected Bibliography

BOOKS

Allen, Sheila, *New Minorities, Old Conflicts: Asian and West Indian Migrants in Britain.* New York: Random House, 1971.

Barrie, W. D., *et al., The Cultural Integration of Immigrants.* Paris: UNESCO, 1959.

Beijer, G., *Rural Migrants in an Urban Setting.* The Hague: M. N. Nijoff, 1963.

Bussey, Ellen, *The Flight from Rural Poverty: How Nations Cope.* Lexington, Mass.: D. C. Heath, 1973.

Eisenstadt, S. N., *The Absorption of Immigrants.* London: Routledge and Kegan Paul, 1954.

Fitzpatrick, Joseph P., *Puerto Rican Americans: The Meaning of Migration to the Mainland.* Englewood Cliffs, N. J.: Prentice-Hall, 1971.

Glazer, Nathan, and Daniel Patrick Moynihan, *Beyond the Melting Pot: Negroes, Puerto Ricans, Jews, Italians, and Irish of New York City*, 2 ed. Cambridge: MIT Press, 1970.

Gordon, M. N., *Assimilation in American Life.* New York: Oxford University Press, 1964.

Hauser, Philip M., ed., *Urbanization in Latin America.* New York: UNESCO, 1961.

Hernández Alvarez, José, *Return Migration to Puerto Rico.* Berkeley: Institute of International Studies, University of California, 1967.

Kuper, Hilda, ed., *Urbanization and Migration in West Africa.* Berkeley: University of California Press, 1965.

Mangin, William, ed., *Peasants in Cities.* Boston: Houghton Mifflin, 1970.

Mayer, Philip, *Townsmen or Tribesmen: Conservatism and the Process of Urbanization in a South African City.* London and Capetown: Oxford University Press, 1961.

Morrison, Peter A., *Population Movements and the Shape of Urban Growth: Implications for Public Policy.* Santa Monica, Calif.: RAND Corporation, 1972.

Rogler, Lloyd H., *Migrant in the City: The Life of a Puerto Rican Action Group.* New York: Basic Books, 1972.

Rose, Arnold, *Migrants in Europe.* Minneapolis: University of Minnesota Press, 1969.

Simić, Andrei, *The Peasant Urbanites.* New York: Seminar Press, 1973.

Taeuber, Karl E., and Alma F. Taeuber, *Negroes in Cities.* New York: Atheneum Press, 1969.

ARTICLES

Abu-Lughod, Janet, "Migrant Adjustment to City Life: The Egyptian Case," *American Journal of Sociology*, 67 (July 1961), 22–23.

Eames, Edwin, and William Schwab, "Urban Migration in India and Africa," *Human Organization*, 23 (1964), 24–27.

Elizaga, Juan C., "A Study of Immigration to Greater Santiago" (Chile), *Demography*, 3 (1966), 353–77.

Fitzpatrick, Joseph P., "Puerto Ricans in Perspective: The Meaning of Migration to the Mainland," *International Migration Review*, 11 (Spring 1968), 8–9.

Goldstein, Sidney, and Kurt B. Mayer, "The Impact of Migration on the Socio-Economic Structure of Cities," *Sociology and Social Research*, 50 (October 1965), 5–24.

Levine, Ned, "Old Culture—New Culture; A Study of Migrants in Ankara, Turkey," *Social Forces*, 51 (March 1973), 355–69.

Mayer, P., "Migrancy and the Study of Africans in Towns," *American Anthropologist*, 14 (June 1962) 576–92.

Rose, Arnold, and Leon Warshay, "The Adjustment of Migrants to Cities," *Social Forces*, 36 (October 1957), 72–76.

Shannon, Lyle W., and Magdalene Shannon, "The Assimilation of Migrants to Cities," in Leo F. Schnore, ed., *Social Science and the City*, pp. 49–75. New York: Praeger, 1968.

Taeuber, Karl E., and Alma F. Taeuber, "The Changing Character of Negro Migration," *American Journal of Sociology*, 70 (January 1965), 429–42.

——"The Negro as an Immigrant Group: Recent Trends in Racial and Ethnic Segregation in Chicago," *American Journal of Sociology*, 69 (January 1964), 374–82.

Thompson, Peter Omari, "Factors Associated with Urban Adjustment of Rural Southern Migrants," *Social Forces*, 35 (October 1956), 47–53.

Tilly, Charles, "Migration to American Cities," in Daniel Patrick Moynihan, ed., *Toward a National Urban Policy*, pp. 152–66. New York: Basic Books, 1970.

21 ● Images of the City

 Cities serve as dwelling places, but they are also places to sing about, to be lonesome for, to eulogize or condemn. Few people are neutral about the city. They love it or hate it, yearn for it or yearn to leave it. Sometimes the sentiment is directed at "the greatest little town in the world." Sometimes it is a broad pro- or anticity bias, or sometimes the focus of feeling is on a single city. "Hell is a city much like London," observed the poet, Shelley,[1] while others, with Samuel Johnson, have felt that "when a man is tired of London, he is tired of life; for there is in London all that life can afford."[2] Ralph Waldo Emerson said, "New York is a sucked orange," while Phyllis McGinley concludes her poem:

> Ah! some love Paris,
> and some, Purdue.
> But love is an archer with a low I.Q.
> A bold, bad bowman, and innocent of pity.
> So I'm in love with
> New York City.[3]

These are just a few of the many manifestations of the emotions and nonrational attitudes aroused by cities.

Obviously, it is difficult to measure urbanism as a state of mind, and certainly it is impossible to apply any precise yardstick to such reactions. Nevertheless, it is important that we describe what is known of the sentiments and symbols attached to cities, if only to avoid possible attitudinal biases that may color research on urban life. It is a sociological truism that what we believe to be real has real consequences, and our beliefs and feelings about the city become factors that influence our behavior.

In this chapter we shall consider various forms of urban symbolism,

---

[1] "Peter Bell the Third," Part 3, stanza 1.
[2] James Boswell, *The Life of Samuel Johnson,* entry for September 20, 1777.
[3] "A Kind of Valentine," *New York Times Magazine* (February 1, 1953).

together with the cultural and historical backgrounds of some of the ideas given expression by the symbols. Particular attention will be given to the development of urban and antiurban attitudes in the United States and their consequences for urban policy.

Varieties of Urban Symbolism

Symbols of the city are of many types and cover a wide range from so-called high culture to popular culture. Images of the city and attitudes toward urban life may be expressed in philosophy, literature, music, art, and other physical representations, as well as in religious ideology.

Levels of Urban Symbolism

The main currents of thinking about the city by European intellectuals in the past two hundred years have been described as falling into three major ideological streams.[4] "The city as virtue," a notion associated with the Enlightenment philosophy of the eighteenth century, was expressed by Voltaire, Adam Smith, and the German philosopher Johann Gottlieb Fichte. By the early nineteenth century the problems associated with an emergent industrialism had begun to manifest themselves and a view of "the city as vice" was reflected in the works of the French physiocrats, the Romantic poets, and important thinkers such as Fourier, Ruskin, Marx, and Engels. By midnineteenth century some intellectual adjustment to the industrial city had taken place and the city was now viewed as "beyond Good and Evil." None of these three ways of viewing the city has disappeared from current European (or American) thought, but one or another has tended to become dominant in the context of the cultural and economic conditions of a particular period. Broad intellectual stances toward the city were always forming and re-forming and doubtless there will be still other widely held views in the future.

MUMFORD'S TYPOLOGY AND THE INDUSTRIAL CITY   The most influential critique of the city is that of social historian Lewis Mumford, who is concerned particularly with assessing the impact of technology on the ultimate value of urban life. Mumford, following the scheme of his mentor Patrick Geddes, posited four major recent technological eras: the *eotechnic,* based on the use of wind, water, and wood as power, which dominated western Europe from the tenth to eighteenth centuries; the *paleotechnic,* based on the use of coal and iron, which became important in the eighteenth century and dominant by the end of the

---

[4] Carl E. Schorske, "The Idea of the City in European Thought: Voltaire to Spengler," in Oscar Handlin and John Burchard, eds., *The Historian and the City* (1963), pp. 95–114.

nineteenth and is equivalent to the early Industrial Revolution; the *neotechnic,* based on the use of electricity and the lighter metals such as aluminum, which began in the 1880's and is now dominant; and the *biotechnic,* which

refers to an emergent economy already separating out more clearly from the neotechnic (purely mechanical) complex, and pointing to a civilization in which the biological sciences will be freely applied to technology, and in which technology itself will be oriented toward the culture of life. . . . In the biotechnic order the biological and social arts become dominant: agriculture, medicine, and education take precedence over engineering. Improvements, instead of depending solely upon mechanical manipulations of matter and energy, will rest upon a more organic utilization of the entire environment, in response to the needs of organisms and groups considered in their manifold relations: physical, social, esthetic, psychological.[5]

Mumford also posits a typology of urban growth and decline: *eopolis,* the village community; *polis,* the city formed from adjacent villages; *metropolis,* a large city dominating the other communities in its region; *megalopolis,* the ever-larger entity which is economically parasitic on the rest of the society; and *nekropolis,* the "dead" city. Significantly, Mumford regards the last three, the most urban stages, as destructive of human welfare and civilization. He does not believe, however, that the destructive urban cycle is initiated only by modern industrial technology, that is, with paleotechnic developments, for he devotes a great deal of attention to ancient Rome and other urban centers which declined into nekropolis without experiencing industrialism. However, he stresses that the industrial advances of the paleotechnic and neotechnic periods have enormously expanded the number and influence of very large cities; hence, the threat to fundamental human values has been greatly increased. According to Mumford, our cities are now at the megalopolis stage, and, unless brakes and widespread planning are applied to urban growth, nekropolis will be the result.

A brief discussion cannot do justice to the richness and complexity of Mumford's work. Certainly he assigns many positive functions to cities, but his main line of thought makes it clear that he regards the city, especially the contemporary large-scale city, as antithetical to man's happiness and fullest development. For Mumford, the ultimate values include (1) relatively small-sized communities so that "human scale" can be preserved in social and economic activities and (2) "organic" relationships between man and the environment. Thus, he has advocated the planning of "regional cities" that will necessarily be limited in size and scope, and the reorientation of technology from mechanical

---

[5] Lewis Mumford, *The Culture of Cities* (1938), pp. 495–96. Mumford's more recent books expand on but show no fundamental change in his point of view: *The Urban Prospect* (1968) and *The Myth of the Machine: The Pentagon of Power* (1970).

productivity to the service of man, that is, biotechnic technology. Although one may agree with Mumford, one must also recognize that his equation of urban-industrial development with materialism and decline is essentially a value judgement.

THE CITY IN FOLK AND POPULAR MUSIC   The tendency to view the city in symbolic terms is not restricted to sophisticated elite groups; it is also expressed by the great mass of people in many aspects of popular culture and also in urban folklore. Botkin, the distinguished folklorist, has maintained that his colleagues have been going to remote rural areas to gather folk songs and stories while neglecting the urban folklore at their doorsteps.[6] Defining folklore as "a body of traditions, collective symbols and myths, folkways and folk-say, rooted in a place and in ways of living and looking at life,"[7] Botkin collected a large amount of such material from newspapers, memoirs, travel writings, interviews, and recordings. He found that American cities possess a folklore that has grown up around landmarks, streets, neighborhoods, place names, nicknames, local speech, foods, festivals, and the like.

Botkin regards urban folklore as particularly interesting because it illustrates more fully than rural folklore the interchange between "folk" and "popular" art. As a pure form, folk art is oral, has limited acceptance, and is diffused by noncommercial and nonacademic media, while popular art is written, has wide acceptance, and is diffused by commercial mass media. Botkin's anthology includes the song "St. Louis Blues," which we cite as an excellent example of the fusion of folk and popular elements.

A more recent analysis indicates how additional forms of folk music have been incorporated into popular urban commercial entertainment.[8] For various reasons, including population movements and new working rules in the music industry, the surviving musical folk traditions of the Ozark and Appalachian regions began to be widely played about the time of World War II. In the process the music itself underwent some changes but its idiom and style also affected the larger musical scene, resulting in "country-western" music. Much of its audience consisted of "urban hillbillies" to whom the "sin-sex-booze" themes of country-western represented the problems they faced in their recent urban migration.

The country-western lyrics face aspects of the current world of the urban hillbilly with directness unusual in popular song. And they are not "ballads" in the sense of narratives about the events. They are direct statements by the participants, with whom the listener identifies. The lyrics deal with the "real"

[6] B. S. Botkin, ed., *Sidewalks of America* (1954), pp. vii–x.

[7] *Ibid.*, p. vii.

[8] D. K. Wilgus, "Country-Western Music and the Urban Hillbilly," in A. Paredes and E. J. Stekert, eds., *The Urban Experience and Folk Tradition* (1971).

world of current life and the "real" problems. The world and the life are accepted, but they are not approved of. Seldom, as in "City Lights" (1958), is the contrast between the rural and the urban scene made explicit . . . ; but the contrast is implicit and sometimes suggested musically and symbolically.[9]

This music also has a much wider mass audience, as indicated by the sales volume of country-western music and the periodic appearance of individual songs on musical "hit parades."

VISUAL SYMBOLS OF THE CITY   The physical attributes of cities are so diverse that it is difficult for people to form an overall description, even of a given city, except by shorthand symbolic representation. Thus, the Golden Gate Bridge "stands" for San Francisco, the French Quarter for New Orleans, and the downtown skyline for New York City.[10] Preliminary investigation of the visual form in which urban residents perceive their cities suggest that they do indeed seek condensation and focus.[11] Lengthy interviews with long-time residents of Boston, Jersey City, and Los Angeles disclosed that in each city almost all of the sample had vivid images and associated sentiments composed of space and breadth of view, historic landmarks, vegetation and water, and so on. In fact, the residents of Los Angeles expressed dissatisfaction at the scarcity of easily identifiable focal points in their city. The spatial image of the city is related to its physical characteristics, but the image is not an accurate map. Thus, none of the Bostonians, even the ones born and raised in the district, included in their image of the city the large triangular area between the Back Bay and the South End, while they all included the Boston Common and certain other features.[12]

The process of condensation of visual images of the city is widespread and probably universal. Thus, a recent study of Tripoli, a contemporary Lebanese market city with a long preindustrial history, indicated that residents constructed a pared-down image of their city in response to questions similar to those which had been asked of the Boston, Jersey City, and Los Angeles residents noted above.[13] However, the elements the Lebanese selected for their image-building were rather different than those of the Americans, leading the author to conclude that, in addition to visual cues, sociocultural associations are important in forming urban images. Traditional Muslim attitudes emphasize the importance of private domestic life and deemphasize the public display

[9] *Ibid.,* pp. 156–57. For a description of the treatment of the city in another musical genre, see Paul Charosh, "The Home Song," in Sylvia F. Fava, ed., *Urbanism in World Perspective: A Reader* (1968), pp. 449–56.

[10] Anselm L. Strauss, *Images of the American City* (1961), p. 9.

[11] Kevin Lynch, *The Image of the City* (1960).

[12] *Ibid.,* ch. 2.

[13] John Gulick, "Images of an Arab City," *Journal of the American Institute of Planners,* 29 (August 1963), 179–98.

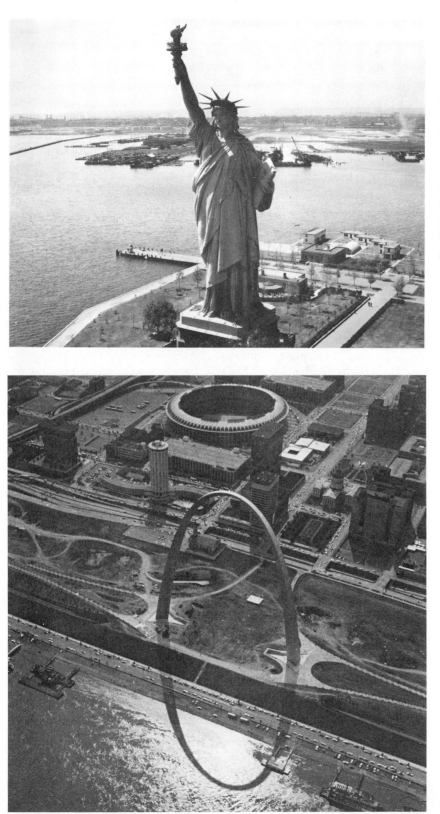

The famous landmark, symbol of a city: The Arc de Triomphe, Paris (left top); Christ on the Mountain, Rio de Janeiro (left bottom); The Statue of Liberty, New York City (right top); The Gateway to the West, St. Louis (right bottom). (French Government Tourist Office; Varig Airlines Photo; The Port of New York Authority; George W. Gardner)

of wealth or distinction. Civic consciousness and service are not highly regarded or developed. Domestic architecture and governmental buildings therefore did not figure prominently in the Tripolitans' perception of their city. In their images, they visualized few individual building or landmarks, but mentioned sections of the city in which distinct activities were carried on to which they had attached important values.

The City in Literature

Literature, which allows sentiments and values to be freely projected, is a rich source of urban symbolism. It may be a direct expression of pro- or antiurban views, but the more subtle views of the city expressed in the choice of adjectives and the themes and moods created are equally important. The city may, of course, be simply a locale for a novel or poem, but often it is an integral part of the action.

The symbolic aspects of the treatment of the city in literature are probably as old as both cities and literature. Thus, among the ancient Roman authors in the period up to the end of the first century A.D., one finds Juvenal referring to Rome as a "great sewer" and Horace describing "that bit of hell/Known as big city life." The general view is summed up as follows:

> The chorus of writers, one and entire,
> Detests the town and yearns for the sacred grove.[14]

Our discussion will focus on the literature on American cities since students will have greater familiarity with these works. Interestingly the largest American city has been, like Rome, a favorite target of the literary scene. Analysis of American fiction dealing with New York City from 1846 to 1937 reveals that the city is consistently portrayed as evil either because it offers temptations and inducements to immoral behavior or because of the disintegrating effects of the desire for wealth and social prestige which allegedly characterize urban society.[15]

THE CITY IN THE WORKS OF MELVILLE, HAWTHORNE, AND POE   In a recent review of the intellectual history of the United States, Herman Melville, Nathaniel Hawthorne, and Edgar Allen Poe are described as having "bad dreams of the city."[16] In their novels and stories of city life before the Civil War, "the city scene was a backdrop for frightening experiences, personal defeat, icy intellectualism, heartless commercialism,

[14] For an extended discussion and examples of the views of Roman literary figures, see Susan F. Lowenstein, "Urban Images of Roman Authors," *Comparative Studies in History and Society,* 8 (October 1965), 110–23.

[15] Eugene Arden, "The Evil City in American Fiction," *New York History,* 35 (July 1954), 59–79.

[16] Morton White and Lucia White, *The Intellectual versus the City* (1962), ch. 4.

miserable poverty, crime and sin, smoke and noise, dusk and loneli-
ness."[17] The following dialogue, occurring on the arrival of rural newcomers to a large city, is illustrative:

The ladies are first of all struck by the hardness of the pavements. "Are they so
hard-hearted here?" asks Isabel. And Pierre replies: Ask yonder pavements,
Isabel. Milk dropped from the milkman's can in December, freezes not more
quickly on those stones, than does the snow-white innocence, if in poverty it
chance to fall in these streets." Isabel complains; "I like not the town" and
asks "Thinks't thou, Pierre, the time will ever come when all the earth shall be
paved?" And Pierre answers: "Thank God that never can be!"[18]

After the Civil War such major authors as Henry James, William Dean
Howells, Frank Norris, and Theodore Dreiser all expressed distaste for
the city. Although the literary realism of Howells and the naturalism of
Norris and Dreiser differed in style from the vivid mood interpretations
of urban evil by Hawthorne, Melville, and Poe, the former also evaluated
American urban life in ultimately negative ways. Thus, Howells, "one of
our most eminent novelists of urban life, ended his career living in New
York but looking wistfully at the American village and the German
city."[19]

Some of Norris' and Dreiser's titles, *The Octopus, The Titan, The Pit,*
are suggestive of the human alienation and degradation they saw as one
consequence of the large-scale organization of the city. It is important to
point out that they were writing during the period when American cities
had their highest growth rate, accompanied by manifold social problems
as well as a greater gap between rural and urban life styles.[20] Their
novels and poems had a basis in reality, but they transcended reality and
transformed it into a world view.

THE CITY IN THE TWENTIETH-CENTURY NOVEL Analysis of twentieth-
century novels about American life reveals that the city is a central
theme.[21] Many modern novelists perceive the city as the distinctively
contemporary way of life and try to distill its essential meaning by
"revealing how it [the city] creates and definitely marks the people living
in it."[22] This intention distinguishes "city novels" from those in which
the place is relatively unimportant or irrelevant to the unfolding of
character or plot.

There are at least three contemporary types of city novel. (1) The
"portrait" study reveals the city through a single character, usually a

[17] *Ibid.,* p. 37.
[18] Herman Melville, *Pierre,* cited in White, *op. cit.,* p. 39
[19] White and White, *op cit.,* p. 116.
[20] Arthur M. Schlesinger, *The Rise of the City, 1878–1898* (1933), p. 77.
[21] This discussion is based on Blanche Gelfant, *The American City Novel* (1954), ch. 1.
[22] *Ibid.,* p. 4.

country boy who is discovering the city as a way of life, as in many of the novels of Theodore Dreiser and Thomas Wolfe. The change in character of the young person as he submits to city life or rebels against it reflects the author's evaluation of the personal impact of urbanism. (2) The "synoptic" novel, in which the city itself is the hero, attempts to present the totality of urban life and describe varied social worlds, many social relationships, and the tempo of change. John Dos Passos' *Manhattan Transfer* is a well-known example of the synoptic novel. (3) The "ecological" city novel limits itself to a particular section of the city and focuses on the impact of urban life on a particular group. Thus, James Farrell's novels deal with Irish-Americans on the South Side of Chicago and Edith Wharton's with the upper class in fashionable areas of New York. In all instances the city novel is symbolic, for "in creating a unified impression [the author] uses particularized incidents as a means of arriving at underlying truths about city life. He offers an interpretation and judgment of the city—a way of seeing and evaluating it as an ordered pattern of experiences consistent with the inner principles of its being."[23]

The City in Religious Ideology

The theme that the country is better than the city—or vice versa—frequently has had religious overtones. Thus, the biblical statement that "the Lord God planted a garden eastward in Eden"[24] has sometimes been interpreted as indicating the divinely designated superiority of the country: "God the first Garden made, and the first city Cain"[25] or "God made the country, and man made the town."[26] Hughes has pointed out that ruralites and urbanites may each regard themselves as the pure followers of religion and notes that few, if any, of the great religions have avoided some conflict between these divergent rural-urban images of the "ideal man."[27] In the United States, for example, the major Protestant churches "are rooted in rural America, linked to rural institutions, made up of rural-bred people."[28] This rural base has fostered an antagonism to the typical large American city with its alien races, nationalities, and religions. Petersen contends that the antiurban animus among Protestant denominations is more deeply derived, however,

[23] *Ibid.,* p. 6.

[24] *Genesis,* 2:8.

[25] Abraham Cowley, "The Garden Essay V" (1664).

[26] William Cowper, "The Task," Book I (1785). The Cowley, Cowper, and similar quotations are traced back to the Genesis passage in John Bartlett, *Familiar Quotations,* 11th ed., p. 111.

[27] Everett Hughes, "The Cultural Aspect of Urban Research," in L. D. White, ed., *The State of the Social Sciences* (1956), p. 262.

[28] William Petersen, "The Protestant Ethos and the Anti-Urban Animus," in Robert Lee, ed., *The Church and the Exploding Metropolis* (1965), p. 63.

and is essentially opposition to the "modernism" and change that large cities represent.

In contrast, the ideology of the Islamic religion has been described as urban.[29] The nonurban Bedouin tribes were disparaged in early Islam; an important group among the early converts were the town merchants. Muslim religious practices require a fixed settlement, a Friday mosque, and forty adult males to conduct the Friday services, conditions which, for the seventh-century Arabia in which the religion developed, were urban. The concept of *hijrah*, uprooting oneself and moving to the city, derives from Muhamad's flight to the city of Medina, and in the early development of Islam was an important way of indicating one's submission to Islam's religious doctrines.

The Subjective Side of American Urbanization

In a stimulating reader, Strauss has commented on how little is known about "the subjective side of American urbanization."[30] In this section we will suggest a deep-seated antiurbanism in American society, as evidenced by the general use of rural reference points in American life, by the history of antiurbanism among American intellectuals, and by the widespread currency of certain beliefs about American suburbs.

Ruralism as the Standard

A recent historical survey of opinions about community life in the United States notes that agrarianism—the belief that "a rural life, particularly one rooted in agriculture, is also the most humanly valuable"[31]—has remained strong despite the marked decline of rural farm population. Thus, Wright attributes to the urbanite "a vicarious life sterilized by machinery,"[32] and similarly, Brownell states, "The decline of the human community as we see it today corresponds to the decline of rural culture and economy."[33]

The three major characteristics of agrarianism have been noted as (1) the belief that the farmer is independent and self-sufficient; (2) that the agricultural economy is the basic one—economic "agrarian fundamentalism" and, most important, (3) that the agricultural life is natural

[29] F. Benet, "The Ideology of Islamic Urbanization," *International Journal Of Comparative Sociology,* 4 (September 1963), 211–26.

[30] Anselm L. Strauss, "Urban Perspectives: New York City," in his *The American City: A Sourcebook of Urban Imagery* (1968), p. 18.

[31] David R. Weimer, ed., *City and Country in America* (1962), p. viii.

[32] Frank Lloyd Wright, "When Democracy Builds," in Weimer, *op cit.,* p. 314.

[33] Baker Brownell, "The Human Community," in Weimer, *op cit.,* p. 325.

and good.[34] Such a prorural point of view has an antiurban reverse image. Sometimes it is indirectly reflected, for example, in the belief that unemployment is an urban and not a rural problem.[35] More often, "spokesmen held that commercialism, frillish affections, uncalloused hands, or too great attention to comfort or leisure corrupted man and sapped his virtue and morality. Farmers followed a sanctified calling."[36]

There is considerable evidence that ruralism is the yardstick by which Americans judge what is desirable and undesirable. That rural attributes, whether real or alleged, should set the standard in an age when the great majority of Americans are urban dwellers is a further indication of the ideological nature of the measuring device. There are, for example, numerous "rural survivals" in American urban life.[37] Thus, Americans regard living in single-family homes as more prestigious than living in apartment houses, and home ownership is preferred to rental. The high status assigned to living-room fireplaces—even those that are "false fronts"—and the acceptance of casual farm clothing—including blue jeans—by urbanites are other instances exemplifying rural standards.[38]

Our stereotype of the personality and behavior of the "ideal man" also emphasizes rural characteristics. Tomars suggests that presidential candidates seek to identify themselves with farm origins or rural occupations to establish that they are "real" Americans.[39] In a more precise and comprehensive manner, William E. Henry concluded, after surveying concepts of the "normal" or "good" man, that even in professional psychological literature, such concepts are built around notions of simplicity and stability associated with a quieter life than that of the city.[40] In a provocative article entitled "Are Cities Un-American?"[41] William H. Whyte observed that although the United States is more urban than ever in a statistical sense, there appears to be a growing alienation between the city and what most people think of as the American way of life. A major cause of the physical and social decline of American cities, according to Whyte, is poor city planning which reduces urban amenities so that those who are able to do so leave the city for a more attractive environment. However, Whyte also suggests that

---

[34] Wayne Rohrer and Louis Douglas, *The Agrarian Transition in America: Dualism and Change* (1968), p. 28.

[35] *Ibid.,* p. 103.

[36] *Ibid.,* p. 29.

[37] Adolph Tomars, "Rural Survivals in American Urban Life," *Rural Sociology,* 8 (December 1943), 378–86.

[38] *Ibid.,* and Botkin, *op. cit.,* p. ix.

[39] Tomars, *op. cit.*

[40] Cited in Hughes, *op. cit.,* p. 266.

[41] *Fortune* (September 1957), pp. 123–33. Reprinted in The Editors of Fortune, *The Exploding Metropolis* (1958).

unimaginative city planning may be a symptom of a general lack of interest in and care about cities.

It is the contention of this book that most of the rebuilding under way and in prospect is being designed by people who don't like cities. They do not merely dislike the noise and the dirt and the congestion. They dislike the city's variety and concentration, its tension, its hustle and bustle. The new redevelopment projects will be physically in the city, but in spirit they deny it—and the values that since the beginning of civilization have always been at the heart of great cities.[42]

The History of American Viewpoints on the City

One way of determining whether there is pro- or antiurban bias in the United States is to examine the historic trend of opinion. Significantly, no studies have concluded that the weight of past and present opinion is prourban, although several studies have concluded that the underlying trend has been antiurban, or at least ambivalent.

However, the studies also show that there have been important changes in the nature of antiurbanism. Generally speaking, antiurban sentiment was at a minimum in the colonial and early national periods when cities were small and dominated by rural customs and interests. During the nineteenth century, as cities grew in size and power and became increasingly differentiated from the countryside, distrust of the city mounted.The many difficulties attending rapid urban-industrial growth fostered the association of city life with social problems, but cities also conferred many benefits and were clearly an increasingly important part of the American scene. For these and other reasons, although cities continued to be subjected to criticism, a new dialogue between ruralism and urbanism began, from which twentieth-century American attitudes toward the city are emerging. Only in the last generation have most urban residents been urban-born.[43] And while this fact alone does not diminish the ability to formulate myths about the nonurban milieu, it may alter their nature.

ANTIURBANISM AMONG INTELLECTUALS   The Whites' historical study of opinion among intellectuals in the United States concluded that

enthusiasm for the American city has not been typical or predominant in our intellectual history. Fear has been the more common reaction. For a variety of reasons our most celebrated thinkers have expressed different degrees of ambivalence and animosity toward the city. . . . We have no persistent or pervasive tradition of romantic attachment to the city in our literature or in our

---

[42] William H. Whyte, "Introduction" to *The Exploding Metropolis*, p. vii.
[43] Rohrer and Douglas, *op. cit.*, p. 5.

philosophy, nothing like the Greek attachment to the *polis* or the French writer's affection for Paris.[44]

Since the Whites' survey dealt with writers, philosophers, and members of the professions, it does not necessarily reflect popular opinion. Nevertheless, the prevalence of antiurbanism among the most literate and thoughtful segment of society, many of whom were themselves city residents, is noteworthy.

The Whites' catalogue of antiurban thought begins with Thomas Jefferson, who said in his *Notes on Virginia* (1784), "The mobs of great cities add just so much to the support of pure government as sores do to the strength of the human body."[45] Jefferson advocated that all Americans should cultivate the land, except those workers—carpenters, masons, blacksmiths—whose products or skills were needed by farmers themselves. He suggested that, to curb urban growth, raw materials be sent to England for manufacturing. It was only after the War of 1812 made it clear that domestic manufacturing centers were necessary for national survival that Jefferson abandoned his opposition to the creation and development of cities in the United States. Ultimately, then, he accepted cities as a necessary evil.

Other facets of antiurbanism were displayed somewhat later in the nineteenth century. For transcendentalist philosophers Ralph Waldo Emerson and Henry David Thoreau, antiurbanism was part of a metaphysical system in which Reason and Nature, supposedly rural characteristics, were exalted over Understanding and Artifice, the urban characteristics.[46] The transcendentalists flourished in the first half of the nineteenth century, but later philosophers representing such diverse systems as idealism and materialism also reacted negatively to the city.[47] Josiah Royce (1855–1916), an idealist, urged that large cities should be abandoned in favor of a "higher provincialism," for he believed that "freedom . . . dwells now in the small social group, and has its securest home in the provincial life. . . . Apart from the influence of the province . . . the individual loses his right, his self-consciousness, and his dignity."[48] George Santayana, the Spanish-born materialist philosopher who grew up in the United States and lived there until middle age, held that man's natural civilized state is agricultural and that men are reduced to proletarian status as "an unhappy effect of the monstrous growth of cities, made possible by the concentration of trade and the multiplication of industries."[49] For Santayana the ideal city was a rural center.

[44] White and White, *op. cit.*, pp. 1–2.

[45] Cited in *ibid.*, p. 14.

[46] *Ibid.*, ch. 3.

[47] *Ibid.*, ch. 11.

[48] Josiah Royce, *Race Questions, Provincialism, and Other American Problems*, cited in *ibid.*, p. 183.

[49] George Santayana, *My Host the World*, cited in *ibid.*, p. 187.

Although the reform movement in American cities in the late nineteenth and early twentieth centuries was founded on acceptance of the city, the direction of reform also expressed a rural nostalgia. The Whites credit William James, the pragmatist, as the inspiration of the movement to study the city carefully as a basis for effectively improving it. Robert Park, the influential urban sociologist at the University of Chicago, Jane Addams, the social worker who founded Hull House settlement in Chicago 's slums, and John Dewey, the philosopher, are regarded as carrying out the pragmatic doctrine of James.[50] Significantly,

they wanted to decompose the city into spiritual units that would emulate village life. This is evident in Park's idealization of the primary group, in Jane Addams' hope that the settlement house would help fill the urban void, and in Dewey's plea for a revival of localism in his *Public and Its Problems*. All of these figures in the Age of Reform stressed the importance of community and communication in re-creating a livable urban life, but they sought to inject into the city the kind of face-to-face community they knew in their own small villages and towns in the nineteenth century, before the radio, the automobile, the airplane, and television made less neighborly forms of communication possible.[51]

THE CHANGING FOCUS OF ANTIURBANISM   The Whites found that significant changes in points of view toward the city occurred over time, despite the persistence of the antiurban theme. During the eighteenth century, opinions of rural and urban life were relatively balanced and nonpartisan. Thus, Benjamin Franklin, the leading Philadelphian, and J. Hector St. John de Crèvecoeur, an agrarian writer, praised both the city and the country.[52] This is perhaps explained by the absence of marked contrasts between town and country in physical appearance or way of life during the period. Even by 1800, the largest city, Philadelphia, had reached only 70,000 in size. There were no city guidebooks and few "exposés" of urban life.[53]

The most virulent antiurbanism flourished in the nineteenth century, as the transformation wrought by industrialization, heavy immigration, and rapid growth became evident. The decades just before and just after the Civil War witnessed the heaviest rates of urban growth in American history. Between 1840 and 1850 the urban population grew by 92 percent, thereby almost doubling in ten years, while the following decades, 1850–1860 and 1860–1870, had urban increases of 75 percent and 59 percent, respectively.

[50] *Ibid.*, chs. 9 and 10.

[51] *Ibid.*, p. 216

[52] *Ibid.*, ch. 2.

[53] Bayrd Still, "The History of the City in American Life," *The American Review* (Bologna, Italy), 2 (May 1962), 20–37.

The intellectual grounds of antiurbanism shifted after the Civil War. Before the war, cities were attacked because they were *too civilized,* that is, they did not measure up to the prevailing notions of romanticism which valued unspoiled nature above all else. Unspoiled nature was a reality which was easily accessible to most Americans before the Civil War. "This does not mean that traditional romanticism can be expressed only in a period which is preponderantly nonurban, but it does suggest that it can flourish as the preponderant intellectual style only under such circumstances."[54] In 1800, only about one-twentieth of the American people lived in cities, but by 1870, a quarter of them lived in such places.

As a predominantly urban society emerged after the Civil War, intellectuals came to realize that any hopes for civilization would have to be realized in the city.

But they were not satisfied with mere possibilities. Urban intellectuals therefore turned upon the American city and criticized it for not living up to its possibilities and its promise; and as a result we find the growth of a city-based attack on the city itself, all in the name of the very things that a real romanticist would have scorned: science, sophistication, and order.

After the Civil War, cities were attacked because they were *not civilized enough.*

For the generation of post-Civil War intellectuals, for realists and pragmatists and naturalists, American city life was not deficient because it was artificial, rational, self-conscious, or effete. On the contrary, it was too wild, too vulgar, too ostentatious, too uncontrolled, too gaudy, too full of things that disturbed the sensibility of the fastidious. . . and too chaotic for scientifically ordered minds who sought a planned social order.[55]

Changes in rural-urban attitudes were also evident in the popular media. In the 1840's and 1850's, cities had become large enough, numerous enough, and different enough to be the subject of intensive interest and attention in the popular press. In 1847, *Hunt's Merchant Magazine* began an extensive series of articles on cities and towns. Phelps' *Hundred Cities and Large Towns of America* appeared in 1852, while popular fiction described the mysteries and miseries of town life.[56] By the middle 1860's, curiosity was replaced by concern over urban problems, but toward the end of the nineteenth century such concern was tempered by a realization that the urban trend was irreversible and, in many ways, beneficial. Thus, although the evils of the city continued to be portrayed luridly in popular fiction, another side of the urban coin was shown, too. Clyde Fitch's play, *The City,* appearing in 1909, contains the lines: "What the city does is bring out what's strongest in us.

[54] White and White, *op. cit.,* p. 226.
[55] *Ibid.,* pp. 229, 227.
[56] Still, *op. cit.,* pp. 24–25.

She gives the man his opportunity, and it's up to him what he makes of it."[57] In the latter part of the nineteenth century, the change in popular portrayal of the farmer from "the sturdy yeoman" to the "hayseed" is also noteworthy.[58] The increasing prosperity and political power of urbanites, coupled with economic problems on the farm as agricultural mechanization and specialization outmoded the traditional self-sufficient family farmstead, contributed to a sense of rural inferiority, frustration, and unrest which expressed itself in several political movements in the post-Civil War period.[59]

HORATIO ALGER AND THE CITY   An imaginative analysis of the materials of popular culture, 55 of the best-selling juvenile novels by Horatio Alger, illuminates another aspect of antiurbanism during the latter part of the nineteenth century. The late R. Richard Wohl, a specialist in urban history, indicated that the Horatio Alger novels were an instance of the "country boy" myth in American society.

. . . The country boy as a symbol has evolved into an intricate tradition, a truly "urban pastoral". . . .The beneficial attributes which flow from rural boyhood are supposed to design a character which lasts a lifetime. . . . At bottom, as everywhere within the limits of this span of folklore, an invidious distinction between the "country" and "city" is stressed. The tacit contrast is between the presumably artificial and superficial (hence morally dangerous) childhood in the city, and the deep-seated virtues and sturdy manliness infused in the countryside.[60]

Wohl's analysis shows that the Horatio Alger novels linked the "country boy" with the American dream of success and upward social mobility. Alger's first best-selling novel was published in 1868, and succeeding books (he published well over a hundred in all) on the theme of the country boy's rise from "rags to riches" in the city continued to appear until Alger's death in 1899. This period coincided with extensive urban growth in the United States, partly through a vast rural-to-urban migration. There was no lack of real problems and real fears in American cities at this time. In this setting Alger's novels were immediately and hugely successful, reaffirming as they did traditional American values with the country boy coming to the city and "bound to rise." But Alger's novels went further, for they merged the country boy with the boy who knew

[57] Cited in *ibid.*, p. 25.

[58] Schlesinger, *Paths to the Present*, p. 229.

[59] *Ibid.* See also the brilliant study by Henry Nash Smith, *Virgin Land: The American West as Symbol and Myth* (1950), which examines the shattering of the image of the American West as a Garden of Paradise.

[60] R. Richard Wohl, edited by Moses Rischin, "The 'Country Boy' Myth and Its Place in American Urban Culture: The Nineteenth Century Contribution," *Perspectives in American History*, 3 (1969), 86.

how to function effectively in the city. Also, his heroes, though originating in the country, were committed to the city.

In part, Alger's novels succeeded because they were well written and did not preach to his young readers, but more importantly, he used authentic, realistically detailed urban backgrounds. Early in his writing career Alger was asked to write suitable stories for the residents of the Newsboys' Lodging House in New York City, and for the rest of his life "the Lodging House was a second home to him. He befriended the boys, lived and played with them, and used them as a perfectly representative audience on which to test his stories."[61] By describing the mechanics of living in the city, including the pitfalls to be avoided, Alger was both entertaining and instructive. His version of the country boy provided "literary guidance and therapy for youngsters by the millions not quite prepared to bridge the gap between rural traditions and urban realities."[62]

THE MYTH OF SUBURBIA   Nothing better illustrates the emotional and ideological component in our view of community life than the springing up of beliefs about new community forms as these forms emerge. The major new community form of midtwentieth-century America is the suburb, and a structured set of beliefs has been devised to form "the myth of suburbia," which includes as its components (1) a landscape of new one- and two-family homes, shopping centers, and schools; (2) a young (25 to 35 years of age), transient, upwardly mobile population made up of "organization men" and their families; (3) a very active social life, both in terms of formal, organized groups and in terms of informal neighboring and kaffeeklatsching; (4) a population homogeneous in age, income, and outlook, which, when coupled with the active local social life, makes suburbanites conformists; (5) and a "return to religion," a swing to Republicanism, and the raising of traditionless children by young mothers whose own mothers are far distant geographically and whose husbands spend long hours commuting to the city.[63]

This description of the suburbs is more fiction than fact, for there is no single type of suburb.[64] There are old "main line" suburbs and equally old "street-car" suburbs; "bedroom" suburbs and "industrial" suburbs; and upper class suburbs, blue collar suburbs, and suburban slums. Suburbs also vary greatly as to which racial, religious, ethnic, age, or social-class group predominates, and many suburbs include a very heterogeneous population. Suburban life styles vary from family-centered to hedonistic, and there is no evidence that important intellec-

[61] *Ibid.,* p. 123.
[62] *Ibid.,* p. 81.
[63] Bennett M. Berger, "The Myth of Suburbia," in his *Looking for America* (1971).
[64] See Chapter 11 of this text for an amplification of this point.

tual or social effects result specifically from suburban residence itself.[65]

Despite the numerous studies indicating how different the suburbs actually are from the fiction of middle class homogeneity and stultifying conformity, the myth of suburbia persists and has only recently shown some signs of alteration. One reason for this persistence is that it allows for a critique of industrialization, standardization, and mass culture. In projecting an image of "cookie-cutter" suburbs and "cookie-cutter" lives of frantic togetherness, critics of the suburbs are attacking the "chrome idols" of materialism. Needless to say, suburbanites themselves may have a very different evaluation of their lives and goals, for the critics are often upper middle class intellectuals for whom the "city" is the place where civilization resides.

In the broadest sense it appears that the suburban myth of harmony, greenery, and cultural kitsch is the contemporary staging ground for the long-standing American preference for rural life. In the modern age, when, through the sheer lack of farm experience on the part of the vast majority of the population, agrarianism has lost its force as a normative standard, the familiar dialogue between ruralism and urbanism may peter out. In place of the nineteenth-century discussions of whether the city or the country is more "civilized," we may have discussions of whether urban or suburban life is more "cultured." In place of the city-versus-the-country debate we may have the city-versus-the-suburb argument. This does not necessarily mean that suburbs are replacing the country in the sense of being rural; it does mean that the suburbs, like all community forms, have the power to arouse emotions and partisanship. As new community forms arise, they become invested with symbolic meaning and enter the arena of public opinion.

After studying the political structure of suburbs, Robert Wood, a political scientist, concluded that it represented a renaissance of the small-town and village ideal.[66] Suburban governments, according to Wood, are typically small, ineffective, and expensive, unsuitable for coping with metropolitan-area problems. Yet suburbanites stubbornly resist efforts at consolidation into larger governmental jurisdictions, and small-scale suburban governments are, in fact, proliferating. Wood points out that the attachment to suburban government is ideological, stemming from a belief that the small community produces the best life and the best government.

---

[65] See Herbert J. Gans, "Urbanism and Suburbanism as Ways of Life: A Re-Evaluation of Definitions," in Arnold Rose, ed., *Human Behavior and Social Processes* (1962), pp. 625–48; Joseph Zelan, "Does Suburbia Make a Difference: An Exercise in Secondary Analysis," in Sylvia F. Fava, ed., *Urbanism in World Perspective: A Reader* (1968), pp. 401–8; Bennett M. Berger, *Working Class Suburb* (1960); and Herbert Gans, *The Levit-towners* (1967).

[66] Robert C. Wood, *Suburbia—Its People and Their Politics* (1958), ch. 1.

Suburbia, defined as an ideology, a faith in communities of limited size and a belief in the conditions of intimacy, is quite real. The dominance of the old values explains more about the people and politics of the suburbs than any other interpretation. Fundamentally, it explains the nature of the American metropolis. . . . If these values were not dominant it would be quite possible to conceive of a single gigantic metropolitan region under one government and socially conscious of itself as one community. The new social ethic, the rise of the large organization, would lead us to expect this development as a natural one. The automobile, the subway, the telephone, the power line certainly make it technically possible; they even push us in this direction.

But the American metropolis is not constructed in such a way; it sets its face directly against modernity. Those who wish to rebuild the American city, who protest the shapeless urban sprawl, who find some value in the organizational skills of modern society must recognize the potency of the ideology. Until these beliefs have been accommodated reform will not come in the metropolitan areas nor will men buckle down to the task of directing, in a manner consonant with freedom, the great political and social organizations on which the nation's strength depends.[67]

It has become increasingly difficult to maintain the myth of suburbia as evidence mounts, from the 1970 census and other sources, of the diversity of suburbs and the increasing resemblance, in terms of both structure and problems, of older suburbs to cities. Crime and delinquency rates have been rising rapidly in many suburbs, and they, too, are faced with the problems of drugs, welfare, pollution, traffic congestion, and unbalanced budgets. Office decentralization has accelerated in many large metropolitan areas, and some shopping centers have become miniature downtowns in the range and variety of goods and services they offer, as well as locales for vandalism and burglary and congregating places for "undesirables." "Black suburbs" have become increasingly important, although this trend does not appear to be accompanied by racial or economic integration, despite the mounting attack on suburban exclusionary zoning. Both the professional literature and the mass media have begun to reflect this new view of suburbia.[68]

While the focus of community ideology was on the suburbs during the period of public awareness of metropolitan emergence, now, in the era of the mature metropolis, that focus has shifted to the New Towns, the large planned communities of which Reston, Virginia, and Columbia, Maryland, are notable examples. New Towns represent a new policy for

---

[67] *Ibid.,* pp. 18–19.

[68] John B. Orr and F. Patrick Michelson, *The Radical Suburb* (1970); Scott Donaldson, *The Suburban Myth* (1969); "The Suburbs: Frontier of the 70's," special issue of *City,* 5 (January–February 1971); "Suburbia: A Myth Challenged," cover story in *Time* (March 15, 1971); "The Outer City: U. S. in Suburban Turmoil," a series of five articles in *The New York Times* (May 30–June 3, 1971); Charles M. Haar, ed., *The End of Innocense: A Suburban Reader* (1972); and *Report of the President's Task Force on Suburban Problems* (1968).

the same set of needs expressed earlier in the image of suburbia. There is the same antiurbanism, the fear and distrust of the city, expressed now in the desire to control and manage urban growth and density by carefully precast new communities. As with suburbs, in New Towns there is also the same concern with diversity, the containment of conflict, and the maintenance of outward harmony and equality.[69]

Summary

We have introduced in this chapter one aspect of the qualitative study of the city, namely, the city as the focus of values, attitudes, and ideology. Belief systems about the city are expressed in such diverse forms as social philosophy, religion, music, art, and literature, and range in level of sophistication from the almost cosmic formulations of Lewis Mumford to the best-selling Horatio Alger novels and popular country music. Apart from the intrinsic fascination they hold, these symbolic representations of the city are real insofar as they have consequences for urban policy and behavior. The fact that statistical measures can seldom be applied to them does not mean that subjective reactions to urban life are closed to understanding.

Throughout its history the United States has been characterized by an antiurban bias, as the Whites' survey of American political, literary, and philosophical thought indicates. Ruralism is the standard while the city is associated with disorganization, decay, problems, and crises. Despite the fact that the majority of Americans are city dwellers, the antiurban bias has persisted, altering its focus to include suburbia as part of the "good life." As additional community forms, such as New Towns, emerge, they too become incorporated into the ideological dialogue of "the city versus the country."

Bibliography

BOOKS

Cohen, Erik, *The City in Zionist Ideology.* Jerusalem, Israel: Institute of Urban and Regional Studies, The Hebrew University of Jerusalem, 1970.

Coser, Lewis, *Sociology Through Literature.* Englewood Cliffs, N.J.: Prentice-Hall, 1963.

Curtin, Philip D., ed., *Africa and the West: Intellectual Responses to European Culture.* Madison: University of Wisconsin Press, 1972.

Donaldson, Scott, *The Suburban Myth.* New York: Columbia University Press, 1969.

[69] See Sylvia F. Fava, "The Pop Sociology of Suburbs and New Towns," *American Studies,* 14 (Spring 1973) 121–33.

Downs, Roger, and David Stea, eds., *Image and Environment: Cognitive Mapping and Spatial Behavior.* Chicago: Aldine, 1973.

Gould, Peter and Rodney White, *Mental Maps: Where Would You Really Like to Live.* Baltimore, Md.: Penguin, 1973.

Lynch, Kevin, *The Image of the City.* Cambridge: MIT Press, 1960.

———, *What Time Is This Place?* Cambridge: MIT Press, 1972.

Marx, Leo, *The Machine in the Garden: Technology and the Pastoral Ideal in America.* New York: Oxford University Press, 1964.

Mumford. Lewis, *The Culture of Cities.* New York: Harcourt, Brace, 1938.

Parades, A., and E. J. Stekert, eds., *The Urban Experience and Folk Tradition.* Austin: University of Texas, 1971.

Schmitt, Peter J., *Back to Nature: The Arcadian Myth in Urban America.* New York: Oxford University Press, 1969.

Strauss, Anselm, ed., *The American City: A Sourcebook of Urban Imagery.* Chicago: Aldine, 1968.

———, *Images of the American City.* New York: The Free Press, 1961.

Trachtenberg, Alan, Peter Neill, and Peter C. Bunnell, eds., *The City: American Experience.* New York: Oxford University Press, 1971.

Venturi, Robert, Denise Scott Brown, and Steven Izenour, *Learning from Las Vegas,* Cambridge: MIT Press, 1973.

White, Morton, and Lucia White, *The Intellectual Versus the City,* Cambridge: Harvard University Press and MIT Press, 1962.

ARTICLES

Adrian, Charles A., "A Comparative Typology of Urban Government Images," pp. 247–62 in Brian Berry, ed., *City Classification Handbook: Methods and Application.* New York: Wiley-Interscience, 1972.

Arden, Eugene, "The Evil City in American Fiction," *New York History,* 35 (July 1954), 59–79.

Benet, F., "The Ideology of Islamic Urbanization," *International Journal of Comparative Sociology,* 4 (September 1963), 211–26.

Berger, Bennett, "The Myth of Suburbia," in his *Looking for America.* Englewood Cliffs, N.J.: Prentice-Hall, 1971.

Charosh, Paul, "The Home Song," in Sylvia F. Fava, ed., *Urbanism in World Perspective: A Reader,* pp. 449–56. New York: Thomas Y. Crowell, 1968.

Fava, Sylvia F., "The Pop Sociology of Suburbs and New Towns," *American Studies,* 14 (Spring 1973), 121–33.

Gulick, J., "Images of an Arab City," *Journal of the American Institute of Planners,* 29 (August 1963), 179–97.

Foley, Donald, "British Town Planning: One Ideology or Three?" *British Journal of Sociology,* 11 (1960), 211–31.

Howe, Irving, "The City in Literature," *Commentary,* 51 (May 1971), 61–68.

Koenigsberg, Marvin D., "Urban Development: An Introduction to the Theories of Lewis Mumford," in Sylvia F. Fava, ed., *Urbanism in World Perspective: A Reader,* pp. 564–80. New York: Thomas Y. Crowell, 1968.

Love, Ruth Leeds, "The Fountains of Urban Life," *Urban Life and Culture,* 2 (July 1973), 161–208.

Maurer, Robert, and James Baxter, "Images of the Neighborhood and City among Black, Anglo and Mexican-American Children," *Environment and Behavior,* 4 (December 1972), 351–88.

Mizruchi, E. H., "Romanticism, Urbanism, and Small Town in Mass Society," in Paul Meadows and E. H. Mizruchi, eds., *Urbanism, Urbanization, and Change,* pp. 243–52. Reading, Mass.: Addison-Wesley, 1969.

Whyte, William H., "Are Cities Un-American?" *Fortune,* 56 (September 1957), 123–33.

Wohl, R. Richard (edited by Moses Rischin), "The 'Country Boy' Myth and Its Place in American Urban Culture: The Nineteenth Century Contribution," *Perspectives in American History,* 3 (1969), 77–159.

Petersen, William, "The Ideological Origins of Britain's New Towns," *Journal of the American Institute of Planners,* 34 (May 1968), 160–69.

Thomas, John L., "Utopia for an Urban Age: Henry George, Henry Demarest Lloyd, Edward Bellamy," *Perspectives in American History,* 6 (1972), 102–34.

SOCIAL ASPECTS OF URBAN HOUSING AND REDEVELOPMENT

22 ● Housing

Although its postcards may picture historical monuments, office buildings, and entertainment, to its residents the city is primarily its housing and residential neighborhoods. The adequacy or inadequacy of a city's housing goes far in determining the quality of life for people who live there. The city's social structure, moreover, is affected in important ways by the spatial distribution, interrelations, and prestige of its residential neighborhoods. In choosing a residence—or in having little choice of where to live—a household chooses not only the comfort or discomfort its home offers, but status or lack of status in the eyes of others.

Urban housing must be approached from a number of directions. First we will look at three in-depth studies of particular communities to see how social scientists attempt to discover relationships between the housing environment and social life. Then we look at a variety of specific relationships between housing and family life. The third approach we will consider is housing as an economic good, also a sociological approach because of what it reveals about values and systems of allocation. How housing is produced and distributed in the United States will be described from this point of view. Finally, to give some perspective to the housing problems of the United States, we will briefly review housing conditions and policies in some other parts of the world.

The assistance of Maynard Robison in preparing material for the housing chapter and for the following chapter on planning is gratefully acknowledged.

Urban Neighborhoods and
Their Housing

A Mobile Home Community

Idle Haven[1], a mobile home park with two hundred households, is located in the San Francisco Bay Area. The mobile homes, up to 24 feet by 60 feet in size, as large as small three-bedroom houses, are relatively inexpensive to purchase. Most cost between $6000 and $10,000 new, including all furnishings, even framed reproductions on the walls.[2] Rents for the plots on which they are placed are about $100 per month, with utilities.

In contrast to the young families who predominate among mobile home residents nationwide, most Idle Haven residents are retired or, if still working, in late middle age. The median income of the retired falls in the $2000 to $4000 range, with Social Security the largest single source. The median household income of those who are employed falls in the $10,000 to $14,000 range;[3] in many cases both husband and wife work. Most Idle Haven residents are working class: 33.9 percent of the men are craftsmen or foremen, 9.8 percent operatives, and most of the retired men held similar manual occupations.[4]

Johnson argues that older working class people fulfill a broad range of their needs in Idle Haven. The community offers those who wish to take part a variety of social opportunities—a swimming pool used more by residents' grandchildren than by residents themselves; card parties; Sunday breakfasts; crafts. Neighbors are reliable sources of aid in times of need; for example, some healthier residents exchange housekeeping services for token payments.

At the same time, many people moved to Idle Haven to avoid social problems or perceived threats to their status. The severe shortage of park spaces allows park managers to exclude blacks and other minority-group families, despite their obvious need for this sort of housing bargain. Moreover, the park has a rigid set of rules regarding upkeep of the small lots and the mobile homes themselves, even requiring that homes more than five years old that are sold be moved out of the park.[5] In effect, these rules allow the park manager to evict any resident she sees as undesirable. A six-foot-high fence surrounding its seventeen acres symbolizes the community's insulation.

---

[1] Sheila K. Johnson, *Idle Haven: Community Building Among the Working-Class Retired* (1971). "Idle Haven" is a fictional name. For further discussion of mobile homes, see pp. 621–22 below.

[2] *Ibid.*, p. 37. These prices pertained in the 1960's.

[3] *Ibid.*, p. 33.

[4] *Ibid.*, p. 27.

[5] *Ibid.*, p. 170.

Thus, Idle Haven provides security—less financial than social—for its residents, many of whom had felt threatened by changes in their former neighborhoods, particularly by the presence of blacks. But that security has other costs. Bound by their desire for protection to the manager's ability to exclude people from the park, and frequently having invested most of their savings in a mobile home, Idle Haven's residents are subject to financial exploitation particularly when selling their mobile homes, and, to harassment or isolation, if they fail to fit into the somewhat stifling social system.

Life in Pruitt-Igoe

Residents of Pruitt-Igoe,[6] a St. Louis Public Housing project, are unable to obtain either the security or the respectability they desire. Pruitt-Igoe's thirty-three eleven-story buildings, with almost 2800 apartments, were first occupied in 1954. By 1959 the project had become a scandal in St. Louis because of vacancies, severe problems of crime and vandalism, and its extraordinarily uninviting, institutional appearance. By 1970, Pruitt-Igoe had deteriorated so badly that a drastic plan to renovate the project, including partial demolition, was begun. In June 1973, the St. Louis Housing Authority voted to close down the project entirely and relocate all tenants, subject to approval from the Department of Housing and Urban Development.

When Lee Rainwater studied Pruitt-Igoe, 9952 people lived there; 3067 adults and 6,895 minors. Of the children, 70 percent were under twelve, and the average number of children in households with any children at all was 4.28. Women headed 62 percent of the families, and two and a half times as many adult women as adult men lived in the project. Only 45 percent of the families were entirely self-supporting, and median income from all sources was $498 per capita. Almost 100 percent of the project's residents were black.[7] To a degree that is perhaps unique, Pruitt-Igoe housed families who had no other place to live in. Many of its original tenants came from urban renewal areas cleared by the city. Even of these, who presumably had lived in St. Louis's worst housing, there was a proportionately very high number of large families and families without adult males.

Eighty percent of the residents interviewed liked their apartments more than those they had lived in before,[8] and those apartments were

---

[6] Lee Rainwater, *Behind Ghetto Walls, Black Family Life in a Federal Slum* (1970). Rainwater and his colleagues carried out an intensive study of Pruitt-Igoe and the lives of its residents in 1963–65, focusing on problems of poverty rather than on housing problems as such.

[7] Data from *Ibid.*, p. 13.

[8] *Ibid.*, p. 14.

livable by any standard. Pruitt-Igoe's vacancy rate[9]—20 to 25 percent—reflected the severe insecurity that the residents felt because of physical danger and danger to their self-respect. Over half the residents interviewed mentioned problems like these:

> The elevators are dangerous . . . . Bottles and other dangerous things are thrown out of windows and hurt people . . . Little children hear bad language all the time so they don't realize how bad it is . . . The laundry areas aren't safe; clothes get stolen and people get attacked . . . The children run wild and cause all kinds of damage . . . . A woman isn't safe in the halls, stairways, or elevators.[10]

Rainwater argues that these problems do not result from the physical design of the project, although its lack of facilities, the fact that elevators stop only at every third floor, and other design factors have some effect. Rather, racial discrimination and lack of economic opportunities make it impossible for the project's residents to live lives considered normal for Americans:

> Lower-class people are constrained to live among others who are equally marginal in economic terms, and in the community that grows up in this situation, a premium is placed on the exploitation and manipulation of peers.[11]

In a way, the disastrous history of Pruitt-Igoe, hardly typical of public housing as a whole, is the reverse of the exclusivity of other residential neighborhoods. Pruitt-Igoe became a refuge for families excluded from the rest of St. Louis. Most importantly, its problems reflect the failure of American society. The scandal of Pruitt-Igoe points dramatically to the unfinished business of America to provide jobs and opportunities for people to break out of the cycle of poverty and discrimination.

An Upper-Middle Class Suburb

Crestwood Heights, studied by Seeley, Sim, and Loosley in the 1950's, is an upper middle class suburb of Toronto.[12] Its massive single-family houses reflect both the values of its residents and their ability to buy the environment they want. To Seeley, Sim, and Loosley, Crestwood Heights residents are strongly oriented toward achievement. For the men, this means success in their jobs as business executives or professionals; for the women, the goal is success in systematically cultivating their personalities and taste and the family's status. Thought, energy, and

---

[9] *Ibid.*, p. 11. Of the two-bedroom apartments, 35 to 40 percent were vacant, reflecting the greater ease with which small families find privately-owned housing.

[10] *Ibid.*, pp. 10–11.

[11] *Ibid.*, p. 371.

[12] John R. Seeley, R. Alexander Sim, and Elizabeth W. Loosley, *Crestwood Heights* (1956).

money are expended so that the children, too, will follow these norms of achievement.

Property provides an important source of identity for Crestwood Heights residents:

The new item is accepted into the family circle and incorporated into its life pattern. But it is not fully integrated until display has brought about its validation as property. The rug, or the painting, or the drapes are "shelter," not at the margin between bodily exposure and survival, but on the dividing line between discomfort and psychological well-being.[13]

The residence is not expected to be permanent; as the family moves up the social ladder with the man's promotions, it also moves to higher status houses. In the meantime, the house serves to separate the family from outsiders, except when encounters can be carefully arranged. Then it serves as a stage on which the family can confirm its success and advance itself socially. The living room and dining room are reserved for entertaining and impressing visitors, and day-to-day family life centers

Partial demolition of the Pruitt-Igoe housing project began in 1972, culminating its 18-year history as an officially-described social, physical, and financial "disaster." (St. Louis Post-Dispatch)

[13] *Ibid.*, p. 47.

603

on the den or rumpus room, now more frequently called the family room. Living and dining room furniture are chosen with great care. The house even provides privacy for individual family members, thus playing an important part in socializing the child:

> The Crestwood child is never integrated into a kinship group to anything like the degree that children in other environments [slums, lower-middle-class homes, and so forth] are identified with their kinship groups. The Crestwood child sleeps alone; usually in his own room . . . . The personality norm held up in gradually increased detail before the Crestwood child is that of the individuated person who can and wants to separate himself from his kinship group and establish a new family unit.[14]

Crestwood Heights, Pruitt-Igoe, and Idle Haven reflect a part of the immense variety of interactions between housing and economic forces, social class and status, varying life styles and family life. The frameworks that have been developed for studying those relationships provide the beginnings of an understanding of housing patterns.

Housing and Family Life

Interactions between housing types and family life are complex and pervasive. Three sorts of relationships have been of particular interest.[15] First, necessity and suitability of particular housing types for particular life styles have been widely explored; social scientists came to see this question as important after World War II, when suburban areas began to grow rapidly. Second, the observation that families have different housing needs at different times has stimulated studies of relationships among family life cycles, housing, and residential mobility. Third, social scientists, public health officials, and urban reformers have long been concerned with the effects of inadequate housing on family life.

Housing Types and Life Styles

A number of social scientists have found patterns in which densely settled, perhaps deteriorated, areas facilitate lives of groups who place a high value on interaction beyond the nuclear family.[16] Prior to its demolition for urban renewal, Boston's West End was a densely occupied neighborhood of somewhat run-down houses, inhabited mainly by work-

---

[14] *Ibid.*, pp. 61–2.

[15] For very useful summaries and interpretations of the available evidence on patterns of interaction between housing and family life, see William Michelson, *Man and His Urban Environment, A Sociological Analysis* (1970).

[16] See, for example, Herbert Gans, *The Urban Villagers* (1962); Peter Willmott and Michael Young, *Family and Kinship in East London* (1957), discussed in chapter 23; and Peter Marris, *Family and Social Change in an African City* (1962).

ing class, Italian-American families. In *The Urban Villagers,* Gans reports his study of the relationship between their values and their environment. The urban villagers prized loyalty to relatives of one's own generation and expressiveness within the peer group, rather than upward mobility and achievement in the wider society. "Total immersion in sociability" of an informal kind was the norm. Within the home,

> The kitchen was normally the main arena of social activity. The living room was used mainly to house the television set and, when visitors came, to allow the men to separate themselves from the women and carry on their own conversation.[17]

The West End's physical environment facilitated the pattern of informal sociability. Its density—more than 150 dwelling units per net residential acre, compared to eight or fewer in most suburban areas—made frequent casual meetings with acquaintances unavoidable, a pattern reinforced by intermixture of stores and housing. The housing's design also facilitated interaction; from their windows, residents could observe goings-on in the street and talk with passers-by. The West Enders valued these characteristics of their neighborhood: "They had little use for the newer suburbs. They described these as too quiet for their tastes—that is, without street life—and occupied by people concerned only with trying to appear better than they are . . . ."[18]

In contrast, suburban areas seem to facilitate life styles focused on the nuclear family. Suburban life styles, as they have frequently been characterized, involve relative equality and intensive interaction between husband and wife; family-oriented activities, such as care for the house and grounds, cookouts, and active physical recreation; and orientation of women toward children and home and away from work possibilities.[19] Some observers have also stressed more intensive neighboring in suburban than city areas. Some of these aspects of a suburban life style, clearly, are connected to density and housing types.

This is not to argue that those physical characteristics *cause* a suburban life style. In his study of Levittown, New Jersey, Gans found most of the residents desired a way of life centered on the nuclear family and home *before* they moved to the new development. In some cases, moreover, they wanted to get away from intensive interaction with relatives outside the nuclear family, and the move to Levittown enabled them to do so. Interestingly, Gans found two groups who were dissatisfied with the move: upper middle class people who wanted the schools to provide a better education than they did; and working class people,

[17] Gans, *op. cit.,* p. 20.

[18] *Ibid.,* p. 22.

[19] In the early years of suburban growth after World War II, many social critics attributed a wide variety of changes in American life styles to the influence of suburban living. For a discussion of the variety of suburban life styles see Chapter 11.

including some who missed intensive interaction with the extended family. The conclusion that certain life styles are lived more easily in given physical environments thus seems warranted.

Stages in the Family Life Cycle, Residential Mobility, and Housing Types

The congruence between housing types and life styles is closely related to differing housing needs at various stages of the family's life cycle. In turn, changes from one stage of the life cycle to another account for a great deal of residential mobility within metropolitan areas.

Some evidence points to the idea that single-family homes are the most suitable environment for raising children, independent of life style. Such houses, with their own yards, allow mothers to supervise children's play from kitchen windows, in contrast to the situation in high-rise buildings, where children must be kept indoors, accompanied to play, or left unsupervised. Life in apartments, moreover, may restrict play to quiet activities. One British study concluded:

> While it is true that people who live in flats suffer more from noise disturbance than people who live in houses, this is not the main complaint. More important is the restriction people feel on making noise themselves. This affects their whole pattern of leisure and makes for more sedentary hobbies such as television viewing.[20]

Ease of raising children, in fact, is very frequently given as a major reason for moving to suburban areas. In a survey of a New York suburb, reported by Harold L. Wattel, 48 percent of the residents interviewed indicated they had sought "a good place to raise children."[21]

Some evidence supports the idea that dense apartment environments are most suitable for young adults and childless older adults. Such households do not need space for children's play and may place a higher value on convenience than do families with children. In a study of residents of newly constructed high-rise apartments and rehabilitated town houses, Janet Abu-Lughod found older couples were over-represented. However, few had changed their housing types in moving; only 27 percent had lived in either one- or two-family houses.[22] As apartments become available in suburban areas and car ownership becomes nearly universal, apartment developments in central cities may

[20] Margaret Willis, "Living in High Flats," London County Council, Architects Department (1955), quoted by Michelson, *op. cit.*, p. 99.

[21] Harold L. Wattel, "Levittown: A Suburban Community," in William Dobriner, ed., *The Suburban Community* (1958), p. 290.

[22] Janet Abu-Lughod, "A Survey of Center City Residents," in Nelson Foote et al., *Housing Choices and Constraints* (1960), pp. 387–447.

lose their attractiveness to both young and older childless adults.

Housing needs of the elderly have been studied more extensively, and several countries have attempted to develop housing particularly suited to their needs. Historically, the proportion of the elderly living in their own households, away from children or other relatives, has increased. By 1960, 83 percent of American men and 70 percent of American women 65 or older lived in their own households.[23] A survey reported by Beyer, moreover, indicated over 80 percent of the elderly desire independent housing arrangements, although over half want to be near relatives.[24] The desire for independence, the increased possibility of infirmity and illness, and the need to remain active raise the question of exactly what sort of housing is most suitable for the elderly. It would appear that no single housing-type provides the answer. Those who are healthy and active need easily cared-for, inexpensive, and conveniently located dwellings. The somewhat infirm need the choice, at least, of their own dwellings in situations where meals and minor housekeeping aid can be provided. In both cases, the elderly need accommodations arranged to facilitate social life. Recognition of this need has resulted in development of age-segregated housing. Whether age-segregated housing or specially-designed housing integrated in broader contexts better meets the needs of the elderly, however, remains an open question.

Residential mobility—the movement of households from one housing unit to another—is one means by which families adjust their housing to changing needs, as well as the basic mechanism relating housing submarkets to one another. One of the most ambitious studies of residential mobility, Rossi's *Why Families Move*,[25] provides considerable insight into the relationship between residential mobility and the family life cycle. Although the study is now over twenty years old, there is little reason to believe the basic relationships Rossi found have changed.

Annually, one of every five American households moves, a proportion that has remained relatively constant over the years. Some of these moves, of course, can be explained by the founding and dissolution of households; another part are moves to other cities as the household's head changes jobs; and a third group results from eviction or physical destruction of the dwelling. In Rossi's study, these three reasons accounted for 39 percent of all moves,[26] leaving a majority of moves, from one dwelling to another within the metropolitan areas, unexplained.

Rossi studied these unexplained moves through extensive surveys in four Philadelphia neighborhoods. He found that tenure, the legal status under which a housing unit is occupied, is an important determinant of

[23] Glenn H. Beyer, *Housing and Society* (1965), p. 417.

[24] *Ibid.*, p. 428.

[25] Peter Rossi, *Why Families Move* (1953).

[26] *Ibid.*, p. 134.

mobility. As one might expect, renters are considerably more mobile than owners, and renters who wish to own their own houses are very mobile. Owners, of course, have less reason to move since they can modify their housing to make it more suitable or spacious. Surprisingly, location plays a minor role in residential mobility; Rossi found moves intended to decrease commuting distances infrequent; nor was nearness to friends or relatives an important determinant of mobility.

Complaints about space inside the dwelling were by far the most important reasons for moving. Large, young families moved most frequently because they had the most difficulty meeting their housing needs. During the first ten years of its existence, the family typically undergoes growth through the birth of children. At the same time, its income is usually more limited than it will be later. Thus, much residential mobility results from the difficulty larger, younger families have meeting their need for space.

Effects of Substandard Housing

It is widely believed that deteriorated housing and neighborhoods create ill health, personality problems, juvenile delinquency, and other social ills. An impressive volume of evidence indicates a relationship between substandard housing and various health and and social problems. In a few cases poor housing causes problems directly: peeling lead-based paint, eaten by children, causes lead poisoning; tuberculosis is likely to occur unusually frequently in crowded dwellings with poor ventilation and limited sunlight. In most cases of association between "pathologies" and poor housing, however, what the cause is has not been established. Causes of particular problems may be quite complex. For example, in a study of the relationship between crowding in the dwelling and children's school performance, Michelson found that whether a child shared the room in which he did his homework was insignificant:

Much more important in this context than physical crowding and lack of personal privacy is the use that people make of the space they have. Significantly higher scores were found among children whose homework was done in rooms devoted *at that time* to only quiet pursuits.[27]

One of the most methodologically sophisticated studies of relationships between poor housing and health and social problems was carried out in Baltimore between 1955 and 1958.[28] Comparisons were made between a test sample of 300 families who had moved to a Public Housing project and a control sample of 300 families residing in a deteriorated section of the city. Both groups consisted of low-income

[27] Michelson, *op. cit.*, p.158.
[28] Daniel M. Wilner, et al., *The Housing Environment and Family Life* (1962).

black families, and the families were matched by size of dwelling unit, family size, members' ages, and so forth. For many problems, the Baltimore study found no significant difference in incidence between the rehoused families and those who remained in deteriorated housing. However, more neighboring and mutual assistance between neighbors and somewhat better social relations within families were found among the rehoused families, who also reported fewer quarrels and more sharing of household tasks and leisure activities. Most significant were lower morbidity rates—rates of illness—in the test than in the control group, particularly among children. In school promotions, the housing project children made a better showing than the control group, although this difference may have resulted from different policies of the various schools attended.

The Baltimore study showed the difficulty of establishing causal relationships between poor housing and "pathologies." That such relationships are difficult to establish, however, does not mean they do not exist. In *Slums and Social Insecurity,* Alvin Schorr summarizes the available evidence:

The type of housing occupied influences health, behavior and attitude, particularly if the housing is desperately inadequate . . . . The following effects may spring from poor housing: a perception of one's self that leads to pessimism and passivity; stress to which the individual cannot adapt; poor health and a state of dissatisfaction, . . . and difficulties in household management and child rearing. Most of these effects, in turn, place obstacles in the path of improving one's financial circumstances.[29]

Housing Supply—An Overview

As we have seen, houses and neighborhoods play extraordinarily important roles in their residents' lives. Housing can hardly be considered just another consumer good bought and enjoyed to one extent or another. It must be seen as a consumer good peculiar in obvious but nonetheless important ways. First, housing lasts a long time, normally through several generations of use; as a result, most housing that families move into in any given year is "used," and changes in the housing stock—the sum of existing housing—can come about only slowly. Second, housing requires uniquely large expenditures. In 1970, the Bureau of Labor Statistics estimated housing would require 23.5 percent of the budget of a four-person family and 34.6 percent of the budget of a retired couple, both living in urban areas at "intermediate" standards of living.[30] Only

[29] Alvin Schorr, *Slums and Social Insecurity* (1963), pp. 31–32.
[30] Bureau of the Census, *Statistical Abstract of the United States* (1972), p. 351.

food rivaled housing as a proportion of the household budget. Housing is further unique in being tied to the land on which it is located. Vacant housing in areas with declining populations and few jobs does nothing to satisfy needs in growing areas.

In this section, characteristics of the American housing stock, as measured by the 1970 Census of Housing, will be discussed briefly; the institutions by which the United States produced housing will be outlined, as will their performance during the 1960's; finally, relationships among housing submarkets, particularly the nature of housing discrimination, will be discussed.

American Housing—General
Characteristics

The decennial Census of Housing provides basic information on the American housing stock. Although nationwide figures obscure important differences between regions of the country and the kind of housing available to various income and ethnic groups, they do give a picture of the overall nature and quality of American housing.

Table 22.1 presents data for 1970 and 1960 indicating some major changes. The total number of housing units rose to almost 69 million in 1970, an increase of almost 18 percent. Since the total population increased only 13 percent, additional housing was available. This accounts for the decline of 14.8 percent in the number of units recorded as overcrowded. The availability of new housing also accounted for the substantial decline, 52 percent, of units with deficient plumbing, adequate plumbing being defined as piped hot water, a flush toilet, and a bathtub or shower.

Another significant feature of United States housing as a whole is the continued rise in the number of homeowners, 22 percent more being recorded in 1970 than 1960. Most owner-occupied units are single-family homes. There are indications, however, that home ownership percentages may be leveling off with rising housing costs and a larger proportion

TABLE 22.1: U.S. Housing Stock, 1970 vs. 1960*

	1970	1960	Percent Change
Total Housing Units	68.6	58.3	17.7
Total Occupied Units	63.4	53.0	19.6
Owner Occupied	39.9	32.8	21.6
Renter Occupied	23.5	20.2	16.3
Overcrowded Units	5.2	6.1	−14.8
Units with Deficient Plumbing	4.7	9.8	−52.0

*Numbers in Millions
SOURCE: *HUD Challenge* 11 (July 1971), p. 31, derived from the Censuses of Housing, 1970 and 1960.

of our population not yet having reached their peak earning years: in 1970 almost two-thirds of all housing units were owner-occupied, compared with 62 percent in 1960, 55 percent in 1950, and 44 percent in 1940.

REGIONAL VARIATIONS   Much of the history and current trends of urbanization in the United States is reflected in regional variations among various housing indicators shown in Table 22.2.[31] Thus, the South and West have the highest percentages of increase in year-round housing units and concomitantly, the highest percentages of housing units built since 1960. However, they also have the smallest median number of rooms per dwelling unit, 4.9 and 4.8, respectively. This is due to the high proportion of apartments among new dwelling units, especially in California and Florida. Surprisingly, the Northeast is the least crowded of the regions, having only 6.3 percent of its dwelling units occupied by 1.01 or more persons per room, a standard measure of crowding. Possibly this reflects the "thinning out" of dense central city population in the Northeast and lower suburban housing densities.

The North Central states have the highest percentage of owner-occupied units of the regions, but in most other housing characteristics, the North Central region more closely resembles the Northeast, which is to be expected in terms of the regional sequence of urban-industrial development in the United States. The South has the highest level of crowding in housing, but in many ways is "catching up," as witness the high housing construction rates already noted. This reflects, among other factors, the growth of industrial cities in the South.

For blacks, the highest home ownership rate was in the South, where about 47 percent of black housing was owner-occupied. Rates for blacks in other regions were 42 percent in the North Central states, 40 percent in the West, and about 29 percent in the Northeast. The lower percentage of black home ownership in the Northeast is partly explained by the

[31] For a description of these urban trends, see Chapter 3, pp. 56–62 and pp. 82–84.

TABLE 22.2: Characteristics of United States Housing, by Region, 1970

Location	Year-round units, change, 1960–70	Median number of rooms	In bldgs. built 1960 or later	Owner-occupied	1.01 or more person per room
U.S., total	19.9%	5.0	25.0%	62.9%	8.0%
Northeast	14.4	5.2	17.6	57.6	6.3
North Central	14.5	5.1	21.1	68.0	7.1
South	25.1	4.9	30.8	64.7	10.0
West	28.1	4.8	31.1	59.0	8.1

SOURCE: U.S. Bureau of the Census, *City and County Data Book, 1972.* Washington, D.C., Government Printing Office, 1973, pp. 6–7.

fact that nearly half of all housing occupied by blacks there is in the New York metropolitan region, where home ownership rates in general, and for blacks in particular, are traditionally low. In the New York metropolitan area, only 18 percent of black housing is owner-occupied; in the city itself, the rate is only 16 percent. For all New York households, the rates are 37 percent for the metropolitan area and 24 percent in the city.[32]

CITY AND SUBURBAN HOUSING   Earlier discussions in Chapters 3, 10, and 11 detailing the concentration of the American population into metropolitan areas and, within them, into the ever-enlarging suburban "ring," will have prepared us for the revelations of the 1970 Housing Census. For the first time in United States history the suburbs had more housing units than either the central cities of metropolitan areas or the nonmetropolitan areas (mainly small towns and rural communities). Suburban housing units totaled 23.9 million compared to 22.6 million for metropolitan central cities and 22.1 million in nonmetropolitan locations. As Table 22.3 indicates this represented an increase of over 30 percent in suburban housing units, far higher than the increases in central cities or in nonmetropolitan areas. The housing increase in nonmetropolitan areas was influenced by the increased popularity of "second homes" and trends in migratory housing.

In all locations the increases in the housing inventory outstripped the growth of population, an indication of overall improvement in housing quality. Another reason for the greater increase in housing than in population is that fewer young married couples were living in a parental home in 1970 than in 1960, and more young people were living alone, as were elderly individuals who no longer had a family to care for.

By every criterion suburban housing is superior to central city housing,

[32] Social and Economic Statistics Administration, Bureau of the Census, *We the Americans: Our Homes* (revised May 1973), p. 6.

TABLE 22.3: United States Housing Inventory, by Metropolitan and Nonmetropolitan Location, 1970 vs. 1960 (numbers in millions)

Location	1970	1960	Percent Change in Units	Percent Change in Population
Total Units	68.6	58.3	17.7	13.3
Metropolitan Areas	46.5	38.6	20.4	16.6
Central Cities	22.6	20.4	10.5	5.3
Suburbs	23.9	18.2	31.4	28.2
Nonmetropolitan Areas	22.1	19.7	12.4	6.5

SOURCE: *HUD Challenge* 12 (July 1972), p. 31, derived from the Censuses of Housing, 1970 and 1960.

TABLE 22.4: Housing Characteristics, Cities and Suburbs, 1970

	Central Cities	Suburbs
Units for use		
year-round	22,600,000	23,900,000
Built		
1960-70	18.5%	32.7%
1950-59	19.1	27.2
1940-49	14.4	12.4
1939 or before	48.1	27.7
With air conditioning	38.2	40.1
Occupied Units	21,400,000	22,500,000
Population in		
housing units	61,800,000	73,700,000
Median number rooms	4.7	5.3
With clothes washing		
machine	60.4%	77.3%
With clothes dryer	31.2	52.5
With dishwasher	15.4	27.0
With food freezer	16.6	28.7
With TV	94.8	97.2
Two or more cars	26.2	44.7
Owner-occupied housing–		
median value	$16,400	$20,000
Renter-occupied housing–		
median rent	$90	$114

SOURCE: Social and Economics Administration, Bureau of the Census, *We the Americans, # 3, Our Homes* (revised May 1973), and *# 7, Cities and Suburbs* (May 1973).

as shown in Table 22.4. There is a wide range of housing in suburbs, as in central cities, but the overall comparisons are revealing. Suburban housing is, of course, newer, almost a third having been built since 1960, compared with less than 20 percent of central city housing. In fact, almost half of the central city housing was built in 1939 or earlier, attesting to an aging housing stock. Suburban homes are larger than those of the central city; the median number of rooms in suburban units is 5.3 meaning that half the units have more than 5.3 rooms and half have fewer rooms, while the central city median is only 4.7.

Table 22.4 also provides some glimpses of suburban life style. Much higher proportions of suburban homes have washing machines and clothes dryers, indicating the availability of space to keep these large appliances and the need to provide one's own facilities in a less-densely settled environment. These appliances are also marks of affluence, as is the greater prevalence of dishwashers and food freezers in suburban homes. On the other hand, the fact that almost half (44.7 percent) of suburban housing units have two or more cars probably falls into the category of a necessary expense, considering the unavailability of public transportation in most suburbs.

Housing Quality

Prior to the 1970 Census, the Census Bureau attempted to classify housing units as "sound," "deteriorating," and "dilapidated." Not surprisingly, the placement of units in these categories by Census enumerators was haphazard at best.[33] In 1970 the presence of certain plumbing and kitchen features were used. These criteria, which are more easily measured and are reliable, indicate a dramatic improvement in housing quality over the decade, as already indicated in Table 22.1. The Census measures of general quality tend to confirm the picture of a steadily improving housing stock. This picture corresponds to what we know about housing expenditures. Since the end of World War II, such expenditures have grown more rapidly than for most other consumer items. In effect, American households have been willing to spend a larger proportion of their increased incomes on improved housing.

Increased quality, however, reflected not only changing consumer preferences, but the unavailability of land zoned for development of inexpensive houses, a particularly severe problem in larger metropolitan areas. In 1973, for example, the Regional Plan Association of the New York area estimated that "only about one family in five can afford the lowest-cost housing units that can now be built in the Region."[34] One important reason was that almost all vacant land in the region is zoned for construction of houses on at least half-acre lots. In contrast, 60 by 100-foot lots predominated after World War II, when half the region's population could afford new houses in suburban locations.

More recently, a detailed study of the nation's housing quality was undertaken by the Joint Center for Urban Studies of Harvard University and the Massachusetts Institute of Technology. They reported that at least one-fifth of the nation's families were "housing-deprived."[35] Of the 13.1 million "deprived" households, 6.9 million were so classified because of physically substandard housing (inadequate plumbing or heating), 5.5 million because of an excessive rent burden, and over half a million because of overcrowded conditions. In the New York metropolitan area, 28 percent of the households were classified as housing deprived, as were 25 percent of the Newark metropolitan area residents.

Others have attempted to rank cities on a variety of measures of

---

[33] For an excellent discussion of the problems of available data on the quality of housing, see Henry Aaron, *Shelter and Subsidies* (1972).

[34] William A. Caldwell, ed., *How to Save Urban America* (1973), p. 18.

[35] David Birch, *America's Housing Needs: 1970–1980* (1973).

TABLE 22.5: Housing Quality, Summary City Rank*, 1970

San Jose	1	Kansas City	16
Philadelphia	2	Milwaukee	17
Portland	3	Dallas	18
Minneapolis	4	Miami	19
San Diego	5	Indianapolis	20
Denver	6	Houston	21
San Francisco	7	Boston	22
Seattle	8	Atlanta	23
Baltimore	9	Cleveland	24
Phoenix	10	Pittsburgh	25
Buffalo	11	Cincinnati	26
New York	12	Chicago	27
Detroit	13	St. Louis	28
Washington	14	New Orleans	29
Los Angeles	15	Newark	30

*geometric mean of five measures
SOURCE: John Tepper Marlin, "City Housing." *Municipal Performance Report*, 1:2 (November 1973), p. 6.

housing quality. A recent study by the Council on Municipal Performance used five measures: (1) housing cost relative to income; (2) plumbing adequacy; (3) market efficiency (the relationship between overcrowding and the vacancy rate); (4) change in racial segregation in housing; (5) discrimination (the relative amounts blacks and whites pay for rent).[36] Their results indicate that none of the 30 cities covered ranked high (or low) on all five measures. Thus, San Jose and San Francisco show the least residential discrimination against nonwhites, but their residents pay a very high proportion of their incomes for housing. Of the 30 cities, only Detroit, Philadelphia, and Phoenix were above average on all five measures. Denver, Minneapolis, and Seattle are the only three cities that rank among the best five on two measures without being among the worst five on any of the other three. Therefore, as the report indicates, the summary rankings shown in Table 22.5 should be viewed cautiously. Despite the variability that might apply to an individual city's ranking, their overall conclusion is well taken: "our housing measures confirm what casual observers have long maintained—that the public policies of the nation and its cities have not produced consistently good results in housing in any major central city in the United States."[37]

[36] John Tepper Marlin, "City Housing," *Municipal Performance Report*, 1 (November 1973), 3–33.
[37] *Ibid.*, p. 6.

Housing Production and Subsidies

Ultimately, the quality of housing occupied by a nation's families depends on the amount and quality of housing it produces. A vast number of components go into the production of housing. Vacant land must be available, accessible, and provided with utilities. Materials in large quantities and great variety are needed, as are many types of skilled and semiskilled labor. Regulations governing construction and occupation of housing—zoning and subdivision ordinances and building and housing codes—must be workable and efficiently administered. Finally, because only a few owners can afford to purchase housing outright, long-term loans must be available to finance both rental and residential housing. Unlike some other countries, the United States has never suffered extended shortages of most of these inputs. Production of adequate housing for the population has been limited mainly by the unavailability of financing and by costs too great for most households' incomes to absorb.[38]

SINGLE FAMILY HOMES   Since the 1920's, resident-owned single family homes have been, by all evidence, the housing type preferred by most American families. Following World War II, housing production and financing institutions brought such housing within financial reach of a majority of American families.

Prior to the Depression, typical homeowners' mortgages were provided by savings and loan associations, banks, or insurance companies.[39] Required down payments amounted to 40 or 50 percent of the house's value, so potential homeowners had to accumulate considerable cash.

Established in 1934, the Federal Housing Administration (FHA) insured lenders against defaults.[40] Over time the experience with FHA-insured mortgages showed lenders that long-term loans to middle-income homebuyers, requiring small down payments, were excellent risks. By the 1960's, families purchasing homes worth two-and-one-half times their annual incomes—the amount lenders and the FHA normally approve—could obtain FHA-insured mortgages for up to 95 percent of the house's value, for a period of thirty years. Over time, the example of FHA financing had revolutionized "conventional" mortgage financing.

The federal government, then, has played a critical role in making financing for home purchases available to middle-income Americans.

[38] For an interesting historical study establishing this point for Boston in the period 1850–1960, see Lloyd Rodwin, *Housing and Economic Progress* (1961).

[39] Mortgages are loans secured for real estate. Should the borrower default on his payments, the lender may foreclose—taking title to the property—as a means of recovering his losses. Most housing is purchased with the proceeds of mortgages.

[40] For discussion of the institutional changes summarized here, see Aaron, *op. cit.,* pp. 77ff.

Federal income tax laws also encourage homeownership; they allow homeowners to deduct mortgage interest payments and local real estate taxes from their taxable incomes, and do not require them to report the income represented by use of the house. Prior to World War II, when federal income tax rates were low, these benefits were of little consequence. By 1966, however, the annual subsidy they represented had climbed to approximately seven billion dollars,[41] by far the largest amount of any housing subsidy. These benefits go primarily to higher-income homeowners, because the tax savings those in higher tax brackets receive through any deduction are proportionately higher than those received by families in lower tax brackets. Higher-income home-owners may receive subsidies of as much as 50 percent of their shelter costs through these income tax law provisions.[42]

FEDERAL PROGRAMS FOR LOW- AND MODERATE-INCOME HOUSING   The mortgage financing and tax benefits described above, benefiting mainly those of above average income, are not generally thought of as subsidies, although that is their effect. The term housing subsidy is generally applied to direct federal expenditures for housing and these have been directed at families below the level of affluence.

Since the New Deal, the federal government has assumed more and more responsibility for providing decent housing for low-income families.[43] The first such commitment was made in 1933, when the Public Works Administration began to construct low-rent housing, primarily as a means of increasing employment. The goal of providing decent housing for all families was adopted more firmly in the Housing Act of 1949, which included the statement: "The Congress hereby declares that the general welfare and security of the Nation and the health and living standards of its people require . . . the realization as soon as feasible of the goal of a decent home and a suitable living environment for every American family." In the Housing and Urban Development Act of 1968 Congress reaffirmed these goals and made them more explicit:

The Congress finds that the supply of the Nation's housing is not increasing rapidly enough to meet the national housing goal, established in the Housing Act of 1949 . . . . The Congress reaffirms this national housing goal and determines that it can be substantially achieved within the next decade by the construction or rehabilitation of twenty-six million housing units, six million of these for low- and moderate-income families.

Despite these escalating commitments, Congressional and public support for programs to provide decent housing for low-income families

---

[41] Aaron, *op. cit.*, p. 53.

[42] *Ibid.*, p. 61.

[43] For a particularly useful discussion of these programs, see The President's Committee on Urban Housing, *A Decent Home* (1968).

has been equivocal at best. While the right of middle- and upper-income homeowners to obtain subsidies through the income tax laws is taken for granted, programs to provide decent housing for low-income families have operated under constant attack.

The oldest such program is Public Housing, instituted in the Housing Act of 1937. Independent local agencies called Housing Authorities plan, construct, own, and manage developments under Federal guidelines. The Federal government pays for the projects through annual contributions. As a result, rentals need cover only operating costs. Only low-income families are eligible for Public Housing apartments.

By 1971, over 1,000,000 Public Housing units had been completed. About one-fourth are located in cities of 500,000 or more, and 49 percent are located in cities of less than 100,000. Thirty-six percent—the largest regional proportion—are located in the South. In 1970, Public Housing tenants had a median family income of $3636, just over half the nationwide median for all families. Seventy percent of Public Housing tenants were black, although almost 50 percent of new tenants were white. These proportions reflect two facts: particularly in large cities, many Public Housing projects have been built in all-black neighborhoods. Black tenants, with fewer economic opportunities and very few other opportunities for decent low-rent housing, have tended to remain in Public Housing longer than whites.[44]

Public Housing has had a very bad image. Problems like those of Pruitt-Igoe are widely publicized; communities like Forest Hills, in Queens, New York, react violently to the prospect of a project's being built nearby. Such images and events reflect Public Housing's problems, if in a distorted way. The program, first, has been crippled by its own requirements. Construction cost limitations have limited the facilities housing authorities could include. Because maintenance expenses had to be met from rentals paid by very low income families, housing authorities generally have constructed easily-maintained buildings, but frequently ignored playgrounds for children, essential shopping facilities, and even adequate elevators.

Realities of local politics have also crippled Public Housing. In *Politics, Planning and the Public Interest*,[45] Martin Meyerson and Edward C. Banfield traced the planning process for Chicago's first projects built under the 1949 Housing Act. In 1949, the Chicago Housing Authority presented to the mayor a proposal for 40,000 units, 15,000 of which would be located on vacant land, mainly in outlying, all-white neighborhoods of the city. Residential segregation rapidly became the major

[44] Data from Aaron, *op. cit.,* pp. 113–16.

[45] Martin Meyerson and Edward C. Banfield, *Politics, Planning and the Public Interest* (1955).

issue in determining where the projects would be located. Under Federal law, the Chicago City Council had to approve each site. White aldermen, forty-eight of the Council's fifty members, refused to accept projects in their areas, apparently because they opposed integration. As a result, Chicago's Public Housing was built on small sites in already black areas. In order to build the number of units for which funds had been allocated, families had to be moved and low-rent housing destroyed. High-rise projects had to be built rather than low-rise structures more suitable for families with children. In turn, high-rise structures, because they cost more than low-rise, left less money within the statutory cost limitations for playgrounds, community rooms, and other facilities.

The pattern Meyerson and Banfield found in Chicago has been repeated in city after city. Racism and the opposition of business interests have limited Public Housing's ability to provide decent housing for low-income families. Despite these limitations, apparently most projects are successful. As evidenced by long waiting lists of applicants in many cities, Public Housing provides low-income families with far better housing than they could obtain otherwise.

TABLE 22.6: Percentage of New Private and Public Housing Units Inside and Outside Central Cities, 1962–1967

	Private		Public	
Year	Central cities	Suburbs	Central cities	Suburbs
1962	39	61	79	21
1963	38	62	82	18
1964	37	63	74	26
1965	34	66	70	30
1966	34	66	76	24
1967	33	67	83	17

SOURCE: U.S. Bureau of Labor Statistics, *Changes in Urban America*, Bureau of Labor Statistics Report # 353, 1968, as cited in Neil Gold, "The Mismatch of Jobs and Low-Income People in Metropolitan Areas and Its Implication for the Central City Poor," in Commission on Population Growth and the American Future, *Research Reports*, Volume V, *Population Distribution and Policy*, Sara Mills Mazie, ed., Washington, D.C.: Government Printing Office, 1972, p. 471.

Table 22.6 indicates the recent location of public housing units. It shows the intrametropolitan location of new housing units built between 1962 and 1967, as compared with new private housing units built in the same period. The data show that nearly two-thirds of new private housing is built in the suburbs of metropolitan areas, compared with less than one-quarter of the public housing units. "The reason why so little public housing is produced in the suburbs is because the suburbs do not want the poor and are free to exercise their prejudices simply by not authorizing the development of such housing. Hence the government's chief vehicle for producing low-income housing in urban areas is being used to cement racial and class patterns."[46]

Since the late 1950's, Congress has legislated a number of other programs aimed at providing housing for "low-income" and "moderate-income" families. These programs have attempted to involve private enterprise in construction, financing, and management; their proponents sought not only to increase production but to reverse the traditional opposition of business interests to low-rent housing programs. A number of programs were aimed at making the urban renewal process more workable; for example, by providing grants and low-interest loans to homeowners to enable them to rehabilitate their houses. Congress also attempted to formulate a set of programs that would be more flexible than Public Housing—serving all families who could not afford new housing on the private market.

None of these programs resulted in much production until the late 1960's. By 1968, however, a more workable set of programs had been developed: the 236 Program, which insures loans to profit-oriented and nonprofit organizations for construction of rental and cooperative housing, and subsidized payments on those loans so the effective interest rate is 1 percent, had produced 124,000 units by 1970. The 235 (j) Program provides similar subsidies to enable moderate-income families to purchase new and rehabilitated housing; by 1970, 131,000 units had been purchased under the program which was expanding rapidly with an additional 457,000 units projected by July 1973.[47] By 1970, construction of housing under the various subsidy programs had become an important proportion of all new construction. In that year, over 1,400,000 new units were started, excluding mobile homes, of which 400,000 were subsidized, mainly through the 236, 235 and Public Housing programs.[48]

Severe administrative problems, however, had occurred, particularly in applying the 235 Program to rehabilitate older housing. Apparently, FHA appraisers have attributed far more than their true value to many homes sold to moderate-income buyers under the program. Aaron notes that, under the program:

The buyer who qualifies has little incentive to bargain for a good selling price. He must pay 20 percent of adjusted income toward his mortgage; the government pays the rest . . . . An eligible family is unlikely to delay its move from squalid housing by haggling over price.[49]

[46] Neil Gold, "The Mismatch of Jobs and Low-Income People in Metropolitan Areas and Its Implications for the Central-City Poor," in Commission on Population Growth and the American Future, *Research Reports,* Volume V, *Population Distribution and Policy,* Sara Mills Mazie, ed., (1972), p. 470.

[47] Aaron, *op. cit.,* p. 187ff.

[48] House Committee on Banking and Currency, Papers submitted to Subcommittee on Housing Panels, Part I, June 1971, p. 69.

[49] Aaron, *op. cit.,* p. 139.

Many observers have long argued that low- and moderate-income families could better be provided with decent housing through "housing allowances," rent vouchers or cash subsidies that would enable them to purchase good housing on the private market. The Rent Supplement program, providing such subsidies to a small number of families, was passed by Congress in 1965; it represented a first step toward "housing allowances," and various experiments have been carried out, mainly to determine how such a program could avoid inflating prices and rents of existing housing. The 235 Program's administrative difficulties seemed to confirm the idea that "housing allowances" would work more efficiently and justly.

Early in 1973, the Nixon administration announced its intention to suspend all subsidized housing programs, committing no more funds until they had been thoroughly reviewed. It argued that costs were more than the Federal Government could afford and that the present programs could not be equitable—although 40 percent of the population was eligible for one or another subsidy, only a small proportion of that number would benefit. The Administration has not, however, proposed any expansion of "housing allowances." Whether the programs would be reformulated, or replaced with programs serving the same income groups, or whether the Federal commitment to decent housing for low- and moderate-income families would simply be abandoned was unclear.

MOBILE HOMES   During the late 1950's and the 1960's, mobile homes developed as another way of meeting the housing needs of lower middle income families.[50] From 1955 to 1961, about 100,000 mobile homes were produced annually; by 1971, this number had grown to 485,000, 20.8 percent of all housing units built during that year.[51] Construction of mobile homes large enough for year-round family living dates from 1955, when the ten-foot-wide unit was introduced. A 1965-66 survey of mobile home purchasers confirmed the idea that mobile homes developed as a resource for lower middle income families.[52] Mobile home family heads were younger and less well-educated than household heads in the general population. The median annual income was $6,700, and the largest number of mobile home families were headed by skilled or semiskilled workers. The majority of mobile home families, as one might expect, were small. In some states, a large proportion of mobile homes were occupied by elderly people.

The mobile home industry has grown up almost entirely outside other housing institutions. Efficient and inexpensive production underlies its

---

[50] A mobile home may be defined as "a movable or portable dwelling constructed at a factory, to be towed on its own chassis, connected to utilities, and designed without a permanent foundation for year-round living." Margaret J. Drury, *Mobile Homes* (Revised edition, 1972), p. 3.

[51] *Ibid.*, p. 6.

[52] *Ibid.*, pp. 17–30.

success. Savings are achieved through factory assembly, using inexpensive labor and materials very economically; but the mobile home industry is hardly capital-intensive. The durability of mobile homes is an unknown; lenders apparently accept a ten-year useful life as realistic, but poor quality and durability, particularly of interior finishes and plumbing, may result in problems for owners.

The mobile home has not been legally recognized as residential housing in most states. As a result, it has not been subject to building and housing codes, and it has been licensed like an automobile and taxed as personal property rather than as real estate.[53] Mobile homes have usually been financed through short-term personal loans, like automobile loans, rather than through mortgages. Because interest rates on such loans are higher than those on mortgages, there has been no shortage of financing for mobile homes.

In the survey cited above, 61.5 percent of the mobile homes surveyed were located in mobile home parks; 38.5 percent outside such parks. In many areas, mobile home parks have been allowed only in areas zoned for industry or commercial uses, or banned altogether. As a result, many parks are located at the rural-urban fringe, at the edge of metropolitan development. The failure of localities to provide for mobile home parks has created shortages of space for mobile homes, particularly in northern metropolitan areas. As a result, mobile home owners often must buy their homes from dealers who can provide park spaces. Johnson comments on the "closed parks" that result:

A closed park usually offers prospective residents a choice of several different mobile homes (although these are often different models by the same manufacturer) in several price ranges. However, the price of such mobile homes is usually several hundred, and sometimes several thousand, dollars more than the buyer would have to pay if he bought the same model from an independent dealer . . . . Evictions or decisions to move or sell out pose other problems. In many of these parks the mobile homes are installed in such a way that it is not feasible to move them . . . . Instead, he [the mobile home owner] must sell his mobile home subject to the park owner's approval or he must sell it back to the park's owner and they will then resell the unit to a new tenant, usually at a substantial profit to themselves.[54]

Because of problems like these and high transportation costs, mobile homes are not really very mobile. Like the residents of Idle Haven, residents of other parks may be trapped in situations where they are subject to considerable financial exploitation.

---

[53] Many local governments have excluded mobile homes, arguing that their residents do not pay a fair share in local taxes. Because parks are taxed as real estate, and mobile homes themselves are taxed in various ways, mobile home owners may pay taxes equal to those they would pay if their homes were taxed as real estate. See *ibid.*, pp. 123–27.

[54] Johnson, *op. cit.*, pp. 168–9.

Despite their low cost, mobile homes have not served the United States' lowest income groups; seemingly, as long as they are financed by short-term loans and park spaces are in short supply, mobile homes will be beyond the reach of most low income families. Nor have they served minority families. In 1966, fewer than 2 percent of mobile home residents were black; apparently, virtually all mobile home parks are segregated.[55]

Problems in Housing Submarkets

Parts of the housing stock, of course, are not equally available to all households. Within each metropolitan area, the housing market is really a variety of submarkets for different housing types, at different prices, serving households of differing sizes, preferences, and incomes. Every metropolitan area's housing market is further divided into black and white markets, separated by more or less impassable barriers. Exclusion of other ethnic groups may divide housing markets further.

Housing economists have frequently used the concept "filtering" to explain relationships among housing submarkets. In its broadest sense, "filtering" refers to both money and people; it is the downward movement in the prices or rents of existing housing units as newly constructed units come on the market and prove more attractive to higher-income families; and it refers to shifts in occupancy whereby the older units are occupied by lower-income groups.[56] This most common concept of filtering carries important policy implications: if prices of existing housing units decline and lower-income groups obtain better housing as a result, then construction, even of very expensive units, will improve housing available to the whole population. If, on the other hand, prices do not decline, or lower-income families are not able to take advantage of such price declines, then addition of expensive units to the housing stock will do little to improve the housing of lower-income groups.

How well filtering works in American metropolitan areas is not clear. A great many units added during the past decades have gone to house newly formed households. Between 1950 and 1970, the number of households in the United States grew by 20,000,000[57] or two-thirds the number of net additions to the housing stock. Two less obvious but equally important causes also limit the working of filtering: housing deterioration and discrimination. Housing abandonment also affects the filtering process.

---

[55] *Ibid.*, p. 165.

[56] William G. Grigsby, *Housing Markets and Public Policy* (1963) provides a very useful discussion of the various concepts of filtering.

[57] U.S. Bureau of the Census, *1972 Statistical Abstract, op. cit.*, p. 38.

Housing Deterioration

Housing deterioration is a major obstacle to effective working of the filtering process; if units deteriorate rapidly, occupation of them by lower-income groups will not improve the quality of those groups' housing. Because data on housing quality are so poor, the extent of housing deterioration, nationally or in any city, is difficult to judge. Clearly, however, older units will deteriorate rapidly without constant maintenance; and when overcrowded.

Recently, several studies have examined problems of maintenance and deterioration, seeking how older housing in central cities might continue to serve a useful purpose for the next decade or two. In 1968-70, Michael A. Stegman studied Baltimore's inner-city housing market.[58] Five percent of the housing was dilapidated, and 25 percent was deteriorating. Low-income families were about four times as likely to live in dilapidated housing as non-low-income families; and black low-income families were twice as likely to live in poor housing as white. Between neighborhoods whose original characteristics—housing types, density, and so forth—are very similar, housing quality varies from relatively good to terribly inadequate.

Stegman found Baltimore's low-rent housing market is not dominated by "slumlords," that is, owners of many units who reduce maintenance to make exorbitant profits. About one-fourth of the inner-city rental inventory is owned or managed by about fifty professionals, but the remainder is owned by a large number of small and middle-sized investors. Management is the key to success in this market. Rents are low, leaving little margin for unusual expenses. The best managers, generally relatively large owners, operate very efficiently; one landlord, for example, paid only $51 for hot-water heaters that cost $135 retail. Reliable long-term tenants are an important and sometimes scarce resource for good management. The "competent investor . . . would rather forego part of the rent than lose an otherwise good tenant."[59] Vacancies can be disastrous, causing not only loss of rents but vandalism. Several larger landlords estimated vandalism costs at 15 percent of total rents. One common sort of vandalism is stripping copper pipes from plumbing systems for sale to junkyards.

Lending institutions have essentially withdrawn from the inner-city

---

[58] Michael A. Stegman, *Housing Investment in the Inner City: The Dynamics of Decline* (1972). Stegman defined "inner-city" as officially defined "poverty" areas. See also, George Sternlieb, *The Tenement Landlord* (1966); and Sternlieb, *The Urban Housing Dilemma* (1970) conducted for New York City Housing and Development Administration, 1970. Stegman's findings in Baltimore largely confirm Sternlieb's in Newark and New York, despite the fact that the housing stocks in the three cities are made up of rather different types of housing.

[59] Stegman, *op. cit.*, p. 125.

housing market, making financing with which to purchase or rehabilitate houses difficult or impossible to obtain. Some of Baltimore's worst maintained properties are owned by people who inherited them and have no interest in retaining them, but are unable to find buyers. Occasionally, larger owners themselves finance purchases by tenants through "purchase money" mortgages, although such purchases usually involve inflated prices.

A number of solutions to the problem of housing deterioration have been suggested and attempted. Sternlieb argues that resident-ownership is a key to saving older, inner-city housing, and Stegman explores the idea of cooperatives to own and manage housing. For over a decade, the Federal government has supported "Concentrated Code Enforcement" programs, attempting to maintain and improve the quality of existing housing in delineated neighborhoods. None of these solutions, however, has proven consistently effective.

Housing Abandonment

In recent years, the problem of rising operating costs, the inability of tenants to pay increased rents, and increasing physical deterioration have led to more and more abandonment of central city housing by owners and, eventually, tenants as well.[60] Owners stop paying real estate taxes, making repairs and buying fuel, in effect walking away from their buildings. Eventually, as conditions become intolerable, tenants move out, leaving vacant shells subject to fires, vandalism and theft of pipes and other components. From one perspective, this process might be seen as encouraging; as the overall housing stock improves, the worst housing, it might be argued, drops out of the market altogether. However, abandonment seems to affect not only the worst housing, but buildings that could serve as decent housing for some years to come.

After completing the only nationwide study of housing abandonment yet, the Urban League concluded abandonment reflects the emergence of what it called "crisis ghettos," areas in which very low-income families are becoming more and more concentrated as those who can move away do so. Social problems become more and more concentrated and housing deteriorates more and more rapidly.

Although abandonment of buildings is alarming, particularly because units that are not the worst in the housing stock are lost in the process, it does not seem to account for a major proportion of losses from the housing stock during the 1960's. Total losses during the 1960's have

---

[60] See particularly George Sternlieb, "Abandonment and Rehabilitation: What Is to Be Done?" in House Committee, Subcommittee on Housing Panels, *op. cit.*, pp.315–72; and National Urban League, *The National Survey of Housing Abandonment*, David Stoloff, Project Director, New York: The League, 1971.

been estimated at 6.1 million units, compared to 3.7 million units lost during the 1950's and 8.5 million projected losses during the 1970's.[61]

Losses of units from the housing stock increased during the 1960's, and are expected to increase during the 1970's, for a number of reasons. The housing stock is aging; the number of units over 30 years old increased from 15 million in 1940 to 21 million in 1950, 27 million in 1960, and 29 million in 1970. Although the useful life of mobile homes is not known, any unit over ten years old may well be beyond further use. Governmental action accounts for an important part of losses. Clearance of highway paths during 1967–1970, for example, accounted for loss of nearly 50,000 units annually; federally-funded urban renewal programs have accounted for annual losses of as many as 40,000 units in recent years; and enforcement of local health and housing codes results in an unknown, but undoubtedly substantial, number of losses each year. Loss of units from the housing stock affects low-income families most directly. Most frequently, their homes are demolished and they are forced to move. Loss of low-rent units, moreover, reduce the housing choices open to low-income families and results in their paying increased rents.

Housing Discrimination

Perhaps the most important impediment to smooth working of housing markets is housing discrimination. Far more than any other group, black Americans have been the victims of housing discrimination. While neighborhoods have excluded Spanish-speaking families, families of Asian backgrounds, Jews and Catholics, such patterns of discrimination have been far less pervasive than exclusion of blacks, and have not resulted in the same inability of even high-income families to buy good housing in desirable locations. The high degree of black-white residential segregation in American cities cannot be explained by reference to low black incomes. Taeuber and Taeuber conclude:

. . . the net effect of economic factors in explaining residential segregation is slight. Their power in explaining residential segregation diminishes as differentials between the races in the quality of the housing they occupy, in the occupations they hold, and in the rents they pay also diminish. Economic differentials diminish but residential segregation persists.[62]

Rather, housing discrimination creates dual markets, one housing market for blacks and one for whites, with almost impermeable boundaries.

The effects of housing discrimination can be seen in the quality of housing blacks occupy. In every region of the country a much higher

---

[61] Subcommittee on Housing Panels, *op. cit.,* pp. 17–19, 106.
[62] See Karl E. Taeuber and Alma F. Taeuber, *Negroes in Cities* (1965), p. 94.

proportion of blacks than whites occupy housing below minimum standards; this is especially true in the South. However, when regional data are classified according to the type of community, as in Figure 22.1, it becomes evident that in large metropolitan centers black housing is superior to that occupied by blacks elsewhere. Thus, in the large central cities of the North and West, 9 percent of nonwhites occupy substandard housing, compared to 4 percent of the whites. The absolute percentages rise, as does the disparity between nonwhites and whites, by noncentral city location and by region, reaching the greatest contrast in the smaller cities, towns and rural areas of the South. There, 61 percent of nonwhites live in substandard housing compared to 16 percent of the whites.

Because of discrimination, moreover, blacks must pay more than whites for equivalent housing. The 1968 report of the President's Commission on Urban Housing concluded:

. . . in 1960, an urban white family with three children had to earn $4,100 annually to afford standard housing, based on allocating 20 percent of their gross income for shelter costs. In contrast, a nonwhite family of the same size had to earn $5,500 to afford the same standard of rental housing.[63]

Housing discrimination was institutionalized in American real estate

[63] President's Commission on Urban Housing, *A Decent Home* (1968), p. 42.

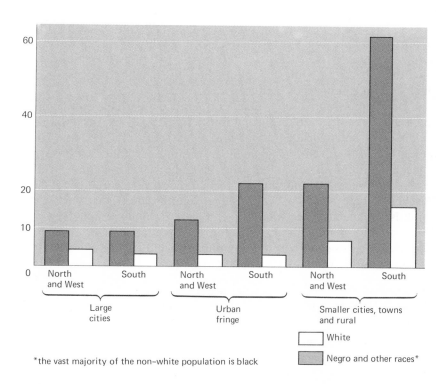

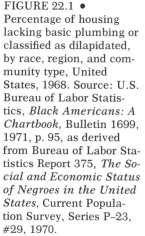

FIGURE 22.1 ●
Percentage of housing lacking basic plumbing or classified as dilapidated, by race, region, and community type, United States, 1968. Source: U.S. Bureau of Labor Statistics, *Black Americans: A Chartbook,* Bulletin 1699, 1971, p. 95, as derived from Bureau of Labor Statistics Report 375, *The Social and Economic Status of Negroes in the United States,* Current Population Survey, Series P–23, #29, 1970.

*the vast majority of the non–white population is black

practices in the decade following World War I.[64] Restrictive covenants, clauses attached to deeds requiring that a property owner never sell or rent to blacks, were required by the FHA for mortgage insurance until 1949, when the Supreme Court ruled such covenants unconstitutional. The real estate profession made maintaining segregation a matter of professional ethics, and many members continue to do so.[65] FHA and professional support for segregation was justified by the argument that the presence of blacks in a neighborhood lowered property values. In this way, discrimination could be rationalized as based on recognition of community values, but not racist in itself. Various studies, however, have shown that market values of property in integrated neighborhoods respond to market forces. Laurenti dealt with this question by comparing neighborhoods at various price levels, where blacks had entered, with matched all-white neighborhoods. He found prices tended to rise at the same rate or faster in newly integrated neighborhoods than in neighborhoods that remained all-white. Because only part of the housing stock at any price level is available to blacks, the same quality housing may be worth more to them than to whites.

Because of discrimination, residential mobility of black families into previously all-white neighborhoods frequently takes the form of "invasion and succession." Black neighborhoods expand from a central core into surrounding white neighborhoods, which frequently become all-black after a time. In some circumstances, invasion may take the form of "block-busting." Once a block or small neighborhood is "opened" to blacks, real estate agents and residents, apparently, are usually willing to rent or sell to blacks. "Opening" the neighborhood, however, is frequently seen as unethical, and may be carried out by "block-busters," soliciting sales from whites by telling them the neighborhood is turning black and their properties' values will decrease.

In *Managed Integration,*[66] Molotch described a perhaps more typical process of succession taking place in the mid-1960's in South Shore, a middle-class neighborhood about ten miles south of Chicago's Loop. Succession in South Shore began at the community's northwest corner, adjacent to already black neighborhoods, and proceeded southeastward. In 1954, foreseeing the possibility of racial succession, a number of local clergymen established the South Shore Commission. Exactly what the Commission's goals were was subject to considerable, although muted, disagreement. Nonetheless, both conservative and liberal members supported a strategy of attracting whites to South Shore, and trying to limit the number of black residents, particularly poor black families. A

[64] Luigi Laurenti, *Property Value and Race* (1960), reviews "Theories of Race and Property Value," including the justifications for discrimination used in the period after World War I, pp. 8–27.

[65] Rose Helper, *Racial Policies and Practices of Real Estate Brokers* (1969).

[66] Harvey Luskin Molotch, *Managed Integration* (1972).

Tenant Referral Service helped whites find housing in the neighborhood. Its services were also available to blacks, but its existence probably did not speed black movement into the community:

> ... by serving blacks as well as whites certain advantages accrued to the commission besides the wherewithal to placate black and pro-Negro members. Because TRS never sought out potential black tenants, it may be that those Negroes who applied for TRS services would have attempted to move into South Shore anyway; by having blacks apply through TRS, some could have been discouraged from moving into the area .... TRS could screen out tenants who were considered lower class or otherwise undesirable for the community. These persons could be told there were no vacancies or encouraged to locate elsewhere.[67]

Despite rapid organizational growth of the Commission, racial succession in South Shore proceeded as rapidly as in areas less well-organized. No panicked flight of white residents occurred. Rather, white families who moved, for the same reasons that cause families to move from any neighborhood, were replaced by black families. South Shore could not compete in the white housing market, because better housing choices were available to whites in suburban areas. In the black market, bounded by discrimination, the area competed effectively. Although some poor families were among blacks moving to South Shore, the majority resembled the white families they replaced; this pattern confirms Taeuber and Taeuber's finding that blacks moving to white neighborhoods tend to have educational and occupational status and incomes as high as or higher than the whites they replace.[68]

During the late 1950's and the 1960's, the Federal government and some state and local governments passed laws attempting to reduce housing discrimination. Most important, the Civil Rights Act of 1968 declared, "it is the policy of the United States to provide, within constitutional limitations, for fair housing throughout the United States" and outlawed discrimination in a range of transactions to be broadened over a number of years. In the same year, the Supreme Court held that the Civil Rights Act of 1866 is still enforceable and bars all racial discrimination, private as well as public, in the sale or rental of property.

Despite these laws and rulings, there is little evidence that housing discrimination has decreased significantly or residential integration is increasing rapidly. In a recent survey study, Bradburn, Sudman, and Gockel[69] found integrated neighborhoods more common than is often

---

[67] *Ibid.*, p. 119.

[68] Taeuber and Taeuber, *op. cit.*, pp. 163–64.

[69] Norman M. Bradburn, Seymour Sudman, and Galen L. Gockel, *Side by Side: Integrated Neighborhoods in America* (1971).

believed. Nineteen percent of the nation's population lived in such neighborhoods, the boundaries of which were defined, essentially, according to local customs. However, the median percentage of blacks in such neighborhoods was 3 percent, and many neighborhoods had so few blacks that most white residents did not know of their neighborhood's integration. Thus, although the percentage of "neighborhoods" that are integrated may be substantial and increasing, the proportion of black families living in such neighborhoods remains very small. For the foreseeable future, most black families will live in segregated neighborhoods and pay more for equivalent housing than white families with comparable incomes.

Urban Housing in Other Countries

To understand the quality and distribution of housing in the United States, it is helpful to view, even if briefly, the housing of other countries. This provides some basis for a comparative perspective and evaluation. In contrast to the United States, many countries, especially in northern and western Europe, provide a large amount of planned, subsidized, and managed housing. Housing is viewed as a responsibility of the government. In the developing countries, where funds for housing, as for other basics of urban living, are in short supply, the distinction between the housing of the "haves" and the "have nots" is very sharp. In Mexico City, for example, the deluxe Pedregal section is magnificent by any standard, but on the other side of town are ugly and congested slums much worse than even the poorest slums in the United States. Similarly, Bombay and Calcutta's modern apartment houses are impressive and provide the most vivid contrast with the lean-tos and shacks and the "street-sleepers," who have no habitation at all.

The Soviet Union

During its almost sixty years, the Soviet Union has suffered housing problems almost unimaginable to Americans. Before the 1917 Revolution, workers' housing in the few Russian industrial cities was miserable. A 1908 survey of St. Petersburg workers, for example, found 44.4 percent of single and 7.1 percent of married workers occupying a single bunk and sharing room and other facilities.[70] At the same time, members of the small urban middle and upper classes enjoyed housing standards comparable to those of Western cities.

---

[70] Timothy Sosnovy, *The Housing Problem in the Soviet Union*, New York: Research Program on the USSR (1954), p. 265.

TABLE 22.7: U.S.S.R. Urban Dwelling Space Per Capita in Square Meters*

Year	
1923	6.45
1926	5.85
1932	4.94
1937	4.17
1940	4.09
1950	3.98

*1 square meter = about 10 3/4 square feet
SOURCE: Timothy Sosnovy, *The Housing Problem in the Soviet Union,* New York:
Research Program on the USSR (1954), p. 269.

The Revolution brought almost immediate improvement in the housing of the poor, the result of expropriation and redistribution. From 1920 until 1950, however, urban housing deteriorated markedly, as Table 22.7 makes clear. Ada Louise Huxtable has described the deterioration more vividly:

A middle-class apartment of six rooms, built about 1910, might have been occupied by a single family of a mother, father and two children as late as 1920. In the 1920's, with the influx of population to the cities and the deterioration of the housing stock, that family would have been reduced to three rooms. The other three rooms would have been shared, at first by relatives. By the mid-1920's, as housing shortages increased, the six rooms were occupied by six families, using the communal kitchen and bathroom. After World War II, with its mass destruction of housing, there were thirty-five people in these same six rooms. Fragments of families shared rooms; all shared the one inadequate, refrigeratorless kitchen and antiquated bath and toilet. Waiting for a single stove, some cooked all night for the next day's meals. Conditions were unspeakable; maintenance was a losing battle; it was a nightmare existence.[71]

The deterioration of Soviet housing can be traced to a number of causes. First, urbanization proceeded very rapidly. In 1920, the urban population was 20 million; by 1930, it had grown to 29.3 million; by 1939 to 55.9 million; and by 1950 to 66 million.[72] Soviet policies discouraged investment in housing and emphasized heavy industry and war-related production. Finally, World War I, the 1918–21 Civil War, and World War II resulted in destruction of vast amounts of housing. For example, between 1910 and 1924 Leningrad lost one-third of its frame houses, destroyed for fuel.[73] During World War II, 1700 towns and cities were 50 to 100 percent destroyed.[74]

[71] Ada Louise Huxtable, "Building the Soviet Society: Housing and Planning," in Harrison E. Salisbury, ed., *The Soviet Union: The Fifty Years* (1967), pp. 240–75.
[72] Sosnovy, *op. cit.*, pp. 262, 103, 203.
[73] *Ibid.*, p. 39.
[74] Huxtable, *op. cit.*, p. 240.

During the 1950's, the Soviet Union began a concentrated attack on the problem of urban housing through massive industrialized construction. Mass-production methods were necessary not only to produce large numbers of units quickly and cheaply, but because World War II left the country with a severe labor shortage. Single apartment developments include thousands of standardized units and standardized buildings. Typically, large prefabricated wall and floor panels have been used, although some completely factory-built rooms, which can be stacked within frames to form buildings, have been used. Kitchens, interior finishes, and other elements have been more functional than attractive.

The Russian housing program, thus, developed quite rapidly, and was characterized by shoddy construction in many units built during the 1950's. Five-story walk-up buildings were typical; joints between walls and ceilings often leaked; plumbing was inadequate; and developments were planned in unimaginative and unattractive ways. By the 1960's, however, standards had risen. One American observer wrote:

In the period from about 1958 to the present, the quality of Soviet housing has improved steadily. The residential structures now being erected would be acceptable *as low cost housing* anywhere in the world, including the United States.[75]

American observers of a project under construction in 1970 wrote:

Lazdynai is located in the northwestern part of Vilnius, capital of Lithuania. The project is designed to provide housing for almost 42,000 people. It will consist of 189 hectares and a population density of 367 people per hectare (150 per acre) . . . .
Floor space per flat will range from 32.7 to 78 square meters (345 to 840 square feet) . . . .
Housing in the area is being built primarily with 5-and 9-story large concrete panel blocks of flats . . . although twelve-story and . . . sixteen-story residential towers are also under construction.
The appearance of the Lazdynai project is significantly better both in quality and scale than those visited in Moscow; the only possible exception being the very high-rise apartments. The community social amenities . . . were the best seen during the Delegations's visit. There are day-care buildings, schools, shopping centers, and movie theaters. The retention of surrounding woodlands around the housing blocks is successful in giving a natural, human scale quality to the project.[76]

During the 1960's, over 23,000,000 housing units were built in the Soviet Union. Current production is over 2,500,000 units annually. Eighty

[75] A. Allan Bates, "Low Cost Housing in the Soviet Union," in Melvin R. Levin, ed., *Exploring Urban Problems* (1971), pp. 255–66.

[76] Department of Housing and Urban Development, *HUD International Brief,* #3, "The Housing Industry in the USSR" (March 1971), p. 9.

percent are built by state-owned companies, 20 percent by housing cooperatives. Rents, which do not cover construction costs, average 4 to 5 percent of family income, compared with 17 percent in the United States.[77]

Sweden

Like the Soviet Union, Sweden faced rapid urbanization, starting at the beginning of this century, with a terribly inadequate housing stock.[78] Despite some efforts of government and cooperatives, until World War II Sweden's housing stock was made up overwhelmingly of units built for profit by investors. Small units predominated; in 1939, 52.4 percent of units in 49 urban districts had one room and a kitchen; and 25.9 percent had two rooms and a kitchen.[79] The first nationwide housing census, carried out in 1945, found 21 percent of all households and 40 percent of all households with children living in overcrowded dwellings; over-

Construction of a residential section of a new town, Togliatti, on the Volga in the Soviet Union, shows use of prefabrication. Plans call for 155,000 residents, mainly workers in the new automobile plant. Theaters, hotels, schools, shopping and social facilities, and a recreation complex are also being erected. (Novosti from Sovfoto)

[77] *Ibid.*, p. 2; and Huxtable, *op. cit.*, p. 240.

[78] For an overview, see, for example, *Housing in the Nordic Countries,* by the relevant ministries of Denmark, Finland, Iceland, Norway, and Sweden, (1968); and Paul F. Wendt, *Housing Policy—The Search for Solutions* (1963).

[79] Wendt, *op. cit.*, p. 67.

633

crowded was defined as housing two or more occupants per room, not counting kitchens.[80]

Sweden has attacked its housing shortage through a variety of programs, many of which have become models for other countries with mixed economies, including the United States. During World War II, the government began granting mortgage loans to private builders, municipalities and nonprofit groups, and purchasers of homeowner housing; and guaranteeing private loans on the same properties. Capital subsidies were granted to reduce rents. Ceilings were set on rents and profits as conditions for obtaining these aids.

To complement the programs designed to stimulate construction, rents of certain groups—low-income families with children and elderly and handicapped persons—were subsidized. In 1965, 200,000 families, or almost 10 percent of all households, received such housing allowances.[81] Finally, rents have been controlled in urban areas since World War II, in privately-owned units not aided by government loans.

Sweden's comprehensive set of housing programs has proven effective in improving housing conditions. By 1960, only 8 percent of all households and 18 percent of households with children were crowded, by the standard mentioned above. During the 1960's, larger units, particularly single-family homes, grew as a proportion of new units completed. Despite this progress, however, Sweden's housing shortage has not been eliminated. Effective demand is high because incomes have risen steadily since World War II. Sweden's median household size, moreover, is very small. In 1960 only 39 percent of households were families with children. Household sizes continue to decrease with continued prosperity, so that Sweden expects 605,000 more households in 1975 than existed in 1960.[82] Finally, housing has had to compete for investment resources with industries needed to improve Sweden's ability to compete effectively in international markets.

Squatter Settlements

During the 1960's alone, some 200 million people moved into the cities of underdeveloped countries in Asia, Africa, and Latin America, adding to the growth brought about by rapid natural increase.[83] Neither governments nor economies in those cities are capable of providing housing, even at very primitive standards, for such numbers. In most cities of the

---

[80] *Housing in the Nordic Countries, op. cit.*, p. 184.

[81] *Ibid.*, p. 193.

[82] *Ibid.*, p. 206.

[83] This section draws from John F. Turner, "Uncontrolled Urban Settlement, Problems and Policies," in Gerald Breese, ed., *The City in Newly Developing Countries* (1969), pp. 507–34.

underdeveloped world, the results have been "squatter settlements," occupations of land disregarding planning and building regulations and ownership. Table 22.8 indicates the extent of those uncontrolled settlements. In Dar es Salaam, capital of Tanzania, over a third of the city's

TABLE 22.8: Extent of Uncontrolled Settlements in Various Cities in Developing Countries

Country	City	Year	City Pop.*	Uncontrolled Settlement Total*	Uncontrolled Settlement As % of City Pop.
AFRICA					
Senegal	Dakar	1969	500	150	30
Tanzania	Dar es Salaam	1967	273	98	36
Zambia	Lusaka	1967	194	53	27
ASIA					
China (Taiwan)	Taipei	1966	1,300	325	25
India	Calcutta	1961	6,700	2,220	33
Indonesia	Djakarta	1961	2,906	725	25
Iraq	Baghdad	1965	1,745	500	29
Malaysia	Kuala Lumpur	1961	400	100	25
Pakistan	Karachi	1964	2,280	752	33
Rep. of Korea	Seoul	1970	440**	137**	30
Singapore	Singapore	1966	1,870	980	15
EUROPE					
Turkey	Total Urban	1965	10,800	2,365	22
	Ankara	1965	979	460	47
		1970	1,250	750	60
	Izmir	1970	640	416	65
NORTH AND SOUTH AMERICA					
Brazil	Rio de Janeiro	1947	2,050	400	20
		1957	2,940	650	22
		1961	3,326	900	27
	Brasilia	1962	148	60	41
Chile	Santiago	1964	2,184	546	25
Colombia	Cali	1964	813	243	30
	Buenaventura	1964	111	88	80
Mexico	Mexico City	1952	2,372	330	14
		1966	3,287	1,500	46
Peru	Lima	1957	1,261	114	9
		1961	1,716	360	21
		1969	2,800	1,000	36
Venezuela	Caracas	1961	1,330	280	21
		1964	1,590	556	35
	Maracaibo	1966	559	280	50

*thousands
**dwelling units
SOURCE: U.N. General Assembly, *Housing, Building and Planning, Problems and Priorities in Human Settlements,* Report of the Secretary General August 1970, Annex III, p. 55, as cited in *Urbanization,* sector working paper, World Bank (June 1972), p. 82.

population are squatters. Similar percentages obtain in Calcutta, Karachi, and Seoul. Half of Ankara's population live in the squatter settlements, the "gecekondu," whose name describes an over-night housebuilder. One and a half million of the residents of Mexico City live in "colonias proletarias," known originally as "barrios paracaidistas," or "parachutists' neighborhoods."

Squatter settlements vary greatly in level and type of physical development and security of tenure.[84] At one end of the continuum are easily removed shelters, the residents of which have no guarantee that they will not be removed today or tomorrow. A recent article described one such settlement in Jakarta, Indonesia, made up of bamboo-framed cardboard shacks.

About 400 people live there, mostly unseen because of the Dutchbuilt flood embankment that hides them from Jakarta's wealthy residential section, Menteng, which begins about thirty yards beyond the tracks . . . .

[84] See the typology developed by Turner, *op. cit.,* p. 514.

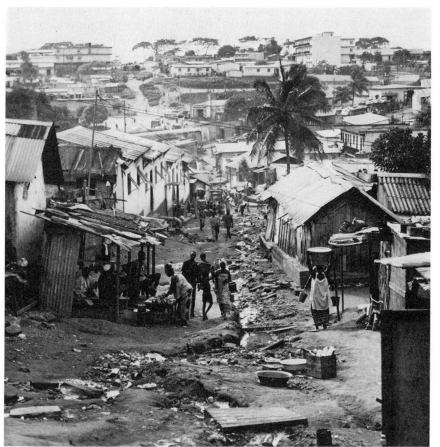

Housing the "have nots"—(top) new housing stands near slum housing in Caracas, Venezuela; (center) mud and straw houses in the poorest district of Karachi, West Pakistan; (bottom) view of the African quarter of Abidjan, Ivory Coast. (United Nations)

They have no electricity, no clean water, no sewers. Some two-thirds of Jakartans make less than 75 dollars a year. The city says nearly three-fourths live in dwellings considered inadequate and unsafe—in conditions that most Americans would not see, let alone experience, in a lifetime . . . .

One day it happened that

. . . several hundred people were burned out of their cardboard shacks along the canal. They were trucked to the outskirts and told to go back to their villages. Some did. But by late afternoon dozens had walked the four miles back and were poking through the charred ruins.[85]

In underdeveloped countries richer than Indonesia, particularly in Latin America, squatter settlements may be far more secure and comfortable. The Cuevas barriada,[86] in Lima, Peru, is one such settlement. It was established by three hundred families in an organized invasion of state-owned property in 1960. As is frequently the case in Latin America, where squatters have achieved considerable political power, Cuevas was legally recognized in 1961, and its residents' tenure was secured. Cuevas' houses are in the process of construction, carried out by their owners, sometimes with the help of paid construction workers. The majority occupy plots about 27 feet by 54 feet; walls surrounding the lots are normally built first. By 1965, the population had grown to about 12,000 in about 2000 households, mostly young nuclear families.

In 1965, Cuevas' residents had average household incomes of $1030, slightly higher than the average for Lima and three times Peru's average. The nameless Jakarta settlement and Cuevas, thus, represent far different phenomena. The four hundred people in Jakarta have been driven to the city by severe overcrowding on the land and the impossibility of making enough money to survive in rural areas. In the city, they have found few opportunities—one finds work, when he can, as a construction laborer at seventy-five cents to a dollar a day; others vend vegetables or fish door-to-door in wealthy sections, making a dollar or two a day. Cuevas represents a more desirable process of urbanization. Opportunities for employment and income in Lima far exceed those in rural areas of Peru. Per capita income in 1967, in the city as a whole, was $350, three times that of the rest of Peru and four to five times that of Indonesia. Housing institutions, however, are inadequate. Minimum standard dwellings cost only $1500, but minimum interest rates are 9 percent and the cheapest available building lots cost $750 to $1000.

[85] James B. Sterba, "The Jobless and Their Problems Jam Asian Cities," *The New York Times* (March 20, 1973), p. 12.

[86] Horacio Caminos, John F. Turner, and John A. Steffian, *Urban Dwelling Environments* (1969), pp. 131–44. Lisa Peattie, *The View From the Barrio* (1970) provides a detailed view of life in a squatter settlement in Ciudad Guayana, Venezuela, in which Peattie, an anthropologist, lived for some time.

Residents like those of Cuevas, as a result, have gone about building homes for themselves outside traditional property and housing institutions.

Summary

This chapter has presented, first, several examples of housing in diverse neighborhood settings, indicating the central role played by housing in defining, although not causing, the variations in life styles. The way in which housing types interact with various phases of family life similarly indicates that house type is the stage that facilitates or constrains the "playing" of specific roles. The effect of substandard housing on its residents is a question of special interest in this regard.

Our consideration of the characteristics of housing in the United States revealed several paradoxes. Despite substantial increases in housing quality, especially in suburban areas, large numbers of the American people remain ill-housed and housing deterioration and abandonment are problems. Despite the government's many programs to provide decent housing for low and moderate income families, no reliable methods have been found for achieving this end, and increasing numbers of Americans have resorted to low-cost mobile homes. Despite the advances and breakthroughs in providing housing for black Americans, they still pay more for inferior housing. Finally, comparing the United States with other countries such as the Soviet Union, Sweden, and developing areas, we find that there are fundamental differences in the physical problems faced as well as in the underlying values and priorities.

Selected Bibliography

BOOKS

Aaron, Henry, *Shelter and Subsidies*. Washington, D.C.: The Brookings Institution, 1972.

Abrams, Charles, *Man's Struggle for Shelter in an Urbanizing World*. Cambridge, Mass.: The MIT Press, 1964.

Bradburn, Norman, Seymour Sudman, and Galen Gockel, *Side by Side: Integrated Neighborhoods in America*. Chicago: Quadrangle Books, 1971.

Building the American City. Report of the National Commission on Urban Problems, Washington, D.C.: Government Printing Office, 1968.

Downs, Anthony, *Federal Housing Subsidies: How Are They Working?* Lexington, Mass.: D.C. Heath, Lexington Books, 1973.

Feagin, Joe R., Charles Tilly, and Constance W. Williams, *Subsidizing the Poor: A Boston Housing Experiment.* Lexington, Mass.: D.C. Heath, Lexington Books, 1972.

Fried, Joseph P., *Housing Crisis, U.S.A.* New York: Praeger, 1971.

Johnson, Sheila K., *Idle Haven: Community Building among the Working-Class Retired.* Berkeley, Calif.: University of California Press, 1971.

Lansing, John B., Charles W. Clifton, and James Morgan, *New Homes and Poor People: A Study of Chains of Moves.* Ann Arbor, Mich.: Institute for Social Research, 1969.

Mandelker, Daniel R., *Housing Subsidies in the United States and England.* Indianapolis, Ind.: Bobbs-Merrill, 1973.

———, and Roger Montgomery, eds., *Housing in America: Problems and Perspectives.* Indianapolis, Ind.: Bobbs-Merrill, 1973.

Michelson, William, *Man and his Urban Environment.* Reading, Mass.: Addison-Wesley, 1970.

Molotch, Harvey Luskin, *Managed Integration: Dilemmas of Doing Good in the City.* Berkeley, Calif.: University of California Press, 1972.

Newman, Oscar, *Defensible Space: Crime Prevention through Urban Design.* New York: Macmillan, Collier Books, 1973.

Pétonnet, Colette, translated by Rita Smidt, *Those People: The Subculture of a Housing Project.* Westport, Conn.: Greenwood Press, Inc., 1973.

Pynoos, Jon, Robert Schafer, and Chester Hartman, eds., *Housing Urban America.* Chicago: Aldine, 1973.

Rainwater, Lee, *Behind Ghetto Walls: Black Family Life in a Federal Slum.* Chicago: Aldine, 1970.

Saltman, Juliet Z., *Open Housing as a Social Movement: Challenge, Conflict and Change.* Lexington, Mass.: D.C. Heath, 1971.

Schorr, Alvin, *Slums and Social Insecurity.* Washington, D.C.: Social Security Administration, Department of Health, Education, and Welfare, 1963.

Stegman, Michael, ed., *Housing and Economics: The America Dilemma.* Cambridge, Mass.: The MIT Press, 1970.

———, *Housing Investment in the Inner City: The Dynamics of Decline.* Cambridge, Mass.: The MIT Press, 1972.

Sternlieb, George, and Bernard Indik, *The Ecology of Welfare: Housing and the Welfare Crisis in New York City.* New York: Transaction Books, distributed by E.P. Dutton and Co., 1973.

———, Lynne Sagalyn, and Virginia Paulers, eds., *Housing.* New York: AMS Press, 1973.

———, *The Tenement Landlord.* New Brunswick, N.J.: Rutgers University Press, 1969.

———, and Robert W. Burchell, *Residential Abandonment: The Tenement Landlord Revisited.* New Brunswick, N.J.: Center for Urban Policy Research, Rutgers University, 1973.

Wilson, James Q., ed., *Urban Renewal: The Record and the Controversy.* Cambridge, Mass.: The MIT Press, 1966.

ARTICLES

Abrams, Charles, "Housing Policy, 1937–1967," in Bernard Frieden and W.W. Nash, eds., *Shaping an Urban Future: Essays in Memory of Catherine Bauer Wurster.* Cambridge, Mass.: The MIT Press, 1969, pp. 35–47.

Cagle, L.T., and Irwin Deutscher, "Housing Aspiration and Housing Achievement: The Relocation of Poor Families," *Social Problems*, 24 (Fall 1970), 243–56.

Canter, D., and R. Thorne, "Attitudes to Housing: A Cross-Cultural Comparison," *Environment and Behavior,* 4 (March 1972), 3–33.

King, A. Thomas, and P. Mieszkowski, "Racial Discrimination, Segregation, and the Price of Housing," *Journal of Political Economy, 81* (May/June 1973), 590–606.

Leeds, Anthony, "The Significant Variables Determining the Character of Squatter Developments," *America Latina*, 12 (July/September 1969), 44–85.

Mangin, William, "Squatter Settlements," *Scientific American,* 217 (October 1967), 3–11.

Michelson, William, "Human Interaction with the Physical Environment," *Encyclopedia of Social Work,* 1971 edition, 290–304.

Portes, A., "The Urban Slum in Chile: Types and Correlates," *Land Economics,* 47 (August 1971), 235–48.

Stegman, Michael, "The New Mythology of Housing," *Trans-Action* (now *Society*), 7 (January 1970), 55–62.

Turner, John F., "Uncontrolled Urban Settlement: Problems and Policies," in Gerald Breese, ed., *The City in Newly Developing Countries.* Englewood Cliffs, N.J.: Prentice-Hall, 1969, pp. 507–34.

Yancey, William L., "Architecture, Interaction, and Social Control: The Case of a Large-Scale Public Housing Project," *Environment and Behavior,* 3 (March 1971), 3–21.

23 • Urban Planning

Urban planning, also commonly called "city planning," is a means of directing cities' physical and social growth and change to provide a more healthy, pleasant, and prosperous environment. Most broadly, planning has been defined as "a method for delineating goals and ways of achieving them."[1] Urban planning can emphasize physical, social, or economic aspects. "Metropolitan planning" attempts to apply the same methods to metropolitan areas as a whole; "regional planning" applies similar techniques to an even broader area, but usually emphasizes provisions for economic growth more than does urban planning. This chapter will not deal with economic planning or physical planning, except tangentially. Thus, we will not discuss such topics as locational costs, the occupational and income base of communities, or architecture, site planning, and urban design, important as these and other aspects of planning may be.

Our focus will be on social planning, itself a large topic. As Warren points out, there are two orientations to social planning. They differ in how they relate the planning process to the sociopolitical context in which it occurs.[2] The first social planning model is abstract and rational. It holds that the planning process should be confined to the technical problems at hand, such as, getting the low-income housing built, installing more public facilities for educational and medical care; at the same time it accepts, or at least ignores as not amenable to planning, the values and priorities guiding the planning process. In contrast the second model involves directly "attacking 'social problems' through concerted purposeful effort"[3] and is therefore characterized as concrete and processual. Thus, planners participate in the sociopolitical process and attempt to alter the governing values and priorities, at least in some measure, rather than accepting them as given. American urban plan-

---

[1] Julius Gould and William Kolb, eds., *A Dictionary of the Social Sciences* (1964), pp. 503-4.
[2] Roland Warren, "Two Models of Social Planning," in his *Truth, Love, and Social Change, and Other Essays in Community Change* (1971), pp.54-71.
[3] *Ibid.*, p. 55.

Some problems for urban planning: traffic congestion in Istanbul, Turkey (top) and smog enveloping the towers of Manhattan (bottom). (top—Turkish Information Office, N.Y.; bottom—Aero Service Corporation)

ners have tended to employ the second model more frequently in recent years, and many of the case studies described in this chapter illustrate this model.

Substantively, social planning can be applied to a number of fields, among them urban education, housing and slum clearance, transportation, welfare and social services, community organization, and medical care. In addition to studying urban (or metropolitan or regional) planning, social planners are also typically trained in a traditional discipline, such as, sociology, political science, economics, public administration, or law. Most urban planners are employed by municipal, county, state, or federal government, although some are employed by private groups, firms, colleges and universities, and some are independent consultants.[4]

The Birth of American Urban Planning[5]

Many cities have at one time or another been "planned," as frontier settlements, fortresses, market places, capitals or religious centers. But modern urban planning is a product of the late nineteenth and the twentieth centuries. It is one current in a very broad and diverse worldwide movement toward planning.

In the nineteenth century, social thinkers began to perceive that industrialization could overcome man's poverty, and that society's problems would no longer result so much from scarcity as from social institutions' inability to properly use industrialism's immense productive power. Socialist thinkers and, later, socialist states, proposed and used "planning" to replace the market as a means of allocating productive resources and consumer goods. Capitalist thinkers and states used "planning" to overcome inefficiencies and injustices created by market mechanisms and to make those mechanisms work more smoothly. Later, newly independent nations saw planning as a means of using their limited resources to produce the fastest possible economic growth.

Beginnings

American urban planning, like European, grew up in response to problems caused by the rapid, chaotic growth of cities. The seventeenth and eighteenth centuries saw the foundation of Philadelphia, Washington,

---

[4] For a description, updated annually, of employment patterns of urban planners, see "Employment Outlook for Urban Planners," *Occupational Outlook Handbook,* U.S. Department of Labor, Bureau of Labor Statistics.

[5] Much of this section is drawn from Mel Scott, *American City Planning* (1969).

Savannah, and many other cities, where detailed and often beautiful plans are still visible in street and building arrangements.[6] These were essentially architectural designs, often geometric in form. But in the decades preceding and following the Civil War, American cities grew at such extraordinary rates that public planning was virtually precluded. In the 1880's alone Chicago grew by 600,000, New York City and Brooklyn together by 540,000, and Philadelphia by 200,000. The smaller cities of Minneapolis and Omaha grew by, respectively, 251 percent and 360 percent.[7] Horse-drawn, steam, and electric streetcars allowed city workers to reside farther from their workplaces, leading to even more rapid growth in urbanized land area. As important, a dominant ideology of unrestrained competition made it impossible for city governments to control growth, with often disastrous results for some urban residents.

Between 1890 and 1920 two major streams of civil reform converged to create American urban planning, particularly land use planning. On the one hand were local business elites, concerned with obtaining the benefits of economic and population growth for their own cities. In the 1880's, a fierce competition developed over which major city would host the Columbian exposition commemorating the 400th anniversary of the discovery of America. Chicago's appointment in 1890 and her 1893 Exposition led to one vision of the properly planned city. Magnificent railway stations and public buildings provided entry to an orderly and prosperous commercial center. From the center, treelined parkways would lead to preserves of nature on the periphery, providing recreation and quiet for the city's residents. By 1900, such techniques of urban design had come together in the "City Beautiful" movement.

At the same time, local business elites were concerned with more practical problems, problems that if fully addressed would often actually require higher property taxes, even though lower taxes were generally sought. In many cities, speculative builders and land subdividers ignored orderly plans for city expansion, requiring wasteful installation of sewer and water mains and expensive payments when streets were built across developed property. Businessmen and property owners were also concerned with events that might affect the "tax base," the value of taxable real estate in a municipality.

On the other hand were settlement house workers and others concerned with conditions affecting the poor. Tenement house districts were subjected to intensive study. They were found to have incredible densities—986.4 persons per acre in one area of New York in 1894;[8] housing units with terribly inadequate light, air, and sanitary facilities; and no

---

[6] See John W. Reps, *The Making of Urban America* (1965).

[7] Scott, *op. cit.,* p. 2; Adna Ferrin Weber, *The Growth of Cities in the Nineteenth Century* (1899), is a classic study of the growth of cities during this period.

[8] Scott, *op. cit.,* p. 10.

parks or playgrounds. Beginning in 1889 in New York, American cities began to impose minimum standards for construction of tenements. Parks in urban areas became a major concern of planners.

These two concerns, for displaying and insuring the city's business success and dignity on the one hand and for uplifting the poor and Americanizing foreign immigrants on the other, have often been in opposition. American urban planning has attempted to serve both ends, usually serving the former far more successfully than the latter, and the tension between them is still evident today.

In 1917, fifty-two landscape architects, engineers, and members of other professions founded the American City Planning Institute, later called the American Institute of Planners. By that date, a doctrine and set of legal tools for urban planning had been developed. These early professional planners stressed, above all, the economic value of city plans.[9] Plans led to local government efficiency, as public buildings, streets, and utilities could be provided in the most economical manner and paid for by orderly repayment of long-term bonds. Planning and expenditure for civic improvements were seen as increasing investment in a city and thereby increasing its property tax base. Thus, Nelson P. Lewis, writing in 1916,[10] argued that construction of Central Park had caused the value of surrounding properties to increase at a rate four times New York City's average between 1858 and 1873. Planning was seen as making more efficient business possible through easier transportation and healthier and more satisfied workers.

The early advocates of city planning also claimed it would benefit the poor. But over time and with a gradual change in the makeup of their leadership, planners altered their priorities. In their efforts to win acceptance from businessmen, some planners by 1916 seemed to have given up earlier commitments to the poor. The first National Conferences on City Planning, held in 1909 and 1910, dealt pricipally with planning as a means of solving social problems; after 1911, however, the conferences were dominated more and more by architects and landscape architects little interested in housing and other social reforms. The annual conferences held major sessions on housing only once between 1912 and 1931.[11]

Earlier, many planners had looked to German models of ways planning could be used to improve living conditions for the poor. Various German cities had used "excess condemnation" to acquire land outside their borders, made profits by holding this land until development surrounded

[9] John Nolen, ed., *City Planning* (1916), includes arguments by many of the era's most important planners.

[10] Nelson P. Lewis, *The Planning of the Modern City* (1916), pp. 175-84.

[11] James G. Coke, "Antecedents of Local Planning," in William I. Goodman, ed., *Principles and Practice of Urban Planning* (1968), pp. 21-2, 26. See also Scott, *op. cit.*, pp. 127-33.

it, and used these profits to build low-rent housing. In Nolen's 1916 *City Planning,* however, Frederick Law Olmsted, perhaps the most prestigious city planner of the time, decisively rejected the German models.[12]

Thus, urban planning has received probably its most important support from the larger local business establishments and property holders. Alan Altschuler has related business control of urban planning to the fact that it, unlike other sorts of planning, has received acceptance in the United States:

> The opponents of planning have recognized the difference [between local urban planning and national economic planning] by focusing their attention on national rather than local planning efforts. Businessmen have been the primary patrons of the urban planning movement in America since its beginnings. As the planning movement has matured, moreover, fewer and fewer large property owners and executives have seen anything ironical about their providing the primary base of political support for local land-use planning while continuing bitterly to oppose anything remotely resembling national economic planning. The major reason for the survival of this apparent inconsistency has probably been that leaders of property-oriented groups have lacked confidence that they could control planning at the Federal level under the President.[13]

By 1920, legal tools had been created to insure orderly development of each major aspect of the city. First of all, zoning was rapidly becoming American urban planning's most important tool. Zoning is the division of a municipality or other jurisdictions into districts and the regulation within those districts of the height and bulk of buildings, the area of the lot that may be built upon, the density of population, and the use of buildings and land for trade, industry, residences, or other purposes. Typically, early zoning plans established districts for single-family homes, apartments, businesses, and industry. Later, homes would be prohibited in industrial areas as well as vice versa, and immensely detailed and complex zoning ordinances would be developed. With these controls, local political figures gained significantly in power, and the "selling" of zoning variances became a source of municipal graft. During the 1920's, many cities and towns adopted zoning without developing comprehensive city plans; in many cases zoning's popularity stemmed from the fact that it stabilized and insured the value of upper- and middle-income residential properties.

A second set of tools regulated traffic and utilities. By 1920, the problem of enforcing street plans had been solved in most states, and urban planners were developing principles of street design and traffic control. Utilities, of course, were controlled either by public ownership or by conditions of franchise contracts.

Finally, urban planning concerned itself with providing public facili-

[12] Frederick Law Olmsted, "Introduction" in Nolen, *op. cit.,* pp. 14-16.
[13] Alan Altschuler, *The City Planning Process* (1965), pp. 323-24.

ties of all sorts. After the 1890's, under the influence of the Chicago Exposition, some cities planned magnificent civic centers. Interest in such centers continued, but at the same time planners and other reformers worked to regularize procedures for all sorts of public construction. City planning commissions, the most common governmental form for planning, were established in many cities. In the widely followed Standard City Planning Enabling Act of 1927, such commissions were separated from politics by nonpartisanship and long-term, overlapping appointments.

In urban planning doctrine, comprehensive plans, general documents looking forward ten or twenty years and covering land-use, circulation, and public investment, were to provide bases by which particular proposals could be judged. In many cities, however, zoning plans and other measures were adopted without comprehensive plans or with plans so general as to be meaningless, often, apparently, because discussion and adoption of meaningful comprehensive plans would cause endless political difficulty. Later, many planners were to attribute many of their profession's difficulties to this fact.[14]

Precedents of the 1930's[15]

The 1930's saw a major break in the course of American politics. Starting late in 1929, the United States suffered her most severe and prolonged depression; by 1933 the national income stood at less than half what it had been in 1929.

The New Deal established a real if very ambivalent public commitment to provide decent housing for the poor.[16] In 1934 the National Recovery Administration began building Public Housing in a number of cities. The first priority of the new program was to provide employment in construction; provision of housing was an important but secondary consideration. In 1937, a Public Housing program was approved by Congress. It was placed under control of local authorities; the principle was established that Public Housing should be available only to families for whom the private market could not provide housing; and the notion of demolishing one slum dwelling for each unit built was established.

In their attempts to deal with masses of unemployed people, local, state, and Federal authorities and voluntary agencies found it more necessary than ever before to try to coordinate their efforts. During the Depression's early years, social workers, government officials, and voluntary agencies laid the foundations for "social services planning." After

---

[14] T.J. Kent, *The Urban General Plan* (1964).

[15] See, particularly, Scott, *op. cit.*, pp. 270-367; and Arthur M. Schlesinger, Jr., *The Coming of the New Deal* (1959).

[16] On the changing nature of that commitment, see Alvin Schorr, *Slums and Social Insecurity* (1963).

World War II, structures for planning welfare and health expenditures were built on these foundations, and during the 1960's some urban planners would begin to work with social welfare planning agencies.

Urban Planning after World War II

In the postwar period, urban planners developed new and more sophisticated legal and analytical tools. Zoning was refined to influence land-use and architecture in very specific directions. Some larger cities established historic districts to control demolition and alteration of the exteriors of buildings in areas of historical interest. In many areas, zoning ordinances were used to encourage suburban builders to construct "planned unit developments," including clustered houses, row houses, sometimes apartments, and substantial open space, rather than single family houses on individual lots.

Conflicts arose over many suburban governments' use of zoning. By the late 1960's, large areas around major cities had been rezoned to require single family houses on large lots. Civil rights groups, liberals, and some planners have pointed out that such zoning excludes poorer people, particularly blacks, by making only expensive housing available. Suburban governments frequently argue that large-lot zoning is necessary to avoid having to provide services for groups—specifically low-income families in low-value houses—whose property taxes would not pay for those services. At the same time, urban and suburban governments often use zoning to compete for commercial and industrial land uses that more than pay in property taxes for the services they require.

By 1970, zoning and similar controls had become extraordinarily subtle tools for accomplishing almost any purpose related to land use. The need to regulate urban growth and to open the suburbs to lower-income residents led to discussion of the possibilities of state and Federal land-use policies and controls, a highly charged political issue.

During the 1950's, transportation planners—mainly engineers planning the interstate highway system—developed elaborate means for measuring the need for highways. Some urban planners often found themselves in opposition to highway plans, as they caused difficulties in carrying out municipal plans. Older, established neighborhoods, particularly if they were in poor areas, were sometimes disrupted or demolished by new expressways, whose routes were selected without regard to the very limited opportunities for relocation of the displaced population. By the early 1960's, moreover, it had become evident that the need for highways could not be predicted simply by calculating numbers of people going to work, school, recreation, or shopping. Rather, new roads

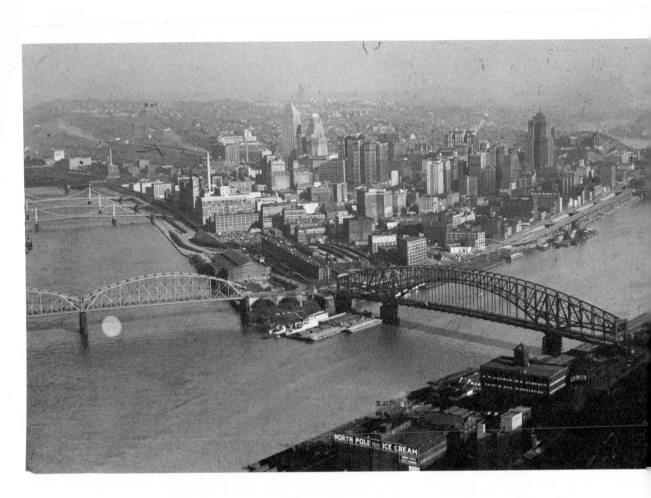

themselves generated development in new areas and, even within older areas, generated auto travel that might not otherwise have taken place. By 1970, urban planners had developed techniques for modeling these relationships with the aid of computers. Some concerned themselves with the need to build fewer highways and more mass transportation facilities.

From the 1950's until the middle 1960's, "metropolitan government" was a topic of intense concern among some planners and civic reform groups. With the growth of postwar suburbs, it seemed that tax base, housing, and transportation problems could not be solved as long as responsibilities were divided in each metropolitan area, among dozens of municipalities and scores of school, water, sanitation, police, and park districts. These concerns were not new; as early as the 1890's a concerted, if unsuccessful, movement for metropolitan government had taken place in Boston. Nor were they limited to the United States. A greater London government was formed in 1963, and Toronto has had one of the most successful experiments in metropolitan government, established in 1953. In the United States, however, this most recent movement for metropolitan government seemingly faced overwhelming

The rebuilding of Pittsburgh's central business district, the Golden Triangle, has altered the appearance of the city. The photo on the left was taken in 1948, the one on the right in 1973. (Associated Photographers, Inc.)

odds. Suburban communities were reluctant to become involved in central city problems; and newly powerful groups in cities, particularly blacks, frequently failed to see why they should submerge their numbers and power in wider governments. Some successful metropolitan governments have been formed; Indianapolis and Miami have them, for example, and also Jacksonville, where the black community was mainly in support of the move. In general, however, the movement has not had wide success. More frequently, such problems have been solved by associations of governments or creation of limited-purpose governmental districts. Transportation districts in many metropolitan areas are the best examples of the latter sort of solution.

By the late 1960's, the profession of urban planning had grown to considerable proportions. In 1954, 187 graduate students had been enrolled in urban planning programs. By 1968, 2500 students were enrolled in urban planning studies and 875 professional degrees were awarded.[17] Sixty schools offered graduate studies.

---

[17] Thomas E. Nutt and Lawrence E. Susskind, "Prospects for Urban Planning Education," *Journal of the American Institute of Planners,* 36 (July 1970), pp. 229-41.

Planning for Whom?—A Case Study of Minneapolis

During the 1960's, a number of studies reported problems of the profession. One of the most interesting is Altschuler's case study of planning in Minneapolis and St. Paul from 1958 through 1962.[18] Altschuler found there was relatively little interest in planning on the part of politically significant groups. One of the cases he related is that of the "Plan for Central Minneapolis."

During the middle 1950's, Minneapolis businessmen and politicians, concerned about the likely impact of the Federal highway program, the growth of suburban shopping centers, and the departure of several corporate headquarters to the suburbs, sought to revive an inactive planning department by recruiting a planning director and assistant director from other cities. After a year of research by consultants, the planners became convinced that proper handling of traffic was the key to continued prosperity for downtown Minneapolis. In the "Plan for Central Minneapolis," they proposed construction of a large parking garage at the edge of the downtown district; a traffic ring; closing alternating streets to create "superblocks" and pedestrian malls; and tight controls over the sorts of businesses that could locate in various parts of the downtown area.

Their proposals, however, had little apparent effect. Politicians and other city officials opposed the parking garage proposal because it would have required immense expenditures. Downtown businessmen felt most aspects of the plan were impractical and imposed unduly rigid controls on private property. In fact, only one part of the "Plan" was put into effect: a proposal to limit downtown Minneapolis's most important shopping street to pedestrian and bus traffic.

To Altschuler, the experience in Minneapolis raises two important questions about planning. First, he questions whether planning in fact has significant effects. Central Minneapolis has continued to prosper, but this seems to have resulted far more from its own characteristics than from the work of planners. Second, and even more important, Altschuler questions whether planners serve any real "public interest" in their attempts to find constituencies interested in working for realization of their plans. This question goes to the heart of the relationship between planning and politics. In the Minneapolis case, Altschuler questions whether the expensive parking facility and expressway the planners proposed would not have drawn resources needed elsewhere for purposes at least as worthwhile; and why the planners did not pay attention to such obvious needs as low-rent housing to replace the 19,000 units that would be cleared for the freeway and other downtown projects.

Altschuler is a political scientist rather than a planner. The com-

[18] Altschuler, *op. cit.*

promises of "comprehensive planning" principles that he discusses are understandably viewed differently by some pro-business members of the planning professions. However, they have not so much disputed the facts of cases like those he discusses as reinterpreted them.[19] Nonetheless, strains caused by the difficulty of upholding professional planning principles while building local constituencies are readily evident in the literature, history, and current practice of urban planning.

Urban Renewal

Despite increasingly sophisticated techniques in zoning and transportation planning, the urban renewal program—both in what it accomplished and what it failed to do—seems to have had more profound effects on post-World War II urban planning in the United States. Urban renewal has led planners to attempt "social planning," to apply planning techniques to insure high employment, the availability of social and health services and other elements of urban residents' welfare. Urban planning has become answerable to black and Spanish-speaking minorities as well as other communities.

Title I of the Housing Act of 1949 created the urban renewal program. The act provided Federal aid to local authorities to acquire land, relocate its commercial and residential tenants, demolish its structures, and sell it to private developers for redevelopment according to approved plans. Legally, state urban renewal enabling legislation provided for the first time that the power of condemnation could be used for public purposes —rebuilding privately-owned commercial areas, for example—as well as for public uses like schools or publicly-owned housing.[20]

The idea of urban renewal was supported by a working coalition of liberals and planners, who saw the program as a means of dealing with slums, on one hand, and major investors on the other. Before the end of World War II, insurance companies and other major investors foresaw both a lack of opportunities to invest in housing and the possibility of a major recession after the war. They looked to urban renewal as a means of obtaining centrally located sites for apartment investments. Local real estate and business interests in many cities saw the program as a means of protecting their investments—whether in department stores or in housing—from the decline of the city around them.

The 1949 act also provided for low-income housing. It authorized

---

[19] Several writers in F. Stuart Chapin and Shirley F. Weiss, eds., *Urban-Growth Dynamics* (1962), make such arguments.

[20] Urban renewal has been studied rather extensively. Martin Anderson, *The Federal Bulldozer* (1965), and Scott Greer, *Urban Renewal and American Cities* (1965), are general studies of the program. Jewel Bellush and Murray Hausknecht, eds., *Urban Renewal: People, Politics and Planning* (1967), and James Q. Wilson, ed., *Urban Renewal* (1966) are collections of key articles, data, and arguments on the program.

construction of 810,000 units of Public Housing by 1954, or 135,000 per year. Construction of these units was seen as necessary for families to be moved from urban renewal sites. Unfortunately, Public Housing, both nationally and in most cities, failed to receive the political support necessary to bring about construction of the numbers of units needed by families relocated from urban renewal sites and, after 1956, highway paths. Herbert Gans has summarized the results in terms of their effects on emptying and rebuilding slums:

The slums cannot be emptied unless and until there is more low-cost housing elsewhere. Private enterprise cannot afford to build such housing. The traditional solution has been to rely on public housing, but thanks to the opposition of the real-estate men and the private builders, it has never been supplied in large enough amounts. Even then, it had to be located in the slums, because other city districts were unwilling to give over vacant or industrial land. In order to minimize clearance, public housing has had to resort to elevator buildings, and in order to protect itself from the surrounding slums, it has constructed fenced-in projects. In order to satisfy its powerful opponents that it was not wasting tax money on n'er-do-wells, it has had to impose institutional restrictions on its hapless occupants, and in order to avoid competition with the private housing market, it has been forced to expel tenants whose income rises above a certain level.[21]

Thus, the urban renewal program has failed to achieve its major purpose, to help those who lived in slums. In fact, it has caused a major reduction in the supply of low-cost housing. The National Commission on Urban Problems has estimated that 1,054,000 dwelling units were demolished by public action connected to Federal programs by 1967, and it cites a National Association of Home Builders estimate that all public actions resulted in demolition of 2.38 million homes between 1950 and 1968 and private action in the demolition of an additional 2.35 million units.[22] Urban renewal itself appears to have caused more than 500,000 of these demolitions. At the same time, only 460,000 units of low-rent Public Housing were built in the eighteen years between 1949 and 1967, despite the 1949 call for construction of 810,000 units by 1954.

For low-income families relocated from urban renewal sites, the reduction in the supply of low-cost housing has been expensive at best. Available data suggest they have obtained no better housing after relocation than before and have paid somewhat greater proportions of their incomes for it. The impact of urban renewal on nonwhite families, over half those relocated, has been substantially greater than its impact on white families.[23]

[21] Herbert Gans, *People and Plans* (1968), p. 32.

[22] National Commission on Urban Problems, *Building the American City* (1969), pp. 82-83.

[23] See U.S. Housing and Home Finance Agency, "The Housing of Relocated Families," in Wilson, *op. cit.,* pp. 336-52, and Chester Hartman, "The Housing of Relocated Families," in the same book, pp. 293-335, and Hartman's "Displaced Persons," *Society* 9 (July/August 1972), pp. 53-65.

Nor does the urban renewal program appear to have succeeded in its other major goal, rebuilding central cities by making them more attractive to investors, shoppers, and residents. Scott Greer argues that those projects that have succeeded would have succeeded as private real estate investments.[24] In other cities, or in poorer locations in the same cities, renewal authorities have been unable to find private investors for already acquired and cleared renewal land.

Given these failures, the questions arise of why the program has been continued and how it has been used. Local authorities have put urban renewal to a wide variety of uses. Perhaps most commonly, it has been used in attempts to revive downtown areas by ridding them of poor and black residents and unsightly land uses and providing new commercial space and housing. Civic, convention, and office centers have been built in many cities, although others have found no private market for such land.

CASE STUDIES IN CHICAGO AND BOSTON   The program has also been used to upgrade the neighborhoods of urban institutions. In the late 1950's Rossi and Dentler studied urban renewal in the Hyde Park-Kenwood section of Chicago, where the University of Chicago is located.[25] The University was designated by the city to plan renewal for the neighborhood. Its purposes were to "stabilize" the neighborhood to insure that its staff could continue to live in Hyde Park-Kenwood and to provide for institutional expansion. To Rossi and Dentler, the University's planners succeeded in the former but failed in the latter.

In South West Hyde Park, a Neighborhood Redevelopment Corporation was formed, and was dominated by the University. Its principal target was a two-block area of rather run-down homes mainly owned by black residents. After much discussion, the Corporation succeeded in obtaining the property, but its actions left considerable bitterness in the area. Rossi and Dentler's findings seem to indicate that, at least in South West Hyde Park, "stabilizing" the neighborhood, in effect, meant removing not only certain buildings but certain people.

Urban renewal was applied elsewhere in mainly residential neighborhoods, using various subsidy programs to build "moderate income" housing on cleared sites. Keyes studied urban renewal in Boston during the early 1960's when these techniques were employed.[26]

He also studied Charlestown, a low-income Irish community. It has old housing, very low rentals, and is well-organized in informal groups, although the community has few formal organizations. In the late 1950's, a plan had been developed which would have required clearance of much of Charlestown's housing. In 1960, planning work for Charles-

[24] Greer, *op. cit.*, pp. 170ff.

[25] Peter H. Rossi and Robert A. Dentler, *The Politics of Urban Renewal* (1961).

[26] Langley Carlton Keyes, *The Rehabilitation Planning Game* (1969).

town began, but this plan had to be abandoned because of public opposition. Eventually, after extensive conflict among the Boston Renewal Authority and various Charlestown groups, a plan was developed which, to Keyes, ideally served the needs of the community. It included removal of an old, unsightly elevated railroad; very extensive rehabilitation, which was possible without forcing families to move because the original rents were very low; and construction of new housing on scattered sites, originally vacant or occupied by the area's very worst buildings. To Keyes, the Charlestown project was successful because there were no groups seen as "undesirable" by those who participated in the planning process.

The Washington Park Urban Renewal Project is located in Roxbury, Boston's largest black community. Keyes saw Roxbury's major interest groups as the black "elite," middle-income people most of whom live in upper Roxbury; blue-collar workers; and the "black proletariat." The latter two groups live mainly in lower and middle Roxbury, and Keyes distinguishes them not so much by income as by life style. "The black proletariat," apparently, is considered "undesirable" by other members of the community.

Planning in Washington Park resulted in a project which removed much of the area's low-cost housing, to the satisfaction of the upper Roxbury elite and many of Roxbury's blue-collar workers. Assurances were given that relocation would be carried out sensitively, but no detailed plans were revealed during the planning process. Keyes writes of the project:

> The passivity of those about to be bulldozed offers a striking contrast to the kind of response that such a proposal would have drawn forth in Charlestown. Moreover, with the rise of Black militancy in the middle 1960's, it is doubtful that such a clearance proposal could be made today without evoking either massive resistance or the demand for much firmer guarantees of relocation housing.[27]

Little work has been done on the effects of urban renewal in smaller cities and few studies have followed renewal projects much beyond the completion of planning. Nonetheless, the available studies seem to point toward a reason why the program has been continued despite its lack of success in rebuilding slums or saving cities: urban renewal has frequently been useful to various interest groups who wish to remove "undesirable" neighbors and who would benefit from the federal subsidies.

The Federal government has attempted to deal with the problems of urban renewal mainly through better coordination rather than by attacking the problem of low-rent housing supply. Starting in 1954, cities

[27] *Ibid.,* p. 183.

participating in urban renewal were required to develop "Workable Programs," including housing codes, comprehensive plans, plans for relocation, and plans for citizen participation. The Housing Act of 1959 authorized assistance for much broader planning through the "Community Renewal Program," which provided grants for cities to make broad studies and long-range plans for renewal, rehabilitation, or preservation of their entire areas. During the 1960's, Federal subsidies were instituted for "moderate-income" housing; such projects were frequently developed by nonprofit community groups. In 1966, the Model Cities program was passed, calling on selected cities to plan coordinated attacks on their physical and social problems. Its purposes were exceptionally broad:

to rebuild or revitalize large slum and blighted areas; to expand housing, job, and income opportunities; to reduce dependence on welfare payments; to improve educational facilities and programs; to combat disease and ill health; to reduce the incidence of crime and delinquency; to enhance recreational and cultural opportunities; to establish better access between homes and jobs; to improve living conditions . . .

These programs have created numerous job opportunities for urban planners and provided an entry for the poor into the planning process. As important, they have brought the profession into different contact with poor, particularly minority communities. During the 1960's, planners began to recognize such communities' problems could not be solved by approaches like urban renewal, that dealing directly with problems like lack of job opportunities and poor schools was essential. Particularly after the shortcomings of the urban renewal program became evident, some planners finally turned to a type of "social planning" that attempted to attack such problems directly.[28] Others developed models of planners as advocates for poor communities faced with renewal or other programs.[29]

Legislation in other fields has followed the urban renewal program's attempt to deal with problems through coordinated, if sometimes unrealistic, attacks. Psychiatrists and others interested in mental health have attempted to launch a coordinated attack on problems of mental health associated with poverty.[30] Perhaps most significantly, the conceptions on

[28] See, for example, Leo F. Schnore and Henry Fagin, eds., *Urban Research and Policy Planning* (1967), and Edward M. Kaitz and H.H. Hyman, *Urban Planning for Social Welfare* (1970).

[29] See Paul Davidoff, "Advocacy and Pluralism in Planning," *Journal of the American Institute of Planners* 31 (November 1965), 331-38; and Lisa R. Peattie, "Reflections on Advocacy Planning," *Journal of the American Institute of Planners* 34 (March 1968), 80-88.

[30] Leonard J. Duhl, ed., *The Urban Condition* (1963) includes articles representing this position.

which the antipoverty programs of the Johnson administration were founded drew heavily from the experience of urban renewal.

In helping to carry out urban renewal and some of the social welfare programs instituted during the 1960's, urban planners continued to suffer the tension between planning as a means of benefiting communities' dominant groups and planning as a means of benefiting the poor and dispossessed.

Some Examples of Planning Abroad

Not surprisingly, urban planning abroad reflects an immense variety of economic, political, cultural, geographic, and intellectual factors. To describe them in any systematic way is impossible here, but several examples of how various factors interact to produce varying types of urban planning will be presented briefly. Urban planning is a complex process and therefore simple transferrals of planning strategies from one nation to another are seldom possible; the answer to "why don't we do it like them?" is usually "because we are not like them"! In many European countries, for example, the government at the level corresponding to our federal government has much more central authority; power at local political levels (state or city in United States terms) is relatively unimportant and hence there is little opposition to central planning and, in fact, the central government builds most of the housing. In some European countries like Britain and Sweden the central government also can buy and hold land for later coordinated development or for permanent "greenbelts."

Some of the history and problems of Britain's New Towns policy shows one way an industrial nation has attacked problems of "slums," housing, and the growth of huge urban areas. Other industrial nations have used new towns in similar ways, but none has built them on a scale equaling Britain's effort. For example, the well known new towns around Stockholm, including Vallingby, have a total population of less than 200,000, and Tapiola, near Helsinki in Finland, has a population of 17,000. Britain's new towns have a population over 1,500,000.

Israel's population settlement and distribution policy, which has included founding "development towns" for recent poor immigrants, represents a response to very different circumstances. Although these circumstances are unique, the way they have been reflected in Israel's policies reveals the complexity of any decision about investment in urban areas. Israel's attempt to use new settlements to develop outlying and underdeveloped regions has parallels in several countries, as does the dominance of her major cities. Thus, Brazil has built its new capital, Brasilia, in an effort to open its vast interior to development;

and Venezuela is building Cuidad Guyana, in the primitive eastern region, in an effort to bring that region into the nation's economic and political life. Even economically advanced countries have problems similar in some ways; many of France's urban planners have concerned themselves with reducing the extraordinary dominance of Paris.[31]

The problems of Indian urban areas, finally, require very different sorts of planning. Calcutta's efforts to build up her economy and to provide even slightly improved living standards contrast brutally with the "problems" of richer countries.

La Defense, a new 1,700 acre city about three miles from Paris, is planned to house 80,000 people and is to be linked to Paris by an extension of the Metro. (French Government Tourist Office)

New Towns in Britain

In Britain by 1972, development of 32 new towns had begun under auspices of the New Towns Act of 1946. Over 1,500,000 live in new towns, which are planned for an eventual population of 3,000,000.

The idea that new towns should be developed in Britain was formulated most clearly by Ebenezer Howard in his 1898 book *Tomorrow: A*

---

[31] Lloyd Rodwin, *Nations and Cities: A Comparison of Strategies of Urban Growth* (1970), reviews problems of regional development in Venezuela, Turkey, France, and Britain.

Peaceful Path To Real Reform.[32] Howard, a court reporter by occupation and with little political power or wealth, was appalled by what he saw happening to the British working class. The percentage of the population living in cities had grown from 20 percent to 80 percent during the nineteenth century, and growth had been very heavily concentrated in London and a few industrial cities. Good housing and open space were beyond the means of workers, and they were often forced to spend hours each day journeying to and from work. It seemed to Howard that whatever gains in wages migrants to the cities received were taken up by increasingly expensive rents.

Howard proposed what he called "Garden Cities," which were to combine the best features of city and country life. They would be built in rural areas and surrounded by "green belts" so access to nature could be preserved. All dwellings would have gardens, and the cities would have maximum populations of about 30,000 so all their facilities would be easily accessible. Employment and culture—advantages of the city— would be provided by locating factories and facilities for culture in the Garden Cities. Thus, the Garden City would provide a complete and healthy life for its residents.

Howard's proposal addressed not only living conditions of the working class but also the "Land Question," seen by many at the time as a major social injustice. Socialists and liberals, including some leaders of the Liberal Party, saw the growth of urban land values, caused by city growth, as a uniquely unearned sort of wealth, one that should belong to the public. Howard's proposal dealt with this problem by setting a limit on dividends investors in Garden Cities would receive. Profits beyond that limit would be used to pay for public services.

Although they were widely discussed, Howard's ideas had relatively little practical impact until World War II. In 1901, he and supporters began Letchworth, the first experimental Garden City; and in 1923 they began Welwyn. But both grew slowly. Industries were difficult to attract, and house rentals higher than Howard had conceived. Both Garden Cities were plagued by lack of capital, which placed them largely in the hands of lenders.[33] Political concern with living conditions of the working class, meanwhile, was focused on the problem of building low-rent housing inside cities.

During the late 1930's and the years of World War II, however, a broad consensus developed that both the housing problem and the problem of London's immense size could best be handled through new towns. At the same time, forces far more powerful than the Town and Country

---

[32] Howard, Ebenezer, *Tomorrow: A Peaceful Path to Real Reform* (1898), republished 1902 and since as *Garden Cities of Tomorrow.*

[33] Frederic J. Osborn, *Green-Belt Cities* (1946, reissued 1969), discusses Letchworth and Welwyn in detail from an advocate's point of view.

Planning Association, which represented Howard's views, defined their own interests in new towns. Declining areas like the north of England and much of Wales were interested in using new towns in conjunction with favorable treatment for industries to provide jobs and halt the exodus of population toward London and the Southeast. City governments which had built low-income housing in the interwar period found land increasingly difficult to obtain, and the prices higher; and so they too were interested in diverting population outside the cities. Perhaps most important, a succession of governmental commissions recommended dispersal of the population of London as the best way to deal with its housing problems. In the 1945 election campaign, all three major parties—Labour, Conservative, and Liberal—endorsed a new towns policy. After the Labour victory, the New Towns Act of 1946 was passed; by 1951, fourteen new towns had been designated.

Britain's new towns have been used for a variety of purposes.[34] Ten, including eight of the first fourteen, have been designated in the London region, in the effort to improve housing and reduce the city's congestion. Glasgow's two new towns, East Kilbride and Cumbernauld, have also been directed to reduce congestion in the city's slums, perhaps Europe's worst.

Other new towns have been directed toward economic as well as housing problems. Corby, between London and Liverpool, was designated primarily to house workers in a major steel factory. Cwmbran, in South Wales, was designated on a site attractive to new industry, to provide both jobs and housing for residents of nearby economically depressed coal-mining valleys. Newton, Aycliffe, and Peterlee were designated in the effort to redevelop County Durham in northeastern England. The northeast as a whole has been one of Britain's most depressed areas for decades, as mechanization reduced coal employment.

Given this variety of purposes, judgments on the success of Britain's new towns are difficult. Nonetheless, it may be asked whether Britain's new towns have realized their stated goals.

One of the most important purposes of the new towns is to provide good housing at low cost. A substantial amount has been built—196,000 units in all the new towns by 1972. Despite substantial government subsidies, however, rents in the new towns have been substantially higher than those in housing developed by local authorities, "Council Housing," and in older, private housing. These facts are not surprising. Local authorities had built many units in the interwar period, when costs were far lower, and could subsidize rents in post-war housing with profits on

---

[34] Among other descriptions of the way the program has operated, see Lloyd Rodwin, *The British New Towns Policy* (1956), and Ray Thomas, *Aycliffe to Cumbernauld* (1969). The latter provides particularly useful discussions of new towns' problems.

these older units. Further, rents in most privately owned housing have long been controlled. But higher rents in the new towns have had a striking effect on the compositions of their populations. Immigrants to the new towns have been overwhelmingly young families, a very high proportion in their twenties. Thomas describes this situation:

> Young people in their twenties face special difficulties in getting accommodation except in the new towns. Their incomes are relatively low so that they are unlikely to be able to raise the capital or a mortgage necessary to buy a house. Since the war there has been little new privately rented housing. Young people do not find it easy to get a council dwelling. They are not qualified in terms of length of residence to be near the top of any council waiting list, and they are not likely to already have enough children to get special priority. But none of these difficulties lay in the way of getting a new town house. It seems likely that the age structure of the new towns is only partly a consequence of the fact that they are new. It is much more the product of the housing situation.[35]

The relatively high new town rents have also affected the class and occupational compositions of new town populations. Most of the new towns have a somewhat higher proportion of managers and professionals than the areas from which their residents came, and a lower proportion of low-income workers. Thus, subsidies contributed to new towns have benefited mainly groups with incomes somewhat above the national average. At the same time, the occupational and income ranges are narrow; their residents are overwhelmingly skilled industrial workers and lower level white-collar workers. During the 1960's, policies directed at making the new town populations more representative of the total British population were adopted.

A second major purpose of the new towns was to provide jobs for their residents, and thus reduce the extent of commuting. The new towns have been successful in attracting employers, although several have inadequate ranges of employment. The new towns have been more successful in attracting industrial than higher-level jobs. As a result, many new town workers cannot afford to live in the relatively expensive new town housing, and many residents commute to white-collar or professional employment outside the towns.

In Glasgow's new towns, the interrelated problems of housing and employment are severe. Rents in Scotland, historically, have been very low, so few who held rent-controlled apartments moved to the new towns of East Kilbride or Cumbernauld. Few of the jobs in East Kilbride or Cumbernauld are white-collar. As a result, in 1966, 23.6 percent of the employed residents of East Kilbride and 31.8 percent of those of Cumbernauld commuted to Glasgow, and 12.4 percent of East Kilbride and 10.7 percent of Cumbernauld workers commuted from Glasgow. Only 7.4 percent of residents of London's new towns commuted to London and

---

[35] *Ibid.,* pp. 827-8.

only 2.8 percent of London's new towns' jobs were held by London residents.[36]

More generally, the new towns were proposed as means of providing more wholesome family life than congested cities could provide. That they have realized this less measurable goal seems questionable. In the early 1950's, Michael Young and Peter Willmott studied family life in a low-income neighborhood of London and in a new town where many of the residents came from the neighborhood.[37] They found the move, while providing an improved physical environment, had also disrupted many important patterns of working-class family life. Because mainly young couples with children moved, the young wives lost emotional and practical help their mothers provided, particularly with child care. Young married men lost the companionship neighborhood pubs had provided. Much higher rents and commuting costs strained family budgets, so little money was left for wives' travel to visit relatives or for recreation, nor were many recreational facilities available in the new towns. Moves to the new town, in short, seemed to have destroyed some of what was worthwhile in working-class family life.

In the two decades since, growing prosperity and maturing of the older new towns may have solved some of these problems. Car ownership in Britain has increased from 2.3 million in 1950 to 11.5 million in 1970, so many new town residents have mobility for leisure as well as work; several new towns, in fact, have severe parking problems. Still, women may be more isolated and less able to find work than in the cities. Teenagers, now a high proportion of the population in the earlier new towns, still have inadequate recreation opportunities. Perhaps more important, as noted above, Britain's new towns have failed to serve her lowest-income families.

Population Distribution in Israel

The settlement of Jewish immigrants in Israel since independence in 1948 has taken place under unique circumstances.[38] Israel's planners and government have had to deal with unpredictable patterns of immigration, a land with few agricultural or mineral resources, and severe military requirements essential to the nation's survival. In the short run,

---

[36] Thomas, *op. cit.*, p. 917.

[37] Michael Young and Peter Willmott, *Family and Kinship in East London* (1957).

[38] This discussion will deal only with the period up to 1967. After the Six Day War Israel was faced with entirely new planning problems caused by control of territories inhabited by a large Arab population. How she will handle these problems is not yet clear. Data for the discussion up to 1967 are drawn from Erika Spiegel, *New Towns in Israel* (1967); Erik Cohen, *The City in Zionist Ideology* (1970), and Ann Louise Strong, *Planned Urban Environments* (1971).

these problems have been dealt with successfully: Israel has kept her promise to serve as a refuge and homeland for Jews throughout the world. In the longer run, the ways she approached the problem of population distribution have contributed to problems that are hardly unique: those who could live in Israel's metropolitan areas have for the most part been unwilling to live elsewhere, and a class and ethnic division has grown up between European and Asian and African Jews.

Before her independence, 85 percent of Israel's immigrants came from Europe.[39] They were well-educated and had a high proportion of working-age people. After independence, a growing number came from Africa and Asia. They had fewer skills, less education, larger families, and fewer workers. The first problem Israel's planners have faced, then, has been absorbing a population grown from less than 800,000 in May 1948 to 3,000,000 in 1971. How to distribute the Jewish population through the country was an important part of that problem.

In 1948, about 70 percent of the Jewish population lived in Tel Aviv, Haifa, and Jerusalem, drawn to those cities by the urban occupations and backgrounds of European Jewish immigrants. Almost 30 percent of the Israeli population was scattered in farm settlements and a few towns, but even this group was concentrated in the northern and central areas.

Israel's early population distribution plans were formulated under the strong influence of Zionist ideology. Zionism, developed in Europe in the late nineteenth century, called not only for a Jewish return to Palestine, but for a return to the soil. After World War I Zionism was dominated by the kibbutz (collective) movements, which called for creation of very small, largely self-sufficient farming communities, and even for abolition of wage labor. Although they have made up a relatively small part of the population, kibbutz members have retained powerful positions in Israel's politics, and have imparted an anti-big city bias in planning. Israel's population distribution plans have until recently seen urban settlements as a means of providing services to rural communities.

In 1948 Israel's population was distributed in a "polar" way, seventy percent living in the three large cities and most of the remainder in very small settlements. The early distribution plan called for creation of settlements of three intermediate sizes. These policies had only limited success. By 1964 it was possible to reduce the proportion of the three large cities to 43 percent, but almost all of this reduction took place between 1948 and 1951, and the three cities and their suburbs continued to contain much of the population.[40] These facts reflected the failure of other parts of the country to attract residents who could live in the metropolitan areas.

[39] Spiegel, *op. cit.,* p. 27.

[40] *Ibid.,* p. 16, 29. In 1972, the three metropolitan areas contained 43 percent of the population. *Associated Press Almanac, 1973,* p. 698.

In subsequent plans population was allocated to other parts of the country by constructing subsidized housing there and not in the metropolis and by assigning new immigrants directly to that housing. Thus, Israel's new towns and new villages have come to have a population quite different from that of the nation as a whole. Asian and African immigrants, larger families with more dependents, poorly educated people, and later immigrants were concentrated in the new towns and particularly in villages. These towns and villages, of course, were those founded as part of Israel's population distribution policy.

Some Problems of Planning in Calcutta

Urban problems in the United States and Britain, and even in an initially poor country like Israel, are of an entirely different sort from those in a terribly underdeveloped country like India. Above all, the lack of economic resources creates India's immense urban problems, and her planners must pay attention first to using resources in the most efficient way possible. A few of the problems Calcutta's planners face are described here, in order to give some idea of their nature. These examples are drawn mainly from the 1966 Basic Development Plan for the Calcutta Metropolitan District.[41]

Calcutta is the dominant center of northeastern India, by far the largest and most important city in an area populated, in 1966, by more than 150 million people. Within 300 miles lie almost all of India's iron and coal resources and most of her iron and steel industry. Forty-two percent of the urban dwellers in West Bengal and three adjoining states live in the Calcutta Metropolitan District, in 1971 a population of 7,200,000. No other city in the four states has a population greater than 370,000. Calcutta's prosperity, moreover, is critical to India's future.

One set of Calcutta's problems is caused by India's rapid urbanization. In 1966, Calcutta's planners estimated that the Metropolitan District would grow to between 12.3 and 12.7 million by 1986. The reasons for this rapid growth are not difficult to see; Calcutta's per capita income is approximately twice that of India as a whole, although it remains less than $300 per year.

Calcutta's problems of providing for in-migrants are complicated by the nature of the city's site. No part of the Metropolitan District lies higher than thirty feet above sea-level. The highest areas lie alongside

[41] Government of West Bengal. Calcutta Metropolitan Planning Commission, *Basic Development Plan for the Calcutta Metropolitan District* (1966). See also Roy Turner, ed., *India's Urban Future* (1961).

the Hooghly River on alluvial deposits from one to two miles wide. Outside these areas, the land is hardly suitable for urban development without immensely expensive improvements.

One result has been crowding even beyond that of other Indian cities. By 1961, Calcutta Corporation and Howrah, the Metropolitan District's central cities, had densities, respectively, of 73,642 and 46,055 persons per square mile. Manhattan, by far the most densely populated county in the United States, has a density of about 75,000 per square mile, but in Calcutta few buildings rise above two stories.

Housing, as a result, is in incredibly short supply. The average occupancy per room in the Metropolitan District reached 2.99 in 1966. Calcutta's planners have set a goal of providing 40 square feet of dwelling space per person, but recognize that a majority of the city's citizens have far less space. In contrast, the American Public Health Association recommends that a household of two persons have at least 750 square feet of space. The first dwellings in Israel's new settlements, built at a time of desperate shortages, provided 320 square feet per dwelling. By 1967 the average dwelling for poor immigrants in Israel had 580 square feet.

Drainage and sewerage are a second major problem. In 1966, 54 percent of the Calcutta Corporation area had sewers, but very few other areas in the Metropolitan District were sewered. Most utilize "service privies," from which waste is removed periodically. Particularly during the monsoon season, when the city has very heavy rains, these privies cause severe health problems. Cholera and lesser diseases are endemic in Calcutta.

Calcutta's planners argue that such problems cannot be dealt with by building new housing areas. Resources necessary for a meaningful rebuilding program are simply not available. For example, providing even 40 square feet of space per person in permanent housing by 1986 would require construction of 200,000 units to relieve the most severe overcrowding and 1.1 million units to house in-migrants. Even such a program, which would not raise housing standards significantly, would require annual expenditures for housing at least 50 percent greater than those now made throughout India.

In their attempt to make such problems somewhat more manageable, India's urban areas have turned to "community development,"[42] which the United Nations has defined:

The term "community development" has come into international usage to connote the processes by which the efforts of the people themselves are united with those of governmental authorities to improve the economic, social, and cultural conditions of countries, to integrate these communities into the life of

[42] Marshall B. Clinard, *Slums and Community Development* (1966) is an extensive report on urban community development in India, particularly in Delhi, and elsewhere.

the nation, and to enable them to contribute fully to national progress. This complex of processes is then made up of two essential elements: the participation by the people themselves in efforts to improve their level of living with as much reliance as possible on their own initiative; and the provision of technical and other service in ways which encourage initiative, self-help and mutual help and make these more effective.[43]

The urban community development program has as goals such tasks as improving houses and courtyards in bustee—non-permanent housing—areas; installing drains; repairing latrines and finding sites for the installation of new latrines; building concrete floors around communal water taps; and installing lighting fixtures on public paths. Even this modest program has been bogged down by red tape and shortages of funds. Calcutta remains, in Rudyard Kipling's phrase, "the city of dreadful night."

Although little evidence is available on the overall success of the urban community development program, the approach would seem questionable on at least two points. First, the program cannot be a substitute for financial resources. Funds are scarce even for basic public health measures that, while leaving much of the urban population in abject poverty, would still improve individuals' life expectancies. Second, and perhaps as important, the formulation of urban community development glosses over the fact that Indian cities are rigidly stratified in both caste and class terms, resulting in the oppression of the poorest Indians by the not so poor. Thus the urban community development program may well insure that its meager benefits go mainly to the not so poor.

New Towns in the United States

The current development of new towns in the United States, and the planning "problems" associated with them, reveal starkly the contrast between American wealth and Indian poverty.

New towns have been developed less extensively in the United States than in other industrialized countries. In large part this reflects the lesser powers of government in land development. Unlike Britain's government, the Federal government has never taken a major originating role in land development. Unlike the situation in Israel, almost all potentially urban land in the United States is privately owned. Moreover, the United States has never had population pressures—or very rapid

---

[43] Quoted by Clinard from United Nations, Department of Economic and Social Affairs, "Community Development and Related Services" (1960), p. 1.

immigration like Israel's or simple lack of space like many European countries—that require development of new towns. Few American cities lack space for housing development.

Nonetheless, new communities of various sorts have been developed in the United States. Toward the end of the nineteenth century two notable industrial new towns, in this case "company towns," were founded. The Pullman railway car company founded Pullman, Illinois, now within the Chicago city limits, as a model industrial town to house its workers. Pullman was, to say the least, a disaster. As Mohl and Betten note:

Pullman's pervasive paternalism represented an effort to impose social order and moral values on industrial workers while the firm earned extra profits through high rent and utility charges. The company owned all the town's housing, as well as much of its retail business.[44]

These policies contributed to the Pullman strike of 1894, one of the bloodiest labor conflicts of American history.

In 1906 the United States Steel Company founded Gary, Indiana. Unlike Pullman, Gary was founded solely for reasons of industrial efficiency. United States Steel wished to create an integrated industrial center, where iron ore and coal could be manufactured into finished steel products. U.S. Steel was determined to avoid the mistakes and paternalism of Pullman. They wished, rather, to develop a city of prosperous homeowning industrial workers. A subsidiary built several subdivisions in the town's northern section, but the costs of lots and houses were too high for the steel mills' unskilled workers.

Most of Gary's development was undertaken by local groups who took part in the city's first elections and managed to control town politics for several years:

Catering to unskilled, immigrant workers neglected by the Gary Land Company, real estate men and builders put up numerous boarding houses, "barrack-like shacks," and cheap frame homes . . . A typical barracks building was eighteen feet wide and one-hundred feet long and divided into apartments of two rooms, each nine feet square. Without running water or any other modern facilities, these apartments rented for as much as nine dollars per month.[45]

At the time, common laborers' wages averaged 16.7 cents per hour. Thus, Gary, founded to be a model industrial town, had from the start miserable, overpriced slums, the result of real estate speculation and U.S. Steel's unwillingness to provide decent living conditions for its workers.

---

[44] Raymond A. Mohl and Neil Betten, "The Failure of Industrial City Planning: Gary, Indiana, 1906-1910," *Journal of the American Institute of Planners* 38 (July 1972), pp. 202-15. The following material on Gary is drawn from this article.

[45] Mohl and Betten, *op. cit.,* p. 211.

Following World War I, civic reformers began to look toward new towns as solutions to urban problems. The City Housing Corporation, a limited-profit group in New York, began development of Radburn, New Jersey, patterned after Howard's Garden City model.[46] Working two decades after Howard and in a more prosperous country, the Corporation was particularly concerned with properly managing the automobile's impact, using superblocks, the cul-de-sac streets that later became a standard feature of suburban design, and other techniques to control auto traffic. They were concerned to hold down costs so low rents and sales prices could be charged. Row-house construction, duplexes, and fewer auto roads cut costs in their projects.

Radburn is an architectural success. Pedestrian traffic is almost entirely separated from vehicular. "Interior parks," accessible only on foot, provide exceptional space for relaxation and active play. Radburn was built very economically, but as a new community, it failed. No industry was attracted, and Radburn became only a small suburban residential area. Because of the depression, the community was never completed. More important, Radburn never provided good environments for low-income families, despite the Corporation's purposes. As characterized by Stein, even the community's first residents had above-average incomes and mainly white-collar and professional jobs.

During the New Deal, several new communities were begun by various governmental agencies. The Greenbelt Towns, of which three with a total population of about 10,000 were built, were most successful. Built by the Resettlement Administration, the towns were seen as means of drawing unemployed families from urban areas. The actual uses to which they were put were far different. Greenbelt, Maryland, thirteen miles north of Washington, D.C., housed a population of moderate, not low, income. Chosen to reflect the white population of the metropolitan area, 70 percent of the first residents were government workers, 30 percent nongovernment; 30 percent were Catholic, 7 percent Jewish, and 63 percent Protestant.[47] No blacks resided in Greenbelt. After 1940, Greenbelt's focus was changed to accommodate government workers crowding into Washington to meet defense needs, and later parts of the new town became little more than cheap housing. Pedestrian underpasses and "interior parks" were never built in the later sections. By the 1950's, the New Deal's new towns had been sold following specific requirements of more conservative Congresses.

[46] On Radburn and other pre-World War II American new towns, see particularly Clarence S. Stein, *Toward New Towns for America* (1950, reissued 1966). Stein, an architect, was a key participant in the City Housing Corporation.

[47] Stein, *op. cit.,* p. 128; for sociological study of Greenbelt, see William Form, "Status Stratification in a Planned City," *American Sociological Review,* 10 (1945), 605-13, and Form, "Stratification in Low and Moderate Income Housing Areas," *Journal of Social Issues,* 7 (1951), 109-31.

The movement to build new towns in the United States was revived during the 1960's under far different circumstances from those surrounding efforts of the 1920's and 1930's. Very substantial economic growth took place during and after World War II, creating an unprecedentedly large and well-educated middle class. Industrial and other unionized workers earned incomes adequate to support homeownership and other elements of middle class life styles, and real and perceived distances between blue-and white-collar workers decreased. The prosperous majority of Americans found new housing opportunities mainly in the suburbs, whose large-scale versions such as Levittown and Park Forest, contain prototypical features of the later new towns.

In the middle 1960's, private developers' efforts to build new towns began.[48] In part, these new towns reflected growth in the scale of suburban development, to the point where single developments of "town" size could be built. In 1964, Eichler and Kaplan listed fifty-four "new community developments," ranging from 10,000 to 300,000 in projected population.[49] On the other hand, more traditional suburban developments had been severely criticized, as requiring excessive commuting and separating men from their wives and children; as creating class, racial and age segregation; and as creating sterile, insulated life styles.

Among the most successful privately developed new towns is Columbia, Maryland, between Baltimore and Washington. Columbia includes 14,000 acres and is planned for an eventual population of 110,000. Its developer, James W. Rouse, is attempting to build not so much a "new town" as a new city. Plans call for a broad range of housing types and prices, leading to broad ranges of age and income. A variety of industrial, office, and service jobs are to be included, and a very complete range of recreational and cultural facilities is planned. Rouse sees development of new communities like Columbia as important to America's future. In a 1964 interview, he said:

Personally, I hold . . . that people grow best in small communities where the institutions which are the dominant forces in their lives are within the scale of their comprehension and within reach of their sense of responsibility and capacity to manage.[50]

To provide such environments, Columbia will include several villages of 10,000 to 15,000 people, each with two to four neighborhoods of 800 to 1,200 families. Physically, Columbia consists of fairly compact neighborhoods surrounded by recreational and natural areas. Plans call for

[48] In the voluminous literature on new towns, see particularly Edward P. Eichler, and Marshall Kaplan, *The Community Builders* (1967); and Harvey Perloff and N. Sandberg, eds., *New Towns: Why—and For whom?* (1973).

[49] Eichler and Kaplan, *op. cit.,* pp. 185-86.

[50] Quoted by Eichler and Kaplan, *op. cit.,* pp. 55-56.

development of a mass transportation system to reduce dependency on travel by car.

So far, Rouse has had very considerable success. He has managed to attract a wide range of cultural facilities to Columbia, including the Washington Symphony for its summer concerts, Antioch and Howard county community colleges, a theater, a coffee house and other establishments. Forty-five industries, including a General Electric plant which will employ 10,000, have located in Columbia, as have several offices. The Columbia Mall shopping center, on which Rouse depends for much of his long-run profit, provides a wide variety of stores in a very pleasant setting. Moreover, homebuilders to whom Rouse has sold property have built, on the whole, pleasing, if not particularly innovative, neighborhoods of detached and row houses. Housing at Columbia has been open to blacks with adequate incomes to rent or purchase.

Aerial view of part of Columbia, Maryland, showing the large shopping mall, office buildings, and several residential neighborhoods. (Photograph-Property of the Rouse Company)

671

Columbia does not have a broad range of population, and there is little reason to think it will in the future. Of approximately 6000 units completed, fewer than 10 percent are within the reach of moderate-income families, as defined by Federal subsidy programs. Yet 70 percent of the jobs Columbia has attracted are industrial and sales jobs paying under $8000 per year. Many of these jobs, particularly the 2000 jobs located in the Columbia Mall, are held by women whose husbands also work, but few of the industrial workers in Columbia can afford housing there. It seems unlikely that Columbia will accomplish its goal of enabling residents to work in the new town and workers to live there. Moreover, Columbia seems to have attracted proportionately few elderly people and young single adults.

Failures of this sort seem to stem from two causes. First, Rouse, like other new town developers, must operate at a profit. Subsidies adequate to bring housing within the reach of low-and moderate-income families while allowing developers to make profits are scarce. In the long run, however, another factor may be as important. Experience in Columbia and, particularly, in California new communities suggests that new communities were more attractive than standard suburbs—housing values held equal—precisely because they offered buyers the guarantee that their neighborhood's "class image" would be safe from encroachment by lower-income housing.[50] In California, Werthman found that the major value placed on the wide-ranging recreational facilities included in planned communities resulted less from the expectation of using these facilities than from the fact that they "added to the general atmosphere." Thus, California families who purchased homes in new communities were frequently interested in insulating themselves from the poor and other "undesirable" neighbors.

So long as American new towns were developed as mainly private ventures, aided only by mortgage insurance and other aids available to other suburban developers, their failures to provide adequate housing for low-and moderate-income families, particularly those whose heads held new town jobs, might have been seen as of relatively little public concern. The Housing Acts of 1968 and 1970, however, provide substantial financial aids to new town development, and require that new community populations reflect the economic and social populations of their metropolitan areas. Problems like those Columbia has experienced thus become a public issue.

[51] Reported by Eichler and Kaplan, *op. cit.*

Summary

Throughout its eighty-year history, as noted at the beginning of this chapter, American urban planning has attempted to serve both the needs of business and middle-class groups for order and aesthetic values and the more desperate needs of the poor. Despite the fact that planners have generally been as committed to serving the latter as well as the former goals, planning has frequently failed. Sometimes, as in many urban renewal projects, urban planners' work has seemed to harm poor and minority groups. As planning becomes more important with the planning of population distribution patterns and whole new towns, the tension between its desire to create pleasant communities where business will prosper and its desire to provide aid to disadvantaged groups continues. The history of Britain's new towns and Israel's population distribution policies shows American urban planners are hardly alone in experiencing the difficulties of resolving these sometimes contradictory ends.

Selected Bibliography

BOOKS

Altschuler, Alan, *The City Planning Process.* Ithaca, N.Y.: Cornell University Press, 1965.

Bellush, Jewel, and Murray Hausknecht, eds., *Urban Renewal: People, Politics, and Planning.* New York: Anchor Books, 1967.

Burchell, Robert, *New Communities American Style.* New Brunswick, N.J.: Center for Urban Policy Research, Rutgers University, 1972.

Cohen, Erik, *The City in Zionist Ideology.* Jerusalem, Israel: Institute of Urban and Regional Studies, Hebrew University of Jerusalem, 1970.

Eichler, Edward P., and Marshall Kaplan, *The Community Builders.* Berkeley, Calif.: University of California Press, 1967.

Epstein, David, *Brasilia: Plan and Reality.* Berkeley, Calif.: University of California Press, 1973.

Evans, Hazel, ed., *New Towns, The British Experience.* New York: Wiley, 1972.

Evenson, Norma, *Chandigarh.* Berkeley, Calif.: University of California Press.

Ewald, William R., Jr., ed., in three volumes, *Environment for Man—the Next Fifty Years,* 1967; *Environment and Change - the Next Fifty Years,* 1968; *Environment and Policy - the Next Fifty Years,* 1968. Bloomington, Ind.: Indiana University Press.

Gans, Herbert J., *People and Plans.* New York: Basic Books, 1968.

Geddes, Patrick, *Patrick Geddes: Spokesman for Man and the Environment,* ed., Marshall Stalley. New Brunswick, N.J.: Rutgers University Press, 1972.

Goodman, Robert, *After the Planners.* New York: Simon and Schuster, 1971.

Goodman, William I., and Eric Freund, eds., *Principles and Practices of Urban Planning,* 4th ed.. Washington, D.C.: International City Managers Association, 1968.

Greer, Scott, *Urban Renewal and American Cities.* New York: Bobbs Merrill, 1965.

Hall, Peter, ed., *The Containment of Urban England,* two volumes. Beverly Hills, Calif.: Sage, 1973.

Lupo, Alan, Frank Colcord, and Edmund Fowler, *Rites of Way: The Politics of Transportation in Boston and the U.S. City.* Boston: Little, Brown, 1971.

Mields, Hugh, *Federally Assisted New Communities.* Washington, D.C., The Urban Land Institute, 1973.

Miller, David R., ed., *Urban Transportation Policy: New Perspectives.* Lexington, Mass.: D.C. Heath, Lexington Books, 1972.

National Commission on Urban Problems, *Building the American City.* New York: Praeger, 1969.

Osborn, Frederick, and Arnold Whittick, *The New Towns: The Answer to Megalopolis.* Cambridge, Mass.: The MIT Press, revised edition 1969.

Perloff, Harvey S., and Neil Sandberg, eds., *New Towns: Why—and For Whom?* New York: Praeger, 1973.

Reilly, William K., *The Use of Land: A Citizens' Policy Guide to Urban Growth.* New York: Thomas Y. Crowell, 1973.

Rodwin, Lloyd, *Nations and Cities: A Comparison of Strategies for Urban Growth.* Boston: Houghton, Mifflin, 1970.

Scott, Mel, *American City Planning.* Berkeley, Calif.: University of California Press, 1969.

Stein, Clarence, *Toward New Towns for America.* Cambridge, Mass.: The MIT Press, 3rd ed., 1966.

Strong, Ann Louise, *Planned Urban Environments: Sweden, Finland, Israel, the Netherlands, France.* Baltimore, Md.: The Johns Hopkins Press, 1971.

Thomas, Ray, *Aycliffe to Cumbernauld.* London: Political and Economic Planning, 1969 (available in the United States from Committee on Economic Development, New York).

Warren, Roland, *Truth, Love, and Social Change, and Other Essays on Community Change.* Chicago: Rand McNally, 1971.

Wilson, John Q., ed., *Urban Renewal: The Record and the Controversy.* Cambridge, Mass.: The MIT Press, 1966.

ARTICLES

Brooks, Richard, "Social Planning in Columbia," *Journal of the American Institute of Planners,* 37 (November 1971), 373–79.

Buder, Stanley, "The Model Town of Pullman: Town Planning and Social Control in the Gilded Age," *Journal of the American Institute of Planners, 33 (August 1967) 2–10.*

Davidoff, Paul, "Advocacy and Pluralism in Planning," *Journal of the American Institute of Planners,* 31 (November 1965), 331–38.

Heraud, Brian, "Social Class and the New Towns," *Urban Studies,* 5 (February 1968), 33–58.

———, "The New Towns and London's Housing Problem," *Urban Studies,* 3 (February 1966), 8–21.

Mann, Lawrence, "Social Science Advances and Planning Applications: 1900-1965." *Journal of the American Institute of Planners,* 38 (November 1972), 346–59.

"New Perspectives on New Towns," special feature, *Journal of the American Institute of Planners,* 39 (September 1973), 306–25.

Peattie, Lisa R., "Reflections on Advocacy Planning," *Journal of the American Institute of Planners,* 34 (March 1968), 80–88.

Schachar, Arie, "Israel's Development Towns: Evaluation of National Urbanization Policy," *Journal of the American Institute of Planners,* 37 (November 1971), 362-73.

Index

Printer and Binder: The Book Press
79 80 81 82 8 7 6 5 4 3 2